DWELLING PLACE

DWELLING PLACE

A Plantation Epic

Erskine Clarke

Yale University Press
New Haven & London

Published with assistance from the Griffith Foundation.

Designed by Nancy Ovedovitz and set in Electra type by Tseng Information Systems, Inc. Printed in the United States of America.

Library of Congress Cataloging-in-Publication Data
Clarke, Erskine, 1941–
Dwelling place : a plantation epic / Erskine Clarke.
p.   cm.
Includes bibliographical references and index.
ISBN 0-300-10867-2 (cloth : alk. paper)
1. Plantation life—Georgia—Liberty County—History—19th century. 2. Jones, Charles Colcock, 1804–1863—Family. 3. Plantation owners—Georgia—Liberty County—Biography. 4. Whites—Georgia—Liberty County—Biography. 5. Jones, Lizzy—Family. 6. Slaves—Georgia—Liberty County—Biography. 7. African Americans—Georgia—Liberty County—Biography. 8. Liberty County (Ga.)— Biography. 9. Liberty County (Ga.)—Race relations. 10. Liberty County (Ga.)— Social life and customs—19th century. I. Title.
F292.L6C58 2005
305.896′0730758733′09034—dc22   2005003958

A catalogue record for this book is available from the British Library.

The paper in this book meets the guidelines for permanence and durability of the Committee on Production Guidelines for Book Longevity of the Council on Library Resources.

10 9 8 7 6 5 4 3 2 1

To Nancy, Legare, and Elizabeth

CONTENTS

PREFACE

Dwelling Place is a history of two peoples living together on the Georgia coast from 1805 to 1869. It is a single narrative because their lives were linked and interwoven in innumerable and often intimate ways and because this coastal land shaped all who lived along its rivers, by its swamps, and on its islands and sandy hills, even as those who lived there shaped the land itself. Yet *Dwelling Place* is also two histories—one of whites and one of blacks, one of owners and one of slaves. For in spite of all of their closeness and all the ways their lives were bound together on this particular part of the Georgia coast, there was a great divide between those who were owned and those who owned. So great was the distance between them and so different was their experience that *Dwelling Place* is necessarily two histories of one place and one time.

One history centers on the family of Charles Colcock Jones, who came to be known among whites as the Apostle to the Negro Slaves. The other history focuses on the family of Lizzy Jones, the matriarch of one of the most influential and widely connected families of the Gullah-speaking slave community of Liberty County, Georgia. Both families were part of dense networks of relatives and friends who constituted significant parts of each family's history. Both families, in all their own diversity and peculiarities, saw the landscape of Liberty County and understood the stories of the people who lived on its land from very different places and in very different ways.

Dwelling Place is an attempt to tell these two histories in a single narrative, because each history was dependent on the other and cannot be understood apart from the other. One history is of a white family's love for one another and of their love for the beauty of a low-country home. Their story is marked by the bitter irony of good intentions gone astray and of benevolent impulses becoming ideological supports for deep oppression. The other history is of a particular African-

American family's resistance to the degradations of slavery. Their story is marked by the varied strategies of its members—not only open resistance to slavery but also acculturation and relentless negotiations—as they sought to ease the burdens of slavery and to move toward a new future for themselves and their family. Because the study explores the lives of specific individuals and families over an extended period of time, it is a composite biography: the lives of owners and owned are seen overlapping one another and being layered together in complex and interdependent ways, even as they are both located within larger social and cultural contexts.

The narrative begins in 1805 at Liberty Hall plantation, three months after the birth of Charles Colcock Jones and a short time before the birth of Lizzy Jones's second son, Cato. It ends in 1869, when the entire region appeared strangely and, for the blacks, wonderfully changed. The story follows the histories of these two families, and their dense networks of relatives and friends, through a period of immense social, cultural, and technological transformations. These transformations, and the comings and goings of plantation life for more than sixty years, are seen and experienced from above in *Dwelling Place* through the eyes of ruling whites and are seen and experienced from below through the eyes of resourceful slaves and freed people who struggled first against the bitter burden of slavery and then against its legacy of a powerful racism.

Any history, of course, involves not only intense research and analysis but also an act of imagination as the "facts" of research are arranged and interpreted in the mind of the historian. This is true of a history of the whites of Liberty County who left behind an extensive collection of letters and documents. An act of imagination is required to enter their world even with all the richness of their written record, for their nineteenth-century plantation world is distant from the largely urban world of the twenty-first century. The distance is perhaps most clearly felt at those points when we ask, "How could they believe that?" or "How could they do that?"

If an act of imagination is required to enter the well-documented white world of nineteenth-century Liberty County, much more imagination is needed to enter the world of Liberty County slaves. Their written records are few and their voices have been for generations largely suppressed. Yet their story has its witnesses, and the witnesses tell of slave life, of the work that slaves did, and of the community Liberty County slaves built. Some of these witnesses are found in the land itself, as archaeologists have dug in slave settlements or as dams and dikes of old rice fields have appeared on aerial photographs. Other witnesses come from studies of other slave communities and from the history of the institution of slavery itself. A few critically important witnesses are found in slave letters and in slave narratives from Liberty County. Most of the witnesses, however, for the family of Lizzy Jones and its network of relations and friends, come in the letters and in the plantation and court documents of white owners. This white testimony must be approached with special care. But with care, and with collaboration from other sources, an imaginative leap can be made to read what James C. Scott in *Domination and the Arts of Resistance* calls the "hidden transcripts" of the slave settlements in order to tell the story of a slave family and how they saw and experienced a time and place shared with other slaves and with the whites of Liberty County.

"The final presentation of one's research," writes Rhys Isaac in *The Transformation of Virginia*, "should not be primarily a record of the researcher's labors, but a *persuasive reconstruction of the experiences of past actors.*" This is the intent of *Dwelling Place*. What was life like for the white Jones family and their white neighbors on low-country plantations during these years? What was life like for the black Jones family and its dense network of neighbors in the slave settlements of Liberty County during these same years? And how were the lives of both whites and blacks linked and interwoven by the power of slavery and by the responses of particular men and women to that power?

I am grateful to many people for their help in the completion of this study —too many people, I am afraid, to name them all. Gratitude, however, demands that I thank publicly those who provided special assistance. Leon C. Miller, manuscripts librarian, Tulane University, and Wilbur E. Meneray, assistant dean for special collections, Tulane, encouraged me through their professional help and many kindnesses. Tim Browning, director of the library, Columbia Theological Seminary, provided the funding for the microfilming of the Charles Colcock Jones Collection at Tulane and thereby saved me many pleasant but time-consuming trips to New Orleans. Gail DeLoach, the senior archivist at the Georgia Department of Archives and History, was helpful in many ways, but especially with the securing of photographs. Mandi Johnson of the Georgia Historical Society, Savannah, provided much appreciated guidance. Bill Bynum of the Presbyterian Historical Society, Montreat, North Carolina, went out of his way to be helpful. Todd Crumley helped find and photocopy materials from the special collections at Duke University. Doug Minnerly, Richard Floyd, Kyle Henderson, Hunter Camp, and Amy Lehr helped to photocopy several thousand documents from microfilm. Richard Blake checked names, edited the genealogical charts, and prepared the indexes of persons with his usual grace and attention to detail. Bonnie Shoemaker provided assistance in securing documents and ordering materials. Her efficient and cheerful ways as an administrative assistant freed me from numerous responsibilities.

A number of people in Liberty County offered me generous assistance. Over many years the staff in the superior court and in the probate court helped me sort through documents and solve troubling mysteries. Bill Cox, president of the Liberty County Historical Society, shared with me his knowledge of Liberty County history and provided microfilm of the Lambert Foundation documents. Molene Herbert Chambless Burke helped me unravel some of the history of the Baptist Churches in the county. Tom Mueller of the First Presbyterian Church, Hinesville, introduced me to people familiar with the history of the region. Colonel George Rogers of Colonel's Island spent an afternoon with me discussing the island and its history. Joann Clark of the Midway Museum showed me a number of documents in the museum's collection and introduced me to people who helped with specific questions. In adjacent Bryan County, David Long showed me every kindness and shared with me his enthusiasm for low-country history.

I am particularly grateful to those who traveled with me over parts of the low country. Buddy Smith, a crabber, spent a day with me in his boat as we explored the North Newport River. He has an amazing knowledge of the river's life and moods and of hunting, fishing, and crabbing in the low country. Townsend Warren provided much lore about shrimping and crabbing. Chris Hartbarger kayaked with me through the Medway marshes and walked with me around the remaining ruins of Maybank plantation. Ezekiel Walthour drove me around parts of the county, pointed out the locations of a number of plantations, and arranged for me to interview members of the African-American community in the county, including Mrs. LeCounte Baggs, who knew as a child Gilbert Lawson, Jr. My conversation with her was an unexpected gift. An unknown driver of a pickup truck pointed out the way through the woods to the cemetery of the Retreat plantation. Ken Speir walked with me over much of the former South Hampton plantation, showed me where the old plantation house was located, and introduced me to Kip Kirby, plantation manager, Hampton Island, who kindly showed other areas of the former Roswell King plantation. Laura Devendorf talked with me about the history and geography of the area around Sunbury and showed me over the grounds of Palmyra and Springfield plantations. Van Martin recalled what he remembered as a boy horseback riding over the lands of Montevideo plantation.

Ed Loring, whose dissertation in 1976 was on Charles Colcock Jones, was a frequent conversation partner as I labored over nine years on the work of this book. Walter Brueggemann, Dan Carter, and Joe Harvard read substantial parts of the narrative and gave me their welcomed judgments. Marcia Riggs, as a womanist and ethicist, was of particular help as I attempted to understand the struggles of African-American women. She read a number of chapters and provided important bibliographic resources. Griselda Lartey spoke with me about older people as storytellers in her native Ghana. All who know Robert Manson Myers's monumental *The Children of Pride: A True Story of Georgia and the Civil War* will immediately recognize my indebtedness to his astonishing scholarship. Peggy Hargis shared her research on the freed people of Liberty County and helped me identify the family names of former slaves.

The Griffith Foundation provided generous financial support for my many trips to Liberty County and assistance in the publication for which I am most grateful. Columbia Theological Seminary provided generous sabbatical leaves for my work on this project and much encouragement through Presidents Doug Oldenburg and Laura Mendenhall and Deans James Hudnut-Beumler and Cameron Murchison. Larisa Heimert, publisher, Yale University Press, has the remarkable gift of encouraging authors while easing anxieties. Dan Heaton, senior manuscript editor, dealt gracefully with my errors while delighting me with his humor.

Constant and sustaining encouragement came from my wife, Nancy, and our daughters, Legare and Elizabeth. They, even more than friends, listened to my relentless telling and retelling of parts of this narrative. *Dwelling Place* is gratefully dedicated to them.

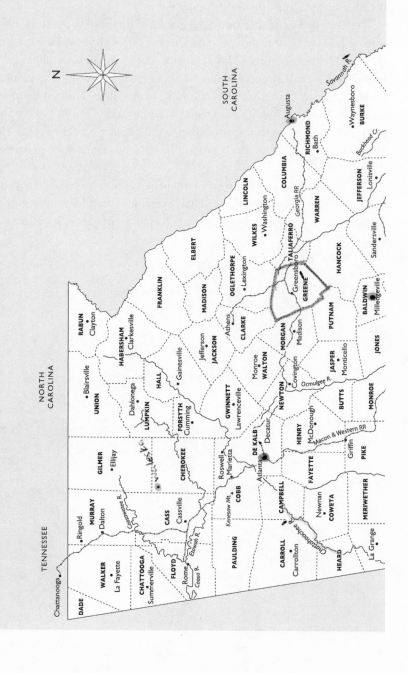

N

TENNESSEE

NORTH CAROLINA

SOUTH CAROLINA

Chattanooga

• Ringold

DADE

WALKER
La Fayette

CHATTOOGA
Summerville

MURRAY
• Dalton

Cossawattee R.

GILMER
• Ellijay

Coosa R.

FLOYD
Rome •

Etowah R.

CASS
• Cassville

CHEROKEE

PAULDING

CARROLL
Carrollton •

Chattahoochee R.

HEARD

COWETA
Newnan •

La Grange •

MERIWETHER

UNION

Blairsville •

Dahlonega •

LUMPKIN

FORSYTH
Cumming

Kenesaw Mt. ▲

COBB

Roswell •
• Marietta

DE KALB •
Atlanta • Decatur

CAMPBELL

FAYETTE

HENRY
• McDonough

Macon & Western RR

PIKE

• Griffin

BUTTS

MONROE

RABUN
• Clayton

HABERSHAM
Clarkesville •

HALL
Gainesville •

GWINNETT
Lawrenceville •

NEWTON

FRANKLIN

MADISON

JACKSON
• Jefferson

Athens •

CLARKE

WALTON
Monroe •

Covington •

MORGAN
Madison •

Ocmulgee R.

JASPER
Monticello •

ELBERT

WILKES
Washington •

OGLETHORPE
• Lexington

GREENE
Greensboro •

PUTNAM

JONES

LINCOLN

TALIAFERRO

HANCOCK

BALDWIN
Milledgeville •

COLUMBIA

Georgia RR

WARREN

Augusta

RICHMOND
• Bath

Savannah R.

Waynesboro •

BURKE

JEFFERSON
Lonisville •

Buckhead Cr.

• Sandersville

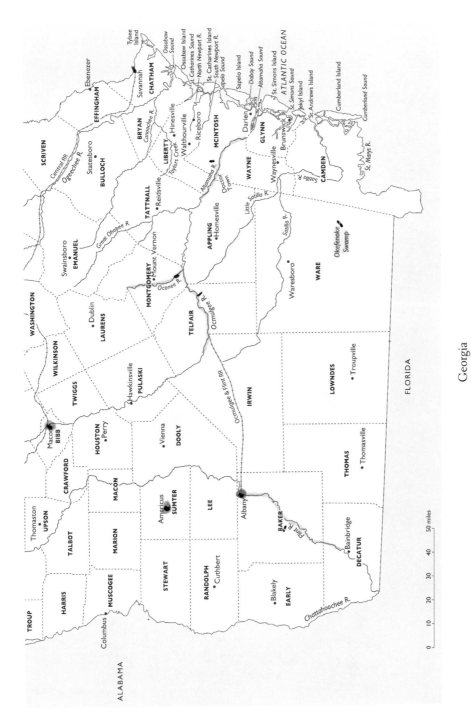

Georgia

Based on Wm. G. Bonner's *Pocket Map of the State of Georgia* (1848)

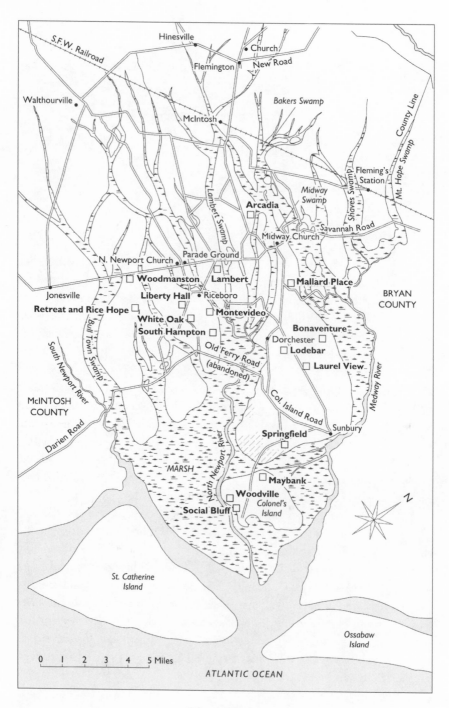

S.F.W. Railroad

Hinesville

Church

New Road

Flemington

Walthourville

Bakers Swamp

McIntosh

County Line

Fleming's Station

Midway Swamp

Arcadia

Savannah Road

Shaves Swamp

Mt. Hope Swamp

Lambert Swamp

Midway Church

N. Newport Church

Parade Ground

Jonesville

Woodmanston

Lambert

Mallard Place

BRYAN COUNTY

Liberty Hall

Riceboro

Retreat and Rice Hope

Montevideo

Bull Town Swamp

White Oak

South Hampton

Bonaventure

Dorchester

Lodebar

Old Ferry Road

Laurel View

(abandoned)

South Newport River

McINTOSH COUNTY

Col. Island Road

Medway River

Darien Road

North Newport River

Springfield

Sunbury

MARSH

Maybank

Woodville

Colonel's Island

Social Bluff

N

St. Catherine Island

Ossabaw Island

0 1 2 3 4 5 Miles

ATLANTIC OCEAN

Liberty County

LIBERTY HALL

Early on a March morning in 1805, as the first hints of dawn touched the Sea Islands and the marshlands south of Savannah, Old Jupiter rose, went out of his cabin, and with a blast from his conch-shell horn announced a new day. The sound filled the early-morning silence of the slave quarters at Liberty Hall plantation and called out the men and women who lived there. Lizzy threw off her blanket and slipped her Osnaburg dress over her shift. Lifting her two-year-old son Lymus to her hip, she hurried toward the kitchen, an outbuilding behind the plantation house. Quickly she stirred into flame the banked coals in the fireplace and began the preparation of a simple breakfast for John Jones. Neither she, nor Jupiter, nor John Jones, nor anyone else on the plantation knew that this day was to bring a crisis for all whose lives were so closely intertwined at Liberty Hall.[1]

Jones was up by the time Lizzy reached the kitchen. He too had heard the sound of Jupiter's horn in the slave quarters, and he had slipped out of bed, leaving his young wife, Susannah, and their three-month-old son, Charles Colcock, sleeping quietly. Jones dressed in his hunting clothes, moved down the hall past the rooms of his other children—daughters Betsy and Susan and son John— and descended the wide plantation stairs. Going into his study, he removed from a cabinet an expensive English-made gun. It had been his first, a gift when he was only twelve. "Old Mrs. Goldsmith," his mother had written from Governor Houstoun's home in Savannah, "has made you a present of a handsome silver mounted Gun, which she begs you'll keep for her sake."[2] Over the years he had used it to hunt the ducks that flew into rice fields at dawn and, loading it with buckshot, to hunt the deer that lived in the woods and swamps that surrounded his plantation home.

Making his way toward the kitchen, Jones could see the slave settlement and fires glowing through the mist of the low-country morning. Sixty-two men, women, and children lived in the cabins that lined both sides of a sandy ribbon of a road. Those who were preparing to go to the fields stood outside around fires warming themselves. Here in the open, in communal yards, they spent most of their time when they were not working or sleeping. In earlier years most low-country slaves had lived in dormitories or mud-walled huts, but gradually rude cabins clustered in quarters or settlements such as those at Liberty Hall had become the norm. They provided some privacy and the possibility for the development of some family life, but they were smoky and dark, had little or no furniture, and were poor places to visit and talk. Except when it was raining or unusually cold, the better place to gather in the mornings and evenings was outside around the fires.[3]

For years Jupiter had been the driver on the Jones plantation, and as he stood by the fire warming his old bones, he knew he was the boss, the master's right-hand man. When John Jones had been away in the 1790s tending to business in the state legislature, his letters to his first wife, Elizabeth, had been full of instructions to his driver: "Jupiter, my dear wife, will be obliged to give the Negroes some corn before Saturday." "Tell Jupiter I expect to see great matters done, as I have left everything to himself." Elizabeth had replied: "Jupiter told me he had finished thrashing that stack of rice, but could not tell me how much it would turn out." And John had written: "Do, my dear, speed Old Jupiter on, and tell him if he wishes to drive for me he must task away and let me see a heap of work done when I return, or I never will trust him again."[4]

Over the following years Jupiter had kept the trust of his master and also of the men and women he lived among in the settlement. His position as driver had required a kind of tightrope performance—he had to convince his master that the work of the plantation was proceeding smoothly and efficiently, and he had to demonstrate to the other slaves on the plantation that he was a buffer between them and the master. He used many strategies to walk this narrow line. No strategy, however, was more important than his cultivation within Jones of a sense of dependence. For Jones knew that without a skilled driver, Liberty Hall would be both unprofitable and also difficult to manage.[5]

No one knew the settlement better than Jupiter. Born around 1740, he had come to the old Jones place, nearby Rice Hope plantation, as a young man, and there he had learned not only the skills of survival in the Georgia low country but also the ways of organizing and managing the work of a rice and Sea Island cotton plantation. With him by the fireside was his wife, Silvey, blind and feeble, who had made her way out of their cabin. They had been together many years and had with them in the settlement their sons Jupiter and Hamlet, their daughter Hannah, and their grandsons Little Jupiter, Augustus, and Prince. A few years earlier, before Silvey was blind, John Jones had rented her to his cousin to work in a neighboring plantation kitchen. Jupiter had used all his skills to get her back to Liberty Hall, and finally Jones had consented. "Make Old Jupiter go to Mr. Dowses and bring old Silvey home and set her to work," Jones had written Elizabeth Jones. Later Jones had sent a message to Jupiter: "Tell him that as he has now got his wife I shall expect he will do his best for me."[6]

As Jupiter looked at the others gathered around the fires, he saw many faces that he had known all his life. Old Monday and Sunbury were here, as were March, April, and May, July and September, November and December. They had all been slaves of the first John Jones and of his widow, Mary, and their names reflected practices from an African homeland. Lizzy, who had hurried off to the kitchen, had come to Liberty Hall in 1801 with her mistress Susannah. With her brother Cassius and sister Willoughby, Lizzy had belonged to Susannah only a year when their mistress married John Jones and they had all moved to Liberty Hall. Susannah's brother, John Girardeau, had willed them to his sister on his deathbed in 1800—with Dick, Paul, Sina, Sary, and little Rosetta, together with land and seven cows and calves.[7]

Jupiter could see even more recent arrivals as he looked at others warming themselves before the fires, eating sweet potatoes cooked in fireplace ashes, or some hominy prepared the night before, or johnnycakes cooked on a long clean board before the morning fires. Abram, Ben, and Jim had come three seasons earlier when Jones had bought them from Captain Forester. Flora, Ishmael, and David had come the next season from Mrs. West's place. But Lucy, July, and Sanco, bought the same year, had already been sold off the plantation and had been little more than temporary laborers for a season and pawns to be moved around in the business of buying and selling slaves.[8]

Of all those in the settlement, however, none were more distinctive than Fanny and her son Marcus and her handsome young daughter Elvira. Only a few seasons earlier, they had been living in Africa. Captured and brought to the coast of their native continent, they had endured the terrors of the passage to Savannah and its slave market. Carried to Liberty Hall by Jones, they were beginning the long process of learning the ways of a slave community that had for generations been creating out of bitter toils a distinct African-American culture known as Gullah. Already Marcus and Elvira were learning the Gullah dialect of the low country and its Sea Islands. In the evenings around the fires they could talk of African ways and memories, and, like so many before them, add their part to the folkways and culture of the low country. Fanny, however, was difficult to understand. She spoke one of the languages of Africa, lacked the linguistic agility of the young, and was learning only slowly a kind of Pidgin English. She did not know it yet, but for the next half-century she would bear as one of the burdens of slavery a kind of isolation as she struggled to listen to and speak a foreign language.[9]

Jupiter began to assign tasks. Late March was the time to begin planting provision crops of corn and peas and, as time allowed, for tilling gardens of potatoes and arrowroot, turnips and onions. Later would come the onerous work of rice and cotton fields, but for now each full hand, whether man or woman, received the familiar task of working a quarter of an acre of provisions, while half-hands and quarter-hands were given proportionally less. As Jupiter assigned these tasks, naming the fields and the sections to be worked, he was performing a central task of a driver that had been slowly evolving in the rice-growing region of South Carolina and Georgia. Already by 1805 several generations of slave drivers had played a key role in the struggle between low-country masters and slaves to name the negotiated boundaries of a task. Masters had used the weapons of the powerful—an organized military, the threats of whip, auction block, and gallows, the claims of superiority, and the styles of speech and dress that intimidate. All these they had used to push out the boundaries of a task, to demand as much work from slaves as could be squeezed out of them. Jupiter and other drivers and field hands had used the weapons of the weak—foot-dragging and playing dumb, gossip that threatened the reputations of owners, and secret scorn for the pretensions of masters; and when the work was heavy and needed to get done, some had run away. All these weapons they had used to limit the boundaries of a task and to reduce the work required of a slave.[10]

The quarter-acre task that Jupiter assigned to full hands on this March morning in 1805 was the outcome of this struggle between low-country masters and slaves. John Jones still liked to think that he possessed some discretionary power, that if he wished he could walk down through the morning mists into the settlement and demand a third of an acre for a task. But for Jupiter and those who stood with him, the quarter-acre task had become a right to be guarded and claimed. Indeed, low-country slaves had extended the task beyond the original rice fields to the cultivation of Sea Island cotton and provisions and to other activities. For full hands, when pounding rice, the daily task was seven mortars. When laying fencing, it was one hundred 12-foot poles. And for a pair of sawyers, the weekly task had finally been settled at 600 feet of pine or 780 feet of cypress.[11]

The landscape of Liberty Hall, like that of other low-country plantations, had encouraged this task system that Jupiter managed. On large areas of the plantation the dark waters of swamps quietly and slowly swirled through forests of giant cypress and black gum and thickets of sweet bay and palmetto. These dark waters provided in cleared areas the means for rice production through an elaborate system of dams, gates, and canals. On higher ground, where the hardwoods and pine had been cut and burned, and where Jupiter and his crews had grubbed out the stumps, Sea Island cotton grew. The task system (unlike the spreading gang system of up-country cotton plantations, with its largely sunup-to-sundown hours) meant that once a task was completed, a slave had the remaining hours of the day for working a garden or raising a pig, for fishing in the river or hunting in the swamp.

Already by 1805 the slaves of Liberty County and the surrounding low country had taken advantage of "after task" time to develop a remarkable if limited informal economy of buying and selling. The pigs and chickens, the marsh ponies and horses, the wagons and cows that low-country slaves owned—they were all the result of this task system. The Gullah culture of Jupiter and Lizzy, of Ishmael and David, of Marcus and Elvira, and of all the other descendants from the nations and tribes of Africa who gathered around low-country fires, was built upon this hard-won system and its informal economy.[12]

While Jupiter was assigning tasks for the day, his son Hamlet was at the stable saddling a handsome English horse. John Jones fancied himself a kind of low-country Cavalier, a gentleman after the English fashion. He was, his grandson later wrote, "Very fond of everything English, importing his horses, hounds, gun, watch, dueling pistols, wines, etc." His English hunting horse was a roan, an animal of large size and spirit that cost as much as a healthy young slave. Jones thought just such a horse was needed for a man of his ancestry and status.[13]

His father, Major John Jones of Liberty County, had been a young South Carolina aristocrat when he came to Georgia to make his fortune. He had an indigo plantation on one of the Sea Islands, and with an expanding slave force he had seen nearby Rice Hope become a prosperous plantation. This first John Jones had been in business with his uncle, Miles Brewton of Charleston, one of the wealthiest men in all the British North American colonies. With a Brewton cousin, the first John Jones had owned warehouses and a wharf in Sunbury, the little port for the growing colony south of Savannah. And there had been other Carolina blueblood relatives: Pinckneys and Hugers, Legares and Swintons, Colcocks and Hutsons. To add to his distinction, Major Jones had become a hero of the Revolution. In the battle for Savannah in 1779, when Patriot forces were trying to retake the city from the British, he had led a charge against the Spring Hill battery, and there, wrote a historian of the state, "in the fiercest and most desperate part of the contest, he was struck by a cannon-ball in the breast, and instantly killed."[14]

Hamlet brought the roan to the plantation house. Jones mounted, took his silver-mounted gun, and rode down the plantation avenue that led to the gate and the sandy road that cut through Liberty County on its way from Savannah down the coast to Darien. At the gate he met his two hunting companions, Colonel Daniel Stewart and James Smith. Stewart, famous for his exploits during the Revolution and the Indian wars that had raged of late in central and south Georgia, was the brother of Jones's first wife, Elizabeth. Smith was a wealthy neighbor whose plantation had been raided only a few years earlier by the Creeks whom Stewart and his cavalry had chased south to the marshes of the Altamaha River. The three men were friends and had often hunted together in the surrounding woods and swamps.[15]

If Jones thought himself a kind of Cavalier figure, with his love for English ways and English goods, his two friends were part of a Puritan tradition that had found its way to the Georgia coast and established itself deep in Liberty County soil. Their ancestors had left Dorchester, England, in 1630 for Massachusetts, settling there for five years before moving on to Connecticut, where they had remained for sixty years. In 1695 a colony had left for South Carolina. There beneath great oaks and beside the black waters of the Ashley River, they had laid out their village and built their meetinghouse. As with most good Puritans, they had prospered—in spite of a sickly climate—so that within two generations there had been a need for new land. Commissioners had been sent to Georgia and, after some negotiations, a grant of more than thirty-one thousand acres had been secured. In this way a colony of 350 whites accompanied by their 1,500 slaves had begun in 1752 a southward trek to what would become Liberty County.[16]

These Puritans were the ancestors not only of Jones's hunting companions Stewart and Smith but also of most of the white planting families of the county. They had found the Georgia coast a good place to settle and at last to put down deep roots. With adequate slave labor the rich soils had offered ample opportunity for the cultivation of rice and Sea Island cotton. Yet as God-fearing Calvinists, they had been aware of the seductions of such a wilderness, and they had immediately set about establishing an organized community. They had declared that they had a "greater regard to a compact Settlement and Religious Society than future temporal advantages." "We are sensible," they had written in their Articles of Incorporation, "to the advantages of good order and social agreement, among any people, both for their Civil and Religious Benefit." At the time of the Revolution the patriotism of these Georgia Puritans had been so ardent that after the war their county had been renamed Liberty.[17]

At the center of this Puritan community stood the church. Almost as soon as they had arrived in Georgia, the settlers had built a meetinghouse in the most central location—halfway between Savannah and Darien. They named it Midway Congregational Church, although it was Presbyterian in everything but name. (All but two of their ministers were to be Presbyterians, and commissioners were sent to Presbyterian courts.) In 1792 a permanent church building had been erected. A handsome meetinghouse with cypress siding, it reflected in its elegant simplicity an ethic that would produce in this rural community a remarkable record of governors and senators, of clergymen and professors, doctors and scientists, judges and soldiers.[18]

The three friends began their hunt. Trails were followed that had brought results on earlier occasions. A buck had been killed between Smith's plantation and Rice Hope. Jones and Stewart had killed two large bucks down toward the North Newport River on the William Peacock place. With several other companions they had jumped and killed a doe and two small bucks nearby. Jones had noted in his daybook that with "two Darkies" to beat the brush and flush the deer, a small buck and doe had been killed as they hunted the deep woods on Colonel Stewart's Cedar Hill plantation. They had no hesitation to kill a doe and thought no more about shooting a fawn than they did about having a lamb slaughtered for a stew. On one occasion, two years earlier, Jones, while hunting alone, had killed one fawn and had captured another and brought it back to Liberty Hall as a pet. He had written it all down in his daybook: the dates of the hunts, his hunting companions, and the places they had found and killed their quarry.[19]

Hunting on horseback in these southern woods and swamps gave them several advantages. They could see over low brush, and the deer were not frightened by the sound of the horses moving through the woods. And when a deer was jumped, the hunters could give chase, which was part of the thrill of the sport. At some point on this March morning, they jumped a deer, and Jones on his roan raced after the fleeting animal. The horse hit a hole or perhaps an obstruction it could not leap, and Jones was thrown violently from his saddle. Carried back to Liberty Hall by his companions, he lay in critical condition with internal injuries. A doctor who was summoned immediately bled him to reduce his racing pulse. Later, as Jones grew worse, mustard plaster was applied to his chest to raise a blister and to revive his vital signs. These familiar medical practices were of no help, and on 28 March, John Jones died.[20]

Joseph Jones, John's younger brother, who had been by his dying bedside, summoned Jacob and Sandy, the slave carpenters at Liberty Hall, and instructed them to build a casket. Using cypress cut from the nearby swamp, they completed the long, narrow box. Friends padded it with cotton and lined it with cloth, while grieving family members dressed the battered body and prepared it for its silent home.[21]

After a night's wake, the coffin was placed in a Jersey wagon for its slow ride to the church. Family and friends rode in carriages, and Jupiter and Lizzy and all those from the settlement walked behind. The road they all traveled was sandy and straight as it headed north. William Bartram, the naturalist, had traveled this stretch of road earlier and had described it as "straight, spacious, and kept in excellent repair by the industrious inhabitants." Large "fruitful rice plantations" could be seen on each side of the road, and light groves had been left, said Bartram, "by the virtuous inhabitants, to shade the road, and perfume the sultry air."[22]

As the meetinghouse was approached, its white steeple could be seen in the distance and its tolling bell heard. A congregation had gathered, and waiting on the front steps for the cortege were the pastor, the Reverend Cyrus Gildersleeve, as well as Dr. William McWhir, a family friend, renowned teacher, and Irish Presbyterian preacher. The funeral service was long. Scripture was read, a few hymns sung, and an extended funeral discourse given. While not particularly pious, John Jones had had some religious experience during his life that had convinced him and the congregation that he could be numbered among the saints of Midway as a full communing member. A few years earlier, after receiving communion, he had written a prayer he had tucked away in his daybook:

> O Lord, I humbly thank thee for giving me another opportunity of commemorating my Dear Saviour's dying Love, this 23rd of April. O my Heavenly Father pardon for Christ's sake, what thou saw amiss in me at thy Heavenly Table. O my blessed God evermore feed me with this bread of life, and receive me into that blessed place where there will be no more sorrow and all tears cease, and everlasting Joy forever more.[23]

After the service, the coffin was carried to the waiting cemetery. Already in 1805 the Midway graveyard had received the bodies of many who had succumbed to the fevers and miasmas of a swampy and mosquito-infested land. White monuments to the dead caught the sunlight beneath great oaks with thick, heavy branches reaching down toward the ground. Among the most recently erected monuments was one over the body of Gildersleeve's wife, with an inscription that read in part:

> She, who in Jesus sleeps beneath this tomb,
> Had Rachel's face and Leah's fruitful womb.
> Abigal's wisdom, Lydia's faithful heart,
> And Martha's care, with Mary's better part.[24]

Close by, a grave had been opened toward the central part of the cemetery and into it the casket was lowered. After a brief prayer, the grave was filled—perhaps by Jupiter and a few of the men from Liberty Hall. Joseph Jones ordered a white marble slab to mark the spot and had inscribed upon it

> Sacred to the memory of John Jones Esquire
> He was Born in Sunbury, Georgia November 25, 1772 and departed this life
> the 28th March 1805 aged 32 years 4 months and 3 days.

Midway Congregational Church
(author's collection)

He was a Dutiful son, an affectionate Husband, a Tender Parent, a fond Brother, a Sincere Friend, a Humane Master, a true Respecter of Religion, and a generous Benefactor to the Poor—

> Yes we must follow soon, we'll glad obey
> When a few Suns have Roll'd their cares away
> Tir'd with Vain life we'll close the willing Eye
> 'Tis the great birthright of mankind to die
> Blest be the bark that wafts us to that Shore
> Where death's divided Friends shall part no more.[25]

For Jupiter and Lizzy and those who lived in the settlement at Liberty Hall, the sorrows of "death's divided Friends" were to come before the grave, as they soon faced a dividing of another sort at a slave sale.

2

RICEBORO

Already before the long walk back from Midway to Liberty Hall, there had been, no doubt, talk in the settlement. Lizzy and the others knew only too well that when a master died, trouble was waiting. Lizzy's previous experience was a familiar part of life in the low country for the black men and women who tilled the fields and harvested the crops and who did the cooking and washing at the plantation house. When her owner John Girardeau had died, not only were Lizzy, her brother Cassius, her sister Willoughby, and five others willed to Girardeau's sister Susannah, but other slaves, together with land and livestock, were willed to other relatives. Tom, Fanny, Abram, Solomon, Jain, and Old Flora had gone to sister Elizabeth Maybank, while Girardeau's niece and nephew had received Harry, Nancy, July, Tenah, Clara, Alphonso, and a young child of Nancy's. Girardeau's wife, Elizabeth, had been left, in addition to lands, all twenty-five of Girardeau's "remaining negroes and stock of horses and cattle, sheep and hogs." John Girardeau's death had thus spelled the breakup of the settlement at his Cedar Grove plantation, and if he had been careful not to divide parents and children, he had arbitrarily divided a network of family and friends who had been living and working together.[1]

In the days that followed John Jones's death, the knowledge of such divisions —and even more bitter ones—must have been discussed around evening fires as they were poked and stirred in the settlement at Liberty Hall. What partings would follow their master's death? Would families be divided? Would friends be sold away? Would those who had lived out their lives as John Jones's slaves have to move from familiar places and answer to other, perhaps more difficult, masters? A new, more intense uncertainty about the future must have entered the world of the settlement and no doubt could be felt up and down the little road with its smoky cabins.[2]

In spite of such uncertainties, life followed its familiar patterns at Liberty Hall. Days began with Old Jupiter blowing his conch-shell horn and assigning tasks, and days ended with supper and talk around evening fires. And every morning Lizzy left the settlement and went to the kitchen of the plantation house. There she prepared meals and, with the house servants Adam, Molly, and Brutus, she swept and cleaned and washed when there was time between her labors in the kitchen.[3]

Joseph Jones took over the management of Liberty Hall as the administrator of his brother's estate. His own plantation, the Retreat, was not far away—it had been a part of Rice Hope—and Joseph was in the process of building it into one of the great plantations of the Georgia coast. If his brother John had thought of himself as something of an English gentleman, a southern Cavalier with expensive tastes for imported goods, Joseph had no such illusions. To be sure, he knew himself to be a gentleman, even an aristocrat, but he was all business. His grandson, decades later, remembered him as "a gentleman of large wealth, and a most successful planter. Just, honorable, charitable to the widow and orphan, he was a man of imperious will, of great personal courage, quick in quarrel, impatient of restraint, intolerant of opposition, and of mark in the community." Born a few months after his father had been struck down by the British cannonball to his chest, Joseph had had his own share of sorrows. The year before his brother died, Joseph had lost his wife, Mary Maybank, and had buried her beside three of their four children: Mary Eliza had lived eleven months, Susanna Maria had lived fourteen months, and Martha Eliza had succumbed to the miasmas of the low country after only eleven months. These little ones and their mother lay in the family cemetery that could be seen from his bedroom window at the Retreat. Such great losses had left him with a tender heart toward the "widow and orphan" and for his own surviving child, Joseph, but his was a tenderness set within the austere code of a patriarch. He expected obedience and discipline even as he offered protection and guardianship to Susannah Jones and her fatherless children.[4]

Joseph hired an overseer for Liberty Hall, a Mr. Warnock, a small farmer from the piney woods section of the county, where the soil was poor and the harvests were small. Warnock visited the plantation every few days, and for the first time in his life Jupiter had to work with a stranger, with someone other than a member of the Jones family. Warnock would review with him the assignment of tasks and the schedule of plantation work, and when someone in the settlement was sick, he would prescribe the treatment—concoctions of various sorts from barks and roots gathered in the woods and swamps and from powders and pills purchased in Savannah. But Joseph Jones was not a planter who would leave an overseer completely to his own judgments and ways—especially an overseer from the piney woods. So on a regular basis Joseph visited Liberty Hall, keeping careful notes in a neat hand of all the expenses, and turning his great energy toward the management of his brother's estate.[5]

Yet in spite of the managerial skill of Joseph, the work of Warnock and Jupiter, and the labors of those in the settlement, all was not well at Liberty Hall. By the winter of 1807, Jupiter and Lizzy and the others who lived in the settlement knew that trouble was brewing. The plantation had not yet recovered from a great hurricane that had come sweeping up from the Caribbean in August 1804. A deadly storm, it had sent a wall of water with a tidal surge over a nearby plantation on Moss Island. The Ashmores, friends of the Joneses, had lost three children, one swept from Mrs. Ashmore's arms, and only the parents and one slave had been washed ashore alive on the banks of the South Newport River. Liberty Hall had not been spared as the storm lashed inland, ruining the rice and the cotton and destroying most of the year's labor. Such destruction had meant that provisions were scarce throughout 1805 and even into 1806 and 1807. Joseph Jones had to order expensive supplies—including wagonloads of corn—to be sent to the people in the settlement. In addition, plantation houses and buildings had to be repaired, and the summer home in Sunbury on the coast had to be largely rebuilt by the plantation carpenter Jacob and his apprentice Sandy. All of these expenses, together with the loss of the crops and income in 1805, had put great strains on the estate and on the plantation's ability to sustain itself. Those who ate their suppers in the settlement knew that times were difficult, for they could hear the wagons rumbling down the plantation avenue to unload at the corn house, and the provisions available for their own cook pots were limited. But what was not clearly known in the settlement was the extent of John Jones's indebtedness. While they had been laboring in the fields, he had been speculating in land and slaves.[6]

As the son of a Revolutionary War hero, John Jones had served in the state legislature and then had followed his friend and brother-in-law Colonel Daniel Stewart in the more lucrative office of county sheriff. Both offices had provided him with opportunities to learn a business that was a passion for many Georgians —the buying and selling of land and slaves. A young Liberty County woman later wrote of planters in the county, "Here generally speaking, it really appears as if to 'make cotton to buy Negroes, and buy Negroes to make cotton' is the dearest wish of their hearts, the sole employment of their noblest faculties. But this is human nature!"[7]

Jones had been elected to the legislature in 1796 as a part of a reform effort in response to the great Yazoo fraud that had involved millions of acres of land in the central and western part of the state. What he had seen in the legislature was what he knew from Liberty County: that fortunes could be made from the buying and selling of land.[8] When he was elected sheriff in 1798, his work had been not so much to apprehend criminals as to oversee the auction of property for back taxes, for the settlement of debts, or for the division of estates. In Liberty County, such property included slaves as well as real estate. The Savannah papers carried his advertisements for the auctions. Typical was one from July 1798:

SHERIFF'S SALES
On the first Tuesday in August next will be sold, at Riceboro, between the hours of X and III o'clock, by public outcry,
The following **PROPERTY**, viz.

All that valuable and well known Rice Plantation, or Tract of Land, in the county of Liberty, in three separate tracts. . . .

600 Acres, in the said county of Liberty, in two surveys, lying on Goshen swamp. . . .

That handsome Situation on Colonel's Island where John Mitchel, Sen., Esq. now resides. . . .

Also the following Negroes, viz. Sambo, Saul, Wally, Pegg, Rose, and Jacob; the fellow Jacob is a carpenter, and has been run away upwards of two years, is still out, and will be sold as he runs. . . .

Two Negroes, viz. Nelly, a young wench, and Prince, a small boy, seized and taken under and by virtue of an execution as the property of the Estate of William Bacon.

John Jones, S.L.C.[9]

And so the ads had run, three or four times a year with different real estate and different slaves all listed over the name of John Jones as sheriff of Liberty County.[10]

In the midst of his work as sheriff and his managing of Liberty Hall, Jones had plunged into his own buying and selling of real estate and slaves. During the decade before his death, he had bought all over Liberty County small tracts of several hundred acres and large tracts of several thousands. Some land had been secured from the state through claims of headrights. Other land had been purchased directly from owners. Sometimes, when a parcel was being auctioned at a sheriff's sale, Jones had had a friend purchase it, and then he would buy it from the friend. And he sold land: three large tracts in 1799 to Charles Ash for $2,500, and in 1803 a nineteen hundred–acre plantation to James Heath for $2,800.[11]

Jones had not been so vigorous in his buying and selling of slaves. To be sure, he had bought Abram, Ben, and Jim from Captain Forester; and Lucy, July, and Sanco had been bought and sold within one year; and Fanny and her children Elvira and Marcus had been purchased in the slave market in Savannah. But the settlement at Liberty Hall had been fairly stable, with most of those who lived there going back, like Jupiter, to slave purchases Jones's father had made before the Revolution.

But the stability of the slave community at Liberty Hall had become increasingly vulnerable. To maintain his cavalier ways and to finance his speculations, Jones had borrowed money from other planters and from merchants in Sunbury and Savannah. Security was demanded, and Jones had begun to mortgage, in addition to his lands, those who lived in the settlement. As pressures increased, he had mortgaged not only those men and women he had bought but also those whom he had inherited from his father and mother: Sunbury, October, November, December, May, and April had been mortgaged. Jacob and Sandy, the valuable plantation carpenters, had been mortgaged. Even Old Jupiter and his son Hamlet had been mortgaged. Jones had paid back many of the debts, and the mortgages had been canceled, but it had all been a juggling act that collapsed when he was no longer there to keep all the buying, selling, and borrowing in the air.[12]

By the spring of 1808, Joseph Jones's business acumen was no longer able to keep the creditors away. As more debts became due and as taxes on the estate mounted, it became clear to him that some dramatic action was needed to satisfy the debts, to preserve Liberty Hall, and to provide some security for the young widow and her children. The answer to the crisis was in the settlement—the men, women, and children who daily heard Jupiter blow his conch-shell horn calling them out of their cabins to the work of the plantation.

The village of Riceboro, the county seat, was located on the main road between Savannah and Darien, several miles south of the Midway meetinghouse and just south of the bridge over the North Newport River. Another road left the village and ran west along the edge of the swamps and marshes that marked the headwaters of the North Newport and from there to the sand hills in the interior of the county. These roads provided ready access to the village and along them came wagons and carts, buggies and carriages, and at night, not a few slaves. A wharf had been built on the river's edge, and to it came a variety of ships that sailed the inland waters along the South Carolina and Georgia coast—schooners with their two masts rigged fore-and-aft; square-stern sloops with single sails; and an occasional brig with its square-sail rig—all of them weaving their way slowly up the river. They carried to the village the products of a wider world bought and sold in Savannah—crockery from England, coarse Osnaburg cloth from Germany, tobacco from Virginia, and rum from the West Indies. The ships took with them as they headed back downstream the products of the plantations: barrels of rice, tightly packed bales of cotton, some timber, and when they were available, butter and eggs, smoked hams and cured beef. So the little boro, isolated as it was along the swampy waters of the North Newport, was nevertheless part of an interdependent transatlantic economy that was largely fueled by slaves like Lizzy and Old Jupiter.[13]

The Riceboro Inn accommodated travelers on the stagecoach and those who had business at the little courthouse. Several stores were also here. They sold hardware and cloth, seeds and medicines, lard and candles, and whatever the owners thought might be needed in a hurry on the surrounding plantations. Their products were generally more expensive than what was offered in Savannah, but they had the advantage of being close to their markets and ready when needed.[14]

Of all the products the shopkeepers sold, none invited more attention than their barrels of rum. Like his neighbors, John Jones had bought rum here to give out in the settlement during seasons of hard labor and on special occasions such as Christmas and the Fourth of July. Rum had the advantage, it was believed by planters, of being both a reward for weary laborers and a tonic for their health. The problem was that rum was also an invitation to trouble, to laziness, to dissipated behavior, and, on occasion, to flight. What infuriated planters was the willingness of the village shopkeepers to sell rum directly to slaves.[15]

The boro, as it was called by those who lived nearby, was like a magnet set in the midst of plantations, irresistibly drawing to it the inhabitants of scattered slave settlements. On Saturday afternoons, after tasks were completed, those slaves with passes from their owners could go to the boro to buy a little tobacco for their pipes, to sell a bushel of corn or some eggs, or to trade a shoat for a basket woven from palmetto fronds and sweet grass during evening hours. The boro was a place to visit, and except for church, it was the primary place in the county where slaves from different plantations could gather without arousing too much suspicion. But nighttime visits were another matter. Those who were bold could slip out of the settlements and make their way to the boro for some rum and illicit pleasures. Patrols of armed planters tried to stop them, but they were employed only sporadically, and planters frequently complained of their inefficiency. What was worse, the shopkeepers, travelers, and sailors all too often aided and abetted those who had stolen away—indeed, complained the planters, sometimes joined with them in drinking and carousing—thereby corrupting the slaves and undermining discipline by being too familiar with them.[16]

As a trusted driver, Jupiter went to Riceboro regularly with a pass, sometimes to get the mail and often to buy something needed on the plantation. He was aware that the village was more than simply a place for slaves to sell their goods on a Saturday afternoon or for some to visit under cover of darkness. He had seen the whipping post by the courthouse and heard the cries of those being punished by order of the court. Indeed, his master, John Jones, during his tenure as sheriff had been responsible for seeing that the orders of the court were carried out and that the jailer used the whip as instructed by the judges, so that many a slave bore the long, thick scars of the whipping post.[17]

Jupiter was also inescapably aware that Riceboro was a slave market. The little boro had no grand marketplace for such a business but simply two unremarkable spots that served as the places for the selling and buying of slaves. One was by the bridge, near the wharf, where traders could stand and offer the sons and daughters of Africa for purchase. The other was in front of the courthouse in the sandy yard shaded by live oaks and their long grieving wisps of Spanish moss. Here the sheriff would gather those to be auctioned, and so it was to this spot, under the oaks and before the courthouse, that Old Jupiter and the others from Liberty Hall were brought in April 1808.[18]

Early on the morning of 4 April, Jupiter gathered a few possessions he had packed, and with old Silvey by his side, went out of his cabin on his way to the boro. With them went their sons Jupiter and Hamlet; their daughter Hannah with her son Little Jupiter; Hamlet's wife, Phillis, and her children Augustus and Prince. They were all part of the first group from the settlement to be sold in front of the courthouse. The sale was not scheduled until the next day, but they had to be there early in order to be inspected by prospective buyers. When they arrived in the boro, they were taken to the gaol, where they were to be kept for the night. Planters from throughout the county who were interested in purchasing "more Negroes to raise more cotton and rice" arrived as well. Some knew the Jones slaves already. Others inspected them carefully. Old Jupiter had to watch their inspection and listen to their questions. Were there signs on their backs or buttocks of whippings, indications that they were troublesome to owners? Were they healthy and strong? "Show me your teeth," they were told. "Let's see your feet and hands." "What about your arms and legs?" "Do you have a hernia?" "Any bulge in your belly?" "Woman, are your children wormy?" "How old are you, boy?" "You know how to hoe in a rice field?" "You good at threshing?" "You know how to guide a plow?" "How old are you, Old Daddy?"[19] Some such slave market questions, now swirling around the gray head of Jupiter, were part of the deep and bitter humiliation of slavery. What could he do to protect his family and those who had for so long been under his care? Jupiter who had spent his life seeing that the Jones plantations flourished, who had announced the beginning of each new day with his conch-shell horn, assigning tasks and seeing that they were done, who had been a buffer between master and slave, using his wit to ease the tasks and the burden of the work, was now powerless to protect even his own children and grandchildren from the degradations and terrors of this sandy place before the courthouse. But the bitter experience into which he was now plunging deeply was the common sorrow of the Gullah people, from whose collective voice was to arise the low-country lament:

> I got to weep at Zion's Court House
> I got to weep there fo' myself
> My dear mother can't weep there fo' me
> I got to weep there fo' myself.[20]

The bidding began the next day at ten in the morning. They were to be sold in lots. The first up were Toney, Betty, August, Jack, and Abby. Joseph Bacon, a neighboring planter, made the highest bid of $1,176 for the five of them. Next came Hannah—not the daughter of Jupiter and Silvey but another young Hannah—and her children Molly and Dick. This Hannah also came from one of the oldest of the Joneses' slave families. She had been born at Rice Hope, her children at Liberty Hall. Captain P. H. Wilkins, with an offer of $380, was the highest bidder and left with mother and children for his plantation near Sunbury.[21]

Next came the largest lot, seventeen in all, and among them stood Old Jupiter and Old Silvey, their grandsons Augustus and Prince, the children's mother, Phillis, but not the children's father, Hamlet, or their Uncle Jupiter or Aunt Hannah. Colonel Joseph Law was a surprising early bidder and ended with the highest bid. His plantation was east of Riceboro, downriver from the village, and was not far from Liberty Hall. Next and last came a lot of eight that included the brothers Jupiter and Hamlet, their sister Hannah, her son Little Jupiter, and Sary, who had belonged to the first John Jones. Once again, Colonel Law was the high bidder. While he was a respectable member of the community of Liberty County planters, and a leader of the Midway congregation, no one had expected Colonel Law to be expanding his workforce with a purchase of twenty-five slaves. What Law knew, however, was that the real purchaser, hiding his identity, perhaps to keep the price from going up, was none other than Joseph Jones himself.[22]

During the following days, as others were brought from the settlement to be sold, Joseph bought openly, no longer using his friend as a front. Included among those purchased was Fanny from Africa and many who had long been owned by the Jones family. But at the end of the purchasing, he had an additional surprise: the twenty-five bought by Colonel Law were to be a gift for Susannah Jones and for the children of his deceased brother. A bill of sale was made over to his sister-in-law and the children. As the patriarch of the family, Joseph Jones was their protector, and these purchases of slaves seemed a wise and prudent way to secure their future and to maintain the family status in the community. A new start could now be made at Liberty Hall, freed from the debts of John Jones and under the careful direction and vigorous management of the hardworking Joseph.[23]

In this way, Old Jupiter and his family were returned with the others in their lots to the settlement at Liberty Hall. Lizzy greeted them, for she—together with all those owned personally by Susannah Jones—had not been subject to the debts of John Jones. Fanny's children Marcus and the handsome young Elvira were there as well, for in 1804 John Jones had given them as a gift to his year-old daughter, Susan. But the settlement was almost half-empty. The cabins of those who had been sold away were reminders that a slave community had been divided and that those who remained were but a remnant of those who had lived there. This remnant—the men, women, and children who were reunited in the settlement in April 1808—did not know it at the time, but they were to form the core of a Gullah-speaking African-American community whose lives would be interwoven with the lives of John Jones's children, grandchildren, and great-grandchildren until a mighty army shook the land.[24]

3

SUNBURY

Among those who walked back from Riceboro and down the plantation avenue leading to Liberty Hall in 1808 was Rosetta, eight years old and a motherless child. She had stood with Old Jupiter as a part of the lot of seventeen and had been subjected to the humiliating examinations of buyers and the bidding for slaves in the sandy yard before the courthouse. Now she returned to the settlement that she had known all her life and to the special supervision of Lizzy. As a young child in the settlement, she had known a life relatively free of work. A slave nurse, an old woman, had taken care of the plantation children while the parents went to the fields, and when instructed to do so, she had given them small jobs around the settlement and the plantation yard—sweeping, gathering eggs, and other work familiar to rural children. But now all that was changing. Rosetta was approaching the age when she would be classified as a "half-hand" and expected to begin learning the routine and work of an adult. This eight-year-old, however, was not destined for working the long rows of cotton or for wading in treacherous rice fields—at least not immediately. Rather she was to be trained as a domestic servant, and she was to begin by being the nurse of the two-year-old Charles Colcock Jones and his five-year-old sister, Susan.[1]

With the two older Jones children—fourteen-year-old Betsy and ten-year-old John—in school in Sunbury, Rosetta had the task of keeping an eye on Charles, helping to amuse him and Susan, and, when he napped, brushing the flies and mosquitoes off him. Unlike so many children of planter families, Charles and Susan did not have an Old Momma, a slave woman whose care for white children nurtured in them deep and special affection. Rosetta was much too close in age to Charles and Susan for them ever to think of her as their Old Momma, but Charles at least would always remember her as his nurse, and she no doubt played a role in shaping his early character. Years later, the child of a neighboring planter, remembering his own nurse, insisted that in "the shaping of character in child life, domestics, whether bond or free, have always exercised more influence than is imagined. . . . Children are largely influenced by the character of the servants to whose care they are necessarily and largely entrusted."[2]

Whatever influence Rosetta might have had on Charles and Susan, the landscape and environment of the low country had a role to play in the shaping of their sensibilities and their deep memories. Much of the children's play at Liberty Hall was outside in the yard and in the gardens that surrounded the plantation house. Susannah Jones, in her grief over the loss of her husband, had turned to her flowers and to her kitchen garden with its neat rows of vegetables and herbs. Here for the next two years, during balmy low-country winters and fragrant springs, the children played and grew. Charles would remember beds on each side of the walk where he would "gather flowers and endeavor to catch the thistle birds when they went into the cabbage heads."[3]

Susannah Jones was thirty in 1808 when her brother-in-law Joseph had to save the family from the consequences of her husband's buying and selling. Pale, with blond hair and blue eyes, she would be long remembered as possessing a "calm sorrowful face." Between visits of family and friends, she spent sad days at Liberty Hall and "lonely desolate nights when the hoot of the large owl would come echoing up from the deep swamp below the family mansion," and the barking of the hunters' dogs "swept fearfully around the corners of the house," reminding her of an earlier hunt and its dreadful end.[4]

Such a setting and such a mood made a lasting impression on young Charles. He would remember his mother taking up her guitar, which she suspended from her neck by a blue ribbon. She "would promenade the east piazza in the quiet evenings and play and sometimes sing." On occasion she would be persuaded to play "some lively air" for Charles and Susan and Rosetta, together with other "little servants to dance upon the grass in the yard." And there were other memories: "I recollect," wrote Charles decades later, "our discovering in the flower garden in front of the house a rabbit's soft bed with three or four young ones, and the Negroes presenting us with young summer ducks which would unceremoniously when let go in the balcony pitch down into the yard below and scamper off." Charles was sure, on recollection, that these activities encouraged an early interest in natural history that would follow him all his life. It also no doubt left deeply embedded in his memory an image of home where whites and blacks lived together and where blacks such as Rosetta brought things to whites, looked after them, and cared for their needs.[5]

Liberty Hall, viewed from the perspective of those who lived in the plantation house and walked on its piazza and in its gardens, was lovely in winter and spring, as all the senses were invited to revel in the charms of the low country. But Liberty Hall was hot and dreadfully muggy in the summer and early autumn, when the heat could be seen rising from the tepid waters of rice fields and flooded swamps, and mosquitoes and gnats swarmed in clouds. Planters had learned early that such seasons were deadly for whites, that miasmas, the noxious emanations from the surrounding waters, filled the air with poison and pollution. Africans and their African-American children seemed for some unknown reason to be able to live in the midst of such miasmas without being as vulnerable to the fevers and agues that struck the whites with violent and deadly results.

Hard experience had taught the planters and their families that their best defense was moving away from such a poisoned atmosphere, and so they went in summer and autumn to the sand hills, where tall pines grew and water drained quickly away and did not stand in fetid pools, or they went to the coast, where sea breezes and salt water kept the miasmas and their fevers largely away.[6] For the African Americans such an absence of white supervision allowed space and time for the nurture of their African traditions, and for the development of their distinctive Gullah culture and of strategies for resistance against white control and white culture.

In late May 1808, Susannah Jones and her two youngest children left Liberty Hall, as was the family custom, and went to their summer home on the coast in the little town of Sunbury. With them went Lizzy and Rosetta. Left behind were Old Jupiter and the remnant of those who had once lived in the settlement. They would be largely on their own under Jupiter's supervision for the next five months, with only an occasional visit from Joseph Jones. No overseer was hired to manage the greatly reduced workforce, and their tasks no longer included the raising of rice but focused now on Sea Island cotton and provisions for the plantation.[7]

Sunbury sat on a high bluff a few miles up the Medway River from St. Catherine's Sound. Protected from the open ocean by the Sea Islands to its east, the town caught both the sea breezes blowing across the sound and the tide as it surged upstream daily, changing the Medway from fresh to brackish waters. In the years immediately before the American Revolution and in the years immediately after, Sunbury had been a thriving little port with its customhouse handling a considerable portion of Georgia's trade. William Bartram, the traveling naturalist, described it in 1773 as "beautifully situated on the main," with a harbor "capacious and safe" and "water enough for ships of great burthen." He had been introduced to "one of the principal families, where," he wrote, "I supped and spent the evening in a circle of genteel and polite ladies and gentlemen." Among the gentlemen of Sunbury at the time of Bartram's visit was not only the first John Jones but also his neighbor Lyman Hall, who in 1776 became one of the signers of the Declaration of Independence. Signing with him was his friend Button Gwinnett, who in earlier years had left his plantation home on St. Catherine's Island and crossed the sound to conduct business and talk politics in Sunbury.[8]

By the summer of 1808 Sunbury had lost much of its commercial vigor. To be sure, its customhouse was still busy and its merchants were now seeking, beyond business with local planters, the trade of an expanding settlement in central Georgia. But the quest for health and not commerce was now at the heart of the town's life. The rhythm of the seasons flowed into the rhythm of the town, as summering families swelled its population with their arrival in June and drained it with their departure in early November.[9]

The little town itself was laid out, like its big sister Savannah, in a neat grid with squares and straight streets, and with wharves along the riverfront. The house to which Susannah took her children in 1808 was located on two bay lots that extended to the low-water marks of the river. Here during the Revolution the British had burned the home of the first John Jones, and here his widow, Mary Sharpe, had rebuilt following the death of her second husband, Major Philip Low, in 1785. Like others, Mary Sharpe had moved between her plantation and Sunbury, and her children, John and Joseph and their younger sister Eliza Low, had spent their summers and falls in the Jones house by the Medway. In 1798 the children had buried their mother, after a lingering illness, in the lot behind the house. She had wanted to follow the practice on many plantations of being buried near the home she loved and not in a distant cemetery. It was this house, made sacred by the mother's grave and family memories, that John Jones had ordered repaired and enlarged following the hurricane of 1804.[10]

Susannah and the children were joined in Sunbury by the children's half brother John and half sister Betsy. They had been in school at the Sunbury Academy and had been boarding with the family of the headmaster, Dr. William McWhir. A native of Ireland, McWhir had graduated from Belfast College and been ordained by the presbytery of that staunchly Presbyterian city. Coming to America at the conclusion of the Revolution, he had settled in Alexandria, Virginia, where for ten years he had been the principal of the local academy of which George Washington was a trustee. Frequently a visitor at Mount Vernon, he was said to have "enjoyed the hospitality of that noted mansion." He had come to Sunbury in 1793, had married a wealthy widow, and had bought nearby Springfield plantation. The hurricane of 1804 had swept over Springfield, and McWhir's losses were said to have amounted to $14,000—enough to buy a fine plantation and supply it with a substantial number of slaves. But McWhir had persisted with his academy located in a two-and-a-half-story building not far from the Jones summerhouse. About seventy pupils attended in 1808, and while McWhir was said to be "a terror to all dolts and delinquents," no one else in the county did more to "impress his character and influence upon the generations in which he lived." Among those so impressed were the Jones children. Young Charles, later his student and still later his friend, wrote of him: "He was the most perfectly social man that I have ever known. Warm and sincere in his attachments, it was a real, heartfelt pleasure to him to be in the society of his friends, and to mingle with men of distinction; and his effort was, by cheerfulness of spirit, and ready and easy powers of conversation, to convert the hour or the day, as the case might be, into one of high social and friendly enjoyment. Fond of children, they never escaped his notice."[11]

Joining Susannah and the children at the Sunbury house were Joseph Jones, his new wife, Sarah Anderson, and Joseph's four-year-old son, Joseph Maybank Jones. Sarah had married Joseph in 1806 (McWhir had performed the service) and had eased the loneliness of the Retreat with its cemetery behind the plantation house. The daughter of David and Mary Anderson, one of the wealthiest planting families along the Georgia coast, Sarah had brought with her, as a part of her marriage contract, thirty-eight slaves to work the rice and cotton fields of the Retreat. When she arrived in Sunbury in early June 1808, she and Joseph had already added one son to the cemetery at the Retreat, and she was seven months pregnant with her second child.[12]

Not far away, in another home facing the river and looking out toward St. Catherine's Sound, was Eliza Low Robarts, the half sister of Joseph Jones and of their departed brother John. Twenty-three years old, possessed of a pretty face and a lively spirit, Eliza was already twice widowed. Her second husband had died only the year before and had left her with their two-year-old daughter, Mary Eliza. They had returned from their plantation home near Greensboro, in the interior of the state where they had briefly lived, to Sunbury to be close to family and friends. The widow and her daughter, like Susannah and her children, were under the care and protection of Joseph Jones. He had thus found himself at age twenty-nine the patriarch of three families. He was determined to hold them together through shared affections and his own indomitable resolve to reap rich profits from rice and cotton fields and from the labors of those whom he called "my people."[13]

During the summer of 1808, as was his practice, Joseph Jones left Sunbury every Monday and made the long ride to the Retreat. There in the evenings he visited with his driver Pulaski, discussed with him the operations of the plantation, and checked on the people in the settlement. In July on visiting the settlement he had found one child sick and noted that "several worms came up her throat." He gave her a dose of calomel and the next day some castor oil. But what had infuriated him was his discovery that Delia, a woman who had come to the Retreat as a part of his marriage contract with Sarah Anderson, was quite sick. "The cause of her sickness," her wrote Sarah, "I never could come till this morning when Pulaski informed me that Caesar had just mentioned to him that she had miscarried" in early June, the week after the Jones family had left the Retreat for Sunbury. "The thing made me so mad on account of her concealing it," Joseph wrote, "that I threatened to give her and her mother both a severe flogging, but they both denied knowing any thing about it and if this be correct she may not as yet have miscarried." Because Delia complained of fever and pain, Joseph made Phillis, the plantation nurse, "use the bitter herbs and give her nitre, laudanum, etc." Joseph found it "somewhat perplexing that our young maids lately married should suffer their modesty to get the better of them so far as to never inform us of their unfortunate situation." According to Caesar, "Delia got scared in the woods which was the cause of her situation, but still there appears to be something novel in their tales. She says she fell over the fence going into the field and all this happened before our leaving home." [14]

Joseph's frustration with Delia and her mother, whom he evidently regarded as being in collusion with her daughter, pointed to the difficulty of managing a large plantation from a distant summer retreat. But what infuriated him, and led him to the threat of a severe flogging, were the concealment and the possibility of an infanticide. Owners had the absolute right, Joseph was convinced, to know all the details of a slave's life—even those details that modesty tried to cover. His patriarchalism demanded obedience and threatened a brutal punishment, but Joseph met in Delia and her mother those who knew how to sidestep his flaring anger. They did not directly challenge his authority but turned on Joseph his own patriarchal code—women, after all, were supposed to be modest about such matters. Moreover, they denied knowing anything about the matter and told a story that left Joseph puzzled by its novelty and by their assertion of a simple accident. Joseph's nephew Charles later wrote that whites "live and die in the midst of Negroes and know comparatively little of their real character. They are one thing before the whites and another before their own color. Deception towards the former is characteristic of them, whether bond or free, throughout the whole U.S." However deceptive they might have seemed to Joseph, Delia and her mother had successfully avoided a flogging by puzzling him and by utilizing patriarchal expectations in regard to women. In this way they cleverly bought themselves time until he departed for Sunbury. [15]

Returning to the coast, Joseph entered into the social life of Sunbury. The

Joneses and Robartses, together with the McWhirs and other friends, were spending a happy summer together by the waters of the Medway. In August, Sarah gave birth to a little girl and named her Mary after her two grandmothers. The baby brought delight to the little circle of family and friends in Sunbury and was no doubt the subject of much attention from her brother and cousins. As their parents hoped, the children formed over the coming years deep and affectionate relationships with one another.

Lizzy and Rosetta lived in simple quarters behind Susannah Jones's summer home. While their lives continued to be filled with work as they saw after the needs of the white family, Sunbury was nevertheless a welcome change from Liberty Hall. Lizzy had grown up at nearby Cedar Grove plantation, and best of all, her husband, Robinson, was living in Sunbury. A servant of Eliza Robarts, Robinson had made, since his return from Greensboro, long trips from Sunbury to Liberty Hall on Saturday afternoons during the winter and spring to see his wife and son Lymus. He would often take with him a bag of soiled clothes and whatever he could bring for his family—some extra rice or corn, a chicken that had been raised, or a rabbit that had been caught in a snare. On Sunday nights he would return to Sunbury and carry with him his clean clothes and the memory of a night and day with his family.[16]

These Saturday-night visits were a prominent part of slave life in the low country, as all over the county little groups of men carrying passes from their owners walked the sandy roads or rode their marsh ponies to visit their "wife house" and families. Like the task system and the slave's right to some personal possessions, the right to marry someone from a different plantation had been secured only through several generations of struggle between owners and the owned in the low country. Many slaves, of course, like Jupiter and Silvey, married someone from within their own settlement and lived together. But many others, like Lizzy and Robinson, had asserted their right to marry someone "off the place." Such an assertion was a bold act of personal freedom. Both the freedom and the burden that went with it shaped much of family life in the settlements and had its impact on the manner in which Lizzy and Robinson related to each other and raised their children. However successfully they were able to manage such arrangements, the summer reunions in Sunbury must have been a better time for them as it offered the opportunity to live together and eased the burdens and the tensions of their weeklong separations.[17]

During the summer and fall, when they were all together in Sunbury, the domestic servants of Susannah Jones and Eliza Robarts had time together not only while they were busy cooking and cleaning and seeing after the needs of

the white families but also after their work was done. With them were the domestic servants of the Joseph Jones family. They too lived in cabins behind the
Jones summer home. Most prominent among them were Jack and Sylvia. Both
had come with Sarah Anderson as a part of her marriage contract with Joseph
Jones, and both were close to her as personal servants. Sylvia was twenty-three
in 1808 and the mother of one-year-old Cuffee. When Mary Jones was born in
August, Sylvia became her nurse, and over time she became Mary's Momma
and then her genuinely loved Old Momma. Because Sylvia was no doubt still
nursing Cuffee, she may have helped to nurse Mary as well. Sylvia apparently developed affection for this little white baby who had been committed to her care,
even as she followed the etiquette of slavery and called her "Miss Mary." Yet however much she might appear as a "Mammy" figure to whites—as a woman who
suckled and reared with affection white children—her affection for Mary was set
within Sylvia's larger affections, and as "Miss Mary" later learned to her surprise,
within Sylvia's larger commitments to own children and her own freedom.[18]

Jack was eighteen and recently married to Lizett, but already in the summer
of 1808 he was showing himself to be a rising leader in the slave community. He
was learning to bridge two worlds—the world of white planters and the world
of Gullah-speaking slaves. He was still learning how to negotiate between those
two worlds, but he had already won the confidence of his white mistress with his
faithful work, good manners, and cheerful spirit. Over time he moved deep into
the white world and probed the cultural sources of its power—its ways of seeing the world, its understanding of nature, time, and space, and its ideas about
human society and the ways human societies should be ordered. By moving deep
into this white world—which was in his lifetime demonstrating its power not
only in Liberty County but also around the globe—Jack came to understand
much about that white world's style of life, its tone and character, and its moral
and aesthetic spirit. He came to believe that in order to resist successfully the
power of whites, in order for slaves to make their way toward freedom, they must
acquire the cultural sources of white power. Over time Jack came to embody a
bitter irony—the belief that black slaves had to become acculturated, that they
had to internalize at a deep level the culture of their white oppressors in order
to resist successfully that oppression.[19]

But Jack was not only learning how to probe and understand the white world;
he was also learning the traditions of an African and African-American world.
And Liberty County, and perhaps especially Sunbury, with its surrounding Sea
Islands, was rich with the traditions of his people. In particular, he was learning
folktales that disguised strategies for resistance. In time, Jack himself became a
master storyteller, entertaining blacks and whites with the adventures of clever

rabbits and foxes, of hungry alligators and buzzards, and of the ways the weak fooled the strong and escaped their powerful clutches.[20]

Summertime in Sunbury meant visits for both whites and blacks to nearby Colonel's Island. Marshes and tidal creeks surrounded its sandy bluffs, and a narrow causeway connected it to the mainland. The causeway, repaired every fall by slaves requisitioned by the county, provided easy access but was also vulnerable to gales and the occasional hurricane that swept over the land. To the north of the island flowed the Medway, and Sunbury could be seen from the northwest end of the island across the intervening marsh and tidal creeks. To the south flowed the North Newport, its waters having cut a crescent into the island at a place settlers named Half Moon. Here the waters ran to forty feet deep and allowed ships of substantial size easy access to the trade of the island.[21]

The island had been settled before the Revolution by a number of families from Bermuda, and for a while it had been known as Bermuda Island. But powerful fevers had struck them, leaving many dead, and the remainder had returned home, leaving behind a Bermuda grass that grew thick in the sandy soil of the island and on the bluff at Sunbury. Other settlers had followed, and among them was the first John Jones, who had an indigo plantation near Half Moon. Here Eliza Low Robarts had been born the day after her father, Philip Low, died in 1785. Scattered across this old Jones and Low plantation, and throughout the island in 1808, were sunken spaces where the indigo vats had been located. The vats, used to ferment the indigo to produce its blue dye, had sent forth a putrid stench that attracted hordes of flies and had made the island an unpleasant and unhealthy place to live. But by 1808 such conditions were gone. The indigo market had collapsed after the Revolution, with the end of British markets and subsidies, and Sea Island cotton had largely taken its place. Visitors in the summer of 1808 found an island noted for its beauty, its healthy climate, and the comfortable summer cottages of white planters. Because a number of colonels from the Revolution and Indian Wars had homes on the island, it had come to be known by the name of Colonel's Island.[22]

The Jones and Robarts families had a number of friends who summered on the island, but the plantation of Major Andrew Maybank was the primary place for their visits. His wife, Elizabeth, was the sister of Susannah Girardeau Jones, and the major's sister Mary had been Joseph's first wife. (It was she who lay with three of their children in the little cemetery behind the Retreat plantation house.) So it was not surprising that the families from Sunbury would go regularly to the Maybank plantation and bring Andrew's and Elizabeth's nephews and nieces to visit them. The Maybanks had no children themselves and regarded young

Charles and Susan and their cousins Joseph Maybank Jones and little newborn Mary Jones with special affection.[23]

Susannah Jones called the Maybanks' summer home the Hut, for it was a simple and unpretentious place. Located close to the causeway, the Hut stood on a sandy rise and looked out across the marsh and tidal creeks toward the mainland. In the distance could be seen the McWhirs' Springfield plantation, and above the marsh grass the masts of sailing ships could be seen moving slowly along as they sailed up the Medway to Sunbury and then returned to St. Catherine's Sound. Live oaks shaded the house from the summer sun, and while the surf could be heard only in the distance on days when it was up, the sea breezes blew faithfully and made it a delightful spot in the summer.[24]

The plantation settlement was located some distance from the Hut. When Lizzy and Rosetta accompanied Susannah Jones and the children to the island, they would meet in the settlement some whom Lizzy had known growing up at Cedar Grove plantation. John Girardeau, in dividing his slaves, had willed Tom, Fanny, Abram, Solomon, Jain, and Old Florah to Elizabeth Maybank at the same time he had willed Lizzy and her brother Cassius to Susannah. And there were others whose connections went back even farther, to John and Hannah Girardeau, the parents of Susannah, John, and Elizabeth. Among these was Clarissa, who was about Lizzy's age. Because she had grown up on the John Girardeau plantation and because she lived to be a very old woman, she was to become a link with earlier generations and a bearer of genealogical information for slave and free. She was one of the first slaves to have an openly acknowledged surname, Clarissa Girardeau, and by that name, different from that of later owners, she showed that she had a history, a memory, and an identity independent of those owners.[25]

Those who lived in the settlement with Clarissa farmed the plantation and raised its Sea Island cotton. During their after-task time, they were able to fish the tidal creeks, cast nets for shrimp, and, when cool weather returned in the fall, gather oysters from the muddy banks of the marsh. By supplementing their diet with these rich sources of protein, they helped make the island a more healthful place, where a Gullah culture could flourish. For summer visitors to the island, white and black, the seafood was a welcome and eagerly anticipated change in menu.[26]

The visits to Colonel's Island, as well as the daily visiting in Sunbury, shaped for slave and free much of the days and nights during the summer and long autumn by the coast. For the slaves, the visits frequently meant more grueling work as additional cooking and cleaning were required for white guests, but it also gave opportunities for being with servants from other households. For whites, the visit-

Dawn over the Medway marshes, looking toward Colonel's Island
(photograph by Van Martin)

ing was at the center of a social life that included for the men sailing, fishing, and hunting and for the women sewing and other domestic activities. On Sundays the little Congregational Church in the town drew some of the inhabitants, while some, slave and free, traveled to Midway.[27]

The summer of 1809 followed much this same pattern. Of special note that summer was the birth of Cato, the second son of Lizzy and Robinson. A strong and healthy child, he was named for the Roman statesman who had taught a love of courage, honesty, and simple living. The Liberty County Cato and the four-year-old Charles Colcock Jones were destined to have their lives closely intertwined in a complex relationship of mutual dependence between a master and a slave whose life would reflect many of the virtues of his ancient namesake.[28]

During that same summer, Jack and Lizett had a little girl. They named her Phoebe. Her name, like Cato's, reached back to Rome, to a classical world in which Phoebe was goddess of the moon. But Phoebe's name also had roots in Africa, where Phiba or Phibbi meant Friday. Like Cudjo, which meant Monday, and Cuffee, which was an African male name for Friday, Phoebe's name pointed to the African practice of day-naming. As such it indicated her father's ability to move between two worlds and two traditions that were converging in the African Americans of the low country. Over the coming years those two traditions warred with each other deep within Phoebe, making her both a valuable and a troublesome slave for her owners. She was to become the personal servant of Mary Jones, the daughter of Joseph and Sarah, and enter a relationship with her even more complex than the one between Cato and Charles. For as the two women grew up—Phoebe a slave, Mary her mistress—their lives were bound together not only in mutual dependence but also in the fierce struggle of two strong-willed women as they encountered one another around questions of power, affection, and independence.[29]

In late spring of 1810, Susannah Jones became ill, and she and her young children moved in May to their Sunbury home. Medical attention was more readily available in the town, and friends were near at hand to offer help. Susannah, however, grew steadily worse, apparently from some debilitating fever. On 10 May she made her will, "being weak of body, but of perfect mind." "I give and bequeath," she wrote, "unto my dearly beloved Son Charles Colcock Jones the following Negroes with their future issue (to wit) Rosetta and Lymus to him and to his heirs forever." Since her daughter Susan had received two slaves from her father, John Jones, Susannah was being sure that the division of her property was fair. "The remainder of my Negroes," she wrote, "I give and bequeath to my two children Charles Colcock Jones and Susanna Mary Jones share and share alike each to receive their respective proportion at the age of twenty one years or day of marriage, which may first happen."[30]

All during June, Susannah grew weaker. The doctor cut her arm with a lancet and bled her, and the children coming into the room to kiss their mother could see the bowl of blood on the nearby dresser. She died the first day of July 1810, and "this first sight of death" for her young son Charles made a deep and lasting impression upon him. Susannah was buried at Midway beside her husband, and her marble tombstone became another reflector of the sunlight amid the shadows of the cemetery's oaks. She had made Joseph Jones the executor of her estate, and on her deathbed she committed Charles and Susan to the care of their aunt Eliza Low Robarts.[31]

Elizabeth Maybank took Susan and Charles to the island, where they stayed for a few months at the Hut. In November 1810 Joseph Jones came for them and carried the newly orphaned children to their Aunt Eliza's plantation outside of Greensboro. Betsy and John stayed in Sunbury with Dr. McWhir at his academy.[32]

In the 1790s a road had been built from Sunbury to the interior of the state with the village of Greensboro in Greene County as it terminus. The rich farmland of middle Georgia was being settled, and merchants from Sunbury were eager to establish posts along the road in order to channel trade through Sunbury. Among those who had business connections in Greensboro was Eliza Robarts's second husband, James Robarts. He had purchased a plantation near the village, and it was to this plantation that Joseph Jones took Charles and Susan. With them went Lizzy and Rosetta. Here they all lived for the next three years. The twenty-five-year-old Eliza Robarts, ever cheerful and attractive, married for a third time shortly after their arrival. Her new husband, David Robarts, a cousin of her second husband, was a cotton factor and commission merchant in Greensboro. He added another strand to the bewildering web of relationships that was being woven among all the Jones aunts and uncles, cousins, and half brothers and sisters.[33]

The Robarts, with the children, moved between the plantation and Greensboro. Charles and Susan began school, and as a six-year-old Charles gave his "first public address" in the little village. During their second year in Greensboro, Charles fell while running and broke a rib on a rock. An abscess formed and injured his lung in a way that was to trouble him all his life. Twelve-year-old Rosetta was his nurse, staying with him from morning until night during his recovery. She had her own ideas about what was needed for his recovery and she would "conceal bread and bacon in her dress and give it to him to eat at night, contrary to the Dr.'s orders."[34] But Rosetta was not entirely preoccupied by her care for young Charles. She was beginning to notice Sam, a young man who was a domestic servant in the Robarts household and who was proving himself to be a favorite of blacks and whites alike.

For Lizzy, being in Greensboro meant that she was able to be with Robinson, who had returned to Greensboro with the Robartses. In late May 1811 the couple had their third son and named him Cassius after Lizzy's brother. It was not unusual for African Americans to name a son after an uncle, especially one on the mother's side, but Cassius represented, like his brother Cato, another classical

Roman name, and in a strange way he too came to embody—at least for his white owners—some of the characteristics of his ancient namesake. The Roman Cassius had led the plot to assassinate Julius Caesar, and Shakespeare had marked him as a duplicitous figure having "a lean and hungry look." The low-country Cassius would always be in the shadow of his older brother Cato, and while Cato was known for his reliability, Cassius came to be suspect, a person who required close watching not only by whites but also by those in the settlements who came to admire him.[35]

The twice-widowed Eliza Robarts became thrice widowed in September 1813. Perhaps after David Robarts's death she had had enough of marrying and burying husbands. Or perhaps prospective husbands did not want to run the risk of marrying a woman, however attractive and well connected, who already had buried three husbands before her twenty-eighth birthday. At any rate, she never married again. She now had three children of her own—Joseph had been born in 1811 and Louisa in September 1813, a few days before her father's death. With these young children and her eight-year-old Mary she once again returned to Liberty County, to her home in Sunbury, and to the protection of her brother Joseph. Her nephew Charles and niece Susan went with her. They went to their Uncle Joseph's Retreat plantation, where they at last found some stability and a place they might learn to call home. Returning with them were Rosetta, Lizzy and Robinson and their children, and all the Robarts slaves.[36]

4

THE RETREAT

The Retreat plantation lay south and east of Riceboro and ran from sandy ground to the swampy banks of the South Newport River. Purchased by the first John Jones before the Revolution, its plantation house, little more than a lodge, had been used as a retreat, a kind of getaway from nearby Rice Hope. Following his mother's death in 1798, Joseph Jones had turned the Retreat into his winter residence. He had torn down the little retreat house, had built in its place his own fine home, and had incorporated into the plantation the lands of Rice Hope. In this way the old plantation house at Rice Hope had quickly fallen into disuse and into the rapid decay that came to all coastal buildings not rigorously maintained.[1]

Encompassing more than 3,100 acres, the Retreat had rich cotton and rice lands and included in its unimproved sections parts of both Bulltown and Rice Hope swamps. With the labors of his growing slave population and with his own inexhaustible energy, Joseph had turned the Retreat into the primary source of his wealth. But he was more than a successful planter, a skilled manager of slaves, and a knowledgeable agriculturist—he was also a careful and shrewd capitalist. Like other wealthy planters in the low country, he invested where he saw opportunity. And what he saw in Liberty County and up and down the Georgia coast during the early decades of the nineteenth century were planters in need of cash. So he lent money to his neighbors and to all who could mortgage slaves or land. He functioned as a kind of informal banker before there was an extensive banking system, and the interest and the foreclosures furnished a steady income that supplemented the wealth that flowed from the Retreat. These financial resources provided the economic foundation for his role as the young patriarch and guardian of his extended family.[2]

Late in the fall of 1813, Joseph traveled to Greensboro to bring Charles and Susan home to the Retreat. With them came Rosetta and Lizzy, with Lymus,

Cato, and Cassius. They came back down the Sunbury Road until they reached Midway, with its meetinghouse and cemetery. There they most likely stopped and walked in the cemetery. Beside the graves of their parents, Charles and Susan would have been able to see the fresh earth that covered the grave of their brother John.[3] He had been a quiet boy who had never seemed close to the family after his father's death, and now at age fifteen he had been buried beside his mother, father, and stepmother under the Midway oaks. Later a tombstone would be erected over his grave with a simple inscription from the Gospel of John:

> For God so loved the world, that he
> Gave his only begotten Son, that
> Whosoever believed in him, should
> Not perish, but have everlasting life.[4]

The travelers turned south on the Savannah-Darien road. Several miles south of Riceboro, Joseph led them off the public highway into an avenue of oaks that ran northeast and provided the initial approach to the Retreat plantation house. The heavy limbs of the oaks reached across the sandy avenue toward one another as if to enclose into Joseph's world all who came beneath them. Coming out from under the oaks, the travelers entered an open area. Going through a gate, they could see roads leading off the avenue in straight lines to cotton and rice fields, neatly dividing the fields and making easy passage for heavy-laden ox carts. They passed through another gate and came to a lawn where sheep grazed. At the far end of the lawn stood the plantation house surrounded by its own fence that enclosed the yard and the house. Joseph had laid out the whole approach to the house, and it was intended to reveal not only his wealth but also his way of seeing the world and giving order to it. The oaks through which he had cut the avenue and the gates he had erected all served as thresholds to pass as they entered the Retreat and the patriarchy of its owner.[5]

The two-and-a-half-story plantation house faced south, was built high off the ground, and was supported by white tabby columns. This familiar low-country style, allowing for a free flow of air and an opportunity to catch any breeze, was thought to be healthier than a house built low on the ground, where the miasmas from the swamps and rice fields might more easily settle. Its height and character also announced, no less than the avenue leading to it, that Joseph was a wealthy planter, a person of authority to be respected and obeyed.[6]

A broad stairway led up to a piazza that stretched across the front and provided, with an equally broad piazza on the back, a popular place for sitting and visiting. A wide hallway, with its polished heart-of-pine floor, cut through the center of the house from the front door to the back, with only the stairs to the upper floors blocking part of the way. At the front entrance, on each side of the hallway, were parlors. One, more spacious and handsomely furnished, was often called simply "the drawing room." Both rooms had brick fireplaces and marble jams. Off from these parlors were wings, smaller rooms—including Joseph's plantation office— with their own slanting roofs. A large dining room held a handsome table long enough for many to be seated and served. Other rooms divided the house into spacious accommodations for many occupants. Garrets on the top half-floor had dormer widows looking out toward the avenue and space for a quiet study or get- away. Various outbuildings, including the kitchen and the cabins for domestic servants, were scattered around the backyard. Beyond them, in an unobstructed line from the back of the house, was the family cemetery.[7]

The horses stopped before the gate to the yard. The household, hearing their approach, had gathered to greet the travelers. Sarah Jones, the mistress of the Retreat, was here with her year-old baby, Hannah Sharp. Standing beside her mother was Mary Jones, now five years old, with her eleven-year-old stepbrother, Joseph Maybank Jones. Every year since her marriage to Joseph, Sarah had given birth to a child. David had been born in 1807 and buried in the Retreat ceme- tery three months later. Mary had been born the next year. Then had come "a fine babe (a girl) ½ after 12 o'clock" in November 1809. "The little spark took leave of this transitory life in three hours after its birth," wrote her father, and was added to the growing number in the cemetery. Susannah, named after her par- ents' recently departed sister-in-law, Susannah Girardeau Jones, had been born on "Saturday night 8 o'clock on the 2nd February 1811." She had "died in Sunbury on the 8th of October 1812 aged one year eight months and six days." Hannah Sharp had been born two months later on "Friday 18th December 1812 4 o'clock p.m." When the travelers arrived at the Retreat in late 1813, Sarah was once again pregnant. Weakened by one pregnancy after another, she must have been able to provide those in her womb only limited nourishment even as her sorrows in- creased with each new burial. Her sad trips to the cemetery at the Retreat evi- dently nurtured her sympathies for those who suffered, and she became known and long remembered for "her unvarying kindness to the poor and needy, which to their dying day embalmed her memory in their hearts."[8]

Standing behind Sarah and the children were the household servants. Sylvia was here, for it was her custom to greet all who came to the front gate. And Jack was here as well. With Sylvia, he was responsible for the running of the house- hold. She had oversight of the kitchen and the preparation of food, in addition to special responsibilities as the Momma of young Mary and little Hannah. Jack served as the butler and majordomo at the Retreat, giving instructions to the other domestic servants. Living with him in the cabin behind the plantation house was the four-year-old Phoebe. During her few remaining years of child-hood, she was to have as playmates at the Retreat young Cato and Cassius, who were now arriving from Greensboro.[9]

When Lizzy and Rosetta were led to their quarters in the settlement, they found many they knew. Following Susannah Jones's death, Joseph, acting as the executor of her estate, had sold Liberty Hall and most of its furniture and had brought to the Retreat all those who still lived in its settlement. Old Jupiter and his wife, Silvey, were gone, buried in the slave cemetery at Rice Hope, but their sons Jupiter and Hamlet were here. Hamlet's wife, Phillis, had died, and Ham-let had taken as his new wife the handsome young Elvira, who had been born in Africa. Their first child, Syphax, was only an infant when Lizzy and Rosetta came to the Retreat in 1813. He later learned from his mother and his grandmother Fanny stories of Africa and their distant homeland. And from his father, Ham-let, he learned about an African-American, specifically Gullah, tradition that reached back through his grandfather Jupiter and his grandmother Silvey to a time before the Revolution. This tradition was still evolving, and Syphax became a part of its future as African Americans were creating out of many languages and cultures, both African and European, a distinct low-country culture. Syphax learned from this African-American tradition the skills of an important trade and strategies for survival and resistance in the land that was to be his home.[10]

The setting of the Retreat—its fields and barns, its smokehouses and clanking cotton gin, its woods, swamps, and riverbank—invited exploration by the eight-year-old Charles. For the next six years, when he was not in school in Sunbury or visiting on Colonel's Island, the Retreat was his home and its landscape a part of his orphaned heart helping to shape his deepest longings for home. Here he would learn to ride horseback, and, like other planters' sons, learn to hunt and fish. While the waters of the South Newport were too broad and swift for a young boy in a boat, the winter swamps and rice fields provided a safe place to mas-ter the handling of a little flat bottom bateau or one of the dugout canoes of the low country. Bright winter days could be spent quietly paddling a canoe through Bulltown swamp, listening to its sounds and watching for a mink to run along a log, or for an otter to swim quickly away, or for a startled deer to leap from a bushy hammock. As he grew older, he was able to hunt the mallards—or En-glish ducks, as he called them—that came into the rice fields at dawn, or to wait at dusk for wood ducks as they flew to roosting places in the swamp. But Charles never became an avid hunter. He grew to be a fine horseman, and he enjoyed long hikes in later life, but he was to become more of a naturalist, an outdoors-man, and a lover of nature than a sportsman. Not that he objected to shooting ducks or deer—far from it, for throughout his life he continued to hunt occasionally. He saw, after all, too many pigs butchered and too many cows slaughtered as a routine part of plantation life to be sentimental about such matters. But he never relished hunting so much as the quiet of the winter woods and the sights and sounds and fragrances of a low-country spring. So during these formative years, when he was home at the Retreat, he was developing a deep love for nature, for its beauty and its mystery, as he explored the landscape of the low country.[11]

Of course the landscape of Liberty County and the Retreat was not composed of nature undisturbed by human activity or human habitation. And while Charles was learning about the landscape of his home, he was also learning about its human activity and those who lived on the land. He was especially close to his Uncle Joseph, sometimes calling him "Father." Joseph, it was later said, "ever sustained to him the relation of a father," and for Joseph's "influence and protection and kindness he was accorded the obedience, respect and affection of a son."[12]

In the evenings Charles could hear his uncle meeting with Pulaski, his driver, to discuss the day's work and the plans for the next day. The two men were the same age and had been boys together at Rice Hope, and Pulaski had been from the first the driver at the Retreat. Named after the Polish count killed fighting the British at Savannah, Pulaski led the men and women from the Retreat settlement as they cleared the land and planted it with cotton, rice, and provisions.[13]

Most dramatic in its impact on the landscape of the Retreat and on the character of its human habitation had been the establishment of rice as a staple crop of the low country. A heavy and bulky commodity, rice had encouraged the development of large plantations throughout the coastal region of South Carolina and Georgia and had played a major role in the emergence of Charleston and Savannah as urban centers capable of handling the processing and transportation of the rice. Unlike the tobacco-growing plantations of the Chesapeake region, the plantations of the low country had high starting costs and required substantial numbers of slaves to begin rice production. The task of turning the Retreat into a rice-producing plantation had thus required many slaves to live in its settlement, and the transformation of the low-country landscape into rice fields had been central to the work of Pulaski and those whom he managed.[14]

The first task for Pulaski and his teams when they had begun their work at the Retreat had been to clear swampland of its virgin timber. Both the Bulltown and the Rice Hope swamps were tributaries of the South Newport, and the soil beneath their slow-moving waters was a mixture of sand, clay, and thick vegetable matter which gave it a very dark color and the name "blue clay." Deeply buried beneath its surface were stumps of cedar and oak, gum and cypress, all supporting in the rich soil a luxuriant vegetation. Great stands of cypress, sweet and black gum, the water tupelo, and the splendid magnolia grandiflora sent their roots deep into the miry clay. Beneath the tall trees in a thick undergrowth were the palmetto and the laurel, the sweet bay and the vines of smilax and briars of various sorts. All of this had to be cleared acre by acre. First a dam had to be built to hold back the water and a ditch dug to let it run off when needed. Then the undergrowth had to be cleared with hoes and mattocks and the trees cut with crosscut saws and axes. Oxen were used to pull the tree trunks and debris into great piles to be burned, and then the ashes had to be scattered to add their richness to the fertility of the soil. Once the clearing was done and the dams and ditches constructed and floodgates properly located, a system was in place for the regular flooding and draining of the rice fields. The dams held back the waters of the inland swamps until needed, then the gates were opened and other dams held the water in the rice fields until it was time to drain them.[15]

This was the system at the Retreat, built by those who lived in its settlement under the supervision of Pulaski, and it required not only constant work to maintain but also grueling work to utilize. In particular, during the steamy months of the summer, the fields had to be drained and the weeds removed, using a broad hoe as each full hand did his or her daily quarter-acre task. This system of rice production in inland swamps was widely used in the coastal sections of Liberty County in 1813, but a new system that utilized the regular rise and fall of tidal rivers had already come to dominate other areas of the low country. In Liberty County, young Cato, Cassius, and Syphax were part of the generation who were to build new dams, canals, and floodgates, this time along riverbanks, to grow the rice of white planters.[16]

Charles watched the work of the plantation and saw the comings and goings of those who lived in the settlement. They were not only shaping through their labors the swamps and fields of the Retreat, but they were also creating with their very bodies and their activities an image of the landscape he called home. They would be—with his Uncle Joseph and Aunt Sarah, his sister Susan and cousins Joseph and Mary—inseparable from his images and experiences of the Retreat and his understanding of what it meant to be at home in its world. Of course he and his sister and cousins were not the only young ones who saw the comings and goings of those who lived in the settlement, nor was he the only young one on the plantation during these years who was exploring its fields and swamps and learning about its landscape. In the settlement Cato and Cassius, not yet old enough to be put to work, were beginning their own process of looking and seeing and interpreting life at the Retreat. And in the yard behind the plantation house, four-year-old Phoebe was beginning to develop her own understanding of what it meant to be black, and what it meant to be white, and what it meant to be the daughter of Jack, the majordomo on a low-country plantation.

Following the Christmas holidays, 1813, Charles and Susan left the Retreat for Sunbury and for Dr. McWhir's academy. They were beginning a period of studying in Sunbury and visiting among various relatives, with the Retreat as their home base and an anchor in their lives.[17]

When they arrived in Sunbury, their Aunt Eliza was there with her children, but Sister Betsy was out on Colonel's Island. She had married in their absence, at age seventeen, and she and her husband, William Maxwell, were living at Orange Grove Plantation at Yellow Bluff on a site that overlooked St. Catherine's Sound. Their home was to become a second home for Charles and Susan, and in time the young couple became another set of "kind relatives" who would love and nurture the orphaned brother and sister.[18]

As students of William McWhir, Charles and Susan had a teacher with high standards who pushed his students to think clearly, read widely, and speak and write persuasively. While he was himself a student of Greek and Latin, and while he hired teachers proficient in the classical languages, he had reservations about making a study of the "dead languages" the center of an educational enterprise in a young republic. This meant that Charles and Susan received what Mary Jones would later call "the rudiments of an excellent English education." In addition to the study of mathematics and the natural sciences, recitations from famous speeches and literature, public addresses, and written essays formed much of the heart of the educational process in Sunbury.[19]

A classmate of Charles's, T. B. Smith, kept his essays written as a young teenager at Sunbury, and they reveal the questions that McWhir had his students address in compositions:

Which is the most beneficial to his country, a warrior or a statesman?
Which has the most influence over the mind of man, music or eloquence?
Are theatres beneficial to a city?
Can misfortune without the concurrence of vice ruin our happiness?
Would it be beneficial for the United States to abolish slavery?
Are the bad effects of war counter-balanced by the good?
Could not the youth of the present time be more beneficially employed than at
    the study of the dead languages?

The questions were intended to be provocative and to engage the students in issues of polity and economics, ethics, and aesthetics. McWhir required his students to set their responses in the context of a debate, to address the positions of an opponent, and to utilize the disciplines of rhetoric, which was understood to be the art of persuasion, in order to make a convincing case.[20]

It is not known how Charles answered question five, "Would it be beneficial for the United States to abolish slavery?" Did he think, when he wrote his essay, of Lizzy and Rosetta, of Old Jupiter and those who had been at Liberty Hall, or of Jack and Sylvia and Pulaski and all those at the Retreat? Whatever Charles thought or wrote, his classmate's essay reflected Charles's own coming struggle with the question.

"Slavery," wrote young Smith, "is one of the most inhuman though at the same time the most beneficial things that ever was introduced into the United States, but more especially the Southern part." "Liberty," Smith insisted, "is a right inherent in all mankind, though without the assistance of African slaves, where would be our commerce?" He granted "his opponents" that "it is against all the feelings of humanity and the principles of independence to deprive our fellow men of that treasure which is their birthright. I must allow that it is a right belonging to man at his birth. Yet Gentlemen, if it is to the interest of the community, surely, it must be beneficial to the Union." And so went his argument, acknowledging slavery to be an inhuman institution, against all the great principles of the republic, but now established and necessary for the happiness, unity, and prosperity of its white citizens.[21]

Such arguments were fundamental to the white world of Liberty County and to the ethos of those who governed its black slaves. Charles grew up hearing these arguments refined and expanded in classrooms and parlors before they were presented to a wider world. And while he was hearing the arguments, he was also learning day by day about the realities of power that the arguments sought to cover and justify—that whites ruled blacks and would not tolerate any threat to their rule or authority. As he breathed deeply the air of the low country, as he came to understand this place as his home, he was also internalizing such arguments as they did their work of shaping the ways he saw the world around him. To be sure, he later resisted mightily the power of these arguments by calling on a religious tradition and alternative vision of human life. But Charles would never escape the arguments or the dispositions induced by them. His sense of what was reasonable, of what was practical, of what was humane and moral was always to find its way home to Liberty County and to its social arrangements. In this way Charles was to face in the years ahead a struggle with a history that was broader than his own and more powerful than he realized. And he was to encounter in this struggle others who were also growing up in Liberty County and who were also breathing deeply the air of the low country—but they were breathing its air as it mingled with the fires of the settlements and with the sweat of hard labor. Cato and Cassius and Phoebe and the other sons and daughters of the settlements were to have their own more bitter struggle with the history of this place and with the arguments that sought to conceal the harsh realities of a land they too called home. And in a way that Charles would never fully under-stand, their struggle was to be not only over the history of the low country but also over its destiny. For in the settlements a future was being imagined that was different from anything that had been seen before in Liberty County. That imag-ining was largely hidden from the eyes and ears of whites, but during Charles's second year at the Sunbury Academy, he and other low-country whites caught a surprising glimpse of what that imagining might look like.

In January 1815, Admiral Sir George Cockburn, who in a daring raid had put to the torch public buildings in Washington the previous August, ordered the British Royal Colonial Marines to land on Cumberland Island to the south of Liberty County. Cockburn did not know of Andrew Jackson's defeat of the British at New Orleans, nor did he know that the United States and Great Britain had a few weeks earlier signed a peace agreement ending the War of 1812. What he did know when he sent the Royal Marines ashore was that the isolated planta-tions of the Georgia coast offered easy pickings for the British navy. What made the invasion so startling for white planters was another British admiral's offer to free all slaves who came on board British vessels and his promise to send them to British colonies in North America and the West Indies. With Royal Marines soon on nearby St. Simons Island, Cockburn ordered his commanders to "bring back with them such negroes as may be willing to join our standard."[22]

Meanwhile, in Liberty County, the operation of the British fleet could be ob-served from Sunbury and Colonel's Island. Charles and his classmates could see the "smoke of merchantmen, captured, robbed, and burnt" by the British, rising from St. Catherine's Sound and the waters south. Local defense was organized, largely under the direction of the now General Daniel Stewart. Joseph Jones was elected captain of the militia, the Liberty County Independent Troop, and led this cavalry south to Darien to face the Royal Marines should they attempt to take the town. Jupiter, the son of Old Jupiter from Liberty Hall, went with him as his body servant.[23]

On the islands the marines were spreading the news that freedom awaited all who wished to leave slavery and board the British ships. At Cannon's Point plan-tation on St. Simons, the British offer was received with some skepticism. The plantation owner John Couper had a reputation for treating his slaves kindly and made his appeal for them to stay. But more persuasive were the warnings of the driver Tom, "a devout Mohammedan from the village of Silla on the Niger in the Foolah nation," who was "held in awe by his fellow slaves." He had been a slave in the British West Indies, and he warned that life was much better on St. Simons than in the cane fields of Jamaica or Barbados. Half of the Couper slaves who were headed to the ships turned around and remained, while sixty took their chances for freedom with the British.[24]

Roswell King, Sr., the Yankee manager of the large Pierce Butler holdings on St. Simons and the Altamaha River, wrote to Butler in Philadelphia of his attempts to persuade his slaves to reject the British offer:

> I tried to reason with some of the most sensible of the Negroes not to be so foolish and deluded as to leave their comfortable homes and go into a strange country where they would be separated, and probably not half live the year out. I found none of the negroes insolent to me, they appeared sorry, solemn, and often crying, they appeared to be infatuated to a degree of madness. While endeavouring to reason them out of their folly, some said they must follow their daughters, others their wives. I found my reasoning had no effect on a set of stupid negroes, half intoxicated with liquor and nothing to do but think their happy days had come. Five old negroes went off that had no work to do only for themselves for these four to fifteen years past. Many others started but were obliged to return finding they were not able to walk to headquarters (Frederica) about 7 miles. Many went off and left their children, others carried off children from their parents and all relations, some left their wives and others their husbands.[25]

In spite of Roswell King's appeal, 138 Butler slaves went over to the British to be settled in Nova Scotia. King, who was well known as a skilled and successful manager, was furious over the decision of so many to seek their freedom. From his perspective they had been treated kindly and had shown a gross betrayal and deep ingratitude by choosing the British offer of freedom. He could explain it only by their "madness" and "folly," by their being "stupid negroes, half intoxicated with liquor." But in the midst of all his rage and ranting, he indicated that he had some awareness of what was happening when he noted they "think their happy day has come."[26]

The flight of slaves to the British was a clear warning to the white planters of the low country that their slaves might envision a different future for themselves than one of continued servitude. Young Charles would remember what happened in 1815, as would his future neighbor and friend Roswell King, Jr. Such a memory would be in great tension with Charles's emerging view of home. If the Royal Marines had come to the Retreat, what would have happened? Would Lizzy and Rosetta, Jack and Sylvia, Hamlet and Elvira, and all the others who made up such an important part of his home—would they have accepted the offer of freedom and abandon their white owners?

Of course there were other signs besides the arrival of the British that those who lived in the settlements were not content with their place in the low-country landscape. Some signs, such as running away, were clear for all who had eyes to see. But in Liberty County there were signs that were not so visible to white eyes, that were camouflaged within the familiar landscape of the low country, and that pointed to a daily struggle for greater independence and a different future. Those signs were embedded in the settlements themselves and in the distinct community and culture being created by the African Americans of the low country.

5

CARLAWTER

When Joseph Jones moved the men, women, and children from the settlement at Liberty Hall into the settlement at the Retreat, he had solved the immediate problem of what to do with them after the sale of his brother's plantation. They had simply become a part of those who cleared the ground, plowed the fields, and harvested the crops at the Retreat. The fruits of their labors, mixed with those from Pulaski's teams, provided for the maintenance of his nephew Charles and niece Susan.[1] The arrangement worked reasonably well for Joseph as the children's guardian, but it was not a very precise financial settlement of his sister-in-law's estate, and Joseph liked to be precise in such matters. The situation was further complicated with the return of Eliza Robarts to Liberty County. As her brother and protector, how was he best to manage her slaves and financial affairs? To address these problems, Joseph decided to purchase a plantation whose character and size would make for an easier management of both the children's and his sister's slaves and finances. The arrival of the British fleet off the coast of Georgia, and Joseph's military responsibilities as captain of the Liberty Independent Troop, delayed him for several years, but in November 1816 he purchased the first of three tracts of lands for Eliza, Charles, and Susan.

Carlawter contained 355 acres and lay on the south bank of the North Newport River, about a mile downstream from Riceboro. Its previous owners had given the tract its name, a clever combination, they no doubt thought, of two family names—Carter and Law. The tract was L-shaped, with one leg running south from the riverbank and the other running east. A settlement was on the place, but no plantation house. On 26 November 1816 Joseph Jones paid $2,000 for the tract—an indication that this was good land—and deeded one half to his sister Eliza and one half to Charles and Susan. Two weeks later he bought the neighboring Cooper tract for $1,000 and also deeded half to Eliza and half to

Charles and Susan. This 399½-acre tract ran straight south from the riverbank and bordered the eastern leg of Carlawter. It had neither plantation house nor settlement, but it did contain good bottomland by the river and rich cotton land in its southern section. Between Carlawter and Cooper, in the empty part of the Carlawter L, lay the 202-acre Lambright tract that was also known as Montevideo for a gentle rise above the river. Joseph had to negotiate for several years before he was successful in securing this tract, but in February 1819 he paid $1,900 and once again deeded half to his sister and half to his nephew and niece. The tract contained no settlement, but it did have rich soil, and on its gentle rise there was a grand site for a future plantation house.[2]

By skillfully combining these three tracts, Joseph created a plantation of 956½ acres capable of producing fine crops of Sea Island cotton, rice, and provisions. In the years ahead, the plantation came to be known simply as Montevideo, but the individual tracts of Carlawter, Lambright, and Cooper retained their names as designated areas within the plantation. Of particular significance for the whole plantation, for its physical and social landscape, was a river swamp with huge live oaks, cypresses, and sweet gums. The swamp stretched along the entire river-front of the plantation and sent a wide arm up a slough that separated Carlawter from Montevideo. This swampy arm would provide an ideal location for rice production and, in its drained upper sections, for cotton fields. It also served as a physical divider between the two tracts and as a reminder of the gulf between those who lived in the settlement at Carlawter and those who were to live in the plantation house that one day would be built at Montevideo.[3]

Joseph did not wait until he had completed the purchases of the three tracts before he moved the people to Carlawter. He put the young carpenter Sandy to work repairing the houses at the settlement. When all was in order, Joseph ordered the oxcarts loaded, and the slaves of Charles and Susan were sent out from the Retreat to join the slaves of Eliza Robarts at their new home by the waters of the North Newport.[4]

Jupiter, the oldest son of Old Jupiter from Liberty Hall, followed in his father's footsteps and was made the driver. He was already fifty-seven when he arrived at Carlawter in 1817, well on his way to becoming the Old Jupiter of a new generation. Because he had no sons, his younger brother Hamlet was his right-hand man and was waiting in the wings for his turn as driver. At the time of the move to Carlawter, Hamlet was fifty-two and Elvira was in her mid-twenties. They brought with them not only their four-year-old Syphax but also a little girl, their daughter Peggy, born in 1815. Old Jupiter of Liberty Hall had clearly been successful in passing on to his sons the skills and prestige of the driver's position.[5]

The move to Carlawter meant another reunion for Lizzy and Robinson. He had gone to Sunbury with the Robartses when Lizzy had gone to the Retreat, and he had had to make the long trips on Saturdays to his "wife house." Sometime during this period of weekday separations, Robinson had been struck with smallpox. He evidently had been quickly isolated, and the contagion had not been spread widely in the community, but he had been left with pockmarks that disfigured his face and an immunity that was to make him a valuable nurse when the disease again struck the county.[6]

At the time Lizzy and Robinson were united at Carlawter, they were expecting their fifth child. Lymus and Cato had been born at Liberty Hall, Cassius in Greensboro, and their three-year-old daughter Sina at the Retreat. Shortly after their move to Carlawter, their son Porter was born. Another healthy and strong child, he was destined, like his brothers Cato and Cassius, to make his own distinctive mark within the Gullah-speaking community of Liberty County.[7]

For Rosetta, the move to Carlawter meant an end to her work as a domestic servant and the beginning of her work as a field hand. But it also meant more opportunities to see young Sam, whom she had gotten to know in Greensboro. Because he was a domestic servant of Eliza Robarts's, quickly establishing himself in a position similar to Jack's at the Retreat, he lived not at Carlawter but in Sunbury during the summer and fall and at the Retreat during the winter and spring. Nevertheless, there were opportunities for them to see each other as he came to visit among the Robarts slaves, and in a short time they were married. Their first child, Lucy, was born in 1820. She was to grow up watching her parents interact with whites and to learn from them ways to move between two worlds.[8]

If the move to Carlawter meant reunions and closer contacts for some, it meant separations for others. The move was, after all, part of an ongoing process of shifting black men, women, and children around as white owners sought to utilize in the most efficient manner their labor force and to accommodate their own particular circumstances. African Americans utilized their own strategies to resist the moves that separated them from family and friends and from familiar places that they called home, but their strategies, however skillfully wrought, were the strategies of the oppressed and not of the powerful. Separations were consequently a bitter part of their lives, and however stable a plantation or a region, the possibilities and all too frequently the realities of separations loomed ever before them.[9]

Among those separated at the time of the removal from the Retreat to Carlawter were Willoughby and Tony. Willoughby, who was Lizzy's sister, went with their children Annette, Cate, and Tom to Carlawter and Tony remained at the Retreat. To be sure, the Retreat was not far from Carlawter, but the separation was real and Saturday nights were short. Fanny, who had been born in Africa, also stayed at the Retreat when her children and grandchildren went off to Carlawter. Because Elvira and her brother Marcus were probably the only ones on the plantation who could speak with their mother in her native tongue, her loneliness must have increased when they went to Carlawter and she was left to struggle with the strange language of the settlement.[10]

These reunions and divisions occasioned by the removal to Carlawter created additional networks of families and friends that transcended plantation boundaries and extended out in many directions. Such networks were common in the low country and grew broader and thicker as the years passed. The African-American population in Liberty County, in contrast to the rising cotton belt in the interior, had a certain stability that was rooted in the geography of the region and in the social character and arrangements of the whites. Most of the buying and selling and moving of slaves, such as the removal from the Retreat to Carlawter, took place within a relatively small area. The distances made it possible for those moved about to remain in relationships with one another. The distances also made it possible for the African Americans of Liberty County to develop a sense of locality, of being attached to a specific place that was larger than the boundaries of one plantation. Kinship and place thus became deeply associated, with one reinforcing the identity of the other. So in an ironic way, planters' arbitrary shuffling and moving around of their slaves within a limited geographical area helped over time to broaden and strengthen an identifiable slave community with its own history and its own traditions. Through their commitments to one another, African Americans were able, as they were moved about, to extend and maintain ties of kinship. The trauma and pain of separations remained, and some separations were distant and permanent, but African Americans were able to create in Liberty County a community of remarkable cohesion as kinship lines, running from plantation to plantation, overlapped in dense networks of relationships.[11]

When Lizzy and Robinson were united at Carlawter, its settlement became their family's home. Here they raised their children, and the children came to associate the settlement with their parents and with those who lived around them and who helped to shape their earlier years. In many ways Carlawter became in time a little village with its own social structure. It had its own leaders and followers, its own manners and habits, and its growing traditions and lengthening memories. The settlement's life, of course, was set within wider worlds and its ways were influenced by other neighboring settlements and the developing Gullah culture of the low country. But Carlawter came to have its own distinct character shaped by the personalities and histories of those who lived there and by its relationship to the powerful world of whites which surrounded the settlement and was a constant threat to it.[12]

Cato was seven and Cassius not yet five when they moved with their parents, older brother Lymus, and little sister Sina into their cabin at Carlawter. The new settlement was much smaller than the one they had grown to know at the Retreat, and it was even more isolated from the world of whites. They would see Joseph Jones on his regular visits during the winter and spring, and in the summers when he came up from Sunbury to visit with Pulaski at the Retreat. But when he was at Carlawter, Joseph mainly conferred with Jupiter, reviewed the work of the plantation, and checked on the health of the people in the settlement. On occasion the brothers saw young Charles, who would come with his uncle for a visit. But because there was no plantation house at Carlawter, and because Jupiter did most of the managing of the plantation, Cato and Cassius were free from the constant watch and influence of whites. This isolation was perhaps more influential in shaping the character of Cassius, for Cato could remember time spent with whites in Greensboro, as well as at the Retreat, and he became more skilled than his younger brother in negotiating the dangers of a white world.

Whatever their future relationship with the white world, Cato and Cassius were a good age at the time of their move to Carlawter to begin learning its landscape and that of its neighboring tracts. They found that the main road to the settlement was little more than an extended avenue that ran east from Riceboro to Colonel Law's plantation. Across the road from Carlawter was the backside, the northernmost section, of Liberty Hall, where Cato had been born. Nathaniel Varnedoe, a young and prudent man of Huguenot descent, was in the process of turning the old plantation once again into a prosperous one. Cato and Cassius could not wander freely over to Liberty Hall, since whites had strict rules about slaves—even young ones—leaving and visiting plantations. But at their age, with their isolation and the light work that was expected of them for a few short years, they had opportunity to explore the Carlawter, Cooper, and Lambright tracts.[13]

The riverbank must have held special attraction for them, with its swamps offering tempting places to explore. Here there were places to fish and to hide and to look for the alligators that liked to lie in the sun on a warm winter's day or that could be heard in early spring roaring their challenges and invitations. The broad slough that separated Carlawter from Montevideo was a particularly good place to spot the gators, and generations of young slaves living at Carlawter were warned not to get caught by those that lay concealed along a muddy bank.[14]

The dark, cypress-stained water of the North Newport also must have held its own fascination for the young slaves as it flowed freely toward the coast and unknown places. Both Cato and Cassius came to know the river well—its moods and character and even its taste as it changed with the seasons and fluctuated with the tides and the phases of the moon.[15] By the time it reached Carlawter, the North Newport had left behind its narrow banks and was spreading out, providing for the brothers a broad horizon and a sense of change and movement that stood in contrast to the scenes of the settlement and its encompassing fields. From the edge of the swamp they could watch ships from far-off places sail slowly up the river to Riceboro, and they could see them sail back down with the tide and disappear beyond a distant bend. And they could watch black fishermen going up and down the river in their canoes and hear stories of those who used little riverboats to slip away to some other plantation or some secret meeting or even some hiding place for runaways. With such scenes and stories, the river and all that floated upon it must have played a role in forming the imagination of the brothers and in shaping the ways they saw and understood the world and their possibilities in it.[16]

Away from the river, Cato and Cassius could discover a network of trails that crisscrossed the land and plantation boundaries. The previous occupants of the settlement (who had been moved or sold away) had created some of the trails that traversed Carlawter, and the new occupants were creating others. Often only hard-to-find paths, they formed an alternative system to the straight roads and plantation gates laid out by whites. Just as the avenue leading to the Retreat revealed Joseph Jones's ideas of order and a world governed by a patriarch, so the trails at Carlawter and neighboring plantations pointed toward the ways slaves saw the world and were shaping it for their own ends. What they wanted were not straight roads, easy for horsemen to patrol or for wagons to traverse, but shortcuts and winding paths that followed the terrain. Some trails led to the river or to distant fields; others crossed fences and provided back ways to neighboring plantations or to the grog shops in Riceboro. Some must have led to secret meeting places in the woods or to a gathering spot in a swamp where a stolen pig could be roasted or a religious service held. Planters knew some of the trails—they, after all, were frequently walking and riding the land checking on crops or hunting. But they knew that there were other trails, largely hidden from them, that provided escape routes for runaways and the means for dangerous communications from one plantation to the next. And so in times of unrest, when runaways were more numerous or cases of arson were reported, whites worried about these trails and the secret world of the slaves they represented, and sought to control their use with stringent laws and patrols of night-riding horsemen.[17]

If these winding trails through the woods and swamps of Liberty County were primary arteries for the life of its Gullah community, nearby Lambert plantation

functioned for decades as its heart. Of all the neighboring plantations that played
a role in shaping the character of Carlawter, none was more important than Lambert. By the time Cato and Cassius moved with their parents to Carlawter in 1817,
Lambert had established itself as a remarkable center of African-American life.
Lambert was located only a few miles from Riceboro off the Savannah-Darien
road, and its influence extended throughout the county and in time reached
deep into the life of those who lived at Carlawter.

John Lambert, a South Carolinian who had been deeply touched by the fires
of the First Great Awakening and the preaching of the Anglican itinerate George
Whitefield, had established the plantation in 1784.[18] A benevolent impulse had
been nurtured by Lambert's religious experience, and on his death in 1786 he left
his plantation in trust for philanthropic purposes. "My will and desire," he wrote,

> is that my estate be kept together and the yearly income applied to any reli-
> gious or good purpose at the discretion of my executors and trustees, for the
> relief of the poor and distressed, or wherever any good or pious purpose may
> be answered in the church of Midway, or any other that may be erected, for
> the carrying on and assisting the intended academy in Sunbury, or promoting
> of any public schools or Seminary of learning; the bringing up of orphans, and
> the like.[19]

Thirty-one slaves were included in his estate, and over the coming years their
labors and the labors of their children and grandchildren provided funds for the
education of poor white children at the Sunbury Academy, for support of white
widows and orphans, and for other benevolent purposes selected by the trustees.
The growing settlement at Lambert (its population more than doubled between
1787 and 1837) was marked by its independence and isolation from white control. An overseer was responsible to the trustees, and on occasion lived on the
plantation, but most years the overseer would visit only two or three times a week
during the winter and spring and less frequently during the summer and fall. In
spite of this isolation, the trustees kept careful financial records that served as
windows for them into the life of the settlement at Lambert and, one might add,
into many other settlements, including the one at Carlawter.[20]

The leading figures at Lambert were not the drivers but a succession of black
preachers who were intermediaries between the settlement and the trustees. The
first had been Mingo, a free man who lived on the nearby Peter Winn plantation.
When John Lambert had first come to Liberty County, he had employed Mingo
to visit his plantation and preach for his people. Mingo had come every week, and
after Lambert's death, the trustees had continued to provide Mingo a small stipend for "coming to the estate and giving the Negroes religious instruction." The

plantation in this way became "a regular place of meeting for the Negroes of the neighborhood who were allowed the privilege of attending." Mingo had received the endorsement of Midway Church, and he had begun to hold meetings across the road from the church near a spring at the edge of a swamp. "Booths of bushes and wide seats, and a raised platform" were built, and here Mingo preached on Sundays between the morning and afternoon services at the church.[21]

Associated with Mingo was Jack Salturs. He had belonged to a series of owners, but had lived for a number of years at Lambert. When Mingo died in 1810, the Lambert trustees purchased Jack for $153, stipulating that the "said Jack have his freedom as soon as his labors together with any monies he may advance, shall amount to that sum with interest." He died in 1813, never having gained his freedom, and the trustees paid his wife the money owed for Jack's work among the people. During Jack's time, a building had been constructed on the plantation for religious service. For a few years after Jack's death, the overseer taught Brown's Catechism to the gathered slaves on Sunday afternoons. But the real successor to Jack was Sharper. During the years that Cato and Cassius were growing up at Carlawter, Sharper became the undisputed leader of the African-American community in Liberty County. For two critical decades, he was the primary interpreter of Christian faith and life to the slaves of the county as he labored "with apostolic zeal" in the settlements of the county. Through his work he became a key player in building a black church and African-American Christianity in Liberty County.[22]

Among those who lived at Lambert were midwives and healers. In the early years of the plantation, Maria attended women in labor and was paid by the trustees for her work. By 1815 Old Lydia had become not only the plantation's midwife but also the nurse for many who were sick in the neighborhood. She was joined by Pluto, who could heal snakebite, and by Scipio, who could cut infected gums with a lancet and pull aching teeth with pliers. They were all practicing a medicine that was a mixture of traditions brought from Africa and skills learned in the low country. Local barks and herbs were used and mixtures of various roots and berries concocted to make syrups and tonics. Those treatments that showed some signs of success were remembered and handed on to become a part of a folk pharmacology respected by blacks and whites alike.[23]

At the edges of this practice of healing and beneath its observations and empiricism lay traditions of magic and a belief in the supernatural. Alongside and sometimes in competition with Mingo, Jack, and Sharper were secret practices and a world of spirits. Root doctors and sorcerers, wizards and witches were looked upon with respect and fear throughout the settlements of the low country. Witches could change their shape at night, slip into cabins, and ride on people's

chests so that the victims awoke feeling not only terrified but as if they were
smothering. "Plat-eye" ghosts and headless spirits came up from the swamps and
marshes on moonless nights to roam the countryside and hide in the dark corners of the settlements. Black cat ashes and bones, graveyard dirt and hair, nail
clippings and bloodroots provided ingredients for powerful powders and potions
that could be used to harm an enemy. Protection from such forces came from
conjure bags worn around the neck and from frizzled chickens kept in the yard to
dig up dangerous charms planted by those who held a grudge against you. These
beliefs and their accompanying practices were part of a secret world at Lambert
and the other isolated settlements of the low country. And they were also part
of an arsenal of strategies to be used against whites when black rage boiled and
the desire for revenge or justice could no longer be suppressed but came rushing to the surface. As such, this secret world was a part of a sacred cosmos, of an
interior landscape of the mind and imagination, which Cato and Cassius were
discovering during their early years at Carlawter.[24]

Whites knew of this secret world of root doctors and charms as they knew
of the existence of the trails that crisscrossed the county. But they knew of this
world largely from a distance, as one would view a faraway cosmos, and they regarded the distance as a part of a cultural divide that separated them from their
slaves.[25] Over and over whites would use this perceived distance between their
world and the world of the settlements as an ideological tool, as a way to justify
keeping blacks in their place. Slaves, it was insisted, were an uncivilized, unenlightened, superstitious people incapable of governing themselves and living as
a free people. But whites were also fearful that if African Americans crossed the
cultural divide, that if they entered deeply into the world of whites, they would
gain access to the power of whites that was rooted in European culture. Consequently, when an open attempt was made in Sunbury in 1816 to teach slaves
to read, it had been quickly suppressed by the state. Reading and writing, after
all, not only provided a dangerous means of communication for slaves but also
opened the way to another culture, to the interior landscape of the mind and
imagination of whites, and provided some access to important sources of white
power. So whites wanted it both ways in regard to what they perceived as this
cultural distance—they were dismissive of the secret world of blacks as primitive
and uncivilized, and they were also fierce in their opposition to blacks' entering
too deeply into the world of whites. In a peculiar way, Charles Jones was to find
himself in the years ahead deeply conflicted by the contradictions of this white
ideology. He would want to transform the world of the settlements with its sacred
cosmos; he would want Cato and Cassius and all the others in the settlements to
be converted at a deep inner level to his way of understanding God, the world,

and human life. But he would also want them to remain in their place in the settlements so that they would be like him in every way except for freedom.[26]

Whatever whites thought of the sacred cosmos of the settlements, it provided slaves important means of resistance. The creation at Lambert and other settlements of an alternative African-American culture, with its own worldview and coherence, was itself a major act of resistance to the hegemony of white European culture. This resistance said that the world of whites, with its straight roads leading to plantation houses and patriarchy, was not the only world or the only way of understanding the landscapes of Liberty County. Trails provided avenues of escape, swamps offered the promise of hiding places, and the imagination of the settlements included the possibility of freedom from white oppression.[27]

Running away was a direct challenge to the world of whites and to their control of the settlements, and stories of runaways, communicated from plantation to plantation, was inescapably part of the world of Carlawter. Sometimes a slave would simply take what whites came to call "French leave." A husband would not return on Sunday from his visit to his "wife house" at another plantation but would remain a few extra days and accept the punishment of a whipping or the denial of some privilege such as free time on Saturday afternoons. More serious were breaks for freedom by runaways who had no intention of ever coming back to their settlements if they could help it. Such breaks were especially common when family members were separated by some distance from one another and running away represented a chance to reunite with family members. Those who ran away were not attempting to overthrow the system of slavery, supported as it was with the overwhelming power of whites in the United States. Rather, flight was a way of escaping the immediate and personal oppression of the system, of making life more bearable for the one who ran—and also for those who were left behind, by putting some limits on white behavior. During the years Cato and Cassius were growing up, they must have heard of many such cases. There was Charles, who had been raised by the Irvine family near Sunbury. When he was sold to a planter in the middle of the state, he "absconded" with a "sorrel horse, saddle and bridle" and evidently headed back for Liberty County. His wife, who had been sold to Savannah, also "absconded," and she was presumed to be hiding with her husband somewhere in the county. Almost a year later their owners were still looking for them and offering rewards in the Savannah papers.[28]

Others had simply wanted to get away, to be on their own and not under the immediate control of whites. The year before Cato and Cassius moved to Carlawter, Joe, who had belonged to the Ward family in Sunbury, was sold to a family in Savannah. A "carpenter by trade, of a yellowish complection," he had made his break from Savannah with Simon, "a young man, about twenty-five years old," who had a "downcast look when spoken to." With them had gone two young women. The four of them had made their way to Ossabaw Island and had been hiding for months somewhere on the south end of the island not far from Sunbury. Joe was finally captured, but again "made his escape." A $125 reward was offered to anyone who would return them all to Savannah. Charles Jones later remembered that it was "no uncommon thing for camps of runaways to be found in different localities in the county, and parties of men called out to break them up and capture them."[29]

Stories of such runaways traveled the trails of the county, were whispered in Riceboro and Sunbury, and were told openly on the long walks back to the settlements after church meetings. Like the stories of the slaves who dared to leave with the British in 1815, the stories of runaways became a part of the memory of a people that was taught in the evenings around fires to the children of the settlements. These stories were not abstractions about human freedom but stories of real people, of Charles, Joe, Simon, and the young women who risked much for freedom. They were stories of courage and sometimes of reckless desperation. Few of the stories had happy conclusions. Many ended with brutal punishments. But they were all stories that helped to shape the imagination of those who lived in the settlements, which helped to provide a vision of an alternative world and a different future. By the time Cato and Cassius moved to Carlawter in 1817, there were generations of such stories to be told, reaching back to a time at Liberty Hall and Rice Hope and to the days before Old Jupiter had been brought from South Carolina. The memory of these and other such stories provided a powerful defense against the attempts of whites to control the imagination of African Americans and to limit their vision of the future to the harsh realities of the present. In the years ahead, Charles Jones learned to his surprise the strength of these memories and how tenaciously they could be utilized to resist white claims.

6

SAVANNAH

In the late spring of 1817, shortly after the move of Cato and Cassius to the settlement at Carlawter, the wind began to blow from the northeast, bringing with it days of rainy weather and thunderstorms. Water in the rivers, creeks, and swamps of Liberty County began to rise, overflowing their banks; rice fields flooded; and, wherever there was a low place, pools of stagnating water began to pulse and quiver with the larvae of mosquitoes. By early June the air was filled with great buzzing clouds of mature mosquitoes as they arose from breeding places to torment all creatures that offered exposed skin and a possible meal of blood.[1]

Among the several species of mosquitoes that filled the low country air that summer were members of the genus *Anopheles*. From the compact head of the female emerged thick spikes of hair, two antennae, and powerful mandibles. Its six legs were bristled and jointed, its wings light and strong, and its back arched for attack. Hunting at night, from dusk to dawn, the female *Anopheles* punctured the skin of victims with her long proboscis and sucked blood until her engorged body turned red. When she bit a person infected with the protozoan species *Plasmodium falciparum*, the *Anopheles* became infected herself with the malaria parasite. When she bit another person, that person became infected. The parasite entered the person's liver, grew, spread into the blood, and invaded the red blood cells.[2]

Of course, those living in Liberty County during the summer of 1817 knew nothing of the *Anopheles* mosquito's role in spreading malaria. They thought that "miasmas," the noxious vapors of summer swamps and rice fields, were somehow the cause of what they called "the bilious remitting" or "country fever" or "marsh fever" or, often, simply "climate fever." What they did know was that Africans and their descendants were more resistant to the fevers, that summer and early

fall was a "sickly season" when no white dared to stay overnight on a rice plantation or near a swamp, and that during rainy summers the fevers spread even to
retreats in the sand hills or on the coast.[3]

On June 21, 1817, a Mrs. Williams who lived at Byne Swamp on the North
Newport died of the fever. The next day Mrs. Samuel Law died of the fever in
Sunbury and a week later, General Stewart's son Edmond died. They were the
first of many who would be struck down that summer as fevers spread from family
to family—Bacons and Walthours, Cuthberts and Elliotts, Wards and Stevens—
so that there was a great grieving throughout the county and the gravediggers
were kept busy at Midway and in the little family cemeteries on the plantations.
Out of the Midway congregation alone, with no more than 340 whites, 39 died
in four months.[4]

Sometime after dusk in late July an infected *Anopheles* entered the Jones
house in Sunbury and bit Sarah Anderson Jones. A low-country doctor in a manual for planters described the course of the disease that soon wracked the body
of Sarah: "Slight chills [are] immediately followed by flushes of heat, which disappear and return every quarter of an hour, or so, the chills becoming shorter,
and the heat increasing, until a fever comes on. . . . Soon afterwards, the whites
of [the] eyes become tinged with yellow, [the] tongue is covered with a brown-
ish fur, [the patient] becomes sick at his stomach, and now and then throws up
bile." Following this onset of the disease, the fever cools, but the remission lasts
only one or two hours, and then the fever returns "as high or higher than it was
before." And so the disease progresses, day by day, with rising and cooling, until
it comes to a crisis.

> When the disease has advanced as far as this, the lips become of a purple color
> and swollen, the tongue dark brown, or black, clammy and offensive to the
> smell, the eyes dry, or red and watery, the urine either very small in quantity,
> or entirely stopped, or of a dark brown color, and has a bad smell. The passages
> are either black, bloody and in quantity, or reddish and watery. The belly feels
> soft and as if it was filled with air, in which state it is said to be tympanitic,
> and sometimes, just before the patient dies, blood will be discharged from his
> bowels, or nose, or mouth.[5]

In such a way the disease ran its painful course through Sarah as her family
watched with distress and increasing anxiety. Physicians tried to arrest the progress of the fevers with the powerful purgatives calomel and jalap, and then with
the Peruvian bark quinine. But the thirty-four-year-old Sarah was weakened from
childbirths and sorrows, having already buried much of her heart with five of her
seven children in the cemetery at the Retreat. The last had been little Hannah
Sharp, "aged three years lacking seven days."[6]

On 9 September 1817 Sarah died, and the next day she was taken in her coffin down the sandy roads that led from Sunbury to the Retreat, where she was buried beside her gathered children.

The death of Sarah cast a pall over the Retreat. Nine-year-old Mary was particularly affected by her mother's death. While her brother John was only two and not old enough to know the meaning of his mother's absence, Mary was of an age to grieve deeply and to feel the sting of death and the pain of separation. She was to remember Sarah as "my own dear mother" and was drawn closer to her father than ever before, giving him the affection and adoration of a motherless child.[7]

For Joseph, the death of Sarah brought not only a remembered loneliness to the Retreat but also questions about his responsibility for those under his protection as the patriarch of an extended family. He invited his sister Eliza to come and see after the children and to make the Retreat her winter home. He also began to make plans for the older children of the family, for their education outside of Liberty County, with its close circle of friends and relatives. Of most pressing concern were his nieces Susan Jones and Mary Eliza Robarts. The teenage girls needed to be introduced to a broader society and to the more sophisticated ways of urban life. Joseph wrote to a cousin in Charleston, Eliza Ferguson, and she agreed, together with her cousin Judge Charles Jones Colcock, to see after the girls for as long as they wished to stay in Charleston.[8]

In early 1818 Joseph sailed with the girls to Charleston. The city was known among its citizens as "the Capital of the South" and they liked to boast that in its harbor "the Ashley and Cooper rivers come together to form the Atlantic Ocean." With Joseph and the girls went Sara Ann Walthour, whose father, Andrew Walthour, was the largest slaveholder in Liberty County. Settled in Charleston under Eliza Ferguson's supervision, the three young ladies took, in addition to directed readings, lessons in music and drawing, and once a week at the school of Mr. Peter Fayotte they were taught the most fashionable dances of their day. In the late afternoons they made calls on friends, mastered the etiquette of tea drinking in parlors and on piazzas, and took walks along the battery with its high seawall. On Sundays at the Circular Congregational Church they meet Pinckney and Legare cousins and could see such political leaders as Senator Robert Young Hayne and Thomas Bennett, soon to be elected governor. Such experiences were as important as their more formal lessons, for their time in Charleston was intended to help refine their manners, to broaden their circle of friends and acquaintances, and to introduce them into Charleston society.[9]

With the girls settled in Charleston, Joseph placed fourteen-year-old Charles Colcock Jones in a Savannah countinghouse in preparation for the life of a merchant. At first Charles worked for Joseph Pelot, a cotton factor and merchant. But

Charles did not like or admire him, and after two years he moved to the counting-house of Nicholas and Neff. Here he became friends with a young Scotsman, Robert Hutchinson, who was a clerk in the countinghouse of his fellow Scotsman Andrew Low. Hutchinson was to become, like his mentor Low, a wealthy man, but in the early 1820s he and Charles were teenagers learning the intricacies of buying and selling cotton and rice on world markets. They also were learning how to keep careful accounts and how to balance a ledger, and, equally important, they were learning an accountant's habits of mind as they internalized values of disciplined work, prudence, moderation, and frugality. Charles's disposition and his love of the Liberty County landscape—its rivers and swamps, its islands and marshes—kept him from ever becoming a pale accountant busy only with income and expenses. But throughout his life he would carry with him an accountant's love of order, a resolve to use time wisely, and an inclination to seek a prudent middle way.[10]

At the Retreat, Eliza Robarts saw after Joseph's three children, Joseph, Mary, and John, and her own two little ones, Joseph and Louisa. Eliza had the help of Jack and Sylvia and her own personal servant, young Sam. Sylvia was John's nurse, and she became Mom Sylvia for the little boy in an even more intimate manner than she was Mary's Momma, for Mary had known and still remembered Sarah Anderson in ways unavailable to the two-year-old John.[11] So they all lived together in this way, blacks and whites, adults and children, for three winters and springs at the Retreat as they followed the routines and rules of plantation life in the Georgia low country. And during the summers and in the fall of these years, they went to Sunbury, and the whites visited among relatives and friends on Colonel's Island, and the blacks made time after their long hours of work for their own visiting, and the five white children grew close to one another under the protection and the affectionate rule of Joseph.

Joseph, however, was lonely in spite of a house full of children and the cheerful company of his sister Eliza. In the summer of 1819 he began to court a young woman, Elizabeth Hart, who was living in Sunbury and whose family had deep roots in low-country soil. Her grandfather, General James Screven, a hero of the Revolution, had been killed during a skirmish near Midway Church, and her family had its own Retreat plantation, across the Medway River from Sunbury, where many slaves produced much rice and cotton.[12]

Joseph's courtship of Elizabeth was short, and in January 1820 they were married by Dr. McWhir. Joseph was forty-one. Elizabeth was a month short of her nineteenth birthday and only three years older than her new stepson Joseph Maybank Jones. Elizabeth was an affectionate and lively young woman and devoted to her husband, but Joseph's relationship with her always carried the marks of an older husband's protection of a much younger wife. At the time of his first marriage Joseph had been only twenty and Mary Maybank eighteen. And when he had married Sarah Anderson in 1806, she had been twenty-three and he twenty-seven. In his relationships with them his patriarchal assumptions and behavior had been tempered by a degree of mutuality, perhaps because they could never think of him as a father figure. But for Elizabeth, who had lost her father when she was thirteen, Joseph filled the role of a fatherly husband, and she would encourage in him the full development of his strong patriarchal instincts.[13]

For twelve-year-old Mary Jones, her father's marriage to Elizabeth appeared as a desertion and as a betrayal of Sarah Anderson's memory. While polite to her young stepmother, whom she must have regarded as an interloper at the Retreat, Mary never gave her the affection of a daughter, nor did she consider Elizabeth a parent to whom obedience was due. "I have been all my life," she wrote ten years later, "pretty much my *own mistress* there being no one but *my Father* to whom I felt it a duty to submit and his great indulgence made his requisitions of the most lenient kind." Mary called Elizabeth "Mother," in deference to her father, but in later years she referred to her simply as "Mrs. Jones."[14]

Elizabeth, as the new mistress of the Retreat, felt the tension with her strong-willed stepdaughter and encouraged Joseph to see that Mary had the education a young lady needed. So six months after his marriage to Elizabeth, Joseph sent Mary to school, not to the Sunbury Academy, but to an academy in adjoining McIntosh County at Barsden Bluff. With her went her older brother, so that neither brother nor sister was with the newlyweds when they went to Sunbury for the summer and fall of 1820.

Barsden Bluff, on the waterway south of Colonel's Island, overlooked Sapelo and Doboy Sound. Located on what was called the Sapelo Main, the little village at the bluff served as a summer residence for local planters and as a launching spot to the plantations on Sapelo Island. An advertisement in the *Savannah Republican* described it as "a healthy and pleasant situation." But Mary evidently did not think it a particularly pleasant place and was homesick. In September, Joseph wrote to encourage her. "Continue to be a good girl," he said "and every body will love you and don't think too much of home as you are acquiring that which will ever make you useful in Society." Mary didn't have, nor would she ever have, much interest in everybody loving her—she was far too independent and too possessed of her own sense of self-esteem. But for other reasons, reasons she herself chose in the years ahead, she sought to be good and to be useful in society. So Mary persevered in her work at Barsden Bluff and began to concentrate on her studies and to develop a love of books and to focus on what she was to call an "intellectual craving." By 1822 she was concentrating on French and geography and writing two compositions a week. "I have commenced," she wrote her father, "translating Telemachus and write French Exercises." [15]

While Mary and her brother Joseph were studying at Barsden Bluff, their cousin Charles Colcock Jones was becoming more deeply acquainted with Savannah. The little city was the metropolis for the Georgia low country, drawing to it much of the trade from its scattered hinterland. General James Oglethorpe had laid out the city in the 1730s with a vision of urban life built upon distinct neighborhoods. At the center of his plan were squares with twenty lots to the north and twenty lots to the south, each lot sixty by ninety feet. To the east and west of each square were four larger trust lots designated for public use. While not all of Oglethorpe's plans had been sustained during the following years, the parklike squares and the surrounding grid of streets had become a mark of Savannah, providing not only an orderly network of thoroughfares and avenues but also a foundation for the growing elegance of the city.[16]

Charles was learning, however, that Savannah, for all of its importance to the Georgia low country, was a small city. In 1820 it numbered only 7,523 residents and had what a later visitor called "a curiously rural and modest aspect" evoked, no doubt, not only by its size but also by its tree-lined streets and shady parks. But it was an energetic city and prided itself on the vigor of its commercial activity. In 1818 the city had sent the steamship Savannah on a pioneer trip to Liverpool, ushering in a new age of transatlantic navigation, and later the city aggressively built railroads into the interior of the state.[17] As a clerk in the firm of Nicholas and Neff, Charles was in a good position to watch this entrepreneurial spirit at work, especially in his mentor William Neff, who had extensive business connections in his home state of Pennsylvania. Charles worked hard, became noted for his energy, integrity, and practical gifts, and gained a reputation as an up-and-coming young man in the world of Savannah's cotton factors and commission merchants.[18]

One aspect of Savannah's life that immediately caught Charles's attention was its slave population and its African-American community. For blacks as well as for whites, life in the city was different from life on the plantation. To be sure, the burdens and sorrows of slavery remained, but the work of urban slaves and the ways they sought to organize their lives were different from the work and life of those who lived at Carlawter and other plantation settlements. In contrast to Liberty County, where slaves outnumbered whites almost three to one, in Savannah the population was almost evenly divided between blacks and whites. Rather than being isolated at a Carlawter or Lambert, slaves in Savannah were part of a complex urban setting where on a daily basis they could interact with whites—

not only with their owners but also with shopkeepers and police, neighbors and strangers.[19]

Most visible in the city were the African-American vendors. They reflected in a large way the market activity that took place in little villages like Riceboro. Women came in from the country to sell the produce of their gardens; men hawked the fish and shrimp they had caught in the creeks and inlets; others sold eggs they had gathered or baskets they had made or game they had snared. Some slaves in Savannah were "hired out" by their owners, returning weekly to their masters or mistresses an agreed sum. While often in the self-interest of the owners, such activities left many whites uneasy. Shortly before Charles arrived in Savannah, a letter writer calling himself Anti-Mulatto had railed in the *Savannah Republican* against "Husksters and Cake-Wenches," accusing them of monopolizing much of the marketplace, driving up prices, and even of taking up paramours "*white*, black or yellow." The grand jury, in its presentments in 1818, had seen "a great evil" in the "granting of badges to colored and black women, for the purpose of hawking about articles for sale." Such complaints revealed not only much about the fears and anxieties of whites but also about the ability of African Americans to create some space for themselves in the city and to vigorously pursue their own interests within that space. For they were not simply slaves and victims of white oppression but a people who were responding to slavery with their own strategies and building their own African-American community and culture.[20]

One of the peculiarities of Savannah that must have struck Charles when he first came to the city was the way slave-housing patterns were different from what he had known in the country. In Savannah, houses of whites were built close to the streets and slave houses were at the backs of the lots. High walls divided the lots and created compounds that kept whites and blacks in an intense relationship with one another so that urban slaves lived among whites in ways that only a few domestics did on the plantations. Such close contacts meant that urban blacks were generally more acculturated to white ways than their country cousins, that they knew more of a wider world and had more opportunities for learning to read and write than those in the plantation settlements. Close contacts, of course, also meant close supervision and constant calls for services. But urban blacks found ways to slip away at night or when whites were not at home. Sheds and stables provided exits from the compounds, and the lanes that separated Savannah's neatly laid out blocks provided convenient and hard-to-police routes throughout the city. Like the trails that Cato and Cassius could follow at Carlawter, the lanes of Savannah served as a means of escape and as places for illegal gatherings and illicit activities. By carefully following the lanes, slaves could make their way to another "yard" for visiting, or go to one of the grogshops that catered to blacks, or sneak down below the bluff of the city to the river's edge, where there were the shanties of those who could hire themselves out in the city.[21]

Among those who used the lanes and hid among the city's black population were runaways. Many came in from the countryside, and others fled a compound to hide in some other part of the city. The Savannah papers carried advertisements for their capture, such as an advertisement that appeared a short time after Cato and Cassius had moved to Carlawter. Ned and Trim had run away from the Mara plantation, which adjoined Carlawter. Their owner, Morgan Mara, advertised that they had forged passes and that with such papers they had a good chance of hiding out in Savannah for an extended period.[22]

Charles had known the handful of free blacks in Liberty County who lived in Riceboro or on nearby plantations. But in Savannah, he found a sizable free black population, almost six hundred in 1820, scattered throughout the city and engaged in a variety of occupations. Many of the men were tailors and carpenters; others were painters, bricklayers, butchers, or barbers; still others were shoemakers or harness makers or worked on the boats that plied the waterways. Women were seamstresses and vendors, washerwomen and house servants. But most of them, both men and women, were "slaves without masters," laborers who toiled in the menial tasks of the city. They all lived in a kind of twilight zone between freedom and slavery, severely restricted in what they could do or how they could dress, but having important privileges denied to slaves—most especially the right to own land and have legal marriages. These free blacks provided a constant reminder that slavery was not the inevitable condition for African Americans. Moreover, they provided important leadership for the African-American community in Savannah and frequently incurred the suspicion and sometimes the wrath of whites for their independence. No free blacks were more conspicuous in this regard than the black preachers of Savannah.[23]

The first and most famous black preacher in the city had been Andrew Bryan. His owner, Jonathan Bryan, had been a neighbor in South Carolina of John Lambert—the one whose will had left Lambert plantation in Liberty County to be used for benevolent purposes. Andrew Bryan had preached at his master's Brampton Plantation on the Savannah River and, after much bitter opposition, had been successful in winning his freedom and establishing the First African Baptist Church in Savannah. On Andrew Bryan's death in 1812, the church had fifteen hundred members and had given birth to two other churches. At his funeral Dr. Henry Kollock, pastor of the lofty Independent Presbyterian Church, "bore testimony to his worth," and five thousand people had gone weeping to Bryan's grave "singing the songs of Zion."[24]

In 1815 Bryan's nephew, Andrew Marshall, had become the pastor of the First African Baptist Church. The son of Bryan's sister and an English overseer, Marshall had been purchased as a young man by Judge Joseph Clay, a leading citizen of the city and a supporter of Andrew Bryan's work at the church. As a personal servant of Clay, Marshall had traveled to the north and had met famous political and intellectual figures in Boston and other cities. Marshall may have had an influence on his master, for Clay had left his judicial position and the Independent Presbyterian Church in 1807 to become pastor of Boston's First Baptist Church. Clay's son Thomas, as well as his daughter Eliza Clay, in time became two of Charles Jones's closest friends.[25]

Having gained his freedom, Andrew Marshall had become a drayman as well as a preacher in Savannah. Marshall had been publicly whipped shortly after Charles had arrived in the city, allegedly for trading with slaves without proper tickets. Behind this public humiliation, however, stood the antagonism of white Baptists who did not like Marshall's independence and, more broadly, the widespread hostility in the white community to black preachers. These preachers, it was feared, were teaching their parishioners to read and to resist white authority. Young Charles took notice of such controversy and later remembered that when prominent whites supported the evangelization of slaves, the work could proceed even in the face of white fears and skepticism.[26]

In time, Andrew Marshall himself began to win substantial white support, and in later years was respected by many of Savannah's whites as well as blacks. With Henry Cunningham, pastor of the Second African Baptist Church, Marshall was an influential leader in the Sunbury Baptist Association, which drew together the African-American Baptist churches of the Georgia low country. Charles did not know it at the time, but in the years ahead he was to become associated with these two black preachers and the Sunbury Association. He came to think of himself as a partner with them in his own efforts to evangelize those who lived in the settlements at the Retreat and Carlawter, at Lambert and Liberty Hall and the other plantations of the Georgia low country.[27]

Charles had felt keenly his loss of a formal education when he came to Savannah to learn the wisdom of the countinghouse and the practices and judgments needed for the buying and selling of cotton and rice. And so he took the path of self-improvement followed by many an ambitious young clerk. "Such was his desire for mental cultivation," it was later written of him, "that the evenings of days of labor and toil were not wasted in idleness or given to pleasure and amusement but faithfully employed in profitably reading the standard works of literature." Jones gave special attention to history "both ancient and modern" and laid the foundation for his later work as a historian. But his work and studies left him exhausted, and in early 1822 he became seriously ill and was reduced "to the gates of the grave." Finally a new physician was consulted, and he suggested a remedy that was successful in "reducing the pulse and controlling the arterial action." Charles began to improve, but only slowly, and for months he knew the helplessness of a child. During this time he had long hours to think seriously about the condition of his soul and his eternal destiny. Following a period of fervent introspection and prayer, he had a deeply moving religious experience that changed the direction of his life and set him on a course that he had not anticipated. As soon as he had gained enough strength, he applied for membership in the Midway Congregational Church.[28]

Susannah Jones had brought Charles to Midway to be baptized as an infant shortly after his father had been killed in 1805.[29] For those in the Calvinist tradition of Midway, Charles's baptism meant that he was a "child of the covenant of grace"—that is, God's grace was a free gift to him that did not depend on Charles's knowledge or his will but came simply out of God's love for him. As an adult, however, Charles had to claim the covenant as his own, for in order to become a communing member of Midway he had to profess his belief that Jesus Christ was his personal savior. Such a claim and profession were not expected to come easily, nor were they to be made lightly. The consequence was that at Midway (and at most U.S. Protestant churches of the early nineteenth century), there were many more people who came to church than there were church members.

Midway Church had two coordinate branches: the church and the society. The society was composed of "subscribers to the Articles of Incorporation." Those who were members only of the Midway Society came to church, believed the doctrines of the church, paid rent for their pews, voted on the minister's salary, and helped to see after the upkeep of the building and cemetery. But since they were not church members, they could not come to the communion table to receive the sacrament of the Lord's Supper or bring their children for baptism, nor were they under the discipline of the congregation. In order to become a full communing member, a person had to stand before the congregation and profess something like this: "I believe God has touched my heart and made me repent of my sins and has created in me a desire to live the life of a Christian. I believe that Jesus died for my sins and through his death has washed away my guilt. From now on, with God's help, I promise to try to live as a faithful discipline of Jesus, following his way and seeking to do his will."[30]

Charles stood before the Midway congregation in November 1822 and made his profession of faith. Standing with him to publicly confess their own faith were his sister Susan and his cousin Mary Robarts, both back from Charleston, and

Charles's uncle General Daniel Stewart, as well as thirty others who had felt their hearts strangely warmed and who had come to make their profession before the congregation. Already closely examined by their pastor, the Reverend Murdock Murphy, and by the members of the church, they represented the largest single group of whites that had ever come before the congregation seeking membership. As such, they were part of an evangelical awakening that had been sweeping the country for some years and that was already being called the Second Great Awakening. The movement was bringing great numbers into the Protestant churches, providing them with a widely shared religious experience, and creating within them a vision for a Protestant America that demanded reforms of society. When the seventeen-year-old Charles made his profession before the congregation, he was joining not only Midway but also this larger evangelical movement, with its distinct piety and its strong benevolent impulse.[31]

Charles's religious experience and its resulting piety committed him to a life of intense introspection. To be sure, the Calvinism of Midway required an outward focus on God, the high and holy One, who was to be worshiped and adored. Personal religious experiences and turbulent feelings, for all of their importance, were not to be the Christian's preoccupation or subject of trust, but only God. Yet because the self was always in danger of wandering onto dangerous paths, because it was fashioned out of fallen nature, a sharp eye had to be kept on the inner life. For Charles this meant a steady gaze at his own heart and motives, a disciplined probing of his feelings, and an awareness of the role of sin in his life. In Savannah, Charles had as his mentor and guide for such introspection his close friend Lowell Mason and his wife, Abigail.

Mason had come from Massachusetts to Savannah in 1813 and, after working as a clerk, had turned to music, his first love, becoming the organist and choir director at the Independent Presbyterian Church. The year Charles joined Midway, Mason published his first tune book, *The Boston Handel and Haydn Society Collection of Church Music.* An immediate success, the book went through many editions. Over the coming years Mason published more than seventeen hundred hymn tunes, some of which were to become deeply identified with the piety of evangelical Protestantism, not only in the United States but also abroad. Among the best known would be Bethany ("Nearer, My God, to Thee"), Olivet ("My Faith Looks Up to Thee"), Dennis ("Bless Be the Tie That Binds"), and Hamburg ("When I Survey the Wondrous Cross"). Charles boarded with the Masons in Savannah, and Lowell Mason was pleased that he had had "a finger in the pie" when Charles was converted and "made over again."[32]

In the summer of 1824 Charles invited the Masons to go with him for a visit to sister Betsy and her husband, William Maxwell, on Colonel's Island. The Maxwells' plantation, Orange Grove, was located at the eastern end of the island at Yellow Bluff and looked out across the marsh to St. Catherine's Sound. In the distance could be seen St. Catherine's Island and, to the north, Ossabaw Island. Mason gave Charles for his reading that summer Jonathan Edwards's great philosophical and theological *Treatise on the Freedom of the Will.* Charles sat in William Maxwell's office, hoping for a sea breeze during hot July days, and began poring over the text.[33] He began a notebook and carefully copied his reflections on Edwards. Orange Grove must have seemed a strange place to be studying the New Englander, there by the marshes and under the Sea Island oaks, with the roar of the breakers in the distance. But Charles frequently remarked in the future that his study of Edwards that summer had "first taught him to think and reason."[34] In his reading of Edwards, however, he had a different intention that summer than learning to "think and reason" — it was to help him know himself and the role of his own will and the workings of the human mind and heart. And the direction his reflections and introspection were leading him was toward a vocational decision, a response to a calling he believed was from God. That calling, he finally admitted to himself the next year, was to become a minister of the Gospel and an active participant in the evangelical campaign to bring salvation to a lost people.

7

SCATTERED PLACES

While Charles Jones was learning about ledgers and the commission business in the countinghouse of William Neff, his cousin Mary Jones finished her studies at Barsden Bluff and moved in 1823 to Savannah. Joseph Jones wanted his daughter to have the kind of education he had provided for his nieces in Charleston — Mary needed to learn the sophisticated ways of urban life and to be introduced more fully to society even as she completed her formal academic studies at the little Savannah academy of the Presbyterian minister Abiel Carter.[1]

The move to Savannah was not easy for the fourteen-year-old Mary, for she had grown to love the marshes and rivers of the low country and the quiet ways of plantation life. Only after she had been in Savannah for some months could she write her father that the "city to me commences to wear a new aspect." It had appeared at first, she said, very lonesome, "but as I gradually became better acquainted with tall brick buildings and flatroofed tabbies and turned to exchange the beautiful and rural scenes of nature for the cramped and conceited works of the city, it appeared a little more cheerful." All too obviously city life — even that of the small and attractive city of Savannah — was not too cheerful for Mary however much she struggled to put the best face on her feelings. "Although it was strange at first to be continually meeting new faces, to hear, instead of the sweet warbler of the grove, the cry of some hoarse fisherman, the change indeed was strange, but I have become quite accustomed to it, and begin to feel myself perfectly at home."[2] In fact, she never was fully at home in the city. Her heart was too much in the country at the Retreat and in its surrounding landscape, and her reaction as a teenager to Savannah was to be repeated in other cities in the years ahead.

What helped with Mary's homesickness, however, was the presence in Savannah of family and friends. Planters and their families flowed in and out of the city, visiting and shopping and seeing after supplies for their plantations. Some planters maintained handsome residences in Savannah as well as homes on their plantations, and not a few successful Savannah commission merchants and bankers owned plantations they would visit during balmy winter weather and during early spring days when the woods were filled with blooming jasmine. Among those who came and went from the city was Mary's cousin Susan Jones, who had married James Audley Maxwell a few months after Mary's arrival in the city. A handsome young man, Audley belonged through his father, Colonel Audley Maxwell, to one of the oldest Liberty County families. They had been instrumental in the establishment of Sunbury and owned a large plantation, Carnickfergus, on the Medway and a summer home, Social Bluff, on Colonel's Island not far from Orange Grove plantation. While wealthy and respectable, the Maxwells carried the embarrassing memory of the first Liberty County Maxwell's suspension from Midway Church for keeping a slave woman as his mistress.[3]

Young Audley was a cotton factor in Savannah and was already making a name for himself in the business by the time of his marriage. He and Susan moved with ease between their comfortable home in Savannah, where Mary and Charles were visitors, and his family's home on Colonel's Island. At Social Bluff they had the front bedroom, and from its windows they could see the wide expanse of the North Newport as it emptied into St. Catherine's Sound. Here in the summer of 1824, Susan gave birth to a little girl, Laura Elizabeth, who quickly won the affection of her two teenaged relatives Mary and Charles. "Laura is certainly a fine child," the eighteen-year-old Charles wrote a few months later to sister Betsy, and then added in a rather surprised way, "I think more of it than I expected."[4]

The Maxwell home served as a gathering place for their extended relations and many friends. Audley's youngest sister Julia was Mary's age, and the two young women soon developed a friendship that was to last longer and be closer than either one of them could have expected. They were all part of Savannah's elite, and they visited with ease among Bullochs and Habershams, Clays, Stileses, and Elliotts. Such a social setting allowed Charles and Mary and their young friends to refine their sensitivities to the rules of etiquette and to finely tune their ears to the coded messages of southern manners. They were learning not simply the grammar of good taste and decorum, so carefully maintained by the guardians of respectability, but a way to safely navigate the dangerous waters of a slave society. They needed to know when to speak and when not to speak, when to be direct and when to be oblique. And they needed to know what could be said only before family, and what one never talked about except in the most restricted circumstances.[5] Learning such manners would play an important part in shaping the character of Charles and Mary and the other young southerners among whom they moved. Indeed, a natural and easy use of such manners, especially in the service of a generous hospitality, was a distinguishing mark of southern elites. Few exceeded the Jones cousins in mastering the nuances of these manners, and in the years ahead few practiced southern hospitality in more winsome ways.

In the spring of 1825, however, Charles was making plans that would place him in a different social and cultural context, one that would demand a different set of manners—those of New England. His decision the previous summer to become a minister meant that he was thinking about a theological education and his own readiness to undertake such an endeavor. His thinking about such matters had been temporarily interrupted when U.S. Senator John Elliot offered to secure a place at West Point for him. But Charles had quickly put that behind him and had pressed ahead in his plans for the ministry. As it happened, Ebenezer Porter, professor at Andover Theological Seminary in Massachusetts, was also a friend of the family. Porter was a frequent visitor to Liberty County, had preached at Midway, and had stayed at General Stewart's plantation. Andover, the oldest theological seminary in the country, had set the pattern for those that followed—a graduate professional institution with a three-year curriculum. The requirement of a college education for admission was intended to ensure that entering students had the philosophical and linguistic background provided by a collegiate education and the general culture and manners taught in the colleges. Charles's problem was that while he had learned about the cotton and rice markets, he knew no Latin, much less Greek. Porter realized, however, that Charles was a well-read young man, that he had received a sound foundation at McWhir's academy, and that he held genuine promise as a minister. He therefore suggested that Charles enter Phillips Academy, also in Andover, in order to prepare himself for an entrance exam into the seminary. Charles left Savannah in April, and on 12 May 1825 he entered Phillips as a nineteen-year-old preparing to take up for the first time a Latin grammar.[6]

Mary stayed in Savannah for another two years. The most important event for her during these years was the marriage of her friend Julia Maxwell to Roswell King, Jr., of St. Simons Island. King's father, Roswell, Sr., had come from Connecticut to the little town of Darien, south of Sunbury, and had established there a flourishing lumber, rice, and cotton business. For eighteen years the senior King had also been the manager of Pierce Butler's vast rice and cotton plantations on the Altamaha River and on St. Simons Island, and it was this Roswell King who had been so furious when some of the Butler slaves had sought their freedom with the British in 1815. When the senior Roswell retired in 1818 to run his own extensive business interests, his namesake had taken over the management of the Butler estates. Only twenty-four at the time, young Roswell followed his father in the supervision of more than 530 slaves scattered over several plantations, some of which were divided by the wide and muddy marshes of the Altamaha estuary.[7]

Roswell, Jr., had thrown himself into the task of overseeing such an estate and soon had made a name for himself as a prudent and skillful manager. He represented a transitional figure among southern planters as they were moving from the austere code of patriarchalism to a paternalism that emphasized owners' solicitude for their slaves. The new paternalism that was emerging was part of nineteenth-century romanticism, and it was increasingly influenced by evangelical sensibilities.[8] Young Roswell was neither a romantic nor an evangelical, and he had no paternalistic assumptions about happy slaves who were content with their lot and grateful for the kindness of their owners. His was more of a utilitarian approach to the management of slaves, a belief that clear rules, fairly and consistently administered with some flexibility, would make for more orderly slaves and a more efficient plantation. But he also thought kindness important: "Slave owners cannot be too particular," he insisted, "to whom he intrust the health (I may say life) and morals of what may justly be termed the sinews of an estate. A master, or overseer, should be the kind friend and monitor to the slave, not the oppressor." In the years ahead, not a few would wonder whether Roswell King, Jr., practiced what he preached.[9]

The wedding of young Roswell and Julia Maxwell was held in October 1825, with Dr. McWhir, a friend of both families, officiating. "I commission you," wrote Charles from Massachusetts to his sister Betsy and her husband William, "to give my congratulations to the bride, and Brother to touch a glass to the groom."[10]

Marriages within such planting families, like deaths within planting families, had an impact on the men, women, and children who lived in the settlements. Julia brought into her marriage slaves she had received as a gift of her father, Colonel Audley Maxwell. And Roswell had been steadily increasing the number of slaves he himself owned. What Julia King did not know, however, when she said her wedding vows, was that among the slaves living in the Butler settlements were three of her husband's children by two different slave women. In the years ahead their presence and their parentage were among the subjects that good manners left unmentioned in the parlors and on the piazzas of St. Simons and Liberty County. It would take an outsider, one unrestrained by the rules of southern manners and eager to make a case against slavery, to publicly acknowledge this side of Roswell King's life.[11]

In early winter 1827 Mary left Savannah and at last returned home to the Retreat. She was a lively and headstrong eighteen-year-old, already well set in her own ways, but she was moving back into a home that had been transformed since 1820, when she had gone away to Barsden Bluff. Joseph Jones and his young wife, Elizabeth, had had four children in the seven years since their marriage — Charles Berrien had been born their first year together; then had come Evelyn Elouisa in 1822, Henry Hart in 1823, and James Newton in 1825. If Mary continued to be polite but cool to her stepmother, she quickly gave her heart to her little brothers and sister. And they reciprocated, looking on her as an affectionate big sister who possessed much of their father's common sense and iron will. Even Charles Berrien, who was his mamma's boy, as an adult looked to Mary in times of crisis rather than to his mother, who always remained, even through her coming sorrows, something of a young bride dependent on others.[12]

Of all the children, however, Mary was closest to her brother John, the only other surviving child of Sarah Anderson. He was a precocious twelve-year-old when Mary came back to the Retreat, and he already possessed a charm that covered a decided tendency to procrastination. He never met a stranger, and all who knew him were drawn to him by the warmth of his personality. Mary tried, without much success, to instill some of her own self-discipline into her brother. His cousin Charles later remarked that he had been a "wayward boy," but that did not keep him from being a favorite of all in the Jones household.[13]

Joseph Maybank Jones, the oldest of all the Jones children, had, after his study at Barsden Bluff with Mary, gone to Savannah and taken up the study of law. While still calling the Retreat home, Joseph Maybank had been elected to the state legislature in 1827 and was soon to enter the debate in the legislature about how the state should handle the Cherokees and their lands in north Georgia. When Mary came home in 1827, he was also thinking about setting himself up as a planter. He had his eye on some land on Colonel's Island for raising Sea Island cotton, and he wrote his father to request a portion of his inheritance in slaves. His father complied and deeded over to his oldest son two families of slaves, twelve in all. Father and son agreed that the slaves would remain under the father's management at the Retreat until young Joseph was ready to start planting. Neither Mary nor anyone else at the Retreat, white or black, knew of this transaction between the two Josephs, and when it was revealed, it was to bring into the open the tensions between Mary and her stepmother, Elizabeth.[14]

In addition to the mother and father and the seven children at the Retreat, Elizabeth's widowed mother, Mary Scriven Hart, was also a part of the household. And of course sister Eliza Robarts and her three children were frequent visitors during the winter months, and other relatives and friends came to enjoy the generous hospitality of the Retreat, so that it was a full and lively plantation home, where good manners were used to lubricate such close contacts and to keep all these relatives and friends from rubbing each other the wrong way. Also needed, of course, was a full staff of house slaves to do the cooking of meals, the washing of clothes, the cleaning of chambers and chamber pots, and the minding of children. Jack and Sylvia had the primary responsibility to see that all ran smoothly—that the meals were prepared on time, that the table was properly set, that the washing and cleaning were done as expected, and that guests were welcomed with grace and efficiency. Among those who helped with these myriad tasks was Jack's daughter Phoebe.

When Mary had arrived at the Retreat, she found that her father had named Phoebe to be her body servant. The mistress was eighteen and the maid seventeen. Both were strong, smart, and talented young women. Both had fathers who were respected and well known for their strength of character, and both had lost their mothers. Both were, in their own circles, elite, privileged daughters of influential fathers. But Mary was free and Phoebe was her slave, and the bitter distance between the slave and the free, between the white and the black, was the fundamental reality of these young women as their lives became bound together and as each inescapably encountered the humanity of the other.

For Phoebe the injustice of this distance and the oppression of its power would long weigh on her like a great lid that kept her emotions under control and caused them to boil with rage beneath a submissive exterior. The consequence was that more than most in the settlements she became a person with two lives—she was the servant on whom her strong-willed mistress would increasingly depend, and she was a restless spirit struggling to be free, to find places where the pressure could safely be released and the rage exposed.

Phoebe learned the art of sewing and became a skilled seamstress. She became as well, in Charles's words, an "accomplished house servant in any and every line: good cook, washer and ironer."[15] But more than all of this, she became the person who best knew Mary's habits, who could best anticipate her needs, and who could most skillfully meet them. Most of the time as Phoebe went about her work, she bit her tongue, choked back her rage, and conquered the impulse of open defiance. Moreover, she generally managed to be cheerful and not sullen or moody. But there was an edge to her, and Mary knew that an impulsive rage lay near the surface of Phoebe's cheerful demeanor, submissive manner, and careful speech.[16]

If Phoebe managed to keep her rage from erupting in front of whites, she was not able to keep from being impulsive in other areas of her life. She had had a child, a daughter Clarissa, when she was barely sixteen, a full four years before most of the women in the low-country settlements had children.[17] Clarissa's father was unknown to the whites and apparently never openly claimed his daughter, and Phoebe was herself not a particularly attentive mother. She had, to be sure, the demanding work of a body servant that took most of the hours of her day. But she never had, as did many slave mothers, a focus on protecting her family or a strong interest in making the life of her children easier. Her restless spirit, so carefully controlled during her long hours in front of whites, sought freedom elsewhere as a part of the bitter price of slavery. If she never fit the image of a "Jezebel" that whites imposed on some slave women—of a troublesome, lusty wench—her fierce restlessness was troubling for whites even as she was valuable to them.[18] For Clarissa her mother's restlessness meant that, even though she was the granddaughter of Jack and the daughter of Phoebe, she was to grow up on the margin and not at the center of the slave community. With the brief exception of a few months, she was never a house servant like her mother and grandfather, and as an adult she lived at the edge of the settlements and was not closely linked to a web of family connections.

By the winter of 1827 Charles had been at Phillips Academy for almost two years. He had plunged into his studies, especially the classical languages: he was already reading Latin and had gotten far enough in his Greek that he hoped to be able to pass the entrance exams to the seminary in late spring. He had been developing habits of hard study and a daily schedule that included morning and evening devotionals and long walks in the New England countryside—during a break, he wrote those at home, he had walked forty miles to Plymouth "to shake down my bones." And he was learning about himself in new ways and about how others saw him. Some at Phillips regarded him as wealthy. They were inclined, he wrote home, to "give a southern man credit for just three times as much as he is worth, and to exact in proportion." "The lady who attends to the affairs at commons hall asked me to tell them who was in the right, the one who said I was very rich or the other who said very poor. I reiterated 'poor, very poor, poor, very poor' as long as my business lasted and came off leaving her crying out for 'rich.'"[19]

But Charles was also homesick for Liberty County. "I am," he wrote sister Betsy, "very often with you at Orange Grove in my dreams by night and my thoughts by day."[20] He sent greetings to General and Mrs. Stewart. "Remember me," he wrote "to Aunt and Uncle Stewart. Tell them I think of them a great deal and would give much to spend time with them as I have in days past."[21] And he thought a lot about those who lived in the settlements—about Rosetta and her family, Jack and Sylvia, Lizzy and young Cato and Cassius, and the others at Carlawter, the Retreat, and Orange Grove. "Please tell the black people," he wrote, "they are remembered." When he learned that old Hannah had died, he was melancholy. She had lived at Liberty Hall and had been purchased by Joseph

Jones in Riceboro in 1808. While she suffered from senility in her last years, she
represented a link with the past. He wrote his sister Betsy:

> Poor Hannah is no more. When such a faithful servant is removed from the
> family we must all feel. Her afflictions were long, and although they appeared
> simple yet to her they were truly afflictions, and she sometimes talked to me
> of religion in such a manner as led me to think she had hope, notwithstanding
> her insanity at times. None can tell but we shall see her happy. Let us look at
> our own hearts Sister, that we improve our talents and seek to be found ready
> when Jesus calls. And that we do not abuse our high privileges and experience
> on death that all our good things were bestowed in this life and find those over
> whom we now rule occupying loftier seats in heaven. Our souls are the same.
> God is no respecter of persons.[22]

Being away from home was allowing Charles to see Liberty County from the
vantage point of New England's rocky landscape rather than across the marshes
and rivers of the low country. The distance provided a new perspective on those
who lived in the settlements while at the same time the distance made him homesick for those whom he loved. Far from home and often lonely, he remembered
the fragility of life, the suddenness with which loved ones could be lost, and he
increasingly began to think of heaven as home, as the place where there would
be no more sorrows or separations. "It is a constant and happy reflection with
me," he wrote sister Betsy, "that I shall one day meet my dear sisters in heaven
where we shall never more part, never more feel affliction and pain, never go
out from the presence of the Lamb."[23]

Such a vision of home would include Old Jupiter and Hannah and the other
saints from the settlements, not as servants but as co-worshippers at the throne
of the Lamb and perhaps as those who would have the best seats at the heavenly banquet. Throughout the rest of his life this vision of heaven provided him,
no less than the New England landscape, a place from which to view Liberty
County and a spot from which to understand its social arrangements and both
its beauty and its deep sorrows. But Charles believed there was a mission to be
accomplished for such an inclusive heavenly home to be enjoyed. "To realize
this felicity, this eternal happiness," he wrote, "I feel there is much to be done,
for we are by nature carnal, opposed to God. We have to watch our corrupt and
unholy hearts."[24] He would spend years peering into his "corrupt and unholy
heart" seeking to discover the sins and illusions that kept him from doing the will
of God, and he would give himself to a mission that he believed was necessary to
bring together all the sons and daughters of Liberty County into such a heavenly
home. But what he would see only in glimpses now and then were the ways in
which his hopes for a heavenly home, his bright utopia visions, were rooted not

only in a vibrant religious tradition but also in the dark soil of his native country and the deep assumptions of white planters.

In the late spring of 1827, having completed his work at Phillips and passed his entrance exams for Andover, Charles returned to Liberty County for his first visit in two years. In Savannah he saw sister Susan and Audley and their Laura, who was already a precocious two-year-old, and her little brother Charles Edward Maxwell, who had been born while Charles was away. At the Retreat he rode down the sandy road under the avenue of oaks to a happy reunion with his uncle Joseph and his growing family, and with his Aunt Eliza and her children. He was particularly glad to see Mary Jones and Mary Robarts — "my two pretty cousins" he called them — and to learn from them the news of the county.[25] Jack and Sylvia were there, as usual, to greet him, and Phoebe too, as Mary's maid. In the evenings, Charles had the chance to see Driver Pulaski when he came up from the fields for his nightly meetings with Joseph and to learn from him about those in the settlement. And there was an opportunity to go with Joseph to Carlawter and see Charles's nurse, Rosetta — she and Sam now had four children — and to talk with Lizzy, who brought back so many memories of old Liberty Hall and of Charles's mother, Susannah. Lizzy and Robinson had had their eighth child — Adam — while Charles was away, and all the children were strong and healthy, a testimony to their resistance to the fevers that struck the whites so violently. Cato was eighteen and was already showing the qualities that would make him a leader in the settlement. As for Jupiter, he was now sixty-seven and was showing his age. His brother Hamlet was soon to follow him as the driver at Carlawter, and like his brother, and their father, Jupiter, before them, he soon was to announce the dawning of each new day with a blast from the conch-shell horn.[26]

Charles was eager to see his sister Betsy and "brother" William. They were in many ways like parents to him, and Orange Grove had been, like the Retreat, a place of stability in his life. But the couple had been through difficult times while Charles was away. Maxwell, who daily drank more than his share of liquor, was a hard worker and one of the most respected men in the county, but he was no Joseph Jones, skillfully expanding his acres and slaves. Maxwell was too impulsive — years earlier he had knocked a man off a horse and whipped him for insulting him and refusing to leave Orange Grove — and while he came from a prominent low-country family, he had the rough edge of a man who worked in the fields beside his slaves and who chewed tobacco and cussed when needed. There had been, however, some bad years and he had gone in debt. A hurricane in 1824, one of the worst ever known on the Georgia coast, had ruined his crops and damaged his plantation, and he was a long time recovering. Joseph had lent him money, but William was still unable to pay his debts, and in 1826 he had had to sell Orange Grove and buy a smaller place, Laurel View, not far from Sunbury.[27] Charles had written him: "Would that your affairs would have enabled you to keep Orange Grove. It is as snug, pleasant, retired place with just the body of land you wanted." But to Charles it was also more. "I look upon it with a great deal of affection, and if it is again visited I shall not fail to attach to every spot its appropriate incident to linger about the fields and the settlement where I have experienced so much delight." The loss of Orange Grove evidently reminded Charles of his orphaned youth and produced in him a "pleasing melancholy" as he remembered "old Liberty Hall."[28]

By the time Charles returned for his visit in 1827, William had been elected sheriff and had had a good year with his crops at Laurel View. So the visit was a happy one, and all the family was able to gather in Sunbury at the old Jones place and at the Robarts home down the street. There were other young people there that summer, and many parties, but Charles began to give special attention to his cousin Mary Jones. He teased her and called her "Her Highness" because of her strong-willed ways and—perhaps to the disappointment of his cousin Mary Robarts—he began to regard Mary Jones as more than a cousin. As his time approached for his return to New England, they agreed to correspond, which was a kind of mutual acknowledgment that their interest in each other was entering a new phase.[29]

Charles left for Andover in the middle of the summer, and Mary remained in Sunbury until the first autumn frost made it safe to return to the Retreat. He wrote her from Andover shortly after he arrived and sent her copies of music by Haydn and Handel that he had secured from Lowell Mason, who had left Savannah and was now living in Boston. "I very frequently wish to spend an hour with you at the piano" Charles wrote, and then added, "or on horseback—pianos and horses and ladies are scarce articles on Andover Hill." And she wrote him about life in Sunbury, which she described as "this delectable spot," and of visits with her friend Julia Maxwell King, who had come up from St. Simons with her little girl Mary.[30]

Knowing her cousin well, Mary Jones wrote that he was perhaps interested in how she was using her time. "The day," she said, "principally in reading, and a little work, but I have grown a very lazy girl of late; my evenings in idleness or something nearly akin to it, conversing with some of our refined village beaux, of whose literary and scientific character we are equally advised." And Charles wrote of his theological studies and of long, disciplined walks in the New England countryside, and how his visit home had been of "great benefit . . . giving me a renewed interest in Georgia as the extensive and interesting field of my future labours."[31]

The most important event for both of them that fall was a spiritual crisis in Mary's life. As a nineteen-year-old, she had been a pious believer and a regular churchgoer all her life, but she had never had a conversion experience. That fall, after much internal struggle, she became convinced not only of her sins but also of God's grace and forgiveness for her personally. She wrote that there had been

> an aching void within, a seeking after that rest which alone can satisfy a sin sick soul. I felt the awful responsibility of being an accountable, immortal crea-ture, and my every day practices but served to convince me of the impossibility of acceptance with a holy and just Almighty. My very feeling and action was in direct opposition to his pure commands, so how should I stand before his great tribunal? But God in his mercy presented a bleeding saviour with the full assurance that whosoever believeth on Him should not perish but have life everlasting. The view itself was life. And I trust, I am now enabled to exclaim, "Thou Lord art my God!" to rejoice in Christ Jesus as my friend, and through his kind mediation, approach the Great Jehovah as my father, to lean on Him for strength sufficient to subdue the evil suggestions of my depraved self, and resist the thousand temptations of an ensnaring world.[32]

Mary was writing her cousin a detailed description of a conversion experience, and in the years ahead she and Charles hoped, prayed, and worked for similar experiences and convictions for all those who lived down the sandy roads of Lib-erty County.

Mary's spiritual crisis, however, was not over. She struggled to understand the implications of such an experience and the continuing conflicts she felt in her heart. Charles, now that he was a first-year theology student in New England, did not hesitate to give her advice about how to probe her feelings and search her own heart. You must, he wrote, deal not in generalizations but in "particulars." Generalizations about what was good and what was evil got no one anywhere. What was needed was a focus on concrete, particular deeds and specific situa-tions. (He would later be dismissive of those who would generalize about slavery, who would say from a distance that it was evil and not look at the particular, concrete realities as he saw them in the settlements of Liberty County.) Charles encouraged Mary to look at her particular actions, to trace those actions to "the particular feeling which originated them, and again this feeling to its cause." In this way, he wrote, "you will presently separate what states of feeling are holy and what unholy in mind, and what situations as to external circumstances are favourable or unfavourable to the proper cultivation of your heart." Above all, he cautioned her not to trust her own heart. "If you do not now, you will very soon know, that it is deceitful above all things and desperately wicked and noth-ing short of the sovereign grace of God can subdue it." For this reason the Bible must be her constant companion and guide, helping her to see through the de-ceptions and illusions of her heart to the realities of her life and of God's judgment and grace. But above all, he warned her not to depend on the excitement of religious experiences "for *evidences* of your conversion or Christian Character, but depend upon the simple and effectual rule which our Saviour gives—'If you *love me* you will *keep my commandments.*' This is your *proof* of conversion and Christian character now and forever."[33]

Charles was spelling out for Mary his understanding of the human psyche and the reason a Christian life is a life of struggle, introspection, and action. Here, in his advice to his cousin, he was identifying his basic assumptions about life that were to guide him as he moved among the plantation houses and settlements of Liberty County in the years to come. But how different were those assumptions from those being worked out by another theological student down the road from Andover at Harvard Divinity School? Ralph Waldo Emerson was also to be an advocate for introspection, for a careful look at the human heart. But his cry became, "Trust thyself: every heart vibrates to that iron string." Rather than being suspicious of one's own thoughts and feelings, wondering about the external circumstances shaping them, Emerson confidently encouraged self-reliant Americans to "believe your own thought, to believe that what is true for you in your private heart is true for all men."[34]

It was not perhaps surprising that one who had grown up in Liberty County— with its settlements and with its manners that hid so much—was more suspicious of the human heart than one who walked the bright and confident streets of Cambridge and Concord. Beyond the theological tradition in which he stood, Charles knew that there were good reasons for whites to deceive themselves, to hide the power and violence that were the foundations for life at the Retreat and Carlawter, in Riceboro and Sunbury. Taking his own advice, he began to wonder what his actions should be in regard to human slavery—and not just any slavery, but the slavery of the settlements in Liberty County; and not just any settlements, but the particular settlement at Carlawter. And what, he wondered, were the feelings that were guiding his thinking and shaping the choices he would make? And what were the external circumstances that influenced his feelings, that nurtured them and gave them their power? During his remaining years as a theological student in the north, he pondered these questions as he thought about the home he loved in Liberty County and about Lizzy and Rosetta, about Cato and Cassius and the others who lived at Carlawter and whose labors paid for his privileges and theological education. How was he to keep Christ's commandments in regard to them?

In the late spring of 1829, Charles returned to Liberty County for his second visit in four years. He found his sister Susan a widow and young Laura and

Charles Edward fatherless. Audley Maxwell had died the previous December, and Susan and the children had moved in with sister Betsy and William Maxwell at Laurel View. Charles grieved with his sister and her children, and worried that Audley had never had a conversion experience.[35] And he talked with Betsy and William Maxwell about their loss of Orange Grove and their new home at Laurel View and William's work as sheriff. But most of his attention was focused on his cousin Mary Jones. They took long walks together down the avenue of the Retreat, going under the outstretched limbs of the oaks to the road that led to Colonel Law's place. They rode horseback over land that they both loved at a time of the year when the wild jasmine filled the woods with its sweet yellow trumpets and the Cherokee rose climbed and tumbled along the roadside with its white blossoms shining against the deep green foliage of the low country. And in the midst of all their friends and relatives at the Retreat, they took refuge and found some privacy, even from Phoebe, in Mary's garret room with its books and chairs and neat desk. In all these places they talked and dreamed together about the future until one night in middle May, after others had retired for the evening, they sat together on the sofa in the drawing room of the Retreat. There Charles asked Mary to marry him and she accepted. They embraced and knelt to "implore God's blessing" upon their "future union."[36]

Charles and Mary needed, however, not only God's blessings, but also Joseph's, and he had made clear on more than one occasion that he disapproved of cousins marrying. Later that night Charles wrote his uncle a note:

My Dear Uncle,
   I can no longer conceal what perhaps you have already discovered — namely, my *attachment to Cousin Mary*. You may be surprised that I entertain *more* than what ought to exist between those so nearly connected by blood relationship, but it is nevertheless true. I was attached to her previous to my residence at the north and I beg you will permit me to pay my addresses to her. You have always, my dear Uncle, exercised the supervision of a *Father* over me in all my affairs, and in this matter, as still holding this relation, I look up to you for your *candid feelings*, and for your direction. I know the family connection existing between Cousin Mary and myself makes the matter more delicate. It is nearer than I ever expected to approach in any matrimonial relation and therefore beg your opinion and direction.
   from your affectionate nephew
   Charles C. Jones[37]

Sometime during the next few days Charles and his Uncle Joseph had a long conversation, and Joseph gave his blessings to the proposed marriage. Mary, who

had not said anything to her father, left with Charles for Sunbury and a visit to
General Stewart, who was dangerously ill. From Sunbury she wrote Joseph at
the Retreat:

Sunbury

My dear Father,

Having learned from *undoubted sources* your *perfect acquiescence* in relation to an event, the most important, I requested Mother to tender you my
sincere thanks for your kindness, and inform you of my sentiments respecting
that subject. Notwithstanding this I still feel it the dictate of *duty* and *affection* thus explicitly to acquaint *you*, my *dearest* and *only* earthly *parent* with my
decision, which is, with *your entire approbation* hereafter to consider Cousin
Charles as my more than relative.

Your ever affectionate
daughter,
M. Jones[38]

Joseph responded three days later:

Retreat May 30th, 1829

My dear Daughter,

I have perused your note on the Important subject you wrote, and can as-
sure you it meets with my cordial approbation.

Tis true that I have repeatedly said that cousins ought not to marry; yet this
kind of objection ought not with a parent to be insuperable. You and Charles
are both old enough to judge correctly in these matters and both members of
the same church.

Should it please God to have you at some future and suitable time united
in the Holy bonds of matrimony, your Happiness will much depend upon a
Reciprocity of Temper in yielding to each other's weakness for poor Human
nature will be frail and subject to *err* and when *this is the case*, I hope from
discretion and good sense you both possess proper allowance will be made.

Wishing you all the Happiness you can desire both Temporal and Spiritual
yr ever affectionate Father,
Jos. Jones[39]

And so the match was made. The young couple had only ten days together before Charles's departure for the North. They found General Stewart dying at
his home near Sunbury. Charles and the old general had made their profession
of faith together before the Midway congregation seven years earlier, and now
Charles stood by the general's bed, reminded him of Christ's gracious promises,

and watched his father's hunting friend and brother-in-law close his eyes in death. Charles wanted to write the obituary, but his remaining time at home was too short. He and Mary paid a quick visit to Betsy and William Maxwell at Laurel View, and then at Midway Church they said their good-byes as Charles got on the stagecoach for Savannah.[40]

"I feel like another man," he wrote from Savannah, "and for you, dear Mary, next to God and Christ, I wish to live. Duty to my Master requires that I should not see your face for some time. . . . But we can pour out our hearts to each other in our letters. We can be companions, although the ocean rolls between us."[41]

8

PRINCETON

Charles did not know it when he left Liberty in the spring of 1829, but the next year and a half were to be the most important period in his life. During the coming months he was plunged into a moral and spiritual crisis the likes of which he had never known and the likes of which he would never again experience. Deeply competing impulses were at the heart of the crisis, each impulse vying for his loyalty, each making its claims on his life. The crisis, at its simplest, was a competition between his sense of duty, with all of its deeply held religious convictions, and his love of his Liberty County home, with all of its associations and memories. The precipitating issue was vocational—what calling should he follow in his ministry?—but the fundamental issue was slavery and his relationship to it. The crisis was intensified, and perhaps made possible, by his distance from home during his coming months in the North and by his exposure to antislavery leaders. But the crisis was also intensified by his sense that duty and home ought somehow to overlap each other, that he ought somehow to be able to do his duty without giving up his southern home with its rivers and marshes, its plantations and people whom he loved.

The trip north was itself a respite. To become engaged to Mary and then to stand beside General Stewart as he died had left Charles emotionally exhausted and ready for the rest that a sailing ship could provide. As the brig headed out to sea, he watched the river ripple with schools of mullet and sturgeon. At sea he delighted in the porpoises that played in the evenings under the bow of the ship, creating a phosphorescence that illumined their bodies and the wake of their passage. They resembled, he thought, "torches borne rapidly through the deep with their flame and sparks trailing after them." He watched a whale breach and spout water in a jet "like an engine, but in a white foamy spray," and he stayed on deck during a storm that left him marveling at the power of God and "the sublimity in such a scene."[1]

Charles landed in Philadelphia, then took the stage to New York and a steamboat to New Haven. After visiting some friends at Yale, he traveled to Hartford, where he spent a day with his friend Catharine Beecher, daughter of Lyman Beecher, the most influential Protestant clergyman in the country. Charles and Catharine had been friends since his early days in Andover, and he knew her to be an educator and social reformer of remarkable strength. She had founded in 1823 the Hartford Female Seminary, an academy for higher education for women noted for its happy atmosphere and rigorous academic standards. Catharine was an early feminist, but one who wanted to expand the role and power of women in the home, where they would shape the future of the republic by carefully teaching and nurturing the children of a young nation.[2]

Catharine warmly welcomed her southern friend who had visited her at the school two years earlier. "She led me," Charles wrote Mary, "to the seat of the Teacher at the upper end of the hall, and said to me as we passed along, with all eyes turned upon 'Mr. Jones,' 'Can you face 120 young ladies?'" Charles did and was immediately struck by the way Catharine insisted that her students "understand the principles of their particular studies." As a reformer she was urging that ornamental education for girls—an education that emphasized painting, embroidery, and piano—be replaced by an education that taught the disciplines of rationality and persistence. In her best-selling *Treatise on Domestic Economy* she later wrote: "The success of democratic institutions, as is conceded by all, depends upon the intellectual and moral character of the mass of the people." And she added, "If they are intelligent and virtuous democracy is a blessing; but if they are ignorant and wicked, it is only a curse." And so, she insisted, there was a need for teachers in the homes and schools of the land who could help raise the intellectual and moral character of the mass of the people. Charles agreed completely with such sentiments, and he wondered about the implications for the "mass of the people" at Carlawter and the Retreat and the other settlements and quarters across the South.[3]

In the afternoon Charles and Catharine rode horseback out to Weathersfield to see the new prison there—an example of the prison reform movement—and then rode slowly back together, "beguiling our way," he wrote Mary, "with interesting conversation" while they admired the beauty of the Connecticut River valley. "It was one of those evenings in spring that almost incline us to wish them no end." The two of them took tea alone and spent the rest of the evening together with Catharine's sister Mrs. Mary Beecher Perkins. The day provided an opportunity for conversation about Charles's own calling and for Catharine to express her strong antislavery sentiments. Perhaps Charles mentioned to her Lizzy or Rosetta or Old Jupiter. He did tell her of Mary and their engagement. He left about nine o'clock, not having met on this trip Catharine's younger sister

Harriett, who in a few months was to join Catharine at the Hartford seminary. Years later, when Harriett wrote *Uncle Tom's Cabin*, she verified her picture of slavery in part by referring to the writings of her sister's friend from the South, Charles Jones.[4]

Charles paid a quick visit to his friends Lowell and Abigail Mason in Boston and then went on to Andover. In spite of his love for much of what he knew of New England, he had already made up his mind to leave Andover and go to Princeton. He wrote Joseph about the reasons for his decision. The weather was bad and the climate "too far north for my constitution." Dr. Porter was in feeble health and there was consequently no professor of ecclesiastical history, the area of Charles's special interest. But the real issue was cultural. "I am rather *too far north*, and should like to get into society a little more southern, or at any rate, a society not so entirely northern." Besides, he wrote, "To graduate from Princeton will help my popularity (if that is to be considered) at home more than to graduate at Andover." Princeton, in its composition and social character, was clearly not so much a Yankee institution as Andover. If Charles were to graduate from Andover, his theological orthodoxy, his manners, and his views on slavery would be suspect at home. "I think," he wrote Mary, that "it would be of advantage to reside among those who are more congenial in their manners and feelings and aims, and at a place where I shall be brought more in contact with the people and the field that shall claim my labours as a minister very shortly."[5]

Charles, however, was deeply ambivalent about New England and its manners and people, and his move south to Princeton was part of the struggle that marked this period of his life. Friends in Georgia worried that during his years in the North he had become a Yankee, with cool manners and distant ways. Some of his friends, Mary had written him earlier, "entertained serious fears lest the cold, calculating temperature of a Yankee climate might chill in your affections those to whom you were and still are ever dear."[6] Even strangers would think him a Yankee and be surprised when they discovered he was from Georgia. Charles, in fact, had come to admire deeply much about New England—especially what he regarded as its orderly landscape and calm and virtuous ways. And if, in later years, he changed his tune, his admiration for New England ways and values was genuine and a part of his intense struggle during his last months in the North.[7]

While Charles was busy making his move to Princeton, Mary was following the familiar routines of Liberty County. She moved with the family to Sunbury for the summer and fall and entered into the social life of the little village. There were visits to Colonel's Island and to the summer cottage of Colonel and Mrs. Maybank to enjoy the seafood served at "The Hut," and to Laurel View to see Betsy and William and Susan and the children. But there were also sorrows to be borne. During the sickly season of late summer and early fall, General Stewart's wife died, her sufferings at the end "being very great." And little Georgia Maxwell, Susan's youngest, was taken with a fever. "The agony of her disease," wrote Mary, "was most heartrending to behold" as the child was in convulsions for up to three and a half hours at a time, and nothing could stop the course of the deadly fevers.[8] And then Mary's closest friend, Hetty Dunwody, was struck down. They had been in school together at Barsden Bluff and had spent time together in Savannah. Seeing "the lonely grave closed upon her" had been a severe shock to Mary. Charles, moved by Mary's grief, wrote back: "We live in a vast charnelhouse. The living fall dead by our side day after day, nor do *we* know but that the sword will smite us next."[9]

After the death of Georgia, Susan took Laura and Charles Edward and went to St. Simons for a long visit with Julia and Roswell King. Betsy and William went with them to the island. With its long beach, balmy fall weather, and the hospitable home of the Kings, it seemed a good place to heal the shock of Georgia's death.[10]

Left behind in Liberty County, a grieving Mary returned to the Retreat in late November 1829 and sat down to write a response to a letter from Charles. He was feeling increasingly agitated by the question of slavery and by the ways it was tearing at him. He felt that he must know Mary's views on the subject. Was she feeling some of the same conflict that he felt?[11]

Writing from her garret room at the Retreat, with Phoebe no doubt nearby, Mary wrote that while she had scarcely formed any definite views on slavery, she would state her feelings. "In many respects my feelings are not unlike your own. With you I think it one of the greatest curses any nation or people should have to contend with. Its effects I think most deleterious to the advancement not only of morals but science, to decided energetic improvement." She also thought it "a great hindrance to the growth of grace in the Christian's heart." The principle of slavery, she insisted, "must be revolting to every feeling and reflective mind and the only efficient obviation of the evil—*total abolition.*"

But even in declaring slavery such an evil, Mary did not think emancipation could be accomplished immediately, and when accomplished, it would take the national government's involvement to compensate slave owners, "for there are not many individuals who would be willing to beggar their dependent families through such philanthropic motives." Then, echoing sentiments not so distant from those of Catharine Beecher on "the mass of the people," she wrote:

> Neither do I think it would at all promote the slave's interest to liberate him in his present degraded state. You might almost as soon contend for the emancipation of all that horde of corruption pent within our common prisons as the

general mass of Negro slaves. I am sure I know not a dozen that I could unhesi-
tatingly say I thought capable of self-government — devoid of every principle of
moral rectitude, divested of all the finer sensibilities of our nature; the master's
scowl or the master's *rod* form the only barrier to the commission of crime the
most atrocious. In their present state what might not be the consequences if
unrestricted by the laws of man; and ignorant and fearless of the commands of
God, they were permitted equally with ourselves to enjoy the rights of freemen?

Mary acknowledged that she felt "greatly dependent upon them for ease and
comforts." But for that very reason "it seems a greater kindness and a more Christian act rather than liberate them, whilst so closely bound by the shackles of in-
nate vice, to seek to raise them first in the scale of moral excellence by a different mode of treatment from what has been adopted hitherto, by treating them
more as rational beings and trying to instill into them virtuous principles." She
would not advocate opening to them the field of science, "for that would only
be awakening them to a sense of their own misery without in any degree bene-
fiting them or advancing their happiness." Rather, she would advocate religious
instruction.

> Teach them to feel that they are immortal, accountable beings. Teach them
> the need of a Saviour and whilst your slaves, teach them the duty of obedi-
> ence from higher motives than earthly displeasure — from Christian principles
> that which the Bible inculcates. I cannot say what would be the result of the
> experience of such a mode of treatment. Many would say it was altogether chi-
> merical and never would accomplish the desired end. I cannot affirm that it
> would be otherwise, but I should be pleased to see it tested.[12]

So Mary, writing from the Retreat with its settlement nearby, spelled out her
position — a program for benevolent reform within the system of slavery. Slavery,
it could be agreed, was a great evil, and the only answer to its evil was total abolition. But abolition was not possible at the present time, nor would it be in the best
interest of those who lived in the settlements. They lacked the internalized disciplines needed for freedom — the virtues and morals required for self-government.
To teach them such virtues and morals, to show them their need of a savior, and
to inculcate a sense of "the duty of obedience" as responsible beings — here was a
high calling worthy of evangelical reformers. Charles would take longer to come
to such conclusions, but Mary's response to his question was clearly the direction in which he was moving.

Charles did not find Princeton all that he had hoped for. It certainly had a
strong southern presence — both the college and the seminary had long been

favorites of wealthy southerners. But the conservatism of the seminary clashed with the theology he had learned at Andover. To be sure, compared with Harvard Divinity School, Andover was hardly a bastion of theological liberalism. At Unitarian Harvard, according to one of its disillusioned students from the South, "The peculiarity of their belief consists in *not believing* . . . the system of the Orthodox."[13] Andover had been established precisely to promote orthodoxy and, with the divinity school at Yale, it had become a center of evangelical reform movements. But its orthodoxy had sought to modify a scholastic Calvinism that still ruled at Princeton.

For Charles the critical difference between Andover and Princeton was closely linked to his own personal struggles and to the spiritual crisis he was facing. The theological question focused on human freedom. How much freedom does any person really have? To what degree do circumstances and the contingencies of one's own birth limit personal freedom? More specifically, does the human will have the power within itself to repent and change the direction of a person's life? Charles identified himself as a Hopkinsian, after the New England theologian Samuel Hopkins. Hopkins had shaped a "New England theology" that had drawn deeply from the wells of Jonathan Edwards's thought and that was particularly well suited for a democratic America. Most notable was an emphasis on what Hopkins called "disinterested benevolence." For Hopkins, the essence of sin was selfishness and self-love. A Christian conversion, however, made possible in a person a disposition for the good of others that did not take one's own interest into account. This New England theology had been a mighty engine for the creation of social reformers, and Hopkins himself had been one of the first in New England to denounce the slave trade as immoral.[14]

In a long letter to Mary, Charles explained to her the difference between the Princeton theology and the New England theology he espoused. The Princeton people, he said, insisted that repentance is a pure gift of God, that the "sinner cannot repent; that he has no power at all to repent. He must do what he can and wait God's time." But the New England theology that Charles held insisted that the inability of a sinner to repent consists in "*disinclination*, and disinclination only. . . . The sinner has all the natural power to repent; he is able to repent. The reason why he does not, is because he *will* not."[15]

So for Charles repentance and belief were largely a matter of the *will*, of volition. One simply had to *decide*, to make up one's mind, to accept Christ as one's personal savior and to change the direction of one's life. Such a theological position was to put him in the camp with Lyman Beecher and other revivalists and social reformers, and with the broad cultural optimism of nineteenth-century America that celebrated the freedom and power of the human will. Here was to be the heart of his pleas with William Maxwell and Joseph Jones and other unconverted relatives. They simply needed an act of will to denounce their love of self and their self-interest and turn to Christ and a new life. And what about Phoebe or Rosetta's Sam or Cassius or the other unconverted ones who lived in the settlements of Liberty County? Were they not also, as Mary said, "immortal, accountable beings" with the freedom to repent and change their ways if they were presented with a direct appeal of the Gospel?

Most pressing for Charles, of course, was the freedom of his own will. Did he have the freedom to decide about the direction of his life, to turn from self-love and self-interest to a concern for the good of others? Most specifically, did he have the freedom to reject slavery, the self-love and the self-interest of a white slave owner, and attack the harsh physical slavery of the settlements? Did the contingencies of his own life—the fact that he had been born in a slave-owning family, that he had been loved and nurtured by slave owners, and that he was a part of a long cultural history that justified human slavery—were all of these contingencies simply "disinclinations" to be overcome with an act of the will? Such questions troubled his sleep, and during the day increasingly occupied his thoughts.

Charles set about addressing the questions in a manner he had learned from his New England mentors—he formed a "Society of Inquiry Concerning Africans." It is, he wrote Mary, *"a matter of no small astonishment that the whole race of Africans as objects of Christian sympathy and benevolence, have been overlooked in Princeton seminary from its foundation, and that even motives of policy have not induced some attention to them."* And so he drew up the constitution and bylaws of the new society, got the approval of his professors, and was elected president. The design of the society was specially shaped to address in a rational and orderly fashion Charles's own spiritual and vocational crisis. The society was to collect "information respecting the condition and prospects of enslaved and manumitted Africans throughout the world, but more particularly those of our own country; to collect information respecting all benevolent societies designed to meliorate the condition of the neglected and degraded portion of the human family." All of this collecting of information was to be done to help Princeton students ascertain "our personal duties and responsibilities" toward enslaved and manumitted Africans and "the manner in which their best interests may be promoted."[16]

Jones was all too aware that most southern whites were not enthusiastic about such questions, that they were in fact deeply hostile to any discussion that hinted at the abolition of slavery. Many ministers, he wrote Mary, "have ruined their influence and usefulness in the Southern states by *injudicious speech* and conduct in regard to the slaves and the general subject of slavery." It was, he said, "highly important that those of us who are anticipating a Southern field of labour should become well acquainted with the subject of slavery, and understand in what way it may be approached, and by course of conduct the best interests of the coloured population and the approbation of the whites may be secured."[17]

Charles struggled to find some reasonable, middle path that was in "the best interests of the coloured population" and that at the same time could receive the "approbation of the whites." Without such a way he would be left with the freedom of a terrible choice—of deciding either for his Christian duty or for the home he loved. What was equally troubling for him was the possibility that his struggle was simply a "disinclination" of his own will to decide for his Christian duty—a disinclination rooted in sin, in his own self-love.

Charles turned his attention for a while to the American Colonization Society as a means of addressing slavery in the United States. It seemed such a glorious scheme, so full of reason and goodwill. The black population of the country would simply be sent back to West Africa, where a "civilized and Christianized republic" could be established in Liberia. There the former slaves could form a powerful republic to suppress the slave trade, open trade with the nations in the interior of Africa, and send from among their numbers missionaries and teachers to reclaim their African brothers and sisters from "their heathenish condition." Charles thought it "a noble design!"[18] And it was noble indeed—unless, of course, you were a slave who wanted freedom in the United States rather than a one-way trip to Liberia, or a white planter who had no desire to lose slave labor. And that was the rub—the scheme carried with it a deep racism that was beginning to be denounced, and it reflected a profound economic and political naïveté.

By the middle of May 1830, with graduation from Princeton looming, Charles felt the pressure building for some decision. He was, he wrote Mary, "uncertain that I should make Georgia my home." He reminded her, "I have always been deeply interested for the Coloured population in slavery in the United States. How it has long been a doubt in my mind whether I ought to return to Georgia and endeavor to do what I can for them there, and also where as God shall give me opportunity, or devote myself at once to them, in some special efforts in connection with the Colonization Society, or in some other manner." He did not know, he said, "which way the scale will turn," and he prayed "for light from on high to shine and make the path of duty plain before my face." One thing he was certain of—it was "high time that our country was taking some measures of some sort whose ultimate tendency shall be the emancipation of nearly three million of men, women, and children who are held in the grossest bondage, and with the highest injustice."[19] Perhaps he was thinking of those who worked the fields at the Retreat or ate by the evening fires of Carlawter.

Charles wondered in frustration why no one was devising and executing measures that would lead to emancipation. He felt that the whole country was dead
on the subject, "while a vast amount of passion and prejudice and self-interest
and difficulty is set in opposition to every attempt to bring it forward." But he
was certain that matters could not stay as they were and that some movement
must take place. He asked Mary to pray for him that God would give him clarity
about the direction he should go. And then he added:

> I am, moreover, undecided whether I ought to continue to *hold slaves*. As to
> the *principle* of slavery, it is *wrong!* It is unjust, contrary to nature and religion
> to hold men enslaved. But the question is, in my present circumstances, with
> evil on my hands entailed from my father, would the general interests of the
> slaves and community at large, with reference to the slaves, be promoted best,
> by emancipation? Could I do more for the ultimate good of the slave popu-
> lation by holding or emancipating what I own? I know not very *particularly*
> how *you feel* on this point. But am inclined to believe that your feelings are
> not much different from mine.

Charles longed to see Mary and he urged her to come north for the summer so
that they could discuss face-to-face these important questions. He was certain
that in "regard to any measures which I may think best to adopt that are reasonable and calculated to benefit the slave population and push forward the Kingdom of Christ, I can be supported so far as *money* is concerned without difficulty."
What he wasn't certain about was whether Mary could follow whatever path he
chose. She had said she would, and she had filled his "heart with joy" when she
told him she was willing for him go where the voice of God called him and that
she would esteem it her highest happiness to go with him. But, he asked, "My
beloved, my dear Mary, *are you* willing to give up all your relatives and friends
for my sake?"[20]

For all of his struggles, Charles was clearly moving toward a decision that
would lead him back to Liberty County as a missionary among slaves. Such a
path seemed to lead to several deeply held hopes—the evangelization of the
slaves to help prepare them for the virtues and responsibilities needed for freedom; the evangelization of slaves for their eternal salvation; and the building of
a home, both an earthly and an eternal one, where blacks and whites could live
together in harmony and mutual affection. Such a course seemed to be the way
to resolve the deep conflicts of his heart and to ease the competing demands of
duty and home. Before he made such a decision, however, he determined to discuss his plan with those most deeply identified with the antislavery movement.

Three days after writing Mary about his struggles, Charles left Princeton for

Philadelphia, Baltimore, and Washington. He had become a great walker during his time in the North, and he set out for Philadelphia on foot. He walked the twenty miles to Bristol and found the countryside dressed in green and cultivated like a garden. White farmhouses with red chimneys, lit by the clear shining of the sun, peered through the green foliage and stirred his admiration. In Bristol, after soaking his feet in cold water, he caught a steamboat on the Delaware River to take him the rest of the way to Philadelphia. Arriving in the city, he went to the meeting of the Presbyterian General Assembly and heard Lyman Beecher preach "one of his *reformation* sermons. The great doctrine of his sermon was 'that nothing could save our country from the various evils which threatened it, but an enlightened and moral *people.*'" Charles kept thinking about those who lived in the settlements in Liberty and how they fit into such a challenge. He talked with Absalom Peters, who four years earlier had led in the establishment of the American Home Missionary Society. They discussed the "condition and prospects of the coloured population of the U. States, and the best method of proceeding in giving them the Gospel, and waking up the public sympathy in their behalf." Peters gave Charles advice about what was needed to start a new movement—that he must develop a careful plan and identify those who would help to carry the plan into effect. Charles took note of the advice, thought about what it might mean for Liberty County, and reported to Mary that Peters had promised that the mission society would support any good proposals for work among the slave population. After a brief discussion with Beecher, Charles left for Washington.[21]

He took a steamboat down the river to the Delaware and Chesapeake Canal, where he boarded a canal barge drawn by horses hitched in a single file. It was a lovely day, and he sat beneath the barge's awning and "enjoyed the cool breeze and the instructive conversation of a China merchant." The canal connected the Delaware River with the Chesapeake Bay, saving a traveler hundreds of miles around the Delmarva Peninsula. Charles marveled at the technological developments of the nineteenth century and the promises they held for a bright future, and he knew that confidence in an expanding technology informed the assumptions of many in the growing antislavery movement. At the bay he boarded the steamer *George Washington* for the run to Baltimore. "Our boat," he wrote, "made between 24 and 26 revolutions of her wheels per minute, and had on 15 or 16 inches of steam."[22]

After a brief stay in Baltimore, Charles took the stage to Washington, where he made his way to the home of the U.S. attorney general, John M. Berrien. A Savannah politician and judge, Berrien was an old friend of Joseph Jones. He knew the influence of the Jones family and its connections in the low country, so when presented a letter of introduction from Joseph, the attorney general gave Charles a warm welcome. He made inquiries about the family in Liberty County and showed Charles every kindness, but when the subject of the Cherokees came up, Berrien's tone changed. He expressed to Charles his satisfaction at the recent passage of the bill authorizing the president to negotiate with the Cherokees "for the sale or exchange of lands and removal West of the Mississippi, and appropriating $500,000 for these purposes." Berrien evidently thought any white Georgian would agree with such sentiments, but Charles expressed his regrets about the bill, for he thought it unjust and an infringement on the rights of the Cherokees. Taken aback, Berrien "put himself to the trouble of entering into some remarks on the right of Georgia to the territory, the misapprehension of the true state of the question in the north, the unnecessary excitement that prevailed in the *Religious* community etc." Charles found Berrien's arguments specious, and he left without receiving an invitation to stay in the attorney general's home. Charles was insulted, evidently considering this slight a serious violation of the code of hospitality inherent in his privileged background. The attorney general soon wrote a letter of apology to Joseph, saying that his busy schedule prevented his offering such an invitation, but Charles accepted the apology grudgingly.[23]

Charles quickly received an invitation, however, to stay in the home of Reuben Post, a New Englander who was the pastor of the First Presbyterian Church in Washington and chaplain of the Senate. There he found a Mr. Evarts, another New Englander, who was the corresponding secretary of the American Board of Foreign Missions. "It will not surprise you, I hope," he wrote Mary, "when I tell you that it does me *good* to meet New England friends and acquaintances."[24] The episode at Berrien's and the warm reception he received from the New Englanders apparently raised a question in his mind. Was there a way that the religious community he had come to know in the North was more his home than the geographical community of Georgia? He certainly found in this religious community, in contrast to Berrien, a welcome and a deep sympathy with his way of seeing contemporary events. Could the religious community represent for him another kind of home—an alternative vision, a broader, less tribal way of understanding home in this world and the next? But of course there was also a religious community at Midway, where his parents and so many friends and relatives lay buried, and where his sisters and fiancée were members.

Charles spent the next day with Ralph Gurley, the executive of the American Colonization Society. They talked about the society, about the young colony of African Americans in Liberia, and about the prospects of the society. Gurley was optimistic about the future and emphasized the moral obligation of every American to address the evils of slavery. The society, Charles concluded, "is gaining ground in the U. States, rapidly, and its colony is very flourishing."[25]

During the next few days, Post showed Charles the sights of the city. They went to the Senate, where Charles saw John C. Calhoun, "not a handsome man, features small, rather slim in person, but an eye full of vivacity and fire, seated beneath rather a heavy brow"; and he saw Daniel Webster and a host of others as well. But he was most impressed with Senator Theodore Frelinghuysen of New Jersey. "His countenance is all benevolence," Charles wrote Mary, and, in contrast to Berrien, he treats "every body with great kindness, I mean *Christian* kindness, and is a most devoted, pious man." Charles saw Frelinghuysen as a great friend of the Indian, for he had made an important speech opposing the removal of the Cherokees.[26]

On the following Sunday, Post asked Charles to preach the morning sermon at the First Presbyterian Church. Charles had with him the sermon he had preached as a part of his examination for ordination. Not surprisingly, the sermon was on Matthew 6:24, a text that addressed the preoccupation of Charles's mind and heart: "No man can serve two masters: for either he will hate the one, and love the other; or else he will hold to the one, and despise the other. Ye cannot serve God and mammon." Senator Frelinghuysen was there, and shortly after the service began Andrew Jackson came in and sat with his wife right under the pulpit. "He looked at me over his specktacles," Charles reported, "with an eye of considerable fire and command, to know who was about to preach." Charles recognized him immediately as the president and liked the old gentleman's appearance very much, with his full head of gray hair. Charles assured Mary that he was not intimated by having the president in the congregation. "Standing up in the presence of God, to deliver the truths of his word to dying men, I found neither time nor inclination to gaze after the man who with his distinctions will be soon laid in the dust, and will appear with me before the King of Kings, the Lord of all; He to answer for the improvement of his opportunity of hearing the word of the Lord spoken; and I, for my faithfulness in delivering it." In the congregation with the president hearing Charles preach on the impossibility of serving two masters was the Cherokee delegation in Washington.[27]

That evening the delegation came to Reuben Post's home. Led by John Ross, the principal chief of the Cherokee Nation, they had come to Washington to fight the removal bill. "Our conversation," Charles wrote Mary, "was chiefly on their controversy with Georgia, the passage of the bill, etc." Charles found them all sensible, well-informed men. "They felt much," said Charles, "and determined to bear with patience every evil that might come upon them, and hold fast their lands and not sell a foot, and if possible carry their cause before the Supreme Court of the U. States." None of those sitting in the Post drawing room could know that in a few short years the friends and relatives of Charles would be leaders in making Cherokee lands the most vigorous and thriving part of Georgia for its white citizens.[28]

Meanwhile, in Liberty County, Mary and her family were back in Sunbury for the summer and fall, having left the Retreat house being painted and readied for the upcoming wedding. Susan and the children left Laurel View in July for an extended stay with the Roswell Kings on St. Simons, and Mary, at her father's urging, was preparing for a visit to Sapelo Island. The Thomas Spaldings of Sapelo had visited at the Retreat, and social etiquette required a return visit.[29]

Mary was reluctant to go, saying that a quiet and retired life had more charms for her than any other. But when she went, she found that Sapelo and the Spalding plantation charmed her. The island, she wrote Charles, was the "most beautiful and romantic spot I ever saw. From the beach which is near a quarter of a mile in width you see the Atlantic rolling at your feet from three points—east, south, and west. We took a moonlight excursion upon it, which I shall never forget. The sublimity of the scene was indescribable." As for the Spalding house, it looked "like the castle of some old feudal lord" and was "seated in the bosom of an extensive oak forest which from its moss clad and venerable appearance seems to have weathered the storms of a century." Mary was also delighted with the beautiful Mrs. Spalding. She seemed to Mary *"almost all* that woman should be— possessing ardent, active piety, great intelligence and a most bewitching kindness and affection of manner."[30] In her description of Sapelo, Mary was apparently inviting Charles to feel as well the charm of the island and the bewitching pull of a low-country home.

Shortly after his evening with the Cherokee delegation, Charles left Washington for Baltimore. With him went Ross and a few members of the delegation. Charles stayed at the home of friends and took an excursion on the new railroad that already had thirteen miles of track laid. His car, pulled by what Charles called "one horse," moved at the rate of ten or twelve miles per hour. It was to him "the most delightful ride I ever had. No motion but that of right on."[31] With no motion but "right on," the train, like the steamboat, was a sign of progress, of advancement, of movement toward an expanding future. Charles was never enthralled by the promises of technology, but he was deeply aware that profound changes were going on around him—changes that would soon be pushing into the Georgia low country and into Cherokee lands—and he shared a widespread optimism about a future that appeared to be arriving on rails.

In the afternoon after his train excursion, he went to see Benjamin Lundy, the antislavery editor of the *Genius of Universal Emancipation*. Lundy had recently met an impressive young abolitionist, William Lloyd Garrison, and had persuaded him to come to Baltimore and join him as the coeditor of the *Genius*. Charles evidently did not meet the fiery Garrison, who bitterly opposed the colonization movement, but he spent the afternoon and early evening discussing with Lundy the antislavery cause and the prospects of the Liberian colony. He left Lundy's home and called on John Ross and another member of the Cherokee delegation. Ross decided to travel with him to Philadelphia.[32]

The two men left the next day. Charles was still undecided about the direction of his life or how he could reconcile the moral and spiritual conflict of his heart. On the boat trip Ross gave Charles an account of Jackson's victory at the battle of Horseshoe Bend and, no doubt, told how the Cherokees had played a role in Jackson's defeat of their ancient rivals the Creeks. Charles and Ross parted in Philadelphia never to see each other again, but Charles had ample opportunity in the future to think about Ross and his efforts to save the Cherokees from a looming tragedy.[33]

Back in Princeton, one thing seemed certain to Charles—his love for Mary and his happy anticipation of their approaching marriage. "I ask from you," he wrote Mary, "indulgence for my numerous defects of character, your earnest prayers, and your affectionate reproofs. Remember that you have but a frail, imperfect man. Expect to see faults, expect to meet trials. All my hopes of whatever happiness is to be found in this vale of tears in the closest bonds of friendship and love are lodged in you." As he prepared to leave Princeton, he assured her "that my affection for you is unabated; that I look forward to our union as the happiest event of my life, leaving out divine things, and that it is my desire and will be my delight and labour to make you a tender and affectionate husband, and do every thing in my power consistent with my higher duties to God, to make you comfortable, and to meet your desires."[34]

Twelve days later he wrote her about his decision and the plan he wished to pursue. He would attempt on his return home to introduce into Liberty County a system of oral religious instruction "for our poor degraded slaves, and thus if the plan succeeds and God opens a door to me, to devote my life to missionary labours among them." He wondered what Mary thought of the plan. "You perceive at once," he said, "that it will be somewhat unpopular, and may excite against me much opposition and that I shall need great judgment and prudence. . . . You will therefore take care of *this* letter and keep to yourself this plan of mine and let me have as early as possible your own views and opinions of it, and of its probable success."[35]

And so Charles made his decision. During the preceding months he had struggled with the divided self of a young man's conscience. He had found his conscience both bound and free—bound by a love of his Liberty County home, bound by all the attachments of the place of his birth and the pull of family and friends, and bound too by the long cultural history that he had inherited and that justified human slavery. But he knew and believed his conscience to be also free—free to decide against home as a remembered and loved place, free to claim a modern homelessness and a broad attachment to an ideal of justice. This claim for freedom was central to his theology and was to be at the heart of much of his mission work and his evangelical appeal to family and slaves.

Charles knew too that his own bondage was in some deep sense linked to the concrete bondage of slaves. What was for him a moral dilemma and spiritual crisis was for Cato and Phoebe, for Rosetta and Sam, and for all who lived in the scattered settlements of the South a bitter struggle of daily life. With the rising of the sun each day, these sons and daughters of Africa knew only too well the bondage of a long cultural history and the struggle for freedom within that history. "How often do I think," Charles had written Mary the year before, "of the number of hands employed to furnish me with those conveniences of life of which they are in consequence deprived—how many intellects, how many souls perhaps, withered and blasted forever for this very purpose!" Their cruel bondage had seemed to him to cast a net over both the enslaved and the enslavers. "What I would not give," he cried, "if our family were not freed of this property and removed beyond its influence!"[36]

Charles's decision to return to Liberty County as a missionary and reformer thus seemed to him one way to negotiate between duty and home, between the bondage of place and its cultural heritage that he felt so keenly and the claims of freedom. A program of mission and reform of the system of slavery, he was convinced, could help to meet the real needs of slaves and, because it would not challenge the foundations of slavery, it also had the possibility of receiving the approbation of the whites. Charles, of course, did not think he was trying to serve two masters, that he was somehow succumbing to a "disinclination" of the will by avoiding a decision for either freedom or bondage. Rather, he thought and he prayed that he was making a decision that bridged the tensions of his psyche and that allowed him to follow a path of faithfulness both to his Christian duty and to the loving home he had been given. What he did not foresee as an earnest young man were the ways his decision would lead him slowly and steadily away from the cause of freedom to the side of bondage.

9

SOLITUDE

While Charles had been struggling in the North with the issues of slavery and his vocational decision, wedding preparations were proceeding at the Retreat. Mary was the apple of her father's eye, and Joseph had kept a number of slaves busy for months painting and repairing the house and making it ready for the wedding of his oldest daughter. Among those who worked on the house was Sandy Jones, the carpenter who as a young man had been an apprentice to Jacob at Liberty Hall. The year before he had had his own wedding to none other than young Phoebe. Their marriage had been a prize for both of them. For Phoebe, Sandy represented the security of an older husband who, as a skilled carpenter, was one of the most respected members of the settlement. Saturdays were free days for him, and he could work for nearby planters or for merchants in Riceboro and keep his wages. And on his side, Sandy had in Phoebe a young wife who was not only winsome and strong but also the influential daughter of Jack. Their wedding had been a simple affair in the settlement. Since Sandy was a church member, old Sharper performed the service. In July 1830, while Mary Jones was away visiting the Spaldings on Sapelo Island, Phoebe had given birth to their son John.[1]

The wedding of Charles and Mary was, in its own way, also simple but of course of a different order from one in the settlement. Elizabeth Jones had the responsibility of seeing that the Retreat was decorated for her stepdaughter's wedding. Smilax vines with long bronze leaves and bright berries were gathered from the nearby woods and woven into garlands around the railings of the piazza and strung over doorways and over pictures in the drawing room and parlor. Winter-blooming camellias were floated in glass bowls and arranged on tables, while the mantles were covered with magnolia leaves—large, shiny, and dark green—mixed with the red berries of low-country hollies. And everywhere candles were placed to cast their soft light. Some had been bought in Savannah and others made on the plantation from beeswax and the fragrant wax myrtles that grew in thick profusion along the edges of Bulltown swamp and by the marshes of the South Newport.

In the kitchen in back of the Retreat, Mom Sylvia directed the preparations of the wedding dinner: beef, venison, and wild ducks, oyster pies and glazed hams, a sweet and creamy syllabub, puddings and jellies, and breads and cakes—all had to be prepared in a timely fashion, and Jack had to see that they were arranged on the tables and sideboards as directed by his mistress.[2]

William McWhir performed the service on the evening of 21 December 1830 in the drawing room where Charles and Mary had become engaged. The night was cold and misty. Years later Charles wrote his son: "We dined at Henry's on Friday, the thirtieth anniversary of our wedding day (nearly a generation), and in the same house we were married. It was easy to recall the past and paint in memory the cheerful scenes of the wedding day and evening. I saw the figures, the countenances, the dress, the smiles, and heard the conversation, and saw myself and your mother too, and the wedding party (but four in number), and our venerable friend performing the ceremony, the supper and all things else—a bright and pleasing vision."[3]

The young couple made their home at Solitude, a plantation home on the North Newport near Carlawter rented for them by Joseph. It was a quiet and secluded place, not too far from family and friends but far enough—an idyllic spot, full of natural, simple charm and with the space and privacy for a couple who had spent so much time apart to be alone together in all the intensity of their love. But with them, of course, were Phoebe and her family, and Lizzy, now growing old, who came from Carlawter to see about the cooking, and Phoebe's young cousin Patience, who came from the Retreat to help in the kitchen and learn the ways of a plantation cook.[4]

Charles and Mary, however, were not together at Solitude ten days before their honeymoon was interrupted with frightening news—Mary's brother Joseph Maybank Jones was dangerously ill. He had left the Retreat a few days after the wedding and had been on his way to Milledgeville, the state capital, when he had been struck with a violent illness at a wayside tavern. Charles and Joseph rushed to him, but it took two days in the gig driving Joseph's horse Wilberforce as hard as he could go. They found him deathly sick with pneumonia. They took immediate charge of him, and a doctor was summoned from a nearby town, but young Joseph grew worse. "He complained of *intense heat*, which was wholly internal, and expressed the intensity of his suffering by comparing it to the 'torments of the damned.'" They used a fan to cool him. He cried: "'My *life* depends on the fan—fan me, fan, fan me.'" He began to pray that God would "smooth his passage to the grave." Charles and Joseph wept as they watched him die in agony, Charles sustained by his Christian faith, Joseph sustained by his stoicism. "Father," wrote Charles, "commanded his feelings astonishingly." They took the body home to the Retreat and buried him beside his mother, Mary Maybank, and his stepmother, Sarah Anderson, and among all the children who now slept in the cemetery behind the house.[5]

And so the marriage of Charles and Mary, which had begun with such joy, was quickly surrounded with sorrow in the death of one whom they loved and with whom they so closely identified. It was for them a reminder of what Charles had written Mary earlier: "Let us be warned. *Earth* is not our *home*. Our affections must be in heaven."[6]

The death of Joseph Maybank Jones—he was a year older than Charles—intensified for Charles and Mary their sense that their time together was a gift. So even in their sorrow they delighted in being together and in the beauty of the world around them. A few years later, on their wedding anniversary, Charles remembered this "springtime of our love" and wrote Mary of the early days at Solitude:

> In wintery morn, with deer and gun
> We walked in fields and leafy woods
> Or drove along the level roads.
> An evening fire our chamber warmed,
> With books and work our circle formed,
> Most pleased of all *to be alone*
> Most pleased to feel that we were *one*.[7]

These quiet days together provided time for them to talk about their hopes for the future and to discuss in detail Charles's plans for his missionary labors among the slaves of Liberty County. On visits around the county Charles began to talk discreetly about his proposals—at first with William Maxwell and Joseph and then with Robert Quarterman, the minister at Midway, and with other friends and family. Some encouraged him, but many thought working among the slaves would be a waste of his time, and others wondered whether such work would undermine discipline on the plantations. Some in the county were openly hostile to his proposals, but they were not influential enough to stop the discussion. Charles, after all, was Charles Jones, and Joseph was not only his uncle but also his father-in-law; besides, there was a host of other powerful relatives who would at least stand with him if he wanted to try an experiment, even a foolish one, in the religious instruction of slaves. What must have eased some minds was the fact that Charles was not only a Jones but also a slaveholder, and with his marriage to Mary he had become a slaveholder of some substance.[8]

Mary, as a surviving child of Sarah Anderson, was entitled to one third of her mother's slaves, together "with the issue and increase of the female slaves." The thirty-eight slaves that Sarah Anderson had brought in 1806 to her marriage with Joseph had grown, through the children of the female slaves, to sixty-five by 1831. William Maxwell and Andrew Maybank appraised these sixty-five men, women, and children in early 1831. From among their number, the appraisers selected twenty-two for Mary Jones.[9]

Phoebe was, of course, among those selected, together with her two children, Clarissa and John. Her father, Jack, was included, as was his brother Robin, Robin's wife, Lizzy, and their children Elsey, Stepney, and young Patience, the apprentice in the kitchen. Forty-year-old Flora and her eight children and one grandchild were picked to go with Mary, as were Tony, Little Caesar, and Adam. Sandy Jones, with his apprentice Syphax (the son of Hamlet and Elvira), had responsibility for constructing the new houses at Carlawter.[10]

Those who were sent to Carlawter from the Retreat moved into a settlement of relatives and former residents of the Retreat. Hamlet had taken over from his brother Jupiter the position of driver, and he now had responsibility for managing the work of more than sixty slaves. Charles hired Strong Ashmore, a neighbor whose father had a store in Riceboro, to be the white overseer and to visit Carlawter on a regular basis.[11] So Charles, in addition to having influential family connections, was known throughout the county as the owner of many slaves.

What was needed, Charles had told Mary, was a cautious, prudent approach to the question of slavery. He was convinced this was the only way any real progress could be made in addressing the great curse of slavery and in bringing salvation to those "held in the grossest bondage, and with the highest injustice."[12] Charles knew the low country too well; it was too much a part of his heart, too deeply ingrained in his manners for there to be any questions on this point: if he wanted to work in the South among the slaves, he had to use not only the wisdom of Solomon but all his knowledge of southern manners, all his family connections, and all of his prestige as a slaveholder to win the necessary approval of the white planters.

What he proposed was the formation among Liberty County planters of a voluntary association for the religious instruction of slaves. Such a plan had proved itself in other reforms—there was a voluntary society for almost every ill in the nation—but it was a plan that had to be sold to the planters. They might have Puritan ancestry, but they lived along Georgia rivers and by Georgia swamps and not in Boston or New Haven. They had formed a Temperance Society and a Library Society and an Education Society, and they had a Domestic Missionary Society at Midway, but they had no Lyman Beecher or Catharine Beecher among them, much less a Gurley or Lundy or a young William Lloyd Garrison. No, they were well educated and widely traveled southern planters with broad interests and concerns, but they were still southern planters, first and foremost southern planters. What more prudent and cautious approach, then, than to get friends and family together and make a proposal? This was precisely what Charles did.[13]

A small preliminary meeting was held in early March, and plans were made for a general meeting later in the month. Robert Quarterman, pastor at Midway (no one could accuse him of anything radical or rash!) joined Charles in issuing the invitations. At the end of March the planters gathered at the little courthouse in Riceboro. Charles, together with the others going into the courthouse, had to cross a sandy yard shaded by live oaks and long grieving wisps of Spanish moss, the very place where slaves regularly stood to be auctioned. Twenty-nine planters came. They represented not only the wealth and leadership of the community but also some of the most distinguished southern families. James Stevens Bullock, planter and president of the United States Bank in Savannah, crossed the yard to the meeting. His grandfather had been the first president of the Provincial Congress of Georgia, and Bullock was soon to marry Senator Elliot's widow and thereby link himself to the Jones clan through their Stewart connections. Bullock's brother-in-law John Dunwody came from his Arcadia plantation near Midway. A graduate of Yale and a leader in the Midway congregation, he was called "Cousin John" by Charles, in the southern manner of reaching out and claiming relatives hidden in the mysteries of genealogy. Odingsell Hart, the wealthy brother-in-law of Joseph Jones, made the trip from his plantation on the Medway River. Barrington King, brother to Roswell, Jr., and a handsome, energetic young man, arrived from his nearby plantation South Hampton. And of course Joseph was there, as was William Maxwell. All in all, it was a distinguished group of wealthy, pious, and good citizens. But it was also unquestionably a cautious group of white planters who were the owners of hundreds of slaves.[14]

Charles looked them over with all the earnestness of a young minister. How different they were from those with whom he had met the previous summer in Washington and Baltimore to discuss the issues of slavery!

Evangelism was his theme, and his text was "Go ye into all the world and preach the Gospel to every creature." "All the world," Charles reminded his listeners, included not only foreign shores and distant climes but also Liberty County, and "every creature" meant not only white planters but also black slaves. Evangelism, Charles insisted, was a task that was laid upon every Christian, a responsibility that could not be avoided. Because black slaves, like their white owners, were creatures of God "moving onward to the retributions of eternity," they needed the Gospel presented to them with saving power. They needed their hearts changed and their morals reformed. Could there be any doubt about this, he asked, when one looked at those who lived in the settlements of Liberty County?

> They lie, steal, blaspheme; are slothful, envious, malicious, inventors of evil things, deceivers, covenant breakers, implacable, unmerciful. They are greatly wanting in natural affection, improvident, without understanding and grossly immoral. Chastity is an exceeding rare virtue. Polygamy is common, and there is little sacredness attached to the marriage contract. It is entered into for the most part without established forms, and is dissolved at the will of the parties: nor is there any sacredness attached to the Sabbath. It is a day of idleness and sleep, of sinful amusements, of visiting, or of labor. They are generally temperate through necessity; when ardent spirits can be obtained, they will freely drink it. Numbers of them do not go to church, and cannot tell us who Jesus Christ is, nor have they ever heard so much as the Ten Commandments read and explained. Of the professors of religion among them, there are many of questionable piety who occasion the different churches great trouble in discipline, for they are extremely ignorant, and frequently are guilty of the grossest vices.[15]

Even the sympathetic white planters who shared such views must have thought Charles an arrogant young minister with much to learn about the human condition. But he felt that if he had to be prudent in regard to the evils of slavery, he could be zealous for moral rectitude, he could talk about chastity and Sabbath observance and temperance and biblical knowledge. In later years, when his missionary labors were well established, his message to planters was filled with a deep sympathy and a respect for those he had come to know in the settlements. But for now this zealous spirit, this high-handed arrogance, suited his purposes well. He could focus on the morality of the slaves, he could call attention to all the behavior of blacks that offended white sensibilities and that called for remedial action. Such an approach was intended to appeal to white planters, for it meant a major thrust of evangelization would be to socialize the slaves of Liberty County into the morals and manners of white society.

But if Charles knew how to count the sins of the slaves, he also could accuse the planters as well—with, to be sure, a cautious, prudent accusation. There would be no hint that they were "men-stealers," or that they were involved in an "inhuman abuse of power," but he could say that they had not been responsible as masters. If their black slaves were ignorant and destitute, if they were "a nation of heathen in our very midst," the planters needed to recognize that they had done very little on behalf of the religious welfare of their slaves. It would not do for them to dismiss the problem by saying that Africans or African Americans were somehow incapable of receiving religious instruction. That clearly was not the case, for God had "made of one blood all the nations of men that dwell on the face of the earth." It could not be plainer that "all men have one common origin, and that all are capable of exercising proper affection toward God." Charles resisted any racial assumptions about differences between blacks and whites.[16] The differences—and he thought they were great—were a matter not so much of race as of class. Black slaves were part of the "mass of the people" of whom Catharine Beecher had spoken with such suspicion. If white planters had doubts about the unity of the races, about the common origin of all races, they needed only take notice of the black slaves around them who understood the Gospel and lived lives of exemplary Christian piety.

In this way Charles left behind the tensions that had been tearing at his heart during the preceding months. The issue he set before his friends and neighbors was not a competition between Christian duty and home—the issue now was the religion and morals of black slaves and the responsibilities of white owners. To deal with this issue he proposed that a new work be begun for the slaves of Liberty County.

His plan was for the planters to form themselves into a voluntary association and "take the religious instruction of the coloured population into their own hands." They would appoint teachers from among their number who would go to stations located near several plantations, where the slaves could come for instruction and worship. There during the week and on the Sabbath the teachers would "communicate instruction *orally*, and in as systematic and intelligible a manner as possible, embracing all the principles of the Christian religion as understood by orthodox Protestants, and carefully avoiding all points of doctrine that separate different religious denominations." The teachers would not be sent to any plantation without the "cordial consent of the owner," nor would they appear except at those times specified by him. The wishes and arrangements of the owners were to be "consulted and complied with." Teachers were to "confine themselves to the *religious instruction* of the Negroes wholly." They were not to "intermeddle with the concerns of the plantation in any manner, nor repeat abroad what their ears hear, or their eyes see on them." In addition to the work of the teachers, Charles proposed, not unexpectedly, that "a missionary may be employed to take a general supervision of the whole, occupy Sabbath stations, preach also during the week on plantations, and assist in framing courses of instruction." The planters gathered at the courthouse had, of course, little doubt about the person Charles had in mind to be the missionary to "these heathen" in their midst.[17]

Such a plan was a way to secure, Charles thought, what he had told Mary the year before was essential for success—both "the best interests of the coloured population and the approbation of the whites."[18] His proposal was tailored to calm the fears of white masters: the teachers would be local slaveholders, members of the association, who had self-interest as well as community pressure to safeguard their activities; the instructions would be oral, free from the dangers of teaching slaves to read or write—which was, in any case, illegal; the content would be orthodox Protestantism, exempt from denominational squabbling and safe from the radicalism that often infected the unorthodox; and the activities and conditions of the plantations would be off-limits, beyond the interests or concerns of the visiting teacher or missionary.

But Charles did not stop with these words of assurance. He had to expose himself even more; he had to press on and show his friends that his plan was not only safe but also beneficial. Such religious instruction would encourage a better understanding among both masters and slaves of the relationships that existed between them. In particular, there would be "greater subordination and a decrease of crime amongst the Negroes." Whites had no reason to fear that religious instruction would promote revolts or the desire for freedom and equality. Just the opposite was the case. The teachers themselves would supplement the patrol system, which, at any rate, was "not efficiently executed now." (Few Liberty County planters wanted to ride about at night keeping an eye on the blacks!) The simple presence of a white man, however, at "stated times amongst the Negroes," would "tend greatly to the promotion of good order." The plan, said Charles, seemed "to carry our security in it." But more than this external show of authority, there would be an internal change in the heart of the slaves. They would come to accept the authority of their masters: they would think like slaves, act like slaves, and be slaves. "We believe," said Charles, that the authority of masters "can be strengthened and supported in this way only; for the duty of obedience will never be felt or performed to the extent that we desire it, unless we can *bottom it on religious principle.*" Here was the key to the complete subordination of the slaves, the way to have their faces grow to fit the masks of obedience that they wore to hide their resistance to bondage. If the blacks would come to believe that obedience to white owners was a religious duty, that submission to their masters was an obligation owed to God, then the authority of the planters would be built upon a solid rock. If, however, blacks resisted that religious principle or substituted another for it, then the authority of masters would be established upon the shifting sands of power and fear.[19]

Charles then took a final, dangerous plunge—he assured his friends and neighbors that in addition to encouraging good order and subordination among their slaves, religious instruction of blacks would provide economic advantages for slaveholders. A faithful servant, he said, "is more profitable than an unfaithful one. He will do more and better work, be less troublesome, and less liable to disease." Of all the things he said, of all the words he wrote, nothing was to come back to haunt him more than this. His work would never be free from the suspicion that at its heart it was guided by economic motivations, that it was an attempt to increase the profits of the planters. Charles knew only too well that he was in dangerous waters and quickly moved to point out that the salvation of the slaves was the primary goal of religious instruction. While economic self-interest might be a powerful motivation in the hearts of white planters, the purpose was the salvation of the slaves' souls. "The great object for which we would communicate religious instruction to them," Charles declared, "is that their souls may be saved. To this all other objects should be subordinated." Charles believed that. It was fundamental for him. It colored all his perceptions about who he was and what he was about. It gave him courage and patience in trying times and covered his life and his work with grand illusions.[20]

In concluding his address to the planters, Charles spoke of their responsibility to their slaves. In the providence of God, the blacks had been placed under their care. For this reason they had the heavy responsibility of providing their slaves with religious instruction. Perhaps answering the doubts of his own heart so recently torn by indecision, Charles declared that slavery itself could be justified if one soul were saved. Speaking as a slaveholder and illustrating the great distance that separated him from those who lived in the settlements, he assured his white listeners that it is "certain that the salvation of one soul will more than outweigh all the pain and woe of their capture and transportation, and subsequent residence among us." His sentiments and focus had come a long way from his conversations in Hartford, Washington, and Baltimore. They had come home to Liberty County.[21]

Charles had made his point. He had covered the ground carefully, step by step, so that in the end his family and friends were convinced, and the Liberty County Association for the Religious Instruction of the Negroes was formed. They organized that very day. (Charles had all the details carefully arranged so that they had little to do but agree.) No one was surprised when Charles was called to be the missionary. For years he would receive no compensation for his labors. His personal wealth would give him the necessary economic freedom for this Liberty County experiment. His wealth—drawn from the toils of Hamlet and Rosetta, Cato and Cassius, Phoebe and Jack, and all the other "hands employed to furnish me with those conveniences of life of which they are in consequence deprived"—such wealth would allow the association the necessary time to gain the strong support of the community.[22]

The association was the first of its kind in the South, and, as might be expected, it met with initial difficulties. Few people seemed to believe that it would last or that it would be able to accomplish its goals. There was a "general indifference," and while influential planters joined, there were only twenty-nine who signed the constitution. Additionally, there was continuing opposition that showered nothing but ridicule or contempt upon the whole project. The greatest difficulty, however, was Charles's own inexperience and the teachers' lack of training. Faced with these difficulties, Charles accepted a call, after only a few months, to be the pastor of the First Presbyterian Church in Savannah. He did this, he later recalled, "with the understanding that, whenever I felt prepared, I might withdraw from the church and return to my chosen field."[23]

In the summer of 1831 Charles and Mary moved to Savannah and took up residence with the family of William King, the brother of Barrington and young Roswell King. The Kings provided a warm and welcoming place for Charles and Mary, and they also found room for Mary's personal servant Phoebe. Because Mary could not do without her, Phoebe had to leave behind at Carlawter her husband and her two children: six-year-old Clarissa and John, who was just turning one.[24]

Charles plunged into his work in Savannah, preaching three times on Sundays and giving special attention to the blacks of the city. One of the services on Sunday was designated as specifically for the blacks, and Charles made friends with the black preachers in the city, including Andrew Marshall at First African and Henry Cunningham at Second African. He became particularly close to Cunningham, who invited him to preach at Second African and who evidently cleared the way for Charles to preach in some of the other African Baptist churches of the city. These were important contacts for Charles, for the black Baptist preachers at the independent black churches in Savannah had an influence that spread throughout the low country. Cunningham had been one of the founders of the Sunbury Baptist Association, which included the church at Sunbury and the Newport Baptist Church near Riceboro. In the coming years Charles was closely connected with these congregations and preached from their pulpits regularly.[25]

While Charles was busy with his pastoral work, both Mary and Phoebe were unhappy about being in Savannah. To be sure, there was a lively social life, even for Phoebe. She was becoming interested in the church and was beginning to attend regularly. And there were errands to run, and in the evenings after work she could see something of the city. But she missed her home and especially her children. "Do my dear sister," Mary wrote Betsy Maxwell, "whenever you write, mention the health of Phoebe's children as she appears anxious about them and it is her only means of hearing from them." And Mary Robarts wrote back, "Tell Phoebe her chicks are well." But Phoebe, perhaps as only a body servant could, evidently was putting pressure on Mary for them to return to Liberty County.[26]

Mary did not need much encouragement. At the end of October she gave birth to Charles Colcock Jones, Jr., and within a few weeks she, Phoebe, and little Charlie were back in Liberty County for an extended stay at the Retreat and Solitude. Charles wrote regularly and made quick trips to Liberty, but he was unhappy to be separated from his wife and young son. "My dear Mary," he wrote her, "it seems as if my affection for you increases with the days of our marriage state; I never, never wish to be separated from you a day, and I have had a struggle in my mind to know whether my affection for you is not exceeding that to my Saviour and his cause."[27]

Charles's work, however, kept him busy. Shortly after Mary left Savannah with Phoebe and Charlie, Charles left the city for the Presbyterian synod meeting in Columbia, South Carolina.[28] The meeting provided an opportunity for Charles to be with some of the leaders in the church who were to be his colleagues for years to come. Moses Waddel, the president of Franklin College (a few decades later the college became the University of Georgia), was a leading member of the synod, as was Alonzo Church, who soon followed Waddel as president. Thomas Smyth, the scholarly young pastor of the Second Presbyterian Church in Charleston, was there. He and Charles had been at Princeton together and over the coming years they became close colleagues. Charles met for the first time George Howe, who had left a position at Dartmouth and had recently accepted a professorship at the seminary. Outside of his family, no one was to be closer to Charles during the coming years than this New Englander. But at this meeting of the synod in 1831, his closest colleague was Benjamin Gildersleeve, editor of the *Charleston Observer*, a widely circulating religious periodical. Gildersleeve's father had been the pastor of Midway Church, had baptized Charles, and had made the first serious effort by a pastor of Midway to reach out to the slaves of Liberty County.[29]

Gildersleeve continued his father's interests in the evangelization of the slaves, and he and Charles immediately set about bringing before the synod a resolution to that end. Columbia, however, was not a hospitable place for such a resolution, and strong voices in the city, fearing anything that might hint of emancipation, made known to the synod their opposition. Charles made a speech addressing the fears and shaped the resolution to meet the challenge head-on. Why, he asked in the resolution, "will the religious instruction be emancipation? Do not the majority, perhaps of our citizens who make this objection, consider slavery sanctioned by the Bible?" If they sincerely believe this, "why then do they hesitate to have the Bible, the whole Bible, and nothing but the Bible, preached to their servants?" But what if they believe the Bible does not sanction slavery? What if they believe the Bible leads to emancipation? "Then our answer is but a word. Shall thousands, and even millions of immortal minds be sacrificed at the shrine of cupidity? Which ought to prevail for the good of mankind, for the glory of our country, for the prosperity of the cause of God—principle or interest? Right or wrong? Let the enlightened conscience of the philanthropist, of the patriot, and of the Christian, return the answer."[30]

Then Charles showed that he had not so quickly forgotten what he had learned in New England, that he shared a widespread confidence in the future, with its trains and steamboats and spreading evangelical Protestantism. What was feared in the religious instruction of slaves, he wrote, was the moral influence of Christianity, "which we cannot possibly avoid, do what we may. It is folly to contend against God. Christianity is ultimately to prevail on the earth, and in due course of time, will reach our servants." If emancipation, feared by those who object to religious instruction, were to come "by the preaching of the Gospel, happy are we in believing that it could not come in a more gradual, in an easier, nor in a safer way. It will be the work of the Almighty, the effect of the Divine principles of His word, which, in their operation, while they impel the master to the end, will restrain the servant from all acts of precipitate violence to attain it. And thus may the Glory of the removal of the evil be laid at the foot of the Cross." So Charles named slavery an evil—an evil that could best be abolished by the influence of Christianity that could not, in any case, be successfully resisted.[31]

The synod passed the resolution and ordered that it be published in the *Charleston Observer*. Some proslavery forces were furious over what was said in the resolution, and Charles soon felt the wrath of at least one powerful political leader in the Palmetto State. But for now he had gotten the resolution through the influential Presbyterian synod and there was time to see something of Columbia and its state legislature. A Charleston cousin, Judge Charles Jones Colcock, took him to see the impeachment of Thomas Cooper, the president of South Carolina College. The charge against Cooper was "on account of his *infidel* principles"—Cooper, a staunch proslavery advocate, represented the lingering twilight of eighteenth-century rationalism—but state politics, Charles noted, were of course deeply involved in the proceedings. Judge Colcock asked for a copy of the synod resolution and shared it with several friends in the legislature.[32]

Charles had an opportunity to visit with William Capers, the Methodist leader who was doing more than anyone else to organize the extensive Methodist mission work on the plantations of the South Carolina low county. Capers, who was serving the Methodist Church in Columbia, did not like the provincial little town. He said having to live there was "like shutting up a man in a birdcage" and told Charles "that the Devil was the headman in Columbia." But he encouraged Charles and told him about the ways the Methodists were going about their work and how they were winning the support of some influential planters.[33]

Charles also had an opportunity to see the new Presbyterian seminary in Columbia. Modeled after Andover and Princeton, it was designed to have a specific southern mission—"to light up another sun which shall throw still farther west the light of the gospel, to shine upon the pathway of the benighted, and those who have long groped in the dim twilight of unenlightened reason."[34] A local mansion, Ansley Hall, had been purchased for the seminary, and additional buildings were planned for an expanding student body. Charles, perhaps anticipating his deep involvement in the life of the seminary, wrote Mary that "the whole establishment is fine."[35]

While Charles was away in Columbia, Mary was visiting friends and family in Liberty County and showing off son Charlie. It was clear to her that she did not wish to live in Savannah, and she and the baby stayed in the country until early summer 1832. Phoebe was glad to be with Sandy and her children and was no doubt even more reluctant than Mary to return to Savannah. But she was expected to go as Mary's personal servant, and for the next five months she lived in the city with Charles, Mary, and little Charlie. When Charles was away, Phoebe slept on the floor in Mary's room and had responsibility for looking after Charlie at night. When she rose from the floor to care for the little white child, she no doubt thought of Clarissa and John, whom she had had to leave in the care of others at Carlawter.[36]

In the fall, a short time before they all returned to Liberty County, Phoebe had a conversion experience. "We have reason to bless God," Charles wrote Betsy in October, "for his merciful visitation of our servant Phoebe. She hopes that she is a Christian and *thus far* the evidence is very satisfactory, and it has been now more than a month since her conversion." Charles hoped, if their lives were spared to return to Solitude, "to do the people on the plantation some good."[37]

In a few weeks, they were all back in Liberty County. Shortly thereafter, Phoebe, having already been examined by the session, joined Midway Church with fourteen other slaves and eight whites. With her, making a confession of faith that day, was Mary's brother John Jones.[38] God seemed to be answering the earnest prayers of Charles and Mary and preparing a way for Charles to link at last his Christian duty with his Liberty County home. What was now before them was to establish their own plantation home at Montevideo and for Charles to begin his work as a missionary among those who had as their only home the settlements of Liberty County.

————————•—•————————

10

MONTEVIDEO AND MAYBANK

Early one morning before Christmas 1832, Charles and Mary left Solitude and rode on horseback to Montevideo. The frost on the fields at Solitude was already beginning to melt, and the crisp morning air held the promise of a beautiful low-country day. They had been dreaming for some time about a place that would be theirs, and as they rode slowly along the sandy road together they knew that the time had finally come for them to begin building a home. Turning off the road that led to Colonel Law's place, they went down a wagon trail past a small pond with willows and cattails. The pond marked the upper end of the slough that separated Carlawter and Montevideo, and the wagon trail, almost a mile long, held the possibility of becoming an avenue equal to that of the Retreat. Charles and Mary rode to a spot above the North Newport and dismounted where a gradual rise provided a view of the river and a splendid place for a plantation house. Looking around they saw a sweet, never-failing spring and an open field running down to the river's edge. They talked of their hopes for this place spread before them, for they had been here before and their hearts had already settled on this hillside. The field with its broom straw became in their imaginations a lawn of thick Bermuda grass; and they imagined that over there, away from the river along the edge of the woods, fruit trees and a vegetable garden could be planted, while over toward the house site there was room for a flower garden, for roses, phlox, and verbena, and for arbors with jasmine and Lady Banksias. Where the house would be built they could envision a wide sandy yard with camellias, aza-leas, and tea olives under the shade of oaks, and there in the sun was a place for a kitchen garden with beds of thyme and sage, oregano and rosemary.[1]

As they looked around them, the site not only captured their imaginations but also evoked something deep within Charles and Mary, something almost ances-tral and primitive, although they of course would never have named it such. For them it simply seemed a welcoming place with its open landscape on a gentle rise above a flowing river. On this December morning the site seemed welcoming because of the beauty of the woods, fields, and sky reflected in the dark waters of the river and because the whole scene conveyed a promise of harmony, security, and abundance. Yet as they stood there together Charles and Mary could not have imagined how during the coming years this spot above the river would become home to them, a place of deepening memories and seductive beauty.[2]

From the time Joseph had purchased the three adjoining tracts of Carlawter, Montevideo, and Cooper for Charles and Susan and his sister Eliza Robarts, it was clear that if Carlawter was the place for the plantation settlement, Montevideo was the place for a plantation home. But if Montevideo was going to be a working plantation under Charles's supervision, some family negotiations had to take place. Joseph bought back from Eliza her share in the property and secured for her the Hickory Hill plantation not far from Sunbury. He then gave Eliza's portion of the three tracts to Mary.[3] "Your gift," Mary wrote her father, "adds another to the numberless proofs I have ever received of your tenderest solicitude for my welfare. To me you have indeed been the best and kindest of earthly parents, and if the warmest affection of your Daughter is any return for all your care and trouble . . . you have not an ungrateful child."[4]

In the meantime, Charles and his sister Susan agreed that Susan's slaves would stay at Carlawter under the supervision of Charles and that if in the future there were a division of the land between them, then Susan would get the Cooper tract and Charles the Montevideo tract. In this way the three tracts became available not only as a home for Charles and Mary but also as a working plantation of almost a thousand acres. They took the name of Montevideo and made it the name for the whole plantation, for all three tracts combined, indicating that Carlawter was to be a part of Montevideo under the control and authority of those who lived in the plantation house.[5]

Joseph's generosity and the family's negotiations were not, of course, without their impact on the settlement at Carlawter. Decisions by white slave owners that seemed reasonable, orderly, and even generous often seemed just the opposite, even disastrous, in the settlements. The purchase of the Hickory Hill plantation for Eliza Robarts meant that her slaves, who had been moved to Carlawter in 1817, were moved—once again—out of the network of family and friends that had been established over of a period of more than sixteen years. In particular, it meant that Lizzy and Robinson would be separated and that Robinson would have to make the long Saturday afternoon trip from Hickory Hill to see his wife and children. To be sure, their older children were now adults—Cato was twenty-four, Cassius twenty-two, and Porter already sixteen—but their youngest child,

Adam, was only eight, and Lizzy was getting older and her health was not good. For them Joseph's gift to Mary was less a sign of generosity and parental affection than simply another indication of the arbitrary character of white power.[6]

Work began on the Montevideo plantation house in February 1833. Phoebe's husband, Sandy, had responsibility for the construction following a sketch outlined by Charles. Sandy stood in a tradition of slave carpenters (he had been an apprentice to Jacob at Liberty Hall) that combined the carpentry skills of Africa and Europe. He not only knew how to use hammers and saws, augers, gimlets, and chisels, and when to use a jackplane or a fore plane or a joiner plane, he also knew how to solve problems. He knew how to look at a task and figure out how it could be done and done right. Working with him as his apprentices in 1833 were Syphax and Porter. Syphax, who was almost twenty, was already becoming a skilled carpenter, and Porter was demonstrating that he was not only a strong young man but also smart and reliable. Working with them in hauling and digging and sawing and making shingles were other men from the settlement.[7]

Sandy built a wharf that ran out into the river not far from the slough that divided Carlawter from Montevideo. Cypress logs had to be cut, trimmed, held in position in the river current, and then pounded down into the river mud with heavy mallets before wide planks could be laid down and attached to them. It was hard and heavy work, especially in February, but the sturdy wharf they built allowed the river schooners and sloops that ran from Savannah to Riceboro to unload nails and building supplies and later to load cotton and rice.[8]

The house that was built at Montevideo — it was later significantly enlarged — was a comfortable two-story dwelling, built off the ground in low-country fashion, with a piazza that stretched across the front and faced the river. Over the coming years, the piazza became a special spot for the Jones family and their guests. Its familiar design — drawing on European, African, and Caribbean influences — had evolved over the years in response to the low country's climate and culture. Its long sloping roof provided shade for the downstairs rooms, and its wide porch was a place to sit and enjoy any cool breeze that might come up from the river. The piazza at Montevideo was a place for visiting, for talking about what was happening in the county, and for remembering old times and old friends. Here Lizzy and Jack and Phoebe and Patience would serve tea in the late afternoon to the whites who persisted, long after most Americans, in keeping the British tea-drinking ceremonies: a tea table would be set with a silver teapot, and around it the Jones family would visit with their guests, drink tea and eat toast or some cake from the kitchen, and follow the etiquette of long-established custom.[9]

Over the coming years Charles and Mary would be able, while taking their tea, to look out from the piazza onto a low-country world: they would watch the river flow, hear the night wind in the pines, and see the moon rise above the trees. The piazza provided over the years a good perspective on the changing landscape of Montevideo—a lawn was planted that eventually ran down to the river, gardens were laid out as the couple had dreamed, and orchards were established. And from the piazza Charles and Mary also observed as year followed year the growing order and harmony of a working plantation: they heard in the distance the clank and clang of the plantation's gins and mills, the thud of rice being pounded in mortars, and the voices of the black men and women who made Montevideo a place of comfort and beauty for all who lived in the plantation house.

What Charles and Mary heard and saw from their place on the piazza was what they came to identify as home—a particular place, a home place, Montevideo, that was associated at the deepest levels of their being with all those whom they loved and that was embodied in a landscape that evoked joy, gratitude, and wonder. But what they heard and saw with such deep satisfaction was also a social order based on hierarchical assumptions. Montevideo became for Charles and Mary a place of responsibility for those who lived at Carlawter—responsibility for Hamlet and all who rose to work when he sounded the conch-shell horn, for Jack and Phoebe in the house, for Lizzy and Patience in the kitchen, and for Sandy, Syphax, and Porter as they went about their carpentry. They all needed, it seemed from the perspective of the piazza, proper control and management. They all needed their clothing and food supplied, their health attended to, and their religious life instructed and nurtured. Such was the view for Charles and Mary as they drank tea in the late afternoon and looked out over Montevideo. Deep beneath such a view, often hidden in the recesses of their imagination, was a realization that what they were seeing was the source of their wealth.[10]

For Sandy, Syphax, and Porter, and for all the others who built Montevideo, the counterpoint to the piazza was the open space before the cabins at Carlawter, where they gathered, winter and summer, around open fires to eat from simple bowls the peas and rice, the corn bread and greens of the settlement. Here around the fires—like the first Old Jupiter and those who had lived at Liberty Hall and Rice Hope—they talked, told stories of Africa and ancestors, sang their spirituals and other songs, did their flirting, warned their children, and whispered the secrets of the settlement. Here, in the secure space of the settlement, they spoke what could not be spoken before whites except in the disguised form of gestures, rumors, folktales, and songs. Here over the years they rehearsed what they wished to say to those who sat on the piazza and would not be able to say—without great danger—until the land shook with a mighty army.[11]

Those who sat around the fires also had a view of Montevideo. They too could see the landscape of the low country. By their fires they knew moonrise and star-rise, and sometimes they could see day a' comin'.[12] No less than those who sat on the piazza, they could hear the sounds of the river changing with the seasons and the weather—in the spring, when the swamps were flooded and the slough full, they could hear the river rushing by cypress and black gums, and in the fall, or when the summers were dry, they could hear only a quiet, distant murmur creeping up from the dark waters to mingle with the sounds of the plantation during the day and to provide at night the melody for the disparate music of low-country creatures.

But what they heard and saw from around the fires was also radically different from what was heard and seen from the piazza, and it was in many ways more complex, more deeply ambiguous and conflicted than what was seen and heard over tea. For those who lived at Carlawter, Montevideo was a place of deep oppression, of arbitrary power and claims of superiority. Yet because Montevideo included the settlement at Carlawter within its boundaries, the plantation was also home for them, a place of family and friends, and increasingly, with its cemetery, a place of ancestors. From around the settlement fires, Montevideo could be seen as a place of heavy labor yet a place of beauty created by that labor; a place of boundaries, of harsh limits to their freedom, yet a place whose boundaries provided some protection against an even more hostile world of white violence and power. To be sure, they knew the boundaries of the plantation to be porous, knew that they were penetrated by secret paths that led to neighboring plantations, to hidden gathering points, and to Riceboro, with its access to illicit pleasures. But porous boundaries also meant that the violence and power of a white world could come pouring in upon them, overwhelming whatever protection might be provided by the paternalism of Montevideo.[13]

So Montevideo was a place and a landscape that could be—like a painting or a book—seen, read, interpreted in different ways depending upon where one sat and what one remembered. This meant that Montevideo did not evoke one meaning or one image in the minds of those who lived there, but many meanings and many images. It also meant that during the next thirty-five years Montevideo would be contested ground, that there would be a struggle—between those who sat on the piazza and those who sat around the fires at Carlawter—over whose interpretation and whose lengthening memory of this place more accurately reflected the realities of a plantation home.[14]

On 17 January 1834, shortly after Mary and Charles had moved into Montevideo, their uncle Andrew Maybank died without issue. "Uncle Maybank" had been especially close to Charles and Susan when they were orphaned. Their mother, Susannah Girardeau Jones, had been the sister of Andrew's wife, Eliza-

A sandy road near Montevideo plantation (author's collection)

beth Girardeau Maybank; and Andrew's sister Mary Maybank had been the first
wife of Joseph Jones. Thus, while no blood relation to Charles, Susan, or Mary,
Andrew regarded them as if they were his own children, and he looked on Laura
and Charles Edward Maxwell as if they were his grandchildren.[15] As a young man
in South Carolina, Andrew had gone through the humiliating experience of di-
vorcing his first wife. Such an unusual procedure, which required an act of the
state legislature, had left him a man of gentle temperament and benevolent disposition. He had returned to Colonel's Island and the plantation of his father,
Colonel Andrew Maybank, and there had risen to the rank of major in the militia and had become a successful planter, owning sixty slaves at the time of his
death.[16]

   Andrew Maybank was buried at Midway, where he was a respected member,
and the tombstone placed over his grave read: "His Christian life was active and
exemplary, and at his death he bequeathed a large portion of his estate to charitable purposes."[17] As is often the case in such circumstances, Maybank's will was
more complex than what was conveyed on his tombstone.

   In the first item of his will, he left cash and stock to the American Tract Society
and the American Board of Commissioners for Foreign Missions. Both were benevolent societies closely associated with Andover Theological Seminary, with
Lyman Beecher and other evangelical reformers. In the second item, he be-

queathed to Laura and Charles Edward twelve slaves and "their issue to them and their heirs forever."[18]

In the third item Maybank gave and bequeathed "to the Rev. C. C. Jones and Mary Jones, and their children, the following property: viz. All my lands on Colonel's Island.... Also the following Negroes: Fanny & Prince, and their children Agrippa, Titus, Phillis, and Niger; also driver Andrew and his wife Mary Ann, and their children, viz. Charles, Sylvia, Gilbert, Dinah, George and Delia; also to them and their heirs forever, with their issue. Also my carpenter Sandy to them and their heirs."[19]

In the other items, eight slaves were given to Robert Quarterman, pastor of Midway; four went to Joseph Jones by way of the estate of Joseph Maybank Jones; "my fellow Andrew" was given to Mary Robarts; and "my fellow Harry" was given to Louisa Robarts. Two slaves—"Kate, a good house servant and fellow Solomon"—went to a young neighbor. Cora and her children he gave to Charles "to dispose of as he thinks proper." The rest of his property—lands, slaves, farm animals, farm tools, boats, household items—were to be sold and the proceeds were to be given to the new Presbyterian Theological Seminary in Columbia. Charles was made executor, with responsibility to see that the instructions of the will were carried out.[20]

So in this way Charles found himself—only three years after his return home from the North—not only the owner of a second plantation and fifteen more slaves but also responsible for the sale of eighteen men, women, and children. Charles had written Mary from Andover that the more he looked at slavery, "the more enormous does it appear." Slavery, he had said, is a "violation of all the laws of God and man at once. A complete annihilation of justice. An inhuman abuse of power, and an assumption of the responsibility of fixing the life and destiny of immortal beings, fearful in extreme."[21] Now as the executor of Andrew Maybank's will, Charles had, as he had never before had, "the responsibility of fixing the life and destiny of immortal beings." He did not appear to find it "fearful in extreme," but he did make arrangements that seemed to him the most humane way to proceed.

Charles talked to Cora, whom, along with her three children, he was "to dispose of" as he thought proper. She wanted to be sold to John B. Bacon in order "to be with her husband in Savannah." Charles negotiated with Bacon and made the sale for $1,000.[22] At the same time, he had an ad for an "Executor's Sale" circulated, and on 5 March 1834 fourteen slaves were brought from their home on Colonel's Island to the courthouse in Riceboro to stand in the sandy yard under the oaks and experience the humiliation and terror of a slave sale. Old Clarissa Girardeau was among them. She had belonged, with Lizzy, to the parents of Charles's mother, Susannah, and had been given to their daughter Elizabeth Girardeau Maybank. Standing with Old Clarissa before the courthouse was her daughter Rachael. Rachael's son Andrew had been the one willed to Mary Robarts, and Rachael's daughters Sally and Sue had gone to Joseph Jones, as had Sally's son Jack and Sue's son Aaron. So Old Clarissa knew, as she stood beneath the long grieving wisps of Spanish moss in Riceboro, that her family on the island, her grandson and granddaughters and great-grandsons, had already been divided.[23]

Planters had gathered from around the county for the auction, but most were neighbors from the island or from Sunbury and nearby on the mainland. There was much to be auctioned—everything from land and slaves to a fine new boat to silverware to a wharf in Riceboro. The slaves were put up in the first lot. They were all to be sold together except for Old Clarissa and Old Tom, who, in the appraisal of the estate, had been declared of no monetary value because of their age. When the bidding began, it became immediately clear that a gentleman's agreement had already been reached between Joseph and Charles. Joseph bid the appraised value for the lot—there would be no bargains here—and they were sold to him. Then came Old Clarissa and Old Tom. Charles bought them together with ten cows, ten calves, twenty-seven hogs, fourteen geese, and four beehives. The two old slaves were returned to their home on the island, and Clarissa was to be able to stay with her daughter and grandchildren at the Retreat whenever she wished and could get a ride there. (No one at the sale could have imagined that the old woman would live another twenty years!) The rest of the estate was quickly sold to neighbors, and all of the proceeds of the auction were used to establish the Maybank Endowment at Columbia Theological Seminary.[24]

Charles and Mary had known their new plantation as "The Hut," a name given by Charles's mother, Susannah. But such a name, though it reflected the simple character of the summer cottage on the place, seemed somehow inadequate for a fine plantation. And so they named it Maybank in honor of the one who had been so kind to them when they were children and so generous to them in death. The main body of the plantation was situated on the northwest end of Colonel's Island overlooking marshes and the mouth of the Medway River, but its 700 acres also included a 150-acre tract on the southern edge of the island. This tract, located where the North Newport River had cut a crescent into the island, carried the old name Half Moon.[25] Here in the deep water of the Half Moon, ships could dock to load Maybank cotton or unload supplies from Savannah. Years after Andrew Maybank's death, Charles wrote in his journal, "We must ever hold Uncle Maybank in grateful remembrance for bestowing upon us this quiet and healthful retreat, where we reared and educated our children until prepared for college, and where we have experienced unnumbered mercies from above."[26]

In early June 1834 Charles and Mary made their first of many annual moves from Montevideo to Maybank. They adopted the old pattern and left the miasmas of Montevideo, as their parents and grandparents had left those of Rice Hope, Liberty Hall, and the Retreat, for the healthier climate of the coast. With them in 1834 were Charlie and his little brother Joe, who had been born the previous September. Before the family left Maybank in November to return to Montevideo, Mary was pregnant with their third child, Mary Sharpe.[27]

When they arrived at Maybank in 1834, they were welcomed by Andrew the driver. He and his wife, Mary Ann, had come to Maybank in 1826 with their children Charles, Sylvia, and Gilbert. They too had stood beneath the oaks at Riceboro to be auctioned by the sheriff. Their previous owner, James Holmes, had borrowed money from Andrew Maybank and had mortgaged Andrew and his family as surety for the loan. When Holmes defaulted on the loan, Maybank foreclosed on the mortgage, and the sheriff brought the family to Riceboro for their sale at "public outcry at the Court House in Riceboro." The "said Negroes" were "knocked off to Andrew Maybank for the sum of one Thousand Dollars which was the highest and best bid that was made." Since their arrival at Maybank, Andrew and Mary Ann had had three more children: Dinah had been born in 1828, George in 1830, and Delia in 1833.[28]

Andrew, who was twenty-six when he came to Maybank, was a large and agile man with powerful hands that were already thick and tough from swinging a hoe and handling a plow. So hardened were his calluses, he could pull a roasting oyster from the fire and shuck it in his hands. While he was not good with numbers, he knew about cotton and corn and how to manage a plantation, and so he became the driver at an early age. "Andrew is such an intelligent man," a neighboring planter later wrote Charles, "and one of principle—it is a pleasure to see his work."[29]

Andrew and Mary Ann were island Gullahs—"genuine Africans" they were sometimes called. The settlement where they lived was some distance from the Maybank plantation house and was tucked away under oaks and palmettos near a bluff that overlooked the marsh. This meant that of all the isolated settlements, of all the settlements that saw whites only on occasion during part of the year, none was more isolated than that at Maybank. Andrew and Mary Ann lived in this settlement for more than thirty-seven years; they raised their children here and buried one of them in its sandy soil; and they came to think of this place overlooking the marshes of the Medway as their home. Here they knew the smell of the marsh and how the dawn wind could stir the palmettos as the sky in the east began to pale over St. Catherine's Sound. Here at their little settlement they would sit with others around evening fires to rest from the day's labors, and, year in and year out, tell in their Gullah dialect the secrets of their world while listening to the sounds of the marsh and the distant surf.

With the isolation of Andrew and Mary Ann there would come remarkable contradictions to their lives—or at least apparent contradictions. As ones who had stood in the sandy yard at Riceboro, they knew only too well the harsh realities of slavery and the arbitrary ways of white power, and they were to have occasion to experience again such harsh realities. Yet they had at Maybank a freedom of spirit that was not crushed by the confines of slavery; they had within their little island world a cultural freedom, even a freedom of movement on the island and in the marshes, that marked their daily lives and the routines of their years. Yet strangely they and their children, of all the Joneses' slaves, were to be the most loyal to their white master and mistress when years later Federal ships appeared off the coast. Of course, it may have been precisely their isolation that made such loyalty possible. Perhaps their distance from Charles and Mary kept them loyal when others, who knew the ways of whites more intimately, were eager to get away from the benevolence of kind owners.

Living at the settlement, in addition to the fifteen slaves Charles and Mary inherited, were the twelve slaves left to Laura and Charles Edward Maxwell by Andrew Maybank and seven given to them by their grandfather Audley Maxwell. Among the Maybank slaves was Jacob, who had made a break for freedom ten years earlier. He had been a young man at the time, in his early twenties, and he had left his wife, Cora, and daughter Sary to head for Savannah, where his father lived. By hiding out in the slave quarters in the city, he had remained free for a few months before being caught and returned to the island. By the time Andrew Maybank died, Jacob and Cora had had another four children. In the evenings around the settlement fires, he could tell of his escape from the island, about life in Savannah, and about how he had paid dearly for his freedom with lashes of a whip.[30]

Montevideo and Maybank each had a distinct environment that shaped the character of the plantation and those who lived on it. Montevideo was a river plantation, with its river swamps and slough. And while it had plenty of sand, it also had rich alluvial soil, especially where dark waters had slowly swirled and left behind the decomposing wealth of past summers. Maybank, on the other hand, was a Sea Island cotton plantation, as different from Montevideo as Montevideo was different from the plantations on the rolling hills of middle Georgia.

Colonel's Island—with the other Sea Islands that stretched along the South

Carolina and Georgia coast—had been formed by ancient geological forces, especially as fluctuating sea levels had deposited layer upon layer of sediment. These islands stood as barriers between the open ocean and the mainland, and they had their own maritime environment.[31] William Bartram, the eighteenth-century naturalist, had visited Colonel's Island in 1773 and had probably roamed over what was to become Maybank Plantation. In his *Travels* he described what he found:

> The surface and vegetable mould here is generally a loose sand, not very fertile, except some spots bordering on the sound and inlets, where are found heaps or mounds of sea-shell, either formerly brought there by the Indians, who inhabited the island, or which were perhaps thrown up in ridges, by the beating surface of the sea: possibly both these circumstances may have contributed to their formation. These sea-shells, through length of time, and the subtle penetrating effects of the air which dissolve them to earth, render these ridges very fertile; and, when clear of their trees, and cultivated, they become profusely productive of almost every kind of vegetable.

Bartram described the thick maritime forest that covered the island and "the great variety of trees, shrubs and herbaceous plants" that thrived in its soil. Most notable were the Sea Island oaks, massive and strong enough to withstand the hurricanes of many centuries, and especially valued in the making of keels for sailing ships. In Bartram's time the island was still home to the black bear, the cougar, and the southern red wolf. By the time of Andrew Maybank's death those species had been long gone, but other animals remained, including deer, raccoons, rabbits, bobcats, otters, and minks. And the birds! They were beyond counting, especially during spring or fall migrations, when the island was a resting place along the Atlantic flyway.[32]

To the north and west of Maybank, and to the south of Half Moon, were salt marshes with a maze of tidal creeks running through great plains of cordgrass—*Spartina alterniflora*—the backbone and lifeblood of the marsh. Green in the summer, brown in the winter, the cordgrass endured twice-daily flooding as the tide rose and twice-daily drought as the tide flowed out. Its roots held the thick black mud of the marsh, and the detritus of broken and decaying wracks of the cordgrass fed a great chain of life. Mullet and sheepshead, flounder and shrimp, crabs and oysters, conchs and clams all flourished in the creeks and along the mud banks and provided an important source of food for those who lived in the Maybank settlement. This marsh became a great schoolhouse for the male children of the settlement and of the plantation house at Maybank. Charlie and Joe, during each summer and fall they spent at Maybank, learned to study the marsh objectively and to collect and analyze marsh life, but young Charles and Gilbert and the other sons of the settlement were the ones who learned the ways of the marsh most intimately, as they lived on its edge and explored its recesses.[33]

The varied landscapes of Montevideo and Maybank had a profound influence on Charles and Mary, on the ways they saw the world and understood their place in it. Charles had developed as a boy a love for nature as he had explored the woods and swamps of the Retreat, and as he had roamed the oak forests and shell ridges of Maybank and Orange Grove. And Mary had grown to love "the beautiful and rural scenes of nature" and to delight in the sights and sounds of a winter's walk down a sandy road.[34] To be sure, both of them had experiences of what they called, in the language of nineteenth-century Romanticism, "the sublime." Charles had experiences that struck his heart and mind with the overwhelming power and majesty of nature and nature's God, that filled him with awe for the beauty, vastness, and grandeur of a storm at sea or a starry winter's night in New England. And Mary, when she visited Sapelo Island, had declared the "indescribable sublimity" of a "moonlight excursion."[35] Such experiences of nature reminded them of God's power and might and filled them with awe when they thought of standing before such a God. But it was not so much these sublime moments that shaped their hearts and minds as the ordinary moments, their daily experience of the beauty of the low country and the picturesque character of the landscape of Montevideo and Maybank.

When Charles and Mary looked across the landscapes of their plantations, they saw not simply economic opportunities but specific places—Montevideo and Maybank—and these specific places were living works being shaped by a vision they shared of the good and the beautiful. As sentient beings they delighted in what they saw when they looked across the lawn at Montevideo to the flowing waters of the Newport, and they found deep joy in the smell of the marsh as they rode to Maybank and felt for the first time each year the wind bringing them the rich fragrance of their summer home. They grew to love sitting on the piazza at Maybank and having as a family their evening devotions. The summer twilight would linger around them like an old friend reluctant to leave so pleasant a place before slipping away, and the Medway marsh would glow and then blush as it welcomed the shadows of the night. Evening by summer evening, the family would watch these transformations of the marsh and listen to the sounds of a low-country night that slowly enveloped them. These ordinary experiences and these familiar landscapes of their daily lives—these were what they treasured.[36]

In it all Charles and Mary experienced the presence of God. They knew, of course, that what they saw was not a perfect world. They knew at some deep level that the harmony and order and quiet, the peace and beauty of Montevideo and Maybank, were only partial. Sin, sickness, and death were all too real along the banks of the Newport or by the Medway marshes for a sentimental romanticism to flourish.[37] Moreover, they knew at least in their heads that the prosperity of the plantations was built upon slavery—a social system, Charles was to say over and over again, that was rooted in the fallen character of humanity. In the same way, they believed the landscape itself—the rivers and the gardens, the marshes and the woodlands, and all that crept upon them or flew above them—was marked by the harsh realities of a fallen world, that, in the words of St. Paul, the "whole creation groaneth and travaileth in pain" (Romans 8:22). But when they looked at the world around them in all its brokenness, they saw a God of goodness and beauty whose grace and love, whose redemption of a groaning world, was finally and most completely revealed and accomplished in Jesus Christ.[38]

This vision of the world and of God's activity in it was at the heart of their spirituality. To confess Jesus as their personal lord and savior was for them a way of seeing the world, a way of knowing the depth of the world's brokenness, and a way of seeing from afar the wholeness of a new heaven and a new earth and the hope for a new home where there would be no more pain or suffering, death or separation. Because it was a new way of seeing, the confession of Jesus meant for Charles and Mary a new way of living. Their devotional life, Charles's missionary labors and Mary's support of them, their arrangements for the running of their plantations, their treatment of their slaves, and Charles's advocacy on behalf of slaves were all rooted in this confession and its resulting spirituality.

But if Charles and Mary believed that their spirituality shaped what they saw when they looked around them, they were less well aware of the ways the landscape itself, with its history and social arrangements, shaped their spirituality and their understanding of God. Like the cypress and live oaks that grew along the river, their spirituality was rooted in the landscape and the history of the low country. Their spirituality was part of a rich Christian tradition reaching back many centuries and stretching across many cultures, but it was also a spirituality that reflected the particular contours of land and life in the low country. So how they saw the world around them was shaped by their faith; and their faith was shaped by the world around them.[39]

This dynamic and reciprocal relationship between their faith and their low-country home was to have a profound impact on the work Charles was beginning to undertake at the very time the house at Montevideo was being constructed and the Maybank plantation was being inherited. Because his spirituality was so deeply rooted in the physical and social landscape of Liberty County, Charles's missionary work was deeply ideological. It served to distort and hide the bitter realities of slaves, as when he would speak of masters and slaves being "spiritual brothers" in ways that concealed the power of the masters. And his work served ideological purposes by legitimizing the power and wealth of those who lived in the plantation houses and by supporting the social order that kept them and their children as the rulers of those who lived in the settlements.[40]

But strange to say, his missionary work also played a part in challenging these ideological purposes and the assumptions that supported them. For there was in his preaching and in what he taught an alternative vision, a vision that called into question the slave sales in Riceboro and the slave settlements on the plantations and all the social arrangements that made whites owners and blacks owned. It was this alternative vision that had troubled his heart in Andover and at Princeton and that informed his report to the synod in Columbia. His work never embraced the vision in its fullness, but it served to strengthen those in the settlements who saw through the limits of his work to a promise for a new day and for a new ordering of the social landscape by the waters of the Newport and the marshes of the Medway.[41]

11

THE STATIONS

Charles began his missionary work the same month he and Mary rode over to Montevideo to survey the landscape for their new home. He had already sent a notice to the planters, and word had been circulated in the settlements of an interior section of the county that he would hold a service on the next Sabbath at the Fraser station.[1]

Leaving Solitude early on the morning of 9 December 1832, Charles rode ten miles to the appointed meeting place. The sandy road he traveled gradually took him away from the swamps and low-lying areas of the county toward a gravelly hill where longleaf pines grew to great heights and water drained quickly away. Planters had discovered that it was a healthful area, largely free from the miasmas that infected the rice fields and swamps, and some families had built summer homes in the neighborhood. Among them was Simon Fraser, who donated four acres for a meetinghouse. When Charles arrived at the Fraser station on this early December day, there was as yet no building, but the planters had begun a subscription for a meetinghouse that would serve the white families at their retreats and as a station for the new missionary of the Liberty County Association for the Religious Instruction of the Negroes. The spot was one of seven places designated, after some negotiations, as stations for the work of the association during the coming year.[2]

Between 150 and 160 slaves had left the surrounding settlements that morning and had walked to the station to hear what this missionary might have to say to them. Charles was pleased to see such a crowd when he rode up. Getting off his horse, he greeted those whom he knew. They gathered around and he opened the meeting by stating to them the great desire that he "had long had of preaching the Gospel to them; that such preaching might be blessed to their true conversion, and they would be expected to second my efforts, by good attendance, and attention, and orderly behaviour." Charles had thought carefully about how to begin his work, and he had decided that he should begin at the beginning with a series on the book of Genesis. And so on this first Sabbath, his subject was "The Creation—Genesis 1." Their behavior, he noted, was decorous, their attention good, and the meeting was "marked with quietness"—all of which greatly pleased him. He left them in the afternoon "much animated for my work."[3]

The next Sabbath he was back at the same station and was greeted by a larger gathering of about 200 slaves. He began by reviewing the previous lesson and found that they "seemed to have retained it very well." He taught them Cowper's "beautiful hymn beginning: 'There is a fountain filled with blood'" and then turned to Genesis 2, with its story of how God rested on the Sabbath after God had created the Garden of Eden and made Adam out of "the dust of the ground, and breathed into his nostrils the breath of life; and man became a living soul." Charles read to them that God had made Adam to fall into a deep sleep, and had taken a rib from Adam and made woman, and had brought her to Adam, who had said "This is now bone of my bones, and flesh of my flesh." And Charles then read: "Therefore shall a man leave his father and his mother, and shall cleave unto his wife: and they shall be one flesh." Such a text provided a focus on the Sabbath as a day of rest, and on the "primitive state of man and the institution of marriage." He knew it was too much for one day, but he felt it necessary to at least introduce all the subjects.[4]

Charles had thought carefully not only about the subject of these first sessions but also about his pedagogy, about how a white missionary could best teach slaves who could not by law be taught to read. As a Calvinist, he was convinced they needed to know the Bible and its story of salvation. What, he had wondered, was the best mode of oral instruction that would inform their minds, touch their hearts, and reform their lives? The method he developed during these early days was later fine-tuned, but he followed its basic approach throughout the rest of his ministry.[5]

On this second Sunday at the Fraser station, he began, after a few hymns and a prayer, by reading the text slowly and deliberately but in "a lively fashion." He then gave a brief exposition of the story of Genesis 2, essentially retelling the story in his own words. He used "Scripture cards," large posterlike pictures of a Bible scene to make the story more vivid. During the coming sessions there would be scenes of Adam and Eve being driven from the Garden of Eden; of Noah, the Ark, and the animals; of the Tower of Babel; and of Abraham and Sarah journeying in the Promised Land with camels and donkeys. The cards, produced by the American Sunday School Union, provided pictures of far-off places and memo-

Scripture card used by the Jones family (courtesy of the Presbyterian
Historical Society, Presbyterian Church [USA], Montreat, N.C.)

rable scenes that could help shape the imagination and interpretation of a text.
"The eye," Charles believed, "greatly assists the memory."[6]

Next came questions and answers from a catechism that Charles wrote specifically for the text being studied—a method that was to be closely associated with
his name and his missionary labors. Charles asked those gathered at the station:
"Is it lawful for us to do any work on the Sabbath day?" And then he had them
say together: "No, excepting works of necessity and mercy." He asked: "After man
was made, how came he to be a living soul?" And they repeated: "God breathed
into him the breath of life." "What does that teach us?" Charles asked, and they
said in unison: "That God gives life and He only."[7]

The questions that most concerned his students, however, were those that
dealt with Adam and Eve. He found that there was "great interest manifested in
the audience on the subject of marriage," and he was glad, for he believed that

"fornication and adultery are their crying sins."[8] Charles asked: "What did God say to them?" And the students said together: "Therefore shall a man leave his father and mother and cleave unto his wife." "What does God mean by this?" Charles asked, and again the students said together: "That a man must love his wife more than all other persons." "And does God require the same love from the wife to the husband?" "Yes, the same."[9]

Charles then asked questions and gave answers that must have been heard at many levels by those who lived in the settlements and knew all too well about slave sales in Riceboro and about wills and estates that could send a spouse to distant plantations.

> Q. And what more did God say?
> A. And they shall be one flesh.
> Q. And what does God mean by this?
> A. That they are never to be parted while life lasts.
> Q. Is it lawful for a man to have more than one woman or a woman more than one man?
> A. No, it is not lawful.[10]

With such questions and answers, Charles was using the familiar pedagogy of the catechism, a pedagogy used for generations by whites as a way to instruct children and those new to the church. Charles had himself learned the Westminster Shorter Catechism as a young person, and he liked the method—the questions and answers could be sharply focused and carefully constructed; and memorization, he believed, was an important avenue to the heart and a way of shaping and informing one's understanding of the world and God's ways with the world. Such a method with its drills also seemed the best way to teach those who could not have a Bible or a devotional text as a resource, but had to depend on what they could remember. Moreover, the responses of hundreds of men and women speaking together in unison gave an authority to the answers that Charles would never have alone. Their united voices saying, "They shall never be parted while life shall last" was a way for the students to gather the questions and answers and claim them also as their own. What Charles did not clearly realize, however, was that the biblical story, and even the questions and answers with their tight constructions, could not be controlled once they were set loose. Those hearing the questions and those repeating the answers would give their own interpretations to the stories. They would remember and interpret what they heard only as it was filtered through their lives in the settlements, through the conversations around evening fires, and through the traditions that they brought with them to the stations.[11]

Charles believed that if the biblical stories and the catechism were an avenue to the heart, the heart itself must be opened if a lesson was to be internalized and owned by his listeners. And so he turned after the questions and answers to what he called "Practical Remarks." "Having filled our *heads* with the *sense* of the Word," he told those gathered before him, "let us strive now to fill our *hearts* with the duties, etc." The Sabbath, he said, is a gift of God for man and beast. It is a day of rest for the body. "How sweet is Sunday to the labouring man and beast." The day is also a gift of rest to the soul, he told his flock, when worldly cares can be laid aside and holy things taken into the heart. Because the Sabbath is such a gift, we ought to bless God for it and keep it faithfully.[12]

As for marriage, it is, Charles said, between one man and one woman, and its foundation must be love. He spoke of its "perpetuity." A man and woman becoming "one flesh" means, he emphasized, that they are never to be separated. They take each other "for better or for worse." No matter if one partner "is old, or sick," they are not to separate. "It is their lot, they must remain together." Only death or adultery were causes for separation. Moreover, the marriage should be lawfully contracted so that everyone would know that the couple should "live together as man and wife." Then he asked those gathered before him: "Are you lawfully married? Have you more wives than one?" If so, he said, it is a sin, it is adultery. "Will you live as a heathen? As brutes?" "Abhor such wickedness. It ruins character. . . . Repent."[13]

In this way, following this pattern, Charles lectured to the slaves of Liberty County during the following months. He met with them on Saturday afternoons and Sundays—one place on Saturday and another station on Sunday. During the winter and spring, he met them at the Fraser station, at the Baptist Church at North Newport, where up to five hundred would gather, at the Cross Roads near the parade ground, where hundreds more would gather, at Midway and at his own home at Solitude for those from Carlawter and other nearby plantations. When summer came and with it the dangers of miasmas and fevers from the swamps and rice fields, meetings were held at the Baptist Church in Sunbury and in the Sand Hills at the little village of Walthourville, which, like the Fraser station, was found to be a healthy spot during the sickly season.[14] Week after week Charles moved through the early chapters of Genesis. Week after week he asked questions: "Why did Cain hate and murder Abel?" "Did God determine to save Noah?" "How did God cause the work to cease at Babel?" "What was the character of the men of Sodom?" "How is Abraham a blessing to the world?"

And week after week he led his students as they said together: Cain hated Abel because Abel "was a holy man." "Yes," God determined to save Noah, "and he gave him warnings." God caused the work at Babel to cease "by making the people speak different languages." The men of Sodom were "exceedingly wicked." And Abraham was a blessing to the world because "he preserves for us the True Religion, the Bible, and his children first preached it to us, and he is the father of our Lord."[15]

And week after week Charles gave some "Practical Remarks" about what the lesson had to teach those who lived and worked on the plantations of Liberty County. Abraham, he said, was a good master. "He loved his servants and desired them to live in peace, and it was ever his delight to teach them the fear of the Lord." And while Abraham was a very rich man, he was "not above looking after the comfort and peace of his people. He was not above giving them religious instruction, and guiding them in the ways of God." "Learn then, my friends," Charles told the slaves, "what masters need to make them good *masters. It is religion*; pray therefore for your masters that God would give them new hearts and make them like to Abraham. And do nothing yourselves to [arouse] their tempers, and lead them away from that which is good." Charles taught his listeners that the greatest blessing "that can come upon a plantation is a pious, holy master." And what about slaves? What servants also need is religion: "This will make them kind to each other, faithful in their families; faithful and obedient to their masters; fearing God and working righteousness." "Whenever I see trouble on a plantation," Charles said, "I see and know that they need *religion* there." He encouraged those who had come from surrounding settlements to "Pray therefore for your unconverted brother servants, old and young, that God would bestow on them new hearts." And when he told the story of Abraham, and Sarah, and their slave Hagar, he said they "all sinned greatly," and he noted "the influence of masters and mistresses over servants": Abraham and Sarah had abused Hagar and led her to sin, and she had consented. And he appealed to his listeners to resist such abuse: "No, no my friends," he said, "you are made for higher service."[16]

In all of his reading of the Scriptures, his questions and answers, and his "practical remarks," Charles was struggling to transcend the racial assumptions that marked so much of southern white culture, indeed of U.S. and European culture. He wanted to treat those who gathered before him as "friends," as those who were "immortal beings" possessed of "immortal minds." Yet he read the texts and interpreted their meanings as a white southerner, a white southern master of slaves, who had been deeply touched by the evangelical and reform impulses of his day. What he found in Genesis supported slavery and did not call into question an economic and social system founded on the ownership of men, women, and children. And yet what he found in Genesis and the stories that he told could become weapons for those who lived in the settlements. If masters wanted slaves to work on the Sabbath, could slaves not protest that was against the law of God? And if masters persisted, could not their reputations be hurt in the community or could not their abuse of the Sabbath be resisted openly? And if masters threatened to divide a husband and wife, could not slaves protest by saying: "They are never to be parted while life lasts." Such weapons were all too obviously the "weapons of the weak"—they could not stop an indifferent or determined owner—but they were nevertheless weapons for a people glad to get whatever weapons they could find.[17]

In July 1833 Charles began a second, parallel series of Bible lessons—this one on the Epistle to the Hebrews. While he used the same format, and developed a catechism to work through the epistle, Hebrews must have seemed tame compared with Genesis and its stories of murder and floods, of sodomy, incest, and intrigue, of burning cities and slaves set free. "In what language were the books of the New Testament written?" he asked. "In the Greek language" was the response of the slaves. And Charles explained why:

Alexander the Great in 334 B.C. overran Western Asia introducing the manners and customs and language of the Grecians and founding Greek colonies in various parts. After his death his empire was divided into four parts, and the Greek still continued to prevail, and did prevail and was universally spoken in and around Palestine.[18]

It all sounded a little too much like notes from Andover or Princeton and he never used the Hebrews catechism again after that first summer. But for all of its stilted character and for all of its voices from distant classrooms, this series of lessons also showed something important about Charles's assumptions and his approach to the slaves. He wanted to teach them so that they could know the biblical story, and he was committed to giving them the best he could muster. Some whites might complain that such teaching was "casting pearls before swine," but for Charles it was his duty to men and women fully capable of understanding and interpreting the Bible. There was in his seriousness, even in his paternalism, a respect for his students. The respect, to be sure, was set within the confines of a southern world and worldview and always flowed downward from his position of power and authority. Yet even as the respect flowed from such lofty heights, it was felt by many of the slaves of Liberty County, who came in increasing numbers to hear him and to learn from him in the years ahead. As time would tell, they received his respect not as a gift, not even as the duty of a paternalistic white preacher, but as nothing less than their due.[19]

Because Charles could not be at all the stations each week, he worked through the association to see that each station had an organized Sunday school with a white superintendent and a coterie of white teachers. At the little village of

Walthourville, the wealthy planter and Yale graduate John Dunwody was the superintendent, and his wife, Jane Bulloch Dunwody, was one of seven teachers who taught each Sunday the scholars who came from the nearby settlements.[20] At Sunbury, Joseph Maxwell (the brother of Julia Maxwell King and brother-in-law of Susan Jones Maxwell) was the superintendent with nine teachers, seven women and two men. At Pleasant Grove, Barrington King from South Hampton plantation was the superintendent and taught with his wife, Catherine, and with Mary Jones and John Ashmore. In neighboring McIntosh County, where Liberty County planters summered at Jonesville, a class met at night during the week for an hour or an hour and a half, with John Mallard as the superintendent and with four or five teachers. At these and other stations, the religious instruction of the slaves was, as Charles had hoped, an effort that extended beyond his work as a missionary to the community of white planters. For the next thirty years white planters and their families were to be involved in teaching, week after week, those from the settlements who wished to learn from whites about the Bible, the church, and Christianity. Most who lived in the settlements were not interested, and not a few, no doubt, were decidedly hostile to the whole project. But over the years a substantial number participated—more than 20 percent of the total slave population in the county in 1845. And those who did participate became the foundation for the growing slave membership in the churches that reached, by 1845, one fourth of the whole slave population in the county—what Charles would call "A very large proportion indeed, and a majority of the adult population."[21]

Charles knew, however, that the white teachers needed help. The task that was before them was formidable and their teaching resources few. What they needed, he was convinced, was a carefully prepared catechism designed specially for the religious instruction of slaves. Charles tried some that had already been written, but they were intended primarily for little children or omitted too many areas of Christian faith and life.[22] And so he set about, almost as soon as he began his missionary labors, to write a catechism that would be "well adapted" to the slaves' conditions and circumstances. He published in 1834 *A Catechism for Colored Persons*, a manual containing "an *intelligible and systematic view of Christian Doctrine and Practice*," and of such a length, 108 pages, "as to occupy some considerable, though not unreasonable time in going through with it."[23] In 1836 he began publishing in the *Charleston Observer* a "Historical Catechism" on the four Gospels of the New Testament. He began with John the Baptist. "In what wilderness did he come preaching?" "The wilderness of Judea." "And what did he preach?" "Repent ye for the Kingdom of Heaven is at hand."[24] And then Charles had questions and answers on Jesus, his life and public ministry. "Who was the mother of our Lord?" "The Virgin Mary." "In what city did she live?" "In Nazareth." "Of what King's family was she?" "King David's family." "Was she rich or poor?" "Poor." In this way Charles moved through the life of Jesus, teaching the story of his birth, of his baptism and his temptations in the wilderness, of his calling the disciples, and of his miracles. He wanted those who lived in the settlements to know biblical history. He felt it was the best he could do for those who by law were kept illiterate, who were kept from reading "the word of life."[25]

The supply of *A Catechism for Colored Persons* was soon exhausted, and Charles revised it and republished it as *A Catechism of Scripture, Doctrine and Practice, for Families and Sabbath Schools, Designed also for the Oral Instruction of Colored Persons.* Intended for both blacks and whites, this catechism soon became widely used throughout the South and was translated—without the sections on slavery—into three other languages for use on the foreign mission field.[26]

Nothing that he ever wrote would be so widely used as this catechism and nothing would bring him greater criticism.[27] He intended it to be a clear, evangelical presentation of the Christian faith. God is presented as the creator and lawgiver who offers salvation to humanity through the death of God's son Jesus Christ. Working against God is Satan and his fallen angels. Humanity, fallen through Adam's sin, is saved through belief in Jesus Christ. "It does not matter," Charles wrote in a commentary on an answer, "what country one comes from, whether we are from the East or from the West, the North or the South. It does not matter of what *colour* we are, whether of white, or brown, or black. It does not matter of what *condition* we are, whether rich or poor, old or young, male or female, bond or free. Jesus is able to save *all* who come into him." It was orthodox, evangelical Protestantism that covered 150 pages of questions and answers and commentary. But set within this evangelical presentation of the faith was a social vision of the relationship of parents to children, of husbands to wives, and of masters to servants. Four pages were given specifically to the "duties of masters and servants."[28]

Beginning with a presentation of God's omniscience, the catechism constructed a paternalistic order in which the slave's place and behavior were carefully defined and restricted.

Q. Is God present in every place?
A. Yes.
Q. What does he see and know?
A. All things.
Q. Who is in duty bound to have justice done Servants when they are wronged or abused or ill-treated by anyone?
A. The Master.

Q. Is it right for the Master to punish his servants cruelly?
A. No.

Masters, it was said, should not threaten their servants and should provide them with religious instruction. Slaves were told that there is one Master of all in heaven who does not show favor to earthly masters for they will have to "render an account for manner in which they treat their Servants."

But if masters had their duties, slaves also had theirs:

Q. What command has God given to Servants, concerning obedience to their Masters?
A. Servants obey in all things your Masters according to the flesh, not in eye-serve as men-pleasers, but in singleness of heart, fearing God.
Q. What are Servants to count their Masters worthy of?
A. All honor.
Q. How are they to do their service of their master?
A. *With good will*, doing service unto the Lord and not unto men.
Q. How are they to try to please their Masters?
A. Please them well in all things, not answering again.
Q. Is it right in a Servant when commanded to be sullen and slow, and answer his Master again?
A. No.[29]

Nothing that Charles ever wrote was to be quoted as often as these questions and answers on these four pages of his catechism. All of the other 150 pages would be largely ignored by his critics, because these few lines seemed to open up the world of his assumptions—whites and blacks each had their place in society and each had their responsibilities: whites were owners and masters; blacks were slaves and servants. What these lines revealed, it would be said, was the purpose of his missionary work—to teach black slaves to be obedient to their white masters.[30]

In addition to lecturing at the stations, organizing Sunday Schools, and writing catechisms, Charles conducted religious services and preached most weeks. Preaching was a daunting task for him, though one that he relished. How was a white planter to preach good news to slaves? Charles was convinced that his preaching had to be adapted to the slaves who had been culturally deprived, neglected by white ministers, and left illiterate because of the laws of the state. Yet he believed that with "proper pains" he could "speedily carry them, ignorant as they are conceived to be, to the limits of our actual knowledge of the doctrines of Christianity: and what is more, make them know and feel it." Such preaching, Charles believed, was a difficult task for a white man—let no one think, he insisted, that any ignorant white could preach to slaves. Success demanded "well educated and as intelligent ministers and good preachers" as the church could supply.[31] In the same way, if a minister was of the opinion that "any sort of sermon" would do for black congregations, "let him try it," Charles warned, "and he will presently be of another mind." Black congregations, he said, were "good judges of a good sermon," as well as "proud enough" not to accept poor preaching. Charles insisted that it was necessary for the preacher administering to slaves to "study just as profoundly, and as extensively, as he who preaches to whites."[32]

Charles's first step in preparing a sermon for a black congregation was to study the "habits of thoughts, superstitions and manners" of the slaves so that he could try to bridge the gulf that separated him from those in settlements. He was aware that he did not know those who lived in the settlements at a significant depth and that the gulf that separated him from them was wider than the slough that separated Montevideo from Carlawter. For this reason he spent long hours studying the history, traditions, and folkways of African Americans.[33] He turned to studies of West Africa—John Beacham's book on the Gold Coast and the Ashanti, Lieutenant Frederick E. Forbes's work on the Dahomey, Thomas Birch Freeman's *Journal*, and John Duncan's *Travels*. But during the early years of his work, he turned above all to the reports of John Leighton Wilson, a friend and missionary at Cape Palmas. Wilson and his wife, Jane Baynard—he was from South Carolina, she from Georgia—had freed their slaves, paid for their way to Liberia, and helped finance the settlers in their pioneering efforts. Wilson wrote letters and reports home, and many of them were printed in the *Charleston Observer*. They were not simply the pious stories of a missionary, but careful studies of African history and culture that were to win Wilson a place in the Royal Oriental Society of Great Britain and be gathered together into his encyclopedic *Western Africa: Its History, Condition, and Prospects*.[34]

It was not African history, however, but African-American history that demanded most of Charles's attention as he tried to bridge the gap between the white preacher and the black congregations of Liberty County. Charles ordered and read everything he could find: reports and pamphlets, rare books and obscure records.[35] But the most important thing he did was to visit among and talk to those who lived in the settlements. And he talked to no one who was more helpful than Sharper, the black preacher who lived at Lambert, the center of the Gullah-speaking community of Liberty County.

Sharper stood in the line of black preachers hired by the Midway congregation and was the most respected man in the settlements. "He has been preaching the Gospel to his colored brethren," Charles wrote, "for almost twenty years, with fidelity." Sharper had been able to learn to read a little, and Charles found that he had "a wonderful command of Scripture in his prayers and sermons, which he has stored up in his long ministerial life." [36] But he not only knew the Scriptures, he also knew his people, and he must have wondered how to respond to this eager young missionary in a way that would be best for those who lived in the settlements.

Sharper knew the Jones family only too well—his wife and his children belonged to Joseph Jones, and Sharper spent as much time as he could at his "wife house" at the Retreat. And now, since Andrew Maybank's death, Charles was the owner of Sharper's son-in-law, the carpenter Sandy Maybank, who was married to Sharper's daughter Mary Ann. [37] So Sharper knew all about Charles, and he must have known what was being said in the settlements about this young white man who owned slaves and was so eager to preach to them and teach them the Bible and be a pastor to them. Sharper evidently decided that the best thing he could do was be a mentor to Charles, to be an interpreter for him about life in the settlements and an intermediary between the world of the white preacher and the black slave. "He gives me," said Charles, "more insight into the nature of my work amongst the Negroes in one conversation, than I gain in the observation of weeks. The ground is all familiar to him, and I esteem it a privilege and a blessing, that we labor together in the same field." Charles urged other whites who were working among slaves to find such a person as Sharper as a mentor. Through them the missionary "will arrive at knowledge, from which the colour of his skin, his station and general association, exclude him; and knowledge which he ought by all means to possess." [38]

Charles, however, believed that he must not only know his people, he must also know his text. Every day in his study at Montevideo and then at Maybank he read the Old Testament in Hebrew and the New Testament in Greek and then reviewed a variety of commentaries on the texts. Charles worked hard on his sermons and spent hours preparing them. [39] But he never seemed to wonder how owning slaves might influence how he read and interpreted the text. He soon learned, however, that a text could be understood one way if you were used to having tea on a piazza and another way if you sat around fires in a settlement.

Charles wrote his sermons in full manuscript form. There would be no outline to be given flesh and blood while he was preaching—much less a noteless or extemporaneous sermon! No, he wrote it all out with a handsome hand and on narrow paper, but with a clear threefold division: an introduction of three to six pages, an exposition of the text that often ran to more than fifty pages, and a conclusion of five to ten pages on what had been learned. Sermons intended for black slaves should be, he wrote, "plain in language, simple in construction, and pointed in application, and of any length *from a half hour to an hour and a quarter*, according to the subject and interest of the people."[40] Whites later remarked to Charles that they found his sermons easier to understand because he had spent so many years preaching to slaves.[41]

When Charles began preaching, he sought to make his delivery "grave, solemn, dignified, free from affection, hauteur, or familiarity, yet ardent and animated."[42] He was suspicious of any kind of emotional excesses and had written Mary from Princeton: "We should not lay very great stress upon particular high states of excitement in social or public worship, where it may in some degree be the effect of external circumstances. . . . The most satisfactory evidence of true Christian character is *habitual frame of mind towards God*."[43] He reflected the habits and dispositions of the white members of Midway. They wanted, after all, sermons suited for their neat meetinghouse: logical, solid as a heart-of-pine, and with a simple grace. Such a theological position was, of course, well suited to maintain control and order with a large assembly of slaves, and Charles expected a "dignified and restrained" response from his black listeners. There were to be no "*audible* expressions of feeling in the way of groanings, cries, or noises of any kind." He wanted no "amens!" to his sermons, no moaning that could spread through the congregation with a low hum gathering strength until it struck like lightning over the waving marsh. Of course, with more than a fifty-page manuscript, any such worries may have been unnecessary. Still, in spite of his sermons' cerebral character and subdued tones, Charles had a passion and pious zeal that reached out to the heart as well as the head. And somehow, strange as it seems, in the preaching and the listening, at least some of the gulf between the white preacher and the black slave was bridged.[44]

Charles's consuming theme was the conversion of lost souls from sin to salvation. The subject was for him the great theme of the Scriptures, the message to the nations, and good news to those who knew all too well the nearness of death and the familiar trails to the graveyards of Liberty County. He had sermons on "Salvation Is of the Lord," on "The Resurrection of the Body. The Fact. The Author. The Time and Manner. The Nature," on "The Folly of Deferring Repentance." He preached sermons that were intended to comfort: "God Is Love," and to encourage: "The Common People Heard Him Gladly." And he preached sermons that warned all who had ears to hear—"The Wicked Shall Be Turned in to Hell, and All the Nations That Forget God."[45]

There were other sermons, however, that were aimed more directly at those who lived in the settlements. Charles began in early 1833 a series of sermons on the duties of servants to earthly masters. Built around the stories of biblical slaves, these sermons were intended to "inculcate respect, obedience and fidelity to masters, as duties, for the discharge of which they as servants would have to account to God in the great day."[46] One sermon was on Eliezer, Abraham's servant, who was a model slave: he took care of Abraham's property, he would not offend God by becoming a thief, and he was a faithful and diligent worker. He was all that any good master would want, and his reward was great not only in heaven but also on earth, as he was chosen to be the chief among Abraham's slaves. Standing in contrast to Eliezer was Gehazi, Elisha's servant, whose behavior was a warning to all disobedient and unfaithful slaves: he was a thief, a liar, and completely untrustworthy. He was all that any good master abhorred, and for his sins God had made him a leper and a wanderer among the desert places.[47]

The most famous of all the biblical slaves was Onesimus, the runaway slave of Philemon, and Charles decided, four months into his missionary labors, that he would preach on this runaway. He left Solitude in early March 1833 and rode to Midway, where a large congregation of slaves had gathered at the stand across the road from the church. He lectured in the morning on the second commandment—about not making or worshiping graven images—and he denounced the charms and sorcery of the settlements and said that they were used for wicked purposes to fool a superstitious people.[48] In the afternoon he turned to "The Story of Onesimus." The stand was in the woods and the slave congregation sat around Charles under "booths" or bush arbors. "I dwelt chiefly on the *character* of Runaways," he reported in the *Charleston Observer*. He spoke of the "*folly, the impropriety, the impolicy* of their course." What could they expect to gain by taking off for the swamps or Savannah? Charles then went on to speak of "the *duty* of all to suppress the wickedness, never to conceal or harbour a runaway etc." As he spoke, he began to notice the faces of his congregation: "By the countenances of the audience, the subject was evidently disagreeable. Some endeavoured to sleep, others to look away, and many got up and left the ground." Their reactions caught him by surprise, for the county was known for having few runaways—there was in Liberty County, Charles believed, "doubtless less running away than in any other population of like size in the State." What he was discovering, or at least getting a glimpse into, was the world of the settlements where running away did not seem like wickedness but a bold bid for freedom. Moreover, those who came to church did not want to hear running away condemned by a white preacher. After the meeting, one man came up to him and said: "That is not Gospel at all; it is all Runaway, Runaway, Runaway." Another said, "The doctrine is *one-sided*," and many said "they would never more come to hear me preach." Charles was apparently stunned and simply noted: "Thus we parted."[49]

Those who walked out of the service and those who angrily confronted Charles afterward were taking a risk—they were engaging in a dangerous and amazing display of open resistance to a powerful white slaveholder. Perhaps because Charles was preaching at the stand, in space they considered to be theirs and had been theirs since Mingo had first preached there years earlier, perhaps for this reason they had the freedom for open dissent. Or perhaps their freedom was rooted in the voluntary character of the service itself—they did not have to be there if they did not want to be, nor did they have to listen or accept if they did not wish to listen to or accept what Charles had to say. Such a spiritual freedom was certainly fundamental to Charles's theology. Or perhaps at some level they respected Charles and trusted him with their anger and open resistance in spite of what he had said. Those who remained, he noted, "seemed to remain more from personal respect to the Preacher, than from any liking to his doctrine." Whatever the sources of such open resistance, what was clear even to Charles was that the resistance was a challenge to the theological presuppositions and paternalistic assumptions that informed his work. His understanding of the Bible, his authority as an interpreter of its texts, was being called into question. Even the authority of the Apostle Paul seemed to be challenged, for they said the story of the returned runaway was "not the Gospel." An alternative theological perspective—a Gospel that did not support slavery and its oppression—was being claimed by those who walked out of the stand and by those who rejected and denounced what Charles had said.[50]

Charles had not attempted to answer the criticism, but had gone about his work "as though nothing had happened." In a short while most of the displeased slaves were back at the station listening once again to him. Two years later he reassured the association that "with an increase of knowledge they will hear such preaching now." But he never preached on Onesimus again. And he realized that some slaves continued to object to him as a preacher because he was a slaveholder and "his people have to work as well as we." The whole experience was an important lesson for him, and he warned others who might try to preach to slaves that it was inexpedient and unfair to dwell on the duties of slaves. The experience revealed to him something of the hidden life and perspectives of the settlements and something about how far he could go as a white preacher. Duties could be mentioned, but not too often. Christian ethics generally applied, he later said, would meet most of the needs of a Christian people without "harping" on the duties of slaves to masters.[51]

12

THE MALLARD PLACE

In late March 1833 Charles left home on his horse Shannon for a presbytery meeting in St. Marys, about a hundred miles south of Riceboro on the Georgia-Florida line. The presbytery, the regional church court of Presbyterian ministers and lay elders, was a required meeting for Charles as a minister, but it was also an opportunity for him to discuss his work with other ministers and with planters who would be attending the meeting as elders.[1]

As Charles left Riceboro he met the Reverend James McDonald, a Baptist missionary of the Sunbury Association who was going to Darien for a revival meeting. As they rode along together, Charles had an opportunity to talk with McDonald about his work and about the Baptist churches in the area, all of which were overwhelmingly black. Charles was developing a close working relationship with the Baptist ministers of the low country, especially Samuel S. Law, who was the white pastor of the North Newport Baptist Church. Law's salary was largely paid by the wealthy planter George Washington Walthour, one of the few whites who was a member of the congregation, but the black membership was large and influential in the settlements. Young Cato from Carlawter was a member—as were many from the settlement at the nearby Retreat—and Cato was quickly becoming a leading member of the congregation.[2]

When they arrived in Darien, Charles met Nathaniel Pratt, the local Presbyterian minister. They rode together to Pratt's new home on the Ridge, an elevated area outside of Darien overlooking the marshes and creeks of the Altamaha estuary. Pratt was a graduate of Yale College and Princeton Theological Seminary and was married to Catherine King, a sister of Roswell, William, and Barrington. The Pratts, like Charles and Mary, were in the process of developing their home and had laid out gardens and fruit trees. They already had an organ in the parlor—it had cost a handsome $400—and Pratt had a study in a neat cottage

140

designed specifically for his books and desk. Charles thought that with Pratt's "attention and northern taste" they would soon have a comfortable home. Pratt was to become one of Charles's closest friends, and in a few years he and Catherine named a son Charles Jones Pratt.[3]

Charles and Pratt intended to ride horseback to St. Marys, but crossing the Altamaha was treacherous. The previous day rising waters had almost drowned several people trying to get across the muddy, surging river on a little flat-bottom ferry, so the two ministers decided to hire a sailboat to take them the seventy miles to St. Marys. Sailing out of Darien the next day, Charles found the intercoastal waters a delight, and their passage south gave him an opportunity to see the large plantations on St. Simons and Jekyll, two of the great Sea Islands of the Georgia coast.[4]

Arriving in St. Marys after two days of sailing, they went to the home of Pratt's brother the Reverend Horace Pratt. His home, a Greek Revival mansion, was not, Charles would later write, "a clerical house, but the very contrary." Pratt's wife, Jane Wood Pratt, he found "a modest, and somewhat reserved woman in her manners, not at all handsome, but very intelligent and pious." She was also, like increasing numbers of pious women in the South, interested in the religious instruction of slaves. Charles already knew that in Liberty County most of the teachers of slaves were white women, and he was pleased to have an opportunity to discuss with Mrs. Pratt her own work in St. Marys and in the little schoolhouse she had in back of their home. She was in the midst of writing "Scripture Sketches for Colored Persons," which was soon published in the *Charleston Observer*. The sketches were of biblical slaves and were intended to show "that servants are not forgotten in that holy book." The stories of these slaves were in the Bible, she said, to show slaves how to follow the model of faithful servants and how to avoid the paths of unfaithful ones. She wrote of the faithful Eliezer and the unfaithful Ziba; the faithful Obadiah and the unfaithful Gehazi; and, of course, there was Onesimus, who "robbed his master and ran away" and was an example, she wrote, of "a wicked and unprofitable servant."[5]

Charles did not know when he sat in the elegant parlor of the Pratt mansion, but he was soon to take public issue with one Mrs. Pratt's sketches—that of Hagar, the slave of Abraham with whom Abraham committed adultery. The problem was that Mrs. Pratt did not include in her sketch that "the mischief did not *begin* with Hagar, but with her *Mistress first* and her *Master second*." Slaves today, Charles would write in the *Charleston Observer*, are exposed to the same abuse. Any preacher to slaves, he said, must tell the whole truth else the slaves will come and say: "Why did you not speak of Master and Mistress too, and shew their evil deeds?" But when the truth was told, Charles said, and Abraham's and

Sarah's abuse of Hagar was recounted, he had found that her story "was one of great power" among the slaves. To his horror, years later Charles was to find such truth telling about the sexual abuse of a young slave woman to be necessary in his own household.[6]

The presbytery meeting the next day was largely devoted to the issue of the religious instruction of slaves. Charles delivered an address "On the Moral and Religious Condition of our Coloured Population" in which he reviewed once again what he regarded as the degraded condition of the slaves and their great need for owners who would attend to both their religious and physical welfare.[7] What was most gratifying for him, however, was an address by the wealthy planter Thomas S. Clay.

Clay was a "tall, dignified, handsome, refined, polite, and most engaging" man, and his plantation, Richmond-on-Ogeechee, was home to some two hundred slaves. An elder at the Bryan Neck Presbyterian Church a few miles south of Savannah, Clay had come to the presbytery meeting to present a "Detail of a Plan for the Moral Improvement of Negroes on Plantations."[8]

Clay began his address by referring to the importance of preaching in the churches and teaching in the Sabbath schools. But what immediately caught the attention of Charles was Clay's insistence on evening meetings on the plantations, where the "resident planter and his family" would gather "his people" together shortly after sundown "in a well lighted room, appropriated to the purpose, with comfortable seats." Then there would be hymns and Bible reading, a short lesson on one of the parables or on a biblical character, and evening prayers. Such services, held every weekday, would demonstrate the planter's interest "in the well being of his servants," would have an influence on both the whites and blacks gathered together, and would keep the slaves from roaming abroad at night to the injury of their health and morals. Already, said Clay, four or five large plantations in his neighborhood were having these evening services, and the plantations were becoming model communities.[9]

Clay then turned to the planter's responsibility for the physical welfare and comfort of his slaves. "Our physical habits," he said, have "a vast influence" on our moral habits; the two cannot be entirely separated, for "Man is a physical as well as a moral being, and this fact must always be kept in view" in the planter's efforts to elevate the character of the slave. Clay reminded the presbytery that the "Gospel . . . commands us to feed the hungry, clothe the naked, and shelter the houseless, as well as preach to the poor." Slaves needed, he said, nourishing food, adequate clothes, care when they were sick, and housing that allowed for some privacy and cleanliness. Slave marriages needed to be encouraged and honored, and slave husbands needed to be restrained from striking their wives, a right, Clay said, the husbands regard as inalienable. In this way, and in great detail, he outlined the responsibilities of benevolent planters for their slaves.[10]

Charles listened carefully to what Clay had to say—it was all precisely to the point, Charles thought, and coming from a layman, and especially from a successful and wealthy planter, the address was noteworthy and would encourage other planters to consider their responsibilities for their slaves. Much encouraged himself, Charles returned to Liberty County after the presbytery meeting ready to take up the work not only of preaching and teaching but also of visiting in the settlements and talking with planters about their responsibilities.

Shortly after his return home, Charles wrote Thomas Mallard, one of the members of the Association for the Religious Instruction of Slaves and a deacon and selectman at Midway Church:

> Dear Mr. Mallard:
>   If it is agreeable and convenient, I will preach for your people on Wednesday evening next.
>   Respectfully And Truly,
>   Your Friend,
>   C.C.J.[11]

Mallard agreed to Charles's proposal and sent to the settlement an announcement of the meeting. At the appointed time, those who had been laboring in the fields and in the barns and kitchen of the plantation made their way to the meeting place.

Standing in the parlor of the Mallard plantation house, Charles looked around a large but unpretentious room papered in a pattern of curious figures. Light from candles and the wide fireplace danced off the room's two windows and revealed the faces of the Mallard slaves. Charles looked at them and they looked back at him. What was he to make of them and they of him?[12]

Major and Pompey knew Charles best. Major was a watchman, a kind of deacon for the black members of Midway, and among the watchmen he was the most influential. When there was trouble in the settlements among members of the congregation, he often went with Sharper to mediate feuds between husbands and wives or conflicts between neighbors. And Major had had his own sorrows, for a few years earlier his wife had been carried by her owner to Burke County. The session at Midway, after making inquiries, determined that there was little likelihood that she would be returned to the county or to her husband. She must be treated as dead, they decided, and Major had been given permission to remarry.[13]

Pompey was also a watchman, but he was better known as the driver at the Mallard plantation and as a man of great energy. He was only thirty when Charles arrived for the evening meeting, but he was already making a name for himself as a man of some property. He later reported that Thomas Mallard had allowed him to plant "all the land I could work," and that "I used to hire men to work for me sometime."[14]

Among those crowding into the parlor was Bess. She had been converted shortly after Charles had begun his missionary work and was soon to join the Midway congregation. Although a young woman when Charles first visited the plantation, she became a "mother" of the church, a female leader of the black members of the Midway congregation, and she soon started a Female Prayer Service for the women in the Mallard settlement. Over time Charles came to think of her as an "old & sincere friend."[15]

Harry Stevens came up from the settlement for the meeting. Most people called him "Dr. Harry" because of his knowledge of herbs, roots, and barks that could ease a bruise or heal a wound or rid a child of worms. He was, however, a carpenter by trade, reportedly the best in the county. Moreover, he was in a way a kind of civil engineer, a person who knew how dikes should be constructed to hold back the river waters when they rose suddenly and how trunks should be built to properly drain a rice field. And on top of all of this, he was a good church member respected by blacks and whites alike. He was married and had a family at the Charlton Hines plantation toward the interior of the county.[16]

And there were others who came into the parlor or stood in the hall or outside on the piazza. Charles could see Maum Willoughby, the cook, whose husband Dublin lived on another plantation. She would laugh and say to the Mallard children that before greeting Dublin on a Saturday afternoon as he came to his "wife house," she "always looked to see what he had brought in his bag for the family." And there was Grace, who was married to Billy on Mr. Walthour's place and was always having trouble with him. And there was "Daddy Jack," who had been married for no more than a month before he and his wife "had divided blankets." He had returned to his bachelorhood and would at night "rake aside the fire coals and then spread his blanket upon the ashes of the hearth."[17]

And so they gathered around the parlor not as unnamed slaves, the sons and daughters of the dark earth who were to labor for a time for named white masters before returning unnamed and unknown to the earth. Rather they gathered as men and women with names and distinct personalities and particular histories and a shared human hope that they would not be forgotten — Major and Pompey, Bess and Maum Willoughby, Dr. Harry and Daddy Jack. These particular men and women, with others in the settlement, were the ones who came to hear what

Charles had to say to them, and they were the ones who would determine in their own minds and in their conversations together what he was about and how they would respond to him and to his message.[18]

Charles looked back at the faces before him, saw signs of fatigue from the day's labor in the fields or the kitchen, and thought that while the Sabbath services accomplished much, "the people absolutely required more." They needed, he thought, to be visited and instructed where they lived. They needed, just as their white owners needed, their minister to perform the duties of a pastor. But as he looked around, Charles also knew that he needed to visit them if he were going to know the actual "extent of his field," its destitutions, and the moral and religious condition of the people. Such visitation would allow his sermons to have a "more direct and personal application," his pastoral relationships a "more familiar and intimate" quality, and his influence a "more extended and powerful" authority. Above all, however, he hoped his visits would convince them that he was sincere and wanted to be their friend and pastor.[19]

Because the meeting was held on a weekday night, only slaves from the Mallard plantation were allowed to attend. Jones thought this an important rule in order to maintain the support of planters. He never gave "any notice whatever to the Negroes on other plantations, or on the Sabbath, that meetings will be held during the week on such and such plantations." Such a rule helped to ensure order among the slaves and avoided the appearance of a dangerous nighttime meeting. "It is a household affair altogether," he later wrote, "and the people are little disposed to embrace such an assembly for bad purposes. If any of them wish to do evil on the plantation, they can choose another night and another occasion just as conveniently." Twelve years after this first meeting at the Mallard plantation, Charles could report to the planters of Liberty County that of "some hundreds of meetings held on plantations at night, there never has occurred a single instance of riot, of theft, or unruly conduct, within my own knowledge, nor have I ever heard a complaint of any such thing."[20]

Thomas Mallard had selected his parlor as the place for the meeting. Over the coming years plantation parlors were common places for Charles to have his evening services, and he found that such a location had both advantages and disadvantages. On the one hand, meeting in parlors was more comfortable than in the "houses of the people which are generally too small, or in plantation houses [buildings] of one kind and another which are open, cold and uncomfortable." (Charles particularly disliked meeting in cotton houses because of the danger of fire and because they were dusty and it took time to set up benches and get them ready for a service.) On the other hand, looking around the Mallard parlor, Charles could see that many from the settlement were not at ease in such a setting. "It is rather a strange place to the field hand," Charles wrote of the Mallard parlor, "and there is no little incongruity between their dress and appearance, and that of the Planter's family, furniture, etc."[21]

Charles believed that those who lived in the settlement wanted some free space, some place they could claim for their own, for their place of worship. "It appears to me," he wrote in the *Charleston Observer*, "exceeding desirable, that on all plantations where the expense can easily be borne, that a convenient house for the worship of the Negroes should be put up. A plain clap board house would answer very well." Charles acknowledged that on some plantations there were "Praise Houses," little buildings or bush arbors that the slaves had constructed for their own use, and he occasionally used them, but he thought something more substantial was needed—a regular plantation chapel. He soon put Sandy Jones and Syphax and Porter to work at Montevideo, and they built a neat chapel with a belfry and bell. And later at Maybank, Charles had Sandy Maybank build a school for the white children that was also used as a little chapel. But these were the exceptions in Liberty County, for few planters would be swayed by Charles's insistence that it was their duty to have their own chapels.[22]

When Charles looked around the Mallard parlor, he saw not only Major and Pompey and the others who attended church at nearby Midway, but some who were never there. Among these were "worldly persons" and even church members who were habitually absent from "the house of God," and some who had been suspended or excommunicated from Midway—there was Joe, who was excommunicated for adultery and had recently been restored to membership; and Hetty and Betty, who had been suspended for fighting with each other.[23] But there were others—the aged and the infirm—who were unable to make the short trip from the Mallard plantation to the Midway station. Charles felt a special obligation to all of these who were "strangers to the house of the Lord," and much of his pastoral visitation was aimed at reaching them.

The worship service began with singing that drew to the house all who had not already arrived. Charles was a good singer, and he delighted in singing hymns with his plantation congregations. Thomas Mallard prayed and read the Scripture lesson while Bess and Dr. Harry, Maum Willoughby and Daddy Jack, Joe and Hetty, and all the others watched him and listened to his words and interpreted through their own experience what they were seeing their master do and what they were hearing their master say. There was another hymn and then Charles preached a short homily. A closing prayer followed, and another hymn, and the service was over. Bess, together with a few inquirers and those under "serious impressions," remained behind. Charles spoke to them about their religious experiences, gave them encouragement and counsel, "administered reproofs" to those who had strayed, and sought to settle any disputes that were brought to him.[24]

When the last of the congregation had left the parlor, Charles went out into the night to visit in the settlement. The plantation buildings that he passed were laid out so that everything, as far as possible, was under Thomas Mallard's eye as he looked from his front door. Charles walked by a yellow clay smokehouse across from the plantation kitchen. In the light from the Mallard parlor and front hall, he could see cotton storage houses and other outbuildings just beyond the sandy front yard. A gin, powered by a horse that tread round and round, stood silently waiting another day for its rattling chain to turn hickory rollers and separate the cotton from the seed. Going beyond the stables and carriage house, he came to the settlement. People were sitting around outdoor fires whose flames lit the night, and light flickered from fireplaces through the open doors of cabins. Charles walked down the sandy road that ran through the settlement. On each side of the road were two-room cabins. They were made of sawed lumber loosely covered with cypress clapboards so that "only the thickness of a single board kept out the winter's air and cold." Through the darkness he could see behind the cabins small gardens, rice ricks, and little storage houses, and he could smell the chicken coops and pigpens that were nearby. Charles visited in the cabins of the aged and sick. A lone candle and the fire from a clay hearth lit each dwelling. The sick lay on crude beds whose mattresses were made of the gray moss from the surrounding swamps. Standing beside these beds, with the shadows and light dancing around him, Charles reminded the sick of the gracious promises of the Gospel, asked them if they put their trust in Jesus, and offered a prayer for their health and salvation.[25]

Charles did not want to neglect any who lived in the settlement. He wanted somehow to cross the deep divide that separated him from Daddy Jack and Maum Willoughby and all the others who lived in the two-room, smoky cabins. "People," he wrote Mary, "cannot bear to see themselves, or friends or anything with which they are connected treated with neglect or contempt. It is all the same whether they be rich or poor, for you know that the poor have feelings and can be pleased and offended as well as the rich. We must therefore remember this, and treat all with politeness and attention." Charles wanted to exhibit in the settlements a politeness that came from the heart and that was "dictated by Christian benevolence." Such benevolence, Charles hoped, would be a bridge across the divide between a white preacher and black slaves. Of course Charles thought it would be, at least for the present, a bridge only the white preacher could cross as he sought to enter empathetically into the world of the settlement. Those who lived in the cabins were to stay in their place and learn the ways of the visiting white preacher until he recrossed the bridge to his own place of privilege. And even when Charles thought himself on the slave side of the bridge, he remembered that his civil relationship with his parishioners was "peculiar" and that he consequently had to maintain in all his relationships with them "the dignity and respect of his *civil station.*" He could not, even as he sought to enter empathetically into their world, "forget that they are *servants,*" or that he could not "elevate them to his standing." So he visited among them for a while as a person of privilege, and then he returned to his accustomed surroundings, where he hoped and prayed for the time when blacks would be ready to cross the bridge and assume the responsibilities of freedom. And in his accustomed surroundings he also hoped and prayed for a time when whites would be ready to allow them the journey. In the meantime, he wondered, "Who can estimate the calm, sanctifying, and saving influences of such visits both upon the pastor and the people?"[26]

After visiting in the cabins Charles returned to the Mallard parlor to sit before the fire and talk with Thomas Mallard and his wife, Eliza. Charles understood such conversations, which he made a regular part of his plantation visits, to be an important part of his pastoral efforts. If the spiritual welfare of slaves was linked, as Thomas Clay had emphasized, with their physical welfare and comfort, then Charles must arouse the conscience of slaveholders, he must persuade them to realize that the way slaves were housed, fed, clothed, and disciplined all had an impact on their spiritual lives and on the ways they heard the preaching and admonitions of whites. Slaves, he said over and over again, "have eyes and feelings and a natural discernment of consistency of character." And, he noted, slaves watch their masters carefully: they are "keen observers of the character of their masters, and their testimony to the rectitude of that character is as good as any that can be obtained, for their condition not only prompts them to observe it narrowly, but furnishes them with the best opportunities of doing so."[27]

If a master does not render his slaves "that which is just and equal," if he does not take an interest in them "body and soul," then they will quickly see through his professed piety and interest in their spiritual welfare:

> If the planter *grinds* his people—endeavouring to get *as much* out of them, and give *as little* in return to them as he possibly can; if he pays little or no regard to the quality and quantity of their food, any further than interest dictates; if he does not respect and cherish their efforts to assist themselves; if he permits them to live immorally; if he makes the neglect or omission of *his work* the greatest crime which they can commit, and calling for the severest punishment; and if he inflicts that punishment without reproof or gentleness; if he gives religious instruction with the *evident design* of promoting his worldly

interest by making them more obedient to *his* commands; if he is *one way* in the *"Praise House,"* and *another* in the *Field*; God in the House and *mammon* out of it, the sooner he resigns his office of religious instructor, the better for himself and his people.[28]

Charles wanted to convince the planters that religious instruction "requires *religious treatment.*" And, he wrote in the *Charleston Observer*, "religious treatment must be universal; it must have respect to the Negro himself, his family, his house, his food, his clothing, his labour, his correction, his every interest, soul and body, for time and eternity." Only in this way would masters follow the biblical injunction: "Masters render to your servants that which is just and equal."[29]

When Charles returned to the Mallard parlor after visiting in the settlements, he spoke not simply in these broad categories about what was "just and equal" but in specific terms—using, of course, his good manners and his sensitivity about what could be said and what couldn't. And what was most immediately obvious from a visit to the settlements of Liberty County was the need for better housing. Charles told Mallard and the other members of the association that the settlement houses were frequently "small, low to the ground, blackened with smoke, often with dirt floors, and the furniture of the plainest kind." Privacy was impossible under such conditions. Charles insisted that planters had not simply self-interest but a religious duty to improve the housing conditions of their slaves. He asked Mallard and the other members of the association how they expected religion or morality to thrive in squalid settlements. Poor housing, he insisted, resulted in poor morals—crowding two or more families in one house "scarcely large enough for one family," mingling up "husbands and wives, children and youth," banished the "privacy and modesty essential to domestic peace and purity" and opened wide the door "to dishonesty, oppression, violence and profligacy." Every slave family on a plantation, "whether consisting of only husband and wife, or parents and children, or *one* parent and children, should have a *house of its own, in undisputed and undisturbed possession.*" The houses should be "convenient and comfortable" and "properly partitioned off, and well ventilated, and neatly whitewashed, and sufficiently large to accommodate the families resident in them; and furnished with necessary articles for household use." Special attention needed to be paid to the welfare of the slave children and different sleeping apartments provided "for boys and girls as they become more advanced." Thomas Mallard agreed with Charles on this point, and he would arrange, when slave children were "half grown," to have one or two "shed-rooms" or "leantos" built on the back of the family's cabin in order to provide some privacy.[30]

Then there was the question of clothes for slaves. How easy it was for planters to let their slaves go about in rags, a bit of this and a bit of that, an occasional old coat or dress discarded as useless by a white family. It could all be so easily justified by saying they were Africans and accustomed to going about half-naked. Charles himself believed that the slaves were "exceedingly inattentive to the preservation of their clothing" because of their African traditions. He insisted, nevertheless, that masters had a duty of both providing clothing and requiring slaves to care for them. On the Mallard plantation, as was the general custom in the county, slave seamstresses made most of the clothes. At Montevideo and Maybank, Phoebe was given increasing responsibility for the daunting task of cutting out and sewing the clothes for a rapidly growing population at Carlawter and the Maybank settlement.[31]

And there were other duties Charles discussed with his fellow planters. "Servants should be provided," he insisted, "with *abundant food*, and that wholesome and good, and as diversified as it can conveniently be made."[32] And they should have their own ground to till: "as much ground to plant for themselves during the year as they can profitably attend; and also the privilege of raising poultry and hogs; indeed every privilege and opportunity allowed them to make themselves comfortable and to accumulate money."[33] And slaves ought to be provided with good medical care that went beyond a prudential concern for the health of one's laborers and valuable property. The "old and infirmed and crippled and useless," all those who no longer had economic value to planters, were not to be put away and ignored in some little cabin in the woods where they would have to care for themselves in their weakness. They were rather to be treated with dignity and provided with proper medical attention.[34] Nor were planters to overwork their slaves. Masters, said Charles, had a duty "to lay upon their servants *that labour only which is just;* allow time to enjoy the comforts of life and to do something for themselves, and preserve to them *sacredly the rest of the Sabbath.*"[35] And Charles also began to speak to masters about their duty not to separate families and about how the planters could encourage family life in the settlements. This was a subject he returned to over and over again, and in a few years he gave special attention to marriage and family life in the settlements. In time, however, he was to learn through the bitter experience of a family in Carlawter how deeply he himself was implicated in the practices of human bondage, even as he sought to work within the system of slavery to make it more humane.

All of these matters Charles discussed with Thomas Mallard and other planters. Sitting together in comfortable parlors or on cool piazzas, they would review their responsibilities as Christian masters. Agricultural journals in the South had been advocating many of the same reforms that Charles called for, though the journals generally spoke of how such reforms would improve the life and productivity of a plantation.[36] Christian masters, however, had more than self-interest to consider. They had to start thinking of their slaves as a part of their households for whom they had responsibilities as they had responsibilities for their wives and children. Like the ancient Hebrews and Greeks and early Christians, paternalistic masters needed household codes of conduct that regulated the relationships between husbands and wives, parents and children, and masters and slaves. For Christian masters, there were the straightforward words of St. Paul to guide them in their relationship with their slaves: "Masters, give unto your servants that which is just and equal; knowing that ye also have a Master in heaven."[37]

While Charles and Thomas Mallard were having their conversation before the parlor fire, another conversation was no doubt going on in the Mallard settlement. Pompey and Bess and Dr. Harry and Maum Willoughby must have stirred and poked the evening fires that burned before the settlement cabins and talked about what they had just seen and heard. This conversation, beyond the ears of the missionary and the master, no doubt involved some evaluation of Charles. What was this young white man about coming to the plantation and visiting in the settlement? Was he a friend to the slave or simply another white man doing his part to keep blacks in the settlements and whites in plantation parlors? Whatever the conversation that followed Charles's visit, there was no single and unified response to him. Some evidently came to regard him as their most important friend in the white community, a person to whom they would turn in times of need. Others evidently wanted nothing to do with him and looked on his work with great suspicion. One thing, however, must have been clear to them all—Charles was not introducing religion to the settlements. When Charles walked into the settlements, he was not walking into a kind of religious vacuum. On the contrary, he was walking into a world filled with a rich diversity of religious life and practices, some of it open and some of it secret. He was walking into a place that had its own sacred cosmos that had existed long before Charles returned from Princeton to begin his missionary labors. In 1833 Charles was only beginning to catch a glimpse of the strength and diversity of this sacred world, and he was only beginning to realize that he would never fully penetrate its mysteries or understand its power.

13

The Arbors

By 1833 Sharper had traveled around the county for twenty years with a freedom known by few other slaves. As the black preacher hired by the white Midway congregation, not only was he widely known and respected, but he also carried with him the authority and sanction of the most important institution in the county. Such freedom allowed him to know the settlements as did perhaps no other person. "The ground is all familiar to him," Charles wrote, as over the years Sharper had ridden "from three to eight miles in the evenings" to visit and preach in different settlements. During such visits and around nighttime fires after worship services, the black preacher had opportunities to talk with those who had been born in Africa and to see the ways traditional African beliefs and practices were a part of life in the settlements.[1]

When Sharper visited Sunbury he could talk with Ben and Sally, who were from Africa and would say when it thundered, "maulin a bumba," and who, no doubt, could remember how marriages were performed, children were named, sacred meals were eaten, and the dead were buried. And Sharper could hear stories in Sunbury of a slave ship coming into the little harbor; and when the slaves saw they were not in Africa, the stories said, they had taken wing and flown home.[2] At the nearby Seabrook plantation of Benjamin Scriven, Sharper could talk with a parishioner, a member of Midway, Dublin Scribben. He was from Africa and would teach his black neighbors an African dance song, "Rockah mh moomba," that would be remembered years later.[3]

And there were other Africans, some of whom bore on their bodies the long or narrow marks of their tribes and some of whom had been only recently captured and illegally brought into the country after the international slave trade had been outlawed.[4]

By the 1830s, however, the number of people born in Africa was only a small part of the black population of Liberty County. In contrast to Brazil or Cuba or even Jamaica, where there had been a steady flow of Africans to buttress traditional African cultures, there had been for decades no large-scale infusion of Africans into Liberty County. This meant that in Liberty County traditional African cultures had been undergoing a transformation into an African-American culture, most specifically into the Gullah culture of those who lived in the slave cabins of the low country.[5] Within that culture, however, Sharper could see not only Africans scattered among the settlements but strong reminders of African traditions and practices. He could see woodcarvings—walking sticks and spoons, bowls and grave markers—that were clearly African in their beauty and design. And at Carlawter he could see the work of Lizzy's son Cassius, who made sweet-grass baskets for fanning rice, for carrying cotton, and for storing peas, and whose work reflected the remembered art of the Ashanti and the technical skills of the Dahomey. Most powerful of all the African survivals encountered in the settlements, however, were the beliefs and rituals that had their roots in a distant homeland and that had been transplanted, adapted, and cultivated in the landscape of Liberty County.[6]

No one in the settlements represented the traditions of Africa more fully than the conjurers who could hurt an enemy or aid a friend.[7] The conjurer was one who had access to the power of another world and whose work explained misfortune and adversity. In 1842 Charles wrote of what he could see of this secret life in the settlement: "They believe in second-sight, in apparitions, charms, witchcraft, and in a kind of irresistible Satanic influence. The superstitions brought from Africa have not been wholly laid aside." A conjurer could make a person suddenly become sick or could provide a powerful love potion or heal those who had had spells cast upon them. Most conjurers lived in the settlements and were known and often feared by their neighbors. But shortly after Charles began his missionary work, Sharper had his position and authority challenged by a powerful conjurer who was evidently a runaway slave who had come to the county to hide along its rivers and in its woods and swamps.[8]

Word spread through the settlements of the conjurer's power, and people began to slip away to see him and to pay him for working his magic. The conjurer's influence grew, and more people turned to him. Charles wrote that the conjurer turned "the ignorant people crazy; cheating them out of their time and money, creating quarrels and confusion among them, and leading them into trouble." Charles referred to him as "that *ridiculous Conjurer*," but the conjurer was dangerous to the ordered ways of the county. Whites knew that a conjurer, Gullah Jack, had been implicated in 1822 in the attempted Denmark Vesey slave revolt in Charleston. More recently, Nat Turner had led his bloody rebellion in Vir-

ginia guided by religious visions. For Charles the danger with all conjurers—
and now especially with the conjurer hiding in the nearby woods—was in their
"pretensions to courage, to divine protection, to the exercise of peculiar power
in consummating their own plans. . . . They avail themselves of the passions and
prejudices of the poor people and thus fit them for their own purposes. They proceed to predict events, or to see visions and dream dreams, or to give out *charms*
of various kinds and for various purposes."[9]

The driver at Laurel View plantation, Samuel Elliott, one of the wealthiest
and most enterprising men in the settlements, had recently become a member of
the Sunbury Baptist Church when the roving conjurer appeared in the county.
At first some in the settlements thought Elliott was in cahoots with the conjurer,
for he seemed to believe in his charms and power. But Elliott, who evidently
found the man a charlatan and a fraud, was laying a plan for his capture. With
Elliott's help the white authorities were able to take the conjurer and ship him
out of the county. "The foolish and ignorant people that trusted in him," said
Charles, "were brought to shame."[10]

Belief in conjurers, however, did not fade. Generations later a former slave
living near Sunbury said of his youth, "deah sho wus conjuhin," and another told
a story of an "ole man roun yuh wut wuz cunjuhed an hab lots uh trouble wid his
eyes. He dig roun his yahd tuh see ef any does is buried deah. Attuh a time he fine
a dawl baby buried unduh duh doe step. Its two finguhs wuz stuck in its eye. Duh
man tro duh dawl in duh ribbuh an duh trouble disappeah." Still others spoke
of meeting ghosts on the road or in a house and declared that being born with a
caul (a membrane over the head) provided one with the ability to see spirits.[11]

Sharper, as the black preacher visiting in the settlements, had to contend with
the conjurers and with the charms that they used, which were widely feared.
He united, said Charles, "the most fearless exhibitions of Divine truth, and ex-
posures of their wickedness." He was a man a little below middling stature,
with a "smooth, benevolent forehead, and of a pleasant countenance." When
he preached, a slight impediment gave a distinctive character to his speech and
"added to the interest of his address." The consistent theme of his sermons was
God's love for all people, and over and over again he declared, "Christ died to
save sinners." When he prayed his language soared and carried the people with
it. After Charles's early sermon on creation, Sharper prayed:

> The old man went down upon his knees, with the whole congregation, in the
> sublimest and most overwhelming descriptions of God and address to Him,
> drawn from the Bible, and the deep feelings of his own soul, he brought God
> down in our midst, he placed us, bowing in his awful presence, as our God,

Creator, King, Redeemer, and final Judge. The silence of death reigned; we had impressions of the Divine Majesty and glory during that prayer, which we never had before.[12]

And when Sharper visited in the settlements and talked with the sick and the troubled, with those who were struggling with the burdens of the day and the fears of the night, the sum and the heart of the old man's spiritual counsel was "Trust and believe in Christ." Here, he said, was a rock in a weary land and a balm in Gilead. He consequently had wide influence in the settlements, and a large number of those who lived in the settlements looked upon him "as their spiritual Father, while all held him in veneration."[13]

But in spite of all of his efforts, the conjurers continued to make their charms and to mix their potions and to explain adversity and to promise help. One charm might be buried in a path or under the door of an enemy, where it could "exert a fatal influence." Another might allow its possessor to break into a smokehouse or kill a master's pig in the woods "without detection." Still other charms could be used "to remove sickness" or to work a "meditated revenge" on enemies or to make a person, in the face of danger, invulnerable. And what helped to make the magic so powerful was that a single charm could be used for multiple purposes—a person could use the same charm to heal a friend and hurt an enemy. The secret was in knowing how to make a charm with a bunch of "hair or wool, crooked sticks, glass of bottles, rusty nails, roots, etc. prepared in size and quality and with various incantations, suitable to persons and circumstances."[14] Years later a former slave in Sunbury, when asked how charms were made, said "Dy make em uh haiah an nails an frum lots uh tings." And another former slave who had lived near the South Newport River remembered how charms were worn for protection:

> These keep othuh folks frum wukin cunjuh on em too. They's made of haiah, an nails, an graveyahd dut, sometimes from pieces of cloth an string. They tie em all up in a lill bag. Some of em weahs it round wrist, some of em weahs it roun the neck, and some weahs a dime on the ankle. Then ef somebody put down cunjuh fuh em it tun black an they get anothuh one tuh wawd off the evil. Some of em has a frizzled chicken in the yahd. People do say they kin dig up cunjuh an keep it frum wukin genes yuh.[15]

Of course charms and conjuring could also be used against whites as a means of resistance and revenge. For a people with no military or legal power, the powers of a secret world could be evoked to hide a feast in the woods or to defend a family from separation or to strike back at a cruel master. What whites most feared were

Liberty County grave markers (Margaret Davis Cate Collection,
courtesy Georgia Historical Society, Savannah, Ga.)

poisonous roots and concoctions that could be slipped into foods or stirred into
drinks. Stories of such poisonings were whispered in parlors and on piazzas, and
over the years more than a few slaves in the low country had been charged and
executed for poisoning or attempting to poison white owners or overseers.[16]

Not as dangerous to order or as secretive as the world of conjurers and charms,
but nevertheless disturbing to whites and many pious blacks, was the world of
entertainment in the settlements. The "chief amusement" in the settlements,
Charles later wrote, "and that to which they become passionately fond is *dancing.*" Protestants believed dancing, by whites or blacks, was an amusement of the
world and not a practice for members of the church. Those who had had their
hearts changed were to live different lives from the worldly, and this meant that
they were to abstain from dances, which led to temptations and sin. "We know,"
Charles wrote, "what evils attend the amusement in elevated society. Those evils

are aggravated and multiplied among the poor and labouring classes." In particular, for those who lived in the settlements Charles believed dancing to be "a dissipating, demoralizing amusement," and it was "so viewed by those who are the really serious, virtuous and pious among them." He had found that their "dances are not only protracted to unseasonable hours, but too frequently become the resort of the most dissolute and abandoned, and for the vilest purposes." [17]

Sharper no doubt knew of such dancing—there was the buzzard lope and the camel walk, the fish tail and the snake hip—and he no doubt had heard of the secret drums that would call the people to sneak away for a dance, even to so far away a place as St. Catherine's Island. "Dey beat duh drums on St. Catherine," an elderly black from Sunbury would remember. "Den dey heah it at Harris Neck an folks deah tell all ub us yuh bout duh dance. We all go obuh tuh St. Catherine in a boat an dance an dance till mos daylight." In the settlements themselves, such dances often followed a corn shucking or were at Christmas or on New Year's Eve. There were fiddlers in the settlements, people whom Charles considered neither "sober" nor "devout persons." [18]

Some planters, however, thought dancing a good diversion for the slaves and sponsored dancing as a reward at the end of a hard season of work. Roswell King, Sr., before his own religious conversion, even thought dancing better for the slaves than preaching by black slaves like Sharper, which could get out of hand. The dancing allowed a diversion for the people and kept them from focusing on more troubling matters. He had written Pierce Butler in Philadelphia:

> There is one plan I cannot forbade proposing (it is not much Expense) which is to send me a *full dozen Fiddles* that will cost from one to two dollars each. I must try to break up so much preaching as there is on your Estate. Some of your Negroes die for the Love of God and others through feir of Him. Something must be done. I think Dancing will give the Negroes a better appetite for sleep than preaching.[19]

The most common musical instrument in the settlements, however, was not the fiddle but the banjo—an instrument that most likely had its origins in African musical traditions. A long neck gourd, grown in one of the settlement gardens, would be selected and carefully dried. It needed a straight neck and as round a head as possible. About a half-inch above the level of the neck, the head of the gourd would be cut, a cat hide stretched across it, and a hank of horsehair used for strings. With the music from such a gourd banjo, African Americans in the low country had been dancing and singing for years by the time Sharper was making his visits to the settlements.[20]

Like the sweetgrass baskets and the Gullah dialect, the music of the settlements represented something both old and new. The dancing that Sharper saw and the singing that he heard were expressions of a remembered cultural style—a cultural style that lay beneath and united all the diverse cultures of Africa represented in the settlements. At the heart of this remembered cultural style was a rhythmic and percussive music that permeated everyday life.[21] Charles found that those who lived in the settlements sang "very often about their business or of an evening in their houses." Phoebe and Patience would sing as they washed clothes or snapped beans in the yard; others would sing as they chopped cotton or shucked corn or harvested rice or rowed boats.[22] Rachael, who was born at Maybank in 1833, later sang to a white baby as she rocked him:

> By oh baby go sleepy!
> Maumer ketch one raaaabit,
> Bile um sweet for baby!
> Rock um by baby go sleepy,
> All de bread an' de cheese I git,
> Put um up for de baby!
> Maumer ketch one raaaabit,
> Bile um sweet for baby![23]

This lullaby, sung first no doubt to a baby in the settlement, was at the same time African in its rhythm and something new that was being created out of the experience of African Americans. Rachael was going to give the baby extra food to eat, something that would be special for a child in the settlement—bread, cheese, and rabbit. Singing such a song in her Gullah dialect, she was drawing together with passion and pathos traditions from Africa and Europe and creating a distinct cultural tradition that reflected the social and material realities of the settlements.

In a similar manner, Sharper was leading the people of the settlements as they helped create a world of African-American Christianity. In Liberty County this world was taking institutional shape around the black preacher and watchmen at Midway and the watchmen at the Baptist churches at North Newport and Sunbury. But much of the vitality of African-American Christianity flowed from the bush arbors built near the settlements and near the churches and from the "hush arbors" built in secret places. In these simple structures, often little more than a gathering place in the woods, different worlds overlapped and sometimes collided: the world of Africa and the world of Europe; the worlds of conjuring and entertainment and the world of Christian piety and discipleship.[24]

As Sharper visited the plantations, he would preach and pray and sing with the people in the arbors. And from these simple places, and others like them across the South, there flowed a river of song of amazing depth and beauty—

the spirituals of a people held captive, the cries of the heart of those who lived in the settlement at Carlawter and at Maybank, at the Retreat and at the Mallard Place, and in all the smoky slave cabins of the South:

> My God is a rock in a weary land
> weary land
> in a weary land
> My God is a rock in a weary land
> Shelter in a time of storm.[25]

The spirituals were the catechisms of the arbors—they taught the stories of the Bible from Genesis to Revelation. There were spirituals about the Old Testament patriarchs:

> O wrestlin' Jacob, Jacob, day's a-breakin':
> I will not let thee go![26]

And there were spirituals filled with the bloody imagery of Judgment Day:

> And de moon will turn to blood (Thrice)
> In dat day, O-yoy [a sort of prolonged wail] my soul!
> And de moon will turn to blood in dat day.[27]

And in between spirituals from Genesis and Revelation were spirituals that told about crossing the Jordan River, about King David, and about a valley of dry bone. And from the New Testament there were spirituals about Mary and Jesus, about disciples and about the parable of the wise and foolish virgins. The spirituals not only taught these biblical stories, they drew the singers deep into the stories and made the biblical stories a part of the experience of the settlements:

> See how they done my Lord
> done my Lord
> done my Lord
> See how they done my Lord
> An' He never said a mumblin' word.[28]

The catechism of the arbors, however—unlike the ones written by Charles—did not tell about Onesimus or sing: "Servants obey in all things your Masters according to the flesh, not in eye-serve as men-pleasers, but in singleness of heart, fearing God." Rather, there was another biblical story that was sung and memorized by the people: "Go down Moses, tell ole Pharaoh to let my people go!"

Often using a call and response for questions and answers, the catechism of the arbors allowed the singers to memorize and internalize the message of the spirituals that took the singers through the life of faith.[29] The seeker had to "walk this lonesome valley," and the converted had to be watchful lest they strayed and the Lord come unexpectedly:

> Brudder, keep you lamp trimmin' and a-burnin,'
> Keep your lamp trimmin' and a-burnin,'
> Keep your lamp trimmin' and a-burnin,'
> For dis world most done.[30]

And for the believers, there were words of comfort and words that reassured the singers that Jesus knew the sorrows of the settlements:

> Nobody knows de trouble I see
> Nobody knows but Jesus,
> Nobody knows de trouble I've had
> Glory hallelu![31]

Permeating these songs of sorrow that told of burdens and troubles was a remarkable joy that gave courage and invited resistance to the degradations of slavery.[32] This joy was also a part of the catechism of the arbors, and it was rooted in a vision of a different future, of a new heaven and a new earth, where there would be no more masters or mistresses, no more slave sales in Riceboro, no more whippings, no more illness, no more death, no more partings. By offering a vision of a different future, the catechism of the arbors was insisting that life in Liberty County was not part of some eternal, unchanging order but was going to change. A day was coming, this catechism taught, when the land would be healed and there would be no more slough separating Carlawter and Montevideo—indeed, on that jubilee day there might even be a great reversal, when the last would become the first, when those who sat around fires in the settlements would sit in the best seats at the banquet of the Lord.

As Sharper visited in the settlements he could not only hear the spirituals as they were sung in the arbors and around the evening fires, but he could also hear religious songs and see religious dances that were in their tone and character even closer to Africa than the spirituals. The ring dances and shouts of Gullah people had been remembered from a distant homeland, infused with Christian imagery, and transformed into a seedbed for the spirituals. More incantation than song, the shouts were mystical and powerful, drawing the singers into a kind of ecstasy as emotions from deep currents surged like a turbulent sea. A number of dancers would form a circle and move counterclockwise to a rhythmic step: feet flat on the floor, heels tapping, hips swaying, shoulders stiff, arms close to the body, hands forward with palms up as a supplication, and all the while an undulating flow of song:

> Day, day Oh — see day's a-coming
> > Ha'k 'e angels
> Day, day Oh — see day's a-coming
> > Ha'k 'e angels
> Oh look at day (ha'k 'e angels) — Oh Lord
> > Ha'k 'e angels
>
> . . . . . .
>
> Who that a-coming (ha'k 'e angels) — Oh Lord
> > Ha'k 'e angels.[33]

Sometimes there was even more dramatic participation in the song. In "Down to the Mire," dancers took turns in the center of the ring on their knees, heads touching the floor, rotating with the circle while the passing shouters pushed the head "down to the mire."

> Sister Emma, Oh, you mus' come dow to de mire.
> Sister Emma, Oh, you mus' come dow to de mire.
> Jesus been down
> > to de mire
>
> . . . . . .
>
> Lowrah lowrah
> > to de mire
> Jesus been down
> > to de mire.[34]

Those who had been down to de mire often came up ecstatic, believing they had been converted. And for any who wanted to join the Midway congregation, it was Sharper's responsibility to talk with them to try to discern the spirit that had been at work in them. And what made the discerning process more difficult was that many who had been down to de mire had also had dreams that had convinced them that they had seen the light, that God had touched their hearts and saved their souls. Charles would also hear them tell of their dreams. A man came to him "professing to be under some convictions of sin" and said: "Last night I dreamt that two *white* ladies, all dressed in white, with smiling faces, said to me, will you come with us and serve the Lord? I answered — I am not ready. Said they, you must get ready and come, and with that they vanished out of sight." Another man, who had been excommunicated, wished to be readmitted to the church. He went to a watchman and told him a dream he had had: "He fell into a hole, and that was full of fire. A white man appeared and took him out, and told him to go and tell T. the watchman." The watchman recalled telling him "I could not take his dream; it was no evidence of any reformation. The man flew into a rage. Now," said the watchman to him, "I know *better than ever*, that *there is no repentance in you*." Another had dreamed that a child, living in another settlement, was going to die, and the child died. And still another said that "she must believe in dreams, because they were the means of her conversion." She had dreamed "that a man had told her she was going to hell," and soon after "her friend had a peculiar dream, and these two combined, first led her to serious reflection."[35]

Charles found these dreams "mild and unexceptionable, compared to numbers that they tell," and he noted that "many place unbounded confidence in dreams, visions, voices and the like." What Charles was learning as he visited in the settlements and talked with Sharper and the watchmen was that there existed in the settlements a "regular system of dreaming for various purposes":

> Their dreams for admission into the Church are very nearly the same, which shows how they come by them. When they wish for a favor, or have a spite against any one, they dream for it, and very often very ingeniously. They have what they call *travels*, or *travails*. These, so far as I understand them, partake of the nature of *Revelations*. Allied to these are their *trances*, and *visions*, and *voices*. They encourage each other in these follies, and their religious teache[r]s especially, for dreams, travails, visions, etc. are powerful engines in their hands for the accomplishment of their designs whatever they may be.[36]

Charles's response, and the response that he recommended to others, was to be careful in the manner of "overthrowing their superstitions" in order not to provoke those who had had the dreams. When a person had had a dream that led to a conversion, Charles would respond: "On that point we have little to say, God may or may not have been in that dream. We cannot tell. Let us pass that by for the present and inquire if you have heartily repented, etc." Charles urged those attacking "their superstitions" to do so "sympathizing with them in their little opportunities of knowing better, and clearing up every thing from the Bible, so that they can not but see the error." But he noted the preacher and watchman "will find professors of religion among the Negroes, as stubborn in holding on to false hopes, and false evidences, as among any other people. He will find them too, as opinionated, and as fond of an *easy way* to Heaven as other men."[37]

Charles did not hesitate, however, to preach against conjurers, charms, and dreams. In a sermon on "Simon the Sorcerer," he said the story of Simon teaches us "what we are to think of sorcerers, wizards, and witches." We are, he said, "to look upon them as deceivers. They pretend only to do wonders, and tell fortunes and give charms. . . . And we may defy all of them in the world to tell our fortunes, what is coming to pass, to make us well or to bewitch us, by their old roots and rusty nails and hair and wool and old bags and sticks and marks and mutterings. They lie and do not [tell] the truth as it was with Simon." What they are after, Charles warned his congregation, is your money.[38]

After the sermon, Pompey, the watchman and the driver at the Mallard Place, told him that some of the "people found fault" with him "because he preached against *Sorcery, Witchcraft, etc.*" Pompey said, "there was a great disposition in black people to hold on to their sins, and to be religious too; but that was impossible." He then added: "As black a man as he was, he would not give up his hope in Jesus for the whole world." And when Charles spoke against dreams, he over heard someone say after the service: "I don't care what he says; can any body make me believe that I did not see *my dream*, nor hear *the voice* that came from God to me? Did I not see it with *my own eyes*, and hear it with *my own ears?*" The experience of the slave was providing a way of knowing, a way of interpreting life and religion, which claimed its own authority and that resisted the way of knowing and the authority of the white preacher.[39]

Such resistance convinced Charles—and perhaps Sharper encouraged him to think this—that a "religious teacher *cannot always meet and put down a superstition. He must depend upon a gradual increase of knowledge. When light enters the mind, darkness will vanish.*" What Charles expected "the light" to teach was a modern dismissal of superstition, a dismissal that flowed most strongly from the Enlightenment's confident smile of reason. But Charles was also reflecting the Calvinist tradition in which he stood and which could be seen in the simple, plain features of the Midway meetinghouse. This tradition insisted that the heart of sin was not so much unbelief as idolatry: the making of a god out of that which is not God. For the Calvinist, the Creator of the heavens and the earth could not be manipulated. Magic, however, was regarded as precisely that—an attempt to manipulate God. And nothing troubled Calvinists more in this regard than the sacraments. They wanted no hint of magic connected with baptism or the Lord's Supper. Being baptized either by sprinkling or by immersion, Charles insisted, did not save a person. He tried to "refute the notion, dearly cherished by many, that there is a virtue, an almost saving efficacy in *the mode*, in *the water* applied to the person." It did not matter if the Reverend Robert Quarterman sprinkled water on the head of a man at Midway or if the Reverend Samuel Law plunged a woman down into the dark waters of the North Newport as the tide turned to carry her sins away; if the person did not have a new heart, nothing was gained.[40]

In the same way, Charles worried that "some entertain erroneous notions" of the Lord's Supper, with "some of them believing it a kind of *saving ordinance.*

If they can eat the bread and drink the wine, all is safe." But what concerned Charles the most were special meals held at night, in gatherings they called the "Society," where "they have had suppers consisting in the substantials of rice, fowls, bacon, etc. which have been viewed by them in the light of *the Sacrament!* at which colored watchmen have presided. Most awful!" The Societies were the gatherings in the bush arbors of church members and inquirers not yet baptized, and they represented an almost secret institution in the settlements. Their sacred meals may have been an adaptation of the love feasts of the New Testament revived by the Moravians, but they also may have reflected a tradition from west Africa of sacrificial meals. Whatever the antecedents of the meal, Charles found it "most awful!" and "pernicious" because some watchmen were involved and because the claim was made that the meal had a sacramental character. He evidently saw in the meal not only a ritual that was blasphemous—by claiming to be something sacred, by claiming to put the participants in contact with the holy—but also a ritual, a social drama, that was subversive. This nighttime meal was enacted without the authority of the white church, and as such it had the potential of nurturing a vision of an alternative world where whites were not masters and blacks were not slaves. To make matters worse, watchmen had not only participated, they had presided at the meals. A secret world—incorporating into it biblical images, Christian theology, and Christian leaders—seemed ultimately more threatening to the established order of Liberty County than a world of conjurers and charms.[41]

In late May 1833, as Charles was leaving his study, he saw a man riding toward the house. It was Sharper's son, bringing news of his father's death. Sharper had eaten some plums, still too green in May, and he had been struck with a violent affliction of the bowels. Medicine had been administered, and had appeared to help, but he shortly fell into a "kind of stupor, and rapidly declined in strength." Some older members of the church came and prayed with him, and he revived enough to say, "By the grace of God I am what I am, and his grace which was bestowed upon me, was not in vain." Then his strength failed, and he died shortly afterward. The son asked Charles to have the funeral on the next evening.[42]

Charles left home on horseback an hour before the sun set and reached Midway just as the moon rose, three quarters full. He drew up his horse by the wall of the cemetery and for a few moments surveyed the "City of the Silent." He looked at the graves and vaults of his father and mother, of other relatives, and of "many, very many friends." Some of the stones were "whiter than marble in the moonlight, and others but dark forms under the shadow of trees." How easily, he thought, "might ignorant and superstitious minds be wrought upon by such scenes." There were "graves, tombs, railings, vaults—all that we meet with in grave-yards: lights and shadows intermingling, every object indistinct, and ever changing in outline."

Charles had been told that the funeral would be held at the Old Field, so he rode on north of the church about a mile. He turned off the road and entered an old plantation avenue that led to the settlement where Sharper had lived as a child. The settlement was gone, abandoned years earlier, and only the foundations of the cabins and the old graveyard remained. Here Sharper's parents and other relatives were buried, and here, in this sacred place of ancestors, the old preacher had picked out his own gravesite, where he would rest undisturbed until Judgment Day. Charles stopped his horse and awaited the arrival of the funeral. He looked and saw "not a living thing in the extensive field. Dark woods skirted it on every side. It was a perfect solitude on the earth." An owl hooted down in the deep swamps and was answered by another. Charles could hear in the distance the low rumbling of a plantation mill. But no one arrived. After about an hour, he called out, and his voice echoed far and wide, but no one answered. He rode back to the road and met a man who told him that for "the convenience of the people the funeral would be held at the Church."

Hurrying back to Midway, he found "between three and four hundred Negroes, already assembled." They were sitting and standing quietly on the green before the church, while on the edge of the gathering were fifteen or twenty horses held by their owners. Charles was the only white man present. The moonlit scene with the white meetinghouse and the silent people on the green, he thought, "partook of the mysterious." The wall of the cemetery ran out of the moonlight into the shadow of the church and lost itself in dark woods. "We seemed," he thought, "to be in a mysterious world; the living had come to commune with silence and the dead." Overcome by the power of the scene, he waited silently for the arrival of the body.

Finally, they could hear the oxcart moving quietly down the sandy road. As it came toward the church door, the people rose and followed it. The procession came to a stop. The old members of the church, together with Sharper's sons, lifted the coffin off the cart and placed it on a bier a few steps before the church door. Charles mounted the steps, and the people gathered around. "The blue heavens," Charles wrote, "were stretched over us, and the moon was our chandelier." A soft "tremulous voice," as if "afraid to break the silence, commenced the song." Charles prayed and then took as his text: "Blessed are the dead which die in the Lord, from henceforth: Yea saith the Spirit, that they may rest from their labors: and their works do follow them." He spoke of the eternal world and of the glories of "our exalted Redeemer." And then he spoke of Sharper, of the old man now in Heaven, resting from "his labors among them, as a friend, a brother and a Minister." And as he spoke the people "wept and wept aloud." And Charles himself choked with emotion and found tears coming again and again.

Charles concluded the sermon, another hymn was sung, and the benediction was given. Then the "lid was removed and they passed around the coffin, and took a last, a farewell look of their dead Minister. The moon shone full upon his face, forever fixed in death. Many were the tears there shed—many were their farewells and their expressions of sorrow." The lid was replaced, the coffin put back on the oxcart, and the body was "committed to his Sons" to carry it to the silent field of the old settlement. As Charles and the crowd watched, the cart moved through the shadows of the surrounding oaks. All around was "the rich, heavy foliage of the forests . . . wet with dew and hanging in silvery masses." The cart came out of the shadows. The moonlight illumined a road of white sand running before them toward the old settlement and its cemetery. Sharper's family, now by itself, may have sung as they walked along with the creaking cart one of the most beautiful of the spirituals:

> I know moonrise, I know star-rise,
>   Lay dis body down.
> I walk in de moonlight, I walk in de starlight,
>   To lay dis body down.
> I'll walk in de graveyard, I'll walk through de graveyard,
>   To lay dis body down.
> I'll lie in de grave and stretch out my arms;
>   Lay dis body down.
> I go to de judgment in de evenin' of de day,
>   When I lay dis body down;
> And my soul and your soul will meet in de day
>   When I lay dis body down.

The little procession turned off the road and went down the ancient avenue toward the settlement. When they arrived at the chosen spot, the sons dug the grave, lowered their father to his resting place, and tossed the sandy soil on the old preacher. With these and perhaps other private rituals they committed their father to the place of his ancestors and to the Savior whom he had trusted.[43]

14

Columbia

As the executor of Andrew Maybank's estate, Charles found that he had continuing responsibilities for the management of the legacy left to Columbia Theological Seminary. The money that had been collected at Riceboro from the sale of Rachael and other Maybank slaves to Joseph Jones, from the sale of cattle and hogs and beehives and silverware and real estate—all of the money had gone into a legacy for the seminary and Charles had to oversee its investment for several years until the estate was finally settled. Such a responsibility, together with his publications and work for the religious instruction of slaves, made him not only well known throughout Georgia and South Carolina but also a churchman of increasing influence. In 1835, at age thirty, he had been elected a member of the board of directors of the seminary, and the Synod of South Carolina and Georgia had appointed him chairman of a committee to investigate the possibilities of a "Southern Union for the Religious Instruction of the Slaves."[1]

Charles was clearly the one behind the proposed "Southern Union," although a number of prominent clergymen and laymen—including Thomas Clay—were on the committee. The plan was to form a regionwide benevolence society—modeled after those he had come to know in New England—which would coordinate and encourage missionary work among the slaves. The society would be composed only of southerners who were desirous of reforming slavery and making the experience of slavery into one of religious and moral training for African Americans. It all sounded reasonable and prudent to Charles, but he had not anticipated the hostility such a proposal would evoke among the radical defenders of slavery, who feared "religious meddling" with the institution and any movement that might challenge the prerogatives of masters. And nowhere would the hostility and opposition be stronger than in South Carolina.[2]

In late October 1835, Charles left Liberty County to attend a meeting of the seminary's board of directors in Columbia and to present to the synod the report on the proposed Southern Union. He sailed from Savannah to Charleston in order to visit with friends in the city and to take advantage of the new railroad that was already reaching from Charleston toward Augusta and Columbia.[3]

His ship sailed quietly into the Carolina port on a clear fall morning and came to its mooring at Adger's Wharf. Charles hurried down the gangplank and down cobblestone streets to the home of his elderly cousin Eliza Ferguson, who received Charles with the warmth and hospitality of a doting aunt. He had visited with her on his travels to and from the North, and she was eager to hear all the news of Joseph and his family, and especially of Sister Susan, who had lived with her while a student in Charleston. Charles was especially eager to talk with friends and relatives about their views on the religious instruction of slaves, for he sensed that if Charleston could be won to the cause, then the way would be opened throughout the South for a sustained and comprehensive campaign. The growing sectional dispute over slavery he found particularly troubling, and he was finding himself more than ever convinced that the religious instruction of slaves was the only safe and sane way for the nation to extricate itself from the morass of slavery. The previous summer he had written William Plumer, an influential Virginia clergyman, that religious instruction must be accomplished "as *speedily* as possible. Our salvation from sore evils, from divine judgments, depends upon it. The Religious Instruction of the Negroes is the *foundation* of permanent improvement in intelligence and morals in the slave-holding states." Charles wrote Plumer that such instruction was "the *only entering wedge* to the great and appalling subject of slavery. The *only sun*, that appearing through the dark clouds, will shed down pure and holy light, and if the Institution of Slavery is to be abandoned, will cause the nation to relax its hold and gradually and peacefully lay it off and then sit down in delightful repose." Such perspectives, however, were precisely what some in South Carolina feared in regard to religious instruction. They wanted no "entering wedge" on the subject of slavery, and the only thing they found appalling was the growing antislavery clamor in the North.[4]

Judge Charles Jones Colcock (the cousin Charles had met in Columbia two years earlier) called on Charles, as did Mrs. Bowen, the Episcopal bishop's wife. Charles went to see Thomas Smyth, the pastor of the Second Presbyterian Church, and met with Smyth's father-in-law, James Adger, reputed to be the wealthiest man in the city. He talked with them all about his missionary labors and about the duty of southern Christians to provide for the religious instruction of the slaves. Smyth shared Charles's sentiments and was himself later accused in Charleston of being an abolitionist. Such a charge was, of course, far from true, although Smyth did think slavery an evil that ought to be removed "as soon as God in His providence should open the way." [5]

What made Charles's visit to Charleston timely was a publishing campaign initiated by abolitionists in the summer of 1835. Less than six months after Charles had visited Benjamin Lundy (the antislavery editor of the *Genius of Universal Emancipation*) in 1830, Lundy's colleague William Lloyd Garrison had launched the *Liberator*, in which he called for the immediate abolition of slavery. Garrison declared in the first issue:

> *I will be* as harsh as truth, and as uncompromising as justice. On this subject [of slavery] I do not wish to think, or speak, or write, with moderation. . . . I am in earnest—I will not equivocate—I will not excuse—I will not retreat a single inch—AND I WILL BE HEARD[6]

Interestingly, most of those who had heard Garrison's challenge in 1831 were New England conservatives who immediately attacked him. Among the most vehement opponents of Garrison was Joseph Tracy, editor of the *Vermont Chronicle*, who denounced immediate abolitionism as revolutionary and a product of the fanaticism of the French Revolution. Slavery, Tracy insisted, should be a "preparatory school for freedom." And he pointed to Charles's new missionary labors and the work of the Liberty County Association for the Religious Instruction of the Negroes as models for what needed to be done on the long road to freedom.[7]

By the summer of 1835, however, southerners were taking note of the growing strength and vehemence of abolitionism. And nowhere was this note taking more vigorous than in Charleston, where a mob broke into the post office, gathered all the material that was thought to have been sent to the city by abolitionists, and burned it in a great bonfire. A "Committee of Twenty-One" leading citizens, with Judge Colcock as chair, had been appointed to investigate the abolitionist threat to the city. The committee had called for laws that would allow authorities to seize and destroy "all incendiary publications which may be brought into this State, calculated to excite domestic insurrection or to disturb the tranquility, happiness and safety of the people." All of this excitement did not bode well for the proposed Southern Union, but what made matters more difficult for Charles was the direct attack that had been launched against the religious instruction of slaves by the fiery planter and political leader from Edisto Island, Whitemarsh Seabrook.[8]

Seabrook, a graduate of Princeton, was the president of the Agricultural Society of South Carolina and had been a longtime promoter of scientific methods of agriculture and slave management. The previous year he had been elected lieutenant governor of the state and had been successful in securing legislation that had tightened restrictions on the times and places blacks could worship. In 1834 he had published *An Essay on the Management of Slaves, and Especially, on their Religious Instruction.* His essay contained a dismissive account of Charles's work, of the synod's report on religious instruction that Charles had written in 1831, and of Thomas Clay's "Detail of a Plan for the Moral Improvement of Negroes on Plantations," which Clay had presented to the presbytery in St. Marys in 1833.

Seabrook's attack on Charles began with an attack on the clergy generally. "The intermixture of plantations and the employment of *any one* whose profession it was to teach the word of God" Seabrook deemed filled with "insuperable objections." Clergy, he admitted, had an important function in society so long as they were kept "rigidly within the limits of their station." Reflecting the Deism of an earlier generation, he thought the clergy dangerous because they are "comparatively deficient in the practical knowledge of mankind" and because they are "subjected to no positive control." A "few of our reverend friends," he wrote, "in their *behaviour* and *teachings,* apply the same rules to the black as the white man," and they were thereby laying "the foundation for opinions inimical to the peace of the State." In regard to the synod's report on religious instruction, he found that it contained "the foundation argument on which the emancipationist proposes to erect the superstructure of his schemes." The synod's plan was "sophistical and illusory," and if it were adopted, then "the reign of fanaticism and misrule will have commenced." As for Thomas Clay's proposal presented to the presbytery, Seabrook wondered if it had been "suggested by a Tappanist," referring to the followers of the antislavery philanthropists Arthur and Lewis Tappan. He suggested that Clay, a "Utopian projector," was "in his heart an Abolitionist."[9]

Seabrook may not have known that Charles and Clay were slaveholders, although that seems unlikely in the little world of the South Carolina and Georgia low country. What he apparently did not know, or certainly acknowledge, was that Clay was a successful planter—much more successful than Seabrook, the expert on scientific management of a plantation. At any rate, Charles evidently thought Seabrook a pompous South Carolinian whose claims to speak for the South were not only pretentious and arrogant but also dangerous. Such an image was reinforced by a visit with Henry Laurens Pinckney.[10]

Pinckney, whose newspaper the *Mercury* was one of the leading papers in the South, was the U.S. congressman from Charleston. With his brother-in-law U.S. senator Robert Young Hayne, Pinckney was part of a particularly powerful association of political leaders—including Hugh Swinton Legare, who later served as U.S. attorney general and U.S. secretary of state—associated with the Circular Congregational Church. As president of the congregation, Pinckney wanted to explore the possibility of Charles's accepting a call to become the church's pastor. It must have been a tempting offer to Charles, for the congregation was one of the most influential in the South and included among its members—in addition to Pinckney, Hayne, and Legare—many of Charleston's oldest and most respectable families: DeSaussures and Porchers, Bennetts and Vanderhorsts, Hutsons and Perroneaus, and a host of others. To accept a call to such a congregation would provide an opportunity to nurture a concern for the religious instruction of slaves in the heart of a city that called itself the Capital of the South. But Charles's heart was in Liberty County, and he put the subject of a call aside. What he was interested in learning from Pinckney was the attitude of the city toward religious instruction. What Pinckney told him was not encouraging.[11]

The political excitement, Pinckney said, that had surrounded the Nullification Controversy had "almost wholly ceased throughout the state, and the leaders have gone to making money, or into good offices, or are seeking such." Pinckney thought that a "spirit of speculation" pervaded the city, "and some say they want to pursue a policy which will make the South independent of the North." What was causing excitement now was "the Abolition question," and, Charles wrote Mary, "sorry am I to inform you that the cause of Religious Instruction has been most seriously injured":

> Mr. Pinckney observed that the people here were disposed to run *into extremes.* Very true. The Methodist missionaries have suffered some hindrances, by having some Plantations closed against them, and the whole community here will bear on the subject nothing but the *most delicate touches.* Nothing can be attempted until the fever cools. The Prints, and the Pamphlets, written here on the subject of Abolition, take the highest ground, in relation to slavery. Some go so far as to justify it *in the abstract,* and to say that it is *no* moral evil, *no* curse, but an *absolute blessing,* and *must be perpetual!*

Charles noted that in spite of such radicals there were "colored schools" in all the churches of the city and that they "taught orally every Sunday." Still, Charles was not encouraged by what he was hearing. In his conversation with Pinckney and Judge Colcock and with such religious leaders in the city as Smyth and the Episcopal minister William Barnwell, he learned that they approved the proposed Southern Union for the religious instruction of slaves. "But," he wrote Mary, thinking no doubt of Seabrook and his supporters, "there is strong opposition to Religious Instruction in this state with many."

Charles evidently saw a radical defense of slavery emerging, a claim that slavery was no curse inherited from the past but a positive good to be defended at all costs. And he saw this claim as being rooted, ironically, in the old revolutionary Deism that lingered in South Carolina. "The truth is," he wrote Mary, "as Mr. Pinckney and others say, the state is divided into two parties, the *Religious* and the *Infidel*. The infidel Party, though many of them pretend to approve religion, are opposed to it *in every form*." Charles believed that the person responsible for such a situation was Thomas Jefferson's old friend Thomas Cooper, the president of South Carolina College. "Dr. Cooper," Charles insisted, "is their Father. That old man has done this state more evil than fifty years can remove. He has a world of iniquity to answer for in poisoning the State with his infidel principles. And yet, wonderful to tell, he says, he believes the Bible and is as good a Christian as any body!"[12]

Such, Charles believed, was the source and character of the opposition to religious instruction of the slaves. On the one side of the debate stood those who believed that slavery, as he had written Plumer, was a "great and appalling subject" and that religious instruction was essential for the religious and moral training of slaves to prepare them for future responsibilities as they walked their long road toward freedom. Such a position, with its biblical defense of slavery and its accompanying paternalism, was, Charles believed, the best defense against those who called for the immediate abolition of slavery. On the other side stood those who argued that slavery was an *"absolute blessing and must be perpetual!"* This was an argument of infidels, of the irreligious, who would increasingly claim scientific justification for their position. (They would soon be arguing that blacks were a separate species from whites and that there must have been a dual origin of the races.) Pinckney told Charles that there was some talk—encouraged no doubt by Seabrook—in the state legislature to forbid "every kind of instruction of the Negroes—even *Religious instruction!*" Charles thought that "the infidel may embrace this present state of excitement in this way to stab religion. But they will rue the day." He did not believe the legislators would act in such a reckless manner, but if "they do, they will for that act be given up to frenzy. They will by it, produce division in the South, and convert thousands of Northern men, now with us, into immediate Abolitionists."[13]

The visit to Charleston was important to Charles, for, he said, "I now know how matters stand." Pinckney warned him that "every man who was interested in and engaged in doing any thing for the Negroes, was in a 'ticklish' situation." Charles responded that "my friends had never accused me of rashness in my operations, and that it was best in periods of excitement to yield to the storm, until it was passed." And so he prepared to leave Charleston affirming that "God reigns," and that only God "can order things as they should be."[14]

Charles left Charleston at six in the morning. He was delighted to be riding on the train, for not only was it a novel way to travel, but it also showed that southerners did not wish to be left behind as progress and technology came rushing across the nineteenth century. He and his traveling companions occupied "an apartment in one of the cars, cushioned with cloth, and a large grass mat on the floor." They sat "socially around as in a Parlour, and had a most delightful time of conversation." The train reached at times the astonishing rate of 25 miles per hour and was "swifter than a race horse." After a trip of 60 miles, they left the train and took the stage for the last leg of the journey, arriving in Columbia at three in the morning. They had taken twenty-one hours to travel about 120 miles — scarcely four hours by train to travel the first 60 miles and more than sixteen hours by stage to travel the last 60.[15]

When the question of a Southern Union for the religious instruction of slaves was taken up by the synod, Charles was not surprised when action on the proposal was postponed indefinitely. His visit to Charleston had prepared him for such an outcome and for those who said "that the time was not right for such an organization," given the "excited state of the country." Local organizations, such as the one in Liberty County, were thought best for the times, rather than a regionwide union. Charles concurred, for he could see in the synod a growing commitment to religious instruction and to the paternalistic assumptions that informed his work.[16]

If Charles was not surprised by the synod's action on the Southern Union, he was surprised when he was nominated for and elected to a professorship in ecclesiastical history and church polity at the seminary. He was certainly not well prepared for such a position — he had no background in either subject other than his studies at Andover and Princeton. But the case that was pressed on him was that he could "do more good for the Negroes, by directing the minds of the young men [at the seminary] to them as a field for pastoral and missionary labours," than he could by his "own direct labours" in Liberty County. Such a call, Charles thought, he had to take seriously. His own preference was obviously to stay in Liberty County and continue the work he had begun there, but his theology and his deepest convictions compelled him to listen carefully to the call of the synod to determine whether it was God's call on his life.[17]

Charles, however, was not about to make a quick decision on such an important matter. He hurried home to talk with Mary and with other members of his family. Sister Betsy clearly did not want him to go — he was needed in Liberty County, she said, and besides, the circle of loving family members would be left with a gaping hole if Charles and Mary left with the children. At first Charles agreed with them, and for the next year he went about his missionary labors in Liberty County and the development of Montevideo and Maybank as if he would stay in the county. But by the fall of 1836 pressure was building for him to accept. The issue for him was once again, as it had been at Princeton, a question of duty and its relationship to home. Was it his duty to accept the call to Columbia, to leave Montevideo and Maybank, to separate himself from so many whom he loved, and to give up his evening visits to the settlements of the county? Duty, a sense of moral obligation rooted in his love of God, seemed to be drawing him to Columbia and saying that he must disregard personal inclinations.[18]

Mary was willing to go, but she was clearly not happy about the thought of leaving her plantation home. "I have been thinking a great deal of your decision in relation to Columbia," she wrote him in November 1836, "but my mind has been calm in prospect of the result. Have we not asked wisdom and direction of our Heavenly Father as to the way of *duty* and will He not lead us in a *plain path?*"

Mary drew the line, however, at "selling out" plantations and people in Liberty County. Charles was wondering whether he should do just that if he were to accept the call to Columbia—should he rid himself of all "planting interests" and put Montevideo and Carlawter and Maybank behind him? Friends discouraged such a course. And Thomas Clay, back from a long stay in New England, said that such a step "would undo almost all that we have done." To be a convincing advocate for religious instruction, one needed, evidently, to be a slaveholder. Besides, selling out would confirm the suspicions of Seabrook and others that the movement was at its heart antislavery. For Mary, it was even simpler— she did not want to break the ties to home. "I should not like," she told Charles, "to sunder the chords that have bound us so long and happily—for go where I will, like the captive bird I expect to sigh for the native air where I sang my sweetest song." So a year after he was elected to the professorship, Charles finally said "yes" to the call to Columbia but concluded to hire good managers to look after Montevideo and Maybank.[19]

Charles and Mary decided that the family should go overland to Columbia in order to manage with some ease all of the trunks of clothes and boxes of books they wished to carry with them. Having said their goodbyes, they left Montevideo early on the morning of 1 February 1837. Charles, riding his horse Shannon, led the way down the avenue and on to the road to Riceboro. Behind him came Jack, driving the family's carriage. Inside were Mary, five-year-old Charlie, three-year-old Joe, and Mary Sharpe, who was not yet two. With them was Jack's niece, nineteen-year-old Patience. She was single, had no children, and had since childhood been trained to be a cook and domestic servant. The carriage was a four-wheel vehicle enclosed with wood, glass, and cloth, and it provided its occupants some protection from the February weather. And so they went, stopping in homes open to travelers, five days in all, until they arrived in Columbia and were warmly received by George Howe and his new wife, Sara Ann Walthour.[20]

Howe, a widower, and Sara Ann, a widow, had married the previous December at the Walthour plantation, not far from Riceboro. The marriage had drawn Howe deep into the circle of Liberty County families and had anchored the New Englander to his adopted southern home. Sara Ann had gone to "finishing school" in Charleston as a young woman with Sister Susan and Cousin Mary Robarts, and it had been to her home in Walthourville that Mary Jones had gone to give birth to Joe in September 1833. A week before Howe's marriage to Sara Ann, he had turned down the professorship of sacred literature at the new and well-financed Union Theological Seminary in New York City. "I must now say," he had written the trustees of Union, "that it appears still my duty to cast in my lot and earthly destiny with the people of the South, among whom I have made my home. When I accepted the Professorship I hold, it was with the hope that I might be the means of building up the wastes, and extending the borders of our Southern Zion." Such a motive, he said, still held him to Columbia. "Though our institution must be a small one through the present generation, and yours will be large, it is important, it is necessary, whatever be the fate of our beloved country, that this seminary should live." If he were to leave, Howe thought, it would jeopardize the future of the seminary. "If I remain," he wrote, "though the field of my efforts must be small, and I must live on in obscurity, we may yet transmit to the men of the next generation an institution which will bless them and the world." Such was the character of the seminary to which Charles was committing himself and his family. And in Howe he would have not only a distinguished Old Testament scholar as a colleague, but a New England friend who was now, through his marriage with Sara Ann, the owner of a plantation in Liberty County with more than fifty slaves.[21]

After staying several days with the Howes, Charles and Mary moved the family into a suite of rooms at the Clark Hotel. Patience stayed with them at the hotel, but Jack they sent back to Montevideo. Such was the confidence they had in him that Jack went alone with the carriage on the long trip home.[22]

Hotel rooms were not Montevideo, but Charles and Mary tried to make the best of their new situation. Columbia they found to be a place of some contradictions. It was a young city with a rough edge to it, but it had some of the polish of low-country culture that had been transplanted to the state capital. "There is good society in Columbia," Charles wrote Sister Betsy, "but not a great deal of it." What was more disturbing was the lawlessness of the place and the continuing influence of infidelity that flowed from South Carolina College. Charles thought that city was filled with "a great many wicked people," that murder was not uncommon in the city, and that if committed by the well-connected, it was not punished. "There is a great deal of corruption in this Town of Columbia,"

Charles wrote after having been there a few months, and he added, "I see very little in it that makes it a desirable place for residence."[23]

But Charles also found Columbia an interesting place, and even a beautiful place in the spring when the dogwoods and azaleas were in bloom and the tea olives perfumed the air. And not least among the city's attractions was the intellectual stimulation available with Howe as a colleague and conversation partner. Moreover, Columbia had young James Henley Thornwell, who was the professor of logic and belles lettres at the college. "He is a man of fine talents, and a Christian," Charles wrote, "and if nothing untoward happens to prevent, he must rise to eminence." And there were others as well whom Charles found good friends— Robert Barnwell, the new president of the college, and Stephen Elliott, an Episcopal minister who had recently been elected the college's professor of sacred literature. (Elliott had visited at Montevideo and was known as a strong supporter of the religious instruction of slaves.) And there were laymen closely associated with the seminary: businessmen Abraham Blanding, William Law, and Gilbert Snowden and Judge H. W. DeSaussure. They all, together with their families, showed great kindness to Charles and Mary and the children and sought to make them feel at home in the city.[24]

But for all the attention that was given them, the family was homesick for Montevideo and Maybank and for all who lived at the Retreat and Sunbury. Three months after they arrived, Charles carried Mary and the children and Patience back to Montevideo for an extended stay at home. Returning to Columbia by himself, Charles was miserable. "My dear wife," he wrote Mary, "why do we ever consent to separate for a day? Every time I am away from you, I resolve it shall be the last. My spirits, my heart, are heavy as lead." In the midst of his loneliness, Charles's own sense of inadequacy as a professor grew. "My exercises of late in the seminary," he wrote Mary, "have been pleasant, but there is no one that knows, but myself, how utterly incompetent in every respect, I am for the station they have placed me in." He wondered if he should resign and, like many a young professor, he was surprised that his lectures were "looked upon with any interest on the part of the students. There are many of them that know just twice as much as I do."[25]

As soon as classes were over in July, Charles headed for Maybank, where in the evenings he could sit on the piazza with family and friends and watch the shadows lengthen over the Medway marshes. During the days he gave himself to hard study so that he might be a step or two ahead of his students on his return to Columbia, and on the weekends he preached and taught at the old stands. He was determined not to return to Columbia unless a house could be found for his family, and during the long break he learned from Howe that a place had been secured. So he made up his mind to give the seminary another go, to see whether it really was his vocation to be professor of ecclesiastical history and polity rather than a missionary to slaves.[26]

In October, Charles was back in Columbia, teaching and making preparations for the family to join him in December, but he was as miserable and uncertain about being there as ever. "It is indeed a question if I am doing as much for the Religious Instruction of the Negroes *here*," he wrote Mary, "as I was doing at home. If the seminary was *larger*, I might do more, but small as it is, and is likely to be, it is a question." And the separations from Mary and the children left him lonely and despondent: "My darling wife," he wrote from Columbia, "I love you a thousand fold more now than the hour I first embraced you and called you *my own*. My youthful passion for you is still a passion, but it has increased with the lapse of years: it carries in it the strongest, tenderest friendship. Words cannot describe my attachment to you. . . . All of that heart which is mine to give, I give *to you*."[27]

After two months alone in Columbia, Charles returned to Montevideo to bring Mary and the children to the rented home that was now waiting for them in Columbia. Coming with them were Patience, Jack and his wife, Marcia, Rosetta's and Sam's daughter Lucy, who was seventeen, and Phoebe's daughter Clarissa. With the rented house and the servants, Charles and Mary were at least giving the appearance of trying to make a home in Columbia.[28]

There was much about Columbia that was more inviting for the family as they began a new year in the little city. A house, even a rented one, was far better than a suite of rooms in a hotel, and Jack and the other servants not only provided their skills and hard work in making the household run smoothly, they also added reminders of Montevideo and Carlawter with their Gullah accents and all the associations that swirled around them. Certainly kind friends, especially the Howes, did all they could to make them feel at home and a part of Columbia. And there were visitors from the low country—Bullocks and Kings, Robartses and Dunwodys. But best of all was the presence of Mary's brother, John Jones, at the seminary. He had had a conversion experience while a student at the college in Athens and had determined to follow Charles's path into the ministry. John was a regular guest in their home, and he helped Charles with his work in a Sabbath school for slaves that Charles started down by the river.[29]

Still, in spite of their efforts and the efforts of their friends, they were homesick. Letters arrived that evoked for them the sights and sounds of the low country and reminded them of faces and voices of family and friends. Sister Betsy was the most faithful correspondent. Big sister that she was to Charles (she sometimes called him "my child"), she longed for them to return to Liberty County. She told of the comings and goings at home, and, while not a gossip, she was a good storyteller and a persistent believer that Charles's place was in Liberty County. She wrote that she and William Maxwell had hosted the wedding for their friends Abial Winn and Louisa Ward at the Maxwells' new plantation home, Lodebar. It had been a grand occasion, with friends and family from far and wide. Tables had been set on the piazza, and the dining room sideboards had been loaded with hams and tongues, wild ducks and turkeys, sauces, oyster pies, and eight different kinds of puddings, together with preserves and cakes and three pyramids with jellies and syllabubs. And if such a feast were not enough to tempt one to come hurrying back home, there was the call of duty and the cries from the settlements—all the people, said Betsy, wanted Charles to come back and help "them on the way to God their Heavenly Father."[30]

If the pull of Liberty County were not enough to make Charles and Mary restless, they had a continuing concern about the character of the city, about its lack of piety and of the polished ways of the low country, and they wondered about the influence of such a setting on their children. And to make matters even worse, the Presbyterian Church was in the midst of a national division, and the uproar was having its effect on the seminary. Old School Presbyterians, staunch defenders of orthodoxy who were firmly lodged at Princeton and in most of the South, had accused New School Presbyterians of having absorbed too much theology from New England Congregationalists and of having abandoned too much of Presbyterian polity in their enthusiasm for interdenominational benevolence societies. Moreover, it was clear that the New School faction was much more hostile to slavery and that a number of abolitionists were a part of the New School. Charles liked none of it—the charges or the countercharges. He had, after all, studied at both Andover and Princeton. His irenic spirit, his experience of working with different denominations, and his piety all left him less than enthusiastic about denominational divisions.[31]

It consequently came as no surprise to any who knew Charles that, following the summer break of 1838, he returned alone from Liberty County and announced his resignation. "I have come to the conclusion," he wrote in October, "that it is duty to return to my old field of labour." Ever since the synod first called him to the seminary, he acknowledged, "my mind has been unsettled, and ofttimes harassed and distressed, and my family has been moved from place to place at the loss of a great deal of domestic comfort and enjoyment." His official reason for his resignation was that he was more fitted and could do more in his old field than at the seminary. All of his qualms about life in Columbia he kept private. And as for the church controversies, he wrote Mary, "I sigh, my dear wife, for relief from the conflictions of party: for my old & quiet field of labour. If there is any curse to be dreaded in a church, it is the introduction of Heresy & and the consequent array and war of party." [32]

And so in December 1838 Charles left Columbia and hurried back to Liberty County, where he intended to take up once again his work among the settlements and his life at Montevideo and Maybank. He had given the call of synod and its accompanying duty its chance in Columbia. But another call—a deeper, more familiar, and more insistent voice—had never left him. This voice he now followed with a new eagerness as he returned to the landscape of home and to the duties of missionary labors. What he would find on his return was, of course, that life had not stood still in the settlements while he was away. Even in Carlawter.

15

CARLAWTER II

When Charles had first taken his family to Columbia in February 1837, the men, women, and children from Carlawter had come and stood in the yard at Montevideo to say their goodbyes. Standing among them was Lizzy. She watched as Charles, riding on Shannon, led the way down the long avenue, followed by Jack driving the carriage. It had been thirty-six years since Lizzy had left her own childhood home at Cedar Grove Plantation to go as a young woman to Liberty Hall with her mistress Susannah Girardeau. As she watched Charles riding down the avenue, she may have remembered the morning in 1805 when his father, John Jones, rode off for his fateful hunt. Certainly over the years she had seen many comings and goings of the white family, and she knew only too well how her life and the life of her family had been shaped by such leave-takings and homecomings and by the decisions made by white masters and mistresses. From slave sales in Riceboro, to summers in Sunbury, to sojourns in Greensboro, to time at the settlement at the Retreat, to the move to Carlawter, to the separation from her husband, Robinson, when the Robartses' slaves had been moved from Carlawter to Hickory Hill—all of these important moments in her life bore the marks of white decisions and white power.[1]

As the carriage had moved out of sight, Lizzy returned to her work. Charles had left Colonel Law's son Joseph as the manager of Montevideo, and there had been careful instruction about the work of the plantation.[2] Lizzy, however, had not been in good health for several years, so her workload was now lighter, confined primarily about the plantation house. She had to dust books and sweep the sandy yard, and on warm days air pillows and quilts.[3] With Jupiter she had become one of the old ones in the settlement. He had been made the gardener, with responsibility for keeping the crabgrass out of the flowerbeds and for pruning the roses and for seeing that the birds did not eat the strawberries in the spring or get in the young fig trees in the summer. He would turn seventy-seven that year, and he knew that his life was drawing near its end. So he had gone into the woods and he had found a young oak and, after carefully digging it up so that the roots were intact, he had planted it in the bend in the avenue. He said he wanted it as a way "to be remembered by."[4]

It had been twenty years since Joseph had moved them from the Retreat to the settlement at Carlawter, and during those years Carlawter had been taking on its own character as a village among the settlements of the Gullah people. With its close ties to the settlements at the Retreat, at Maybank, at Hickory Hill and Lambert, Carlawter had its own rhythms of work, its own ways of doing things, and its own growing memory of fields that had been cleared and barns built. But during the coming years nothing was to mark Carlawter so much as a distinct community as would its spreading web of family relationships. Networks of kinship, long present, became increasingly dense as children raised in the settlement began to marry.[5]

Lizzy and Robinson had eight children living at Carlawter in 1837. Lymus, the oldest, was thirty-two; Adam, the youngest, was twelve. But it was their three middle sons — Cato, Cassius, and Porter — who were becoming central figures in the life of Carlawter. Cato, who was twenty-eight, had become after Jack the person in the settlement closest to Charles. They had walked the fields together, and Charles, who had become a great walker during his time in the North, would brag to Cato that he could outwalk him. But Cato was the one who knew the land most intimately, who knew the secrets of the woods and of the river in its seasons. And while he knew the land belonged to Charles, he would look on it as somehow being his own, not in a sentimental way, but as a landscape that reflected the work of those who lived and labored upon it.[6]

Cassius, like his brothers Cato and Porter, was a big man. He was strong and evidently handsome, and he was becoming, in addition to a good field hand, an excellent basket maker — work that brought him some money when he sold baskets in Riceboro or to a neighboring planter. Adapting patterns and techniques rooted in West Africa, he would split the leaf stems of a cabbage palmetto and with a knife shape them into a uniform size. Turning the smooth outer surface of the stems to the outside, he would weave them into a basket that had a fine polished look. He could also take sweet grass and make a light, flat basket for fanning rice. And in the afternoons after completing his tasks, he could cut green branches, and then around evening fires he could make stick baskets from them that would grow tight and strong as the branches dried and shrank. For these stick baskets with their many uses, neighboring planters would pay 37½ cents each. Over the years his basket-making skills allowed Cassius to accumulate substantial possessions—including a mare, a colt, and a buggy—that rivaled the possessions of anyone who lived at Carlawter except those of his brother Cato and the plantation carpenters. But Cassius also had a hot temper, and while he kept it under control most of the time, it could flare suddenly and sometimes get him into trouble. He also had a way with women—and that too could get him, and also others, into trouble.[7]

Porter, who was twenty in 1837, was continuing to learn the carpentry trade. His primary teachers had been Sandy Jones at Carlawter—who had learned the trade from old Jacob at Liberty Hall—and Sandy Maybank at Maybank. In 1837 all the carpenters, including Syphax, were spending much of their time at Maybank building new cabins for its settlement and various outbuildings for the plantation.[8] But they also had work to do at Montevideo. They cut trees down at Maybank, dragged them with oxen over to the North Newport, and, when the tide was flowing their way, floated them upriver to Montevideo, where they cut them into lumber with a pit saw. It was all hard and demanding labor, but the carpenters were steady workers and over time they built building after building.[9] Porter, like the other carpenters, could hire himself out on Saturdays, and in this way he too was beginning to earn some money and accumulate some possessions.[10] He was also beginning to take notice of Patience, who worked in the kitchen with his mother. He was, no doubt, pleased when her sojourn in Columbia turned out to be relatively short.

Lizzy's husband, Robinson, would have to make the long trip from Hickory Hill for his Saturday night visits to his "wife house" and to see his family at Carlawter. Traveling with him was Rosetta's Sam, the majordomo for Eliza Robarts's household. By 1837 Rosetta and Sam had five children, and in the evenings around the settlement fires the children could hear stories from their mother about how Rosetta had been Charles's nurse and how she had looked after him when he was a sick, recently orphaned, little boy.[11] Their oldest child, Lucy, was learning from her parents the ways of a domestic servant, and her parents could see that she was becoming a young woman of considerable inner strength who—even under the burden of slavery—was able to carry herself with dignity. In the coming years deep lines would begin to mark Lucy's face, each line telling of the troubles she had seen; but her face would also come to reveal a remarkable strength, the strength of one who had looked straight into the heart of slavery and had not been overcome.[12] In 1837, however, she was sixteen and smooth-faced, and young men were beginning to notice her. One in particular, Charles the son of Andrew and Mary Ann at Maybank, would began to pay her special attention. But first she had to spend time in Columbia with Patience and with Phoebe's daughter Clarissa to help with the housekeeping.

Hamlet continued to be the driver at Carlawter, and, like his father, Jupiter, and his brother Jupiter before him, he would announce each new day with a blast from the conch-shell horn. Elvira had died in childbirth in 1826, but Hamlet had five children by her living at Carlawter—Syphax was the oldest—and he had another three children from his first wife, Phillis, and they too were a part of the settlement.[13] When Charles had left for Columbia, he had placed increased responsibilities on Hamlet, for although Joseph Law had been made manager, Hamlet was to run the day-to-day work of the plantation. "Do tell Hamlet," Charles would write when away, "the moment he gets through picking over his cotton to *push on fast as he can in ginning*," and later he wrote: "Tell Hamlet as soon as Syphax is done at Lodebar to set him to work repairing the chimneys to the Negro houses."[14] But Hamlet was getting old—he turned seventy-two the year Charles left for Columbia—and it was increasingly difficult for him to see after all the many matters regarding the order of the plantation and the health and welfare of the settlement. It was a situation made for trouble, and trouble had already begun to stir at Carlawter. At the center of it were Phoebe and Cassius.

While continuing to serve as Mary's personal servant, Phoebe had been developing her skills as a seamstress. Twice a year Charles would buy cloth in Savannah and have it delivered by sloop to the wharves at Maybank and at Montevideo. In the spring big bolts of coarse Osnaburg linen would arrive, and in October bolts of woolen cloth would be unloaded. For winter undergarments there were bolts of flannel, and for the women who worked in the plantation house, rolls of printed calico arrived in the spring to be made into dresses and aprons. Charles, wanting to be just to his servants, ordered six yards for each adult—one yard more than the normal practice in the low country.[15] While some families at Carlawter and Maybank apparently made their own clothing from the cloth, Phoebe had the primary responsibility—under Mary's supervision—for cutting out and sewing most of the pants, shirts, and dresses for the people. Of course she had help— Rosetta spun the thread and helped with the sewing, as did others around the plantation house. But Phoebe was the skilled seamstress—she was the one who took the measurements for size, who saw that the patterns were closely followed, and who sewed the cloth with tight stitches. Such skill made her even more valuable to Mary, who continued to depend on her for many things.[16]

Phoebe, Sandy, their child John, and Phoebe's daughter Clarissa lived in a cabin near other members of Phoebe's extended family. Her father, Jack, and his wife, Marcia, were nearby, as was Phoebe's recently widowed uncle Robin. Although Phoebe was eight years older than her cousin Patience, they had become good friends working together around the plantation house until Patience left for her sojourn in Columbia.[17]

Sandy was frequently away from Carlawter, sometimes at Maybank for an extended period and at other times at another plantation when a neighboring planter hired him for some special project. He was also growing older—he was at least twenty years Phoebe's senior—and Phoebe was growing restless in their marriage. Cassius, who had evidently been courting Hamlet's daughter Peggy, began to pay special attention to Phoebe. Before long she was "sharing his blanket." [18]

It was impossible, of course, to keep such a development a secret in a small community such as Carlawter and even in the larger community that surrounded it. Sam, the immediate successor to Sharper, reported to the session of Midway what was being said about Phoebe. She was cited to appear before the session, and Nathaniel Varnedoe from Liberty Hall was designated to determine whether the charges were true. Three months later Phoebe was excommunicated, and Cassius and Phoebe began to live together as husband and wife. Six months later their first child was born, a boy whom they named Cassius. [19]

The affair may have taken a heavy toll on Sandy—certainly living in the tight little community at Carlawter must have been difficult for him. His health quickly gave way, and the next year he was reported seriously ill. He lived another few years, but he was never well again. [20]

As Charles was preparing to leave Montevideo on one of his return trips to Columbia, Peggy asked to speak to him. Charles wrote Mary at Maybank what he had learned: "Place no confidence whatever in Phoebe. She is now as artful & as great a thief & liar as ever, and she & her husband are linked in & support each other in all theft that they can commit." Peggy, he said, had told him that Phoebe was trying to obtain false keys to pantries and storehouses. "Do not," Charles warned, "let her have the handling of any keys about the house." [21]

Mary could hardly believe such a report. Phoebe, after all, was her personal servant, she was the daughter of Jack, and Mary was dependent on her in innumerable ways. "What could have induced Peggy to tell you what she did?" Mary asked Charles. *"Please write me* as your letter creates great concern in relation to Phoebe. She has done very well indeed thus far." [22]

Charles responded with more details. Peggy had told him that Phoebe had cut a piece of paper to fit the shape of a master key and had sent to Savannah to have a copy made, that Phoebe's "husband had sent to town also for a key to the corn house, and that they were both dishonest. She assured me there was no mistake." But Charles did not want to concern Mary unduly while he was away, so he added: "Give yourself no uneasiness, my dear wife; yet with such a representation it is as well to be careful, but not more so than you ordinarily are, for our principle is to lay no temptations in the way of our servants." He was glad to hear that "they have all behaved well. I believe they will continue to do so, and you will have no trouble."[23]

Within three weeks, however, Mary wrote him back: "There is no dissembling the truth—we have a *wicked & corrupt* set of Negroes at Montevideo, but I will tell you all when you come home." She assured Charles, "You must not think that they give *me* any trouble. I have got along very quietly." And she said that, in contrast to his daughter, "*Jack* has been very attentive to all his business."[24]

And so the matter stood. Mary later remembered the episode as an example of what a master or mistress had to pass through when "attempting to assert the supremacy of their own authority." She recalled "feelings of mortification, disappointment, and absolute anguish of spirit." But the experience taught her to "consider these trials not as peculiar to myself but as actually belonging *to* the sin and ignorance which everywhere pervades the present state of our domestic relations. We must try and be kind and oft times forbearing, not exacting and suspicious whilst we do maintain cheerful and constant obedience—*this* to those in any subordinate situation is not only requisite to peace but happiness."[25]

The whole episode, following as it did Phoebe's unfaithfulness to Sandy, left Charles suspicious of her. He was never dependent on her the way Mary was, and her behavior was a challenge to his image of himself as a benevolent master. If he could not keep his own "household" in order, how could he preach to others about theirs? An uneasy truce developed between Charles and Phoebe, but the next time he left for Columbia he sent Phoebe to work on a neighboring plantation, and he took Clarissa to Columbia to help with the housework and to be under the supervision of her grandfather Jack.[26] As for Cassius, he continued to live with Phoebe—they had a daughter, Jane, in 1838 and another son, Prime, in 1840—but he had two other families as well. He and Peggy had a son, James, in 1842, and had a daughter, Nanny, on a neighboring plantation.[27]

In May 1837, shortly after Mary had returned with the children from her first stay in Columbia, Jack came to Mary early in the morning and told her that Lizzy was very sick. She "complained of great pain in her bowels which had suddenly swollen up during the night." Jack said they had given her "such remedies as we knew to do good," and she seemed to be relieved. Mary ate a quick breakfast and, taking Charlie and Joe with her, she went immediately to Carlawter and found Lizzy lying before the fire in her cabin. Her sister Willoughby was with her. "She appeared very weak," Mary wrote Charles, "but told me she had eaten her supper & drank her coffee as usual." Mary, finding Lizzy's pulse weak and her extremities cold, sent Willoughby running back to the plantation house to tell Jack to send some laudanum and mustard, by which she hoped to stimulate Lizzy's system. In the meantime, Mary lifted Lizzy up and gave her some "some strong hot, catnip tea which she drank with perfect ease but said, 'Mistress, I am done. I shall never do any thing more.'" Mary said, "Lizzy, if it is the will of God, I hope you are willing & ready to go." She replied, "Yes mam, I am willing & ready to go. I put all my trust in *Jesus Christ*. I look to Him." Mary, following the familiar ritual with the dying, white or black, said, "Do you indeed feel Lizzy that your sins are forgiven & that you have taken Christ for your own Saviour?" She answered, "Yes mam, I look to Him alone and I am willing & ready to go." Mary then laid her gently back down, "telling her how happy I felt to hear her talk so, for Christ was our compassionate and almighty friend." Lizzy said, "I am very weak" and turned on her side; and "the catnip tea poured from her mouth." Mary heard "the death rattle in her throat, saw a few contortions of her face, a low murmuring sound of the voice & her soul was in Eternity." All that Mary could feel or say was "Lord Jesus receive her spirit."

Willoughby had not yet returned with Jack, and no one else was in Carlawter. Robinson was at Hickory Hill, and all of Lizzy's children had evidently gone to their work thinking that the medicine Jack had given their mother had revived her. Mary was alone with Lizzy's body, except for little Charlie and Joe, who "were weeping bitterly & saying 'Is Mom Lizzy dead? Dear mother, where is her soul? Has her soul gone to God? Mother she does not move. Oh! Mother will we too die!'" For a half an hour, with "the poor little fellows crying around me over the lifeless corpse of poor Lizzy" they waited for Jack and Willoughby. "*Death & Eternity*," declared Mary, "were then *realities* & never did I feel more the responsibilities of *owners*."[28]

Charles was moved to tears when he received Mary's account of Lizzy's death. "Poor Lizzy," he wrote Mary. "Though the scene was so peculiarly trying, yet I rejoice that you were with her, and were enabled to converse with her. I lament her death for she was a quiet, faithful Negro, & one of the oldest on the plantation." Charles thought Lizzy's professions were sincere and that "she is now in a better world." He agreed with Mary about the responsibilities of owners. "We should indeed feel our responsibility as *owners* more; nor should we forget to make efforts for their salvation, while they are in health." He regretted that "we are prone to procrastinate, and to crowd all our conversation, & prayers, and their salvation, in the compass of a few brief & painful hours, immediately preceding death." As for Charlie and Joe, they "never before *saw death!* May God sanctify the scene to them!"[29]

Mary wrote no details of Lizzy's funeral. But whatever the rituals performed at her grave, Lizzy's burial in the plantation cemetery meant that for her children

and grandchildren—and during the coming years for her great-grandchildren
—Carlawter was a place of ancestors. The network of family relationships that
marked Carlawter as a little village included not only the living but also ancestors who were now part of the land and the landscape.[30]

A year after his mother's death, Porter began courting Patience in earnest.
Patience had from an early age worked in the kitchen with Lizzy and had learned
from her something of a developing African-American cuisine. Porter had opportunities, no doubt, to learn something of Patience as he had seen her at work
with his mother and as they had been together in the evenings around the fires
at Carlawter. In the summer of 1838 it had become clear that the white family
would not be going back to Columbia to make it their home and that Patience
would be staying at Montevideo and Maybank. Before the next Christmas the
young couple were married. They had joined Midway together in February 1835,
and during the coming years both were faithful and responsible members of
the church. Indeed, responsibility was to be a characteristic that marked both of
them as they went about their work and their lives.[31]

Patience was large, big-boned, and stout—her shoes were "the *largest* woman
size" available in Savannah. Perhaps growing up around the plantation kitchen
had provided the nutrition needed to reach her size. At any rate, her size reflected
her growing stature in the slave community. She was very close to her uncle Jack,
and her husband, Porter, was becoming a skilled carpenter who was already filling in for an ailing Sandy at Carlawter and who one day was to replace Sandy
Maybank as the chief carpenter of the Joneses' plantations. Patience was herself
beginning to replace her cousin Phoebe as Mary's closest personal servant. Such
a replacement did not come quickly—it would not be complete for years—nor
was it apparently something that Patience sought. Rather, this slow process of replacement had more to do with the ways the two cousins responded to slavery
and how they negotiated the complex relationship of mutual dependence between mistress and slave.[32]

In remarkable ways, Patience came to embody her name. Unlike Phoebe, who
had to struggle to conquer her impulse to open defiance and whose rage lay near
the surface of her cheerful demeanor, Patience was a self-possessed woman who
met life with a deep composure and with a capacity to endure the burdens of
slavery. A white visitor at Montevideo and Maybank would remember her "with
pleasure" as "adept in her art, reliable, and refined in manner and conduct."[33]
Her way of resistance, her struggle, was to see after the welfare of her family.
Rather than rage against the system, Patience tried to work the system in such a
way that her family was protected from the harshest aspects of slavery. She wanted

her children to have the best food, housing, and clothing that she could provide, and she wanted them to have a stable family life with her and Porter. Of course Phoebe also wanted these things for her family, but she was never able to give herself to these concerns in the way in which Patience was able. On the other hand, like Mom Sylvia at the Retreat, Patience was no "Mammy"—no hefty cook who smiled and was happily submissive.[34] Rather, she was patient, doing what she could for her family, and when freedom came, she was to show where her deepest loyalties lay. These differences between the two cousins in time played out in their family histories, as each sought to resist in her own way the degradations of slavery.

About the same time that Porter and Patience were marrying, Cato was also courting a daughter of Jack's, Phoebe's half-sister Betsy, who lived at the Retreat and who worked as a domestic servant under the tutelage of Mom Sylvia. After Phoebe's mother, Lizett, died, Jack had married Marcia, and in 1838 they had three adult children living at the Retreat. (Charles rented Marcia from Joseph so she could live with her husband both at Montevideo and when Jack went to Columbia.) Betsy was nineteen when she married Cato in 1839, and he was thirty. The next year they had their first child, Rinah; then would come Ned, and finally Madison, named for his uncle, Betsy's brother. Cato and Betsy would never live together—he would have to make the trip to his "wife house" at the Retreat on the weekends. But they were devoted to each other and managed through their devotion to face all the stress and hardships of their separation.[35]

Cato and Betsy's marriage was followed the next year by that of Lucy, Rosetta and Sam's daughter, to Charles, the son of Andrew and Mary Ann at Maybank. Because Lucy worked in the house, she traveled with the white family between Montevideo and Maybank. While at Maybank, she and Charles could see each other regularly. In 1840 they married, and in 1841 they had their first child, Tenah, who in time became the personal servant of little Mary Sharpe Jones.

So the first generation at Carlawter, the generation that could remember Liberty Hall, that knew John Jones and Susannah Girardeau and old Jupiter and blind Silvey, this generation began to pass as the second generation began to marry and to have children. Jupiter and Hamlet did not long survive Lizzy, as they, with others, passed over Jordan and were buried in the cemetery at Carlawter.[36] In this ebb and flow, the complexity of kinship was deepening as lines of relationships stretched out from family to family, frequently crossing one another.

By 1839 Carlawter had become a community, a specific place in the Georgia low country that was a part of a larger world of southern slavery and its economy. Here men and women lived and worked together and watched their children and grandchildren, and those of their neighbors, grow up and marry. Here along its sandy street and around its evening fires stories were told, memories were lengthened, traditions were developed, and the bonds of kinship were tightened. To be sure, larger, distant forces of economics, politics, and technology continued to affect the lives of all who lived here. Yet the Gullah community that was built at Carlawter played a fundamental role in shaping how those who lived in the settlement saw and interpreted the world around them. And equally remarkable, Carlawter itself was composed not simply of a mass of slaves but of distinct men and women, people with names, with diverse personalities and personal histories—Cato and Cassius and Porter and Phoebe and Patience and Lucy and all the others who found their lives and their lots cast in this particular place under the bitter burden of slavery. During the coming years each of them, in his or her own way, would seek to negotiate the deep waters of slavery as they looked toward freedom's distant shore.

16

SOUTH HAMPTON

When Charles sent Phoebe to a neighboring plantation in late 1837, it was to South Hampton, where Barrington and Catherine King lived with their nine children. Catherine King needed some additional domestic help in preparation for a move of their family in late April 1838. By the time Phoebe arrived at the plantation, Barrington King was in the midst of selling South Hampton and turning his considerable energies toward the creation of new wealth spun from cotton mills built on the rolling hills of North Georgia.[1]

John Ross and the other members of the Cherokee delegation whom Charles had met in Washington in the summer of 1830 had been unsuccessful in preventing the state of Georgia from taking their lands. They had succeeded in getting the U.S. Supreme Court to rule in their favor in one case, but President Andrew Jackson had disregarded the court's order, and by 1838 the Cherokees were being forced to leave their lands and to travel their Trail of Tears to a reservation in Oklahoma. (Ross's wife, Quatie, was one of some four thousand who died along the way.) A state lottery had already provided for the division of the Cherokee lands, and the up-country was about to become the most populous and prosperous part of the state, as whites were poised to rush in and take the land secured by the military power of the United States.[2] Even in distant Liberty County, the impact of the violent and bloody removal of the Cherokees was substantial, as its upheavals broke in upon the old stability of the population and set in motion removals of another sort from plantation houses and settlements in the county.

Already in 1829, Roswell King, Sr., had traveled on horseback throughout the up-country on behalf of the Bank of Darien. His purpose had been to explore the region and the possibilities of a branch bank near the newly opened gold mines of north Georgia. What he found north of the Chattahoochee River was a region of hardwood forests, fertile valleys, and rushing streams. In 1832, following the first lottery for sections of the Cherokee territory, he had purchased a sizable tract of land and had begun making his plans for a village and mill as he awaited the removal of the Cherokees. In 1838, as some seven thousand U.S. troops began rounding up the Cherokees and confining them in "collection forts," King moved to a site just north of the Chattahoochee on Vickery Creek, not far from the bustling little town of Atlanta. Other families from the low country soon joined him in his newly created village of Roswell, and all of them were closely connected to the Joneses of Montevideo. Among them was Major James Stephens Bulloch, who arrived in the spring with his wife, Martha Stewart, daughter of the old general Uncle Daniel Stewart. After a two-week trip from Savannah, "Cousin" John Dunwody of Arcadia plantation near Midway Church arrived with his wife, Jane Bulloch, the sister of the major. The Reverend Nathaniel Pratt and his wife, Catherine King—Roswell Sr.'s daughter—came from Darien so that Nathaniel could establish a Presbyterian Church in Roswell. And Barrington King left South Hampton in April with his wife, Catherine, and "9 children, 8 servants and 6 horses," to join his father and the others from the low country in the establishment of a new community and a new industry. By 1840 the Roswell Manufacturing Company had 28 whites working the looms of its cotton mill. By 1844 there were 75, and soon after more than 110. And by the mid-1840s Barrington Hall, Bulloch Hall, and Dunwody Hall—all elegant Greek Revival mansions—had been built, as well as Roswell King's handsome two-story Primrose Cottage, the Pratt's home Great Oaks, and the Roswell Presbyterian Church. Fourteen miles away, near the new village of Marietta, James Smith, who had been with Charles's father on his fateful hunt in 1805, built his up-country home of Welham. These removals, and others that followed, stretched the lines of kinship from Liberty County plantation houses and settlements to the mansions and slave cabins of a nascent New South.[3]

Already railroad lines were pushing rapidly across Georgia, the largest of the states east of the Mississippi. By 1843 the Central Railroad connected Savannah with Macon in the middle of the state. Two years later the Georgia Railroad linked Atlanta to Augusta, where there were rail connections to Charleston. At the same time the Western and Atlantic Railroad was pushing across the center of the former Cherokee territory to link Atlanta with Chattanooga and the railroads of Tennessee, while other roads connected Macon with Atlanta and still others were reaching from Macon toward the rich, unsettled lands of southwest Georgia. This transportation revolution meant not only a new mobility for people and goods but also new ways of investing capital, new ways of seeing the world as it went rushing by train windows, and new ways of thinking about the future as the sound of the train whistle began to be heard across the state.[4]

a

b

c

d

Roswell homes (all courtesy Georgia Archives): (a) Barrington King home; (b) James Bulloch home; (c) John Dunwody home; (d) the Reverend Nathaniel Pratt home

For Barrington King, the move to Roswell meant a change in investment from his low-country plantation to an up-country cotton mill. South Hampton, with its 1,950 acres, was located a few miles downriver from Montevideo and had come to King in 1822 through his marriage to Catherine Nephew of Ceylon Plantation in neighboring McIntosh County. Under King's supervision South Hampton had become one of the most prosperous plantations of Liberty County. He had needed, of course, a sizable labor force to build a thriving rice plantation, and this need had also been largely met by his marriage to Catherine Nephew, for she—like Susannah Girardeau and Sarah Anderson and Sarah's daughter Mary Jones—had brought a number of slaves into her marriage.[5]

Those who lived in the settlement at South Hampton had accomplished the grueling work of converting river swamps along the North Newport into wide rice fields with embankments, canals, and floodgates. Giant cypresses, black gums, and tupelos had been felled, and their stumps had been left in the mud, where they would remain as silent reminders to future generations of the massive labor required to clear the swamps. When the North Newport was low, ditches had been dug in the mud at the water's edge and the earth thrown up into embankments fifteen feet in breadth at the base and five feet high. Then the cleared land had been divided with smaller embankments into fields of convenient size and connected by canals and by floodgates built by the plantation carpenters Jacob and Peter.[6]

Unlike the older method of raising rice on inland swamps at the Retreat, the resulting river fields at South Hampton had a reliable supply of water that could be readily controlled. When the tide pushed upstream in the spring at the full moon, the gates would be opened and the fields, already plowed and planted, would be easily flooded through the series of canals and gates. This "sprout flow" of water stayed on the fields for a week and then when the tide was out, and the river level had dropped, the fields would be drained to allow the seeds to sprout. Once the young sprouts had established themselves, the gates would be opened for the "stretch flow," when the fields were flooded for about a month to kill any grass that might grow in the sun. And when the weeds that grew in the stagnant water needed attention, the gates were opened again at ebb tide and the fields drained. Barefooted men and women then plunged into the muddy rows of rice and hoed the weeds two and sometimes three times during the coming weeks in the summer sun. Finally the "harvest flow" came, with its tepid and teaming waters to support for two months the ripening rice and to keep the stems from becoming long and leggy. When this flow was drained in mid-September, once again barefooted men and women went down into the mire, this time to reap the rice with sickles. The rice, after being left on the stubble to dry for a day or two, was gathered into small sheaves and carried on the heads of the laborers to rice barns, where the sheaves would be threshed and the rice winnowed and pounded.[7]

Such a system of rice production had brought substantial wealth to Barrington King and had provided him with the resources to undertake his up-country adventure in manufacturing. With his vision of the future increasingly dominated by images of fast-flying shuttles and expanding rail lines, he had sold South Hampton in 1838 to his brother Roswell King, Jr., for $22,000. Included in the price were forty-two slaves from among the men and women who lived in the South Hampton settlement. The proceeds of this sale and the sale of other slaves were invested in the Roswell Manufacturing Company and in his elegant new home, Barrington Hall. In this way Barrington King parlayed his rice wealth into a new career as a southern manufacturer, and the family of Roswell King, Jr., became neighbors and among the closest friends to those who lived at Montevideo. Roswell would become "Uncle Roz" to Charlie, Joe, and Mary Sharpe, and Julia Maxwell King would be "Aunt Julia" to them.[8]

Roswell King, Jr., had managed the Butler estates on the Altamaha and St. Simons Island for twenty years when he retired as manager and moved with his family to South Hampton in 1838. He was a complex person whose complexity was hidden beneath a remarkable candor and matter-of-fact way of seeing the world that often cut through the cloud of southern manners that were intended to conceal as well as soothe. He had gained a reputation as a skilled manager of slaves, and his "manner of expressing himself" had become almost legendary among rice planters by the time of his move to South Hampton. On keeping slaves from running away, he had written ten years earlier: "No Negro, with a well stocked poultry house, a small crop advancing, a canoe partly finished, or a few tubs unsold, all of which he calculates soon to enjoy, will ever run away." On punishing slaves he had insisted: "The lash is, unfortunately, too much used; every mode of punishment should be devised in preference to that, and when used, never to lacerate." This was particularly true of young slaves, he said, who like "all young persons will offend."[9]

King valued efficiency above all things in the management of a plantation and thought that it required not only hard work and careful planning but also a flexible spirit and a commitment to innovation. So a quest for efficiency marked his treatment of slaves—what was efficient was good; what was inefficient was bad. When a concern for the welfare of the slaves led to the efficient production of rice and the efficient management of the plantation, then such a policy, he thought, should be pursued. And when a harsh lesson needed to be taught for the efficient control of slaves, then such a lesson was necessary. On one occasion, when several slaves had tried to escape from Butler Island into the surrounding marsh and swamps, he had used the novel punishment of pouring cold water over them on a January day. One of those so punished, a twelve-year-old boy weakened by worms, died a few days later evidently from the shock to his system.[10] And there were other dark sides to King that threatened his efficiently run plantations—most particularly his treatment of his own children who lived in the settlement, and of their mothers whom he had abused as a young man before his marriage to Julia Maxwell. When he left the management of the Butler estate to take up residence at South Hampton, he left three of his own children as slaves by the muddy banks of the Altamaha.

If King's youthful passions, linked to his power as a white manager, had been a threat to an efficiently run plantation, he allowed no parental affection—or even sense of responsibility—to intrude on his decisions as a planter and slave owner. At stake, of course, were issues other than personal feelings. Mulattoes, children with a white parent—even a powerful white father such as Roswell King—were not included in the classification of "whiteness" that had been carefully constructed over the years, first in British North America and then in the United States. For King to treat his mulatto children as other than the property of the Butler estate would have been a challenge to the racial assumptions and ideological foundations of slavery. White had come to mean free and privileged in the United States, and anyone with any African ancestry could not be white.[11]

Roswell and Julia had five white children at the time of their move to South Hampton. The oldest two—Mary and Audley—grew especially close to Charlie, Joe, and Mary Sharpe at Montevideo. Mary King, who was eleven in 1838, was already showing a lively, independent spirit and giving hints of the beautiful young woman she was soon to become. Fun loving and affectionate, she was especially close to her cousin Laura Maxwell, the daughter of Charles's sister Susan Jones Maxwell and her late husband Audley. In a few years sister Betsy wrote to Laura that Mary King "is as gay as a lark, and at the head of all mischief and fun; your grandmother [Maxwell] said the other day that she expected Mary would never be satisfied at home again unless she had a crowd with her; she always wants to go somewhere or must have company." Since Laura was also a cousin to Charlie, Joe, and Mary Sharpe, she and her brother Charles Edward acted as links drawing the King and Jones families close to one another and making them more than simply neighbors.[12]

Audley was nine at the time of the move to South Hampton, and he and Charlie soon became close friends. Together they explored the swamps and woods around their plantation homes and the marshes, creeks, and rivers that surrounded Colonel's Island; and together they learned to hunt and fish and to ride their marsh ponies down the sandy roads of Liberty County. Possessing an affectionate and winsome disposition, Audley was more like his mother, Julia, than like his father, Roswell, although he loved order and neatness and in time was to become a successful planter himself. Some years after the move to South Hampton, his father wrote to Charles: "Audley comes up fully to our expectations and is mother's main man, but for me, there is too much precision in him, too much a man of rules: if a thing cannot be done according to rule, it cannot be done at all. He does not enjoy his breakfast unless his hair is perfectly brushed. I want a man that will tumble out of his bed, half awake; and direct, but as he gets older these will wear off." But then the father added: "You must not infer from what I said about Audley that he does not come up to our expectations. He fills my shoes now. But a man to get along these times must be erratic. With me if a thing could not be done by the rule, I adopted one of my own, and seldom failed." [13]

As for Roswell King himself, he quickly became a part of the little circle of friends and relatives that moved between Montevideo and Maybank, the Retreat, Lodebar, the Mallard Place, and the other prominent plantations of the county. He was accepted as an eccentric who not only spoke his mind in often memorable ways but was also something of a know-it-all. Sister Betsy, who had known him for years, on one occasion showed him some strange fish brought from Florida's tropical waters. "For the first time in my life," she wrote, she "heard him say he never had seen such things before—something wonderful for him, for he has always seen or known everything no matter what you show him or say." [14] Still, many of his neighbors and friends found him an attractive and interesting person. Even Charles—who knew him as an unconverted, worldly man with a hard edge—was drawn to him and found in him a friend. And if King ignored his own children whom he left in the slave settlements on the Altamaha, he was a favorite of the white children, who delighted in his eccentricities. Robert Mallard, the youngest son of Thomas Mallard, would remember him with affection:

Uncle Roz', as he was called, was immensely popular with the young folks. For one thing, he was a mortal coward where horses were in question. He would travel up and down the river in his canoe, rowed by his black singing oarsmen, between the plantation and summer homes, but nothing could induce him to get into his wife's carriage to go to church, or even for a neighborhood visit; if he went at all, he was an outrider, on the step behind, ready to get off the moment the horses became restless. [15]

For her part, Julia Maxwell King was a cheerful, pious, and good neighbor to the Joneses and sought to be a kind and benevolent mistress to her slaves. She and Mary Jones had been friends since Mary's student days in Savannah, and Julia remained close to her sister-in-law Susan Jones Maxwell. Her piety was always in some tension with Roswell's quest for efficiency, and their family life and to some extent the character of their children reflected the tension between the competing values of the parents. But Roswell supported her insistence that the family have daily devotions, and he became a participant at Bible reading and prayer, including those times on Colonel's Island when they gathered as a little community with the Joneses and other neighbors. "He deeply honored the piety of his wife, a lovely Christian woman," Robert Mallard remembered, and he "helped her in his peculiar way. 'Come, Julia, get the books,' he would say (she had family worship). It was never neglected, nor he absent."[16]

When Julia's father, Colonel Audley Maxwell, died in 1840, he divided his 1,900-acre plantation on Colonel's Island into three parts—with one part going to Julia King, one part going to his son Joseph Maxwell, and one part going to his grandchildren Laura and Charles Edward. The Kings turned their part into Woodville Plantation, their summer home, while Laura's and Charles Edward's part, which contained the old Maxwell plantation house, was known as Social Bluff. In this way, the Kings became neighbors to Charles and Mary and their children not only at Montevideo but also at Maybank. And Laura and Charles Edward, with their mother, Susan, had with Social Bluff a plantation home that they could call their own.[17]

Colonel Maxwell divided not only his land but also his ninety slaves. Those who went to Julia became, like their white owners and other King slaves, a part of the world of Montevideo and Maybank, visiting in the settlements and sharing the rhythms of life and work on low-country plantations. Over the coming years webs of kinship were stretched along the roads and paths between Carlawter and the settlement at South Hampton, between the cabins on the marsh at Maybank and those along the banks of the North Newport at Woodville and Social Bluff.[18]

The leading figure in the South Hampton settlement was Paris, the driver, who had been the driver for Colonel Maxwell. Roswell King had great respect for him and for his skill in the growing of Sea Island cotton and rice and in the management of a large labor force. Paris was eventually included in Roswell's will, not only as a valuable slave to be willed to heirs but also as a recipient of an annual stipend of $30. Like many drivers, Paris was a large man, powerfully built, and he commanded respect from whites and blacks alike. He was also a pious man, a leading watchman at the North Newport Baptist Church, and the sexton at the little church at Pleasant Grove that was located on the southern end of South Hampton. During the coming years, he came to be closely associated with Charles's missionary labors.[19]

Susan Jones Maxwell, as Julia's sister-in-law, had with Laura and Charles Edward visited the Kings frequently at their St. Simons home and at Butler Island. She was no doubt delighted when South Hampton was purchased and the King family moved near to her brother Charles's Montevideo. But Susan's life had its own important developments in that year. In November 1838 she became the wife of Joseph Cumming, a widower with four children, the oldest of whom was eighteen and the youngest eleven. Suddenly becoming the mother of four new children must have been a challenge to her. With Laura, who was fourteen, and Charles Edward, who was nearly thirteen, she had five teenagers to see after, plus an eleven-year-old: a daunting task even for a mild-mannered woman.[20]

Sister Susan—as Charles, Betsy, and Mary often referred to her—had grown into an attractive woman who enjoyed a wide circle of friends. Yet she tended to linger in the background and not make her presence felt in the way in which the widely read Mary would do with her strong opinions, or Betsy would do with her laughter and her hospitable and affectionate embrace of family and friends. Susan was certainly dependent on strong male relatives and lacked much of the self-confidence of Mary or Betsy, especially in regard to the work and management of a plantation. Being an urban woman whose life was deeply involved in the social circles of Savannah no doubt shaped much of her character. And when she was in the country, she was for most of her life the guest of others— her uncle Joseph, her sister Betsy and brother-in-law William Maxwell, her sister-in-law Julia and Julia's husband, Roswell, her brother Charles and sister-in-law Mary, and then in later life her daughter Laura and Laura's husband.[21]

Susan's passivity, however, should not be exaggerated. She could give wise advice when needed to her children and stepchildren, and even to her confident Uncle Joseph and brother Charles. Moreover, when troubles came, when the world that she knew was turned upside down, she found within herself courage to face a new order and the will to do hard physical work for her family and friends.[22]

If Susan tended to linger in the background in her circle of family and friends, just the opposite was the case with Laura. When her mother married Joseph Cumming, the fourteen-year-old was already demonstrating the playful spirit and good humor that were to draw people to her all her life. She was developing a self-confidence and a grace that were to make her a most attractive young woman. In a few years her uncle Charles wrote to William Maxwell that Laura "has created quite a sensation among our young gentlemen." And that "sensation" was long lasting, as various "beaux" hovered around her for years until her marriage at age thirty-two. Her brother Charles Edward was a studious and thoughtful child, and as a young man he was always attentive to his mother and sister, but he lacked the good health and robust constitution of his younger cousins Charlie and Joe. He did, however, hunt, fish, and ride with them at Montevideo and Maybank, and he and Laura were loved and regarded by Charles and Mary as if they were their own children, while the childless Betsy and William Maxwell also looked on them as their own.[23]

When Susan married Joseph Cumming in 1838, she was entering a circle of another prominent Georgia family. His father had been the first mayor of Augusta after its incorporation and president of the Bank of Augusta, and his mother was a relative of Thomas Clay. His sister Anne had in 1836 married General Peter Skenandoah Smith, whose father was a business partner with the fabulously wealthy John Jacob Astor.[24] Susan's marriage, however, like so many other marriages of white masters and mistresses, was to have consequences for those who lived in the settlements. It was not long before Joseph Cumming decided that he should take responsibility for the management of his wife's property, including her slaves, as well as those who belonged to Laura and Charles Edward.

When Charles and Mary had begun the construction of their home at Montevideo, Charles and Susan had agreed that if there were ever the need for a division of the property given them by Joseph Jones, Charles would get the improved section of Montevideo and Susan would get the Cooper tract. Following her marriage to Joseph Cumming, the Cooper tract was separated from Montevideo to form White Oak plantation. (Charles bought a tract west of Carlawter from a neighbor and kept Montevideo approximately the same size as it had been before the division.) In the meantime, Charles and Susan divided the slaves that had come to them through the gift of Joseph Jones—those of John Jones's slaves whom Joseph had purchased at the Riceboro courthouse in 1808. Susan got the first lot of slaves, which included the family of Hamlet by his first wife Phillis; old Jupiter, who was soon to die; and the family of Lizzy's sister Willoughby. In addition, Susan had as a gift from her father the children of Elvira, Hamlet's second wife, which included Syphax the carpenter and Peggy, who was a domestic servant and who later had a child by Cassius. Altogether twenty-two men, women, and children were moved from Carlawter to the new settlement at White Oak. Prince was made the driver at White Oak, following in the steps of his father, Hamlet, his uncle Jupiter, and his grandfather Old Jupiter, who had blown the conch-shell horn at Liberty Hall. From the settlement at Maybank, Joseph Cumming removed twenty-three slaves who had been gifts to Laura and Charles Edward from Major Andrew Maybank and from their grandfather Audley Maxwell. These were sent to the nearby Social Bluff settlement. Fortunately, these two moves were not far from the familiar settlements at Carlawter and May-bank. But for the children of Hamlet and Elvira and all the others whose lives had been bound up with the slaves of Charles and Mary, the moves were simply another indication that they were regarded as valuable resources that could be allocated according to the situation and needs of white owners.[25]

Charles did not hesitate to name Cato the new driver at Montevideo. While he was not the oldest of Lizzy's sons and while he was not, like Prince, a descendant of earlier drivers, Cato was clearly the man for the job. Charles trusted him and trusted his judgment. He belonged to the North Newport Baptist Church, was faithful in attendance there and at the plantation meetings, and was soon to be made a Watchman. Over the years he had shown himself to be a skilled worker who had internalized at some deep level a discipline and a self-confidence that made him a leader. And while he would wear the high leather boots and the greatcoat that were symbols of his authority and carry over his shoulder the "cotton planter"—a "short whip with heavy handle and tapering thong, plaited in one piece"—he would not, Charles believed, abuse his authority and become a tyrant in the settlement. To be sure, his relationship with his brother Cassius and with Phoebe was to be tumultuous and troubled. But Cato's long service as the driver at Montevideo would be marked by his ability to gain and keep the trust of those who lived in the plantation house and of those who lived in the settlement. He would be Charles's right-hand man, and he would also be the one who would lead Carlawter as the settlement sought to create as much free space for itself as possible within the confines of slavery and to protect itself from the threats of outside intrusions into its life. The absence of a sustained white presence at Montevideo during much of the year, and later the almost entire absence of the white family for five years, would provide a context for Cato's leadership and for Carlawter's development into an even more tightly knit village among the village settlements of the Gullah people.[26]

17

MIDWAY

Charles returned to Montevideo in early December 1838 as a man about to begin the happiest and most productive period of his life. He felt that he had been set free from his work at the seminary to go home to his calling as a missionary among the Gullah people and to live once again above a flowing river and beside a waving marsh. Above all, however, he would be free to be with Mary. He had missed her terribly when he was in Columbia and she was in Liberty County, and he had filled his letters to her with increasing expressions of love and longing. "You are my own darling Mary," he wrote from Columbia. "Separated from you, I am ever restless, homeless, lonely, desolate, and I look forward with the most delightful anticipation when, if it shall so please a merciful Providence, I shall embrace you and take you once more, the wife of my youth, the mother of my children, the joy and comfort of my life, to my bosom: and then I will tell you over and over the constancy and ardour of my love."[1]

Charles's experience in Columbia had turned his attention more sharply than ever to issues of marriage and family life, and to the relationship between husbands and wives. These had long been subjects of great concern to him, lodged most deeply perhaps in his own quest for home, but they were issues that now came to a focus in his own life and in his work in the settlements.

When he had been a student at Princeton, Charles had written Mary a series of letters on marriage that, taken together, were intended to form a sort of marriage manual for the young couple. The letters reflected the boldness and confidence of a young man, a single seminarian, who knew all about marriage and family life because he had studied such matters at Andover and Princeton. Yet beneath his pretensions—and he was never again so pompous as he was when he was writing these letters—he had distilled from his readings a vision of marriage and family life that, tempered over time, was to inform his hopes for his Liberty County home and his relationship with Mary.

He had begun by emphasizing that their marriage would depend "very much upon the degree of our intellectual cultivation, and the pains which we take to maintain and advance it." They should share, he insisted, a disciplined schedule of reading and study and conversation for their mutual improvement and piety. They were to seek to create a hospitable home, free of gossip and undue inquiry into other people's business, one that was respectful of the poor as well as the rich. Great restraint was to be used in what was to be said to others—especially about personal family matters—in order to avoid an unbecoming familiarity. On the other hand, as husband and wife they were to be open and confiding to one another. They were to be "true and best friends," having at the heart of their relationship an intimate friendship that was grounded in mutual respect and in a fervent love that sought the good of the other. Such respect, Charles wrote, was particularly important in *"little things."* These, Charles said, "make up the greater part, by far, of our lives. Pass no reflections upon personal appearance, upon intellectual powers, nor do anything that will serve to cherish the thought that we are in any way contemptible to each other." "The sum of the whole," he wrote, "is that we must at all times and in every thing treat each other with the greatest delicacy and respect. Let us feel this, and actions will spontaneously be delicate and respectful."[2]

Mary received and responded to the letters with appreciation, sometimes with amusement, and on occasion with strong disagreement. She thanked Charles for the thoughtfulness of the letters and for the time he had spent writing them, assuring him that they would serve as a "textbook to which I may ever turn when the duties and circumstances of life call for such assistance and direction of conduct as they amply afford." But she was amused when he tried to inform her about women's underwear, about the dangers of corsets and stays, which, Charles feared, tended "to destroy that fullness of the chest in all its parts, which is the distinguishing beauty of the female person." Mary thanked him for his interest in what might make her flat-chested, but she let him know that she knew much more about such matters than he. And while he spoke of husband and wife as *"heads* of a family," he also wrote that wives were finally to be submissive to their husbands as commanded in the biblical texts. To this Mary replied that the biblical texts "do not imply I should suppose any thing like the absolute servility of a slave but that enlightened and cheerful acquiescence which reason and religion would approve." And then she added:

> *For myself,* I do *not know* what kind of a submission I shall yield *by and by.* I would hope however that will be other than that which merely a selfish policy dictates. *Experience* has taught me but little of the *grace* of obedience. As you may know, I have been all my life pretty much my *own mistress* there being no

one but *my Father* to whom I felt it a duty to submit and his great indulgence made his requisitions of the most lenient kind. So you must not be surprised if you sometime have to bear with the *self-will* of a spoiled child. You must not *scold* too *often* at all events.

And on one occasion when Charles had "scolded" her for what seemed to him a certain fickleness and attributed it to the female character, she had responded in kind: "[your] unwarrantable attack upon my sex, with an accusation of characteristic changeableness is what I shall not here discuss, not that I am in the least convinced of the truth of your insinuations, but that like all other time-strengthened delusions it would require reason, substantiated by fact, to prove its fallacy; and this would occupy rather more time and space than comports with my present design."[3]

By 1838 Charles had learned what Mary's brother John would later say about her: "She was not afraid of her own opinions," and "the fear of man brought no snare to her." She was obviously not easily intimated by "time-strengthened delusions" with regard to the role of white women.[4]

Mary would have to express, of course, her "own opinions" in a social and cultural world that assumed that wives were to be submissive to their husbands and that assigned carefully defined roles to women. Such roles, after all, were part of ancient household codes. Greek and Roman philosophers had taught such codes, which also had been incorporated in some of the letters of the Apostle Paul. "Wives, submit yourselves unto your own husbands, as unto the Lord," was regarded as an apostolic injunction as surely as "Servants be obedient to them that are your Masters, according to the flesh." Mary accepted this injunction, but she resisted any implication in it that would make her anything less than a fully responsible human being endowed with the capacity to know right and wrong, with the right to act on her convictions, and with the ability to manage when needed the practical matters of a plantation.[5]

Mary, perhaps ironically, employed the traditions of evangelical piety to resist a narrow definition of the role of white women. In particular, she called upon an evangelical understanding of her duty before God and upon the evangelical expectation that a Christian live, as she wrote to Charles, "a life of usefulness in one way or another to my fellow creatures and consequently of happiness to myself." When Christian duty and usefulness were linked to the particular circumstances a woman might find herself in—when duty and usefulness were linked to demanding "providential arrangements"—then the narrow confines of a white woman's place and role could be resisted. Mary consequently did not hesitate to inform her brother John, when death left a woman responsible for the man-

agement of a nearby plantation, that she did "not believe in ladies' assuming responsibilities—but when the Lord is pleased to lay them upon them, I do not
see why they should not trust him for grace and strength and go forward in their
performance."[6]

What had clearly emerged by late 1838 in Charles and Mary's marriage was
a relationship marked by mutual dependence and affection. Over the coming
years their love would deepen their youthful passion for one another, but not,
as Charles said, "tame it." And their letters would be filled with expressions of
deepest respect and love—a love that, while always reflecting their spirituality,
never was afraid of sensuality. When away from Mary, Charles would write that
he longed to embrace her and "smother" her with kisses. And after another absence he wrote: "I shall be ready to eat you up for joy and love. I do not wish to
meet you in public, but somewhere, where we may give expression to our overflowing affection." And Mary would write Charles: "Of one thing only am I assured: that you alone possessed and now possess the first, the only, the undivided
affection of my heart." Such was the character of Charles and Mary's love for
each other and of their hopes about their life together. Their understanding and
their experience of marriage were foundational for their vision of family life and
of the home they were seeking to create together at Montevideo and Maybank.
And their own marriage and home would be the background providing underlying assumptions in Charles's concerns for the marriages and homes of those
who lived in the settlements, whose labors, sorrows, and struggles made possible
so much of the comfort and sweetness of life for those who sat on the piazzas at
Montevideo and Maybank.[7]

Charles resumed his missionary labors shortly after his return to Liberty
County in December 1838. He immediately drew up a "regular plan of instruction and operations for the Winter and Spring." At Midway, where a religious
stirring was beginning at the Mallard and other nearby plantations, he began
a "series of *Historical and Biographical Discourses.*" Beginning with the call of
Abraham, he sought to "make the people acquainted with the most remarkable
of God's dealings with the Church and the world" and with "the lives of eminent Saints," always "keeping the Saviour prominently in view as the great sight,
the hope and foundation of acceptance with God." At the North Newport Baptist Church, where in earlier years he had conducted a series on the "principal
portions of the Gospel," he began a series of "Expository Lectures on the Book
of Acts." At Pleasant Grove, near South Hampton, he began a doctrinal series
and moved systematically, week after week, through the doctrines of the fall,
depravity, atonement, election, regeneration, and perseverance, "together with

such purely practical subjects as were suggested in the progress of the series."
Do not think it strange, he said in his report to the association, that such doctrines should be present to "untutored minds." The doctrines were themselves
an essential part of "Divine truth" and were accessible to all. Instructors, whose
grasp of theology was more than a superficial acquaintance with its nomencla-
ture, could lead the people into these deep waters, "depending upon the self-
evidencing power of the truth itself," and upon the "Holy Spirit, who has immediate access to the understanding and affections of mankind."[8]

As Charles went about his teaching, preaching, and visiting in the settlements
during the winter and spring of 1839, religious stirrings began to spread. A number of young people, who had been attending the Sabbath schools established by
the association around the county, began to show signs of conversion and were
beginning to be inquirers for membership at Midway, at North Newport, and at
Pleasant Grove. And the stirrings were not limited to the youth or to those who
lived in the settlements but were also beginning to be felt among older people
and among those who lived in the plantation houses of the county. At this point,
however, Charles's intensive work was interrupted in late spring. Not only was the
season of dangerous miasmas approaching, but Charles was also elected by his
presbytery to go to the meeting of the Presbyterian General Assembly in Philadelphia. Charles and Mary decided that rather than go to Maybank for the sickly
season, they would take the family north for the meeting of the assembly and for
an extended vacation. Mary's brother John Jones, who was graduating from the
seminary in Columbia, agreed to come home to his father's new summer home
in Walthourville and to spend the summer and early fall as the missionary in
Charles's place.[9]

Charles and Mary left Savannah for Philadelphia in the brig *Philura*. Sailing
with them, in addition to their three children, were Mary's seventeen-year-old
half-sister Evelyn Jones, who hoped the travel would improve her health. They
all hoped that the salty air and sea breezes would provide a relaxing time, but
the voyage turned out to be a miserable experience for all. The little sailing ship
had to struggle through stormy weather, and for eight days they were all seasick
and longing for some solid, immovable ground under their feet.[10]

In Philadelphia, Charles attended the meeting of the Old School Presbyterian
General Assembly and noted that the recently expelled New School Assembly
was nothing but "an *abolitionist body*." After the assembly, the family took the
train to Harrisburg through what Charles called "the finest farming country I
have ever seen." Then they crowded onto a canal boat with "a miserably wicked
and ill mannerly set" as the family traveled to visit friends at the village of Wilkes-

Barre. They spent a week in Princeton, where Charles preached at the college and in the town, and everywhere they went people asked him about his work and about the conditions of the slaves in the south. They were in New York for the Fourth of July celebration—a great rowdy affair that left twenty or thirty dead. The Joneses, with the "respectable part of citizens," stayed at home and left the wild celebrations to the "*lower orders*, the Irish, Dutch, Negroes, sailors etc."

The pastor of the city's old Brick Presbyterian Church, Gardiner Spring, asked Charles to speak one Sabbath evening and "give to his people some account of the religious instruction of the Negroes, in the South." Charles happily agreed, but soon after he had commenced speaking, "a man began to speak aloud and become unruly." Evelyn Jones was frightened and thought "they would have an abolition mob," but as the man "would not behave himself, they turned him out in short order, neck and heels." Charles thought his unruly behavior an indication that the abolitionists were "going down among the lower classes of society" and that the "respectable keep clear of them."[11]

They left the city and followed the trail of the respectable to Saratoga Springs, where they saw friends from the South and a great fashionable crowd "from all parts of the world." From Saratoga Springs they went to Niagara Falls—a fatiguing journey by train and stage—and then to Montreal and Boston and out to Andover, where they spent several weeks visiting old friends and recuperating from their travels.[12]

Everywhere that they went Charles sought to learn what he could about the abolitionist movement. He wanted to "make some acquaintance, as intimate as possible, with the publications, the general spirit and design, the standing and influence of those persons who of late years, have been so violently assailing the character, and the domestic institutions of the South." He visited bookstores and "the principal Depositories" of the abolitionists, read Garrison's *Liberator* and other newspapers and periodicals, and "inquired particularly of individuals, in private and in public station, concerning the whole movement." His conclusions confirmed his previous impressions: "the good sense and Christian feeling of the Free States, were far from being perverted; or from having any serious impression made upon them, in favor of modern abolition doctrines." With such conclusions, Charles and the family turned toward home and arrived safely at Montevideo in October 1839.[13]

While the family had been away, the religious stirrings that had begun the previous winter had prospered under the leadership of John Jones. The young seminary graduate had followed the pattern set by his brother-in-law Charles and had been busy preaching, teaching, and visiting in the settlements. The number of inquirers, those preparing for church membership, had grown steadily, and throughout the county there was a new attentiveness to religion and much "conversation on practical piety."[14]

Charles took up his missionary work immediately, throwing himself into a busy round of preaching and teaching and visiting in more settlements than ever before. John, who moved in with them at Montevideo, continued to work with Charles and to be a part of the efforts to encourage the revival fires that appeared to be breaking out in the county. As more inquirers began to press for church membership, Charles decided that a new strategy was needed to avoid excitement and "bodily exercises" taking the place of true repentance and conversion. What was needed, he thought, was for the watchmen to play a more central and organized role in assessing the readiness of those who came for church membership and in encouraging and disciplining those who were members. He consequently organized a regular watchmen's meeting for Midway and one for the North Newport Baptist Church.

By 1840 the office of watchman had been an important, but rather informal, office in the churches of the county for several decades. Working with Sharper and the other early preachers, the watchmen had reported to the white session at Midway or to the white preacher at North Newport on cases needing discipline; they also had been leaders of worship, especially with the prayers before services. But they did not meet as a group at any of the churches, as did a board of deacons or a session, and this is what Charles decided was needed. The approval of the white members was secured, and the watchmen evidently responded favorably to the proposal.[15]

On 8 March 1840, twenty-nine men from twenty-three plantations gathered for the first meeting of the Midway watchmen. Six of them, including the preacher Toney Stevens, were named selectmen to act as a kind of executive committee for the watchmen. Among them was Pompey, from the settlement at the Mallard Place, and Charles, the blacksmith on the plantation of Sara Howe's brother George Washington Walthour. (When the North Newport watchmen met, Paris, the driver for Roswell King, was the first among equals—there being no official black preacher—and Cato was numbered among the watchmen.) Charles explained that the purpose of the meeting was to "receive reports of the state of religion from the different plantations under their care" and for the watchmen to consult about the "best means for the support and prosperity of religion." The meetings would allow them to encourage one another and to give advice to one another "in cases of difficulty," to report poor members "that may need some assistance," and to pray together "for a blessing on the church." Central to their task was "to receive reports of cases of discipline." When they were able, they were to dispose of such cases, and when disciplinary cases called for action by the white session or congregation, then they were to prepare all the facts in the case for a formal presentation.[16]

Charles conducted the watchmen's meetings as he would a meeting of a white session—parliamentary rules of order were followed, and in cases of discipline careful procedures were observed in regard to witnesses and evidence and the rights of the accused. Such practices, he believed, were important for nurturing black leaders for the church and helping them learn the orderly ways of church government. As such, the meetings were aimed at acculturating the black leadership into the virtues and practices Charles believed were necessary for self-government. The practices of self-government—even on the limited basis that was allowed in the watchmen's meetings—could be, Charles believed, a way for the black leadership to begin to internalize the disciplines required on the long road to freedom.

Toney Stevens and the watchmen no doubt met such efforts with mixed feelings. On the one hand, the meetings provided opportunities for them to gather as a group, to organize themselves, to make decisions as leaders of a community, and to grow in self-confidence—all important opportunities for an oppressed people who lived in a society structured to teach them subservience and the need for white governance. At least in this area, limited though it was, there was some space for public leadership and self-government. Moreover, their work could help to bring some order to their community threatened constantly by the disorders of slavery.

On the other hand, the meetings must have seemed one more tool of white control—a way of co-opting the black leaders into white ways of doing things. Cooperation with the white missionary meant, after all, cooperating with the oppressor, for, as it was said of Charles, "his people have to work as well as we."[17] Perhaps most significant, the watchmen's meetings, with Charles presiding, could be seen as subversive of the informal authority structures that had emerged in the Gullah community.

Apparently Toney and the watchmen decided for the art of the possible and sought to use the meetings and the work of the watchmen for their own purposes. By organizing as a group, they carved out visible, public space within Liberty County for black leadership, for decision making about the issues in the community, and for formal procedures for settling disputes among themselves. Much of this had been done before by the white session at Midway or by the little coterie of white members at the Baptist churches. With the watchmen's meetings, black leadership in the county had a new role and a new visibility.

The watchmen met monthly, generally after a Sunday service, and heard re-

ports and conducted their business. Sometimes there were differences to be settled between church members. Pompey, at the Mallard Place, had a falling out
with Peter, the driver at the Quarterman Baker plantation. Toney, Charles the
blacksmith for the Walthour plantations, and Joshua, another selectman, met
with them, and the two men were reconciled. A few months later, Peter was in
another dispute, this time with the driver Paris from a Walthour plantation. Another committee was appointed, and the men were reconciled. Such cases took
some of the watchmen's time, but the great focus of their work was on trying to
stabilize marriages and family life within the radical disorders imposed by slavery.
In turning to this task, the watchmen did not have the formal participation of
slave women who, like white women, were not allowed to assume any office in
the church.[18]

Traditions of marriage and family rooted in the different cultures and nations
of Africa had been assaulted by the tearing of men and women out of their home-
lands, by the living conditions and housing patterns in the settlements, by the
early ratio of many men to few women, and by the harsh and often arbitrary decisions of whites in the buying, selling, and moving of slaves. In the eighteenth
century as a Gullah community had begun to be created generation by generation, new patterns of marriage and family life had slowly begun to emerge as men
and women struggled to create the Gullah-speaking African-American family.
By 1840 the results could be seen at Carlawter and Maybank, at the Retreat and
the Mallard Place and the other settlements of the low country.[19]

Some couples, like Andrew and Mary Ann at Maybank, lived together in the
same settlement and raised their children together under the same roof. Other
couples—such as Rosetta and Sam, and Cato and Betsy—lived out their lives
separated during the week and were together only when the husband came to
the "wife house" on Saturday nights, yet they managed to remain faithful to one
another and to create families of significant strength and cohesion. Some, like
Phoebe and Cassius, evidently worked out a way to remain together as a married couple even as the husband had acknowledged wives and children at other
plantations; other couples in similar situations accused each other of infidelity
and declared that they were no longer married. Still others—like Old Jupiter at
the slave sale in Riceboro in 1808—had to face the bitter humiliations of not
being able to protect a spouse or children from the power of whites, or they had
to endure the trauma of separation when a spouse or children were sold away or
removed. All of them had to find a way to negotiate their lives and relationships
in a system in which the state did not recognize slave marriages.

For the state, the primary relationship of black men and women was with a
master or a mistress, not a husband or wife. Owners needed the freedom to con-

trol their slave property according to their own economic interests. The recognition of slave marriages would have limited that control and would have left owners open to the charge that they were frequently "putting asunder" what "God had joined together." The churches, on the other hand, had begun to insist on the sanctity of slave marriages. To be sure, no white member of Midway was ever disciplined for "putting asunder" what "God had joined together" in the marriage of blacks—that would have presented a crisis to the system of slavery and would have challenged owners' absolute control over their slaves. But by the nineteenth century, Midway and other churches in the low country were seeking to impose church discipline on black members as a way of supporting the marriages of those who had no protection under state law. The tensions created by attempting to uphold marriage within a system that worked directly against it could be seen in the records of Midway. Time and again, the session had to decide what to do when a spouse was removed or sold away. And over and over again, the session had to decide that a spouse must be treated as dead because it was unlikely that a husband or wife would ever be returned to the county. Under such circumstances, the one remaining was said by the Midway session to be free to marry again.[20]

The work of the watchmen was in large part to try to uphold slave marriages under these constant attacks and to find ways to strengthen the families of the settlements. Month by month Toney and the watchmen heard reports of men and women, church members, who were struggling with issues of fidelity. To be a church member required not only a conversion experience and a confession of faith but also a promise to try to live according to the norms and expectations of the Christian community in Liberty County. Much of what the watchmen did was to provide moral guidance for the slave members and structures for reconciliation when there were troubles between husbands and wives. The discipline that the watchmen administered, often invoking the authority of the white session or congregation, had as its purpose the shaping of the character of the community, the reconciliation of those who were alienated from one another, and the restoration to full church membership of those who had been disciplined. Their use of discipline was soon felt at Maybank and the Retreat and among the house servants of Betsy and William Maxwell.

Sandy Maybank, who was married to Sharper's daughter Mary Ann at the Retreat, was frequently hired out to do carpentry work on neighboring plantations. While working on the W. Q. Baker plantation, he took up with Mag, and they had a child, Peter. Word of their relationship was reported at the watchmen's meeting, and after formal charges and the testimony of the watchmen Joshua and July, the case was turned over to the white session, where Sandy was excommunicated. He and Mag had another child, Mary, and he evidently continued to maintain two families for several years. But in time he became convinced of the sin of such a practice, and while he continued to see and support his Baker family, he began to live faithfully with Mary Ann and in this way was received back into the church.[21]

At Lodebar, the William Maxwell plantation, the cook Miley was married to Isaac, who lived on the neighboring plantation of Mellon Bluff. Working with Miley was Louisa, a younger woman. The two women had joined the church together in 1839, and Charles had sent word to them: "Tell Louisa and Miley, that the great work of living *as Christians* has just begun, and I hope they will be faithful, and not draw back, or give occasion to any to find fault." But within a year the women had a serious falling out. Isaac, on his Saturday visits to Lodebar, had begun an affair with Louisa. The case was reported to the watchmen. Witnesses were called. Testimony was given. And Louisa and Isaac were excommunicated from the church. Such a liaison evidently caused great tension between the two women, who had to live and work together. In time, however, Louisa repented of her relationship with Isaac and through the recommendation of the watchmen was restored to membership in the church. But Isaac was another matter. Charles called him an "unprincipled fellow," and later in a rage Isaac beat Miley so severely that she lost most of the sight in her one good eye. So bad was the beating, wrote Betsy, that it would have been better for Miley if Isaac had "broken her neck." Perhaps their shared troubles with Isaac brought the two women closer together, for Louisa was a gentle nurse to Miley following the beating, and later Miley cared for Louisa after she almost died from childbirth.[22]

Because he met with Toney and the watchmen, Charles heard all of these reports and the testimonies of the witnesses, and in his visiting in the settlements he was frequently called upon to help settle disputes between husbands and wives, not only of church members, but also of others who wanted an outside arbiter. He consequently decided that a series of sermons on marriage was needed for the instruction and encouragement of the people. Preaching at Midway and at the North Newport Baptist Church, he addressed such crowds that the decision was made that only the married could sit on the lower floors of the churches and the single were assigned the galleries.[23]

Marriage, he told the congregations, is an honorable estate, created by God for the "peaceful and successful propagation of the human species on the earth" and for the "happiness and comfort" of the marriage partners. He denounced polygamy and insisted that marriage be between one man and one woman. Those who marry should do so intelligently, with affection for one another "with their own consent" and "with the open and full consent of *Parents* or *Guardians*." A marriage service should be a public ceremony that honors marriage and gives public support to those who are marrying. He denounced fornication as a sin against one's own body, and he quoted St. Paul: "To avoid fornication, let every man have his own wife, and let every woman have her own husband." As for divorce, only the adultery of a partner provided a lawful reason to leave a spouse and marry another. But he said nothing about when a husband or a wife was sold away.[24]

In February 1841 Charles preached on the authority and the duties of husbands, first at North Newport and then at Midway, before packed congregations. God created the husband the head of the family, Charles said. But the husband must exercise his authority over his wife intelligently, knowing the rights of his wife: "His wife has a right to have her own opinion and speak her own mind on all subjects. She has a right to inquire into and to know every thing concerning their character, business, and welfare in life. She has a right to worship God as she pleases, and to maintain her authority over her own children and household and she has a right to see her friends and enjoy their society in reason." A husband is to exercise his authority "honorably and justly," "tenderly and rationally," "benevolently," "piously," and "affectionately."[25]

With the authority of husbands, Charles said, come the duties of husbands. And the first duty was that of love, which "lies at the foundation and comprehends and insures all others." They are to give themselves, and their entire affections, to be the "peculiar possession" of their wives. They are to show their love in their looks and in their words. The husband "will avoid wounding and irritating remarks, bitter and sarcastic reflections. He will not dwell upon faults, nor magnify them, nor delight in scolding and faultfinding." Husbands are not to say things like "they have a hard lot in married life," or "they shall never have an opportunity for a second wife," or "when their wife dies, they intend to form a connection with such and such an one!" "This," said Charles, "is cruel!" But the love of the husband is to show itself in actions that are kind, in behavior that supports a wife in her work, and in tender care when she is sick. A husband is to protect his wife: her person from danger and violence; her character from any who would assail it; her interests from any waste or injury. He is to provide for his wife and see that she lives in as comfortable a home as he can provide and that she has a full share of all of his possessions. And he is finally to present a pious and holy example for his wife, praying with and for her, for her life in this world and in the world to come.[26]

What did Charles's congregations think when they heard these sermons? Surely they thought about a husband being sold away, or they wondered how a husband was to protect a wife being whipped or assaulted by an owner. It must have seemed as if a big low-country alligator was right in front of the pulpit, thrashing its tail and showing its teeth, as Charles pretended not to notice it. Yet those who came to hear him preach on marriage did not walk out as they did when he preached on Onesimus. Rather, they packed the two churches and evidently found in what he had to say something they could use in their own struggles as men and women, husbands and wives, who had to face daily the power and appetite of the thrashing gator.

If, in his sermons to slaves, Charles could not bring himself to mention slave sales in Riceboro or divisions of estates or the power and abuse of owners, he did not fail to address these issues when he made his published reports. The duties of owners, he told Liberty County planters, was "to assist" their servants "in the pursuit of peace, justice and purity." And to do this, they needed to begin by providing *"sufficient and separate accommodations for the families of their servants."* Charles had made the rounds of the settlements in the county, and he knew all too well the wretched conditions in which many families struggled to live. "Every family on a plantation," he insisted, "whether consisting of only husband and wife, or parents and children, or of *one* parent and children, should have a *house of its own, in undisputed and undisturbed possession.*" Bad housing led to bad morals. "The crowding of two or more families, or parts of families into one house, and that perhaps scarcely large enough for one family; the mingling up of husbands and wives, children and youths, banishes the privacy and modesty essential to domestic peace and purity, and opens wide the door to dishonesty, oppression, violence and profligacy." How, he asked the planters, can "religion or morality thrive" under such circumstances?[27]

Nor did he hesitate to insist that planters "should *not separate, nor allow the separation of husband and wife, unless for causes lawful before God.*" Marriage, he told them, is a divine institution to be held sacred among any people. "Does an owner presume," he asked, "to contract or annul the marriages of his servants at his pleasure and for his own interest and convenience, or by any of his own arbitrary regulations?" If so, "He shall answer it to Him, who hath said, 'what therefore God hath joined together let no man put asunder.'"[28]

Charles wanted—at least at one level of his consciousness—slave couples and slave families to enjoy in the settlements a marriage and a family life that reflected from a distance the orderly, comfortable, loving, and mutually supportive family life that he knew at Montevideo and Maybank. Indeed, that was what he saw when he looked at Jack and Marcia, at Andrew and Mary Ann, at young Patience and Porter and young Lucy and Charles. They, and other families like them, Charles believed, were essential for the good ordering of society and for the stability, peace, and happiness of the community. Their success as couples and families he regarded as models for others. To be sure, as he made clear in his reports to planters, he was not naïve in regard to the forces that worked against slave families. It was just that he hoped that the religious convictions and self-interests of planters were enough to subdue the thrashing gator before his pulpit.

18

MAYBANK

In late spring 1841, a little caravan set out early in the morning from Montevideo for Maybank. The carriage driven by Jack led the way down the avenue, followed by two oxcarts loaded with carefully packed barrels of sugar and flour, with trucks of clothes and with boxes of household items needed for the next five months at the island home. Traveling with the family in the carriage was James Dubuar, a native of Aurora, New York, and recent college graduate. Charles had hired him to be the children's tutor, and the coming year was to be for Dubuar a kind of sojourn in an exotic land before returning to the North and theological studies at Union Theological Seminary in New York.[1]

As they turned out of the avenue and made their way toward Colonel's Island, Dubuar could look out of the window with the eyes of a newcomer at the passing landscape: the dark waters of cypress swamps reflected the sky and occasionally the white plumage of a snowy egret or a wood ibis wading in the water; live oak forests with thick undergrowths of palmettos, hollies, and yucca threatened any who would try to penetrate their secrets; and in open areas, black men and women could be seen everywhere spread out across cotton fields and along the dams and canals of rice fields.

The little caravan moved slowly down the sandy road, for the oxen were deliberate and plodded carefully along, pulling their heavy carts. With such a pace they did not approach the causeway leading to the island until late in the day. The marsh, stretching out to the north, had already turned green, and now in the afternoon sun it glowed as shadows were beginning to ease their way across its wide expanse. The hot fragrant breath of marsh mud and grass greeted the travelers and gave Dubuar hints of what might await all who would spend a summer and fall on a Georgia Sea Island.[2]

Jack turned the carriage into the avenue at Maybank. An old oak framed the

gate and provided a natural entry to the plantation. They went beneath its arching trunk and moved down the sandy avenue past several outbuildings—including the cabin where Patience and Porter lived—and came to a clearing where
a new plantation house awaited them. During the preceding year the old Hut
had been torn down, and a new house had been erected on an elevated foundation of handmade bricks brought from Montevideo. Sandy Maybank had been in
charge of the construction, and working with him had been not only his apprentices Syphax and Porter but also Toby James, the son of driver Plenty James at
old Liberty Hall. (Charles had worked out an agreement with Nathaniel Varnedoe so that Toby was apprenticed to Sandy to learn the arts and to develop the
habits of a carpenter.) Andrew and his crew from the settlement had helped with
the construction during the winter months after their cotton had been picked
and sent to market on a river schooner.[3]

The new house was a handsome cottage, two stories, built off the ground in
low-country style. Situated under the spreading branches of Sea Island oaks, it
too, like the old Hut, looked out onto the marsh of the Medway through a line
of oaks. A broad piazza stretched across the front of the house, and a hall, almost
eight feet wide, ran through the center of the house from front to back. Charlie
later described the house as "ample and very comfortably furnished." It had room
not only for the family, for Charles's study, and for the children's tutor, but also
for the many guests who would spend weeks with them during the summer and
fall. As with the Hut, the piazza was to be a favorite gathering place, and on its
east end the family and their guests would take their meals in good weather and
have their evening prayers. Here they could enjoy the sea breezes that generally
rose about ten in the morning and lasted until the evening, when the wind would
shift and blow from the land during the night bringing with it all the sounds and
fragrances of the nighttime marsh.[4]

A short distance from the house, outside its immediate yard, Charles had had
a little schoolhouse built for the children that he also used as a chapel for the
people in the settlement. Here Dubuar set up his classroom and began the formal
education of Charlie, Joe, and Mary Sharpe. They were joined every morning
during the week by the older children of Roswell and Julia King, who rode over
from their nearby summer home, Woodville. Mary King, already a lively and fun-
loving fourteen-year-old, was the oldest among them and may have felt a little too
old for Mr. Dubuar's lessons. Audley had only recently turned twelve, and he and
Charlie, who would turn ten in October, were the closest of friends, although
Fred King was closer to Charlie's age. Willie King was a studious little eight-year-
old, the same age as Joe. Mary Sharpe, at six, was the youngest in 1841. Rossie
King, who was a year younger than Mary Sharpe, was to join them the next year.[5]

Mr. Dubuar began his classes at eight in the morning with an opening prayer and ended them at two in the afternoon, Monday through Friday. (When they retuned to Montevideo in the fall, he began at nine and ended at three.) The only vacations were the Fourth of July, Washington's birthday, and three days at Christmas. All the children carried their lunches as if they were far from home and ate at the little schoolhouse, a practice that no doubt gave more time to the parents for their own study and activities. Charles and Mary oversaw the curriculum, and during the next seven years a series of young college graduates taught the children English literature and composition, Latin grammar and classics, natural sciences, and mathematics through trigonometry and beginning calculus. On Monday mornings they would read compositions they had written the previous week and recite some famous speech or some excerpt from some important literary or historical works. Memory work was regarded not as wasted time but as a way for the children to internalize the values and style of an upper class, to develop an ear for the beauty of the English language, and to master the rules of rhetoric and the art of persuasion.[6]

Such an education was necessary, Charles and Mary were convinced, for Christian gentlemen and Christian ladies. It had as its goal not only the imparting of knowledge but also the shaping of character and the preparation of their children for usefulness in society. For the boys, it meant an education that prepared them for college and professional work. For Mary Sharpe and Mary King, it meant an education that informed their hearts and minds, refined their manners, and prepared them for the responsibilities of home and family.[7]

Charles and Mary were not alone among the planting families of Liberty County in seeking such an education for their children. Indeed, such an education was a part of the ethos of a community long nurtured in the values and pieties of Calvinism. Scattered all around the county were little plantation schools where other children were being prepared for a life of usefulness and distinction. Most notably was the school at the LeConte plantation, where John and Joseph LeConte, under the watchful eye of their brilliant father, had been prepared for their future role as two of the nation's leading scientists. Charles had been a frequent visitor in the LeConte home, admired greatly the botanical garden of the boys' father, and may have used their school as a model for the one he established for his children at Maybank and Montevideo.[8]

However important the learning that went on in the little plantation schoolhouses, the learning that took place after school was equally significant. The whole plantation at Maybank—and to a lesser extent at Montevideo—was a schoolhouse for curious and highly disciplined children, especially the boys. The marshes, with their creeks teeming with life; the woods and ridges of the island, with eagles, owls, and migrating warblers; the beaches of nearby St. Catherine's, with their shells and various pipers, willets, and curlews; the Indian mounds and shell middens that lay waiting with their hidden treasures; the river swamps at Montevideo, with their deer and turkey, alligators and otters, wood ducks and mallards—all invited exploration and increasingly sophisticated analysis that asked what is here, why is it here, and what is its nature?[9]

Charles and Mary encouraged such explorations and questions by their children and modeled a love of nature that delighted in the beauty of the low-country landscape and that found in the world around them the evidences of God's creative power and goodness. Charles himself taught them astronomy, not only so that they would know the names of the evening stars that shown so brightly and of the constellations that moved across the nighttime sky, but also in order for them to feel the wonder and awe of God's majesty and of God's created universe.[10]

The boys' exploration of their environment was encouraged by their hunting and fishing. Both Charlie and Joe soon became avid hunters—and Audley and the other King boys were frequently their companion—advancing from bows and arrows to shotguns and rifles. They learned how to wait for ducks at dawn where oaks dropped their acorns in slow-moving waters and where blinds could be built at the edge of rice fields. They learned how to distinguish the track of a buck from that of a doe and how to sit quietly and call a strutting tom turkey in the spring and how to jump-shoot clapper rails and ricebirds. And in the marsh creeks that flowed in and out with the tide before Maybank and in the river at Half Moon, they caught whiting and flounder, bass, sheephead, and even croakers, and in the winter they went after shad, knowing its roe to be a delicacy, and when the drumming season began in the spring and fall, and they were old enough, they joined others in the rivers and inlets catching the big fish.[11]

Joe was as avid an outdoorsman as his brother, but increasingly his attention and efforts were focused on hunting and fishing in order to study what he shot or caught. Robert Mallard later wrote of him: "His gun and fishing-pole, like the net of the entomologist, were to him valuable chiefly as instruments with which to procure specimens for dissection and investigation, in which work he had the zealous aid of every Negro on the plantation." Many a beautiful specimen fell to his gun. A wood ibis with its white plumage and bald head was carefully embalmed with arsenic and mounted with a wood rat placed in its long bill. Ducks and geese, herons—including the great blue—and a roseate spoonbill were stuffed with cotton as specimens. The same fate awaited curlews, with their sickle-shaped bills, and plovers and orioles and many a migrating songbird. A squirrel was mounted with a peanut in its mouth. Rats from the marsh and barnyard were caught and stuffed, and innumerable bugs that thrived in the low country were gathered and preserved. A large rare kite, with its long, deeply-forked tail, was a prize of one day's hunting, and a great horned owl that had hooted once too often in the swamp was shot from its perch and mounted with wax eyes and with its wings outstretched. They all went into the museum Charles had Sandy Maybank build for the children at Maybank, where the specimens were carefully examined on worktables and the birds compared to descriptions in Nutall's *Ornithology* and labeled in Latin. Joe often dissected what he brought to the museum, and at a very early age he began to make careful sketches of what he saw—a practice that was to be valuable to him later in life.[12]

Charlie joined Joe in the gathering of these wild specimens, but his interests were focused more sharply on the shell middens and Indian mounds, where he found arrowheads, spear points, and scrapers, hatchets, mortars and pestles, fishing plummets and hooks, and pieces of pottery on which "various images were curiously wrought." His prize find, however, was a burial urn of "graceful outline" measuring "fifteen inches and a half in height, nine inches in diameter in the widest part, and ten inches and a quarter across the top." Charlie had found the vase in an upright position in a small shell mound on the island. Its surface was imprinted with ornate geometrical designs, and when he looked within there were the "bones of a young child." All of these artifacts intrigued him and stirred his imagination as he arranged them in the museum. They made him wonder about the mother whose child was buried in the urn and about those who had once lived on the island and hunted its woods, who had gathered such huge numbers of oysters and clams from the adjoining creeks and marshes, and who had now vanished from the earth. "We question," he later wrote, "but there are no voices of the past in the ambient air."[13]

Mary Sharpe also had her corner of the museum where she would put her treasures, more modest in scope than those of her brothers and consisting of what was considered more appropriate for a young lady—no marsh rats or skeleton in a burial vase for her! She would have rather a "small piece of linen from the pyramids of Egypt" and a "few owl feathers" from an "old owl from the pyramids" brought to her by a visiting missionary. And there would be shells and fossils brought by her father for her to see and wonder over, but she would not shoot, catch, or dig for any items to place in her corner of the museum.[14]

For all the children, but especially the boys, the museum was a place to teach them how to look and look again and analyze and think about what they were seeing. And in remarkable ways, the boys' busy activities connected with the museum nurtured interests that came to shape their lives and vocational choices. Charlie would become a lawyer, but his passion would be as a historian and as a kind of early archaeologist exploring the ancient ruins of the aboriginal people of Georgia. More than 150 years after the little museum was built at Maybank, his research on the *Antiquities of the Southern Indians, Particularly of the Georgia Tribes* (first published in 1873) would be reissued and declared a "landmark publication," and his collection of artifacts begun at Maybank would find their way to the American Museum of Natural History and to the Peabody Museum at Harvard. Joe would become a doctor, but his passion and the focus of his life would be as a scientist who would seek to understand the causes of disease, especially malaria and yellow fever, and he would gain an international reputation as an advocate for public hygiene as a way to combat the ravages of epidemics. As for Mary Sharpe, she was equally bright and disciplined as her brothers, but as a woman her vocational choices were limited. She would become an affectionate wife and mother, a leader of women in the church, and a person of uncommon good sense and strong character. Her gender, and the circumstances and the contingencies of her birth, limited her freedom to explore other options and to choose other paths.[15]

The education of the children, of course, did not go on only in the schoolhouse and museum or in the surrounding woods and marsh. Much was taught and much was learned on the piazza when Jack and Phoebe and Patience served tea in the late afternoon and when the family and guests gathered for dinner. At such times the manners of elite southern whites were carefully instilled in the children, as was their position as young masters and young mistress. And much was also taught when Charles read to the family in the evenings when they gathered before the fireplace in the parlor as the weather began to turn cold. These evening gatherings were especially memorable for the children. Years later Mary Sharpe wrote:

> This early cold always carries me back to Maybank. Well do I remember the first fires that were kindled in the fall, and how we used to gather around the hearth—Father reading aloud, Mother knitting or sewing, Brother Charlie sitting upon the floor with a bunch of wire grass and ball of flax thread making mats with *Taddy* at his side (or else sinewing arrows), Brother Joe with his paint box and some megatherium skeleton model before him, and I think I used to make mittens or sew my hexagon quilt. Sometimes a hoarded stock of chinquapins would engage the attention of all the children, each one counting his store.[16]

Charles and Mary in their disciplined life of study and work were themselves models for the children. In 1841 Charles, in addition to his missionary labors, was busy completing his *Religious Instruction of the Negroes in the United States.*

For years he had been gathering books, pamphlets, and reports on the slave and free black population in the United States. The book provided a historical sketch of religious instruction from the earliest colonial period to 1842, a summary of "the Moral and Religious Condition of the Negroes," a call for the church to "Attempt the Improvement of the Moral and Religious condition of the Negroes in the United States, by Affording them the Gospel." The study was earnest and patronizing, as one would expect, but it was also filled with valuable reports, summaries, and observations that would be used for years by historians.[17]

Mary was also a model of disciplined work for her children. In the early years of her marriage she read widely, largely under the direction of Charles, and saw after the increasingly complicated work of a plantation mistress. She was particularly interested in the education the children were receiving, and she would continue to be a deeply engaged critic of their work even when, in college, the boys were making names for themselves as scholars. She always pushed them to express themselves clearly and simply—especially encouraging Charlie to abandon a florid and pompous style that marked his early efforts. And Mary had a special concern that Mary Sharpe's education, though limited by her gender, be full and rich. She wanted her, for example, to master French: "I am anxious," she would write, "for your thorough knowledge of the language and that you should speak as well as read and write it." Later she would warn Mary Sharpe: "How degrading to the intellect is the way in which *young females particularly* spend their time! With the mass of mankind there seems very little conscientious appreciation or improvement of the talents—for which they will have to render an account."[18]

Clearly time was a gift and resource to be used frugally and responsibly. All of the family would learn to sing vigorously the hymn of Charles's friend Lowell Mason: "Work, for the Night Is Coming!" Day by day Charles and Mary modeled for their children a belief that disciplined work was both a religious responsibility and the only road to distinction. "All excellence," Charles would write Charlie, "is the fruit of careful, persevering labor." And Mary would confess that the "monitor within" was always reminding her: "There is something to be done." Disciplined work, rooted in a sense of duty, was a lesson all three Jones children were to master.[19]

Along with their parents, the influence of the children's close relatives, especially their Aunt Betsy and their grandfather Joseph, helped to shape their characters and interests. Betsy regarded the children, together with Laura and Charles Edward Maxwell, as her own and treated them with great affection, an affection that they returned in equal measure, for she was to them a second mother. Married when she was only seventeen, Betsy had little formal education—only a few years under William McWhir at Sunbury—and would always be, in spite of her prominent connections, a countrywoman known for her hospitality, plainspoken ways, and sense of humor. She may have been dyslexic—she would write in a terrible hand "Jhon" for "John"—or she may have simply spelled as she spoke with her low-country accent—consistently writing "both" as "boath." Years later John Jones wrote of her: "There was in her a most marked individuality of character. . . . I have never known anyone who has left behind them more distinct impressions of what they really were. None who knew her can ever forget the intense humanity that pervaded her whole nature; the bold generous heart, her willing, helping hand, her transparent candor, her quenchless zeal in all good works, her ardent devotional spirit, and her unshrinking piety faithful to God and man. Is it any wonder that she was loved and honored by all who knew her?" What she provided the children as they were growing up was a sense that they were loved and honored for who they were. She would speak to them frankly and tease them and encourage them and always let them know how much she cared for them.[20]

Their grandfather Joseph contributed something else to the children's growing years. He was for them Captain Jones, the honored patriarch, and in him and in his affection for his grandchildren they had nurtured a sense of belonging to an extended family and being connected to a particular place over the generations. In him they found the security that comes from being linked not only to a geographical place but also to a social place and to a history that had shaped and been shaped by the landscape of the low country.[21]

Charles and Mary hoped that all of these influences would lead above all to the conversion of their children. "Oh! How holy should we be in heart and in life," Mary wrote Charles, "striving daily by precept and by example to lead our own beloved ones to the lamb of God, who taketh away the sins of the world." Morning and evening prayers, daily Bible reading, faithful attendance at church, and their own example—these were the ways the parents hoped to lead their children to Christ. As the children grew older, Charles and Mary would feel an increasing anxiety for their children's conversion, and this concern played a growing part in their relationship to all three.[22]

For the children themselves, all of these influences came together to help shape their understanding of who they were and of their place in the world. Fundamental for them would be a Calvinist insistence on the value of ordinary life—an insistence that permeated the air of Maybank and Montevideo. This focus on ordinary life meant that home and family—not a cathedral or even a meetinghouse—constituted sacred space, especially as that space was marked by disciplined family prayer and devotions. The ordinary occupations of men and women—including those of doctors and lawyers, scientists and historians, housewives and mothers—were seen as vocations, as calls of God, that had dignity and possessed spiritual worth and contributed to the public good. In the coming

Low-country oxcart (from *Drums and Shadows*, photograph by
Muriel and Malcolm Bell, Jr., used by permission of Muriel Bell)

years the Jones children would give themselves to their callings with remarkable
discipline and profound identification with their work. Laziness they would regard as a sign of ingratitude and as harmful not only to the individual soul but
also to the community. All the elements of their education and nurture would
help to shape in the children personalities possessed of an intense consciousness
of personal worth and self-respect, a powerful sense of vocation, and a feeling of
great privilege and immeasurable responsibilities and duties. Not incidentally,
all of these characteristics were well-suited for paternalistic elites in a slave society who felt that without their governing hand and benevolent impulses, chaos
would be set free to rule the land.[23]

While the children of planters were being educated in this manner, another
kind of education was going on in the settlement at Maybank. Gilbert, the third
child of Andrew and Mary Ann, turned fifteen a few weeks after James Dubuar

began his classes. Every morning on his way from the settlement to the stables, Gilbert had to pass the little schoolhouse, and he no doubt heard on a regular basis Charlie and Joe, Audley and Mary King, and the others reciting or working on their different lessons of which he could have no part. And he must have watched with some amazement the stuffing and mounting of animals in the museum. Certainly he, with others in the settlement, kept an eye out for arrowheads and spear points and other relics of the original inhabitants of the island, for a reward was possible for a good find.[24]

All of these familiar patterns of daily activity were part of the structure of the plantation, the way life was ordered at Maybank, and that order had an educational purpose—to teach Gilbert that he was a slave, that he was to go when he was sent and to come when he was called; that he was to walk past the schoolhouse and the museum as a spectator and not go in to learn their lessons or acquire their power. And he was expected to do this without murmuring or complaining, but cheerfully, as one who acknowledged at a deep inner level that this was his place and these were his duties. Such indoctrination had behind it the power of the familiar, of everyday practices at Maybank and Montevideo.[25] Yet in spite of such indoctrination, there must have been anguish for Gilbert and a sense of deprivation among all the children of the settlement who had to walk past the schoolhouse and hear the lessons being taught and know that they could not be included. And never would their resistance to the indoctrination of the plantation be clearer than when freedom came. Then they would flock to the schools for the newly freed people and with great sacrifice seek education for themselves and their children.[26]

But there were other lessons that had to be learned in 1841. When Gilbert reached the stables, he had lessons under the direction of his older brother Charles, who was teaching him how to drive the gig, the little two-wheeled, one-horse carriage that Gilbert would use to make the long trips to Riceboro to pick up the mail or to go to Montevideo to get something needed on the island. It had been decided in the plantation house that Gilbert's vocation, his calling, would be that of a "rider," and, like his brother Charles, a driver of oxcarts and a general handyman rather than a field hand. This meant that he had to learn from his brother how to care for the horses in the stable and how to be sure the oxen were properly fed and watered. He needed to know how to put on a harness so that it would not rub the horse, and how to hitch an ox to a cart without getting gored or kicked, and how to navigate an oxcart so that it would not tip over with a full load of cotton or plantation supplies.[27]

Gilbert would become in time particularly skilled in handling the oxen that were the primary draft animals at Maybank and Montevideo, and at Arcadia, too.

The oxen were adult male bovines—generally Durhams or Devons—that had been castrated and were less excitable than horses and mules. A yoke of these oxen in their prime had roughly the same amount of pulling power as a span of large draft horses, and while they were easier to train to the line and to voice commands than horses, they had a tendency to pull against each other. Gilbert learned, however, that if he tied their tails together, they would pull together as well as any horses. He also learned that their short legs and cloven hooves made oxen particularly useful on a low-country plantation. With their short legs they could ease around huge stumps left to slowly decay in cleared fields. And unlike the cupped hooves of horses and mules, the oxen's cloven hooves did not create suction as they plodded through muddy fields or along flooded roads. They were consequently much less likely to get bogged down in swamps or rice fields or when spring rains spread swampy waters over sandy roads.[28]

Perhaps being drivers of oxcarts influenced the way Gilbert and his brother Charles learned to see the world. As the carts moved slowly but steadily around the plantations, hauling manure from the cow pens and bags of cotton from the fields, and as Charles and Gilbert loaded and unloaded the carts, they both grew to be patient and strong men who met the world as it came their way and persevered. In time Charles became known for the dignity with which he carried himself, and in his old age his broad shoulders would still reveal the strength of his youth, even as his face showed that he had seen more than his share of hardship and sorrow. Gilbert, like his older brother, grew into a steady and reliable man who did not easily change his ways or his course once he had set upon it. He wore in the future a pocket watch with a chain and used it to check the time when he had to drive the gig or carriage to get someone from the stage or later the train. The watch helped to make him punctual, and consequently he was regarded as all the more reliable.[29]

With Charles and Gilbert in the Maybank settlement was young Niger, who was beginning to receive a different kind of education. During the coming years he would be designated the fisherman, and while he would have other work to do as well, it was fishing, shrimping, crabbing, and gathering oysters that would be his primary vocation until the Federal ships began to appear off the coast. This meant that of all the people who lived at Maybank, white and black, no one would know the marshes and their creeks or the rivers and their inlets like Niger. Much of his early education would be focused on learning to navigate his bateau through the winding creeks of the marsh that were a labyrinth for the uninitiated. He found, as he went out day after day, the deep holes in the creeks where the young shrimp would gather as the tide went out, and he learned how to make a shrimp net and cast it just before the tide turned. And he learned how to make simple basket traps for crabs. Most of the year he would use a fish head in the basket for bait, but in the fall and spring, when the females were molting and shedding their shells, he would put a big male in the basket, and female "peelers" would come crowding in seeking a mate. And Niger would take these soft-shell crabs to Patience, who sautéed them and stacked them on a big platter for the dining room table at Maybank, although no doubt not a few were carried to the settlement. And Niger learned how to fish for trout in the creeks, and for spots during their fall run, and how to use fiddler crabs—they darted everywhere over the marsh mud—to catch the highly prized sheephead that tended to nibble with their big incisors rather than swallow the bait. "Niger succeeded in procuring some fine fish for two dishes; we had also an excellent oyster pie," Charles wrote; the oysters, no doubt, had also been gathered by Niger from their muddy beds.[30]

Except for those in the plantation house, the young women in the settlements did not have as many opportunities as the men to learn specialized work such as belonged to drivers, carpenters, riders, or fishermen. Phoebe, Patience, Lucy, and a few others worked as cooks and seamstresses, chambermaids, and personal servants. But Andrew's and Mary Ann's daughters Sylvia, Dinah, and Delia, along with most of the young women in the settlements at Maybank and Carlawter, were taught to labor in the fields, plowing the ground, planting the seeds, hoeing the weeds, and harvesting the crops. To be sure, they had to learn how to handle a plow and make a mule turn to the right or left by calling "gee" or "haw," and how to swing a hoe and carry on their heads a bundle of rice or bag of cotton, but their work was generally limited to the most routine and often burdensome of agricultural labor.[31]

Despite the schoolhouse's being closed during the days of the week to those who lived in the settlement, it was open in the evenings as a chapel for their prayers and worship. And it was open on Sunday afternoons as well, the one time during the week that Gilbert and Niger and those who worked the fields or washed clothes were invited in for a lesson. Joining them were young and old from the settlements at nearby Woodville and Social Bluff who wished to take part in the Sunday school. Mary Jones and Julia King were the primary teachers, although when Charles was not away preaching and teaching, he often conducted the lessons. And as the Jones children grew older, they too joined in teaching biblical stories and their father's catechism to old and young alike. The lessons that they taught followed the pattern at the various stations, but Mary and Julia frequently added another subject to their lessons—they read news reports from the *Charleston Observer* and other religious papers. Most often they read reports from missionaries, especially those of John Leighton Wilson from Cape Palmas and then Gabon, which, while couched in the piety of the mission movement,

Woman pounding rice in Liberty County
(courtesy Georgia Archives)

were rich in details about the history, traditions, and current events among the
Kru and Grebo of Liberia, the Mpongwe of Gabon, and other peoples of the
regions. Such reports must have been windows to a wider world for those who
lived in the settlement—as they were windows for those who lived in the plantation house at Maybank. Indeed, the reports may have been one of the strongest
drawing cards to the Sunday school for a people largely isolated on an island and
kept from learning to read and write. Other worlds were revealed in the reports,
and whatever ideological purposes may have been intended in reading them to
slaves, the hearing of the reports provided important reminders that the way life
was ordered at Maybank was not the way life was ordered everywhere, that whites
were not always owners and blacks not always slaves. Such other worlds undercut white attempts to control the imagination of the settlements and to prevent
the imagining of subversive alternatives that could challenge the current arrangements on the plantations.[32]

And so the education of the children and young adults who lived in the settlement at Maybank proceeded day by day, as did the education of those who lived in the plantation house. But there were other elements to the education in the settlement, elements that were more secretive and not as obvious as the education for their work or the education in the Sunday schools and worship services. These were the lessons taught by parents and other older ones around the evening fires in the settlement by the marsh. As the night wind stirred the ancient oaks and the sound of the surf rolled in the distance, lessons were taught about life on a low-country plantation and about how to act around whites. A central message of the lessons was for the children to recognize in whites, even benevolent ones, a dangerous presence. They were to be, said one Sea Island slave, "jus' like de birds when a gunner was about, expectin' a crack ebery minute." Gilbert and Niger and other young slaves were taught to remain quiet or act dumb when questioned by Charles or Mary. Such a strategy was a way to avoid trouble and was a means to protect oneself and one's family and friends. The young were taught to be cautious and act "Jes like the tarpins or turtles." "Jes stick our heads out to see how the land lay." Those who lived in the settlements, Charles wrote in some frustration, "are scrupulous on one point: they make common cause, as servants, in *concealing* their faults from their owners. Inquiry elicits no information; no one feels at liberty to disclose the transgressor; all are profoundly ignorant; the matter assumes the sacredness of a 'professional secret.'"[33]

Gilbert and Niger, Sylvia and Dinah, and all the others growing up in the settlements were taught to use the language of subservience as a strategy of concealing the secret life of the slaves—"massa" or "missus" could be used as terms of address to make owners think the lessons of subservience had been well learned and to hide the lessons of resistance being taught by settlement elders. But such behavior required walking a fine line, and slave children had to learn how far they could go without evoking an angry response. For if a master thought what he was hearing was a sham, if a mistress thought some deception was in the air, they could quickly become outraged. Indeed, many whites believed all slaves were deceitful. Even Charles felt this. He believed that there was "an upper and an under current" in slave life. "Persons live and die in the midst of Negroes," he wrote in the year James Dubuar came to Maybank, "and know comparatively little of their real character. . . . The Negroes are a distinct class in community, and keep themselves very much *to themselves*. They are one thing before the whites, and another before their own color. Deception towards the former is characteristic of them, whether bond or free, throughout the whole United States." Charles believed that such behavior was taught in the settlements, that it was "a habit— a long established custom, which descends from generation to generation." So life at Maybank, as at Montevideo and other plantations, involved deception by those who lived in the settlement and suspicion and surveillance by those who lived in the plantation house. No amount of benevolent intentions on the part of Charles and Mary could overcome this fundamental reality of life on a low-country plantation.[34]

The hidden lessons at Maybank and other plantations did not, however, always remain hidden. What was taught around the evening fires would be made public in veiled and opaque ways to those who lived in plantation houses. And at Maybank and Montevideo, the one who most often did this muffled revealing was apparently none other than Jack, the patriarch of the settlements, the most respected man of the settlements among both whites and blacks alike. Jack did the revealing by being the central storyteller and conveyor of folktales. While he was much more for the Jones family than an Uncle Remus figure—he was too important a part of their lives to be simply an old storyteller—he was apparently the primary one from whom young Charlie learned the Gullah tales he published years later as *Negro Myths from the Georgia Coast, Told in the Vernacular.* To be sure, the primary audience for Jack's stories was Gilbert and Niger, Phoebe and Patience, and the others who struggled daily to make their way through the dangers of slavery. But the stories also provided a way to say to whites what could not be said directly. So stories were told on the kitchen steps to the young whites on the plantation, and they would be remembered and recorded by Charlie.[35]

Some of the stories Jack told appeared to be simply explanations of what could be seen in the landscape of the low country. As the white children sat around him, Jack explained "How Come Buh Alligatur Nebber Sleep Fur From de Ribber Bank." Jack told how Buh Rabbit made trouble for Buh Alligatur—he set the broom grass on fire and made Buh Alligatur rush to get in the water. Buh Alligatur, said Jack, was so mad at Buh Rabbit that "Buh Rabbit faid Alligatur an ribber tell dis day." And because of the fire, "From dat day to dis," Jack noted, "you kin nebber ketch Buh Alligatur sleep fur from de bank; an de fus time eh yeddy [hears] bush crack, er anyting mek rackit, he leggo everyting an fall right in de water."[36]

Some stories provided moral guidance and told the children of the settlement and the plantation house how to live in a community. You should keep your promises for "Anybody wuh gwine back on eh prommus, an try fuh harm de pusson wuh done um a faber, sho ter meet up wid big trouble." And you should not meddle in other people's business because it is a "Bad plan fur stranger fuh meddle long tarruh people bidness." And you should always be a faithful friend because "Eh yent [it doesn't do], in dis wul, fuh man fuh ceive [to deceive] he fren." And when in need, you should turn to your friends, because "Wen you want somebody fuh do you sarbis, call pon you fren, but don't trus you eenemy done um."[37]

But Jack was interested in teaching young Gilbert and Niger and all the others in the settlements about the dangers of life in the low country, and in the muffled language of the stories he gave hints to the white children about the dangers blacks faced. He wanted those in the settlements to know how blacks needed to be always on their guard against whites, and he told stories that not only provided warnings but also taught strategies for surviving and for tricking masters and mistresses. In "Buh Fowl-Hawk an Buh Rooster," Jack told how the hawk came to eat the children of the rooster:

> When Buh Rooster clean forgit Buh Hawk, an leh eh chillun play bout een de grass, befo eh know, down drap Buh Fowl-Hawk, an eh ketch up one er dem same Buh Rooster chillun. En fly off wid um to one big oak tree, an eh pick eh bone clean. Buh Rooster holler, but eh cant tetch Buh Hawk. De chicken sweet. Buh Hawk feel good. From dat day tell now, Buh Fowl-Hawk blan [is accustomed to] pick eh chance an lib off Buh Rooster chillun.

Jack was giving a serious warning to all the parents in the settlements—watch after your children! Watch after your children! Always remember whites might sweep down at any moment and carry them off! Whites live off the children of the settlements, and once they get them, all your crying will not bring them back. In such a dangerous world, Jack insisted, parents should discipline their children: "Do same luk Buh Eagle. Mine you childlun well wen dem leetle; an soon es dem big nough fuh wuk, mek um wuk." Jack's niece Patience took these lessons to heart, but his daughter Phoebe ignored his warnings and would pay a bitter price. And as for the white children, they only found the stories entertaining.[38]

Jack also taught trickster tales that had their roots in west Africa. The tricksters—and Buh Rabbit was the greatest of them in the low country—used their wits to get the best of powerful figures like Buh Wolf, Buh Alligatur, and Buh Bear. In the story, for example, that explained why the alligator stays near the riverbank, the trickster makes the powerful anxious, always listening and ready to slip into the safety of the water at the slightest hint of danger.[39]

In perhaps the most daring of his stories, Jack told the children—and perhaps the adults on the piazza heard it too—how the two antagonists Buh Wolf and Buh Rabbit competed for the affection of a "rich an berry pooty" gal. Buh Rabbit tricks the wolf into letting him ride him to the woman's house, where the victorious rabbit calls out: "Wuh you tink er me rarruh [father's] ridin horse?" Having been mounted and humiliated before the woman, "Buh Wolf so painful, so bex, an so shame, eh keep on run, an eh nebber come back fur see de Gal no mo."

When the woman "notus how smate Buh rabbit bin," she consents to marry him. In the worst of white nightmares, the weak not only wins the possession of the rich and pretty woman but also humiliates the strong male by mounting and domesticating him.[40]

The world Jack told about in the stories was a harsh world where danger could come sweeping down suddenly from the sky and where the weak could trust the strong only at great risk—even the strong who claimed to be the friend of the weak. His stories were filled with the bitter wisdom of those who knew all too well how arbitrarily whites could act, how indifferent they could be to the interests, affections, and commitments of blacks. Yet the world Jack revealed in his stories was profoundly complex, for the weak could turn against the weak and friend could betray friend. Life in the settlements was not all harmony, nor was it always marked by the solidarity of the oppressed. The powerful in the settlements, especially the drivers, could abuse the weak, especially the women, and those who were weak could adopt the brutal practices of the strong. After Buh Wolf tries to burn up Buh Rabbit in a hollow tree, Buh Rabbit tricks the wolf—who mistakenly trusts Buh Rabbit—into getting into a hollow log. The rabbit then burns up the wolf, showing him no mercy. "Buh Rabbit," said Jack, "leetle fuh true an eh yent strong, but en berry scheemy an eh hab er bad heart." Buh Rabbit knew, however, he was up against a powerful and ruthless opponent in Buh Wolf, who had his own tricks and schemes and his own bad heart.[41]

Such were the lessons taught to Gilbert and Niger and the other children of the settlement, and such were the lessons heard if not understood by the white children. For Jack was telling not simple stories but sophisticated narratives that were open to various interpretations. Charlie and most whites heard in them what they were educated to expect from blacks—amusing, fanciful tales of an ignorant and superstitious people. But for those who had ears to hear, especially those educated in the settlements, the stories explored in depth the character of human life in the low country and provided wisdom for living in a harsh and often arbitrary world.

The education of Gilbert and Niger, of Sylvia and Dinah, and all the others growing up in the settlements at Maybank and Carlawter was thus severely restricted but nevertheless multilayered and rich. Such an education helped to form them not into simple stereotypes—into those whose character was marked by an infantile dependence or whose rage led them to become heroic freedom fighters—but rather into complex personalities of often remarkable cohesion and integrity.[42] During the coming years they would draw on the resources of their education to guide them along various and sometimes competing paths toward a distant freedom.

19

———◆•◆———

ARCADIA

Following his graduation from Columbia Seminary in 1839, John Jones spent almost a year as a part of the family at Montevideo and Maybank. He had been an assistant to Charles in his missionary work and had met with substantial success at the stations and at the North Newport Baptist Church. In the fall of 1840 he was called to the adjoining county to be the pastor of the Bryan Neck Presbyterian Church, a congregation composed primarily of three wealthy planting families —the Clays, the McAllisters, and the Arnolds—and of numerous black slaves.[1]

John was already demonstrating the characteristics that were to mark his long ministry—he had a warm and friendly manner that invited confidence, an ability to empathize deeply with the joys and sorrows of those around him, and an evangelical zeal that was rooted in a genuine and attractive piety. But he was a restless soul, and he would have difficulty staying in one place for very long. He was also —strange to say, in light of his restlessness—a great procrastinator. People came to expect him to be regularly late—it was, he lamented, his besetting sin. Repentance, however, did not change his behavior. He had been late writing a letter ending a relationship with Senator Elliott's daughter, late writing a formal letter for the engagement with his fiancée, and he was late for one of the first church services at Bryan Neck. Friends rebuked him without success. His warmth and good humor, however, covered a multitude of such sins, and those who knew him came in time to overlook what would otherwise have appeared as negligence.[2]

Thomas Clay, with his long-standing concern for the religious instruction of slaves, played an important role in the call of John to be the pastor at Bryan Neck, and it was to his home, Richmond-on-the-Ogeechee, that John went on his arrival in Bryan County. Richmond was an unusually handsome plantation. Frederick Law Olmsted, the distinguished New York landscape architect, visited the plantation on one of his southern journeys and described with enthusiasm the beauty of the place. After passing through the settlement, where Clay had constructed neat cottages on each side of the avenue, Olmsted approached the plantation house. On either side of the avenue, "at fifty feet distant, were rows of old live-oak trees, their branches and twigs slightly hung with a delicate fringe of gray moss, and their dark, shining, green foliage meeting and intermingling naturally but densely overhead." Olmsted stopped his horse and held his breath, for, he wrote, "I have hardly in all my life seen anything so impressively grand and beautiful." He rode on and found a circular courtyard and the "owner's mansion," surrounded by an "irregular plantation of great trees," with one oak that was seven feet in diameter. What Olmsted found was a home well known to Charles and Mary, one where during the coming years they would be frequent visitors.[3]

John arrived at Richmond as a young man about to be married to Jane Dunwody, a family friend. Her maternal grandfather, James Smith, had ridden with Charles's father on his fateful hunt in 1805 and now divided his time between his plantations in the low country and his home near Marietta in "Cherokee Georgia." Her uncle, John Dunwody, moved between his handsome new mansion in Roswell and his Liberty County plantation Arcadia. In December 1840 he visited the Clays at Richmond and made inquiries about the character of the young minister. Dunwody wrote his widowed sister:

> I find he is much beloved by all his congregation. . . . She cannot find a more suitable person; and she will be in one of the best societies in this or any other country. . . . I had a confidential conversation with Capt. Jones. He is much pleased with the prospect of his son's happiness associated with your daughter.[4]

The wedding was held in February 1841, and in this way the Jones family became more closely connected to the Dunwodys and the family of James Smith.

The wedding of his oldest living son was an important moment for Joseph Jones. The captain was growing older, and the cemetery behind the Retreat plantation house now held not only two wives but also fourteen children. During the preceding decade, he and his wife, Elizabeth, had buried four of their little ones beside the four of Mary Maybank Jones and the six of Sarah Anderson Jones. And of their ten living children, the oldest were growing up and moving out of the parental home. So Joseph was beginning to see the shadows of his own life lengthen, and he knew that the time was not too far in the future when he would join those behind the Retreat in his own silent grave. John's wedding made Joseph think of such matters, and within a year, under John's gentle urging, Joseph had a conversion experience.[5]

Joseph's conversion, together with that of William Maxwell, which had taken place a few months earlier, was a cause of great rejoicing for Charles and Mary and for all the other members of the family who continued to look to the Retreat as the old home place, the center of gravity that held all the other scattered homes of the family in place and linked them to one another. Joseph's conversion meant for his pious relatives that even in death the family that was centered in the Retreat would not be divided.[6]

Joseph, as the patriarch of the family, had long held to a kind of stoic outlook on life that was deeply marked by the rationalism of the Enlightenment. When John had been converted during his college days, Joseph had written his son that while John had "chosen that *good part*" that could never be taken from him, he was not to be carried away by religious emotions. "Be steady in your course," urged the father, "and don't let your religious feelings become too enthusiastic." "Religion," wrote the patriarch of the Retreat, "never was intended to lessen any of our lawful comforts here but to make us enjoy them more rationally and do all things to the *glory of God*."[7] Joseph's own conversion did not change these perspectives, or the way he managed the Retreat and his other business affairs, but his conversion did strengthen the side of his nature that was tender and generous toward family and friends and that made many not only respect him but also love him. But of course, Joseph still expected obedience where obedience was due. And he would still act decisively when his will was challenged.

Joseph announced that he wanted to join the Bryan Neck church, although it was more than twenty-five miles from the Retreat. Two other wealthy planters indicated that they too wanted to join. Charles preached the sermon on the day they gathered in the little church, and he took for his text Jesus' admonition: "Lay not up for yourselves treasures upon earth, where moth and rust doth corrupt, and where thieves break through and steal. But lay up for yourselves treasures in heaven, where neither moth nor rust doth corrupt, and where thieves do not break through nor steal. For where your treasure is, there will your heart be also." The text was familiar, but perhaps it made some who heard it turn their thoughts toward those who lived in the settlements. For the little cluster of whites who gathered in the Bryan Neck Presbyterian Church that day owned well over one thousand slaves, who constituted much of their treasure on earth.[8]

Following the sermon the elders of the church met to examine the applicants for membership. "The meeting of session," wrote John, "was most solemn, interesting and affecting. Mr. Stiles asked father to state some particulars touching his conversion, and as father answered for himself he was so much overcome by his feelings and tears that utterance was choked. The examinations were all solemn, close, and satisfactory, and all the applications were sustained." Thomas Clay "was deeply interested," and as he went to welcome Joseph to the church, "he fell upon his neck and embraced him in tears." So Clay, the master of Richmond, and Joseph, the master of the Retreat, stood before the congregation embracing and weeping. And one in the congregation who saw Joseph's tears said: "This must be the work of God, for that man never bowed to mortal; and if conquered now, God has done it." At the communion service following the examination, John and Joseph sat side by side at the long table across the front of the church. "I cannot tell you," John wrote his young wife, "how I felt as I sat by father and together we commemorated the love of a Dear Redeemer."[9]

Six weeks after Joseph joined the church, John sold to his father twenty-three slaves who were a part of John's inheritance from his mother. Joseph paid him $8,400 for them, and John wrote a note to himself: "This morning father and I had a final settlement of our business in the way of slave property—a business for life and I hope not ever to be regretted." John's personality did not lend itself to the management of slaves—he was too easygoing and lacked the personal discipline needed for the efficient use of slave labor. Besides, he had reservations about slavery itself and wondered whether it was not more trouble for white owners than it was worth. So he sold to his father most of those whom he had inherited from his mother, and in this way twenty-three of those who lived in the settlement at the Retreat were not moved from family and friends but continued to live at the place they had come to know as home.[10]

But not only had John inherited slaves from his mother; he had also assumed responsibility for more than thirty slaves whom Jane brought with her into their marriage. After some indecision and investigation, and much advice from his father and brothers and Mary too, he bought Bonaventure, a 2,800-acre plantation on the Medway River, and moved all but the domestic servants to the new settlement he had built on a little knoll where the clouds of mosquitoes were not so thick. A manager was hired to oversee the work of the plantation and to free John from the responsibilities of its immediate supervision.[11]

The purchase of Bonaventure was an indication of the growing wealth of the white families closely connected to the Retreat. Joseph himself had expanded the Retreat so that it now contained more than 4,500 acres, and he had purchased in recent years other valuable tracts and plantations, including the 2,500-acre Laurel View and the 800-acre Lodebar, which he had purchased from William Maxwell. Both Laurel View and Lodebar were near Bonaventure, and both produced fine crops of Sea Island cotton. To these new plantations Joseph had moved families of slaves from the growing numbers who lived at the Retreat.[12]

The number of slaves was also growing at Carlawter and Maybank, as well as at sister Susan's White Oak and Social Bluff. Births exceeded deaths in the settlements by substantial margins, and the number of working hands had passed what was needed for the efficient management of these plantations and their labor force.[13] In addition, Susan, Laura, and Charles Edward had inherited from the children's grandfather Audley Maxwell twenty-two slaves. Susan's husband, Joseph Cumming, managed from Savannah the interests of Susan and the children in Liberty County, but he was in ill health and was not able to do much supervision of the plantations. When he died in 1846, Charles encouraged his sister to buy another plantation where "her people" could be more efficiently managed. After some investigation of various possibilities, Susan purchased nearby Lambert plantation for Laura and Charles Edward.[14]

For fifty years Lambert had been at the center of the Gullah community in Liberty County. Its settlement had been largely isolated from white control except for a visiting manager, and there had developed on the place a fierce independence. Here the early black preachers Mingo and Jack had lived, and here old Shaper had spent much of his time. And here midwives and healers, root doctors, conjurers, and storytellers had practiced their skills and had kept alive memories from a distant homeland. But during the 1830s the plantation had become more difficult to manage. Will had gotten drunk on a regular basis, and Fortune and Toney had been involved in disruptive cases of adultery. But what had been most frustrating for the Lambert trustees had been the actions of Prince, Ned, Summer, John, and Scipio. They had broken into storehouses, stolen provisions, and run away. It was all too much for the trustees, and the decision was made to sell the plantation and its slaves and to put the proceeds in some less troublesome investment, such as the new railroads that were being rapidly built across the state. In this way the settlement at Lambert was broken up, its members scattered among various buyers, and the plantation put on the market.[15]

Not long after Susan bought Lambert, she moved thirty-eight slaves into the old settlement, where Shaper had preached and where Old Lydia had nursed the sick and Scipio had pulled aching teeth with his pliers. Syphax had been sent ahead to repair the cabins that had stood empty between the sale of the Lambert slaves and Susan's purchase of the plantation. Most of those sent to Lambert were slaves who had been inherited from grandfather Maxwell. Among them was twenty-three-year-old William, who was made the new driver for the plantation. For the next twenty years, he would be the leader at Lambert, seeing after much of its cotton and rice production.[16]

Left at White Oak were the grandchildren and great-grandchildren of Old Jupiter and Blind Silvey from Liberty Hall. When White Oak had been split off from Montevideo and Susan's slaves withdrawn from Carlawter, they had gone to the new settlement at White Oak. There Prince had been made the driver, following in the footsteps of his father, Hamlet, his uncle Jupiter, and his grandfather Old Jupiter. With him in the settlement were eight other grandchildren of Old Jupiter and Blind Silvey and ten great-grandchildren.[17]

The growth of the slave families at Carlawter and Maybank meant that Charles and Mary were also feeling pressure for more land. In response, they purchased in 1845 John Dunwody's Arcadia plantation. Located toward the center of the county, not far from Midway Church, Arcadia straddled streams and swamps that were a part of the headwaters for the North Newport. Dunwody had already carefully developed its 1,996 acres, and the plantation was known for the quality of its rice produced on inland swamps. A fine plantation home stood at the end of a straight, oak-lined avenue that ran perpendicular to the main road, which ran west from Midway to the new county seat at Hinesville. The settlement, located close to the road, was to the left of the avenue as one approached the plantation house and helped to provide not only an impressive entrance but also, for those who lived there, easy access to a wider world. Altogether Arcadia represented a splendid addition to Charles and Mary's estate, and while it would never be home for them in the way Montevideo and Maybank were home, it was to provide significant income for them and their children during the coming years.[18]

Charles and Mary moved thirty-one slaves from Carlawter to the settlement at Arcadia in January 1846. The central family in the move, and the one that remained at Arcadia during the various shuffling of people during the coming years, was the family of Jack's brother Robin. This family was to lay the foundation for a community at Arcadia that lasted long after freedom came. Stepney, Daddy Robin's only son, was named by Charles to be the new driver at Arcadia, a position he held until the disruptions of war and then resumed in a radical new form after the war's end.[19]

Such moves as those to Laurel View and Lodebar, Lambert and Arcadia not only demonstrated once again the arbitrary power of whites, but also made Sundays an even more important time for those who lived in the settlements. Sundays provided an opportunity for separated families to gather at Midway or North Newport and have the day together. Because there were morning and afternoon services and lessons, the whole day could be spent at church. Simple meals brought from the settlements would be eaten in the early afternoon, and there would be much visiting among those who had been forced apart. So the very act of going to church was a means of resisting the power of whites to separate families and to control the lives of the black men and women of Liberty County.

If the wealth of the white families connected to the Retreat grew during these years, the fortunes of the younger generation did not immediately flourish with regard to romance and marriage. Charles Berrien—the oldest son of Joseph and

Elizabeth Screven Jones—married Marion Susan Anderson in 1843. The marriage was apparently happy enough, but Marion had an unstable side to her personality that would later, under stress, result in bizarre and criminal behavior. As for Charles Berrien, he had been and evidently remained something of a mother's boy. He lacked his father's drive and business acumen, and he would never be as successful in planting and other business activities as his younger brothers Henry Hart and James Newton. But what he lacked in success he made up for in pomposity. Being well connected became the primary source of his identity, shaping not only the way he saw himself but also the way he saw and judged others.[20]

The day after Charles Berrien married Marion, his sister Evelyn married Marion's brother Joseph Anderson. Evelyn—who had traveled with Charles, Mary, and the children to the North in 1839—was a favorite of family and friends. She possessed a gentle and affectionate manner and enjoyed the company of many friends. But she was in poor health and had been most of her life. Her trip to the North had been in large part an attempt to gain strength and put on weight, but she was frail when she married. And the man she married, like his sister, had an unstable side to his personality. His instability later led to alcoholism and probably to opium addiction, and the misery that would come his way would serve as a warning to all who knew him.[21]

Of all the children of Joseph and Elizabeth Screven Jones, none was more attractive in spirit than James Newton Jones. He had a kind disposition, he looked for the best in others, and, when there were disagreements between friends and family, he sought to be a mediator and reconciler. Moreover, others looked to him as a responsible person who cheerfully sought to do what was best for his family and friends. About a year after the marriages of his brother and sister he became engaged to Mary King, daughter of Roswell and Julia. Mary was, as Betsy described her, "gay as a lark and at the head of all mischief and fun." She admired James, thought he would make a good husband, and said yes when he proposed. The trouble was that she did not love him. He was perhaps too responsible, too agreeable, and too much of a reconciler for her lively spirit. Julia pleaded with her daughter as Mary began to waver and to wonder whether she had made a mistake in becoming engaged to James. Julia said that affection built upon a foundation of respect and esteem "must be productive of happiness." But such parental advice did no good, and Mary King broke the engagement. Julia had to write the letter to James Newton telling him of Mary's decision. "I have a singular letter from Mrs. K to show you," he wrote his sister Mary Jones. "Thanks to a merciful providence," he confessed, "I am able calmly to bear what I once thought I never would."[22]

"Is not Cousin Mary King's conduct *scandalous*," wrote Charles Edward Maxwell. A solemn and sacred commitment had been made and then broken. "I cannot approve or justify that which I honestly believe to be wrong," wrote Mary Jones to her friend Julia. But she assured her that she had no "feeling of ill will or unkindness" to young Mary and that, in spite of the pain, the relationship between the families would not be damaged. In four years Mary would marry Charlton Henry Wells, a handsome young physician, a graduate of Dartmouth and the College of Physicians and Surgeons in New York. It would be six years before a bruised James Newton Jones married the attractive daughter of a neighboring planter. Both marriages would be happy, and both would be short.[23]

Henry Hart Jones was the third child of Joseph and Elizabeth Screven Jones. He possessed in large measure those qualities of his father lacking in Charles Berrien—a quick mind, great energy, and a determined will. As a college student in Athens, he fell in love with Laura Maxwell—as well he might, for of all the women associated with the Retreat, she was not only the most beautiful but also the one possessed with the most playful spirit and the most winsome personality. Like her Aunt Betsy and her cousin Mary King, she loved to tease and to laugh and to tell stories on herself and on friends and family that revealed in humorous ways the foibles and pretensions of the human heart.[24] So it was not surprising that Henry fell in love with her; he was one of many. He told her that he loved her, and she evidently listened to him and wondered what it might be like to be married to him. But for two years he said nothing to Laura's mother, Susan, about his feelings, confiding only to his sister Mary Jones, who, as always, was ready to give advice. Finally he wrote from school in Athens, requesting permission to begin a "correspondence" with Laura that would mean an engagement. Laura, he wrote his sister Mary, responded "in quite a kind and open manner, in which she announced the decision of her Mother with reference to our correspondence." Susan had said no. "Tell Henry," she had said, "I think it best to defer the consideration of the matter until his course of study is completed; he is very young and the delay will not be hurtful, but rather beneficial."[25]

The response was kind and, as with the best of southern manners, it allowed Henry to hear the decision as a practical matter and not as a personal affront that would rupture relations within the family. But as so often with southern manners, Susan's answer also evidently concealed deeper and more troubling matters. The problem was not that Laura was Henry's first cousin once removed, but that Henry at a very young age already had two children by a slave woman in the settlement. She was a mulatto, apparently very attractive and no older than Henry. While much about the character of their relationship (even her name) was hidden behind the protective screen of southern society, one thing was clear

—he was a white male, son of a powerful planter, and she was a vulnerable young woman, the slave of a powerful planter. Power and its abuse were fundamental factors in the relationship, even if there had been an element of consent on her part. She, after all, was a slave in a system that demanded obedience.[26]

By the time Henry finally wrote asking permission to begin a "correspondence" with Laura, he had apparently ended the relationship with the young woman in the settlement. And he had had a conversion experience, which, he later wrote Mary Jones, saved him from "a terrible career of dissipation and wickedness" that "would have cast a blight upon our family and name." During the coming years, he tried to treat the slave woman and his slave children with the respect of a kind master—as we shall see, their relationship was to be extremely complex and difficult to grasp. But once again, certain things were clear—she would become his slave, and his two children would become his slaves. No kindness could overcome the harsh and bitter reality of such a situation, and no respect could penetrate the boundaries that separated a white master from his slave children and their mother.[27]

Two years after having receiving the "no" in regard to Laura, Henry married Abigail Sturges Dowse. Her older brother had been the roommate of John Jones in Athens, and her father was a wealthy planter in Richmond County near Augusta. Henry and Abigail would be married for forty-seven years, until his death in 1893. They would have a happy marriage, although six of their eleven children would die in infancy or as young children. Abigail apparently accepted with equanimity Henry's slave children and their mother in the settlement at Lodebar, where they all lived. And when the slave mother married a man from the Mallard Place, Abigail, as we shall see, helped to prepare a remarkable wedding.[28]

Three weeks after Henry and Abigail married in May 1846, Henry's sixteen-year-old sister Emma eloped with a young Savannah physician, Stephen Harris. Emma was a headstrong young woman, self-centered and used to getting her way. When she failed to get her father's permission to marry Harris, the young couple secretly left the Retreat at night. They made their way quietly through its gates, hurried down the sandy avenue through the shadows of its old oaks, and raced past Midway on their way to Savannah, where they were married. The news of their secret flight and marriage came to the Jones family like the sudden news of a child's death. Only this was the news of the betrayal of parental trust and affection. Joseph was stunned, for the act seemed to him a selfish disregard for the feelings of a father who had shown his child nothing but kindness and love. Even more, the flight and the marriage had been a challenge to Joseph's authority and to the ordered ways of the Retreat; it seemed an impulsive, immature, and dangerous abandonment of restraint and subordination in the quest for self-satisfaction. As such, Emma's action seemed a deep treachery deserving not only condemnation but also banishment from the affections and company of her family.[29]

To be sure, some tried to temper the feelings of outrage. Julia King wrote Mary Jones from Roswell, where she was visiting in the upcountry. The news, Julia said, "came to me like a clap of thunder and of all persons in the world I should have thought that Emma would have been the very last to have taken such a step." Julia felt "most deeply for her parents always kind and indulgent." They were in sorrow now, and Julia thought that Emma's troubles were sure to come. But the past, said Julia, cannot be mended, and a "state of enmity is a state of misery." Julia reminded her friend Mary of Jesus' words to the woman caught in adultery: "Does no man condemn her, then neither do I. Go and sin no more."[30]

Mary Jones would have nothing to do with such counsel or reasoning. She saw the sorrow in her father's eyes and the deep embarrassment and pain caused by the rashness of her young half-sister. Three months after the elopement, she wrote Betsy: "Dear father still looks badly and has no appetite. I fear that he will never recover from the affliction brought upon him by that wicked child. Ah! Few surely know the depths of sorrow and misery produced by this affair and I look upon those who apologize for her conduct as upholding disobedience, ingratitude, and deception." And Joseph took out his will and added a codicil. To my daughter Emma, he wrote, I bequeath five dollars, "with the will and intent that she shall not inherit any more of my property real or personal, on account of clandestinely at night running way with and marrying S. N. Harris contrary to my will, wish, and advice, she being a minor and under parental control."[31]

In the middle of October 1846, not long after having changed his will, Joseph left his summer home in Walthourville for his weekly visit to the Retreat. He conferred, as was his custom, with Pulaski and saw after other business, and prepared to leave. Mom Sylvia walked with Joseph to the gate, where his buggy waited. Van Buren, a ten-year-old who was working around the house, ran ahead to open another gate. As Joseph began to drive the buggy away from the house, his walking cane slipped from the boot of the buggy into a rear wheel, and its clatter frightened the horse. The animal raced away and began kicking back at the buggy. Joseph tried to rein it in, but to no avail. He tried to tear open the back of the buggy to escape but could not get through. As the horse raced toward a sharp turn in the road, Joseph in desperation threw himself out of the buggy toward the grassy edge. The rear wheel caught his hip and spun him around. His head and right side hit the ground with the full force of the racing buggy. Young Van Buren ran up, found his master lying on his back speechless. Nearby the horse, having hit the fence, stood tangled in the harness, looking back at the buggy. Dr. Benjamin King, who had been visiting the sick in the settlement, came rushing to the scene of the accident. He was a local physician, a "confirmed inebriate" and no relation to the Kings of South Hampton.[32] Taking Joseph's arm, he cut it with a lancet, but only a little blood could be drawn. An improvised stretcher was made with a mattress and boards, and Joseph was carefully carried into the drawing room at the Retreat, where he was placed on a mattress on the floor. In the meantime runners were sent to the surrounding plantations and riders went for other doctors and for members of the family.

Charles and Mary were at Maybank enjoying a seafood dinner with their children and with their Aunt Eliza Robarts and cousins Louisa and Mary Robarts when word arrived of the accident. Leaving the children with Mary Robarts, they hurried in the carriage toward the Retreat, with Jack and Gilbert driving. When they finally arrived, they found Charles Berrien, Henry Hart, and James Newton already there, together with their mother, Elizabeth, and friends from several surrounding plantations, all weeping. Joseph was still speechless and almost totally paralyzed. The doctors had now successfully bled him, and they had applied mustard plaster across his chest, on the inner part of his thighs, and on the back of his neck. The plaster was removed and blisters began to form that, it was hoped, would stimulate his system. Charles and Mary immediately took charge—Elizabeth was apparently unable to do much, and Charles Berrien and the other sons were grateful for the arrival of their older sister, who was experienced with nursing the sick.

The next day Joseph rallied in a way that gave hope. But the rally was short, and he soon began to grow weaker. Brother John arrived, as did Roswell King. When William Maxwell, Joseph's oldest friend, came into the room, Joseph looked at him, smiled, and said, "Maxwell." As he grew weaker, the doctors urged that he be blistered on his head. Mary, weeping, took scissors and cut off "his gray and venerable hair." The doctor took the razor "and shaved it smooth, and Mary in pain and weeping put on the blister."

Mary said to Charles, "You must speak to Father on the subject of his soul's salvation—do not delay it a moment longer." Charles roused him up and asked: "Father, my dear Father, is Christ precious to you?" The question "seemed to awaken his mind," and Joseph found strength to answer: "Yes, yes." Charles asked: "Do you put all your trust in Him for salvation?" And Joseph answered, "Yes." Charles told him that "Christ was near to him and would be with him in his hour of affliction." Mary, leaning over her father, said, "Him that cometh unto Christ, he will in no wise cast out."

This exchange was like an "electrical shock" in the parlor. "It brought everyone, black and white, around the bed." The people from the settlement filled the yard and the piazza. Charles told them to "come in one by one and take his right hand and bid him farewell forever." John sat by his father's side and held his wrist so that the shaking might not be too much. And so they came in one by one, men, women, and children. "Good-bye my kind master. Jesus Christ go with you." Some kissed his hand and "most of them wept." Then Pulaski came, "his old and faithful driver." He and Joseph were the same age, had grown up together at Rice Hope, and "were boys together." Now Pulaski "bowed his gray head" on Joseph's hand and "held it there for ten or fifteen minutes in tears of unfeigned sorrow."

The end approached and everyone grew quiet. Charles called on John to pray, and while he prayed, Joseph's "spirit gently took its flight. He fell asleep without a struggle or a groan."

William Maxwell and Roswell King prepared the body for its long sleep. A carpenter made the coffin—a simple and unpretentious one. Friends arrived. Paris, the driver from South Hampton, came "and the Christian man" gave the family "consolation." Plenty James, the driver from old Liberty Hall, also came and offered his condolences. The service was held in the room where Joseph died— the family gathered to the side in the plantation office, friends crowded into the room, and the people from the settlements at the Retreat, at Laurel View, Lodebar, and Carlawter stood on the piazzas and in the yard. The Rev. I. S. K. Axson, the minister at Midway, conducted the service. They sang a few hymns and Axson read from the Ninetieth Psalm: "Lord, thou hast been our dwelling place in all generations."

After the service, the lid was removed and they all said their final good-byes. Charles "put the shroud around him and the winding sheet over his face and the pall covered all." Then Jack and Pulaski, Cato and Stepney, and Sylvia's sons Cuffee and Sandy came and took the coffin out of the parlor and across the back piazza and down the steps. There Charles and William Maxwell "took up the head, John and Charles Berrien, the body, and Henry and James the feet and with slow steps" they bore him to his "house of silence" where two wives and fourteen children awaited him. After a prayer, they lowered him into the grave, and Pulaski took up a shovel and "commenced to cover his master's grave."[33]

Joseph's death was the end of an era. But it was more. A year after Joseph's death, John wrote his sister Mary: "The thought of never meeting him again in those familiar places is a source of bitter, constant anguish."[34] It was as if the gravity that had held a little world together had suddenly been cut off and the Retreat could no longer exert its attractive force on the lives of all those who had looked to it as in some way their home and dwelling place. At an important personal level Charles and Mary could hear in Joseph's last rattling breaths this breaking with place—a sound heard as well by John, Eliza Robarts, and other members of the family. Now the seductive calls of railroad whistles and new places could be heard more clearly and forcefully. To be sure, there would be continuing attachments to Liberty County and to an extended family. During the next fifteen years Montevideo—and to a lesser extent Maybank—would take the place of the Retreat as the old home place for many in the Jones family. But with Joseph gone the old ties would never be so strong, for such was the power of his personality and the character of the old patriarchal order that he embodied.

The whites, of course, were not the only ones who could hear in the death rattles of Joseph the sound of change. Those who came up from the settlement to see Joseph as he lay bruised and dying came not only to see "old master" spread out on the parlor floor but also to witness a critical moment in their own lives and in the life of the settlement. When they came one by one to shake his hand, their tears and their good-byes flowed no doubt from many sources and for many reasons, but surely they flowed most profusely for themselves and for their own waiting good-byes. As they shook Joseph's dying hand, they shook a hand that had never been offered to them in its strength and vitality—Joseph, after all, had thought a handshake with a slave suggested an undue familiarity and was an invitation to insubordination. His hand had been for ruling and not for shaking. So they came one by one, and they took his hand in theirs so that now at the end they could grasp his weak hand in their strong hands. Now finally Joseph could feel their calluses and know in touching them all the labor and sorrows of their lives. Yet this taking of his hand was not so much a moment of triumph for those who lived in the settlement as it was a moment of truth telling, a moment of saying how things had been and how things were. For they took his hand with the bitter knowledge that this man, who had controlled their lives in the past, also controlled them in his looming death. His written will would largely shape their future as his iron will had shaped their past. So tears came, and good-byes were said, and Pulaski buried his old head in Joseph's hand and perhaps remembered the past and thought about the future.

Almost five years later, John brought to the Retreat a new portrait of Joseph. No other white was there, and the settlement had been greatly reduced in numbers. He opened the portrait in the parlor, "in that very room," he wrote Mary, "in which our dear father breathed his last, and it was deeply solemn and sad. It seemed as if he had come back again. I called in Momma and old Pulaski." Mom Sylvia came to view the portrait, but Pulaski was elsewhere. John left for awhile, and when he came back he found Pulaski "bending over the picture in a most solemn attentive manner, and as I entered the room he exclaimed, 'Massa know me, but he wont talk to me. He see me, he know me, but he wont speak to me.'" The old man went out and gathered the people and brought them all in to see the likeness. "And they all evinced in a very quiet manner," wrote John "a remarkable degree of veneration and affection for their deceased master." Pulaski, the old driver who with Joseph had supervised the building of the Retreat, looked until he wept, and said to John: "We are so thankful that you brought old master to see us."[35] Joseph had finally become an old master who could no longer speak or give commands but only see.

20

THE RETREAT II

A little more than a year before Joseph's death, Charles received an invitation to a meeting in Charleston, the old center of fierce opposition to the religious instruction of slaves. As he read the invitation, it no doubt brought back memories of his visit ten years earlier. In 1835 the city had been in an uproar over abolitionist materials sent through the mails, and Whitemarsh Seabrook had launched a bitter personal attack against Charles and Thomas Clay. Henry Laurens Pinckney and Judge Charles Jones Colcock had told Charles that the opposition to the religious instruction of slaves was the work of an "Infidel Party." This party, they had agreed, was rooted in a remnant of Deism among some of the planters and was associated with the old curmudgeon Thomas Cooper at South Carolina College.

With such memories, Charles read the remarkable invitation he had received. A group of leading citizens of the city was inviting "a considerable number of gentlemen" to a meeting in Charleston on the religious instruction of slaves. The invitation had gone only to "South Carolinian gentlemen"—that little club of planters, merchants, and professionals that dominated the Palmetto State. The only exception had been "two gentlemen of Georgia"—Charles Jones and Thomas Clay, the very two whom Seabrook had denounced! They were now being invited to take part in the deliberations and to "furnish their views" because of "their known interest in the subject, and their long-continued personal exertions in this department of benevolence." The invitation suggested that during the preceding ten years some important changes had taken place among Charleston's leaders as they thought about the South's "peculiar institution" and the place and role of religious instruction of slaves in southern society. After consulting with Thomas Clay, Charles decided to make the trip and participate in the meeting.[1]

He left Liberty County for Charleston in early May 1845. Traveling with him was Dr. William McWhir, Charles's old teacher in Sunbury. McWhir had decided that while he had not received an invitation, he would arrive at the meeting and trust that no one would object to an eighty-six-year-old Presbyterian minister hobbling in from Georgia. They stopped in Bryan County at Richmond-on-Ogeechee and were joined by Thomas Clay. The three went on to Savannah and took a ship for Charleston.[2]

Once again as he sailed into Charleston harbor, Charles could see the fine homes and church steeples that stood as proud symbols of the city's fabled wealth and influence. But the city that his ship approached in 1845 was no longer the largest or the richest in the South. During the years that Charles had been preaching at the stations and visiting in the settlements of Liberty County, Charleston had shown little growth. A former resident of the city, now living in New Orleans, soon wrote of the change: "When the Crescent City consisted of a few huts on the low lands of the Mississippi, her sister of the Palmetto State was reveling in the riches of foreign commerce, and in all affluence and property. But now the vision is changed. The noble city on the banks of the Cooper and Ashley looks back to the past with lingering regret," while the Louisiana port moves ahead.[3]

Charles knew, however, that if Charleston had lost its commercial preeminence, it still claimed to be the Capital of the South because of its cultural and political leadership. Moreover, it continued to play a critical role in the slave trade, for the slave markets in the city were doing a thriving business in the sale of low-country slaves for an expanding southern frontier.[4] Charles could remember that when he had been a student of McWhir's in Sunbury, slavery had still been largely confined to the Atlantic seaboard. But now as he sailed into Charleston harbor in 1845, the South's "peculiar institution" was already being established in distant Texas, and slaves in great numbers were being carried to the rich new lands of an expanding South. Charles knew only too well that this steady expansion of slavery, with its appetite for more and more black laborers, was already beginning to destabilize the settlements of the low country and was a growing threat to the stability of the nation itself.[5]

The meeting was held in the Depository on Chalmers Street. As Charles, McWhir, and Clay walked down the short cobblestone street in the center of the city, they passed the Ryan Slave Market, a grim, jail-like building. That day there was within its confines a "likely" group of black men, women, and children being offered for sale. Among them were "Four prime Fellows, field hands and good axemen"; "2 Women, field hands, mother and daughter, very likely"; "a young woman, seamstress and ladies' maid, with her son, 6 years old"; "a colored girl, 17 years old"; "2 single girls, 9 and 12 years old"; "a single Boy, 10 years old"; and "an elderly woman, good cook, washer and ironer." Perhaps some of them saw the three Georgians as they walked to their meeting.[6]

Those who gathered at the Depository also composed a "likely" group, but of a different sort. Presiding was U.S. Senator Daniel Huger, a Unionist who had opposed John C. Calhoun during the Nullification Controversy of the 1830s. With Huger was Joel Poinsett, a former congressman and another Unionist. Educated in England, Poinsett had had a distinguished diplomatic career, had traveled through Russia and South America, and had brought back from Mexico the flower that would bear his name—the poinsettia.[7]

Charles and his Georgia friends could see, however, that Unionists were by no means the only political leaders who had come to the meeting. Robert Barnwell Rhett, the "fire-eater," had come to the city from his James Island plantation. He was to be elected to the Senate after Calhoun's death, and was to earn the dubious distinction of being the "Father of the Secession." The brilliant young lawyer C. G. Memminger also arrived. Memminger's political star was only beginning to rise; at its zenith he would become secretary of the treasury for the Confederate States of America. With them was Charles's friend Robert Barnwell, president of South Carolina College, later to serve as a Confederate senator.[8]

In addition to these political figures, the Georgians saw what looked like a gathering of Charleston's exclusive St. Cecilia Society—Charles Cotesworth Pinckney, Daniel Ravenel, Charles Lowndes, Thomas Pinckney Alston, Grimké Drayton, and Drayton Grimké. They were all wealthy planters, owners of many slaves and many plantations, whose families had long been prominent in the state and had provided leading patriots during the Revolution.[9]

Among those walking into the meeting room were some of the state's most influential clergy. The Episcopal bishop Steven Elliott arrived with the Reverend William Barnwell, the pastor of St. Peters Episcopal Church in Charleston. Both were longtime friends with Charles, and Elliott had stayed at Montevideo on more than one occasion. William Capers, the Methodist minister whom Charles had met years earlier in Columbia, hurried into the room. He had only recently returned from Louisville, Kentucky, where he had been a vigorous participant in the organizing convention of the Methodist Episcopal Church, South. In informal discussions, he could tell how southern Methodists had formed their own church because of their differences with northern Methodists over slavery. As the primary organizer of the Methodist mission to slaves in South Carolina, Capers knew more than anyone in the state about the religious instruction of slaves. Richard Fuller, an influential Baptist minister from Beaufort, came into the gathering having also just arrived in Charleston—he had come straight from the first meeting of the Southern Baptist Convention. Like the Methodists, the Baptists had divided over slavery. Thomas Smyth from Second Presbyterian and Benjamin Gildersleeve, the editor of the *Charleston Observer*, represented, together with Charles and McWhir, the Presbyterian clergy.[10]

So it was a distinguished group that gathered, and Charles must have found it a remarkable group in light of his visit to the city in 1835.

They met for three days as the slave sales went on down the street at the Ryan Slave Market. Robert Barnwell Rhett, Daniel Ravenel, Robert Barnwell, and Senator Huger led an animated discussion. Was religious instruction of slaves in the best interest of the South? If so, what were the best means of providing it? Thomas Grimké reported on his personal practices as a master—he was a model of paternalistic benevolence much like Thomas Clay at Richmond-on-Ogeechee. Rhett told how he was developing piety and good order among his James Island slaves. And reports were read from other planters about how they were providing religious instruction to their slaves.[11]

On the second night, Charles delivered an address "in a very full, clear, and impressive manner." Gildersleeve, reporting on the address, noted that "no individual in the country [is] better acquainted with the subject in its history, its details and its practical bearings than he," and that his "opinions have more weight" than those of anyone else "with the entire Christian Community of every denomination." As if to confirm Gildersleeve's judgment, Charles was asked the next day to write the report of the proceedings. He was given the letters that had been gathered from different planters, and with his notes and other materials he returned to Liberty, where he compiled a seventy-one-page pamphlet on the proceedings and the reports of planters. Meanwhile the sales continued on Chalmers Street as "prime fellows," "likely women," "colored girls," and black children—all objects of white benevolence from down the street—were brought forward, examined, sold, and led away.[12]

The report that Charles wrote, and which was signed by Huger and other Charleston members of a "standing committee," was a rehearsal of familiar themes for Charles. At the heart of the report was the insistence that religious instruction of slaves was both a duty of white southern Christians and an effort that was in the long-term best interests of the South and the nation. The sure results of such efforts were clear: good and obedient slaves, kind and pious masters.

The importance of the Charleston meeting, however, far exceeded the familiar positions advocated in its report. Charles realized that the gathering itself and the character of its participants meant that Charleston, the old center of opposition to religious instruction, had been largely won to the cause he had so long advocated. He found the meeting and the reports gathered "truly astonishing."

The religious instruction of the slaves, rather than being seen as a threat to the white South, now appeared to the most conservative elements of southern society to be a religious duty and a necessary strategy for the future development of a southern homeland. Behind such a shift were religious and cultural changes that had been at work across the South. Evangelical Protestantism was becoming ever more deeply embedded in southern society, providing a worldview and a language that would be powerful ideological weapons for whites in the defense of the South and its peculiar institution. Charles may have realized, as he reviewed his notes of the meeting and put together the report, that during the coming years the primary advocates for the religious instruction of slaves would be increasingly located not in the hinterland of Liberty County but in the Capital of the South. In such a setting the cause's ideological functions could be more fully claimed and utilized. So even as Charles was being praised in Charleston, he could feel a shift in the character of his work in Liberty County. He was no longer a pioneer in a suspect enterprise but the respected leader of a cause that had been adopted by the South's most suspicious and influential establishment.[13]

For three years following the Charleston meeting, Charles continued his missionary work, and his reputation continued to grow among whites, South and North, so that some whites began to refer to him as "The Apostle to the Negro Slave." But Charles had apparently begun to think of himself in different terms. As he had visited in the settlements year after year, as he had taught and preached, baptized and married, comforted the sick, and buried the dead, he had slowly come to think of himself more as a parish minister than as a missionary. "I have long since settled it in my mind," he told Liberty County planters in 1845, "that the place of the Minister is with the people of his charge: and *wherever* they can and are willing to meet with him, there should he be, and quietly and naturally adapt himself to circumstances." Over the years Charles had made a strenuous effort to be "with the people of his charge" in a way that would allow him to know them well and for them to know him and, he hoped, to trust him as one who was genuinely concerned for their welfare. When he had first started his work, after his years of study in the North, he had felt more like a missionary in an alien place. Liberty County had been his home, but he had had a keen sense of the distance that separated him from those who lived in the settlements, and he had known that he had much to learn about the life and ways of the settlements. By 1845, however, the settlements had become more familiar and the roads to the settlements well known and well traveled. Charles felt that he had become a pastor who knew his people by name and who could see around him the signs of his ministerial labors.[14]

Over the years of his work the preaching stations and Sunday schools had evolved from experiments to established institutions. Neat buildings had been built at the stations—the trustees of the Lambert Estate had been generous in contributing funds, and the Presbyterians had built a little meetinghouse at Pleasant Grove for its growing Sunday school. By 1845 the Sunday schools—at Walthourville and Sunbury, at Midway and North Newport, at Jonesville, Gravel Hill, Pleasant Grove, and Colonel's Island—had been faithfully sustained for years by planters and their families, who taught weekly classes for their black students. It had not been unusual for five hundred to six hundred, sometimes seven hundred students to be in the schools on a given Sabbath. And because most of the students had been children, growing numbers of the slave population could recite the Lord's Prayer, knew the Ten Commandments and the Apostles Creed, and could answer the questions of the catechism. Moreover, the Sunday schools had helped to prepare many for membership in the churches of the county, as had Toney Stevens and the watchmen at Midway and North Newport. So Charles watched gratefully as the number of inquirers, of those seeking admission to the church, grew steadily and the church rolls expanded.[15]

A census was taken in the county in 1845, and Charles thought the time was right for a careful study of the black membership in the churches. In 1846 he visited a "large majority" of the plantations (in all but the piney woods sections of the county) in order "to obtain on the plantations from the drivers, watchmen, or owners, an accurate return of all the Negroes who *now are*, or *have been*, in membership with our churches." He visited or made inquiries at 125 plantations, of all sizes. He found 41 plantations on which whites resided only part of the year and 60 "upon which *no white persons reside at all the year around*." As a consequence, he noted, "entire neighbourhoods of plantations" in the heart of the county "are wholly abandoned, not having a *resident* white person upon them from May to November; nor is there in the whole District one regularly organized and active *Patrol*." Under such circumstances, Charles thought, "the people, if they were so disposed, have ample opportunity of doing evil, and our surprise should be, not that there are here and there transgressors, but that the wicked and unprincipled among them do not indulge themselves more frequently." Charles thought that there was "unquestionably an influence for good resting upon the people," and that the planters "should be grateful for it, and pray and labour that it may continue and be of the right kind."[16]

As he had made his rounds to the different plantations, Charles found one of the "influences for good" came from the character of the drivers in the county. He was able to identify seventy drivers who were members of the different churches, with sixty of them being in good standing. Among them were many of the watchmen and leaders in the churches, including Paris from South Hampton, Cato from Montevideo, Pompey from the Mallard Place, Plenty James from old Liberty Hall, Caesar from the George Howe plantation, and Peter from the LeConte's Woodmanston. They, with other drivers, constituted a powerful and influential group within the largely isolated Gullah community. Because drivers held so much power in the settlements, and because they were "exposed to peculiar and strong temptations and have great opportunities of leading improper lives," there should be, said Charles, much gratitude that they are "in so remarkable a manner brought into connection with the churches, and under the restraints of Christian profession and principle."[17]

In conducting his church census, Charles wrote down—and Laura copied in a neat hand—the name of each plantation canvassed and the name of each church member on the plantation and the name of the church where that member belonged. What he found was as follows:

Sunbury Baptist	161
North Newport Baptist	543
Midway Congregational	377
Pleasant Grove Presbyterian	31
Hinesville and Mount Olivet Methodist	21
Congregations outside the county	6
Females	693
Males	446

Charles noted that one denomination usually "took the lead" on a plantation and followed the leadership of owners and drivers. Members were influenced as well by "convenience." (Most of the church members at the Retreat belonged to the nearby North Newport, while most of the church members from the Mallard Place, which was next to Midway, were Congregationalists.) In all the churches membership required not only an extended period as an "inquirer" but also an examination by church officers to judge a person's Christian convictions—did a candidate put all of his or her trust in Jesus Christ and his righteousness? Was a candidate's conversion reflected in changed behavior? Many more people came to church than belonged to church. Only those who had passed through this process became full members who could come to the Lord's Table for communion.[18]

The tax returns for 1844 indicated that there were 4,212 slaves in the district of the county being studied. The church membership was 1,139, which, Charles noted, "embraces about *one-fourth* of the whole number. A very large proportion indeed, and a majority of the adult population." Charles thought few if any regions of the South could claim as church members such a high proportion of its slave population. Even the white population of Liberty County, famous for its Puritan traditions and piety, could not claim such a high percentage of church membership.[19]

Charles believed that church membership, and the conversion experience that was claimed in church membership, was a gift of God as God's Spirit worked in a person's heart and the person made a decision for Christ. But he also thought that certain social factors had contributed to the growth of the churches in Liberty County. No doubt thinking of restless whites pushing toward new frontiers and of what he had seen in the Charleston slave markets, Charles named the stability of the Liberty County population as a positive force for the religious life of the people. Stability provided an opportunity for people—white and black—to nurture their sense of being at home, as well as time to improve their physical surroundings. But home for Charles was also a spiritual and moral resource. For to be genuinely "at home" required, Charles thought, the cultivation of commitments and affections not to abstract ideals but to particular places and to living and breathing human beings. The planters of Liberty County had largely resisted the restlessness of their time, and because Liberty County was their home they had supported and encouraged the religious instruction of the people. And because the people in the settlements had roots in the county and had improving living circumstances, there was, Charles thought, the necessary peace and order needed for the cultivation of their spiritual and moral lives. So Charles concluded: "The moral improvement of every people depends much upon their being in a good degree stationary."[20]

Another positive social factor, Charles thought, in the building up of the churches was the prosperity of Liberty County planters. With their regular incomes, they "are consequently *able* to do more for their people." The "comfort" of the people had improved when prosperous planters had made "some suitable return to those through whose instrumentality" the planters had acquired their wealth. As Charles had made his rounds to the different plantations, he had found that the cabins, the food, and the clothes of the slaves had improved. Slaves now had more opportunities than earlier to till their own gardens, raise their own pigs, sell their eggs and baskets, and make a little money for themselves. More owned their own horses and cows, and some—such as Cassius at Montevideo—even owned their own buggies. Moreover, planters were beginning to see that it was in their own interest to promote the interests and circumstances of their slaves. "The people have something to live for," said Charles, "something to hope for and something to enjoy." Charles observed that on the plantations where the living conditions of the people improved, there was "a greater elevation of character." And he noted that the physical condition of those who lived in the settlements was "an outward evidence of our interest in their spiritual state which others will immediately inquire into and judge us by."[21]

So Charles looked around him in Liberty County, and he saw good things had happened during the years of his ministry. He was not one, however, to overlook difficulties, or to evaluate and not warn. There was much work to do for the religious instruction of those who lived in the settlements, many difficulties had to be faced, and many of the attitudes and practices of the planters had to change. And among the difficulties that he saw, none was more pressing than this: those who lived in the settlements all represented money to the planters. They are, Charles told his friends and neighbors, "in the language of scripture, 'your money.' They are the source, the means of your wealth; by their labour do you obtain the necessaries, the conveniences and comforts of life. The increase of them is the general standard of your worldly prosperity; without them, you would be comparatively poor. They are consequently sought after and desired as property, and when possessed, must be so taken care of and managed as to be made profitable." The consequences, Charles thought, were clear:

> Now, it is exceedingly difficult to use them as money; to treat them as property and at the same time render to them that which is just and equal as immortal and accountable beings, and as heirs of the grace of life, equally with ourselves. They are associated in our business and thoughts and feelings, with labour and interest and gain and wealth. Under the influence of the powerful principle of self-interest, there is a tendency to view and to treat them as instruments of labour, as a means of wealth, and to forget, or to pass over lightly the fact, that they are what they are, under the eye and government of God. There is a tendency to rest satisfied with very small and miserable efforts for their mortal improvement, and to give oneself but little trouble to correct immoralities and reform wicked practices and habits, should they do their work quietly and profitably and enjoy health and go on to multiply and increase upon the earth.

If planters—and Charles clearly included himself among them—faced such dangers because "their people" were "their money," a concomitant danger, Charles thought, also lurked for those who lived in the settlements:

> The difficulty presses in another direction. *The Negroes* themselves, seeing and more than seeing, feeling and knowing, that their owners regard and treat them as "their money"—as *property* only, are inclined to lose sight of their better character and higher interests, and in their ignorance and depravity, to estimate themselves and religion and virtue no higher than their owners do. The saying becomes true, *like master, like servant.*[22]

Charles named in this way the big low-country gator that had always been thrashing around before his pulpit. He acknowledged what must have seemed so obvious to those who sat around the fires in the settlements—that the very character of slavery was deeply and fundamentally hostile to human dignity and welfare. Charles continued to hope, however, that good intentions and benevolent impulses and even the self-interest of planters would be powerful enough to overcome this fundamental hostility, to domesticate the gator and make room for good to be done for those who lived in the settlements. All his careful analysis, all his acknowledgment of the inseparable link between the physical and the spiritual life, and all his labors as a pastor in the settlements did not finally lead him to attack the system, to say with the abolitionists that slavery, with its degradations, must come to an immediate end. The most he was able to do was seek to be a reformer within the system, work to make the system somehow more humane and the life of the slave somehow more bearable. Others, however, as we shall see, would take his work, his reports, and his insights and use them as Charles could never bring himself to do—in a struggle for freedom for all the sons and daughters of Africa who lived in the settlements of Liberty County.[23]

Following his trip to Charleston in 1845, Charles wrote three annual reports for the Liberty County Association for the Religious Instruction of the Negroes. And each year Charles attempted in the reports to evaluate his work and to see whether the time was right to bring this period of his life to a conclusion. The reports for 1845 and 1846 only gave hints of his movement toward a new calling. When he met with the association in January 1848 and gave his report for the preceding year, however, he announced that he had once again accepted a call to become a professor at Columbia Theological Seminary. In contrast to his decision in 1836 to go to Columbia, Charles now seemed ready and even eager to go. His health had suffered a setback after Joseph's death, and his nighttime visits to the settlements had been curtailed. Moreover, the earlier, experimental character of his work in Liberty County had clearly come to an end. He was no longer swimming against the stream of southern white opinion but was sailing with an increasingly powerful current flowing in defense of human slavery. And there were more personal factors as well that influenced his decision—factors that were rooted once again in family, in his commitment to those whom he loved, and in his understanding of home.

The death of Joseph Jones in October 1846 had not only been an emotional trauma for his family, it had also set in motion forces that significantly altered attachments to home for Charles and Mary. Joseph's will, as one would expect, was carefully drawn, and its provision divided his accumulated wealth among his heirs. The 4,500 acres of the Retreat were divided between his sons James Newton and Edwin West, with the widow Elizabeth and the minor children having the right to live in the Retreat house and to a share of the plantation's income as long as they remained single. Charles Berrien, who had already received land from his father, was given 300 acres adjoining his plantation near Walthourville. Henry Hart was given Lodebar, while Laurel View went to his younger brother Andrew Maybank. The Walthourville summerhouse and an adjoining plantation, Wild Woods, went to the widow Elizabeth. "To my beloved daughter Mary," Joseph left the two lots in Sunbury where the old Jones place had been and where Mary and Charles's grandmother, Mary Sharpe (Jones) Low lay buried. "I would leave my daughter more," Joseph had written, but he had already given her Carlawter and a division of her mother's slaves. The same was true for John—he received some land in a distant county, and Joseph said he would have given "my dear son more" except that he had already made a settlement of slaves with him (including Mom Sylvia, who had remained at the Retreat) and had helped him purchase Bonaventure. Furthermore, John had received a "liberal education together with a profession" and was well situated in life. Other relatives—including Charles, sisters Susan and Betsy, and aunt Eliza Robarts—received gifts of money. Joseph's daughter Emma was allotted her $5 for "clandestinely at night running away with and marrying S. N. Harris." As for the 208 slaves who were still owned by Joseph, they were to be evenly divided— along with railroad and bank stock, cash, and other possessions—among the primary heirs (Elizabeth and all her children except Emma). Charles was made attorney for Elizabeth, who was the executrix. This meant that he had responsibility for a division of all those who lived at the Retreat settlement, at Laurel View and Lodebar, and at some of the other plantations. The only exceptions were old Pulaski and his wife, Affy. "My faithful servant and old Driver Pulaski and his wife," Joseph had written, were to remain at the Retreat, where Pulaski was to continue as "senior Driver." In addition, the old man who had grown up with Joseph, who had been his "right-hand man" in the development of the Retreat, and who had wept beside his master as Joseph lay dying on the parlor floor— "faithful old Pulaski" was to receive every year "an extra suit of union clothing and six dollars" from the "joint planters of the Retreat."[24]

William Maxwell, with two other planters, carefully appraised the value of each of the slaves: James, a mason, was worth $1,000; Cato's twenty-six-year-old wife Betsy was appraised at $450, his six-year-old daughter Rinah at $200, and his three-year-old son Ned at $150. Charles then divided all 208 of them into eleven lots of approximately equal worth, keeping parents and their nonadult children together, and apportioned them to the heirs. So, ironically, Charles, after having emphasized the importance of stability, played a central role in destabilizing the old settlement at the Retreat—a settlement whose established ways, kinship ties, and sleeping ancestors reached back to Rice Hope plantation and to the days when slave ships were arriving regularly in Savannah and Charleston. Many of the people in the settlement were soon scattered: they loaded oxcarts with their possessions and traveled the sandy roads of the county to new plantations. Others would leave the settlement in the coming years as Joseph's heirs grew up and married and left home with their inheritances following them. Before the terrors of war would break over the land, the settlement at the Retreat would be empty, all the people gone from its familiar surroundings and many of them gone from Liberty County.[25]

Charles's work as the attorney for the executrix had required that he go through Joseph's papers. One day, shortly before the slaves were to be apportioned, he made a surprising discovery. He found that Joseph's oldest son, Joseph Maybank Jones—who had died intestate in 1831 a few weeks after Charles and Mary had married—had received before his death twelve slaves from his father. Joseph had simply kept his son's slaves, and they and the children of the women were included in those appraised and divided into lots. The problem, Charles immediately realized and Savannah lawyers confirmed, was that Joseph was not his son's only heir—all of Joseph Maybank Jones's brothers and sisters alive at the time of his death, including Mary and John, were to be counted heirs. Charles concluded that Joseph Maybank Jones's estate had to be removed from the estate of his father and settled separately. Elizabeth Jones originally agreed to such an arrangement, but with Charles Berrien's encouragement she changed her mind and insisted that the division precede as if the Joseph Maybank Jones papers had not been found. This Charles refused to do. He immediately resigned as attorney for the executrix, and a few days later Mary and her brother John notified their stepmother that they were challenging that part of their father's will that included the slaves of their brother Joseph. Both sides hired lawyers, and the case was headed to court.[26]

This whole matter was deeply distressing for Charles and Mary, as it threatened to disrupt close and intimate family ties. In his will, Joseph had urged a continuation of that "brotherly and sisterly spirit" which had been exhibited among his children during his lifetime. "I doubt not it will be continued," Joseph wrote, after I have been "consigned to that narrow house allotted to frail man."[27] With the exception of Charles Berrien, such was the case among the children of Joseph—Henry Hart, James Newton, Maybank, Evelyn, and the others were too close to

Charles and Mary, they looked to them too often for guidance and counsel and for support when sick, to be alienated from them.

Matters were different, however, with Elizabeth. She had been so retiring, so much in the background during all the comings and goings at the Retreat and during all the decisions about family matters. Her self-confident stepdaughter Mary, only a few years younger than she, had always taken the lead and been outspoken. Even when Joseph lay dying on the parlor floor, it had been Mary and not Elizabeth who had taken over. Mary had been the one who had knelt for hours by her father's head and who had at the end gently shaved his head for the doctor's blister. Now as the widow and executrix, Elizabeth made her presence known, and the tension between her and Mary came into the open. Elizabeth dug in her heels and absolutely refused to acknowledge the estate of Joseph Maybank. And, to make matters worse, when she had a tall obelisk raised over Joseph's grave, she had carved in its marble side the names of all of his children but Mary and John. Mary and her brother were obviously deeply hurt by this attempt to remove them from among the children of Joseph. The legal matters were eventually settled out of court—with Mary and John (and Emma too!) each receiving a part of their brother's estate—but the rupture with Elizabeth never entirely healed. Mary never again referred to her as anything but Mrs. Jones, and Elizabeth on her part remained decidedly cool and distant toward Mary. John, with his affable spirit, soon made peace with Elizabeth, who had been a mother to him in ways she had never been to Mary.[28]

After her brief efforts at self-assertion, Elizabeth once again receded into the background. Even Charles Berrien would turn to Mary and not his mother when there was sickness or trouble in the family.[29] Charles and Mary soon assumed their roles as patriarch and matriarch in the extended Jones family. But first there had to be a clear break with Liberty County. Joseph's death and the troubles associated with his will made it easier for Charles to accept the call to Columbia and for Mary to consent. Their attention and affections were now focused sharply on the younger generation—on Charlie, Joe, and Mary Sharpe—and Columbia offered the opportunity for the children to continue their educations without leaving home for college or a boarding school. Home would now be defined for Charles and Mary in ways that no longer included the Retreat except as a place of memories and occasional visits.

21

COLUMBIA II

Once Charles and Mary had made the decision to go to Columbia, they had the daunting task of preparing for the move. They now owned three plantations that had to be managed, and with the death of Susan's husband, Joseph Cumming, in 1846, Charles also had the responsibility for the management of White Oak, Social Bluff, and Lambert. So as they prepared to leave Liberty County in 1848, Charles had to think first about what he was going to do in regard to the management of these six plantations and the more than 160 slaves who lived upon them. And Mary had to see after all of the special responsibilities that were hers in regard to Montevideo, Maybank, and Arcadia.

The most critical task was finding responsible managers who not only knew how to raise cotton, rice, and provisions but also knew how to direct and see after the needs of those who lived in the settlements. Charles wrote Susan in late spring of 1848 and told her he had secured for White Oak and Lambert the services of two neighboring planters—Thomas Winn Fleming and Peter Winn Fleming—and that William Maxwell had agreed to look after Social Bluff. Charles gave Susan detailed instructions about the management of the plantations and warned that she must be careful and frugal in order to keep from going deeply into debt. Charles Edward was now a student at Princeton, and Susan, who had little business sense and almost no idea about managing a plantation, had to assume responsibilities she had never had before. From now on—even with the managers—she would have to see about plantation ledgers, about selling cotton and rice, and about buying blankets, cloth, shoes, and bacon for the people of the settlements.[1]

As for Montevideo, Charles had been able to secure the services of Thomas Shepard, a friend who owned a small plantation, Grassy Glade, in nearby McIntosh County. Shepard was a member of Midway and had been a supporter of

Charles's work for the religious instruction of the slaves. His piety—as well as his ability to raise cotton and rice and to keep all hands fully occupied—made him, Charles thought, a good manager for Montevideo. Shepard would later manage White Oak as well.[2]

For the management of Arcadia, Charles hired Irwin Rahn, a Jack of all trades. He could raise cotton, rice, and corn, and he could also make bricks and work as a skilled carpenter. He was a member of Midway, and he and his wife had named one of their sons Charles Jones. The child, who had worms, died of congestion shortly after his father took over the management of Arcadia. While pious and skilled in many trades, Rahn lacked the formal education and sensibilities of the Jones family. Neatness, order, cleanliness, and a good diet were not among his most cherished values. He consequently did better at raising cotton and rice at Arcadia than at supplying pork for Daddy Robin and the others who lived in its settlement. And in spite of having the eye of a carpenter, when he looked at the cabins in the settlement, he failed to notice—as Mary later found to her dismay—that some of them had begun to lean and that the floors in some of them were beginning to give way.[3]

Charles felt most confident about the arrangements he made for Maybank. Andrew was a skilled driver, "an intelligent man—and one of principle," and clearly the leader of all those who lived in the settlement by the marsh. Furthermore, William Maxwell had agreed to see after the place, to confer with Andrew, to handle the marketing of the cotton, and to purchase the necessary supplies for the people. He and Betsy were now living in Sunbury, and they would be going to the island on a regular basis to visit and stay at Social Bluff.[4]

While Charles was making these arrangements for the management of the plantations, he continued his weekly preaching and teaching at the stations. He had been forced the year before to give up the part of his work that he most cherished—the weeknight visits to the settlements of the county. The old childhood wound to his lungs that he had received when he was staying with his Aunt Eliza in Greensboro had evidently started to give him trouble. "I laboured under an irritated and inflamed state of the lungs," he had told his neighbors, "which forbid exposure to the night air."[5]

As for the future of the Association for the Religious Instruction of the Negroes in Liberty County, Charles told its members that the work of the association was now up to them. The work, he said, must "be left to your own consciences and to God, and my prayer is that you may not be found wanting." From its inception, the association had involved the efforts of many people—officers had been elected annually, and many men and women had been involved over the years in teaching Sunday schools around the county. But the association itself was, in the words of Rebecca Mallard, "Mr. Jones' association." Charles was the one who gathered the materials and wrote the reports, and he had been the one who had seen that the meetings were held each year and that the invitations had been sent throughout the community. So when he left, the association itself came to an end. No more reports were issued, and no more appeals to the South for the religious instruction of the slaves flowed from Liberty County. The local efforts that the association had sponsored continued, however, now largely under the auspices of the Lambert Estate and under the direction of the Lambert trustees. During the coming years they hired missionaries who would visit in the settlements and preach in the stations, and they began to pay Toney Stevens's owner $30 a year for his labors as the "coloured preacher" for the Midway congregation.[6]

While these various transitions were unfolding, Mary was busy preparing to move her family to Columbia. Clothes had to be selected and packed in trunks; books had to be boxed; decisions had to be made about what household items would make the trip to Columbia with the family; and the plantation houses at Montevideo, Maybank, and Arcadia had to be prepared for the family's long absence. At the same time that Mary was busy with these preparations, she was also busy with her usual routines. Phoebe and Patience were both pregnant and unable to be as helpful as usual. Moreover, Phoebe's youngest child, Richard Baxter, was sickly and demanding much of his mother's attention. His twin brother had died the year before, shortly after his birth, and Richard had struggled to gain weight and strength. In late summer 1848 Mary wrote Laura that the "protracted illness of Phoebe's poor little Richard" occupied much of his mother's time. Patience's "indisposition," on the other hand, had "through a kind Providence" terminated happily, "as she has added a young Patience to her household gifts."[7]

Mary and Charles were trying to decide in the midst of their packing and familiar routines not only about clothes and furniture but also about which servants to carry to Columbia. They did not want to take Phoebe and Patience—although they were Mary's "standbys"—because of their large and growing families. Jack and his wife, Marcia, on the other hand, were free from the responsibilities of a young family, and they also seemed indispensable because Jack managed so much of the household and because Marcia was a good cook. Moreover, Jack, with his good manners and cheerful spirit, had become a polished and elegant servant whose dignified ways added to the comfort of the Jones family and reinforced the family's image of itself. He was, an acquaintance told Charles, "a gentleman of the old school."[8]

For almost forty years Jack had stood beside the dinner table, first at the Retreat and then at Montevideo and Maybank, and had served those who sat around it.

And while serving, he had listened to the conversations of whites who talked as if he were not there. He knew what whites thought of the Gullah people and how blind whites were to what really went on in the settlements and how deaf they were to what was said around evening fires. To be sure, Jack knew Charles and Mary's kindness and their concern for the welfare of the slave and how exceptional they were among whites. But like Buh Rooster, he knew he had to keep a sharp eye out for Buh Fowl-Hawk; and like Buh Rabbit, he knew he had to outsmart Buh Wolf and Buh Alligatur. More than any of the Joneses' slaves, Jack had probed the character of white culture, and he had come to understand the assumptions of Charles and Mary and how they saw the world. They were, he knew, dependent on his good sense and on the work of Patience and Phoebe and all the others who labored for them. So in a strange and ironic reversal of roles, he had a sympathetic—one could almost say paternalistic—attitude toward these needy whites who couldn't get along without him or without all those who sat by settlement fires in the evening. He was consequently more than a "good and faithful servant"—Charles and Mary regarded him as a friend and as an integral part of their household.[9]

Jack and Marcia obviously could not do all the work needed for the Jones family, so Charles and Mary also decided to take with them Phoebe's eighteen-year-old John and ten-year-old Jane. They were being trained to be domestic servants, and their grandfather Jack could not only look after them but also provide them with training that would help—it was hoped—to offset some of the bad influences of Phoebe and Cassius.[10]

While Charles and Mary were making their arrangements for the move to Columbia, other members of their family were also in the midst of leaving the low country. John Jones had already moved to Marietta in northwest Georgia. Not long after Joseph's death he had visited the upcountry, and friends had urged him to make it his home and the field of his ministerial labors. He wrote his sister Mary that he felt "greatly constrained thus to do, from two considerations."

> First, the peculiar importance of this field which is fast becoming the most populous portion of Georgia, and its great and immediate need of the living preacher. Secondly, the climate has been very beneficial to Jane's health. Marietta I think to be the healthiest village in N.W. Georgia, and said to be the most eligible position for a missionary, commanding many stations by Railroad, and many others in riding distance.[11]

By the spring of 1848 John had bought a home in Marietta and had moved his wife, Jane, and their energetic five-year-old son, Dunwody, to the up-country.

Nearby were Jane's grandparents, James and Jane Smith, who had been such close friends to Charles's parents at old Liberty Hall. Welham, their up-country home, John wrote, was "a quiet, delightful home; its inmates are kind, cheerful, and affectionate. The mansion is the perfection of cottage beauty, and the outer buildings admirably correspond. The whole presents the appearance of order, neatness, and comfort." Also nearby in Roswell were many friends, including the Dunwodys, the Bullocks, the Pratts, and of course the Kings. John and Jane became frequent visitors at the Dunwodys', for John Dunwody was like a father to Jane. "They live," wrote John, "in a comfortable and stately mansion, built of brick."[12]

As for Atlanta, John found it a new society, rough and preoccupied with making money. And with prophet vision he described it as "the village where all the rail-roads meet, and there is such a running to and fro of rail-road cars, that one is most strongly reminded of a verse in Nahum 2:4 'The Chariots shall rage in the streets, they shall justle one against another in the broad ways: they shall seem like torches, they shall run like the lightnings.'"[13]

John's interests, however, were focused not on Atlanta but on the old Cherokee lands—especially those between Marietta and Chattanooga. Cass County, just north of Marietta, he called "the heart of the Cherokee Country, from its superior lands and its abundant mineral ores." He marveled at the fertility of the Etowah River Valley, where low-country families would soon be building fine homes. "This country," John wrote Mary, "is full of life and speculation. Lands are high, and settlers are moving in every day. Men are graduated and estimated very much by their means. Here is a broad field for missionary and ministerial effort. But ministers must expect for many years to work without a salary."[14]

John was soon called as the pastor of the Marietta Presbyterian Church, a position he accepted with the understanding that he would have time to do mission work in the rapidly growing areas of the old Cherokee country. What he found there, of course, was that other missionaries had been there before him. He wrote Mary of a visit to the little town of Rome, with its seven hills in northwest Georgia. "Upon crossing the Coosa at Rome, we entered immediately a rich farm once the property of John Ross the Head-chief of the Cherokees." Seventeen years earlier, when Charles and Ross were meeting in Washington and traveling together to Baltimore and Philadelphia, Charles had written of Ross and other members of the Cherokee delegation: "They felt much and determined to bear with patience every evil that might come upon them, and hold fast their lands and not sell a foot, and if possible carry their cause before the Supreme Court of the U. States." Since then Ross's confiscated lands and fine home had passed through several hands, and now when John visited it, he found it "inhabited by the Presbyterian minister of Rome, Mr. Caldwell and his wife. Keeps a female school in the house so recently the Indian's home." And not far from Rome, John saw "another relic of the past, the old mission house and farm." Here Dr. Elizur Butler, under the auspices of the missionary society begun at Andover, had "taught a school for the Cherokees." Perhaps Butler's experience as a missionary to the Native Americans had made Charles think about his experience and strategy as a missionary to the African Americans. Charles had sought to work within the system of slavery to make it more humane and never tried to oppose it openly. Butler not only protested vehemently the confiscation of Cherokee lands, but he also endured brutal treatment and four years in a Georgia prison for the Cherokee cause. And when he was finally freed, Butler identified so deeply with the Cherokees that he traveled the Trail of Tears to be with them in Oklahoma.[15]

Not long after John had settled in his new home in Marietta, he found a home in the center of the village for his aunt Eliza Robarts, her daughters Mary and Louisa, and the four motherless children of her son Joseph. John thought Marietta would suit his aunt better than Roswell because of "the great convenience of the Railroad." Since the death of her last husband in September 1813, she had looked to her brother Joseph and the Retreat as anchors in her life. Now at age sixty-four, with those anchors gone, she found the courage and the freedom to make a new home for herself and her family in the bustling little village on the outskirts of Atlanta. "Your house is engaged," Charles wrote his aunt as she was preparing to leave Sunbury, "and you will presently be gone from Sunbury and we shall see you no more there."[16]

Eliza's courage and freedom, of course, had repercussions in the settlements of Liberty County. She owned almost forty slaves, and some decision had to be made about what to do with them. After some negotiations, she reached an agreement with her nephew James Newton Jones for him to rent most of those who had been working in the fields at her Hickory Hill plantation. These he moved to the settlement at the Retreat. Among them was Old Robinson, the widowed husband of Old Lizzy. Charles agreed to rent five of his aunt's slaves, including two children, probably to help keep families together. All of these he sent to Carlawter. But Eliza decided to take with her to Marietta six domestic servants. And among these was Sam, the butler and majordomo of the Robarts household. This decision came as a bitter and painful blow to Sam and his wife, Rosetta. They had been married in 1819, and although they had lived at different places for most of the years that followed, they had had their Saturday evenings and Sundays together. By the time of Sam's removal to Marietta, they had five children and four grandchildren living at Carlawter and Maybank.[17]

Sam and Rosetta evidently complained bitterly of the separation—although no doubt with the skill of those who knew the ways and temper of whites. Perhaps they reminded Charles and his aunt of what Charles had been preaching all these years, that husbands and wives were not to be divided. So as a compromise, it was agreed that every year Sam could return to Carlawter for not only the two weeks of Christmas holidays but also for the month of January.[18]

In late September 1848 Charles and Mary set out from Maybank for Columbia with Charlie, Joe, and Mary Sharpe. Journeying with them were Jack, Marcia, John, Jane, and Phillis. In Savannah they took the steamer *William Seabrook* for Charleston. A northeast wind was blowing and the sea was rough. Everyone became seasick except Jack and Jane. "The boat reared up," said John, and "gave him the light head." The steamer and the stormy ocean were new experiences for all those—even Jack—who had spent their lives in the settlement. "New sights and scenes for them all," noted Charles, "and they seemed to enter into them." In Charleston the white family stayed in the Charleston Hotel. The blacks stayed on the ship. Jack was sent ahead the next day with the first load of furniture. The second load went up the next day with the other servants whom Charles led down the streets of Charleston "in Indian file—Marcia in the center with her old cloak and Jack's hat on her head." The following day, the white family boarded the train with the third load of furniture. Tracks had been laid to Columbia since their last trip—no more rough carriage rides were needed. The train left Charleston at nine in the morning and was in Columbia by five that afternoon. George Howe was waiting for them with his carriage and buggy. Jack was there also, "as usual with his broad smile." He reported "that all had arrived safely."[19]

While their house was being prepared, Charles and Mary, together with the children and the servants, all moved in with the Howes, who received them "as relatives." Seventeen-year-old Charlie took the entrance exam and was admitted to the sophomore class of South Carolina College, and fifteen-year-old Joe was soon admitted into the first-year class. Mary Sharpe went to a school for young ladies run by a Mr. Muller. "He has the reputation," Joe wrote his Aunt Betsy and Uncle William, "of being very cross."[20]

Part of the reason for the move to Columbia was for Charles and Mary to continue to supervise the education of the children—especially the boys, as they entered the dangerous years of college, and particularly South Carolina College. To go from the little schoolhouse and museum at Maybank to the college classroom in Columbia must have required some adjustments for the seventeen-year-old Charlie and even more for the fifteen-year-old Joe. But living at home and not on the campus no doubt eased the transition. Moreover, the boys brought with them a personal discipline and intellectual curiosity that had already been deeply instilled in them. "The use of translations of Latin and Greek books read in college," Charles wrote their Uncle William, "is common with the students. They call them by the familiar name of *Ponies*—helping a fellow to jog through his lessons. Charlie says he never will use them, and Joe says he never will, they will aim to employ their own minds and get their lessons *themselves*."[21]

Charles found Columbia "much improved." It is, he wrote home, "a busy time, a great deal of cotton arriving and the Rail Road has as much—if not more—than it can do, both up and down." And the military culture that so marked the state was everywhere visible. "It is as military a state as any in the Union," wrote Charles, and "the Mexican war and the gallant conduct of their Palmetto Regiment has made them more so. Parades and reviews from time to time."[22]

As for his own work, Charles was soon busy at the seminary teaching church history and polity. "We are getting on tolerably well in the seminary," he wrote William Maxwell shortly after he had taken up his responsibilities. "Thus far everything has been very pleasant, only I have more to do than I can do as well as it ought to be done." He especially enjoyed being with the students, two of whom were former tutors for the children at Maybank and Montevideo—William Matthews, a Georgian, and James Rogers, a native of Pennsylvania. Once Charles and Mary were established in their own home not far from the seminary, both of the former tutors took their meals with the family, and "almost any evening," Charles noted, "some of the students drop in and take a cup of tea with us."[23]

And there were others who came to visit and to enjoy a hospitality that had been nurtured in the low country. George and Sarah Howe continued to be their closest friends. She was, Charles noted, "as fat as she can be—never saw her in better health and full of good spirits, and her Lord is not a whit behind her." Sarah's daughter Augusta was married to the young Benjamin Morgan Palmer, the pastor of the Presbyterian Church in the city. Palmer, who had graduated from the seminary in 1841, was already making a name for himself not only as a preacher of great power but also as an intellectual who moved with ease among a circle of intellectuals in the city. James Henley Thornwell at South Carolina College was at the circle's center. He had achieved "hegemony over the institution" of the college and, in the words of a later historian of the university, was "perhaps the most important person connected with the institution during the twenty five years following his arrival." Both Palmer and Thornwell would frequently teach at the seminary—and later be on the seminary faculty—and Charles regarded them as among his closest colleagues in Columbia.[24]

In addition to Columbia friends, there was a steady stream of guests from out of town who came for extended stays with the Joneses. Not long after the family had settled in their new home, General John Cocke of Virginia arrived to spend some time with them on his way back from a visit to his plantation in Alabama. In 1847, when Charles and Mary had been in Virginia for a meeting of the Presbyterian General Assembly, General Cocke had come in his carriage to Richmond and carried them to Bremo, his plantation home designed by his friend Thomas Jefferson. Mary had written Betsy of her impressions of the general. He had told her as they had ridden across the Virginia countryside of his friends "John Randolph, Madison, Monroe, and Jefferson." Mary noted that while "he is himself from a first family of Virginia, I have a far higher encomium yet to pass upon this noble Christian gentleman — universally is it said of him: 'General Cocke lives to do good.' His heart and hand and purse is engaged in every work of benevolence." She believed that he stood "preeminent in his efforts to instruct and improve his Negroes," who she thought "are certainly in advance of any servants that I have ever seen for intelligence." His Alabama plantation was, in fact, a remarkable experiment. He had carried there a group of slaves from Bremo and had arranged for the proceeds of the plantation to go toward their establishment in Liberia as free people. During the coming years the general became a close friend of the Jones family, regularly visiting with them on his trips to and from Alabama.[25]

Almost from the moment of their arrival in Columbia, the family missed their Liberty County home, but visiting friends and family from the low country helped with homesickness. Laura came in the spring for an extended stay. Shortly after she arrived, Charles wrote her Uncle William Maxwell that "many have called to see her, and she has been out to two little social parties. She has created quite a sensation among our young gentlemen. She seems quite popular and admires the town." A little later Charles wrote his cousin Louisa Robarts about some of the social life in the city and his general impressions of Columbia:

> The town abounds in the most beautiful flowers at this season. The gardens are flourishing and much grown since you were here. So are the trees, which improve the appearance of the streets wonderfully. But the society which you knew here retains its identity in a remarkable degree. I cannot say that Columbia altogether takes my fancy as a place to call my home. Am not prepossessed in favour of Carolina notions. Besides it is a town where religion does not appear to flourish, at least not at present.[26]

So, like their experience of Columbia in the 1830s, Charles and Mary again found the city a difficult place to call their home. It still had a rough edge to it, and in spite of many gracious friends such as the Crawfords and the Howes, it seemed to them to lack the refinements of the low country. They were especially concerned by what they regarded as the disorderly and lawless character of much of the city, and by "Carolina notions," which substituted arrogance for personal discipline and the pursuit of excellence.

Still, they could not deny that Columbia had many advantages, especially for their children. Charles wrote John Jones that Joe was "getting on tolerably well in his studies. Rather young, but we could not do better." He was continuing his collections "of minerals, fossil remains, etc, and has some rare specimens. General Cocke brought him some sharks' teeth from his marl pits in Greene Co. Alabama and other things. He has a great passion for these things." Moreover, Joe "made the acquaintance of the greatest naturalist in town, Dr. Gibbs, who has the finest *private* collection of curious remains of one kind and another" that Charles had ever seen. Dr. Richard Brumby, the professor of chemistry and mineralogy at the college, told Charles that he should let Joe "have his way" and that he would "take special pains with him." But Charles worried that Joe's "partiality for these studies may interfere with more solid acquirements."[27]

While Charles and Mary were making their adjustments to Columbia, their thoughts constantly turned toward their low-country home and toward those who lived in the settlements. They worried about the care the people were receiving. Charles wrote Thomas Shepard that he had always gotten "*good* supplies for the people, without being extravagant. You must use your judgment in the matter. Six yards to the grown and in proportion to the children. I think about 500 or 550 yards will be sufficient. Have the clothing shipped to you to Riceboro, and you can then take it to Montevideo, and give out your cloth and shoes there—and then send to Mr. Rahn, for *Arcadia*—and to Col. Maxwell—at Maybank for *Maybank*."[28]

And there were concerns for individuals, especially those who were old. "I do not know if Tony wears flannel," Charles wrote Shepard of the old man who had become the gardener at Montevideo and who suffered from arthritis. "If he does not, let him have a couple of flannel shirts to wear next to his body. The old man will find benefit from them in his pains. He likes a little Tobacco at times." And there was Mom Clarissa—she had been old in 1833, when Charles had bought her from the Maybank estate to keep her at her island home, and she was still spending her days in the settlement by the marsh. "Old Mom Clarissa is fond of tobacco," Charles reminded William Maxwell and added, "when you think of it and it is convenient do get it for her." And young mothers were congratulated. When Phoebe gave birth shortly after Charles and Mary had left for Columbia, they sent word to her: "Tell Phoebe we all wish her joy." "Jane," Charles reported, "is laughing all the time" about the birth of her little sister. Young

mothers, Charles instructed Shepard, should have "everything you deem necessary for them."[29]

Charles worried constantly about adequate food for those in the settlement,
for he evidently sensed that with absent owners the people were most vulnerable
in regard to provisions. He instructed Shepard to "kill a Beef for the people from
time to time, of some kind, as the stock will allow." And a month later he wrote
again: "Give the people beef from the stock as often as you can. Make use of
everything in the Garden in the vegetable way that you fancy, and whenever you
want an extra stew for the people, kill a lamb. I must leave every thing to your
judgment and discretion and feel assured that you will do what is right."[30]

In almost every letter home there were special messages for those in the settlement. "I beg Brother," he wrote his sister Betsy, "to let Andrew and the people at
Maybank know how we are and that we send Howdy for them all by name and
Jack, Marcia, and John and Jane send howdy to all." "Please tell Patience and
Andrew and all the people at Maybank howdy for us. Our servants are all well
and send howdys." And when his old nurse Rosetta was grieving over her husband Sam's removal to Marietta, he sent word: "Tell Rosetta her mistress and
myself will not forget our engagements," meaning apparently their agreement
to let Sam stay at Carlawter during the two weeks at Christmas and during the
month of January.[31]

When Shepard had taken over the management of Montevideo, he had decided almost immediately that the slough that separated Carlawter from the
Montevideo tract needed to be drained and its rich river bottomland converted
into rice fields. It would be a huge task and take several years to complete. Cato
had primary responsibility for overseeing the work, but he received important
help from Dr. Harry, the carpenter and root doctor at the Mallard Place. Dr.
Harry knew all about how canals were to be dug, dikes built, and gates constructed to regulate the flow of water. He was no longer a young man, but he
came over to Carlawter and spent weeks with Cato, giving him and Porter instructions about ditches and dams. Later Charles wrote Shepard:

> Thank my old friend Dr. Harry for me—specially. And when you collect my
> money on my account, I wish you to remunerate him for his pains in coming
> over to Carlawter last fall, and directing and aiding Cato in laying out the
> ditches and dams in the rice field below the buildings. *Do not forget this.* Give
> what you and he may think right. The old man has been a good neighbor to me.

But the old man refused any compensation for his efforts, apparently out of respect for Charles. So Charles wrote back:

Please return Dr. Harry my sincere thanks for his trouble last Fall: it was my desire that he should be compensated, but as he refuses, I must take it as an act of pure friendship. Tell him and his wife howdy for me. It will be a pleasant day to me when I shall be permitted to return to Liberty and see all my black friends again.[32]

But of course, all was not peace, harmony, and friendship between blacks and whites in Liberty County. The removals out of the low country were beginning to undermine the old stability that had marked much of the region. Under stable conditions, much of the resistance to slavery had focused on the development of a distinctive Gullah community and on strategies to ameliorate the harsh conditions of slavery. The task system, the right to marry persons from other plantations, Saturday night visits to the "wife house," and the ownership of personal property—all of these had been important victories for those who lived in the settlement in their long struggle toward freedom. But with the removals intensifying the vulnerability of the community, direct acts of sabotage and resistance became more frequent, and the response of the whites had been swift. Not long before her family left the low country for Marietta, Eliza Robarts wrote John Jones that four runaways had camped on a hammock in the Medway swamp in back of the Mallard Place. "The gentlemen from Dorchester went after them," she wrote, "and found them camped with several of Capt. Mallard's sheep they had stolen. One of the Negroes raised his gun to shoot; Dr. Delegal shot him dead." The others escaped into the swamp. During the coming years, there would be increasing reports of runaways and of barns and even plantation houses being burned.[33]

Open resistance began to find its way even to Carlawter and Maybank. When Charles and Mary had been preparing to leave for Columbia, they had moved Phoebe to Maybank, while Cassius was required to stay at Carlawter and to visit Maybank only on Saturday nights and Sundays. This was a repeat of the strategy Charles had employed in 1837, when he had sent Phoebe to work at South Hampton. He did not want them together to encourage one another in "mischief." After Phoebe's baby was born, however, in late November 1848, she had been given permission to stay at Montevideo for three months. When the time came for her to return to Maybank, Cassius and his younger brother Daniel evidently protested to Shepard in an angry manner. Shepard had responded with some substantial punishment—perhaps by a whipping or by taking away Saturday visitation rights for a period of time. Charles wrote Shepard after having received a report about the matter: "Cassius has naturally a bad temper though it does not show itself often, and your decision both with him and Daniel will have a good effect. We will have crosses with the best—the only thing we must look to is to be *prompt and decided*." In contrast to Cassius and Daniel, their older brother Cato continued as a model of a faithful and responsible servant. "Tell Cato," Charles wrote in the same letter to Shepard, "I will write him shortly, and that it gives his mistress and myself great pleasure to learn that he is getting on well and gives you good satisfaction." But Cassius's anger and resistance were not easily suppressed. Three months later he took "French leave" and, as Cato reported to Charles, simply failed to return to Carlawter after a weekend visit to Maybank. Cassius evidently pleaded illness as the reason for his remaining with Phoebe and for his delay in returning to Carlawter. Shortly after this Phoebe was sent to South Hampton, as she had been earlier, this time to work for Julia King and to stay out of trouble at Carlawter.[34]

In May 1849 Mary came down with rheumatic fever. Vigorous treatment by the doctors in Columbia freed her from the fever but left her very weak. Charles, who had to provide most of the care for Mary, felt his isolation from his extended family. "I think as much as in any sickness since our marriage," Charles wrote Betsy, "I felt we were alone here, for in our sickness and afflictions you and Brother and aunt and our kind cousins have always been with us. But now I had to be all alone—day and night." As Mary showed signs of improvement, the decision was made for her to go to Marietta, where the summers were milder and she could have the attention of her brother John and Aunt Eliza and their families. She traveled by train through Augusta and Atlanta, but the trip was exhausting, and she soon had a relapse. John sent Charles an urgent message that he must come as quickly as possible; his "presence was indispensable," for, said John, "his sister was very sick." Charles, taking Mary Sharpe with him, went "as fast as steam" could take them and found that the fever had returned with a vengeance. It was obvious that Mary needed sustained rest for a full recovery, so the decision was made to spend the summer in Marietta. In July, Mr. Rogers brought Charlie and Joe over in the carriage. They took six and a half days to travel the 238 miles between Columbia and Marietta—"good travel," Charles thought, "on the rough up-country roads."[35]

While her Marietta relatives showed her every kindness, Mary's illness made her long for her low-country home and for the familiar touch of Patience and Phoebe. "The greatest personal privation I have had to endure," she wrote Betsy at the end of the summer, "has been the want of either Patience or Phoebe—tell them I am never [going to be], if life is spared us, without both of them again." And she sent a special message to Patience: "Tell *Patience* I have often remembered what a good servant and attentive nurse she was to me in 1840, and often as I lie down weary and in pain, I say 'Oh! If I only had Patience here to rub me all over.'"[36]

The summer in Marietta gave Charles an opportunity to make a careful evaluation of the up-country and gave him hints of the rapid expansion of people all across the nation. "The people look generally healthy and hard working," he wrote Shepard. "The population of the state is up here." "This is a pleasant climate," he wrote Betsy, "cool nights, no mosquitoes—said to be healthy. The whole population carried away with buying and selling, trading lands and speculation." He traveled with John through much of the old Cherokee country and saw how the trains were transforming the land, and he came to realize as never before the great need for home missionaries among the rapidly growing population. And perhaps as he looked out of the train windows at the Etowah River Valley or saw the ancient sites of the Cherokee nation, he may have remembered his days in Washington, his encounter with the attorney general, and his discussions with John Ross and the Cherokee delegation. And perhaps he remembered how he had not raised his voice in defense of Ross and his beleaguered people once he had returned to Georgia.[37]

Charles and Mary returned to Columbia from Marietta in the carriage with Charlie, Joe, and Mary Sharpe. Their route took them first to Roswell, where they spent a few days with friends admiring their fine mansions. From Roswell they took the winding north Georgia roads that skirted the mountains. They crossed the Savannah River on a ferry, rode to Greenville, and turned east to Columbia. The journey, while exhausting, gave them all a better understanding of the up-country, of its dusty roads, red clay hills, and cotton farms.[38]

The new academic year in Columbia turned out to be not only memorable but also a turning point for the Jones family. Charles's classes went well and there was a large entering class at the seminary. But Charles did not feel at ease in Columbia nor a part of the circle of intellectuals connected with the college and the seminary. He spent almost two years in Columbia before being invited to be a contributing editor of the scholarly *Southern Presbyterian Review* with Thornwell, Howe, Palmer, and Smyth, and he felt slighted by the delay. He was obviously respected and admired by his colleagues, but their respect was for Charles's labors as a missionary and not for his intellectual life. Thornwell, Palmer, and others in their circle were seeking to develop a theology that was guided by natural law, commonsense realism, and Protestant scholastic traditions. They were seeking a theology that avoided what they regarded as the dangerous extremes in American life—an extreme individualism and an extreme organicism. What they were advocating was a theology and philosophy of a *via media*, a middle way, which would serve as both an ideological prop for slavery and a conservative utopian vision for the future of the South. Charles read little philosophy and was not conversant with recent developments in theology—it would have been surprising, after all, if he had been reading German theologians or philosophers while he made his rounds to the stations and settlements of Liberty County. So he felt increasingly isolated from the interests and concerns of his colleagues.[39]

And Charlie was soon isolated at South Carolina College. When Professor Brumby, who had been so kind to Joe, changed a class schedule, the whole class had protested, including Charlie, and boycotted his class. But when the faculty said that they must attend, Charlie alone of the regular students, acting as he thought right and "in the face of his whole class walked into Professor Brumby's recitation room!" The rest of the class was suspended, and Charlie received from the president of the college a respectable dismission. That night the suspended students, whom Charles called "*the rebels*," burned their books in front of Professor Brumby's home and went on a general rampage, parading around the campus with drums and horns, breaking windows and doors, and confirming for Charles and Mary the image of undisciplined Carolina boys. "The class is blotted out of college. Not a man remains," Charles wrote William and Betsy Maxwell. "What am I to do with my son?" Charles wondered. "He is thrown out of the college by the improper conduct of his class. God has some design in all this which we cannot see into yet."

While all this was going on, another crisis was developing in the Jones household. Charlie had been sick earlier in the month with pneumonia, Mary Sharpe was now in bed with it, and Louisa Robarts, who was visiting, was not feeling well. And in the servants' quarters in the back, both Jack and Marcia were also sick with pneumonia. Jack appeared to be getting better—the doctor had come and bled him, and this seemed to have relieved him. Then he had suddenly taken a turn for the worse. Charles was with him day and night. "Almost every dose of medicine he took," Charles wrote, "and every spoonful of nourishment he took from my hands." When his death seemed certain, they asked him the familiar questions addressed to the dying. "He was," he told Mary, "in God's sight but a filthy rag," but "his hope was in Jesus" that "his Saviour was shedding unnumbered mercies all around him."

Jack began to say his good-byes. He told Charles that "it was a blessed thing to have a good master and mistress," and he said "he could not begin to speak of God's mercies to him." They told Marcia that Jack was dying. She was lying dangerously sick on a bed not far from her husband. She could not believe Jack was really dying. It must be a turn in the sickness, she said. Charles helped her to her feet, and she "staggered to him and put her hand on his forehead and cheek and said: 'Jack, you know me?'" "Oh yes, Marcia child," he responded. And then he gave her "his parting counsel in a most clear and touching manner, and begged her no longer to put off her soul's salvation."

Charles called all the household, white and black, to Jack's bedside: his grandchildren, John and Jane, Louisa, Joe and Mary Sharpe. "He took them one by one by the hand and charged them in the Lord and commended them to God." Then Charlie came, once the little white boy listening to Jack's stories about Buh Wolf and Buh Rabbit, Buh Rooster and Buh Fowl-Hawk, and all the other inhabitants of the low country. And Jack said to Charlie, "Oh, my young master, this is my whole heart." And to Mary he said, knowing how she depended on him, "I am so sorry to leave you; I know how you will miss me."

Charles asked him, "Jack, is your mind at rest? Is Christ still precious to you?" "He smiled and raised his hand toward heaven." In this way he died, and Charles wrote William and Betsy, "It is the loss not only of one of the most faithful and excellent, long-tried servants, but of a devoted, long-tried and affectionate friend— to us and to all our family. Jack was one of the family." That afternoon when Charles went to dinner, and Jack was not standing in his place by the table as he had for so many years, but was now "lying dead in the servants' house in the yard," Charles was overcome by emotion. Then "the tears came full and fast and fell down on the tablecloth," and he could not see the carving knife he held in his hand. Charles got up, gave his seat at the head of the table to Charlie, and asked Mr. Rogers to ask a blessing. After dinner Charles wrote home to Liberty County to give the news. "Do be kind enough," he asked William and Betsy, "to let Patience know of her uncle's death, who loved her as his own child." Charles wrote a special letter to Cato. He was to tell his wife, Betsy, who was Jack's youngest daughter, and her brothers and sisters. They had been divided and scattered to different plantations following Joseph's death. And Sister Susan, who was visiting at South Hampton, told Phoebe of her father's death. "Mother read your letter to Mom Phoebe," Laura wrote, "and she was very much affected indeed."[40]

Later, on the evening of Jack's death, Charles and the family sat around the fire in the parlor. They had secured someone to sit up with Marcia during the night, and plans had been made for Jack's funeral the next day. He lay in the servants' house wearing in death "that smile of life" which was "so natural and constant with him." The family stayed up late, talking and grieving together. They all went to their rooms. Charlie banked the fire and went to bed. About half past one in the morning there was a cry: "Fire! Fire! Wake them! You will all be burnt up! Come out! Come out!" Charles and Mary leaped out of bed, and there followed a great rushing to the outside. Charles picked up the sick Mary Sharpe to carry her out. "We were gasping for air," Charles remembered, "and hurried to the front door."

> The boys had come down, and we all went out together. As I came to the door a man met me who I knew not and said: "You cannot come out this way." I was startled for a second. I knew it was the only way. I told him to stand aside, and thrusting him aside, we hastened down the front steps. I was so overcome with the suffocation that I could not hold up my child, but let her fall on her feet. At that instant John was there and said: "master, give her to me." And he took up his young mistress, and Mary and Louisa went over across the street to Mr. Thompson's.

Charles rushed to the back to the servants' quarters, where Jack was lying smiling in his coffin, and with others "bore him out of the servants' house and carried him across the street and laid him down on the sidewalk. Others took up poor Marcia (almost in a dying state) and put her, cot and all, through the window farthest from the fire; and she was covered with blankets and carried over to Mr. Thompson's also." The fire did its work, and the house was soon nothing but smoldering ashes. Rats had evidently loosened the mortar around the chimney in the parlor, providing the source of the fire.[41]

The family lost almost all of their Columbia possessions. Most serious were the loss of Charles's papers and library. Some years later Mary wrote that the fire consumed "much that was truly valuable of our earthly substance."

> It destroyed totally the *priceless treasures* of my *beloved* husband's manuscripts, comprising works for the press, missionary journals, embracing a period of 16 years labour for the Religious Instruction of the Negroes, in Liberty County, Georgia, and throughout the Southern States—Theological Lectures—*Church History*—sermons—Addresses, Letters, etc. etc. together with his valuable library.[42]

She was surely right with regard to his missionary journals, for these detailed descriptions of his work and the people of the settlements could not be replaced. Fortunately, some excerpts had been published in the *Charleston Observer* in the 1830s.

A few days after the fire, Marcia died and was buried beside Jack. Charles made an inventory of their possessions that had been saved: Marcia had thirteen dresses, ten handkerchiefs, one shawl, underclothes, two pair of sheets, six blankets, and one quilt. Jack had nine coats, three overcoats, one cloak, fourteen pantaloons, seven vests, one jacket, four new shirts, and three hats.[43] Charles had a tombstone cut and engraved and placed over their final resting place so far from Carlawter and the Retreat:

John Anderson Jones
A Servant of God
A. 60
And Marcia his Wife
A. 55
Of Liberty County, Ga.
Died
April 17th and 20th 1850
Our Kind and Faithful
Friends
John 6:39–40[44]

PHILADELPHIA

Three weeks after the fire and Jack's death, Charles received a letter from the Presbyterian Board of Domestic Missions in Philadelphia. Charles, the letter said, had been unanimously elected to be the board's new executive. The letter astonished Charles, for he had not sought the position—he did not even know that the board was considering him. Moreover, the position was one of great responsibility, for the board had oversight of more than four hundred Presbyterian missionaries scattered across the United States. The invitation seemed providential.[1]

The letter of invitation and the others that followed from Philadelphia reflected both the confidence and the concerns of a Protestant establishment that had emerged in the United States since the revivals of the Second Great Awakening at the beginning of the century. The United States, it was believed, had a great destiny. That destiny, however, was dependent upon the nation being a Christian nation, and more specifically, a Christian nation imbued with the faith and experience of evangelical Protestantism and the values of a democratic society. Presbyterians—together with their New England cousins, the Congregationalists—believed they had a distinct role in the evangelical campaign for the nation's destiny. They were to bring to the enthusiasm of other evangelicals not only sound theology but also order, learning, and appreciation for the cultural traditions of British and North American Protestantism. Such perspectives—and they were, of course, resented by many—had provided the context for Charles's work as a missionary to slaves. His labors in Liberty County had been within the peculiar confines of slavery. The offer from Philadelphia, on the other hand, was an invitation to a broader field in the cause of evangelizing the nation and providing the moral foundations for a democratic society.[2]

So Charles was once again thrown into a vocational quandary. "If I know my own mind and heart," he wrote Mary (who had returned to Maybank), "I have no objections to remaining in Columbia, no objections to going to Philadelphia, no objections to returning to Liberty County and my old work." His only desire, he wrote, "is to know what is agreeable to God's will. That I desire to be my guide." Homeless as they were in Columbia, with the horror of the fire fresh in his mind, Charles was convinced that "it is vain to endeavor to look anywhere for rest and heaven on earth; we shall meet with sin and its consequences both within and without, go where we may. To go anywhere against God is folly and unhappiness. The true peace of the soul lies in loving God supremely and living to Him. His service must be our delight." Such theological reflections, however, did not lead to easy answers in regard to the call from Philadelphia. He acknowledged that the thought of "no more returning and living at our home in Liberty is very painful." But, he said, "if God be with us, and we are doing His will, He will make a home for us, and may make us happy as we may be in this world where our lot is cast."[3]

He longed to talk with Mary: "I wish you, my dear wife," he told her, "to give this call to Philadelphia a conscientious and candid and prayerful consideration, as I know you will, and then give your views and conclusions." Mary wrote back immediately. She could not, she said, "pretend to interpret the divine will" but could only struggle to discern it amid swirling and conflicting issues. The point is, she wrote, "What is the divine will? Where shall you do most good? Where best glorify God? Where most advance the growing interests of our dear children in their education and the formation of their characters?" She acknowledged the importance of the position in Philadelphia and considered the advantages of having the boys enrolled in Princeton if the family should go to Philadelphia. But she also wondered what it would be like to live in the North at a time when sectional tensions were growing:

I am Southern born and Southern reared; my hopes, my desires, my sympathies, and my interests are with the land of my nativity. I wish my children free from the prejudice of sectional feeling when carried to animosity; yet I want them to love the South and to support and defend her honest rights; and in the event of any national division (which I trust in the goodness of Providence will never take place) I hope they would be found true to the land of their birth. The liberalizing effect of a Northern education is desirable, but not alienation, leading to dishonorable and traitorous conduct.[4]

Others wrote as well and gave their advice. With "so much *sage counsel*," remarked his sister Susan with some amusement, "you will not be at a loss how to decide." But Charles wanted the counsel of others, especially those close to him. From Marietta came a requested letter from John. "I do not feel myself compe-

tent to advise," he said, "but as you have requested my opinion, I answer 'Go!'"
He thought the Philadelphia position the most important in the church, but he
also thought the growing sectional crisis was another reason Charles should accept the position in Philadelphia. Following the Mexican-American War, a fierce
debate had erupted over what to do with the territories ceded by Mexico. "At
the present crisis," wrote John, "we need safe men in high places, both in the
church and state. If as a country and church we hold together, we need safe men
to bind the cords of love and union stronger still, and if we are broken to pieces,
we will especially need safe men to direct and decide and control." Charles was,
John thought, just such a man. Even Betsy and William, who were feeling their
age and wanted nothing so much as the family to return to Liberty—they too
said, "Go!" "It is God's call," Betsy wrote Charles; "you must obey." So after two
months of reflection and listening to what others had to say, Charles accepted
the call to Philadelphia.[5]

The family spent the summer at Maybank preparing for their departure to the
North. Their time together was like a lingering low-country evening when the
shadows lengthen over the land and the marsh wind blows and brings both a
sense of peace and a melancholy mood. Charles and Mary knew that they were
enjoying the twilight of their life together as a family before the boys left the
parental home to be on their own for the first time. Perhaps to keep the melancholy at bay as long as possible, friends and relatives were welcomed to Maybank
to enjoy the summer on the island, and time was found for the boys to enjoy
fishing and sailing. "This afternoon," Mary wrote, Charlie "went to the second
bluff about an hour and a half before sunset and returned with over a dozen of
the finest sort of fish—young drum, bass, whiting, croaker, all of which we are
going to take early in the morning to Sister Betsy," who was at Social Bluff. And
among the women at Maybank, Woodville, and Social Bluff, there was "much
visiting, writing notes, sending butter, berries, and vegetables," and a general enjoyment of one another's company.[6]

But there was also, especially for Mary, a melancholy, an unavoidable sad
note—a kind of whippoorwill calling in the evening—to be heard in the midst
of summer's pleasures. She felt, as many a parent has felt, a sense of ending and
nostalgia for happy days when children were young and their voices filled the
house. Some days she would sit "and silently muse on the past, when our dear
children like a little flock were gathered around us," and she would remember
"our pleasant friends and neighbors, our domestic school, our little social Bible
class."[7] And she would remember the voices of those who were gone, who in the
past had been such an important part of the life of Montevideo and Maybank.

And on one Sabbath day that summer, when her soul was quiet, she remembered what she had been taught at Midway—that the Sabbath itself with family and friends worshiping together was not a burdensome duty but a gift and a foretaste of heaven. Sabbath worship and rest taught her of what was to come—an eternal home where there would be no uprooting and no more parting. She wrote in her journal:

> Never again shall we there encounter the agonizing pains, the heaving, gasping, dying strife which has torn and lacerated our bosoms as we looked upon our beloved friends passing from time to Eternity or as we ourselves with fearful trembling have entered the dark valley and shadow of death, and felt the cold swellings of Jordan dashing upon our unsheltered souls. Oh! No! The blessed Saviour's rod and staff hath comforted and supported them and us and together we shall sit at his feet.[8]

At the end of July, Charlie and Joe left Maybank for Princeton. As they were preparing to leave, they were handed a letter of "parting counsels" from their parents as an expression of their "deep interest" in their sons' welfare and their "sincere affection" for their dear children. The parents wrote that it gave them "pleasure to believe" that Charlie and Joe would adopt their counsel "as rules" upon which to frame their character and regulate their lives. And then Charles and Mary spelled out in detail their expectations for their sons.

Charlie and Joe were to read the Bible twice a day; keep the Sabbath holy; shun any opinion that would lead them to disbelieve or doubt the Bible; and devote themselves to their studies together with a "rigid system of *diet, rest,* and *exercise.*" They were to use their time wisely and not abuse their advantages; abstain from tobacco and ardent spirits; avoid *"profane, Sabbath-breaking, idle, intemperate, immoral and dissipated young men"* and "cultivate and prize the society of young gentlemen of intelligence, integrity, and piety of character."

Thinking, no doubt, of South Carolina College, the parents said there was to be no participation in college riots or rebellions. Charlie and Joe were encouraged always to endeavor to *"respect the feelings and rights and circumstances of your fellow men,"* and they were told to conduct themselves as "well-bred gentlemen, and men of character, dignity, principle, and honor." They were specifically admonished to "refrain from familiarity with persons of low character or inferior stations in society," and reminded to "have self-respect."

In regard to finances, they were to be economical and never run into debt. "If possible, borrow from none. Be careful to whom you lend. Generously give according to your means." In regard to women, they were "to enjoy the refining influences of elevated female society," but they were to "lay aside all flippancy of behavior and excess of manner or dress," and they were to "form no connections" beyond those of friendship.

As brothers, they were to be *"respectful, kind, accommodating, patient, generous, and affectionate to each other*; and under all circumstances of trial or necessity or suffering *stand by each other as nearest friends*; and promote each other's peace, happiness, reputation, and success in life, without envy or jealousy, by every lawful and just means in your power." Finally, they were to *"remember your God and your Redeemer, and the priceless value of your immortal souls, and the near approach of death, judgment, and eternity."*

As the parents sent their sons away, they concluded their letter by reminding them that they were "children of the covenant" who had been dedicated in baptism to God. They commended them to God's "loving-kindness and tender mercy." And they assured them "that we shall ever do all in our power to promote your welfare, and that you will ever have the prayers and true affection of your own dear father and mother."[9]

The letter was long, loving, and full of the admonitions of anxious parents sending their sons off to a distant college. But none of its many "counsels" would have come as a surprise to Charlie and Joe. The letter was rather a summary of what they had been hearing all their lives at home and in the long sermons at Midway. They knew the "counsels" reflected the hopes and values of their parents and Charles and Mary's deep love for their children. What the boys could not have fully realized about the letter were the ways a Calvinist piety was mingled with the morality of an early Victorianism. But perhaps they were able to hear in the letter something else—the ways an elite southern Protestantism hoped to perpetuate itself by instilling in its children the values and patterns of behavior necessary "for usefulness in society."[10]

A few weeks after Charlie and Joe left Maybank, Charles decided that "all the perishable portion of the museum should perish." Charles had found that the "animals had scarcely a hair left on them, and the birds were fast losing their feathers." So Andrew and his son Gilbert were summoned to haul into the yard all that was destined for the flames. They went into the little museum, where a young Gilbert had watched the white children conduct their investigations, and they took the great wood ibis from its perch, carried it to a clearing, and carefully laid it on the ground as the foundation for what would follow. Around the ibis's long legs and beside its "gaping beak with the wood rat in it," they placed the mounted ducks and geese, the herons, and the roseate spoonbill. On top of these they arranged the curlews, plovers, and orioles and all the songbirds. They took the squirrels and rats and tucked them in the pile, leaving one with his head stuck out of the stack "grinning with his groundnut in his mouth," so that Charles

From left: Charlie, Mary Sharpe, and Joe Jones (courtesy Hargrett Rare Book and Manuscript Library, University of Georgia)

thought he looked "determined to save his dinner if possible." Finally the great horned owl was "placed hovering with outstretched wings upon the apex." Then papers were stuffed here and there, and Gilbert applied the torched.

> It was a burning! The papers roared; the feathers fried; the sealing-wax eyes of the birds wept out in melting tears. The cotton ignited; the smoke ascended; and the whole premises were fumigated with vapors of arsenic and burning legs and bills and skins and feathers and cotton and hair and snakeskins! Gilbert snorted and got himself out of the smoke, exclaiming: "Eh! De ting *smell!*"

The flames marked a symbolic end to the old days when the children had been under the watchful eye of their parents, and the burning cleared the way for a new period in the children's life and education. The museum, Charles wrote his sons, "has been good." It had offered them "instructive employment for many an hour" that might have been spent in "idleness and folly." If much of their work had gone up in flames, their father assured them their labors in the museum had provided them with something more permanent—it had given them "a taste for natural objects and habits of observation that will never leave you." The school and the museum had accomplished much. Charlie and Joe were now headed for Princeton. Roswell King had already left earlier in the summer to take Fred and Willie King to Yale. And in a short time Mary Sharpe would have the advantages of "a *polished Philadelphia* school" for young ladies. And at Maybank, Gilbert turned for a while from driving carts and buggies to the burning of all that was perishable in the museum.[11]

Charles, Mary, and Mary Sharpe arrived in Philadelphia in early October 1850. With them were Susan, Laura, and Charles Edward—he had graduated from Princeton and was now a student at the Medical College of the University of Pennsylvania, and his mother and sister had decided to join the family in Philadelphia at least for the winter.[12] Charlie and Joe had already been busy for some weeks with their studies at Princeton. Those in Philadelphia stayed at the American Hotel across from the Old State House, a noisy place whose commotion was particularly annoying to Mary, accustomed as she was to the quiet sounds of the river at Montevideo and the marsh wind at Maybank. And from home there came a letter from brother John in Marietta:

> It does appear so strange to think of you moving so far off from your Southern home. But I do believe you are highly blessed in being permitted to make an honorable and dutiful move out of a slave country, particularly on account of your children. I am becoming less and less attached to that Domestic Institution. What will be the end of the slave question? Much excitement prevails in Georgia about the admission of California into the Union.[13]

While searching for some more permanent accommodations, Charles also began to investigate more carefully the character of the work he had undertaken. The size, scope, and challenge of the work impressed him. The nation was rapidly expanding, the frontier was leaping westward, and everywhere there was a need for new churches to bring the light of the Gospel and the orderly ways of a democratic society.[14]

Charles's early experience in a Savannah countinghouse now served him well. Such training, together with Charles's orderly and disciplined ways, soon led him to discover irregularities in the board's finances and organization. So during the coming months he spent long hours at his desk not only engaged in a voluminous correspondence with missionaries scattered across the country but also putting in order the work of the Philadelphia office. Such long hours at a desk soon began to take their toll on his health.[15]

In early May 1851, Charles left Philadelphia for a meeting of the Presbyterian General Assembly being held in St. Louis. It was his first trip to the American

Charles Colcock Jones (1808–1863) (Charles Colcock Jones Papers,
Tulane University Manuscript Department)

West, and what he saw along the way filled him with wonder and provided him
with a personal experience of the size, energy, and wealth of the country. From
Philadelphia he traveled to Pittsburgh—a two-day trip by train and canal boat.
Pittsburgh he found to be a "City of Smoke, full of iron furnaces and factories,
and every fire made with bituminous coal." Charles thought the city "altogether
unlike the East. . . . Things are done with a rush," he remarked, and "the people
are pushing, and every man seems very independent of his neighbor."[16]

In Pittsburgh he boarded the steam packet *Cincinnati* for his trip down the
Ohio River. He found the river to be beautiful, and he admired the villages along
its banks and the fertile farms that stretched away to the horizon. The steamer
itself was a technological wonder—powerfully churning through the water and
as comfortable as a floating hotel. At Louisville he went ashore and found it a
"Southern city," an "agreeable" one. He sent a telegraph to Mary—another technological miracle; later he exclaimed: "Oh, these telegraphic wires! The wonder
and comfort of the age!" Then boarding another steam packet, he was on to St.
Louis.[17]

In St. Louis he found John waiting for him, having come from Marietta by
way of Nashville. Charles wrote Mary that they rushed into each other's arms,
"the gladdest fellows you ever saw." Charles made his report to the assembly,
using a large map of the country to illustrate the importance of his subject. The

Mary Jones (1808–1869) (courtesy Hargrett Rare Book
and Manuscript Library, University of Georgia)

report was received enthusiastically, and Charles was paid what he called "very
high and extravagant compliments." Later he was nominated for a professorship
at Princeton seminary, a nomination he turned down.[18]

As for St. Louis itself, its growth and vitality astonished him—already almost
ninety thousand inhabitants, more than the size of Charleston and Savannah
combined! And when he thought of the size of the country with its broad and
beautiful rivers stretching thousands of miles, he was amazed. Still, he thought
"the great West" a more pleasant place to visit than live. "So much mixture of
people from all places," he wrote Charlie and Joe, "so much driving, speculating,
selfishness; a world of strangers, a world of changes; moving, pushing, sickening,
dying." But he had to admit: "Many like its ideas of greatness, its excitements,
its adventures, its creations and annihilations."[19]

Charles left St. Louis on May 27. He and John traveled by steam packets down
the Mississippi and then up the Ohio and Cumberland rivers to Nashville. From
there they took the stage and crossed the Cumberland Mountains to Chattanooga, then took a train to Marietta. After visiting family and friends in the little
village, and making a quick trip to Columbia and Augusta, he was at Montevideo
on June 17. I am, he wrote Mary, in "our old and quiet and happy home!"[20]

Happy reunions with relatives and friends quickly followed Charles's arrival, and those who lived in the settlements seemed genuinely glad to see him. But there was disturbing news about Betsy when Charles arrived home. She had been troubled by a mole on her arm and had finally decided to have it removed. Charles Edward, home from Philadelphia, helped with the operation. She was recovering nicely, but the size of the mole was a cause of some concern.[21]

Charles left Montevideo after a stay of two days and hurried to Maybank. Early the next day, as the morning wind brought the sweet smells of a low-country island, and the sun turned the marsh grass to gold, he went upstairs to his old study and wrote Mary:

> Not a sound about the house. Perfect quiet within. But the whole world without is filled with the melody and notes of a hundred birds. Their voices are not silent a second of time. They seem to have entered in and taken possession more perfectly than when we were here. The calmness, the quiet is delightful. The lot looks so grown, so fresh and green. The house all open, so clean and pleasant from top to bottom. Everything just as you left it, and all reminding me of my love, my sweet Mary. If I look out on the flowers and smell their fragrance, she planted and trained them with her own hands; if I look at the trees and the garden with its fruits, its oranges and figs and pomegranates, its pears and peaches and plums and apples, they were all set out under her eye and pruned and fostered by her care; if I walk in the piazza, in imagination she is at my side, and we are leaning in the cool breeze upon the shaded banister, sharing our thoughts and our love together. In the parlor, in the passage, in our chamber, her image is before me. There is not a part of the dwelling—no, not a single part of it—which does not furnish some scene of affection, some moments of love between us. Oh, if you were here, you would know how my heart beats towards you, my own, my dearest Mary! Then my children are associated with all around me too. If you were all here, would I not be a happy husband and a happy father?[22]

Within two weeks Charles was back at his desk in Philadelphia listening to the sounds of the city rumble past his window as he worked on the accumulated stack of mail on his desk. But he was soon alone once again. Mary Sharpe had been seriously ill with a fever while he was away, and her parents decided that she needed the therapeutic waters of some resort. Consequently, while Charles remained at his desk, Mary and Mary Sharpe, escorted by Charlie, left in mid-July for Saratoga, New York. They were as amazed by New York City as Charles had been by Pittsburgh and St. Louis. "Surely civilization with its mighty, transforming power has been abroad in the land," wrote Charlie as he gazed upon Manhattan. And before they boarded their Hudson River steamer, they saw crowds of new immigrants—mostly German and Dutch—in their traditional dress. "Taking them all in all," Charlie thought that "they presented as singular and curious an appearance as one could well imagine." So the travels of the family during the spring and summer of 1851, even while reminding them of home by a river and a Sea Island marsh, showed them much about the great changes that were transforming the nation.[23]

Charles had returned to his Philadelphia desk with a new sense of the importance of domestic missions and the urgency of his work on behalf of the church. Nevertheless, he and Mary were happy when his responsibilities required that he attend a meeting of the Synod of Georgia the following November. They quickly decided that Mary would accompany him, that they would go to Liberty County after the synod meeting, and that when Charles returned to Philadelphia, Mary would remain at Montevideo for most of the winter. She was clearly unhappy in Philadelphia and often miserable. "All," she wrote that year, "is so cold and desolate and cheerless in this land of strangers; not a generous or even a polite emotion seems to move the hearts of those around me."[24]

They left Philadelphia in mid-November and were in Marietta a week later, having traveled by train and ship. They were amazed at how quickly and easily they made such a long trip—and it could have taken less time had they not stopped in Charleston, where Charles preached for Thomas Smyth and talked to John Adger about his work among the slaves of the city.[25]

In Marietta they had a happy reunion with John Jones and his family and with Aunt Eliza and all her tribe. The Presbyterian Church in Marietta was flourishing under John's leadership; its membership had almost doubled the previous year, and the congregation included what Charles called "some excellent low-country families." John's own family now included little Mary Elizabeth, a beautiful and vivacious two-year-old, who was the delight of her parents. Dunwody, however, was giving his parents increasing concern. John had written earlier: "He often shows a strong spirit and a disobedient one." Later he wrote: "Dunwody is hearty, but wayward and gives us much anxiety." And still later John confessed: "He is rather a hard boy and gives us many painful feelings. He was so long an only child that he has become selfish." Dunwody had been for some time showing clear signs of becoming a rebellious "preacher's kid." But Dunwody, in addition to his rejection of his parents' piety, apparently had some learning disorder that made him a poor and restless student. He was destined to live under the long shadow of his father's affable ways and to depend upon his father's influence to open doors for him later in life—even doors that would lead to the most wretched of work.[26]

Charles and Mary hurried to Liberty County after the synod meeting. They wanted to attend the wedding of Mary's brother James Newton Jones, but when they arrived Mary was too exhausted from the trip to go to the wedding—perhaps her wish to avoid her stepmother added to her fatigue. At any rate, Charles went "to represent our branch of the family at the wedding."[27]

It had been six years since Mary King had broken her engagement in such a scandalous manner with James Newton. She admired but did not love him, she had told her mother Julia that summer of 1845. In 1849 she had married Dr. Charlton Henry Wells, a handsome young physician, a graduate of Dartmouth and the College of Physicians and Surgeons in New York. He was, Mary reported to Mary Sharpe after James Newton's wedding, "a most gentlemanly and amiable person, and I doubt not an excellent M.D." And he had in Mary King a wife who was devoted to him and who, said Sarah Howe, "loved him with the most uncontrolled affection."[28]

James Newton, bruised by the broken engagement in 1845, had been left reluctant to risk such rejection and embarrassment again. After his father's death in 1846, he had given himself to the responsibilities of managing the Retreat and seeing after his mother and younger brothers and sisters. He had quickly become, wrote John Jones, "an excellent guardian and manager." In time his success restored his confidence and he began to court Sarah Norman, the daughter of a neighboring planter. She was kind and gentle, clearheaded and forthright, and apparently a beauty, for James Newton had become one of the most eligible bachelors in the county.[29] Their wedding was held in her parents' home in Walthourville. Charles wrote Mary Sharpe a detailed account. There were, he said, three bridesmaids and three groomsmen.

> The bride and groom looked remarkably well. The bride wore a veil falling from the head but not over the face; high-neck dress of satin (I believe) with a lace deep over it. Very becoming and genteel. Her maids were similarly dressed, with silk bodices; and the whole appearance of the bridal array was in good taste and pleasing to all. The room was crowded. Conceive a room entirely occupied all around with seats, and then as many persons as could be crowded into the center space, and you have an idea of our condition. And everybody engaged in the most animated conversation.

At the appointed time, I. S. K. Axson, the pastor at Midway, performed the wedding service. Then the Liberty County Independent Troop—in which James Newton was an officer—having gathered in the yard, fired salutes, "to the consternation of some of the little children, and the great delight of others." Some of the young ladies played on the piano and sang; some of the men retired "from the ladies society" to an adjoining room. At eleven o'clock, dinner was served, and was, wrote Charles, "very handsome." He thought the "whole evening passed off most agreeably," and he told Mary Sharpe that the wedding was like one "you ordinarily attend in our county." James Newton seemed especially happy. "He is thought," said Charles, "to have made a prudent choice."[30]

A little more than two weeks after the wedding, Charles was on his way back to his Philadelphia desk. In the meantime, Joe had arrived at Montevideo, and he would remain with his mother during the winter break.[31] The separation of the family that winter made Charles and Mary more homesick than ever for their old established ways at Montevideo and Maybank. And James Newton's wedding evidently stirred memories in them of their own wedding at the Retreat and perhaps of Joseph and other departed ones whose voices and images seemed to be growing more distant as if they were, year by year, floating farther away from home on the dark waters of time. The day after their wedding anniversary, which came shortly after Charles had arrived back in Philadelphia, Mary wrote him:

> Yesterday, my dear husband, was our twenty-first wedding day! Can you believe it? Oh, that I had the power to recall all the love and mercy that have crowned those departed years! I seem to have been dwelling in a land of receding shadows, and it is with wonder and astonishment that I stop to review the path by which we have been led. "Surely goodness and mercy have followed us all the days of our life"; and I trust we feel a desire to "dwell in the house of the Lord forever"!

Mary acknowledged that only "Sovereign and Infinite Wisdom" knew how "much longer we shall be spared to each other." "I have no desire," she wrote Charles, "to rend the veil which obscures futurity! My husband, my children, my own soul, interests temporal and spiritual—I desire to place all in God's hand, to be guided and disposed of as His righteous will directs." Mary evidently felt in their separation—and her increased worries about Charles's health—the approach of what she had called years earlier "the great separation day."[32]

And in Philadelphia on their wedding anniversary, Charles wrote a long love poem to Mary. He recalled their wedding at the old Retreat and declared: "Blest day that made thee mine!" He remembered their life together and called her "Light of my life! My counselor, my aid/My sweet companion, by kind Heaven made." A month later he wrote John Jones: "I shall have to be set down among the *confirmed, incurable lovers.* In fact, I want to be confirmed, and don't want to be cured!" But he too sensed the lengthening shadows gathering over his and Mary's life together, and he reminded her that "the vale of life, my love, before us lies!"[33]

Brooding upon the past and contemplating their mortality did not, however, preoccupy Charles and Mary—they were, after all Calvinists, who were concerned about being faithful to the responsibilities immediately before them. "Memory," Mary wrote, "is the reigning faculty, and I know usurps too much of time and feeling for happiness or usefulness."[34] So each of them gave themselves to the duties and the busy activities of daily life.

Mary turned her considerable energies to the management of their plantations and to the ordinary details of life in the low country. She ordered new blankets for those in the settlements and instructed Sandy and Porter to repair the back piazza at Montevideo and then to put into good order the cabins at Arcadia. She moved Caesar—one of the younger, single men—into a cabin in the yard at Montevideo to stay with his uncle, old Tony, who was the gardener. "This will be for the comfort of the old man," she wrote Charles, "and protection of the lot." And she complained to Irwin Rahn about the small number of hogs being raised at Arcadia and insisted that their numbers be increased in order "to secure bacon to our people."[35]

Not only did Mary see after the management of the plantations, she assumed the ministerial role of her husband in his absence. She had, of course, been teaching Sunday school for years, but now she began to lead worship at Maybank and to preach. The Apostle Paul, she wrote Charles, says, "Suffer not a woman to teach." But she thought such an admonition must not include a woman's teaching or preaching to "children and servants." For if Paul meant this, then "we are not accountable for their ignorance or their errors." A white mistress, Mary apparently reasoned, could teach and preach as long as no white man was present, but if there were only children and black men and women in worship, then that was another matter. Deep racial assumptions set within the hierarchical world of slavery were apparently loosening for Mary long-established gender roles for white women.[36]

Mary knew that she was making decisions and giving instructions beyond what was usually expected of plantation mistresses. But when she saw something that needed to be done, she did not hesitate to act. "It has been a source of satisfaction to me," she wrote Charles, "to be with our people to instruct them as far as I can and look after their comfort and the interests of the plantation." She was "thoroughly convinced of the necessity of doing so" as long as Charles's duties called him away from home. "I do not believe in ladies' assuming responsibilities," she later wrote her brother John, "but when the Lord is pleased to lay them upon them, I do not see why they should not trust him for grace and strength and go forward in their performance." With all of her decisiveness and energy, John thought Mary more like their father than any of Joseph's other children. She was, said John, the "best representative of a sire who never feared the face of clay."[37]

When Charles received a letter from Mary that winter providing details of all her work and decisions, he wrote back: "Am obliged to you for all the stirrings up to things and duty on the different places." You are, he told her, "a great hand for business." And as for her teaching and preaching, he wrote: "Teach and preach as much as you please in the mode you did. I give you leave. You are a minister. We are one flesh, you know." But he was cautious about her going too far, about Mary's crossing too many boundaries as she assumed some of the traditional responsibilities of a man. "This will do for the occasion," he told her, "but we *will not* carry the matter beyond the family and household." [38]

Mary's visit to the low country was not only a time of duty and responsibilities but also an opportunity for seeing family and friends. She and Joe went to South Hampton for Christmas with the Kings and other friends. And after Christmas there was a trip to Maybank, a kind of "maroon" Mary called it, without all of the comforts they had carried there in the past when oxcarts had been loaded for a summer on the island. But they were not without the bounty of the island— Betsy sent over from Social Bluff a "nice corned beef"; Joe went hunting and brought back a duck and some quail; Andrew brought "a fat young turkey"; and there were oysters Niger had gathered, cold and fresh from the marsh, so that, wrote Mary, "with a dish of fried oysters, rice, potatoes, and turnips, with a dessert of oranges and sugared oranges, we had a very nice *maroon*." [39] But such pleasant time was soon brought to an abrupt end.

A few days after their arrival at Maybank, Mary and Joe drove up in the carriage and saw smoke and found "fires burning low on the ground." Gilbert ran up and cried: "Aunt Patience's house is burned down!" With hearts pounding they looked and found that not only Patience's house but also the plantation kitchen, the poultry yard, the stable, and the fences beyond it "all lay a heap of smoldering ruins." Fortunately, the wind had carried the flames away from the plantation house itself, and it was not harmed.

Patience told Mary what had happened. A spark had caught the roof of the kitchen—an old building with pine shingles. The women working around the house had done what they could to put it out, but the flames spread. Andrew and those working in the fields came running to help. William Maxwell was summoned, and he came rushing with his crew from Social Bluff. A spark fell on the stable, filled with fodder, and it "was like falling in a tinderbox. In one moment the flames rose in the skies and licked around." The roof of the corn house caught. Andrew said that "the Lord helped him and gave him strength. He flew up like a squirrel (to use his own expression) and tore off the shingles." The others kept putting wet blankets on the buildings and fences, and in this way, the fire was finally stopped. William said, "No man in the world could have acted with more promptness or forethought than Andrew." He not only rushed to the roof and with his tough hands tore off the burning shingles, but he also gave instructions to the others to help stop the spreading flames.[40]

The Maybank fire brought back forcefully to Mary—and later to Charles, when he read Mary's account—all the memories and the trauma of the night in Columbia when they had awakened to smoke and flames. True to their theology and piety, they wondered what they should learn from this second fire. They both believed the fire "was from the Lord," who was trying to teach them something. Charles thought that God was seeking "no doubt to teach us over and in a milder form the lesson that all our earthly possessions are held by us at His pleasure; that they are ours to hold for necessary and charitable uses in His fear, but not to keep as an unchanging inheritance." The fire made Charles search his own heart and to wonder whether his long quest for home was a "secret idolatry of heart which still clings to earth for home and happiness." "The Lord," he wrote Mary, "may be revealing our hearts to us, and teaching us that *our home* is in His hand; that He can take it all away in a moment of time; and therefore we must live upon Him, to Him, and for Him; and He and He alone be our portion and our inheritance."[41]

Two weeks after the fire, Mary—having made arrangements for the rebuilding and repairs at Maybank and having replaced what Patience and Porter had lost in the fire—left with Joe for the North and her home in a Philadelphia boarding-house.[42]

The winter of 1852 was a busy and demanding time for Charles. The Presbyterian Church (Old School) was growing at a rapid rate—faster than the general population—and the number of domestic missionaries had now exceeded five hundred.[43] Charles's days, and many evenings, were spent trying to keep on top of his correspondence, and his hand, arm, and shoulder began to trouble him greatly. In addition, there was the constant pressure to raise money to meet the demands of an expanding mission. This meant that he had to travel regularly on the weekends and speak to church groups and preach in various congregations, which meant that he also had to find time to study and write his long sermons and addresses. But all of his labors were taking a toll on Charles's health and making him wonder how much longer he could continue in his work.[44]

During these winter months of 1852, Charlie and Charles Edward were moving toward graduation—Charlie from Princeton and Charles Edward from the Medical College of the University of Pennsylvania. In late March, Charles Edward's mother, Susan, wrote him from South Hampton, where she was visiting: "I suppose I may congratulate you now on bringing off some of the honours."

Charles Edward had indeed done well in his studies and had already made plans to begin his medical practice in Savannah. Susan had rented a fine home in the city—it was built off the ground in low-country style, and the enclosed ground-level rooms were designated to serve as Charles Edward's new office. The young physician was ready not only to enter his profession but also to assume his responsibilities for his mother and his sister Laura.[45]

Mary, however, was worried about her nephew. He had worked such long hours, burning the candle at both ends as he came toward the end of his medical studies. A few days before his graduation Mary wrote Laura that Charles Edward had been "suffering from a severe cold and cough, and looks very thin." She added: "If possible he ought to recruit his health before he enters upon the active duties of his profession." The next week he graduated—with honors—and shortly afterward he set off toward home. He got no farther than Morristown, New Jersey, however, before he was struck with a violent case of dysentery. He had a telegraph sent to his Uncle Charles: "I am very sick with inflammation of the bowels here at Morristown N. Jersey. Come to me and bring me twenty-five dollars and bring Dr. Hodge with you."[46]

Charles and Mary rushed to his side, arriving late in the night. The next morning they wrote Charlie and Joe at Princeton: "We found your dear cousin very ill—glad, glad to see us, as we to get to him. The attack has been exceedingly violent, and his situation is very critical, although we hope for the best." They lavished on him all the love and attention they could and called in another physician. But he did not improve. He is "*critically ill*," they wrote Charlie and Joe the next day, "and we know not how his case will terminate! We must pray and hope for the best. He sends love to you." The next day he seemed a little better, but Charles warned his sons: "A *deathbed, my dear sons, is no place for you to prepare to meet your God!*"[47] Charles Edward died early the following morning.

Charles wrote Susan:

Oh, my sister! My sister! How shall I speak? "The cup which my Father giveth me to drink, shall I not drink it?" Oh, this cup—so unexpected, so bitter, so deep! God writeth you *sonless!* Help her, O my God! Your help, my sister, must come from Him who made heaven and earth—the almighty and compassionate Saviour.

We are in sore dismay and distress beyond expression! Alas, how sudden, how violent past all remedies his disease! Nothing left unattempted, undone. We were with him day and night. He lacked for no attention. All skill was executed in his case. Dear child, his hour had come, and God has taken him. You were spared the agony of the eye and the ear. The kindness of the people is extraordinary. We will do all things the best we can. My dear wife and I are cast down and overborne. He was beloved as a child to us. He died this morning at ten minutes after five o'clock. God only can comfort you and our dear Laura! Pray for us as we do for you. Love, love to everyone.

Your ever affectionate and afflicted, distressed brother. Mary writes this letter with me.

Susan was crushed. Laura became "but the shadow of what she was" and Betsy and William were left "bowed with sorrow."[48]

The family's sorrows that spring, however, were not over. A month after Charles Edward's death came news from Marietta that John's little girl Mary Elizabeth, "the darling of her parents" and Charles and Mary's "pet niece," had died. She had run across her bedroom, tripped over a toy box, and hit her head. At first she seemed fine, but later in the day she began to complain of a headache, and then she began to vomit, and the next day she had died in her mother's arms. John was grief stricken, but he wrote Charles and Mary, "My sorrows are light compared with those of that chief mourner, the stricken and almost inconsolable mother. . . . I now understand the meaning of that verse, 'Rachael weeping for her children and would not be comforted because they are not.'" "O!" he cried, "this cutting off one's heart and putting it in the grave."[49]

The death of Mary Elizabeth added a tenderness and vulnerability to John and his ministry that made many love him. Later in writing Mary about Charles Edward's death, he said that when he lost his "precious baby, my little idol, an unknown fountain of sorrow for myself and other bereaved parents broke forth from my heart." The loss, he said, taught "a lesson which may be imagined, but never known, until we are called to take our own flesh and lay it in the dust." And later when his brother Henry Hart lost a child, John wrote Mary that the loss of a child brings a "sorrow that lives as an exhaustless fountain in the heart. Tears never cease to flow for those little ones and the parent's heart becomes a kind of endless whispering gallery in which their little words and remarks reverberate unceasingly." And then giving an indication of his own continuing grief, he noted that "at times impetuous with emotion and anguish long suppressed, the swelling heart heaves, moaning like the ocean that cannot be at rest."[50]

Charles and Mary were back in Liberty County in late November 1852. Charles had another synod meeting to attend, and he had been invited to speak at the celebration of the Midway congregation's one hundredth anniversary. But a primary reason for the visit was for Charles to see his cousin, Dr. Charles West, and to have a complete physical examination. West's news was not good. While the doctor encouraged Charles to get other medical advice, he was confident about his diagnosis. "I regard your symptoms," he wrote Charles,

> as the first indications that the nervous structure of the spine is becoming *per-manently congested*, the progress of that state leads to paralysis of the arms & hands. This congestion once begun in one limited spot, seldom remains within these limits, but is apt to extend to other portions of the spine producing paralysis also, and once it begins its march of extending to portions now healthy we do not know when it will stop. In fact, it seldom ceases short of the nervous centre, the Brain.

West believed that the disease "had been produced without doubt by great mental effort, without sufficient muscular exercise." He also believed "It has been aggravated without doubt by removal to a colder climate." He recommended that if, after exercise, the debility continued, a surgical procedure be followed to allow for drainage from the "lower portion of the cervical vertebrae" at the back of Charles's neck. The major thrust of what he recommended, however, was that Charles leave his work in Philadelphia and return to Liberty County. There he could rest and exercise, and his nervous system could benefit from the warmth of the climate.[51]

Charles immediately wrote the directors of the Board of Mission and enclosed a copy of Dr. West's letter. He then asked if it would be "consistent with the interests of the Board" to allow him to remain in a "warmer climate during the severer months of this winter and endeavor to recover his health?" The response, which came quickly, was deeply sympathetic but also ambiguous. It appeared that the directors were leaving to Charles the decision about remaining in the South. Two weeks later, in the middle of January, he and Mary left Liberty County for Philadelphia. "Dr. Jones is threatened with paralysis," Eliza Mallard wrote her son Robert, a student at the seminary in Columbia. "Notwithstanding," she said, "he has left for the North."[52]

Charles plunged back into his work for the board, and he felt from every side pressures and responsibilities weighing upon him as his physical condition continued to weaken. He was not ready, however, to bring his work to its end. When the General Assembly met in June, he received permission for a six-month leave of absence to see whether he could recover his health.[53] He decided to spend the summer in Sharon, Connecticut, in a beautiful part of New England where the summers were cool, the villages quiet, and the pace of life could be slowed down. The plan was that Charles and Mary Sharpe would go to Sharon; that Joe would join them later in the summer and escort his sister on some outings; and that Mary would remain in Philadelphia with Charlie, who had spent the previous year working in a Philadelphia law office and was preparing to leave in the fall for law school at Harvard.[54]

Charles was very pleased with what he found in Sharon. "It is an old fashioned, plain New England village," he wrote Mary, "and the inhabitants of the plain, honest, moral, business style." He enjoyed the New England countryside and took long walks every day. "I like the place," he wrote Mary, "so retired and so beautiful." But in spite of the quiet, the rest from his labors, and the long walks, Charles's health did not improve. And he missed Mary terribly. "I cannot bear to be separated from you," he wrote her. He wanted her to join him in Sharon, but when Joe arrived to take Mary Sharpe to Yale for its graduation exercises, Charles decided to go for a quick visit to Philadelphia because, he told Mary, "I love and can't stay from you." He confessed he felt that "love never grows old nor decays." And he thought that their love for each other was "as fresh now as when we first loved and won each other's hearts."[55]

But Charles also had another purpose for making a quick trip to Philadelphia. He wanted to see Dr. Hodge and get "some prescription for my neck, which continues much at the old rate. . . . My impression is deepening that it will take a long time to restore me—if ever. I desire," he told Mary, "to leave it all with God." Mary, however, had already made up her own mind in regard to Charles's condition. "I think my dear," she wrote from Philadelphia, "you must be now convinced that years of rest are absolutely necessary to your restoration *with God's blessing,* and I look forward with great satisfaction to our return to our own home on that account above all others."[56]

While Charles's health thus became a primary motive for a return to their Liberty County home, there were other reasons as well. That summer of 1853 a series of embarrassing letters appeared in the *New-York Daily Times.* Frederick Law Olmsted, the traveler, writer, and future landscape architect, had left Savannah the preceding winter for a visit to the plantations on the Georgia coast. Reporting in the *Times* on what he had found, he told of having visited briefly Eliza Clay's Richmond-on-Ogeechee and of having been charmed by its beauty. He had spent three days at Whitehall, the neighboring plantation of Richard Arnold, where he "found Slavery under its most favorable circumstances." Olmsted had been eager to discover at Whitehall and throughout his travels whether the treatment of slaves was humane and whether the institution of slavery was—as many southerners claimed—an instrument for civilizing and evangelizing slaves. What he had found, he wrote in the *Times,* was that "the mind and higher faculties of the Negro are less disciplined and improved in slavery than in the original bar-

barism of the race." And he concluded that "Slavery, in its effects on slaves, is at war with progress, with enlightenment, with Christianity."[57]

In order to justify his conclusions and to dismiss any charges that he had "observed superficially and judged with prejudice," Olmsted quoted extensively from Charles's final report to the Liberty County Association. In particular, Olmsted pointed to Charles's remarks about slaves' being the property, the "money," of their owners. Because they were "money" for their owners, it was, Charles had said, exceedingly difficult for slave owners to render their slaves "that which is just and equal as immortal and accountable beings, and as heirs of the grace of life, equally with ourselves." Olmsted seized on this and other statements from the report and used them to verify his conclusion that "Slavery, in itself, rendering impossible a strong appeal to the character and happiness of its subject, recognizing him solely in such a manner as produces self-*humiliation*, can tend only to *degradation* of conduct and character."[58] Such use of the report must have been not only embarrassing for Charles but also infuriating. Olmsted's letters, however, were nothing compared to the use made of Charles's work by Harriet Beecher Stowe, the sister of Charles's old friend Catharine Beecher.

During Charles and Mary's second year in Philadelphia, Mrs. Stowe had published *Uncle Tom's Cabin; or, Life among the Lowly*. A firestorm of controversy had followed. Stowe had taken a tradition of sentimental and domestic novels and transformed it into a tool for the most influential antislavery story of the time.[59] And while the novel had quickly become immensely popular, it had also come under bitter attacks from southerners who accused its author of "falsewitness against thousands and millions of her fellowmen."[60]

In response to these and other charges of distortion and deceit, Mrs. Stowe published in 1853 *A Key to Uncle Tom's Cabin; Presenting the Original Facts and Documents upon which the Story is Founded*. And among the "original facts and documents" most quoted were the reports and studies of the Reverend Charles C. Jones.[61] Mrs. Stowe treated Charles with respect, perhaps remembering his early zeal for reform and his friendship with her sister Catharine. "The Rev. Charles C. Jones" is, she wrote, "a man of the finest feelings of humanity, and for many years an assiduous laborer for the benefit of the slave." She called him an "earnest and indefatigable laborer for the good of the slave," and she thought that his *Religious Instruction of the Negroes in the United States* "manifests a spirit of sincere and earnest benevolence, and of devotedness to the cause he has undertaken, which cannot be too highly appreciated." Yet for Mrs. Stowe, Charles's sincerity and benevolent spirit made his support of slavery all the more deplorable. After declaring that he possessed a "sublime spirit," a "mind capable of the very highest impulses," she lamented: "And yet, if we look over his whole writings, we shall see painfully how the moral sense of the finest mind may be perverted by constant familiarity with such a system." And she declared that while it was a "very painful and unpleasant task to express any qualification or dissent with regard to efforts which have been undertaken in a good spirit, and which have produced, in many respects good results," she nevertheless had to conclude that it "is not the *true and pure gospel system*" which Charles had given to the slave. She found that what Charles had taught the slave was that "his master's authority over him, and property in him, to the full extent of the enactment of slave-law, is recognized and sustained by the tremendous authority of God himself."[62]

Such mining of Charles's reports for antislavery purposes, and such bitter conclusions as those reached by Olmsted and Stowe, stirred in Charles and Mary a kind of culture shock and a sense of being aliens in an increasingly hostile northern land. And so the decision was made without regret in the fall of 1853 for Charles and Mary to return to Liberty County and to begin the last years of their life together above the dark waters of the North Newport and by the Medway marshes. They would turn their faces south because of Charles's health and because of the gravitational pull of the low country on their hearts. But they would also go south to home, to the familiar, where there was no sense of dislocation or alienation, where the distance from the North, and the routines of plantation life, would mute what they regarded as the virulent rhetoric of abolitionists. At home, they hoped, the bitter charges of a Harriet Beecher Stowe could be dissipated by the morning wind blowing in from the sea at Maybank and by the night wind coming up from the river at Montevideo.

23

CARLAWTER III

Life in Liberty County had not been frozen in time waiting for Charles and Mary to return to their remembered home. During their five-year absence—from 1848 to 1853—there had been marriages and births, fields planted and harvested, houses built, and barns and homes burned. Sicknesses had struck; death had come to both the young and the old; and black men, women, and children had been bought and sold, divided among heirs, and shifted from plantation to plantation to accommodate the interests and needs of whites.

At Carlawter, across the old slough that separated the plantation house at Montevideo from the settlement, life had no more stood still during these years than it had at any of the other plantations of the county. For those who gathered in the evenings to talk before open fires, the absence of the white family—for what Mary called years of "nonresidence on this place"—meant an isolation and a degree of independence from white control that most who lived there had never known before under the paternalistic care of their owners. To be sure, Thomas Shepard visited the plantation regularly during these years, but he had several other plantations to look after, and he rarely stayed overnight on the place. And when Charles and Mary came for their occasional visits from Columbia or Philadelphia, the visits were generally short, and the master and mistress often spent much of their time at Maybank. They sent instructions about housing and food, about planting and repairs, about blankets to be distributed and ways to care for the sick. But their instructions were sent from afar or given during a brief visit before they were on their way again to distant homes. In this way those who lived at Carlawter had space and time to nurture their Gullah culture and to assert their independence to a degree that had not been known since the early days of the settlement, when Joseph Jones had first moved Jupiter and Hamlet, Elvira and Lizzy, little Cato and Cassius, and all the others to the recently purchased plantation. But of course the independence during those earlier years had never been complete, and the isolation during Charles and Mary's sojourn in far places was never so great that the power—and sometimes the wrath—of whites could not be felt.[1]

With the removal of Jack to Columbia in 1848 and his death in 1850, Cato became the single most influential figure at Carlawter. He was the one who rose early and announced the new day with a bell (the conch-shell horn of Old Jupiter had been long abandoned) and assigned the tasks for the day. Cato wore high-top boots, tough pants and shirts, and during the cold months a greatcoat that reached almost to his ankles. Over his shoulder he carried his "cotton planter," the plaited whip that was a sign of his authority. He owned two horses—Jenny and Bunkum—and often rode one as he moved from field to field to supervise the work of the plantation.[2]

In the fall of 1850, when Charles and Mary left for Philadelphia, Cato turned to the task of getting in the last of the cotton crop—they had already picked fifteen thousand pounds of cotton by the end of October—and to the work of harvesting the black-eyed peas, corn, and sweet potatoes that would provide much of the food for Carlawter during the coming year. And they had the rice from the old inland swamp fields to harvest; by the first of November the women had gathered the sheaves and, in the erect and elegant manner of their mothers in Africa, carried them on their heads to the stack yard. There they had neatly arranged the rice and its straw before the rice house, where it would soon be threshed and winnowed.[3]

Once most of the harvesting was done, Cato turned his attention to the new rice fields off the river: they needed, he knew, more work before they could be planted in the spring. For the two previous winters Cato had been supervising, under Shepard's instruction, the enormous effort of clearing the slough that separated Montevideo from Carlawter. During the first winter he had sent his brothers Cassius and Lymus, Daniel and Adam, and the other men of the settlement into the swampy arm of the river with axes and crosscut saws to fell the old cypresses and black gums, water oaks and tupelos. Charles and Gilbert—who came from Maybank to help—had used oxen to draw the logs together on dry places, and the women of Carlawter had cut the branches and built great flaming pyres of the green wood so that for weeks during that winter smoke had filled the air of Montevideo and its settlement. During the next winter—following the directions that had been given earlier by Dr. Harry from the Mallard Place settlement—Cato had supervised the construction of the long embankment that kept out the water of the river. Wooden trunks, or floodgates, constructed by Sandy

Maybank and Porter, had been carefully placed to allow the flooding and draining of the old slough.[4]

Now in the early winter of 1850, Cato was sending the men and women of the
settlement back to finish burning the remnants of the now well-dried and blackened tree trunks and to complete the digging of canals. To dig the canals, they
had to plunge into the muddy fields and with long-handled shovels toss the heavy
earth to the side to make the dykes that separated the fields. When stumps were
in their way, they used axes and mattocks to grub them loose and oxen to pull
them out. For full hands like Cassius and his brothers the daily task for digging
the canals was between two hundred and five hundred cubic feet, depending on
the number of stumps that had to be removed.[5]

Cato was eager for this demanding work to be finished, and he pushed his
hands hard so that in the spring all would be ready for the planting of rice in the
dark and fertile soil. But he told Shepard that he was worried that the effort to
get the new rice fields ready would put them behind in their planting of corn
and other provision crops.[6]

As they were beginning these winter labors, word came that smallpox had "unexpectedly made its appearance in the most malignant form in Riceboro." Adam
Dunham, a Riceboro merchant, had been in New York purchasing supplies.
When he returned home, he became sick. At first Dr. Benjamin King—still too
fond of his liquor—thought Dunham's illness a bad rash and allowed a number
of visitors to see him. Soon, however, Dr. William McConnell was called in, and
he declared the disease to be smallpox. Dunham confessed to having seen a man
with smallpox in New York, and immediately Riceboro was put under quarantine. Old Robinson, the father of Cato and Cassius and all of Old Lizzy's children, had had smallpox years earlier, and he was called from the Retreat to be the
nurse of those with the disease. Citizen guards were placed around the boro, including the southwestern edge of Montevideo. Sandy Maybank and Porter had
been doing some carpentry work in Riceboro, and for a while there were fears
that they might have contracted the disease, which was beginning to spread. The
guards asked Thomas Shepard to give them up so that they could be kept under
the quarantine in Riceboro, but he refused, saying they showed no sign of the
disease and that he would not allow them to be exposed by being taken back to
the boro. But he worried that some from Carlawter might try to get through the
quarantine and visit in Riceboro—especially the children of Old Robinson—
or sneak through on the way to visit a wife or family on another plantation. He
talked to Cato and insisted that no one be allowed to leave the plantation. Later
Shepard wrote Charles:

I have every confidence in Cato's care and vigilance. He never leaves the plantation and has not seen his wife for several weeks. All communication between *all* being completely stopped. This seems hard upon the men whose wives are abroad but the only safe way of arresting the disease. I have no doubt the disease will soon be terminated.

He had given, he wrote, a special charge to Cato "to keep a bright look out" on his brothers, for there was danger of their getting the disease if they slipped away to the boro to get tobacco and came in contact with their father.[7]

In the meantime, Dr. John LeConte had come out from Savannah, bringing some vaccine, and he had begun to inoculate his family and their slaves. Thomas Shepard and William Maxwell immediately began to do the same, but they had difficulty getting enough vaccine. They consequently took "some vaccine matter" from the scabs that had formed on their own arms and used this for the people in the settlements. Within a few weeks the crisis was passed — nine in the boro had gotten smallpox, and one had died. Those who had contracted the disease suffered terribly, their bodies covered with oozing scabs and pustules. Adam Dunham, who brought the disease to the county, "paid dearly of it," wrote Henry Hart Jones, "in the utter loss of his good looks. His face looks like an infinite number of minute ground moles had been burrowing under the cuticles of the skin."[8]

The smallpox outbreak intensified the long-brewing tension between the merchants of Riceboro and the surrounding planters. The planters were furious that Dunham had exposed the county to an epidemic without quickly acknowledging his contact with the disease in New York. On their part, the merchants felt that the quarantine had been maintained for too long and that their business had consequently suffered unnecessarily. To compensate for their losses, the merchants began to be more blatant about selling liquor to slaves who would slip through the night and come to the little village for some illicit pleasures. The planters responded by organizing for the first time in years a regular nightly patrol to intercept any slaves without a pass from an owner. Henry Hart wrote Charles and Mary that Charles Stebbins and his nephew Richard Lyon, who owned a general merchandise store in Riceboro, were the chief culprits. They harbored, he wrote,

a Negro in their store the other night without a ticket refusing to deliver him up when summoned by the Patrol, who however guarded the doors until half past one o'clock Sabbath morning and took the Negro as he came out. The citizens have taken the matter in hand vigorously and patrols scour the country almost every night. Council will be procured to *prosecute* Stebbins and Lyons on several distinct counts. I expect to mail this letter tonight on an excursion of the above kind with some of my Dorchester neighbors. On Saturday night they intercepted Negroes with whiskey jugs going over the Bryan line for liquor also. There will probably be a general meeting of the citizens on this subject.[9]

Tensions were obviously building not only between planters and storekeepers but also between planters and their slaves; and the unrest surrounding the smallpox outbreak was but a sign of things to come in Liberty County.[10]

Cato's vigorous response to the threat of smallpox, however, had only strengthened Charles's confidence in his driver. A few weeks later, when Cato had become sick with a bad cold and what was apparently a serious sinus infection, Charles wrote him a long letter. He told him to wear warm undershirts and drawers; he should get "Phoebe to cut them out and make them at once and nicely for you." If he lacked any "outer clothing," then Mr. Shepard would get them for him. "You must pay attention to what you eat," Charles told him, and be particularly careful to stay out of bad weather. "We have been together a long time," Charles wrote,

> and I have always had a great attachment to you and confidence in you, and you have always been a good and faithful man to me. And now that we are apart from one another and you are sick it makes me feel a great deal. But I hope you will soon be up again. Be careful of the cold, damp, and changeable weather in February and March. Mr. Shepard will point out some one of the men who can take a look after things when you are not able to be as much about as you wish, and he can take directions from you and make his report to you.[11]

Charles's letter to Cato was in the familiar language of a paternalistic master to a respected slave. They had been "together a long time"—from the earliest days that both of them could remember. They had walked the fields together, talked about crops and the weather together; they had worried together about the sick in the settlements and in the plantation houses; and they had prayed together in the little chapel, at the watchmen's meetings, and at the North Newport Church. Charles had grieved with Cato when Old Lizzy had died, and Cato had helped to carry Joseph's body toward its grave at the Retreat. The two men probably knew each other about as well as a white master and black slave could know one another. Certainly Charles thought so.[12]

Cato responded to Charles's letter with one of his own. He could not write it—when Charles had been learning to write, Cato had been learning about the work of a slave. So Cato had Thomas Shepard to write it for him, and that meant of course that the letter was not fully Cato's, that whatever he said was interpreted by Shepard and written in Shepard's stilted language. But still this letter reflected—as did the other letters Cato wrote to Charles—something of who Cato was and how he saw the world.

> Dear Master
> I received your kind letter, and when Mr. Shepard was reading it to me on the marsh dam, I felt thankful to God for so good a master and it made me feel melancholy to think you and mistress who I knew loved and felt for me was so far away, and the uncertainties of our lives. Maybe we shall never again look on one another, but be this as it may, we know one thing if we live as we ought death cant separate us, though it may do so for a little while.

And later Cato wrote Charles:

> I always feel satisfied that I have a good Shear of your Love and Confidance, but whenever I See you take the time and trouble, to write me your Servant a kind and I may say fatherly letter, it makes me feel more like crying with love and gratitude for So kind a master than any thing else, and always feel it in my heart to say, I will try and be a better Servant than ever.[13]

Cato appeared in these letters and in other aspects of his orderly life to have internalized the ideology of the whites. He certainly knew the familiar rituals of subordination, as he addressed Charles as "Master" and told Charles what he wanted to hear. Day after day, he arose, went out to oversee the work of those who lived at Carlawter, and lived his life in ways that appeared to reinforce the belief that it was natural and inevitable that whites be owners and blacks be owned. Moreover, Cato had played a large role in making Montevideo a successful plantation. He had never participated in an organized revolt—nor, for that matter, had anyone else in the settlements of Liberty County—even though he knew blacks vastly outnumbered whites. He apparently believed at some level that slavery was inevitable, and that the power of whites was of such a character that there was little possibility of overthrowing the system. Maybe he thought that a successful revolution only "grows out of the barrel of a gun" and that slaves lacked the necessary firepower and military organization to challenge white hegemony. Certainly such assumptions were the intention of the Liberty County Independent Troop, with its parades and military exercises. At any rate, Cato's public language, his gestures, his way of relating to whites all pointed toward an acceptance of white authority and its legitimacy. Such seemed to be the power of the ideological forces that had been at work in his life since the day Lizzy had given birth to him in Sunbury. Certainly Charles thought of Cato as a "good and faithful man" to his master.[14]

But Cato's character was not so simple. Years earlier, Charles had written that "persons live and die in the midst of Negroes and know comparatively little of their real character. They are one thing before the whites and another before their own color." Much of what Charles saw in Cato was what Cato wanted him to see. Day in and day out, year in and year out, Cato seemed a faithful servant to Charles. And ironically his faithfulness—especially during these years of Charles's absence—provided greater independence for himself and for those who lived at Carlawter, for as long as Cato was trusted, there was less need for white supervision. From time to time in the years to come, however, Charles was to catch a glimpse of another face behind Cato's familiar smile. The glimpse would not be enough to challenge Charles's image of Cato, and Charles would go to his grave believing Cato a "good and faithful man" to him. It would be Mary's lot, rather, to have a bitter revelation of another world behind Cato's subservience.[15]

So Cato, as he went about his work as the driver at Carlawter, was a deeply complex man. He was neither all internalized subservience nor all clever deception. He seemed to have two competing impulses within his heart and mind—one impulse that said "the settlement is my place in life," another that cried "resist!" During the coming years he sometimes followed one impulse and sometimes the other as he carefully read the signs of the times and the social landscape of Liberty County.

If Cato had become the person in the settlements whom Charles trusted the most, Phoebe had become the person whom Charles most distrusted. His distrust had many roots: her adulterous affair with Cassius in the 1830s that had been so hard on her husband, Sandy Jones; her alleged plot—reported by Peggy—to get keys to the storerooms; and, perhaps most of all, her self-confidence and independence that sometimes took her near the edge of insubordination. She knew how far she could go without provoking harsh punishment, but she would go far enough to irritate Charles and to convince him that she could not be trusted. Moreover, he apparently recognized in her a rage that burned just below the surface of her cheerful manner. He knew that most of the time she kept her anger under control, that she bit her tongue and did not "answer back" when spoken to. But there were times when she could be what whites would come to call "uppity." She could give an occasional look of insubordination even as she went about her work, and she had a way of crossing her arms when something was said to her that she did not like. For all these reasons, Charles felt that Phoebe had to be treated carefully and given close supervision. Over the years Charles's respect for her father, Jack, had apparently acted as a buffer between Phoebe and serious trouble, but Jack's death had left her more vulnerable than ever to the power of her white owner.

Phoebe, however, was Mary's personal servant, and Mary was deeply dependent upon her. Phoebe was a link to Mary's mother, to the Retreat, and to all the associations of Mary's early years. Mary had—for all of her strong will and independence—a reliance on Phoebe that went beyond the pragmatic matters of a plantation household to complex emotions nurtured by memories and associations. Phoebe apparently understood this dependence even as she knew that she was herself dependent upon Mary's emotional attachment to her and protection of her. For decades the two women had lived in each other's presence, and over the years Phoebe had observed her mistress carefully. With the possible exception of her cousin Patience, Phoebe had entered the world of whites more deeply than anyone who now lived at Carlawter or in the settlements at Maybank and Arcadia. Daddy Jack and Mom Sylvia had no doubt talked to her when she was a child, explaining what she saw when she observed white people eating elegant meals at the Retreat and interpreting for her the meaning of what she heard white people saying. As a young woman, she had been close by when Charles and Mary had met and poured out their hearts to each other in the little garret at the Retreat, and she had slept on the floor of Mary's room when the white children were young and Charles was away. For years she had heard Charles and Mary talk with family and friends on piazzas and in dining rooms and parlors, and she had filtered it all through her own experience and her own analysis and her own deep rage at the injustice of it all. So she knew how whites talked and acted, and she understood something of the world of whites that was often hidden from those in the settlements who spent their days plowing fields and harvesting crops.[16]

At the time of Jack's death in 1850, Phoebe had been working at South Hampton under the supervision of Julia King—Charles had sent her and her younger children there, as he had on earlier occasions, to keep her out of trouble when he and Mary were away. Later that summer, when Charles and Mary had returned to Maybank, Mary had sent for Phoebe and the children to come to the island.[17] Clothes had to be prepared for the move to Philadelphia, and Phoebe was indispensable as Mary made careful arrangements for the family's departure. As the time approached for Charles and Mary to leave for the North, Phoebe asked to be sent to live at Carlawter. Cassius had been making the long trip from Carlawter to Maybank to visit at his "wife house" on Saturday nights and Sundays. He had his own little buggy and a mare to pull it—they had probably been purchased with money he had made from selling his baskets—and this had made the trip easier for him.[18] Still, the family was separated during the week, and they wanted to be together at Carlawter. After some apparent hesitation, Charles agreed. This meant that Phoebe would now be sent to work in the fields under Cato's directions and Thomas Shepard's supervision—and not only Phoebe but also her son John and her daughter Jane, who had been house servants in Columbia under the eye of their grandfather Jack. Jane, who was turning thirteen, would join four other young women who were being sent to the fields for the first time.[19]

Shortly after Charles and Mary arrived in Philadelphia with Mary Sharpe, Charles received a letter from Thomas Shepard. William Maxwell, Shepard wrote, who was looking after Maybank, had "sent me Phoebe and her family on Friday last and I have put her right in the field with the rest picking pease and she turns around as though it was fine sport. I hope she wont get tired of it too soon." Phoebe seemed like "Buh Rabbit" thrown into the brier patch, "de place me mammy fotch me up!" She had gotten to be with Cassius, even if it meant "picking pease" rather than sewing clothes. But Shepard was keeping an eye on Phoebe and her family, and within two weeks there was trouble. "I gave John a pretty little brushing," Shepard wrote Charles in mid-November 1850, "which I think will do both him and his mother good for a long time."

> I gave Cato a note to Mr. Rahn and directed him to send it by John that night, as I wanted an answer in the morning. So next morning Cato found that John did not go but kept the note in his pocket and said to Cato that if he could not spare time to send him on an errand in the day time, he would not go at night. Cato knowing I would be there in the morning, did not trouble him till I came. I was well pleased to find he hated a flogging so bad.[20]

Shepard's "pretty little brushing" was a flogging intended to teach John a lesson and to give Phoebe a warning. Shepard wanted John to know that even if he had been in Columbia, and even if he was Jack's grandson, he was to go when he was sent and he was to do what he was told. Neither Shepard's nor Cato's instruction was to be ignored. Equally important, no sass would be allowed. Cato had simply bided his time when his nephew had been "smart" with him and had waited for Shepard to use the whip. The flogging had apparently been both brutal and shocking for the young man, who had so recently been a house servant protected by the reputation and wisdom of his grandfather. While John's flogging may not have been the first at Carlawter, it was the first to appear in the plantation records. It was not, however, to be the last.

As for Phoebe, Shepard was waiting for her to take a misstep. "Phoebe behaves herself very well so far and does her work readily," he wrote Charles, "which I hope she may continue to do, for my mind is made if the very first time she crooks to lock arms, believing it to be the first for her and me too." The whipping of John must have evoked a deep rage in Phoebe and do doubt left her with a searing memory of his agony and perhaps a sense of humiliation that she could not protect her son. But Phoebe knew that Shepard was watching her on his visits to Montevideo and she apparently determined there would be no "first for her" with Shepard's whip. Four months later, in one of Cato's letters to Charles, he said of his sister-in-law: "Phoebe and I get along so, so. So far as yet, she does her work very well, but there is a strong notion now and then to break out. But she knows well enough how it will be if she does, and I am in hopes she will let her better judgment rule her passions." But Cato thought Phoebe had not been a good influence on his brother Cassius—or Cash as he called him.

> As for Cash, I am afraid he has given up himself to the old boy, for since his wife has been with him he appears more petulant and has not only given up going to prayers but I have several times heard him make use of bad words when he was displeased and have shamed and talked to him so often that I have felt it my duty to report him to the church and Mr. Law has cited him before the next meeting.[21]

So Cato acted not only in his role as driver but also in his role as a watchman at the North Newport Baptist Church to try to bring his brother in line. Perhaps he saw some handwriting on the wall for Cash and Phoebe and their family. But whatever he saw, Phoebe's skills as a seamstress were too valuable to leave her picking peas and hoeing cotton.

Mary soon sent instructions for Phoebe to begin making clothes for those in the settlement and for the white family in the North. "If she does her work properly," Mary wrote, "she may remain at Montevideo." But if "there is any difficulty about it," then Phoebe and her youngest children were to be sent down to Maybank, while Cash and Jane were "to continue in the field at Montevideo," where John was also working.[22]

Later that summer, while Phoebe was busy with her sewing, Shepard reported that the "skeets are bad, bad, very bad in the settlements this summer."[23] Much rain had fallen from clouds sweeping in from the Gulf of Mexico, and the swamps, canals, and rice fields of the county had been filled with water that was soon pulsating with the larvae of mosquitoes. By midsummer great clouds of mosquitoes were filling the air, ready to attack any creature with warm blood. The consequence was particularly dire for the elderly and the young in the settlements.

A number of the older ones became sick with fevers—old Tony the gardener, Sandy Maybank the carpenter, Cato's older brother Lymus, and others—for although they had a greater resistance to malaria than the whites, they were not immune to the ravages of the disease. Already that year there had been death among the very old in the settlements. At White Oak, Old Fanny had grown in-creasingly weak during the previous winter. She had been allowed in her old age to leave the Retreat and move to White Oak, where her grandchildren could look after her and where she could be near her great-grandchildren. There in the evenings around the open fires she could tell in her Pidgin English how she, with her children Elvira and Marcus, had been captured in Africa and brought through the terrors of the midpassage to a strange land. She could tell of being bought by John Jones in Savannah and by Joseph Jones at his brother's estate sale in Riceboro in 1808. She had known the deep sorrows and terrors of slavery and the isolation of one who had struggled to learn not only the English of her captors but also the Gullah of the settlements. When Thomas Shepard wrote to Philadelphia and reported that "poor old Mom Fanny died last week," he had "no doubt" that the "old woman is safe in heaven." He had "several times talked to her on the subject of religion and from what little I could understand in her broken English and from the signs she made but what her religious feelings were unmistakably genuine."[24]

In the middle of the summer of 1851, after the mosquitoes had been swarm-ing, Mom Flora became sick and appeared increasingly weak. She had come to the Retreat in 1806 when Sarah Anderson had married Joseph, and she had been moved to Carlawter in 1832 as a part of Mary's inheritance from her mother. Flora and her husband—who lived on another plantation and whose name was never listed in plantation records—had had seven children, and by the summer of 1851 she had twenty-nine grandchildren and one great-grandchild living at Carlawter or Arcadia. As she grew weaker that summer, she "took the notion she was about to die," and she got Thomas Shepard to send someone and "beg Mr. Rahn to let her children come and see her for the last time." Rahn consented to let them go for "a part of a day much to the satisfaction of the old lady." The visit of her chil-dren had "given her new life," and both she and Shepard were of the "opinion she will live perhaps much longer." But within a week "poor old Momer Flora died." Shepard wrote Charles:

> I done all I knew and thought necessary for her comfort and relief. And tried to talk to her the best I knew and ascertain her own comforts in the near pros-pect of death. She said she was willing and expected to go. She had been sick a great while and now no service to herself or others. And it was time for her to be gone. And I hope although her ignorance prevented her from saying all she wished, yet her stay was by faith upon the all sufficiency of an atoning Saviour and her children and sister from Mrs. Jones on the Sand Hill all came to see her before she died.

Charles wrote back to Shepard: "The poor Lady is gone! I saw not much change in her, but she said, she did not think she would ever live to see us return. My conversation to her was pleasant, and my hope is that she had a saving interest in the Redeemer. She was one of the most kind and inoffensive people I ever knew."[25]

For the last years of her life, Mom Flora had been a nurse at Carlawter, looking after the little children in the settlement. When she died, her responsibilities were shifted to Rosetta. Shepard and Cato told her "to take up the switch and go on as she had been doing—attend to the yard and dairy and see that the little ones was regularly fed and nursed by the larger ones and keep them out of the creek from being caught by the alligators." Rosetta was herself still grieving the removal of Sam to Marietta. When Sam had returned to Marietta after his Christmas 1849 and January 1850 stay at Carlawter, Rosetta had become sick. Charles had wondered whether Rosetta's grief "for Sam's going back to Marietta made her sick in part." Then when Sam had not come at Christmas 1850 for his annual visit in the low country, Rosetta had become alarmed. Shepard told her "she must not grieve so much after old Sam." But she said she thought he was "married again in the up country, by his not coming down with his mistress which he might, she said, had done if he wished." Charles sent word to his old nurse that she should "keep a good heart about Sam," and he told Shepard to keep her well supplied in tobacco. He sent her and the other old ones a dollar each, and he also sent a dollar to Patience, but nothing to Phoebe.[26]

Shortly after Mom Flora died, Rosetta was busy looking after sick children—especially the little ones of Phoebe and Cassius. Shepard wrote Charles:

> There has been more sickness this season at Montevideo than any other since I have had charge here, particularly among the children. Phoebe's family has all been sick from big Cassius down to youngest, and the three youngest Albert, Lafayette, and Elizabeth—have really been very sick. I tried first one thing and then another, and after getting all the worms away and the system cleansed, the stubborn fevers in spite of all the horehound and cherry bark and dogwood bark, it would not yield till I got a dollar's worth of quinine before it was broken. Phoebe looks as slank as a whippoorwill yet but she has also missed her fever and are all again up and several of the other families of children has been sick from whom lots of worms has been taken but all better.

Within two weeks nine-year-old Albert was dead and, wrote Shepard, "Lafayette and Jane's cases hangs on . . . and rather the longest now than any other. Theirs has gone into the old fashioned fever and chill." Charles noted in his plantation records that the cause of Albert's death was "worm fever"; the next year he learned that of all the children at Carlawter, those of Phoebe and Cassius were most afflicted with the worms.[27]

Both Shepard and Cato apparently believed that worms—the roundworms *Ascaris* and *Trichuris*, the scourge of slaves—were the primary causes of the deaths. But Joe, in his medical investigations, later reached a different conclusion about such cases. "Do not," he would urge white planters, "attribute the diseases of children in the summer and fall to worms." He noted that at "this period of the year, when children are most liable to climate fever, it is the habit of so many planters to dose them with various drastic and disgusting mixtures, to rid them of worms, under the idea that the worms are the cause of the fevers of this season of year, because, when the children are taken sick, the worms travel away from them through every avenue and in every direction." Joe believed that the explanation of "this striking phenomenon" was that the fever altered the habitat of the worms and caused them to move. The worms had been, he wrote, "quietly housed all winter in comfortable quarters, without exciting any injurious effects upon the unconscious landlords, are suddenly sickened and disgusted with their altered fare and habitations, and beat a precipitate retreat in the most convenient and natural directions." The real disease was climate fever, or malaria, and the proper treatment was to administer a "gentle purgative" to get rid of the worms and then quinine to stop the fever.[28]

The children of Phoebe and Cassius seemed, however, especially susceptible to the worms and to the fevers that caused them to come crawling up the throat and out of the digestive tract "through every avenue and in every direction." And the children's susceptibility was probably linked to their diet.[29] Phoebe was apparently less successful than her cousin Patience—or Rosetta, Lucy, Mary Ann, and most of the other women in the settlements—in providing the necessary nutrients needed to keep the roundworms from interfering with the digestion and health of the children. Lack of adequate food made a child more likely to have an infestation of worms, and the worms, not getting enough food to sustain them and the child, began to interfere with the digestion and absorption of nutrients. In this weakened condition the child became more vulnerable to the ravages of malaria and other diseases.[30]

Perhaps something had happened to Phoebe, perhaps some emotional tie had snapped, when she was taken to live in Savannah with Mary and Charles in the early 1830s, leaving her less able to focus on her children. The move had separated her from young Clarissa and John and had left her deeply anxious and troubled. Or perhaps her restless spirit and largely suppressed rage distracted her over the years—as Buh Rooster was distracted and failed to notice Buh Fowl-

Hawk preparing to swoop down and take his children. Or maybe she did not have in Cassius—with his two families at other plantations—a father who was as interested in providing for his children as were his brothers Cato and Porter and the other fathers who had one family in the settlements. Whatever the source, Phoebe did not focus her energies on caring for and protecting her children in the way that Patience and others did.

A critical issue, of course, for all who lived at Carlawter, was supplementing the food that was distributed by Cato. They received regular provisions of corn, rice, black-eyed peas, and sweet potatoes. And during seasons of heavy work and at Christmas, a cow or ox was butchered, lambs were made into stews, and cane syrup was provided to sweeten porridges and hoecakes. In January and February hogs were slaughtered and smoked to be used as bacon throughout the year. But none of this was enough to provide a balanced diet and adequate nutrients for young children or for those engaged in the heavy work of a plantation. For this reason the gardens, chickens, rice plots, and hogs of the people were critical supplements for the diets of those who lived in the settlements. And hunting and fishing were also important as a way to add sufficient amounts of protein to their diet.[31]

Unlike the island settlement at Maybank, where seafood provided a steady supply of protein, the locations of Carlawter and Arcadia put limits on what was readily available from hunting and fishing. Inland they had no great banks of oysters or marsh creeks teaming with fish and crabs. But many at Carlawter and Arcadia took advantage of what they had. They could fish in the river, in swampy creeks, and in the rice canals. They employed, as did other low-country slaves, hooks and sinkers for catching freshwater bass and bream, and they set out trotlines for catfish, stringing the line along the edge of the river, where the water was deep and the hooks could be loaded down with night crawlers, the fat earthworms that came to the surface of the ground at night when the soil was wet. And late in the summer, when the water was low, the men "churned" together for fish in the canals of the rice fields, wading in the water with flour barrels.[32] Of course there were not only fish but also snakes, turtles, and alligators in the canals and creeks. The snakes were left alone or sometimes hunted at night by torchlight. But the turtles were caught for food, especially the pond slider, a basking turtle that would flop off a log into the water when disturbed. It could easily be caught in a trap baited with a fish head or the guts of a chicken. And on occasion, alligators would be caught with an iron hook attached to a long pole. At low water, when an alligator's hole was exposed, a front leg of the creature would be hooked and the hissing, thrashing gator would be dragged by several men up on the bank, where a brave soul with a sharp axe would sever the powerful muscles in back of the head. Both turtle and alligator—especially the alligator's tail— would go into stew pots.[33]

There was also game to be trapped or shot. Rabbits could be lured into a simple box with a door that fell quickly when jarred. Possums could be caught in a snare; raccoons could be hunted with some of the dogs that were always around the cabins looking for a handout; and wild ducks, geese, and turkey and even deer could be hunted with one of the guns kept in the settlements. Surprisingly, slaves throughout the low country owned or had access to guns. They used them to scare birds out of the rice fields or for their own hunting. Cato owned a gun that could bring down a deer; Stepney used a shotgun to hunt ducks and geese; and Andrew was noted for his success in hunting wild turkeys with a smoothbore musket. Years later archaeologists digging in low-country settlements found not only remnants of guns and musket balls but also the bones of deer and fish and other animals hunted or trapped.[34]

In addition to such game there were blackberries and plums that could be gathered in June and July, and in the late summer children could scramble up small trees and shake loose the wild muscadine grapes that grew at the edge of the woods or where sunlight penetrated the forest canopy. And in the fall, hickory nuts and walnuts could be gathered by those who wanted to take the time to crack the shells and dig out the meat. All these foods added variety and provided important supplements to the diets of those who lived at Carlawter and Arcadia and encouraged in them a spirit of self-reliance and independence from their white owners.[35]

Nevertheless malnutrition visited in some of the cabins, and the most obvious sign of its presence among adults was the dangerous habit of pica: clay eating. "Cross-eyed Titus," who lived at Arcadia, had showed indications of being a clay eater in 1849 when Charles and Mary were still in Columbia. The signs were clear: indigestion and emaciation; pale lips and fingertips; whiteness of the tongue; cold skin; and great fatigue. Mary was convinced that "if not stopped he would become seriously diseased and die." Two years later, in the late spring of 1851, three of the Maxwell-Cumming slaves at Lambert were diagnosed as being afflicted with the habit.[36]

Many physicians thought that the clay eating was a cultural residue from Africa and named the custom *cachexia africana*.[37] But some planters and physicians recognized that a better diet would prevent the outbreak of pica on a plantation. Roswell King, years earlier when he had been manager of the Pierce Butler plantations, had found that an extra "feed of ocra Soup, with Pork, or a little Molasses or Hommony or Small Rice" had so satisfied the children in the settlements that there was "not a *dirt eater* among them." And John LeConte, in his medical investigations of the malady, argued vigorously that a better diet was the best response. Mary and Charles, together with the Maxwells, responded in a way that acknowledged indirectly the need for a better diet—all four clay eaters were sent to Colonel's Island, where they evidently received enough proteins and minerals (especially calcium and iron) in their diets to quench the desire to eat the clay. But two from Lambert were made to wear for a time iron mouthpieces "to prevent access to the poison," and the others were threatened with its use in order to break the habit.[38]

Most of those who lived at Carlawter, Arcadia, and Maybank were able to adequately supplement their diets through their own "after task" efforts. In the afternoons, after their tasks were complete, they could work their corn or rice patch, tend their gardens of turnip greens and rutabagas, okra and arrowroot, peas, melons, and peanuts. "Don't forget," Charles would instruct Thomas Shepard, "to let the people have every chance of planting for themselves."[39] And most did, driven by self-interest and the need to add substance and variety to their diets.

But the children of Phoebe and Cassius continued to show signs that they were not getting enough to eat. The year after their Albert died, Cato wrote Charles:

> All are now well excepting Phoebe and her whole family. They are up and down some one every day with fevers. I have gotten away all the worms from Lafayette, Lizzie, and Victoria, and Mr. Shepard says we must not give them any more medicine, but try and break the fevers with Thumowist [?] Tea, and dogwood and cherry bark. None of them are ever very sick but can't get clear of the fever.

A few weeks later, Shepard wrote Charles:

> Cato mentioned in his letter that the most obstinate cases of fever was with Phoebe's three children Victoria, Lafayette and Lizze. They would in turn miss their fevers from three and four days and then it would return. Poor Little Lizzie had missed hers for four days on the previous to the 9th inst. on the morning of which day she was as usual playing with the children till the fever came on, which Phoebe says she did not think her any sicker than she had often been before with the same fever till in the evening Cato came up and she let him know how restless Lizzie appeared to be, and on his examination found her dying which took place soon after which was no doubt from the effect of worms. Lafayette and Victoria has been more or less sick ever since.[40]

Phoebe later complained bitterly that Cato did not supply enough provisions for the settlement, but most at Carlawter were apparently able through their own hard labors "after task" to secure what was needed in the way of an adequate diet. For in spite of their work in muddy rice fields and down long rows of cotton, in spite of swarming mosquitoes and invasions of roundworms, in spite of all the burdens of slavery on a low-country plantation, the little Gullah community at Carlawter not only persevered but also grew. In 1858 Joe completed a statistical study of Carlawter. He found that between 1834 and 1858 there had been thirty-five deaths in the settlement and eighty-six births, a natural increase of fifty-one in the population over a twenty-four-year period. No doubt the stability of the settlement, its family structures and housing patterns, together with the diet supplemented by the efforts of those who lived at Carlawter, contributed to this remarkable growth of its population.[41]

There was one family, however, that was not included in the statistics for 1858. That was the family of Phoebe and Cassius, and their exclusion, as we shall see, flowed not directly from births, diets, diseases, and deaths but from decisions made by white owners who were famous, far and wide, for their benevolence.

24

ARCADIA II

In November 1851, Irwin Rahn wrote Charles and reported on the crops and conditions at Arcadia. The work that year had been strenuous, and good crops of cotton, rice, corn, and peas had already been gathered. But Arcadia, he said, was not producing all that it might. "I find, as I have been told by 2 experienced planters, that I have not got a sufficient force here to keep up and improve the plantation as I would like." The plantation included 550 acres of cotton land and 600 acres of inland swamp, much of which was in diked rice fields. With its pine barrens, Arcadia was twice as large as Montevideo and almost three times as large as Maybank. Yet, Rahn noted, he had only sixteen full hands to work the plantation.[1]

Charles was convinced that Rahn was right. More could be done at Arcadia. Moreover, Maybank had been losing some of its productivity. The soil was still rich along the island ridges where the old oyster-shell middens added fertility, but most of its land was sandy, and even under Andrew's good management its harvests were not very large.[2] The population in the settlement at Maybank, however, had been steadily growing over the years. The answer seemed clear—good management meant moving people from the settlement at Maybank to the settlement at Arcadia. In January 1852 Charles wrote instructions from Philadelphia:

I wish Prime, Fanny, and their family sent up to Arcadia: Prime, Fanny, Niger, and Harriet occupy Lymus' house; Lymus removed to Montevideo. Big Titus go with Stepney; and Little Titus with Agrippa and Bella; and Clarissa and Patrick take their house; and Phillis and her child take Clarissa's place in Silvia's house until we have two more houses built. When they are built, then Elsie can move with her family to Arcadia. This removal from Maybank had better be made at once, in order that the people may assist in preparing for the coming crop.³

Prime and Fanny had lived at Maybank for years—they were part of Andrew Maybank's estate that had been left to Charles and Mary in 1834. Fanny had been only two years old when she had been taken—a motherless child—to the settlement at the "Hut" in 1800. So Fanny must have had little if any memory before she had been taken to the settlement above the Medway. Prime, however, had been twenty-three when had been brought to the island. He and Fanny had soon married, and in 1824 they had their first child, Agrippa. During the coming years, four more children would be born to them in their little cabin overlooking the Medway marshes—Titus, Phillis, Niger, and Harriett.⁴

When Charles decided to move them to Arcadia, Prime and Fanny had been living together in the Maybank settlement for almost twenty-nine years. With them went their five children, their daughter-in-law Bella (Agrippa's wife), and three grandchildren. They were all, no doubt, glad they had been kept together as an extended family, but once again the move indicated the power of whites to act arbitrarily and to uproot a black family from their home of many years.⁵

Among the others who were removed to Arcadia was Elsey, whose carpenter husband Syphax lived at Lambert. Elsey brought with her to Arcadia their eight children, who represented the union of important families in the settlements. On their mother's side were Elsey's father, Daddy Robin, and her brother Stepney, who were at the center of the settlement at Arcadia. On their father's side was a line that extended from Syphax through his parents, Hamlet and Elvira, to Hamlet's parents, Old Jupiter and Blind Silvey, and to Elvira's mother, Fanny, who had been born in Africa. So it was not surprising that among the children brought to Arcadia by Elsey there was a little Elvira named after her grandmother and a little Stepney named after his uncle.⁶

This shuffling of people to Arcadia meant that the settlement at Maybank would no longer be as large as it had been and that Maybank itself would become increasingly marginal as a source of wealth for Charles and Mary. At the same time, Arcadia would grow in economic importance, regularly producing more cotton and rice than Montevideo. But Montevideo would remain the beloved home, the old home place, for Charles and Mary, and Maybank would remain the summer retreat where they entertained friends and guests and where in the evenings they continued to watch the shadows spreading slowly across the low-country landscape.⁷

If Arcadia would never play an important role in the hearts and imaginations of the white family who owned it, it would become an increasingly important place for the African Americans who lived in its settlement. Indeed, in the coming years the family of Daddy Robin and the family of Prime and Fanny would claim the lands of Arcadia as their own in ways that in 1852 could only be envisioned in settlement whispers and secret songs.

Among those who were already living at Arcadia was Clarissa, Phoebe's oldest child by an unnamed father when Phoebe had been only sixteen. Clarissa had remained at the edges of life in the settlements. Unlike her mother or grandfather Jack, she did not become a valuable house servant. In 1848 Clarissa had her first child—a little girl she named after her mother. The child's father was a man named Oscar from a neighboring plantation, but his relationship with Clarissa had evidently been only casual, for in 1850 Clarissa had her second child, this time by Patrick, a man who was to become her husband. They named their little girl Mag, after Patrick's mother.[8]

Patrick lived at the Quarterman Baker place, which adjoined Arcadia, and he had as a young man a reputation of being something of a rogue. The Midway congregation had suspended him on two occasions, and his reputation raised questions for Charles and Rahn about his becoming the husband of Clarissa. But his master wrote in support of Patrick's appeal. "I suppose you know," Quarterman Baker wrote, that Patrick "has been bad. He has not however done anything very bad which has been proven on him for more than two years within the same time he has been suspended on two occasions but it has not been proven on him to my satisfaction therefore must consider him as not guilty." Clarissa was herself eager to become a member of Midway, but her application was denied until she and Patrick were formally married. When Charles wrote from Philadelphia and gave his approval to the marriage, he also gave instruction that a new cabin was to be built for them so that the family might have some privacy and a place to call their own. Shortly after their marriage, Clarissa was received into the Midway congregation. She and Patrick had another daughter, Chloe, in 1852, and in 1855 they had a son, John, who was named after Clarissa's half-brother. So the great-grandchildren of Jack and the grandchildren of Phoebe would grow up calling Arcadia home and were destined to become laborers who would bear in their dark bodies the sorrows of their people and the heavy burdens of raising cotton and rice before returning to the earth in deep anonymity.[9]

There were, of course, other marriages in the settlements while Charles and Mary were away in Philadelphia. Andrew and Mary Ann's daughter Dinah married Abram, a slave of the Roswell Kings. He lived in the settlement at Woodville, and he and Dinah were to have four children during the 1850s before a bitter separation and death tore them apart and left Andrew and Mary Ann, by then grown old, to look after their grandchildren.[10]

The two most talked about marriages in the settlements during these years when Charles and Mary were away, however, took place not at Arcadia, Carlawter, or Maybank, but on adjoining plantations. At White Oak, Mary—a cousin of Cato's and Cassius's—asked to marry Zadock, a slave of John Barnard on his nearby North Hampton plantation. Thomas Shepard wrote Charles the details of what happened:

> I wrote you in my last that little Mary had a babe. I saw it a short time since for the first and find it instead of being Zadock's pickanniny its daddy is a white man. A short time since Zadock brought me a proper ticket from Mr. Barnard saying if it met my approbation Zadock had his full consent to marry the woman. So I gladly gave Zade my full permission and at the same time congratulated him on the birth of a son, which he appeared to take well and seemed to understand. But lo and behold, when he saw the babe the colour was too bright for him—however, Zade is a pretty accommodating fellow. He told the girl she must not do the like again and took her to wife rough at a venture.[11]

Shepard apparently believed that Mary had, of her own free will, a sexual encounter with a white man—perhaps he thought she had gone to Riceboro on a Saturday night and met there some sailor whose little ship sailed up and down the North Newport. Or perhaps he thought one of the merchants or one of the travelers who stopped in the boro had plied her with liquor and had his way with her. Or perhaps he knew something that he was concealing from Charles—that she had not been a willing participant in a sexual encounter but a victim in the common abuse of black women by white men. Whatever Shepard knew or thought, Zadock apparently knew enough about what had happened to take Mary as his wife and to give her a public admonition—one of the weapons of the weak— that may have acted as some protection for her in the future.[12]

If there was some question or secrecy about the father of Mary's child, there seemed to be no doubt about the father of Henry Hart Jones's two slave children. They had been born at the Retreat when Henry and their mother were teenagers, but since the death of Joseph Jones, the children and their mother had been living at Lodebar, Henry's plantation. Windsor, a house servant at the Mallard Place, had begun courting the mother (whose name remains hidden in the plantation records) and had received permission to marry her. Rebecca Mallard wrote her son Robert Quarterman Mallard of the approaching wedding: "Windsor is to be married to a woman of Henry Joneses almost white with two children that are almost white, also, for I am told, they can scarcely be distinguished from Mr. Jones." Rebecca Mallard evidently had questions about the wisdom of the match—although she apparently had no questions about the father of the children. Some of Windsor's brothers had married "light complicted wives," and Rebecca thought "they very often do badly in so doing."[13]

The plans for a remarkable wedding, however, went ahead. Henry and his wife, Abby, agreed to give a big wedding for the slave couple. Invitations were sent out to whites and blacks, and arrangements were made with the black preacher Toney Stevens to conduct the wedding service at Lodebar. Among the whites who attended were Lou Mallard, the daughter of Rebecca and Thomas Mallard, and her cousin Ann Baker. They were escorted by John Ward, who would shortly be elected mayor of Savannah, serve as president of the Democratic National Convention in 1856, and eventually be the first United States minister to China. Ward did not stay for the wedding, but a number of the Mallard domestic servants came in their best attire, including Josiah and his wife, Henrietta. Rebecca Mallard wrote about some of the details of the wedding:

> Windsor was married on Saturday night at Mr. H. Joneses. Lue & Ann Baker were invited to attend. The invitation was accepted and away they went escorted by young Mr. Ward. He saw them there, but did not remain as he was not invited. They (the girls) enjoyed themselves so well that they did not get back until a little before twelve. Old Toney Stevens married them. Windsor seems to be in fine spirits and is quite a fine servant. . . . They had quite a nice wedding. James & Em & Margaret [went] together. Josiah & Henrietta. Lue laughed & said that Josiah had his horse sent up in order to ride to the wedding.[14]

The wedding appeared a happy occasion for all, black and white alike. Perhaps among the whites no one was happier than Abby, for even though the relationship between her husband and his slave had been years earlier, its memory must have been painful for Abby, a constant reminder to a white mistress of nighttime visits by her husband to the settlement at the Retreat.

And among the blacks, perhaps no one was happier than the slave woman herself, for the marriage provided—once again through the weapons of the weak—at least some protection from abuse. With a husband from the influential Mallard Place, reports of scandalous behavior on the part of her white master could be, if needed, circulated in the community in a way that would undermine Henry's reputation as a pious and respectable citizen. Years earlier Charles had written Mary: "We must strive to have as few difficulties as possible with *servants and dependents*, for through their tale-bearing the influence of many a family is ruined, not to say their respectability. People are not generally aware how much their servants have them in their power." Charles thought that however much "vanity or insolence may look down with contempt on the suffrage of men undignified by wealth and unenlightened by education," slaves seldom "commend or blame without justice." For the slave, the vice and virtue of owners are "easily distinguished." The slave consequently knows the "secrets of a master," for pride and folly generally make the master think he is secure when in fact he is being "inquisitively watched" by the slave, who has a "desire of reducing the inequalities of condition." So for the slave mother, her marriage to Windsor provided some protection, even if that protection should not be exaggerated.[15]

However happy the wedding of Windsor and his bride, tensions were building between blacks and whites in Liberty County. At the heart of black resistance to slavery in the low country had been the creation of a Gullah community and its efforts to ameliorate the harsh conditions of bondage. If there had never been in Liberty County an organized revolt against slavery, there had been over the generations of those who lived in the settlements a steady struggle to limit the power of whites and to create a community that remembered ancestors, affirmed the dignity of blacks, and told stories that taught strategies of resistance. The isolation of the settlements during much of the year and the relative stability of the slave population in the county had played important roles in the creation of the Gullah community and in its adoption of various strategies to resist the degradations of slavery. To be sure, the slave sales under the oaks in Riceboro and the movement of slaves from plantation to plantation within the county were constant reminders of the power of whites and of their ability to act in arbitrary and cruel ways. But African Americans had nevertheless been able to create, within the harsh confines of slavery, networks of families that reached from Colonel's Island on the coast to the river plantations along the North Newport and to Walthourville on the sand hills. Saturday night visiting at "the wife house"; Sunday meetings at Midway, North Newport, and Sunbury; and the Saturday markets at Riceboro and Hinesville had all contributed to the creation and maintenance of a coherent Gullah community with its own worldview and ethos, its own reading of the landscape of the county, and its own ways of challenging the assumptions of white masters and mistresses.[16]

In the 1850s, however, the Gullah community of Liberty County began to come under increasing pressure, as it had in the 1830s with the opening of Cherokee lands to white settlers. Now fertile lands in southwest Georgia were beginning to be opened for settlement.[17] The new lands acted as a magnet—they drew whites toward the promised rewards of rich cotton crops, and they tore blacks away from their Gullah communities that had been built with courage and much sacrifice. By the middle of the decade this magnetic pull of virgin lands was radiating most forcefully into Liberty County along the tracks of an expanding railway system that could easily transport people and materials westward. When the rails of the Savannah, Albany, and Gulf Railroad were laid through the county in the 1850s, the settlements began to be linked more readily to a wider world, and slave families faced new, more radical, and frequent separations.[18] For not only were family members carried away in increasing numbers to live on and work distant lands, but laborers were hired from the Retreat and other plantations to lay the rails, build the bridges, and maintain the tracks of the expanding railroads. Those who were hired out to work on the railroads would spend months away from their homes and would be subjected to harsh new work routines and to the management of those who had no self-interest in their welfare.[19]

As this shaking of old foundations first began to be felt in the early 1850s, a religious revival broke out among both the whites and blacks of the county. And among the various settlements, none was struck more forcefully by religious fervor than the settlement at Arcadia. Toney Stevens had been visiting the plantation regularly, preaching in its little chapel, visiting in the settlement, and generally encouraging the people.[20] Through his pastoral care, some began to feel religious stirrings along the sandy road of Arcadia's settlement. Charles, on his visits home from Philadelphia in June 1851, wrote Mary of what was happening at Arcadia:

> You will be happy to know that a considerable change has passed over some of them of late for the better: Charles and Lucy, Pharaoh, Clarissa, Kate Jones and Agrippa, and Bella and some others. They are more sober, and regular at church and in the house of prayer; and it is hoped they may be under the influence of the Spirit of God.

Lucy, Pharaoh, Adeline, and Bella all applied for membership at Midway and were admitted on communion Sunday, August 1851. Clarissa, Kate, and Charles applied but were not admitted until the next year. Mary Jones was home from Philadelphia on the communion Sunday, May 1852, when Charles—who had grown up in the settlement at Maybank—was baptized and received with eight other slaves into the Midway congregation. (Clarissa and Kate had been admitted the previous January.) Mary wrote Charlie and Joe at Princeton:

> It has been a great source of gratitude to our Heavenly Father that so many from Arcadia have within eighteen months professed religion and seem to be walking worthy of the Christian name—all connected with Midway Church. *Charles* joined the last Communion. My heart felt bursting with love and thankfulness as I saw the great man kneel as humbly as a child for baptism; a true change seems to have passed over him.[21]

Charles—the son of Andrew and Mary Ann—was to become an increasingly important figure in the settlements. As a cart driver and a skilled handler of oxen, he was in demand on all three of the Joneses' plantations during certain seasons of the year. He and his wife, Lucy—the daughter of Rosetta and Sam—came to be regarded by their owners as among the most responsible people in the settlements as tensions between whites and blacks began to come more into the open. During the coming years, Charles and Lucy moved toward the inner circle of elite slaves that included Cato, Porter, Patience, and Phoebe, as well as Andrew and Rosetta.

On the Sunday when Charles was baptized and became a member of Midway, four young white men—all cousins—were also admitted into membership of the church. One of them was Robert Quarterman Mallard. The youngest son of Thomas and Rebecca Mallard, Robert had grown up at the old Mallard Place and later was to write about *Plantation Life Before Emancipation.*[22] What neither he nor Charles knew as they went forward in May 1852 to take their vows before the Midway congregation, was that Charles and Lucy's only daughter, Tenah, was to become in a few short years the slave of Robert Mallard and would eventually be carried with her husband, young Niger the fisherman, far from her low-country home.

If some in the settlements began turning with a new fervor to the consolations of religion, others in the settlements began to turn toward more open resistance as the relative stability of the Gullah community began to be undermined in the 1850s. The long-used tactic of running away was an option chosen by some as the disruptions of the period began to loosen, for increasing numbers, the ties they had to the settlements. Sam Mallard, Robert's older brother, was one prosperous planter who had to face the challenges of runaways during these years. A number of his slaves made a break for freedom during the hardest part of the harvest season in 1852. Led by the slave Barak and his wife, Lucy, they hid in the river swamps for weeks, although apparently they kept in touch with some who lived in the settlements, perhaps getting some supplies and most likely taking some livestock from surrounding plantations. Sam Mallard sent word throughout the settlements that "if they had to be taken, he would give them one hundred lashes apiece." So they began to "come in" and give themselves up. Barak and Lucy were taken to the little jail in Riceboro, where they were held for several weeks as the ringleaders before being sent off to Savannah to be sold. The others, no doubt, were severely punished—most likely with the whip, even if not with a crippling hundred lashes. As for Sam Mallard, he had been greatly troubled by the whole incident. His father, Thomas, thought he had had enough trouble "to make him poor," but his mother, Rebecca, thought "he bore it very well indeed."[23]

Other planters, however, did not fare as well as Mallard. His brother-in-law, Leander Varnedoe, who had grown up at old Liberty Hall plantation, had his plantation home burned in 1852, his family barely escaping with their lives. Mary

Jones reported that the fire was "thought to be the work of an incendiary—a run-away servant belonging to Dr. Way." And there were other suspicious fires around the county during these early years of the decade: a cotton house and sixty bales of cotton, another plantation home, and one of the LeConte's gin houses.[24]

More startling for whites even than these fires was the murder of a planter in the adjoining county of McIntosh. James Houston, whose Peru plantation was on the South Newport River, also planted on Wahoo, a small island near Harris Neck. Miles of marsh surrounded the island and helped to make it one of the most isolated places on the Georgia coast. In June 1852 Houston floated down the South Newport in a small boat and made his way through a winding creek to the little landing near the island settlement. He was carrying provisions for the coming weeks when the work of those who lived in the settlement would be hard and the sun hot. A tall, good-looking man, Houston was a member of a distinguished family, but he was also a drunkard who could fly into a rage and bitterly abuse his slaves. On this early June day, he apparently arrived on the island drunk and began to abuse his slaves with a whip. They watched him and waited. At some point in the early evening he made his way to a little shack, where he collapsed in a drunken stupor. Someone, most likely the driver, came into the shack and, with a blow that would not kill him, hit him in the head with an axe. Others came in and carried him outside to a tree, where his arms where tied up. Then in an act of revenge and of resistance to further abuse, they whipped him to death. They burned his clothes and bedding in order to conceal what had happened and buried him in the thick marsh mud near a creek where "the water ebbed and flowed over the grave." When he did not return to his plantation, suspicious whites went looking for him. They found his battered and decaying body uncovered by the work of the tide and exposed to the hungry elements of the marsh. Thomas Shepard wrote on 28 June to Charles in Philadelphia that three of Houston's men "are now in the Darien gaol awaiting their trial. One of whom is his Driver, acknowledges their crime. Says they had calmly determined to run the risk of the gallows than to be treated as they had been." Irwin Rahn reported in early July that "what gave rise to the nefarious act was making his people work on the Sabbath days." By the middle of July, John Stevens was writing from Palmyra plantation that five of Houston's slaves were "imprisoned (among them a woman), and many others implicated." On 10 August, Rahn wrote again that "those Negroes of Mr. Houston" were "ten in no. in committing the murderous act. The people in the county assembled, holding a court executed five without a legal process of law and it is supposed they execute the balance." An orderly lynching was apparently thought the best way to deal with such an insurrection. Thomas Shepard thought that the whole affair showed how Satan—"old Sambo," he called him—"will (as often as he can) make sin in one work the destruction of others."[25]

Black rage, however, did not always turn against whites or rise in resistance to slavery—often it was directed against other blacks, especially as the settlements were increasingly disrupted. At Arcadia one of the men—Allen—got in a fight with a man named Robert from a neighboring plantation. Plymouth, the driver for John B. Mallard, was able to stop the fight, but not before Allen butted heads with Robert. The blow to Allen's head evidently caused a concussion, and Allen died a few days later. At North Hampton plantation, near Montevideo, a young carpenter was at first thought to have drowned in the dark waters of the North Newport but was later believed murdered by someone in the settlement.[26] And a group of slaves that were associated with the old Mallard Place were involved in a fight that led to death. Charles wrote in his journal some of the details:

> Mr. B. A. Busby's man Anthony was killed Saturday night by a blow on the head with a rake in the hands of Mr. J. L. Mallard's boy Adam, 13 or 15 years old. Woman Betty—W. S. Baker's—implicated—discharged. Boy committed for trial. Done in Dorchester in the night. Anthony died Sunday afternoon. Not a good Negro.

Occasionally someone in the settlements would turn, out of some despair or desperation, not to resistance but to self-destruction. Jim, the driver at Charles Berrien Jones's plantation, had grown up at the Retreat and had been widely respected. When Charles learned of Jim's death, he wrote Charlie:

> Your uncle Berrien has been much afflicted in the loss of his driver, Jim. Little Jim as he used to be familiarly called. Poor fellow—something went wrong on the plantation, his character was implicated, and he seems not to have been able to bear the loss of character and he deliberately loaded the gun, went into a room, lay down, fixed his head on some cotton, cocked the piece, drove the ram rod, put the gun between his feet, kept the muzzle with his left hand in its place under his throat, and then with the ram-rod in his right hand touched the trigger! The load passed through the crown of the head! In this position— unmoved, he was almost immediately found. How sad! He was waiting in the house before we were married, and was very handy in getting my letters to your mother out of the office on mail days and hastening home with them. Thus is the journey of life strewed with light and shade and the shade is often very dark and distressing.[27]

Of course, there was nothing new about any of this. Running away, burning barns, fighting among blacks, and even occasionally the murder of a white and the suicide of a black had a history in Liberty County. But the decade of the 1850s apparently encouraged such behavior as the increasing disruptions of the settlements unleashed long-suppressed rage and new anxieties. In such a context old tensions between blacks and whites took on a growing intensity, and that intensity intruded into the settlement at Carlawter.

In the spring of 1852, Daniel—a brother of Cato, Cassius, and Porter—sold some rice he had raised in his rice patch to some people who lived in the settlement at Oak Hill, the nearby plantation of Solomon Barnard (it bordered White Oak). Daniel's wife lived at Roswell King's South Hampton, and it was Daniel's habit to walk the little road that led from Montevideo and White Oak through Oak Hill to South Hampton. In April, as he walked back to Carlawter, some who owed him for the rice called to him to come to the Oak Hill settlement for a payment on their debt. While he was there, Barnard came up, found him in the settlement, and told him never to come back without his permission. A few weeks later, as Daniel was walking to his wife's house, those who owed him again called him to come to the settlement to receive the balance of his money. He asked whether Barnard was there, and when told he was not, went to the settlement. He was about to leave when Barnard's driver found him and ordered him off the plantation. Daniel left immediately. Later in the day, on his way back to Carlawter, he once again encountered the driver, this time on the road. The driver cursed him and "said he had a great mind to tie him & give him a flogging anyhow." Daniel told him he could do no such thing in a public road. The driver then called some of his men and attempted to capture Daniel, who was able to make his escape by getting across the line into one of the fields of White Oak. Then on a late Thursday afternoon in early June, when Daniel was walking back from his wife's house at South Hampton, Barnard saw him on the road and ordered him into his backyard, where there was a pillory. When Daniel saw the pillory, he realized Barnard's intention and tried to make his escape but was overtaken by Barnard and his brother-in-law, Lowndes Walthour. Barnard beat him over the head and arms with a stick and then put him in the pillory, where he flogged him and kept him confined overnight.

The next day, after Daniel made his way back to Carlawter, he found Thomas Shepard and told him the whole story. Shepard had him strip, and what Shepard found infuriated him. He wrote Barnard immediately, saying, "From all I could judge and as I believe, from the cuts and whales upon his buttock and back, you must have given him at least 70 lashes with all your skill & might." After reviewing the events as told him by Daniel, Shepard wrote that he would withhold an opinion until he heard from Barnard. But he added that even if Daniel deserved a flogging, Barnard had "grossly violated a rule which always exists among good neighbours." And he implicitly warned Barnard that if "you don't see proper to act upon the laws of neighbourship, you will act upon the laws of the Land."[28]

Shepard sent a copy of his letter to Charles, who was preparing to leave May-bank after a short visit home. Charles was even more outraged than Shepard. Barnard, he said, "has acted towards me in *a very unneighbourly manner and for which he can have no excuse whatever.*" If there was a problem with Daniel, then Barnard should have spoken to Shepard, "and he *should have had every reason-able satisfaction, and that promptly.*" But what particularly astonished Charles was that Barnard gave Daniel "an excessive whipping, and that in *a Pillory! I did not know that such an instrument of punishment existed in our neighbourhood!*" If, said Charles, "such a practice of the treatment of servants prevails in other neighbourhoods, it certainly does not in ours; & it is one against which I protest, and to which I shall by no means submit." Charles then used an old ploy that southern whites often used when they wanted to protect a black. "*My property,*" wrote Charles, "*shall be respected and it will be protected.*" Ironically, the whole system of slavery was called upon to defend Daniel, who after all was Charles's chattel.[29]

After his strenuous protest, Charles cooled a bit and went on to say: "It is my full conviction that when my neighbour calmly reviews the matter, unless I am mistaken in his character as a man and a gentleman, he will see cause to regret the course he has pursued." In this way Charles poured oil on these southern waters. He had his letter to Shepard forwarded to Barnard, and it evidently eased the tension between them. Five years later, when Shepard was no longer physi-cally able to manage Montevideo, Charles hired Barnard as the manager for the summer while Charles and Mary traveled in Kentucky and Virginia. Daniel, no doubt, was particularly circumspect that summer.

Daniel—like his brother Cassius—had a knack for getting into trouble.[30] Neither brother ever seemed to learn the lessons that Jack had taught in his folk stories—especially that whites were dangerous and blacks must be constantly on their guard around them. But even their cautious brother Cato found himself caught up in the public tensions between blacks and whites that were build-ing during the 1850s and that could spill over into tensions between blacks and blacks, or whites and whites.

Elijah Chapman, a small planter—his plantation Edgely was near Riceboro— let his cattle out in the spring to roam the woods and forage in the new growth of grass that grew wherever sunlight penetrated the canopy of oaks and pines. When he could not find several head, he began searching nearby plantations and was eventually led to Montevideo by one of his slaves. He wrote Charles what he found and what followed:

In hunting for my cattle in May, there was a large bunch that I could not find. After hunting two or three days I found that they had them in your pasture. In riding over to get the cattle out, I found where they had just killed a black cow of mine and burnt up the hide and offal. And where they had emptied [?] the maw of two more, I took up a part of the hide and showed it to your carpenters that was working on your house. I thought at first that I would not say anything about it knowing what Negroes are. Two or three times one of my boys complained to me about Cato's abuse to him about his telling me that the cattle was killed in your pasture. I told the boy to take no notice of him. On Saturday 17 of November, I sent the boy to Riceboro. Cato met him there and told him the first time he met him hunting for cattle, he would do him so bad that they would have to turn him out of the church or send him to jail he said. Mr. Stebbins son was present when he told him so. The boy would have fought Cato long ago, but I forbid him doing so. I thought it was best to let you know so as we could put a stop to it.[31]

Chapman's "boy" had evidently found a secret place where those from Carlawter had been enjoying a feast by barbecuing three of Chapman's cattle. Cato was furious at the man's betrayal and by his intrusion into the affairs of Carlawter—an intrusion that challenged Cato's authority and his reputation with whites. In Riceboro, before Stebbins's general store, a dangerous fight had been narrowly avoided, even though Cato knew that the consequences would have been severe for him. But what had been at stake for Cato was not only his authority and reputation but also a secret world at Carlawter where stray cattle could be butchered and feasts held out of sight of white managers and owners. That secret world lay beneath the relative calm of Carlawter, where most who lived along its sandy street were dutiful and submissive and where the ideology of slavery appeared to have triumphed. Chapman's letter must have provided Charles a disturbing glimpse into this secret world, where resistance to white authority was not only nurtured but also practiced. No record was left of Charles's response to Chapman or of his questions to Cato. But powerful illusions—rooted in Charles's labors to create calm, peaceful, and orderly settlements—must have shaped what Charles wanted to see when he glimpsed this secret world. For what he was to see on his return to Liberty County—even as he heard distant train whistles helping to transform the county—were images of home, where blacks and whites dwelled together in substantial harmony under the benevolent rule of whites.

25

MAYBANK II

During one of her bouts of homesickness in Philadelphia, Mary had received a letter from Susan Cumming warning her that the home Mary remembered and longed for was no more. "But my sister," Susan had written her, "your home whenever you return to it will be changed. Perhaps your children will be separated from you, you will not direct their education and pursuits and many persons and things which formerly gave you pleasure you will cease to feel an interest in." Home, Susan had reminded Mary, is not something unchangeable, an immutable place, but rather a place in time that is always becoming something other than it had been. Sitting at an old family desk at Social Bluff and looking out on the waters of the North Newport flowing into the sea, Susan had confessed to Mary how "differently everything appears to me now from what it did when this place was first my home." Then the "future seemed joyous and bright," but now "a pall has been cast over it." Still, she said, "how much gratitude do I owe for undeserved mercies . . . and if not self deceived a hope beyond this life."[1]

Mary and Charles were not naïve about such matters. They knew, Charles had written, that their home was not "an unchanging inheritance" somehow immune to the vicissitudes of life. And they were aware that the passage of time in Liberty County—the flow of the North Newport and the tide's regular coming in and going out over the Medway marshes—had wrought, while they were away, changes among their family and friends and on the social landscape of their remembered past.[2] Such musings, however, did not dampen their joy as they began their preparations to return to their beloved low-country home with its familiar ways. They would miss Charlie, who was staying behind at Harvard Law School, and Joe, who was hard at work at the Medical College of the University of Pennsylvania. But Charles and Mary had pride in the accomplishments of their sons and in their promise for usefulness and distinction in society. So leaving the boys in the North was not so difficult for the parents as they made ready their departure for home. As for the eighteen-year-old Mary Sharpe, she would go home with her parents and prepare to enter a lively social life among the planting families of coastal Georgia.

Whatever their sense of alienation from northern society, however irritating and disconcerting they found its growing antislavery sentiment, Charles and Mary did not hesitate to carry home to Liberty County products of northern energy and ingenuity. For weeks they oversaw the crating of furniture and the packing of boxes. A piano bought for Mary Sharpe in Philadelphia and a recently purchased mirror stove from the firm of Hill and Schoch were meticulously prepared for shipment south. Two mahogany and two cherry dining tables—handsomely made by Pennsylvania craftsmen—were carefully crated, as were twenty-six cane-bottom walnut chairs, four rockers, several dresser bureaus, a mahogany study table, two bales of carpeting, a large sofa, and the miscellaneous furnishings of a large and affluent household. With the furniture went boxes of medicines—quinine, alcohol, brandy, camphors of various sorts, cream of tartar, soda, alum, nitrate of potash, calomel, and the ever-present Blue Mass for stomach problems and general ailments. And strange as it may seem, there were also barrels of groceries—a barrel of wheat flour and a barrel of rye flour, a barrel of Irish potatoes and a barrel of green apples, a large can of lard, two bags of buckwheat meal, and a half-barrel of crackers. And there were boxes of currants and citron, almonds and spices of all sorts—including cinnamon, mace, nutmeg, and ginger, the products of exotic lands. And there were boxes of tools and boxes of candles and soap, and most surprising there were eight superior hams, six superior sides, and a half-dozen tongues carefully packed for shipping to a plantation home with its own smokehouses. Finally, there were boxes of books. Some contained histories: *Life of Luther*, *Life of Calvin*, *Life of Wesley*, books on the early and medieval church, and D'Augnige's history of the Reformation in four volumes. Other boxes were packed with biblical commentaries, classics of Puritan theology, and devotional books intended to expand the libraries at Montevideo and Maybank, where Charles would seek to do scholarly work far from the resources of a college or public library.[3]

Furniture, barrels, and boxes were all carried on drays to a Philadelphia wharf and shipped on 25 October 1853 aboard the *Keystone State*. A week later Charles, Mary, and Mary Sharpe left Philadelphia. They reached Colonel's Island on the evening of 7 November and hurried across the causeway as the shadows spread and the evening glow of the Medway marsh began to fade. They turned under the arching oak that served as a gate. As they rode down the avenue, with its thick canopy overhead, they finally saw the lights of Maybank reaching out into the engulfing night to welcome them home. Two days later a river schooner arrived at Half Moon wharf. Andrew and his men were waiting with oxcarts for the furniture, barrels, and boxes.[4]

Although the November frosts made it safe to return to Montevideo, renovations of the plantation house there inspired Charles and Mary to stay at Maybank for the winter. Charles had already sketched a drawing of a much-enlarged plantation home and had, long before the return from Philadelphia, sent instructions for Sandy Maybank and Porter and their young carpenter apprentice William (a grandson of Hamlet) to begin gathering the building materials. Among other things, they were to take men from Carlawter and Arcadia into the swamps to cut cypress, and from the logs they were to draw twenty thousand shingles. Others had been put to work in the brickyard at Montevideo digging clay, cutting and hauling in wood, forming and firing the bricks to be used in foundations and chimneys. After Charles returned to Liberty County and could supervise their work, the carpenters began the renovations and enlargement of the house, and Daddy Robin and others at Arcadia took over the responsibility of cutting cypress logs and drawing shingles. Lumber for the framing was ordered from sawmills in Savannah, brought through the coastal waters and up the North Newport by a river schooner, and unloaded by Cato and his men at the Montevideo wharf.[5]

While the work on the house proceeded, Charles and Mary turned their attention to the interests of a retired couple. Most pressing were the gardens at Maybank and Montevideo. They had been carefully laid out years earlier. At Montevideo oaks and magnolias had been brought from the woods and carefully planted to enhance the approach to the house, and a double row of cedars had been planted along the road that ran past a little pond to the river and the wharf. Jasmine now grew around the piazza and would in early spring mingle yellow blooms with the white blossoms of climbing lady banksias roses. Camellias, azaleas, and tea olives were scattered in places of filtered sun, while in the open were beds of roses, perennials, vegetables, herbs, and Mary's prized bed of strawberries. Trees, shrubs, and perennials had been collected over the years from various places. Some native wildflowers had been gathered on the plantation. Some plants had been purchased in Savannah or ordered by mail. And Charles had brought back from Columbia dahlias, chrysanthemums, Persian honeysuckle, lilies, and roses. But most of their garden had come from cuttings and gifts from other low-country plantations—from the Retreat, from South Hampton and Richmond-on-the-Ogeechee. And from the LeConte plantation had come cuttings of "choice roses," tea olives, purple and scarlet azaleas, and roots of amaryllis.[6] At Maybank there were vegetable and flower gardens and a fine grape arbor, but special attention had been devoted to an orchard so that during the family's stay on the island fresh fruit—oranges, figs, pomegranates, pears, peaches, plums, and apples—would be readily available.[7]

These gardens and orchards had not been neglected during the family's stay in Columbia and Philadelphia—indeed, they had largely come to maturity during those years—but there was much work waiting to be done on Charles and Mary's return. Mary took primary responsibility for the garden renovations. In a long letter to Charlie in the spring of 1854, Charles described Mary's day and work in the garden at Maybank:

> She rises about six in the morning, or now half-past five; takes her bath, reads, and is ready for family worship about seven; then breakfasts with a moderate appetite and enjoys a cup of good tea. Breakfast concluded and the cups, etc., washed up and dinner ordered, Little Jack gathers up his *"weepons,"* as he calls them—the flower trowel, the trimming saw, the nippers and pruning shears and two garden hoes—and follows his mistress, with her sunbonnet on and her large India-rubber-cloth working gloves, into the flower and vegetable gardens. In these places she spends sometimes near two hours hoeing, planting, pruning, etc., Little Jack and frequently Beck and several other little fellows and Gilbert in the bargain all kept as busy as bees about her—one sweeping, another watering, another weeding, another planting and trimming, and another carrying off the limbs and trash. Then she dismisses the forces, and they go off in separate detachments to their respective duties about the house and premises, and she takes a walk of observation and superintendence about the kitchen yard and through the orchard and lawn, accompanied by any friends she may have with her and who may be disposed to take a walk of a quiet domestic nature.
>
> About ten her outdoor exercise is over, and she comes in, sets aside her bonnet, draws off her gloves, and refreshes herself with a basin of cool water, after which she disposes of her seamstresses and looks that the house has been well put to rights and in point and in perfect order—flowerpots dressed, etc. She now devotes herself to cutting out, planning, fitting, or sewing, giving attention to the clothing department and to the condition of the furniture of chambers, curtains, towels, linens, etc. The wants of the servants' wardrobe are inquired into, and all the thousand and one cares of the family attended to.
>
> Meanwhile the yards have been swept, the walk sanded, and Patience has her culinary world all in neat order. The two milk-white cats have had their breakfast, and are lying in each other's paws in the shade on the green grass in the flower garden; and the young dog *Rex*, having enjoyed his repast, has stretched himself at full length in the sun, and ever and anon rolls over and

wallows and kicks his feet into the air. The old turkey hen has spread her young ones like scouts around her, and is slowly picking along the green, and the gobbler is strutting with two or three idle dames in another direction. The fowls have scattered themselves everywhere in the lot, crowing and cackling and scratching; the sheep have finished their early browse, and are lying down beneath the great hickory tree; and overhead and all around is one general concert of birds.

The glorious sunlight, the soft south wind, and the green earth and the blue heavens—Mother sees and enjoys it all; but she is too busy now to come out and take a view. If she has visitors, she is sitting at work and in conversation with them, or for an hour or two before dinner takes her book or pen in hand. But sometimes she indulges in a quiet little doze, and gets up refreshed just before we are called to dinner. This meal she usually enjoys, but is never much of an eater; enjoys her food, but in much moderation.

For an hour or two after dinner she retires, and about the middle of the afternoon makes her appearance dressed for the evening. Then she is full of her uniform cheerfulness, and attracts everybody to her—husband, children, servants, visitors, old and young. The sea breeze is blowing sweetly. Our friends have driven over; the horses have been taken from the carriage, and the drivers have gone to pay their calls in the servants' quarters. The chairs are set out in the piazza, and here we spend a social hour and take tea. Our friends take leave, and then we have family worship. Sometimes they unite with us before they go. We all retire now to our study or rooms, and when the business of the day is over, then Mother enjoys the quiet, and loves to sit up reading and writing and conversing. She says this is the pleasantest part of *the day* to her.

You will recognize all this as very natural—what you have seen many times. Surely our hearts should be full of gratitude to God for all His unnumbered and undeserved favors to us as a family. May we all through riches of grace be saved in a brighter, better, and more enduring world than this![8]

Such, no doubt, was what Charles saw as he observed Mary's daily routine. But it was also surely what he wanted to see—an ideal image of a plantation home that had long shaped his imagination. All was pleasant, orderly, purposeful, and pious. Family, friends, and servants all had a place in such a home and went about their allotted roles with cheerfulness. Even nature itself—singing birds, domestic animals, "the glorious sunlight, the soft south wind, and the green earth and the blue heavens"—seemed to conspire with Charles's ideal of home and its ordinary responsibilities and pleasures. For Charles this scene of domestic tranquillity seemed "very natural"—the way things ought to be. Such a vision had deeply influenced his work as a missionary in the settlements, and such a vision was increasingly to dominate his thoughts in retirement and influence his response to any threats to his idealization of Montevideo and Maybank.[9]

While Mary was busy with her responsibilities in the gardens and house, Charles took up a new work that was to occupy him for the remainder of his life. He had decided to write a history of the Christian church. The idea, no doubt, had come to him while he was in Columbia. As a professor of church history, he may have thought that he had gotten started on the task with his lectures. But it was an immense undertaking—especially for someone located on a low-country plantation far from any major library. Nevertheless, he took up the task, beginning with the Old Testament and God's covenant with Abraham. Day by day he would work steadily in his study, writing with his now shaky hand and ordering books for his library as needed. Charles may never have realized that it was an improbable project, but he no doubt knew that it was an important one for him, providing as it did purposeful work and an intellectual focus for the last years of his life.

In addition to these routines that marked much of their retirement, Charles and Mary also developed—like many a retired couple—an increased interest in their ancestry. Already before their return to Liberty County, Charles had written a distant cousin in Charleston, John Colcock, about Charles's great-grandfather John Jones, who had been killed in the Revolution. And inquires were made among some of the old slaves—who were valuable repositories of information—about what they could remember of Mary's mother and of Charles's mother and her family. Old Mom Clarissa, who lived at the Retreat, reported that Charles's "mother's mother was Miss Hannah Splatt, who was married to Mr. John Girardeau," but the old slave did not know "where and when" they were married or where Charles's grandmother had come from.[10]

A short time after their return, they had gone to the Retreat, a place of such deep memories and sacred ground, and Charles had even paid a visit for the first time in years to old Liberty Hall, where he had been born. He walked into the garden, the same spot, he wrote Charlie, "cultivated by *my mother*." He found the "gate in the same place and the leading walk and bed, on each side the same!" He remembered how as a child he gathered flowers in the garden and how he tried to catch "the thistle birds when they went into the cabbage heads." And he remembered his mother, a young widow, who would take her guitar and walk on the east piazza in the evenings and play and sometimes sing.[11]

So Charles and Mary entered vigorously into their retirement years as they began renovations of home and gardens, tried to fill the gaps in their knowledge of their family's genealogy, and visited the old home places. And Charles, with Mary's support and encouragement, took up the task of writing his church history. As a couple, they were in a way trying to build a new home with their boys now off in the North and coming home only for occasional visits. But they were also trying to re-create the best and the happiest memories of the home they had known as a family—and even more, they were trying to realize the ideal of a plantation home nurtured by piety, friends, and the beauty of a low-country landscape and sustained by the labors of obedient and cheerful servants. To a re-markable extent Charles and Mary would be successful in these endeavors. For a few short years after their return to Liberty County, they made Montevideo and Maybank places of beauty, warmth, and great attraction for the whites who were privileged to call these places home or who were invited there as guests of a distinguished and hospitable family. But their low-country home was no in-vulnerable bastion, and its peace and harmony were to sustain deep blows from nature itself and from within the circle of those who were thought to be not only obedient but also privileged slaves of benevolent owners.

Earlier in the summer of 1854, eight months after Charles and Mary had re-turned to Liberty County, Roswell King died at Woodville, the Kings' summer home on Colonel's Island. His death, Charles wrote, created "a great vacuum in our little community." He had been a gruff and plainspoken man, famous for his aphorisms. He had written Charles in Philadelphia: "one half the boys *raised* these days are like the buttons on the back of a coat, of no use at all because they are kept at home to gratify the parents eye. I would rather have a son of mine cele-brated for *piracy* or a *Cuban Liberator* than for Indolence." William Maxwell, he wrote in the same letter, was "like a Hen on a hot griddle, not being able to keep his cotton down." And of Laura, he reported, "I know from her symptoms [she] is in a fair way of getting a *Touch of the Times*." In spite of his gruffness, his plain talking, his frequent lack of tact and Victorian refinement, he had been a good friend to Charles and Mary. Some of this was no doubt because of family connections through Susan Cumming and her children. But Charles and Mary also felt close to him because the two families had shared so much as neighbors. Their children had grown up together and had studied together in the little plan-tation school, and so it was not surprising that Charles would call King on his death "our old and kind friend and neighbor." Charles and Joe (who was home at the time) "performed the last sad office of friendship, preparing him for his grave," and Susan made his shroud. King was buried in the Midway cemetery, but he had never had a conversion experience and was not regarded as a Christian. Julia was distraught by this and cried to Mary, "Oh, if there was but one word of comfort!" And Charles lamented that from "a spiritual point of view Mr. King's death is a very melancholy one! He died as he lived."[12]

Two months after King's death, as the summer's crops of rice and cotton were maturing in the fields, a huge hurricane came roaring up the Atlantic coast from the Caribbean. As the winds at Maybank increased to a gale, the family prepared for the storm. Windows and doors were made tight. The winds continued to grow in intensity. Charles looked out the house across the Medway marsh, and not a spear of cord grass could be seen above the surging tide. He later wrote Charlie that a "clear rolling sea" was "all around us and reaching away to Bryan, Sunbury, and Palmyra, the whitecaps keeping it in a foam and the driving spray and mist shutting the distant shores from the sight." Soon the trees around the house began "to fall and to lose their branches. The rain drove into the house under the shingles, through the plastering. All hands securing the windows, tying them hard and fast. Servants with tubs swabbing up the water as it pours into the entry and rooms." Shutters on the front of the house were suddenly "blown to with a loud report" shattering glass and allowing rain to pour through the broken panes. "Waiters, sheets, etc., crammed in and water shut out." "There goes the old cedar on the lawn!" wrote Charles. "Poor old fellow, riven from top to bottom, split in two. How the wind roars! The trees are in an agony. Their limbs are torn and twisted off." Andrew appeared at the front door. Charles yelled above the roar of the storm: "Where are the people?" "Every soul came over with me," shouted the driver. "Would not stay behind." They were all in Patience's house, the newest and most secure house on the lot. "Master," asked Andrew, "is this a storm or a *harrycane?*" "*Harrycane*, Andrew, sure," said Charles. As the wind grew more violent, all who were in Patience's house suddenly appeared at the door, having made their way through the fury of the storm. They came in dripping wet. Mary had a large boiler of strong coffee made and gave them all some "so that although most of them were drenched, nobody took cold."[13]

When the storm finally passed, they surveyed the damage. The trees along the avenue were "rent and torn and blown down everywhere." The causeway to the island had been rendered impassable by the tide flowing fiercely over it. Everywhere fences were flat, but surprisingly no buildings were destroyed at Maybank. Reports began to come in, however, of even greater damage inland. At Montevideo a "new cotton house, the barn, a large shuck house put up last year, and the millhouse" were destroyed, and the renovations at Montevideo were much "thrown back" by the storm. And at Arcadia a corn house and a rice house had been destroyed. Similar reports were received of damage at South Hampton, at White Oak, Lodebar, Lambert, and other surrounding plantations. Miraculously no lives were lost anywhere in the county, but crops were badly damaged everywhere. "Our losses in crops and expenses in repairs will be heavy," Charles wrote, "so we must make economy the order of the day." With Charlie at Harvard Law School, with Joe in medical school in Pennsylvania, and with major renovations under way at Montevideo, it was a bad time to lose most of the crop and most of the income for the year. If the storm made "economy the order of the day" for the whites, it made life more vulnerable for those in the settlements, especially for a family at Carlawter.[14]

While no one died from the high winds of the hurricane, the storm left in its wake flooded cisterns and stagnating pools of water. From these arose clouds of mosquitoes, intensifying the misery of a yellow fever epidemic that had already broken out in Savannah. Unlike malaria, yellow fever was primarily an urban disease, for its carrier, the blood-sucking *Aedes aegypti* mosquito, disdained swamps and lakes. Among its early victims in Savannah was Dr. Charlton Wells, the young husband of Mary King. He had left the relative safety of the country to go into the city, saying, "in times of sickness the physician's post of duty claimed him." Night and day he was engaged attending the sick, "most of whom were poor people." Worn with fatigue, he had been drenched when the storm struck and was soon taken with the fever, dying shortly thereafter. Mary Jones wrote Charlie that they had "seen a good deal of him this summer, and a more lovely character is seldom met with: talented and accomplished in his profession, pureminded, gentle, and affectionate, tender and devoted in all the relations of life, reflecting peace and happiness. Who could fail to love and admire one so truly amiable, accomplished, and gentlemanly?" And then she added: "Poor Mary! God alone can comfort and sustain her! They were all in all to each other, devotedly attached." And Sarah Howe wrote of her concern for the widowed Mary, "knowing how she loved him with the most uncontrolled affection."[15]

Charlton Wells was not the only young doctor to fall in the line of duty. Dr. Stephen Harris (it was he who had eloped with Emma Jones, provoking Joseph to strike her from his will) had developed a reputation as a skilled physician and was held in high regard in Savannah. When the epidemic struck the city, he did not flee to the safety of the countryside but stayed in the city, tending the sick until he too was struck down by the fever. Emma was devastated. She would later marry again—to the younger brother of Dr. Harris—but when she died in 1913, she would be buried in Savannah beside the one with whom she had fled the Retreat in 1846. The inscription on her tomb would read: "Her body lies beside the husband of her youth. We have loved in life, and in death we will not be divided."[16]

Emma returned to the summer home of her mother in Walthourville and, while the fever still raged in Savannah, persuaded James Newton Jones, her older brother, to go into the city to retrieve some papers. On his return to the county, he stopped at Lodebar to see his brother Henry Hart. Here the fever, contracted in Savannah, struck Jimma, as he was affectionately called. It began with fever, chills, and muscle aches and apparently followed the familiar pattern of liver failure and jaundice. Hemorrhaging began from the gums, nose, and stomach lining. The digested blood, when vomited, looked black, a kind of "ropy fluid, like coffee grounds mixed with a glairy, shining fluid," while muscle spasms produced excruciating pain. Jimma's hands blackened, and blood settled under his nails. Charles and Mary were summoned from Maybank, and they hastened to Lodebar. At his bedside they joined his mother and his wife, together with William and Betsy Maxwell, Susan and Laura, and Henry Hart and his wife, Abby. The doctor had already bled Jimma and had given him much quinine and brandy. Blisters had been applied to his "legs, thighs, stomach, breast, and arms and back of the neck. Every effort made to bring on reaction." Mary "rubbed his hands and arms incessantly, others his feet." The doctor said there was no hope. Charles knelt and prayed beside the bed. Jimma stirred and repeated to himself the first two verses of the 103rd Psalm: "Bless the Lord, O my soul: and all that is within me, bless His holy name. Bless the Lord, O my soul, and forget not all His benefits." He began to sink. His wife, Sallie, horrified by his slipping away, crawled up on the bed beside him trying to hold him back from death by the strength of her love. "Jimma, Jimma," she cried, "my dear Jimma, speak to me once more. Do you know me? Who am I?" He replied: "*My own dear Sallie.*" Bending her face nearer still, she cried again: "What do you say?" "*My own dear Sallie.*" And with his last act of consciousness, he "turn[ed] over to her and fix[ed] his dying eyes upon her!" His body was carried to the Retreat, where he was buried in the family cemetery behind the house, near Joseph's grave.[17]

So death came among the young couples of the county who—only a few years earlier—had flirted and courted on the piazzas at South Hampton and at the Retreat and at weddings in Walthourville. And while Charles and Mary needed no such reminders, these deaths so shortly after their return home were intimations of "How empty and transitory is *life, the pursuits* of life, the *possessions* of life! How near we are to *God and eternity with all its amazing realities!*"[18]

By the summer of 1856 Charlie and Joe were back in Georgia, beginning their professional careers in Savannah. Charlie had graduated from Dane Law School, Harvard, in the class of 1855, and later that year he began practicing law with the family friend John Elliott Ward, the mayor of Savannah. While he quickly made a name for himself as a rising young lawyer, Charlie also turned to archaeology—his old love from his school days on Colonel's Island. Within three years of his return to Savannah he would publish *Indian Remains in Southern Georgia*, the first of some eighty papers, pamphlets, and books that were to flow from his prodigious research. Joe, on his part, received his medical degree in 1856 and was soon practicing medicine and serving as professor of chemistry at Savannah Medical College. He had already, as a medical student, published four first-rate articles—three in the leading national medical journal, the *American Journal of the Medical Sciences*, and one in the Smithsonian Institution's prestigious *Contributions to Knowledge*. Both of the sons were clearly on their way to distinguished careers, to what Charles and Mary called "usefulness in society." And both were also deeply a part of a lively social life that was centered in Savannah and that flowed out to Maybank and Montevideo and the surrounding plantations of Liberty County.[19]

The most important social event for the Jones family in 1856 was the marriage of Laura Maxwell. She was the beauty of the family, bright, personable, and a lover of a funny story. She would write about the peculiarities of the latest fashions in Savannah, Philadelphia, or New York, or tell of blundering beaux or of a stout Savannah matron who had had leeches applied as a treatment for her rheumatism only to have the leeches curl up and die. Only her Aunt Betsy Maxwell could match her in teasing Laura's dignified and proper Uncle Charles. Laura was well connected—through her mother, Susan, and her father, Audley, and her stepfather, Joseph Cumming—to a bewildering array of low-country cousins, aunts, and uncles. After the death of her brother Charles Edward, she was the owner with her mother of Lambert plantation and of Social Bluff on Colonel's Island, and was the sole owner of forty-two slaves. In addition, White Oak and some other thirty slaves were owned by her mother and were anticipated as part of Laura's inheritance. She had been courted much. Henry Hart Jones had been only one of many to fall in love with her. There had been aspiring young men in Savannah, and a Yankee beau from Philadelphia, and even young Robert Quarterman Mallard had called on her—Laura had called him a "a very smart beau." But the one who finally won her heart was the Reverend David Buttolph, a handsome young man, a native of New York, and a graduate of Williams College and Columbia Theological Seminary. Buttolph had served two years as the associate pastor with Thomas Smyth at Second Presbyterian Church in Charleston before accepting a call as the pastor of Midway Church in Liberty County. Not long after his arrival in the county, he had started courting Laura. Eliza Mallard, on learning of the attention he was giving Laura and knowing her wealth and social connections, wrote with amusement that he was courting "one of the fattest lambs of his flock"![20]

The wedding was held at Social Bluff in June 1856. Mary had written Laura earlier: "And I wish you, dear Laura, to say *to all your friends* in Savannah whom you intend inviting to the joyful occasion that we shall be most happy to entertain them at Maybank. Our hearts and home will be open to them all." It was a generous offer from a loving aunt, but many guests meant long hours and heavy work for Patience and Phoebe and all those who helped them in the kitchen and in the house. The wedding itself was evidently a grand occasion in the familiar style of country weddings, and Patience and Phoebe no doubt were called upon to help prepare some of the low-country delicacies for the wedding feast.[21]

Among those who had been busy with the preparations at Social Bluff was Betsy Maxwell. The wedding day itself, 10 June 1856, had been selected in honor of Betsy and William's forty-fifth anniversary. But Betsy was obviously ill. Her left arm was swollen, and she had a draining wound in her armpit from surgery the previous spring. Five years earlier she had had a mole with an "inky character" removed from her arm. Everything had seemed fine for several years following the surgery, but in February 1856 she had begun to complain of great discomfort with her arm. A tumor was then found in her armpit. She went to Savannah, and there in the home of Susan and Laura, doctors used chloroform and ether to put her to sleep. The deep-seated tumor was found to be larger than first expected, and the surgery was delicate, leaving a large wound. Betsy bore the surgery "with great fortitude," but within a few weeks another tumor had to be removed from her neck. By the time she returned to Liberty County, more tumors had appeared on different parts of her body. In spite of her suffering, she had thrown herself into the preparations for the wedding with energy and interest. She regarded Laura as a daughter—or more as a granddaughter, since as a young wife Betsy had helped to raise Susan and Charles when their mother had died and then years later Laura and Charles Edward had spent many a month with Betsy and William at Laurel View or on the island. So Betsy had found somewhere within her the will and strength to be a part of Laura's wedding. But the effort took its toll on her, and shortly thereafter she was confined to her bed.[22]

William carried her to Dorchester, one of the little summer retreats, where comfortable large homes had been built as some families had begun to tire of the annual move between plantation houses and summer cottages. Abial and Louisa Winn welcomed their old friends into their home (the Winns' wedding in 1838 had been at Lodebar, then the home of Betsy and William). Betsy now prepared for her death. At first she had wondered "if travel or a change of air or springs of some kind" might not be of help. But when the doctor told her that nothing would cure her and that death was not far off, she "yielded to what she saw to be the will of God." She was not alarmed but "made her arrangements for her departure with calmness and clearness and spoke of that departure as of an ordinary event." She made decisions about the distribution of her possessions, giving special remembrances to those whom she loved. She had her hair cut off, for it was impossible for her any more "to comb and put it up," and she gave it to Laura and Mary Sharpe and to the Winns' daughter Lizzie.

As her suffering increased, she refused all but the lightest dosage of opium, for she did not want to be stupefied. She said to Joe, who had come from Savannah to be with his aunt, "I wish to die in my senses." Patience prepared some arrowroot for her, and its soft texture and rich nutrients provided a little strength. Betsy found great comfort in hearing Scripture read and hymns sung around her bed and in prayers said for her. "Her heart," her brother Charles said "was in the Word and worship of God." She was calm and peaceful as she faced her death and looked to "the Rock Jesus Christ." She said, "I trust altogether in my precious Saviour and have no fears," but at one point she began to wonder, as she remembered all her sins, whether she was too confident. Charles said to her: "My dear sister, it is common for God's own children to be tempted of the Devil & of their own unbelieving hearts in days of affliction & death." No one, he reminded her, can count on personal merit or righteousness, but all must depend on God's grace. Betsy said: "Yes, that is what I constantly do and I have comfort and peace."

As her end approached she began to call family members to her bed to give them her parting admonitions and blessings. They came and knelt weeping by her bed, holding and kissing her hand as she spoke to them. "Laura and Mary Sharpe, my precious children" she said. "Joe my son, my dear child," "Sue, my precious sister." And so with tender affection she said her good-byes. To Mary Sharpe she said: "Your Aunty loves you dearly. God bless you my child." To Joe she said: "Joe, my dear Baby, my son, your old Aunty is going to leave you. Let me entreat you to come to Christ. Do not put off your soul's salvation." She sent word to Charlie, who had stayed in Savannah: "I leave my dying farewell for him. Tell him to live not for the world. . . . I beg him not to put off his soul's salvation, and not be carried away by transient pleasures and honors." She thanked Susan and Charles and Mary for their tender care for her; she committed them to God's keeping, and urged them not to grieve too deeply for her. She sent her love and good-byes to those in Marietta and north Georgia—to her aunt Eliza Robarts and her family, to John Jones and his family. When she called William, the old man came and sat beside her on the bed "and took her hand in both his hands and laid it on his cheek and he bowed down his head, convulsed with grief." "William," she said,

> I have tried to be a good wife to you. I have tried to do my duty to you; to keep you from extravagance, to keep things together, to be economical and to make both ends meet. I have prayed for your conversion and God has answered my prayers. I am going to leave you. You will be all alone. Do not stay too much

at home by yourself—go around and see the children. God be with and bless you my dear Husband. We cannot be long separated.

She then drew him to her, kissed him, and said "farewell, goodbye my dear Husband."

Then she called her personal servant Louisa. They had been together as mistress and servant for years. Each had cared for the other when sick, and Betsy had stayed by Louisa's bed days and nights when she almost died of childbirth. Louisa knew Betsy as only a personal servant could know the habits and moods of a mistress. And Betsy knew much about Louisa—about her affair years earlier with Miley's husband Isaac, how she had later repented of it, and how she had been so good to Miley when Isaac had beaten her and had so brutally damaged Miley's eye. Now on her deathbed, Betsy said her good-byes to Louisa, gave her parting advice, and sent messages with her to all "the servants at the plantation."

Betsy's pain now became excruciating and her nausea constant. She prayed to die: "My work is done. Come Lord Jesus, come quickly! Come quickly, Lord Jesus receive my spirit." They gave her ether and chloroform, and she found it a comfort as her end grew near, but her "life ebbed away in the slowest manner imaginable." Finally, early on the morning of 24 July she left "Jordan's stormy bank" and crossed over the river. Charles and Mary were with her, as were Joe and Susan and Laura and her new husband, David Buttolph. William was seated at Betsy's side, holding her hand. Mary reached over and closed her eyes and placed "the napkin about her face." David Buttolph had said a prayer and then, after everyone else had left the room, Mary and Susan began to perform "the last sad offices" of preparing Betsy for her "long rest." Joe rode to Montevideo and had Porter and Sandy Maybank build the cypress coffin and the outer case.

The funeral was held two days later at Midway. A large crowd of whites gathered from around the county to honor a greatly beloved member of their little community. And in the balcony, wrote Charles, were "all our servants from the different plantations, a large number of them." David Buttolph, looking up into the balcony from the Midway pulpit, could see among them Louisa and Miley, Cato, Phoebe and Cassius, and Patience and Porter. They had come to say their own good-byes to a white mistress and to make their own private judgments about her life.[23]

The pallbearers—Charlie, Joe, Henry Hart, and Maybank Jones—carried the coffin out of the meetinghouse to the Midway cemetery. Beneath the massive oaks and the long gray wisps of Spanish moss, Betsy was buried among her family and friends. A plain white marble stone was later erected at the spot. It said to all who stopped to notice it that Betsy's way of dying, like her way of living, was a testimony to a Calvinistic and evangelical faith that had taken root and flourished in the Georgia low country.[24] And her stone shining in the shadows of the oaks and moss of the Midway cemetery served as another painful reminder to Charles and Mary that the home they sought was elusive. Time, like a low-country river, brought change and loss, and even love could not resist its flow or protect a home from time's erosive power.

26

SLAVE MARKET

The sorrows that invaded low-country homes with such violence were not, of course, confined to those who lived in plantation houses but were also a part of life in the settlements. Indeed, disease and death were a part of the wider and more pervasive sorrows of those who sought to make a home under the burdens of slavery's oppression.

A short time after Charles and Mary had returned from Philadelphia in the fall of 1853, they had sent for Phoebe to come to Maybank. She had been hired out in late summer to Mrs. Susan Way, who was home from China with her missionary husband for a short stay in Liberty County. Mary, however, wanted her old personal servant close to her, so Phoebe had been brought to the island to work her magic as a seamstress and to help Patience in the kitchen. Cassius and their children stayed at Carlawter, but Phoebe's son John was brought with her to Maybank and apparently put to work around the house and lot. The previous summer John had left his wife, a young woman at Carlawter, and the overseer Benjamin Allen had not been able to get him to return to her. John thus brought with him a growing reputation as a rogue.[1]

Christmas 1853 fell on the Sabbath, so in order to avoid disturbing "the hallowed day," the Christmas celebration was postponed to Monday, 26 December. Early in the morning, Charles and Mary gave gifts to all those in the settlement and received in return gifts of eggs and "many thanks." Later in the day, Charles and Mary, with Mary Sharpe, went to Andrew's cabin for a Christmas worship service with the people of the settlement. During the service, John left the room in some distress. After the service, Charles and Mary went to John's cabin and found him "suffering from great oppression—difficulty of breathing and hemorrhage from the lungs." Because his situation was alarming and no doctor was near, they sent for William Maxwell. After various remedies were administered,

John had some relief, but he was obviously dangerously sick. As soon as he was able "to receive it," Charles spoke to him about the state of his soul and urged him "to repent of his sins and cast his lost and guilty soul at the feet of Jesus Christ, the poor sinner's only friend." He had been, Mary noted, "a prayerless, wicked, profane, Sabbath breaker and immoral boy and he seemed insensible to his sins and their consequences." About sunset Andrew came running over and reported that John's breath was growing very short. Charles and Mary again rushed "to him and there he was in agony of body, gasping for breath, spitting up blood profusely, apparently nigh unto death and with all the terrors of sin and *eternal destruction filling him with* horror unutterable." John said that "he had *lost his time. He knew the way but he did not care for it,* that he had been a *fool,* that even since he had been so sick he would not pray 'for fear that people would laugh at him and run their rigs upon him and say because he was sick and afraid to die that he wanted to turn to God.'" He confessed that "he never would think upon these things because he believed that he would get well, but if spared he hoped to let the world see that he was a *praying soul.* And then in the most earnest manner, he would entreat the blessed saviour to have mercy on his poor soul." He thanked Charles "for all his kindness and faithfulness in warning and teaching him and trying to bring him to Christ." Mary repeated "that precious passage: 'For God so loved the world etc.'" John said "it was true and he could look only to Christ." "Poor fellow," wrote Mary quoting Psalm 116: "The sorrows of death compassed him and the pains of Hell got hold upon him." And she felt herself the horror of his situation: "Oh! The Anguish of coming to our dying hours with no preparation for judgment and eternity! No Saviour, no Mediator, no Advocate!" No one, she thought, could tell what the result would be, but she hoped that if he were spared "we shall see the evidences of a genuine work of grace on his heart." But she warned her unconverted son Charlie that "a *death bed* is no place for repentance—remorse and anguish for sin are not faith and love to Christ."[2]

John's health continued to decline during the coming weeks. By the first of February 1854, Charles thought, "Poor John is to all appearance approaching that awful event which awaits us all." Charles had been visiting him regularly, "conversing and praying with him." His mind, he reported, "is calm and seems staid on the Lord Jesus Christ—the only support in such trying hours." Charles believed that there had been a great change in John and added, "We sincerely hope it may be the work of God in His infinite mercy to him." John asked to see his sisters Clarissa and Jane, and Charles sent for them at Carlawter and Acadia. After the visit, Jane was allowed to remain at Maybank to be with her brother. John sent "a thousand howdyes, and *goodbye too!*" to Charlie, who at that time was still away at Harvard. And he said that he never expected to see Charlie in this world anymore. "Nothing," he said, "is left for me but to look to the Lord Jesus Christ and to put my whole trust in him."[3]

Two weeks later, John was sitting in a chair with his mother, Phoebe, and his uncle Porter at his side. John's "arms were resting along on the back of the chair and his face sideways on his arms, and neither arms, hands, head nor person moved." Porter called him, but he did not respond. "He touched him, but he moved not. He put his hand to his nostril. There was no breath. He was dead!" He was, wrote Charles, "conscious, calm, collected, reposing his hopes on the Lord Jesus Christ to the last. We cannot decide. God alone knows. But we have strong hope for him. Ten thousand times this, than other wise."[4]

A coffin was built, and they carried John's body in a creaking oxcart to the chapel at Montevideo. The service was at noon, and the people came from Arcadia as well as Carlawter and Maybank to the little chapel. Charles found the service a "solemn and affecting hour." Phoebe and John's sisters "and many others and indeed all were affected. The opening of the coffin and the last look was the touching close." The men bore John to his grave in the cemetery at Carlawter, and the people followed in procession. There they committed him to the ground and to the grace of God.[5]

Jane had been close to her brother—they had spent time in Columbia together and shared a rebellious spirit. She was in many ways her mother's child, having absorbed Phoebe's rage against slavery and its oppression. But the teenager lacked her mother's self-control and her grandfather's wisdom about the ways of whites and about strategies for avoiding their wrath and violence. So Jane had become in the eyes of Charles and Mary another troublemaker, like her brother John before his sickness. It consequently seemed to Charles and Mary that Phoebe and Cassius and their children were becoming not simply irritants but a festering sore in the settlements, increasingly difficult to control and disruptive of the peace, order, and harmony of the plantations. Less than two years after John's death, Mary wrote Charlie: "We have not yet determined what we shall do in reference to *that* family. We wish to act aright. They have always been unprincipled. *Jane* gives constant trouble. Much as I should miss the *mother*, I will not separate them if I can help it. It is a painful and harassing business."[6]

Mary's note to Charlie was an ominous indicator of things to come. Phoebe was obviously a skilled servant who had a special relationship with Mary not only because of her talents as a seamstress and personal servant but also because of the memories and associations that clustered around her. Charles, however, had continued to distrust her, and Jane's behavior had reinforced his images of Phoebe and Cassius's family. As Jane continued to be obstinate and surly, Charles and

Mary had begun discussing what to do about her. If they separated her from her family, they would be betraying all that Charles had said about masters' keeping slave families together. They obviously found the whole matter "painful and harassing," as it intruded into the peace and tranquillity they sought in their low-country home.

Jane may have learned that Charles and Mary were discussing her behavior and were perplexed about how to act "in reference to *that* family," or she may simply have had more than she could stand of Carlawter. At any rate, in August 1856 she made a break for freedom.[7] She probably slipped aboard a river schooner docked in Riceboro, maybe helped by one of the black seamen, and hid on board until the vessel arrived in Savannah. There she was able to blend into the obscurity of an urban black community. Now her previous experience in Columbia came to her aid, for it meant that she was not simply a plantation slave on the run but a young woman with some experience of urban life and with some understanding of strategies for survival. She adopted the name Sarah and began to represent "herself as belonging to a gentleman in the up country who allowed her to find work and pay wages"—a common practice in Savannah.[8]

A Mrs. Dunham, an older woman with connections to Liberty County, was in need of a house servant and chambermaid. Nelson, a house servant of a neighbor's, was asked to help find someone. He made inquiries for several days before Jane met him and told him the story she had fashioned for "Sarah." Nelson took her to Mrs. Dunham. Jane presented herself to her, said she was able to do housework, and agreed to work for $6.50 a month. Jane "behaved herself very well, attending ordinarily well to her duties," but Mrs. Durham found that she was "greatly inclined to be lazy, and at times somewhat impudent in answering back when spoken to with reference to her work." Jane apparently had a place to live in the yard behind the house. After she had been there a few weeks, Jane reported that "her master was in the city and had told her that she must go back with him up the country." She asked for her month's wages, saying she must leave. She was told, "Go to your master and get from him a receipt for your month's wages, and I will pay you." She was also told to ask her master to let her stay a day or two longer in order that another house servant could be secured. "After this she said nothing further about wages or about leaving."[9]

In the meantime, of course, Jane's absence from Carlawter had been discovered. When a search for her was unsuccessful, Charles and Mary faced a new dilemma. They needed to recover their runaway slave, but they could not bring themselves to follow the usual custom of putting an advertisement in the paper. An advertisement—"Runaway slave of the Rev. Charles C. Jones"—would seriously damage Charles's reputation as a successful and benevolent planter. Why would a slave of one known far and wide for his benevolence and for his advocacy of reform run away? In spite of such concerns, a reward of $25 was offered through Charlie, who was by then practicing law and living in Savannah with Joe.

As the search began for Jane, Phoebe and Cassius showed no interest in helping to find out where she had fled. Their apparent indifference infuriated Charles, and their lack of cooperation seemed to him a deliberate challenge to his authority and to his paternalistic assumptions. He believed that they could "have brought her back" if they wished. Moreover, adding fuel to the fire of his anger, they "sold all her clothing, plainly intimating that she is no more expected or desired back."[10]

Slave hunters in Savannah tracked down runaways who were hiding out in the city's black shanties by the river or who were, like Jane, disguising themselves as workers being hired out by their owners. Among the slave hunters in 1856 was a city constable by the name of Jones. He hired spies to be on the lookout for Jane, and in late September she was discovered. About six in the evening on 30 September, Jones went to Mrs. Dunham's house, arrested Jane, and took her — most likely at Charlie's instructions — to the slave jail of William Wright, one of Savannah's most prominent slave traders. Charlie wrote his father the next day and provided the details he had learned about Jane, her employment by Mrs. Dunham, and her arrest. He recommended that no legal action be taken against Mrs. Dunham. "I am persuaded," he wrote, "that there was no intention in the case to harbor the Negro in any manner, shape, or form. A prosecution would be unpleasant, tending to make the matter notorious, and would in every probability be unaccompanied by conviction."[11]

Jane was "just as fat as she can be, with fine ear- and finger-rings, etc." Charlie believed Wright's jail as "safe and comfortable as any in which she can be placed" and calculated, "She would be worth in this market eight or nine hundred dollars." He wondered "whether she should be allowed to come on the plantation again. Her tales of Savannah and of high life in the city would probably not have the most beneficial effect upon her compeers."[12]

Charles was obviously relieved to receive his son's letter. He wrote back immediately. While he agreed that no legal steps should be taken — he certainly did not want to "make the matter notorious" — he did hope "we may yet discover *in what conveyance and by whom she* was taken to Savannah," and he speculated that one of the river schooners had been the means of her escape. One thing was for sure: "We have had trouble enough, and I wish to have no more. She is no more to return to the plantation nor to the county." Charles believed that Phoebe and Cassius were "privy to her movements, and are in good spirits and consider her gone for good." He had decided that neither Phoebe nor Cassius nor anyone else on the plantations was to be informed of Jane's arrest and for good reason:

> We have concluded to dispose of the whole family, but not in Savannah nor in the low country. They must be sold up the country, where they will not come back. It is very painful, but we have no comfort or confidence in them, and they appear unhappy themselves—no doubt from the trouble they have from time to time occasioned. Enclosed is a list of them—to which *Titus* is added— with your mother's estimate, which cannot be far from a correct one. You can copy the list without the sums annexed and show it to Wright, and if you think best to Montmollin also, and learn what their estimate would be, and if they have orders from the up country, and could dispose of the whole family to one owner; for we cannot consent to separate them. If the thing can be done, we will close the matter at once. Should you hear of anyone willing to purchase, you might come to some understanding about it. Make no final contract without consulting us.

The list that Charles sent read as follows:

C. Sr.	[Cassius] Father. Age 45. Good field hand, basket-maker, and handy jobs. (I put him at that; Mother thinks it too low)	800
P.	[Phoebe] Mother. Age 47. Accomplished house servant in any and every line: good cook, washer and ironer, and fine seamstress.	1000
C. Jr.	[Cassius Jr.] Son. Good field hand. Age 20	1000
J.	[Jane] Daughter (in town). Age 18. House servant, good seamstress, and field hand.	900
P.	[Prime] Son. Field hand. Handy fellow. Age 16	800
V.	[Victoria] Daughter. Age 14. Smart, active field hand	800
Lf.	[LaFayette] Son. Age 12. Smart, active boy	800
T.	[Big Titus] Man. Age 29. Field hand and good oxcart man	600
		$6700[13]

The decision was thus made to sell the whole family, and Big Titus, the son of Prime and Fanny, who lived at Arcadia, was also "thrown in" the lot.[14] Why they decided to include Big Titus is not clear—perhaps he was regarded as Jane's husband, or perhaps Charles and Mary wanted to increase the number and value of those being sold. What is clear is that the sale of the family would serve several purposes—it would remove Jane, "the troublemaker"; it would remove a family which had "always been unprincipled"; and it would attempt to keep the family together and thus reinforce the image that Charles and Mary had of themselves as kind and benevolent owners. It is also clear that Charles did not want the family anywhere in the low country, where they might make contact once again with their friends and relatives who lived at Carlawter, Maybank, Arcadia, the Retreat, and other surrounding plantations.

Charlie immediately began the negotiations for the sale. He talked with John S. Montmollin, a prominent slave trader, who told him that the slaves could be sold quickly in southwest Georgia. Charlie talked with Wright, who thought that the market would improve and prices would be better in a month. The estimates given by Mary and sent by Charles must be, Charlie wrote, "subject to greater or less modification. The size, soundness of teeth, etc., are all to he considered."[15] Days and weeks passed, however, and no buyers appeared. Mary began to have second thoughts. She was apparently hesitant to sell Phoebe, who was such a superior seamstress and around whom so many emotions swirled. Charles wrote Mary, who was visiting in Savannah:

> I thought we had determined to part with the whole family, and were only waiting, upon recommendation, a month later for a better sale, until within a few days of your leaving for Savannah, when you appeared to hesitate on account of the inconvenience and trouble that would ensue upon the loss of an efficient house servant and seamstress. Our determination to sell the whole family was based, I believe, on these considerations: (1) An indisposition to separate parents and child, no matter how evil their conduct had been in the premises. (2) The unreliable character of the family, the trouble the mother has always given, and the moral certainty that whenever occasions offer, the same rebellious conduct will appear again. (3) And in case of the sale of the present incorrigible runaway apart from her family, although they have sent her away never to return, the effect upon them in all probability will not be for the better. (4) And lastly, a change of investment would be more desirable than otherwise.

Because Phoebe and her children belonged to Mary, she needed to give her permission for them to be sold. Moreover, Charles did not want to act alone or in an arbitrary manner as the "head of the household." He told Mary:

> I do not wish to influence you in the least degree beyond your own convictions, nor to have you subjected to any inconveniences in your domestic arrangements whatever, and therefore cannot assume the sole responsibility of a decision. *It is the second or third time we have had it in contemplation to sell this family.* The sale of one may prove beneficial to the character and subordination of those that remain. Time only can show. If not, they may be sent after her.

Charles did not believe the family had ever been treated badly by their owners. Had Jane or Phoebe or Cassius any cause for their behavior, Charles said he would feel differently. "But I think they have not. Jane has been treated as our other servants have been, and every effort has been used to reclaim her—and without effect." And so, since the family had no reason for their behavior, he concluded:

> If, therefore, you wish the whole family sold, I have not the least objection. If not, then Jane may be sold and we may wait and see the effect. If for good, we shall be glad; if for evil, then we must meet the evil as best we may. But I have very little hope of any improvement. The *main* objection to the sale of the family, so far as I can see, is the loss of the services of a servant who has given us more trouble, and even now and always has required more watching, than all our servants twice put together. However, I am willing to keep her and do all I can to make her profitable to you—as much so as in times past. I have no objection.[16]

Charles's distrust of Phoebe—in spite of his not wanting to impose his will on Mary—finally had the possibility of leading to some action, and he clearly did not want to miss the opportunity of getting rid of one who had so frequently irritated him and disrupted the peace he sought at Maybank and Montevideo. But his fourth "consideration" about "a change of investment" was also revealing. Expenses had mounted and income had shrunk ever since the hurricane. The year before Jane ran away, Charles had for the first time in his life mortgaged some of his slaves: three of Old Lizzie and Robinson's sons, Lymus, Daniel, and Little Adam; and Old Lizzie's daughter Maria and her son Dick. So a "change of investment" would be more than "desirable"—it would also relieve significant financial pressure that had accrued with the renovation of the Montevideo house and the expenses associated with Charlie's and Joe's educations. Mary agreed with Charles's careful and prudent reasoning, and the efforts to make a sale proceeded.[17]

Within a week, Charles had made arrangements for Phoebe, Cassius, Cassius Jr., Prime, and Victoria to be taken to Wright's jail, where prospective buyers could examine them and consider "the size, soundness of teeth, etc." The twelve-year-old LaFayette had already been taken, with his sixteen-year-old cousin Little Titus, to Savannah to work as a house servant for Charlie and Joe. For some unknown reason, Big Titus had been removed from the lot of those to be sold.[18]

Charles hired Joseph Jackson to be in charge of getting Phoebe and her family to Savannah. Jackson was a small farmer, a rough man, who owned a little place south of the Retreat near the Pleasant Grove church and who had served for a time as the overseer of John Jones's Bonaventure plantation on the Medway. He could be called upon to hunt runaways in the swamp or to catch a slave slipping away at night to visit in another settlement—just the kind of white man needed for the dirty work of carrying slaves to market.[19]

Charles also rode to Arcadia and called the driver Stepney aside. Stepney was a cousin of Phoebe's—they had both been born at the Retreat and had grown up together—but it was better to send him than Cato with Jackson. Cato was, after all, Cassius's older brother. They had explored the world of Carlawter together as boys, and if they had taken different roads in their response to the oppression of slavery, their roads had run side by side for many years. But now the road of Cassius—the handsome, restless one whose anger could flare so quickly—would be parting from the road of Cato, the prudent one who suppressed his anger and worked the system. So Charles followed his own prudent instincts when he sent Stepney and not Cato on this bitter mission.[20]

No letters were written and no records were left to tell how Phoebe and Cassius were informed that they and their children would be sold. They were apparently told on Saturday, 1 November, that they would be taken early the next Monday morning. Nor was any letter written or record left that told how Cassius and Phoebe and their children responded to the news. It was probably with a combination of defiance and grief. Certainly there were no hints of Phoebe's pleading to remain at Carlawter and no indications that Cassius promised to become a dutiful and submissive slave if he and his family were not sold away.[21]

At any rate, there was little time for them to say their good-byes or to make arrangements for the disposal of their possessions. Cassius asked Cato and Porter to give his son James (the son of Peggy, who lived at White Oak and who had been a rival of Phoebe's) and his daughter Nanny (the daughter of another woman on another plantation) "3 small hogs, 3 pots, 1 oven, 1 pail, 1 piggin, 3 plates, [and] 1 new bucket." Cassius sold a colt to his brother Daniel for forty-five dollars and gave him a saddle and bridle. That left Cassius's mare, valued by him at seventy-five dollars; his buggy that had recently been repaired by Prophet at South Hampton; a barrow and a sow; two bushels of rice; a dozen chickens; two hundredweight of fodder; ten bushels of corn; and nine stick baskets that Cassius had made. He asked Charles to sell all of these possessions, pay Cassius's debts, and forward the proceeds to him once he and Phoebe and their children reached their new home.[22]

At four o'clock on Monday morning, a little jersey and a wagon set out from Carlawter. Charles and Mary were up, as were Cato, Daniel, and their sister Sina, who was sick with a recurrent fever. And no doubt Porter and Patience were also up with their children to say their good-byes, together with old Rosetta and her

children and all the others who lived in the cabins at Carlawter. Permission may
have been given for Prince, the grandson of Old Jupiter and Blind Silvey, to bring
the people from White Oak to bid farewell, or perhaps they had come on Sunday. But surely on that Monday morning there were tears that wet the sandy soil
of Carlawter, for even Charles and Mary found it painful. "We have had a sad
day of it," wrote Charles later in the morning, "as you may suppose—the first of
the kind in our lives." But he also wrote that he and Mary "do not wish them sacrificed" with a quick sale that would bring only a low price.[23]

The jersey and wagon went down the Montevideo avenue, turned right on the
little road that led to Riceboro, went past the old courthouse where in former
years so many had been bought and sold, and then turned north on the road
to Savannah. They moved slowly in the morning darkness past Lambert, where
Sharper, the black preacher, had lived and where the slaves of Laura Maxwell
labored in rice and cotton fields. Just as the sun was coming up, they approached
Midway Church. From a distance the sandy road to Savannah and its slave market appeared to run straight through the meetinghouse, with its tall steeple now
illumined by the morning sun. Phoebe may have remembered the day she had
made her confession of faith before the congregation and had become a member, or when she had been excommunicated for several years when she had had
her affair with Cassius while still married to Sandy Jones. More likely, Phoebe's
eyes and her thoughts turned westward beyond the old Midway cemetery to
Arcadia, where Clarissa, Phoebe's firstborn, lived with Phoebe's four grandchildren. Maybe Phoebe was thinking that in spite of all that Charles had said about
keeping families together, a daughter and four grandchildren were not in the
wagon on the road to Savannah. Or maybe she was thinking that even a slave
so privileged as she had been—the daughter of Jack, the personal servant of
Mary Jones, the skilled seamstress—even she could be stripped of her privileges
and sold away. Or maybe she was thinking that she was but a chick left un-
guarded by her father's death and now she was in the clutches of the hungry
fowl-hawk. But who knows what Phoebe thought as she rode along that November morning?

They reached Savannah before the evening and made their way to the house
where Charlie and Joe lived. When they arrived, young LaFayette was confronted
for the first time with the terrifying reality of his parents' and brothers' and sister's being taken to the slave market. He was told that for the moment he would
not go with them to the market but would remain with his cousin Little Titus
to be a house servant for Charlie and Joe. He would not be allowed to return to
Carlawter to say good-bye to his aunts, uncles, cousins, and friends, or to Arcadia
to see his sister Clarissa. Rather, when the time came, he too would be taken to

the jail for an inspection and sale. That evening Charlie went with Jackson and Stepney to Wright's to see "the people located." And so the journey from Car-lawter to the slave jail was made in what Charles called the "least public" and "most speedy" way.[24]

Weeks passed, however, and no purchaser was found. Buyers came and in-spected Phoebe and Cassius and the children but did not buy. For a while, it appeared that a buyer had been secured who wanted Phoebe and Jane as house servants and who would keep the family together. In late November, Mary wrote Charlie:

> Your father and myself think with you that if $4300 can be realized for that family, you had best close the bargain; for their present expense is very great, and increasing. Of course, as we are compelled to sell, we would like to realize their value, but are willing to let them go for less in view of selling all together. We are now much in want of funds to meet our liabilities in bank and for the house. I know that you will do the best for us in this matter. It will be a relief to have the business closed. It has caused me great distress.

But in the end the offer for the family did not appear as advantageous as hoped, and the transaction was not completed. Then on 10 December, Charles wrote Mary from Savannah that Charlie had completed the sale for $4500 cash. "They have all been sold to one person—not to be separated, but remain on his own farm in the vicinity of *Macon*." Charles believed they had been "sold as we de-sired"—that is, as a family—"and of this we should be glad, although more might have been obtained had they been sold separately." Then he added, "Conscience is better than money."[25]

So the deed was done, and Mary wrote: "I am thankful that family is finally disposed of." The day after the sale, Charles began paying off his debts—his bank account had fallen to almost nothing—and he put $2,337.48 in railroad stock as a change of investment. Even Porter and Sandy Maybank were paid for their work on Saturdays during the previous two years. And Mary, now deprived of Phoebe, began shopping for one of the new sewing machines that had recently appeared on the market.[26]

The sale of Phoebe, Cassius, and their children was a moment of self-revelation for Charles. Years earlier, when Charles had been a student at Princeton, he had wondered, in midst of a moral crisis, whether he ought to continue "to *hold slaves*." He had written Mary "as to the *principle* of slavery, it is *wrong!*" and he had asked himself: "In my present circumstances, with evil on my hands en-tailed from my father, would the general interests of the slaves and community at large, with reference to the slaves, be promoted best, by emancipation? Could I do more for the ultimate good of the slave population by holding or emancipating what I own?"[27] His decision to return to Liberty County as a missionary and reformer had seemed to him one way to negotiate between duty and home; it had seemed a bridge between the cultural heritage of a place and people whom he loved and his convictions about the evils of slavery and the freedom of the human will to turn from self-love and self-interest to a concern for the good of others. What was now clear was that his work and his life in Liberty County had not served as a bridge between these competing convictions and impulses but rather as a bridge that had led him away from earlier convictions about the evils of slavery to the unwavering support of a southern home and human bondage.

The sale of the family was a moment of self-revelation because Charles finally knew clearly where he stood. His heart had hardened in regard to slavery. There would be no more clear warnings of the corrupting influences of slavery that had marked so many of his reports during his missionary years. Rather, during the coming years he would take his stand with a southern homeland, where old times would not be forgotten, and where human bondage seemed the only defense against chaos and anarchy and the only promise for a long-sought peace and order.[28]

Yet the sale of Phoebe and Cassius and the children was not only a moment of self-revelation for Charles; it was also a moment of deep self-deception. When Charles wrote Mary in a self-congratulatory way that "conscience is better than money," he seemed to think he had freed himself from any charge of self-interest, and he appeared completely oblivious to the ways in which he had acted cruelly in the quest for the high ideals of peace and harmony. Indeed, he seemed unconscious of the ways in which he was confirming Harriett Beecher Stowe's charge against him. She had written that while he possessed a "sublime spirit" and a "mind capable of the very highest impulses," if we "look over his whole writings, we shall see painfully how the moral sense of the finest mind may be perverted by constant familiarity with such a system."[29]

In late winter 1857, three and a half months after Phoebe and Cassius had been banished and sold, their voices returned as if from the dead to disturb once again the tranquillity of Montevideo and Maybank. On 18 March Charles, having disposed of all of Cassius's possessions except his buggy and having settled his debts and collected most of what was owed Cassius, wrote to Charlie in Savannah:

> Enclosed is Cassius' account. Have delayed until we could sell his mare. Sold last week. Balance to his credit: $84.75, for which you will find a check within

of date, the space left blank for the name to whom the check shall be *paid*. *Insert the name of Cassius' master,* to whom you will please send *the account and check. But first* write to him to *ascertain if Cassius and his family are still with him,* so that there may be a certainty of Cassius' getting his money. Keep copies of your letters, and *register* the letter enclosing the check when you send it. We must use every precaution to get his money to him.

Charles's record of Cassius's account reads as follows:

Account of Property belonging to Cassius left to be given away and to be sold as he desired by his former Master

Articles left to be given to his children Nanny and James
   3 small hogs, 3 pots, 1 oven, 1 pail
   1 piggin, 3 plates, 1 new bucket
   All given by Porter and Cato to Nanny and James a short time after Cassius left.
   The *saddle* and *bridle* was taken by Dan [Cassius's brother]. He said Cassius gave them to him.

Property left to be sold:
   1 *mare*—valued by Cassius at $75. Could not get that price— sold for $50.
   1 *colt:* sold by Cassius to Daniel for $45 and $9 paid on the colt by Dan. Dan gave up the colt and the $9 paid Cassius by Dan was paid back to Dan and the colt was sold for $35.00

		Amount over	$85.00
Hogs: 1 barrow, 122 lbs. @ 5 cents. . . .		$6.10	
1 sow, sold for		5.00	$11.10

Rice: Two bushels rough rice thrashed out by	
Porter sold for 62½¢ per bushel	1.25
Fowls: 2 hens @ 50¢; 2 pullets @ 50¢	
1 rooster @ 25¢; 8 small chickens 75¢. Sold for same	2.00
Fodder: about 200 weight	1.00
Corn: about 10 bushels. 2 bushels given to Plenty to pay	
him for what Cassius owed him on the Buggy.	
8 bushels left sold for 62½ per bush.	5.00
Mr. Audley King—paid for 9 stick baskets @ 37½¢ each	3.37½

TOTAL SALE AND DEBT COLLECTED $108.72½

CASH PAID ON ACCOUNT OF CASSIUS

To Stepney the money loaned Cassius by Stepney when he was going away:	$10.00	
To Prophet for repairs on the buggy $6.00. One dollar paid him by Cassius before he went, leaving to be paid	5.00	
Amount over	$15.00	
To Money paid back to Dan which he had paid Cassius on the colt	9.00	
	$24.00	24.00
Dollars		$84.72½

This amount now due Cassius and sent to his
present master in a check through C. C. Jones, Jr.
Esquire in the Bank of the State of Georgia dated March 18, 1857[30]

Charles, having thus carefully accounted for Cassius's possessions, was ready to bring the whole business to a conclusion. He apparently thought that Phoebe and Cassius and the children were with a planter near Macon in the center of the state. But knowing the ways of slave selling and slave trading, he wanted to make sure that those so recently bought were still with the purchaser. Charles did not know it when he wrote Charlie, but two letters were already on the way to him from distant New Orleans.

The first letter to arrive was from a man named Lilly. Once again Charles wrote Charlie in Savannah:

Enclosed you will find a letter received today which will be as great a surprise to you and Joe as it has been to us. The man Lilly who writes the letter is evidently a Negro trader, and not the permanent owner of the Negroes! The internal evidence of the letter proves it. In addition, I have learned that *Lyons* at the Boro received a *friendly* letter from Old Cassius this evening in which he speaks of not yet being *at home*—dated in New Orleans. My opinion is that they are there on sale! Lilly says *he bought them in Savannah*. This was not the *name* of the man who appeared in the purchase, nor was *New Orleans* his home. Was it not a *planter* near Macon who bought for his *own use* and not to sell again? Here seems to be deceptions wheel within a wheel!

Since Charlie had already written to the ostensible purchaser about the money owed Cassius, Charles thought that they might learn more about what had happened to the family if there was a reply from the one who had signed the papers for the family. In any case, he told Charlie:

> Do not let him know of Lilly's letter. He may request you to send him the money for the people. Do not do so. It will be a roundabout way, and they may never get it. All we wish to learn of him is to know how the game has been played. If we have been deceived by Wright and the purchaser, we have been deceived. We were endeavoring to do the best we could.

Charles then instructed Charlie to send Cassius's money—together with the account of Cassius's possessions that had been sold—to Benjamin Morgan Palmer, Charles's former colleague in Columbia, who was now serving as pastor of the First Presbyterian Church in New Orleans. He was, said Charles, "the only friend I have in New Orleans upon whom I could confidently call in the matter." Palmer was to be told the whole story and of Charles's fear "that the people have fallen into the hands of a trader." Palmer, wrote Charles, could pay the money "over to Cassius and Phoebe himself and then inform us of the fact."[31]

More information was soon to arrive. Charles secured the letter that had been sent to Frederick Lyons in Riceboro. The letter had been dictated by Phoebe and Cassius and written down by someone in New Orleans who apparently did not understand clearly their Gullah accents. The letter was sent to Lyons—Mr. Delions, he was called in the letter—as one white man Phoebe and Cassius trusted and apparently knew well. They probably had over the years taken secret paths at night from Carlawter to the boro, where Lyons had welcomed those who had come under cover of darkness to his store and had sold rum to those from the settlements who had a little money. He had been, the planters believed, all too familiar with their slaves.[32]

New Orleans March 17th 1857
  Pleas tell my daugher Clairissa and Nancy a heap how a doo for me Pheaby and Cash and Cashes son James we left Savanah the first of Jany we are now in New Orleans. Please tell them that their sister Jane died the first of Feby we did not know what was the matter with her some of the doctors said that she had Plurisly and some thought that she had Consumption. Although we were sold for spite I hope that it is for our own good but we cannot be doing any better than were are doing very well. Mr Delions will please tell Cato that what [food] we have got to t[throw] away now it would be anough to furnish you Plantation for one season Mr Delions will please answer this Letter for Clairssa and Let me know all that has happened since I left. Please tell them that the Children were all sick with the measles but they are well now. Clairssa

your affectionate mother and Father sends a heap of Love to you and your Husband and my Grand Children Phebea. Mag & Cloe. John. Judy. Sue. My Aunt Aufy sinena and Minton and Little Plaska. Charles Nega. Fillis and all of their Childdren. Cash. Prime. Laffatte. Rick Tonia [Victoria] [send their love] to you all. Give our Love to Cashes Brother Porter and his wife Patience. Victoria gives her Love to cousin Beck and Miley.

I have no more to say untill i get a home. I remain your affectionate Mother and Father.
Pheobia and Cash

P. S. Please give my love to Judys Husband Plaska and also Cashs love. Phoebe and Cash send a great deal of Howdie for Mr Adam Dunumn and Mr Samuel Braton.[33]

The letter with its greetings to many family members and friends was a reminder that the sale of Phoebe and Cassius and their children had violently torn them away from many whom they loved. Among those to whom greetings and love were sent were Phoebe's daughter Clarissa and her children; Cash's daughter Nancy (or Nanny) and son James; Porter and Patience and their children; and various other relatives at the Retreat and at Carlawter, plus two more shopkeepers in Riceboro.[34] Phoebe believed—the tone of the letter was more hers than Cassius's—that they had been sold "for spite," that there had been ill will and malice on Charles and Mary's part in the sale. Nevertheless, she evoked an ancient piety in interpreting what had happened to them and declared that she hoped "it is for our own good."[35] And that good, she said, could already be seen in the abundance of food available to them in the New Orleans slave market: "please tell Cato that what [food] we have got to t[hrow] away now it would be anough to furnish you Plantation for one season." So even from a distance, Phoebe was challenging the benevolence of Charles and Mary—and the leadership of Cato— by declaring that even in the notorious slave market in New Orleans there was more food available than at Carlawter.[36]

As for Jane, the report of her death seemed matter-of-fact. Perhaps for her parents, who had already lost so many children—including John—and who had been so suddenly carried away from the home they had known all their lives, Jane's death seemed simply one more loss among so many. Charles was more expansive as he thought about Jane and her death in a distant place:

Am truly sorry to learn the death of poor Jane! How soon and unexpectedly has she been cut off—the cause of all that has been done! Would that she had lived and died at home in peace with God and with the world! I have prayed for those people many, many, very many times. I wish them well.[37]

So with Charles's prayers and well wishes, Phoebe and Cassius—together with Little Cash, Prime, Victoria, and LaFayette—disappeared into the massive slave markets of New Orleans. At the time, no one who knew their story could have imagined that in a few tumultuous years there would be a strange reversal. One who had been served most of her life by Phoebe would find herself an exile in New Orleans, and one of those who had disappeared in the New Orleans slave market would reappear in a very different Liberty County.

27

PATIENCE'S KITCHEN

Of all those who lived in the settlements, no one had been closer to Phoebe than her cousin Patience. In many ways Phoebe—who was eight years older—had been like a big sister to Patience, only a big sister whose restless ways Patience would not follow. The cousins had married brothers and had worked closely together for years, cooking, sewing, and serving tea on the piazzas at Maybank and Montevideo. Both cousins had been devoted to Daddy Jack. He had been a kind and loving father to Phoebe, and he was said to love Patience "as his own child." Patience and Porter had named a son after him. Mary Jones had regarded the two women as her indispensable personal servants, and when Mary had been seriously ill in Marietta, she had written, "The greatest personal privation I have had to endure has been the want of either Patience or Phoebe."[1]

But for all of their closeness, Phoebe and Patience had developed over the years personalities as different as their husbands were different. Both of them felt at some deep level a pressing anger—but Phoebe's anger had eaten away at her, while Patience's anger had energized her. Phoebe's anger had made her reckless and had left her vulnerable. Patience's anger had made her wise as a serpent while appearing harmless as a dove. And their anger, while largely turned toward white oppressors, could also be turned toward each other precisely because their lives were so closely intertwined, because the actions of one affected the life of the other, and because they could see in each other hated stereotypes whites used for slave women—the Surly Troublemaker and the Contented Mammy.[2]

If Phoebe and Cassius had seemed troublesome and rebellious to Charles and Mary, Patience and Porter appeared honest and reliable. While Phoebe and Cassius had chafed under the burdens of slavery and Phoebe had been inclined to cross her arms and express open defiance, Patience and Porter had sought through their good manners and efficient work to oil the system of slavery and to make life easier for their family and for those in the settlement. Phoebe and Cassius's road had led them to open resistance and to the slave market in Savannah. Patience and Porter's road led them to veiled resistance and to a capacity to endure the humiliations of slavery without succumbing to its power or internalizing its ideology. Each road was hard and was marked by its own sorrows. Neither road—as roads traveled by slaves—had been freely chosen, yet each couple had decided on which road to walk as they responded to their bondage and to its deep oppression.[3]

Patience had listened more carefully than Phoebe to Jack's stories. She knew that the fowl-hawk—even one with a benevolent look in his eye—could come sweeping down at any moment and snatch its victims away. To meet the challenge of the fowl-hawk, she had mastered the rituals of subordination. To Charles and Mary, Patience's pleasant ways and good manners—her "yes ma'ams" and "yes sirs"—her unfailing attention to her work, and what Mary called "Patience's fidelity of character" had made her a model servant. But for Patience, such deference and fidelity were ways to achieve her own ends—in particular, the protection of her family, her "chicks," from the dangers of the fowl-hawk. Over the years of practicing such art, Patience had taken on the character of her name. She appeared to whites as a Mammy figure—a stout, happy, subservient woman who loved her white family. But beneath such an exterior she was patiently waiting for the time when she could reveal, without danger to her own family, what was hidden beneath her pleasant and deferential ways. In the meantime, this large, strong woman was energized by her anger to become the undisputed master of the kitchen as Charles and Mary sought to make Maybank and Montevideo places of beauty, warmth, and generous hospitality.[4]

Patience stood in a long line of low-country cooks who combined African, European, and Native American traditions into a distinct low-country cuisine. Her mother-in-law, Old Lizzie, had been her primary teacher, but there had been others as well, especially Mom Sylvia at the Retreat. They had shown her remembered dishes fixed in traditional African ways, and how to cook over open fires and in fireplaces. They had taught her how to prepare the foods that came from the gardens and fields, from the woods, rivers, and marshes of the low country, and how to season the foods with herbs from the plantation gardens and with spices brought in Savannah. Mary and Sister Susan and other plantation mistresses also had had their say over the years about how meals were to be prepared in Patience's kitchen. They had provided menus that made the rounds between plantation kitchens, and they had given special instructions about the selection of menus and precise directions about when and how the food was to be presented at the table. Patience had learned from all these diverse sources and had added her own particular touch to her cooking—a touch that had grown out of her own experience in the kitchen and that provided a distinctive character to the food she prepared. In this way she had become, long before the renovations had begun at Montevideo, an African-American Gullah cook of remarkable skill. A frequent visitor at Montevideo and Maybank later wrote of Gullah cooks generally that they "completely distanced" French cooks "in the production of wholesome, dainty and appetizing food," and he remembered with particular pleasure "'Maum' Patience," who "was adept in her art, reliable, and refined in manner and conduct."[5]

Before Patience could begin to work her magic in the kitchen at Maybank or Montevideo, hard and sustained work was required to get food to the kitchen. Rice and corn grown on the plantations provided the basic staples. They demanded the unremitting labors of Cato, Andrew, and Stepney and their crews. For the rice, in addition to the work of building the fields, dams, and canals, sweating men and women had to reap, thrash, and pound the golden grain. As for the corn, after it had been harvested, it still had to be shucked and milled before it could be prepared for bread or grits. The field or red peas, planted along the rows of corn, had to be harvested and thrashed. Vegetables from the gardens— sweet potatoes and collard greens, okra and arrowroot, red potatoes and turnips, eggplant and butter beans, squash, tomatoes, and onions—all had to be carefully tended before being gathered and brought to the kitchen. Strawberries and melons—the Maybank melons were famous around the county for their sweetness—together with fruit from the orchards, had to be gathered at the right moment before being eaten fresh or made into jam or jelly, or before the rinds of the melons could be pickled.[6]

Niger, as the primary fisherman, spent long hours casting shrimp nets, hauling crab pots, digging clams, gathering oysters, and paddling his bateau through winding creeks, seeking special fishing holes. When the weather turned cold, Andrew and Cato oversaw the butchering of hogs. A large hog was hit in the head with a heavy blunt instrument, dipped into a cask of hot water to aid in taking off the bristles, and then hoisted high. Its throat was cut and its blood drained into a large pot in preparation for blood sausage. After its interior was gutted and cleaned, men and women working together washed the intestines, liver, and other organs, rendered the lard, and made the hams, bacon, and ribs ready to be salted and smoked. Charles and Gilbert brought cartloads of hickory to be split for the smokehouse, where the fires had to be carefully attended. Patience used a "large sausage stuffer" bought in Savannah to stuff pork scraps and chopped liver, together with selected herbs, into the washed intestines to make a variety of sausages. When a cow was slaughtered, not only was the meat carefully butchered, but some of the choice cuts were also corned, using salt, sugar, saltpeter, and red pepper, while the hooves were set aside for calves'-foot jelly, and the hide was carefully preserved for tanning. When Charlie or Joe shot wild turkeys, ducks, or geese, or brought home from their hunt ricebirds or quail, older children had to pick the feathers before the birds could be cleaned and made ready for cooking—and the same was true of chickens and domestic geese and turkeys.[7]

For sugar and syrup, patches of sugarcane were cut and the cane was fed into a mill turned by a horse walking around and around. The rollers of the mill squeezed the sweet juice from the cane, and the juice was funneled through a cloth strainer into a barrel. A brick and clay furnace was prepared, and over it was placed a boiler box. The juice was strained a second time as it was poured into the box, where it was brought to a boil and the rising foam was skimmed off. Finally, the syrup was strained a third time as it was poured into barrels for storage or processing into sugar.[8]

The products of all of this effort flowed toward Patience's kitchen to serve not only the needs of the white family—including weddings and funerals and special holidays—but also as the foundation for the hospitality so generously shown to the many guests who came to Montevideo and Maybank. Patience needed both culinary art and extensive organizational skills to get large and finely prepared meals on the table at set times. Lucy—the daughter of Rosetta and Sam and the wife of Charles the oxcart driver—became, after the sale of Phoebe, Patience's chief companion in the kitchen. Young Flora—she turned seventeen in 1856— became their apprentice and was kept busy peeling and plucking, scaling and scrubbing. And there were other younger ones who helped in various ways. While Patience thus had many helpers in and around the kitchen, she had no one who had taken her Uncle Jack's place. He had managed much of the household and had played a major role in seeing that meals were served not only on time but also correctly. Consequently, much of his managing responsibilities had fallen on Patience.[9]

For Patience, as for other low-country cooks, rice was the fundamental dish for most meals. Europeans had long regarded the rice grown on the South Carolina and Georgia coast as the finest in the world. It is, wrote an Englishman, "the best *Rice* which grows upon the whole Earth, as being the weightiest, largest, cleanest, and whitest, which has been yet seen in the Habitable World." Called Carolina Gold because of the color of the ripe grain in the field, it was a long-grain rice of an exceptional fine quality. Before Patience could cook the rice, however, it had to be "graveled" or washed—she would place it in a piggin, slush it around, and carefully pour it into another pail. After several such procedures, and it had been soaked for about an hour, the rice was ready to cook. Water—two parts to one part rice, with salt added—was brought to a boil. The rice was added to the boiling water and cooked over low heat for about twenty minutes. The lid was then removed, the rice stirred and fluffed, and the lid placed back on the pot with a slight opening for the cooked grains to dry. The rice that was thus cooked and brought to the table was, in the words of a South Carolinian, "white, dry, and every grain Separate." Patience's way of cooking rice was a method that reached back to India and had traveled to Liberty County by way of Madagascar, the west coast of Africa, and South Carolina. In contrast to the method developed in China, which produced sticky rice for eating with chopsticks, the method Patience used eliminated loose starch and provided separate grains that were fluffy and white.[10]

Patience frequently made a pilau, or pilaf, with the rice. A chicken or a wild duck or a piece of beef would be boiled with bacon. The broth—with onions and proper spices added—would be used instead of water for the cooking of the rice. Once the rice was ready, it would be placed in a large serving dish, and the meat that had provided the broth would be carefully arranged on top or sometimes chopped and stirred into the rice.[11]

Cakes, puddings, and various breads were also made from the rice. Mary wrote out the recipes in a neat hand as a record for future use. For rice bread Patience would take "1 pint of rice flour, 3 eggs, a heaping spoonful of butter, ½ pint of milk, and 3 teaspoons of yeast powder mixed in the flour." She would mix it altogether and "bake quickly." For simple rice cakes, she would use "3 cups of boiled rice, 2 eggs, milk and a little salt, 1 tablespoon or dessert spoon of butter." She covered the rice with milk, stirred them together, being careful not to mash the rice. She beat the eggs and stirred them in, adding flour enough to make a thick batter but one thin enough to pour from her bowl. She poured the batter in a biscuit tin and baked it in a hot oven until brown and firm on the top. She then cut the rice cake in square pieces, buttered them, and served them hot to those taking afternoon tea on the piazza.[12]

Of course Patience also served sweeter and more elaborate cakes to those having tea on the piazzas at Montevideo and Maybank: ginger cake, lady cake, cheesecakes, and one called flirtation cake, which apparently had some story or at least some hopes associated with it. An eccentric concoction called sea foam cake called for "4 cups flour, 1 butter, 2 of sugar, 3 eggs, and 2 teaspoons sea foam." Pound cakes of various sorts were favorites of those who enjoyed the view of the North Newport flowing by, or of the Medway marshes in the afternoon. A "plain pound cake" called for "3/4 lb. Butter, 1 lb. of sugar, 10 eggs, juice of a lemon, and a glass of brandy." A more adventuresome pound cake—one that came suspiciously close to a fruitcake—took "12 eggs, 1 lb. of butter, 2½ lbs. of sugar, 4 lbs.

of raisins, 4 lbs. of currants, 1 lb. of citron, juice of 1 lemon, 1 spoon ground cinnamon, 2 spoons of nutmeg, glass of wine, glass of brandy, glass of rosewater." These pound cakes would be made at any time of the year and enjoyed with tea in the afternoon or as dessert. The genuine fruitcake, however, was made in the early fall in preparation for the holiday season. Patience laid out on her work-table three pounds of flour, three pounds of sugar, three pounds of butter, two pounds of citron, six pounds of raisins, and four pounds of currants. After tossing and rubbing the fruit in flour, she stirred all the ingredients in a large bowl and added one ounce of nutmeg, one half-ounce of cloves, one half-ounce of cinnamon, one ounce of mace, thirty eggs, and three full glasses of brandy. She then mixed all into a batter and poured it into pans lined with oiled paper dusted with flour. When the cakes came out of the wood oven, she carefully wrapped them in oiled paper for storage. During the coming weeks Mary would keep the cakes moist and fresh by pouring a little brandy over them at regular intervals—she kept the brandy locked in a cupboard with other medicines—until the time finally came to eat them. By then the cakes were a potent force for holiday cheer.[13]

The preparation of such delicacies required of Patience long hours of work, yet her cooking was much more than work—it was a powerful art. She was creating with meticulous care food that delighted all the senses and that nourished human life both physically and spiritually. A simple recipe for "light rolls" she learned from Cora, the cook at Social Bluff, and written down by Mary as "Cora's Light Rolls," gave hints of both the hours involved and her art:

Take half a yeast cake and dissolve it in a cup of luke warm water, letting it stand half an hour. Pour the water off (throw away the dregs) and work into that water flour enough to make a thick batter (about as thick as pound cake batter). Let that batter stand to rise about an hour. When it looks well risen, work it into your flour a pint and a half or a quart of flour with a dessert spoon full of lard and the same of butter and a table spoon of Brown Sugar. This set to rise about nine o'clock at night. At six in the morning work them well again and put them in the pan in which they are to be baked. Let them rise an hour; then bake about half an hour.[14]

If breads and cakes were demanding, so were the meats and seafood, and with these dishes Patience's art reached its pinnacle. When the weather turned cool and Niger came in with his bateau filled with oysters, they had to be shucked before an oyster pie or oyster soup could be made. The oysters, fresh from the cold waters, would be placed close to the fire long enough for the oyster shells to open slightly. Taking up a steaming oyster, the shucker would insert a sharp knife into the opening, give the knife a twist, and pry the shells apart. The oyster liquor would be poured into a pot and the oyster cut out of the shell. Patience would take two quarts of the shucked oysters and mix them with three pints of milk, one pint of oyster liquor, one quarter-pound of fresh butter, three dozen cloves, three blades of mace, and two dozen black peppercorns to make a delicious oyster soup. Or when Niger arrived with a basket of shrimp, Patience would first pick up a shrimp in each hand and using her thumbnails cut their heads off. Once they were all headed, she dropped the shrimp in boiling water for a few quick minutes until they turned pink. After they had cooled, she peeled the shells from the shrimp and removed the dark vein that ran down the shrimp's arched back. The clean, pink shrimp she could send to the table at Maybank cold, or she could mix them with cooked rice and butter, salt and pepper, before baking and serving. When Niger arrived with trout and spots and other small fish, she would generally fry them in a large skillet in grease obtained from frying out fatback. When he brought in a big sheephead or drum, Patience would typically broil it after scaling and cleaning it. As for the crabs, she would drop them live in boiling water and cook them until they turned a rosy pink. Then she and her helpers would begin the laborious task of picking out the sweet meat before it could be made into a casserole or baked with rice or made into crab cakes of great delicacy. But in the fall, when Niger would bring in the "peelers," then Patience would sauté the soft-shell crabs and serve them on big platters to the delight of many guests at Maybank.[15]

High on the list of favorite foods among both family and guests was the game brought from the fields, woods, and swamps of the plantations. Venison was readily available when Charlie or Joe went hunting. In the fall, ducks descended on rice fields in great numbers as targets for eager hunters, and Stepney would shoot not only ducks but also migrating geese in the rice fields at Arcadia. In the spring Andrew would often shoot wild turkeys for the table. All of the game took special preparation and offered their own special flavors to the cuisine of Maybank and Montevideo. No game, however, was as distinct to the low country or seemed to gather up in its body the wild and sweet taste of the land as much as the ricebird—*Dolichonyx oryzivorus*. Louisa Cheves Stoney, the granddaughter of Charles's friend Thomas Smyth in Charleston, later described the peculiar delight of the low-country way of eating ricebirds:

Select the fattest birds, remove the entrails, bake them whole or split them up the back and broil. Permit no sacrilegious hand to remove the head, for the base of the brain of the rice bird is the most succulent portion. Or the birds may be placed in either shape in a round bottom pot with a small lump of butter, pepper and salt, and cook over a quick fire. Use no fork in eating. Take the neck of the bird in the left hand and his little right leg in the right hand. Tear away the right leg and eat all but the extreme end of the bone. Hold the bill of the bird in one hand and crush your teeth through the back of the head, and thank Providence that you are permitted to live. Take the remaining left leg in your right hand and place in your mouth the entire body of the bird, and then munch the sweetest morsel that ever brought gustatory delight. All that remains is the front portion of the head and the tiny bits of bone that formed the ends of the legs. To leave more is to betray your unappreciativeness of the gifts of the gods.[16]

With his growing weakness, Charles was afraid of the tiny bones of the rice-birds, so years earlier he had stopped crushing the backs of their heads with his teeth or putting a whole bird in his mouth, but otherwise he enjoyed enormously the food prepared by Patience's hard work. On one occasion he wrote of breakfast: "Mother has come down. We have just had worship and breakfast is ordered in and such a breakfast—hominy, rice, corn bread, eggs, honey, fresh butter, milk, cream, crackers, johnnycake, potatoes, clabber, flowers and roses in abundance, coffee and all so forth." On another occasion he said: "Niger succeeded in procuring some fine fish for two dishes; we had also an excellent oyster pie and roasted chicken and a dessert. . . . The gentlemen particularly relished the fish and oysters." And Mary would write when company had arrived for dinner at Maybank, "They were all prepared to do ample justice to a joint of boiled lamb, a sirloin of roast beef, a large juicy ham, fish, crabs and shrimp to say nothing of several varieties of vegetables fresh from the garden." And she would tell of having for dinner a "nice corned beef," a wild duck Joe had shot, a turkey presented by Andrew, together with "a dish of fried oysters, rice, potatoes, and turnips, with a dessert of oranges and sugared oranges." It was consequently no wonder that Frederick Law Olmsted—the traveler, writer, and future landscape architect—wrote of low-country cuisine that it contained "delicacies which are not to be had in perfection . . . anywhere else than on a rice-plantation." If such a cuisine had many sources, and if it had behind it the hard labors of many in the settlements, it was the work and imagination of Patience and other plantation cooks that drew the various sources and ingredients together into a coherent and distinct cuisine whose essence was drawn from the rich flavors of the land and from the dark waters and salt marshes of the low country.[17]

Those who lived at Carlawter and in the settlements at Maybank and Arcadia also developed a distinct cuisine with their more limited resources. To be sure, there were direct overlaps between the way food was prepared in the settlements and what was prepared in the plantation kitchens and served in the plantation houses. It would have been surprising, after all, if there had not been such overlap since African-American cooks were doing the cooking in both places. Nevertheless, there were distinctions, and the distinctions had to do with Charles and Mary's ability to command resources—especially of time and food—that were not available to those who were raising the rice and corn, catching the fish and crabs, and doing the cooking in the settlements.[18]

All those living in the settlements had provisions of corn, rice, red peas, bacon, and cane syrup, largely drawn from their own labors, controlled by Charles, and distributed by Cato, Andrew, and Stepney. In addition, milk was often supplied from the dairies, especially to make corn mush for the young children. To these provisions, settlement cooks such as Mom Rosetta added the vegetables they grew in their gardens and the chickens and domestic ducks raised around the settlement cabins. Children gathered wild fruits, berries, and nuts. And the men raised hogs and secured by their own skill and effort fish and game—rabbits, possums, turtles, raccoons, an occasional deer, mullet, and catfish. Because they had so little time for themselves, however, the cooks of the settlements necessarily developed a cuisine that was generally simple and relatively easy to prepare. This meant that such one-pot meals as pilaus, stews, and soups would be especially common and practical. Most of the time the women of each family prepared the food for their family members, but when the work in the fields was especially heavy, a great wooden trencher of rice and bacon would be prepared in the plantation kitchen and taken to those in the field.[19]

The cooks at Carlawter and in the settlements at Maybank and Arcadia made use of a variety of cooking utensils. Cassius and Phoebe, for example, had at the time of their sale "3 pots, 1 oven, 1 pail, 1 piggin, 3 plates, 1 new bucket," which were left for Cassius's son James and daughter Nancy. The pots could be used for cooking rice and grits, soups, stews, and vegetables. The oven could be used for baking in the fireplace. And the pail, piggin, and bucket could be used for holding water or milk. In addition, they no doubt had a variety of baskets made by Cassius that could be used for storage of corn, peas, and rice, and perhaps gourds, which were widely used in low-country settlements as dippers and utensils of various sorts.[20]

Corn and rice provided the two most important ingredients for the settlement cooks. The corn could be used for corn bread—a pint of cornmeal could be mixed with a pint of milk, a couple of eggs, and if available a little soda, and the mix baked before the fireplace. More common were johnnycakes and hoe cakes. For johnnycakes, cooked grits were mixed with a little rice flour and milk and the dough placed on a board before a fire. When those who were working in the fields carried the dough with them and cooked it on a hoe for their lunch, then it became a hoe cake. And of course the grits themselves, a staple in both the plantation house and the slave cabin, were relished, especially for breakfast. A Native

American dish, grits were prepared by pouring water through wood ash to make a diluted lye solution. Ground corn was then soaked in the lye to remove the hulls. After several washings, the grits were ready to be boiled. At Montevideo and Maybank a pint or pint and a half of grits, "after being prepared by divers washings," would be put into a pint and a half of water and boiled rapidly for fifteen or twenty minutes. In the settlements, syrup or butter—when available—would be stirred into the grits with a little salt. A special breakfast would include with the grits a piece of fried bacon or salt pork and eggs from the hens that were kept in coops behind the cabins and allowed to scratch around the settlement.[21]

The pilau of the settlements was hoppin' john—a dish that had its low-country origins in Africa. Rice and red peas were its primary ingredients, with a little bacon or salt pork thrown in, together with an onion and some cayenne pepper, also grown in the gardens around the settlements. The peas would be cooked with the pork and onion until tender and then the rice and pepper added. Collard greens, when in season, were often boiled—with a piece of salt pork when available—and eaten with the hoppin' john. So popular was this combination that it became in time a required meal not only in the settlements but also in the plantation houses on New Year's Day in order to ensure good luck for the coming year.[22]

One of the most nutritious and popular foods of the settlements was the sweet potato. An important source of vitamin A, sweet potatoes were stored in an ingenious manner behind slave cabins, where livestock could not get to them. Hay was scattered on the ground, and on top of it a layer of sweet potatoes. These were covered with more hay, followed by another layer of the tubers, and so on. When sweet potatoes were wanted, the hay would be pushed aside and as many potatoes withdrawn as needed. These were generally baked in ashes, a technique said to enhance the flavor and sweetness of the potato.[23]

Of all that was raised in the garden patches at Carlawter and the other settlements, okra was perhaps second in importance only to the sweet potato. An African plant—like sorghum, red peas, eggplant, and benne seed—okra had made the Atlantic passage to become deeply rooted in low-country cuisine (in New Orleans okra would be called gumbo, after the Umbundu word for the pod, *ochinggômbo*). Easy to grow and prolific, it provided a ready companion for rice in many combinations. When stewed with tomatoes and bacon and cooked with rice, it made a red rice, a kind of okra pilau, to which fish or shrimp or chicken or rabbit or some other meat could be added. Settlement cooks made an okra soup by putting the okra pods into a pot of water with a piece of pork, some tomatoes, and cayenne pepper and slowly cooking the soup for most of the day. Or the okra could be cut into pieces, rolled in some flour, and fried to make a dish of remarkable sweetness.[24]

These familiar dishes of the settlement were supplemented during times of heavy labor and holidays with beef killed "for the people." Charles kept a substantial herd of cattle roaming the woods and fields of the three plantations—in a typical year they would number more than 175, plus another 35 oxen. Indeed, many more cattle were kept than hogs, and beef apparently played as important a role in the diet of the settlements as did pork, which Charles purchased by the barrel in Savannah to supplement those slaughtered on the plantations. "Give the people beef from the stock as often as you can," Charles had written Thomas Shepard in June 1849—and others would be killed in August and at Thanksgiving and at Christmas and New Year's. When a cow was killed at one of the settlements, then the cooks could fix a feast, with roasts and stews and other special dishes. And when stray cattle from another plantation were found in the woods, then a secret barbecue could be held in an isolated place—as Cato had done with Elijah Chapman's cattle—with the men apparently doing the barbecuing. A few slaves kept their own cattle—Cato had six in the mid-1850s. But these were too valuable to be slaughtered and were apparently used primarily for their milk.[25]

The skill of settlement cooks in turning few resources into tasty and often nourishing dishes, however, should not obscure the struggle of the cooks and others to secure adequate and varied food for the families of the settlements. Even under the benevolent and watchful eye of Charles and Mary, food was sometimes scarce. This was especially true in late winter and early spring, when many of the supplies from the previous year had been exhausted and the spring gardens and wild fruits and berries had not yet started to produce. Then the diets of the settlements were often more bland and monotonous than usual—corn, peas, and salt pork; rice, peas, and salt pork—and a rabbit, possum, or catfish would be especially welcome in a stew pot.[26]

During such times of scarcity in the settlements, Patience was in a position to supplement the diet of her family and perhaps of others with food from her kitchen. Leftovers were no doubt frequently available, and her little ones, who played close by their mother until they were old enough to begin work, could be given a plate of pilau or whatever was being cooked. In all of this, Patience had to be very careful in order to maintain her reputation as a dependable person who could be trusted. She could not allow even a suggestion that she was in any way stealing food from smokehouses or from cupboards or from other storage places. All her actions needed to be aboveboard and to appear to be a natural part of her work. Patience was apparently remarkably successful in creating just such an appearance for her kitchen. As a consequence, she was able to provide for her family not only extra food but also some protection from the ravages of slavery.[27]

At the time Phoebe and Cassius were sold, Patience and Porter had had eight children. All of them were alive in 1856, all of them were healthy, and all of them had lived under the protective care of their mother and father in their cabin at Maybank and Montevideo. Patience's hard work in the kitchen and her deferential ways did not flow from a simple fear of punishment or of the slave markets in Savannah. Nor did they flow from a passive acceptance of a white ideology about her place as a slave. Rather, Patience had a kind of pragmatism as she faced the burdens and dangers of slavery. She knew that most of her labors would be appropriated by whites, that most of the food she prepared was being carried to the dining room tables at Maybank and Montevideo and to the piazzas where whites took their tea. But she also knew that her work and her reputation as an artist in the kitchen had a direct impact on her own comfort and well-being and on the comfort and well-being of her family. Her pragmatism thus provided the strategy for her savvy resistance, the resources needed for persevering, and the means for her to guard against the constant threat of the fowl-hawk.[28]

$$\text{---}\bullet\text{---}$$

Montevideo

Charles and Mary moved into the renovated Montevideo in the late fall of 1856 after Betsy's death, at the time that Phoebe and Cassius and their children were sent to Wright's slave jail in Savannah. The master and mistress of Montevideo, eager to be finally settled in their plantation home, had spent part of the preceding winter in the old section of the house while the carpenters, plasterers, and painters completed their work.[1]

Porter and Sandy Maybank, together with their helpers, had substantially enlarged Montevideo. As skilled carpenters they had been able to take a design sketched by Charles and figure how much lumber to order, how to handle the new pitch of the roof, and how to solve the other myriad problems of a major renovation. When they were finished, the two-story house had fifteen rooms, plus the piazzas that functioned in pleasant weather as outdoor areas for visiting, afternoon teas, and evening worship. The house was painted white both outside and inside, and the shutters on each of its thirty-seven windows were painted green. Each window was six feet high and was placed just above one-foot-high baseboards in the ten-foot-high rooms.[2] This design provided every room an open, light, and fresh atmosphere and invited the eye to look outward toward the surrounding gardens. Mary described what could be seen from the house:

> The house is beautifully located, on one side fronting a lawn of twenty or thirty acres covered with live oak, magnolias, cedars, pines, and many other forest trees, arranged in groves or stretching out in lines and avenues or dotting the lawn here and there. On the other front passes the North Newport River, where all the produce of the place may be shipped to Savannah and water communication obtained to any point. In the gardens will be found both sweet and sour oranges and the myrtle orange, pomegranates, figs, the bearing olive, and grapes. . . . Attached to the house lot are a brick kitchen, brick dairy, smoke-

house, washing and weaving rooms, two servants' houses, a commodious new stable and a carriage house and wagon shed, various poultry houses and yards attached, a well of excellent water, and a never-failing spring.

Across the new rice fields—where the old slough had been—Carlawter had also had its improvements. The settlement now contained "a two-story cotton house, gin and ginhouse, barn, cornhouse, ricehouse, winnowing house, millhouses, and fifteen frame houses, a brick shed and yard of excellent clay, and a chapel twenty by thirty feet."[3]

Porter and Sandy Maybank, walking toward Montevideo from the simple cabins at Carlawter, did not see the gardens through a tall window, nor did they view the house from a carriage driving down the sandy avenue. Rather, if the carpenters walked across the rice field dikes early in the morning as light first began to break through the fog rising from the river, or if, after a day's work, they walked toward Montevideo in the evening as shadows stretched across the gardens toward the house, they could see that they had built a place of beauty. They could look toward a plantation house where they knew every room intimately: how joists where connected to beams; how the wide, heart-of-pine floorboards were tightly laid next to one another; and how the doors and window frames were built to exact specifications and carefully placed to enhance the beauty of the house. They had every reason to be proud of their work, for they had built a house that many would admire and not a few would love. But they could see in Montevideo not only a tribute to their skill and hard work but also a bitter reminder of the ways their skill and hard work had been expropriated for the benefit of white owners. So the renovated Montevideo with its gardens and outbuildings could be viewed from two angles, from two perspectives, and these conflicting interpretations of the place would linger long after the house and gardens had returned to the fecund wilderness of the low country.[4]

To this plantation home there came a stream of white visitors in the winter and spring, to be followed in the summer and fall by a similar stream to Maybank. They included the expected family members—John and Jane Jones, with Dunwody and their other children; Aunt Eliza, with her daughters Louisa and Mary and the motherless children of Eliza's son Joseph Jones Robarts; Henry Hart Jones and Abby with their little ones; Sister Susan and Laura and David Buttolph; and the lonely William Maxwell, who would come for extended stays. And there were the old friends who came for visits—Julia King and Audley and his younger brothers and sisters; Mary King Wells, who had developed terrible migraine headaches since the death of her husband, Dr. Charlton Wells; Eliza Clay from Richmond-on-Ogeechee; and Jane Harden—the sister of Joseph and John

LeConte—with her daughter Matilda, who had a stunning figure and whose striking beauty drove Charlie, Joe, Audley, and all the other young men visiting on piazzas to distraction.[5] And there were new friends—a LeConte from Philadelphia, who came to the island to look for a laurel described by the eighteenth-century botanist John Bartram as "found only on Col. Island"; lawyer friends of Charlie's and doctor friends of Joe's; and Mary Sharpe's friend Kitty Stiles from Savannah, who was not only a lively and pious young woman but also a member of a family with prominent social connections up and down the East Coast.[6] All of these guests came to enjoy the well-known hospitality of Montevideo and Maybank, to savor the beauty of winter and spring gardens above a dark river, and to enjoy the smell of the marsh and the sound of the surf on a summer's evening. And the most important single occasion for showing such hospitality during Charles and Mary's retirement years was the marriage of their greatly loved daughter Mary Sharpe.

Mary Sharpe was twenty-one in the spring of 1857. While she was not the beauty or lively wit that Laura was, and while she did not have the stunning figure of her friend Matilda Harden, she was an attractive young woman with much of her mother's strength of character. With sparkling blue eyes like her grandfather Joseph's, she had had her share of beaux. There had been a particularly persistent suitor when she was in Philadelphia. Even after Mary Sharpe had given him a firm but polite refusal, he had not given up, and the next year he had proposed to her once again; she had again politely refused.[7]

When Mary Sharpe had returned to Georgia, she had entered a lively social life full of flirting and matchmaking. After attending a wedding in middle Georgia, she had sent her brother Joe a piece of the wedding cake, together with a sealed enveloped for him "to dream upon." She explained what he was to do: "I have written some names upon the paper and you must not open it until you have dreamed upon it for three nights." He was to write and tell her which young woman on the list had stirred his dreams. But she added playfully: "If you are like me you wont dream at all. I tried to dream but no visions came into my head." She added, however, that their friend Mittie Bulloch was marrying "Mr. Roosevelt of New York." Neither she nor Joe could have dreamed that their friend would become the mother of a future president of the United States.[8]

In the meantime, Robert Quarterman Mallard, the youngest son of Thomas and Eliza Mallard, had completed his studies at Columbia Theological Seminary and had accepted a call to the Presbyterian Church in Walthourville. The congregation in Walthourville was a daughter church of the Midway Congregational Church, and its organization reflected a development that was beginning

Abial and Louisa Winn home, Dorchester (courtesy Georgia Archives)

to trouble all those who loved old Midway. Some planting families were finally growing weary of the annual trek between plantation homes and summer and fall retreats. The Thomas Mallards, for example, had stopped spending the winter and spring at their plantation home near Midway—the old Mallard Place—after they built a fine new home in the little village of Dorchester, not far from the home of Abial and Louisa Winn.[9] By 1855 those living in Dorchester had tired of making the Sabbath trip to Midway, so they had organized the Dorchester Presbyterian Church. This movement away from long-established country churches such as Midway to village churches was taking place throughout the rice-growing region of South Carolina and Georgia. So it had not been surprising when the members of Midway who lived in Walthourville decided to organize their own congregation. The Walthourville Presbyterian Church they built looked in many ways like a smaller version of Midway—a neat meetinghouse whose clear windows and elegant simplicity reflected a Calvinism that had long flourished in the low country.[10]

Robert Mallard was the second pastor called to Walthourville. His predecessor had been none other than the ever-restless John Jones, who had spent less than a year in the village. Grieved by the quick loss of their popular pastor, the congregation had welcomed the young Mallard enthusiastically. Charles heard several of his sermons and thought they were "excellent," and Mary declared that he "certainly possesses eminent gifts as a preacher." Mallard was soon a regular visitor at Maybank and Montevideo. On an early visit to Maybank, he had spent the night

Walthourville Presbyterian Church
(author's collection)

and gone fishing the next morning with Joe. "They returned," Mary wrote Mary
Sharpe—who was in Savannah—"about eleven o'clock with over a hundred, the
best of which I made him take home." Mallard was, like most young men raised
in the plantation houses of Liberty County, an enthusiastic outdoorsman who
enjoyed hunting deer on horseback and fishing the rivers and marsh creeks of
his low-country home. But it was not long before his primary reason for visiting
at Maybank and Montevideo was to see Mary Sharpe. And they were soon very
much in love.[11]

Mary Sharpe wrote a school friend from Philadelphia that Robert had "black
hair and dark complexion; some say handsome, but I do not think so. He is above
medium height." But he was, in fact, quite a handsome young man who had
long attracted the attention of many a young woman. His black hair, olive complexion, and dark eyes reflected perhaps his French Huguenot ancestry. He was,
moreover, also pious and studious and what Charlie later described as manly. He

had had a conversion experience shortly after graduating from college and had joined Midway with three young cousins who had been hunting companions. With them making his confession of faith had been Charles, the oxcart driver who was the son of Andrew and Mary Ann and the husband of Lucy.[12]

Robert and Mary Sharpe did their courting under the watchful eye of Charles and Mary and the many guests who were frequently a part of the Jones household. At Montevideo the young couple could find some privacy by taking long walks together and by sitting on a "rustic seat" behind the line of cedars that ran down to the river. Here they could speak of their love for each other and dream of their life together. Shortly after their engagement, Robert wrote Mary Sharpe: "What a strange life is this upon which we have entered! In my plans for the future I move not alone, nor yet with an indistinct ideal by my side, but with one whose *voice* and *face* and *form* are familiar to me — *my own loved Mary.*" He hoped that a kind providence would grant him his anticipation of marrying her. "What an hour will that be," he exclaimed, "when I shall (as I hope) lead from the altar my own loved bride! The future will have its joys and its griefs, but with another I hope to enjoy the one and to bear the other." Neither he nor Mary Sharpe could know how clearly Robert saw the future and how soon not only the joys but also the griefs were to come their way.[13]

The marriage was held in April 1857 at Montevideo. Two hundred invitations were sent, but of course not all those invited could come. Sarah Howe wrote from Columbia: "Few things in this world would give me more pleasure than to witness the *union* of two young friends whom I not only esteem *but love*. Mary Sharpe has always seemed very near to me, and I can give her my blessing with all the feelings of a mother's heart." But, she added, it was impossible for them to attend. And General Cocke wrote from Virginia that he deeply regretted not being able to attend the wedding of "my dear Mary Sharpe." But many could attend and many arrived long before the wedding itself.[14]

Kitty Stiles arrived in late December and stayed more than three months. Mary Sharpe had spent months with her in Savannah, and they were the closest of friends, so it seemed natural that they should be together as the arrangements were being made for the wedding. But there were others as well. "Cousin" John Dunwody arrived from Roswell in March. His wife, Jane, had died the previous summer, and now his fine mansion in Roswell seemed empty and lonely. Dunwody wanted to visit friends in the low country, and no doubt he went out to see Arcadia, his old plantation home, where he and Jane had lived so many happy years together and where their children had been born. He intended his visit to be short, but he became seriously ill, and for three weeks Charles and Mary had to give him constant attention. Dunwody's son, Dr. William Elliot Dunwody, was summoned to help care for his father, and he too stayed for days. In the mean-time, John Jones and his wife, Jane, with their son Dunwody and younger chil-dren arrived. Jane was the niece of John Dunwody, who had been like a father to her, and she too helped to look after her uncle. And of course William Max-well was there. The old man was missing Betsy terribly, and he did not want to be alone as the plans went forward for the marriage of his dear Mary Sharpe. Altogether, it was a very full household as the preparations for the wedding in-tensified. Patience must have been pushed to the limits of her energy and of her cooking and managerial skills to see that meals were prepared and served at the long dining room table and that the duties of the house servants were carried out promptly and correctly. As for Mary, the mother of the bride, she may very well have wished for Phoebe, the "accomplished house servant in any and every line: good cook, washer and ironer, and fine seamstress."[15] But Phoebe was that very spring in the slave market in New Orleans, where she had buried her daughter Jane.

The guests began arriving in earnest the week before the wedding. While the women visited and worked on the preparations, some of the young men, includ-ing Joe, went in the Kings' little sloop out to St. Catherine's Island for a maroon at "Mr. Waldburg's summer place," a beach cottage owned by Jacob Waldburg, who planted cotton on the large and isolated island.[16]

The wedding itself was held at nine o'clock on Wednesday evening, 22 April 1857. Charles performed the ceremony and used as the text for his homily a pas-sage from the Old Testament book of Proverbs: "I Wisdom dwell with Prudence." It was twilight and the garden at Montevideo was at the peak of its springtime splendor. The white blossoms of the dogwoods reflected the fading light, and the tea olives perfumed the air as the night wind came up from the river, bringing the murmur of dark waters. A few days earlier Charles had noted in his journal that the whippoorwills had begun calling in the evening, and now they added their music to the wedding ceremony. Inside the house a feast had been spread. Wed-ding cakes had been ordered from Savannah, but most of the food—hams and roasts, quail and turkey, shrimp and crab, pilau and pies, pickled peaches, nuts and fruits, fresh strawberries from the garden, together with various breads, jel-lies, and syllabubs—represented the exhausting work of Patience and her crew of helpers.[17]

As Charles and Mary looked around at family and friends illumined by the flickering lights of candles, they remembered their own wedding now so long ago. Theirs had been in December as a cold mist had swirled outside and frost had decorated the windows. But the Retreat had been beautiful with its garlands and blazing fireplaces, and Joseph had had everything put in perfect order for the wedding of his beloved daughter. So many who had been there were now gone. And surely none were missed on this April evening more than Joseph himself and dear Betsy.

On the Monday evening following the wedding, after most of the guests had departed Montevideo, "the people had their wedding feast." Long tables were set up near the river and loaded down with food—no doubt some of it left over from the wedding—and a beef was killed and barbecued over an open fire. It was a day of celebration for those who lived at Carlawter and in the settlements at Maybank and Arcadia after all the frenzied work required for the wedding. And for Charles and Mary it was an occasion to demonstrate not only their benevolence but also their conviction that slavery was a domestic institution, and that servants were a part of the planter's family. For those doing the celebrating, however, there must have been deep anxiety, for they knew only too well that the marriage of whites, like the death of whites, often brought painful separations to those who lived in the settlements.[18]

Shortly before the wedding ceremony had taken place, a marriage contract had been signed. Robert signed for himself, and Charlie, Joe, and Henry Hart Jones signed as trustees representing the interests of Mary Sharpe. The contract was primarily intended to secure the slave property that Mary Sharpe would bring to her marriage. Charles and Mary had carefully discussed the needs that their daughter would have as she and Robert set up house in Walthourville. She would obviously need, they thought, some domestic help, so the decision was made that Lucy and Charles, with their sixteen-year-old daughter Tenah, would go with Mary Sharpe as her property. Lucy was a skilled cook and housekeeper, and Tenah was bright and was quickly learning the work of a domestic servant. The move would mean that Charles would live at Arcadia, while Lucy and Tenah would live in Walthourville. Charles would thus be a part of the throng of men traveling on Saturday afternoons to a "wife house." For Charles, however, this did not mark a significant change, since for years he had been shifted about from plantation to plantation, according to the need for his oxcart and his labor.[19]

Lucy and Tenah would not be enough help for Mary Sharpe, however, even though she and Robert were just beginning to establish their home. So it was decided that Patience's sister Elsey—the wife of Syphax the carpenter, who lived at Lambert—would also be given to Mary Sharpe. With her would go her six youngest children and one grandchild. In addition, Elsey and Syphax's oldest son, Robert, and his wife, Harriett, together with their children Betsy and Matilda, were also given as a wedding gift. Altogether sixteen men, women, and children were given to Mary Sharpe. They included the grandchildren of Andrew and Mary Ann and of Mom Rosetta and Sam. They also included great-grandchildren and great-great-grandchildren of Old Jupiter, who had been the driver at Liberty Hall and who had blown the conch-shell horn when the sky in the east began to pale. Robert's body servant James joined them as one who would help serve the needs of the young minister and his bride. James had grown up in the settlement at the old Mallard Place, where Pompey was the driver and Dr. Harry had long practiced his medical skills.[20]

Mary Sharpe's marriage precipitated not only a wedding gift of slaves but also a general division of property among Charlie, Joe, and Mary Sharpe. Three weeks before the wedding, Charles submitted a tax return for Arcadia. Without formally deeding the property to his children, he listed Arcadia as now belonging to "C. C. Jones, Jun., Joseph Jones, and Mary Sharpe Jones." With its 1,996½ acres were listed "42 slaves" as now belonging to his children. Charles would continue to give general oversight to the operation of the plantation and Mary would continue to be concerned about the health and living conditions of those who lived in the Arcadia settlement, but the profits that flowed from its rice and cotton fields would now begin to be divided evenly among Charlie, Joe, and Mary Sharpe.[21]

A few weeks after Mary Sharpe and Robert's wedding, Mary's half-brother Charles Berrien Jones died, leaving a wife, Marion Anderson Jones, and six children. All of his life he had remained his momma's boy and had kept the pompous ways of one who was not too sure of himself. He had, however, been reconciled to Mary and Charles after the dispute over Joseph's will and had looked to them for the support and guidance of an older sister and her husband. As a kind of peace offering, he had sent Charles the old silver mounted shotgun that had belonged to Charles's father, John Jones. The gun had evidently been kept at the Retreat, and in the division of property following Joseph's death, Charles Berrien had taken possession of it. For their part, Charles and Mary had welcomed Charles Berrien and his family to Montevideo and Maybank, and Mary had gone to be with Marion when she was in labor and when any of the children were seriously ill.[22]

Beneath these calm family waters, however, trouble had been brewing long before Charles Berrien's death. Marion—like her alcoholic brother Joseph Anderson, the widower of Evelyn Jones—had an unstable side to her personality. She imagined insults where none were intended and saw schemes where none were being laid. In all this she found encouragement in her sister-in-law Emma Jones Harris, who still seethed over being left out of her father's will for eloping with Dr. Stephen Harris. And the primary person on whom they focused their anger was Henry Hart Jones. In contrast to an equivocating Charles Berrien, Henry had stood firmly with Joseph in his decision in regard to Emma, whose elopement had been seen as an act of "disobedience, ingratitude, and deception." And while Charles Berrien had managed his planting interests only moderately well, Henry had followed in his father's footsteps in successfully enlarging his holdings of land and slaves. Moreover, when their brother James Newton had died, it was not Charles Berrien, the oldest of the brothers, who had been given responsibility for managing the estate but Henry. All of this was resented deeply by Marion, so it was not surprising that she refused Henry's request to see and pray with Charles Berrien as he lay dying. What would be surprising and shocking to the Jones clan was the "diabolical" plan for revenge that soon began to consume the grieving Marion and that came to fruition in a few years.[23]

Charles and Mary left shortly after Charles Berrien's funeral for a meeting of the Presbyterian General Assembly being held in Lexington, Kentucky. In contrast to the long days of carriage and steamboat travel of a few years earlier, they were able to make the trip by train in only three days, including a stop in Marietta to see Aunt Eliza Robarts and her family and a quick visit with John Jones and his family in Rome, where John was now serving as pastor of the First Presbyterian Church. But the train trip, short as it was in comparison with earlier travel, left Charles exhausted. "Could I have in any degree foreseen how much exhausted he would have been," Mary wrote, "I would never have consented to his coming on to the assembly." But after a good night's rest, Charles was refreshed, and for the next ten days he enjoyed the opportunity of being with many friends from around the country. Thornwell and Adger were there from Columbia, and there were other friends from his Philadelphia days, and from Princeton too. Still, in spite of the pleasure of seeing old friends, his strength was clearly waning. "You have no concept, my dear child," Mary wrote Mary Sharpe, "how feeble your dear father is. I am convinced if ever he is to be permanently benefited, the effort must now be made."[24]

That effort was a trip to Hot Springs, Virginia, so that Charles might bathe in the healing waters of the springs. The "creeping paralysis" of his disease was slowly spreading, and even his heart appeared to be weakening. When they arrived at the springs, Mary wrote, "My hope and daily prayer is that a special blessing may rest upon his use of these wonderful waters—these fountains which an all-wise and gracious Providence has opened here for the suffering and afflicted." For the next six weeks they visited various Virginia springs—Hot Springs, White Sulphur Springs, Rockbridge Alum Springs, Rockbridge Baths—trying different treatments and seeing different doctors. But none of them worked. "Your dear father has not derived the advantage we anticipated," Mary confided to Mary

Sharpe. "At times," she wrote, "he appears very despondent in reference to his future recovery. In all our hours of darkness and sorrow how precious is the truth that if we are indeed the children of *God, loving* Him, all things shall work together for our good! Here rests our faith and hope." So they turned their faces toward home, having completed their last long trip together, and arrived at May-bank in late August 1857.[25]

    While Charles and Mary had been away, Joe and Charlie had spent a profitable summer. Joe had been unanimously elected to a professorship at the University of Georgia, thanks not only to his growing reputation as a scientist but also to the political savvy and hard work of his uncles John Jones and Henry Hart Jones. The position — professor of natural philosophy and natural theology — did not, however, really fit Joe's interests. So after a year in Athens, he accepted an invitation to become professor of chemistry at the Medical College of Georgia in Augusta. He had, however, one momentous event occur while in Athens — he finally had a conversion experience and joined the church, to the enormous relief of his parents and friends. Joseph Lumpkin, chief justice of the Georgia Supreme Court and an elder in the Presbyterian Church in Athens, wrote Charles of Joe's conversion. Among those "rejoicing in the light and liberty of God's children," wrote Lumpkin, was Little Titus, the oldest child of Patience and Porter, who had been selected to be Joe's personal servant. "It was a beautiful incident," Lumpkin said, to see Joe's "boy marching up with his young master to join the church, and commemorating together with him for the first time the New Testament Passover." Little Titus said his "old master's religion was good enough for him."[26]

    For his part, Charlie had been busy with his professional duties. He had become a junior partner in the law firm headed by John Elliot Ward, who only the year before had served as the president of the Democratic National Convention. Charlie had also begun courting Ruth Berrien Whitehead, the daughter of an "extensive landowner and a large slaveholder" in Burke County and the niece of John Berrien, the attorney general who had been so impolite to Charles in Washington in 1830 after they had disagreed over the recently passed bill for the removal of the Cherokees. Now in the late summer and fall of 1857, Charlie and Ruth found themselves falling in love. In January, Charlie announced to his parents that they were engaged.[27]

    As for Mary Sharpe, she told her parents not long after their return that she was in a "special way." The following April, a few days before the Mallards' first anniversary, a little girl was born to the young couple. They named her Mary Jones, after her grandmother. John Jones wrote the new grandfather Charles and sent his blessings: "May mother and babe be blessed and strengthened day by day, and may the little creature live to be a wellspring of joy to its parents and grand-parents! There's nothing like a baby—nothing so humanizing, so concentrating, so softening, so peacemaking. My dear Jane and myself long to see the little wonder." As could be expected, Charles and Mary immediately became doting grandparents. "She is not large," Mary wrote to Joe, "but well formed (particu-larly her head), and fat as a ricebird, is strong and healthy, has never had a colic, and has the best appetite you can imagine." Mary Sharpe, for her part, had "such an abundance of nourishment that she has to nurse one of the little Negroes." So Robin, the youngest child of Patience and Porter—he was named after his maternal grandfather—was brought to Mary Sharpe. She took him in her arms, held him at her breast, and gazed upon him, this little black slave child. Per-haps Mary Sharpe remembered, as Robin eagerly sucked a mother's milk from her, her Uncle John's words: "There's nothing like a baby—nothing so humaniz-ing, so concentrating, so softening, so peacemaking." But perhaps she had other thoughts.[28]

With the birth of their first grandchild, Charles and Mary began to see the growth once again of their family circle after the loss of so many they loved. Charles's illness, however, began to make their own future appear as a "length-ening shadow," and their memories turned increasingly to the days when their own children were about them. For the aging parents, home without the chil-dren and a much-loved grandchild was not their longed-for home, no matter how comfortable Maybank might be or how handsome Montevideo might appear as one walked in its gardens. Mary wrote Charlie in early summer 1858:

> You cannot think how much your father and mother miss their dear children. They are the sources of our greatest earthly comfort and happiness; and al-though we rejoice that they are filling stations of usefulness in the spheres al-lotted them by our Father in Heaven, still home is scarcely home without them. I keep some little memento of each daily in sight. Whilst writing I can look up and see the three little chairs you occupied in childhood, and to my eye they are almost fashioned into images of yourselves.[29]

For Charles and Mary, the members of the older generation were no longer the ones who were missed so intensely; even the memory of Joseph and Betsy was gradually slipping from their minds to emerge only from time to time with spe-cial poignancy.[30] Rather, it was the children who had grown up and left home who now left an emptiness at Maybank and Montevideo. The children's pres-ence was needed for home to be home. In this way, time for Charles and Mary, even in the midst of their disciplined activities, was beginning to be measured by the visits of their children and their newly arrived grandchild.

29

THE RETREAT III

Two years after the death of James Newton Jones from yellow fever, his brother Henry Hart Jones purchased the Retreat from Jimma's widow and from the other members of the family who had some interest in the old home place. All the slaves who had remained in the Retreat settlement were sold to neighboring planters, and Henry brought back to the Retreat those he had inherited from his father, Joseph, together with their descendents. Among those sold was Venus, the wife of Prince, the driver at White Oak. He was the son of the driver Hamlet and the grandson of Old Jupiter and Blind Silvey of Liberty Hall. Venus had been living for years at White Oak—rented out to Susan Jones Cumming in order to be with her husband. While she was the wife of one of the leading drivers in the county, such a position did not protect her. She was soon taken away from her husband to the up-country, to old Cherokee Georgia, where she was to be sold again with others from the Retreat settlement. Eliza Robarts wrote Susan from Marietta, "Tell your servant Prince his wife Venus is dead. The Negroes were all sold at Holly Springs except [Young] Pulaski and his wife." Perhaps her sorrow over the separation from her husband of many years killed Venus. Eliza Robarts did not say anything else about her death—apparently no details were given for a grieving Prince. In any case, the settlement at the Retreat was once again shuffled around and those Retreat families that had been a part of the Gullah community of Liberty County for generations—including Old Pulaski's son and his wife—were being scattered far and wide. The bitter process of breaking apart the Retreat settlement that had begun with Joseph's death was fast coming to its conclusion.[1]

Among those who were removed from the Retreat were two slaves of Eliza Robarts's—Katy and her daughter Lucy—who had been rented for years first to James Newton and then to his widow. In order to accommodate his old aunt,

Charles agreed to rent the two women. The mother and daughter were put to work under the supervision of Cato.

A year after their arrival at Carlawter, Lucy became pregnant—a condition she repeatedly denied even as it became increasingly evident that she was "large with child." Charles instructed Cato and his old nurse Mom Rosetta—who now served as the midwife at Carlawter—"to tell her to take care of herself and see that nothing happened to the child." Lucy, however, continued to deny her pregnancy. Finally on a Friday evening, Mom Rosetta was sent to the laboring woman. When later questioned, both Rosetta and Lucy's mother Katy denied ever seeing a child born and said they had seen Lucy having only "a bad bile." Both older women, Charles wrote, "endeavored to make the impression that she never had a child, and could not have been in a family way." On the following Monday, the woman was examined and "clear evidence" was found that she had "been delivered of a mature child." She denied it vigorously. A physician was called and "pronounced that she had unmistakably been delivered of a mature child." Charles ordered a search, and eight days later a dead child was found tied up in a piece of cloth and secreted in grass and bushes. Once again a physician was called, and he pronounced "it a child come to its maturity." The "wretched mother," confronted with the dead child, confessed. The child, she said, had been born dead when she was alone in her cabin. "She then tied it up in the Cloth," Charles recorded, "carried it down into the bottom, and hid it. Was afraid to disclose it, as she had all along denied it."[2]

Charles was furious. Years earlier, when life in the settlements had been more stable and he had been in the midst of his missionary labors, he had written that "infanticide" was a "crime restrained in good measure by the provision made for the support of the child on the part of the owner, by the punishment in the case of detection, and by the moral degradation of the people that takes away the disgrace of bastardy." More recently, however, as the breakup of the settlements intensified, he had heard of more cases throughout the county. "Awful depravity," he wrote in his *Journal*, "calling for prompt and efficient correction."[3]

After consultation with Charlie, Charles decided to submit the case to the county court. On Charlie's advice, the decision was made not to charge Lucy with murder, which could result in not only her execution, and with it a substantial loss to Eliza Robarts, but also the execution of Mom Rosetta and Katy. Rather, Lucy, her mother, and Mom Rosetta were all charged with concealment.[4]

With Henry acting as their legal counsel, the three women were brought before a panel of judges in Hinesville. The judges found Lucy guilty but agreed to Charles's request that charges be dropped against Mom Rosetta and Katy. They reprimanded and warned the older women before dismissing them. Then on Charles's instructions, "for the sake of impression," the constable gave Katy and Mom Rosetta "a few stripes over their jackets." Mom Rosetta no doubt concealed what she thought of such treatment by Charles, whom she had cared for so tenderly when he was a little boy.[5]

As for Lucy, she was given ninety lashes on her bare back—thirty on the Monday following her trial, thirty on the following Thursday, and then, as the first wounds were beginning to heal, thirty on the next Monday.[6] Charlie wrote his father: "Let me congratulate you upon the correct termination of the legal proceedings against Lucy. The judgment of the court was proper; you have discharged your duty as every good and true citizen is bound to do; and I am happy that your mind is now relieved from the burden of the prosecution." In regard to Katy and to Mom Rosetta, who had been a nurse not only to his father and but also to him, Charlie thought the effect of judgment "is probably better than it would have been had actual punishment have been inflicted. The power of the law is brought to bear, they made to realize the fact of a misdemeanor committed, and a new element of mercy and forbearance impressed upon them. The recognition of this will be a pledge of future amendment."[7]

Lucy was returned to Carlawter the same day she received the last thirty lashes. There her mother and perhaps Mom Rosetta did what they could to ease her pain and treat her raw and bleeding back. Two days later Lucy and her mother were sent from Carlawter to be rented to the railroad. In the meantime, Charles paid for the expenses of the trial, since he and Mary did not wish "Aunt to bear any part of them."[8]

In spite of Henry's skill as a planter, the old lands of the Retreat did not yield what he had hoped. To be sure, the inland rice lands, with their rich "blue clay" of Bulltown and Rice Hope swamps, still produced abundant crops. But the cotton land had become increasingly worn in spite of frequent manuring of fields and rotating of crops. And what made the yields seem more meager than ever were the reports from southwest Georgia, where new cotton lands were producing huge crops. Henry, with a businessman's eye for a good investment, began to explore the possibility of purchasing a plantation in this developing part of the state. In early December 1858 he left the Retreat to find a plantation he could purchase in Baker County. When he returned in a few weeks, he had purchased a large plantation he named Malvern. Within a few weeks of his return, he sent a number of the people from the settlement at the Retreat to Baker, near the southwestern corner of the state. His wife, Abby, wrote from the Retreat that Henry had "carried so many of the Negroes from here, that it makes the plantation look quite deserted. They all went off in fine spirits. It made me feel quite sad parting with them. I am glad they have had such pleasant weather for their journey."[9] Henry was obviously enthusiastic about the possibilities of Malvern, and he convinced his brother John Jones to join him in investing in the rich new lands of southwest Georgia. They soon purchased together another plantation in Baker, this one containing 1,750 acres, and John began to make arrangements for the removal of some of "his people" from Bonaventure.[10]

In this way Henry and John, together with other friends and relatives in Liberty County, participated in the breakup of old slave communities and in the massive movement of African Americans from the settled regions of the South to the new frontiers of an expanding slave society.[11]

Shortly after the purchase of Malvern, Henry put the Retreat up for sale. His aunt Eliza Robarts wrote Charles: "I think Henry is right to move his Negroes to Baker; the Retreat lands are much worn. But it makes my heart sad to think of it: the old homestead of my mother and my brother, with other associations, endears it to me; and I would hate to see it pass into strange hands." The Retreat had finally become a place largely of memories for the Jones family—a place associated with the past and not the future, with Joseph's life and labors and not the hopes and dreams of his descendants.[12]

Henry's plan in regard to his Baker County plantations was to be an absentee owner. And so he began to have built a fine new home in Walthourville not far from where his mother lived, and close to the home of Marion Anderson Jones, the widow of his brother Charles Berrien. Here he intended to have his permanent residence once he had sold the Retreat. Henry also began in the spring of 1859 a strange ritual of gathering the bodies of his dead children into one place. He and his wife, Abby, had lost a beautiful little girl, Ella, in 1853. The child, almost four years old, had died of the croup and had been buried under the oaks in the Midway cemetery. Another child, a little boy, had died shortly before the purchase of Malvern, and he too had been buried at Midway.[13] But a son, Joseph Henry, had died years earlier when he and his mother were visiting near Augusta. Henry now went to the little cemetery where the child lay, had the coffin exhumed, and brought it back to Midway. In late March 1859 Charles wrote in his journal:

M. and myself went to Midway, met Henry and Brother Buttolph with the body of his little son Joseph Henry, removed from Bath, Richmond County. Dead six years. H. raised the lid and look so as to see *the white hair of his little head, smoothed and brushed back!* He never saw him in his illness and death. A father's anxious affection! Said it was a great satisfaction to have seen so much. Would look no further! The case was lowered into the grave by the side of his brother recently buried. M. held the umbrella over my head—we prayed and closed the grave!

Another child, an infant daughter, lay in the little cemetery behind the Retreat not far from Joseph's obelisk and among the roses and jasmine that rambled over the tombs of many children and Joseph's first two wives. In late April 1859 Henry wrote his brother John from the Retreat:

> I rose soon after dawn this morning and proceeded to search for and exhume the remains of our little daughter Evelyn, who died Oct. 5th, 1849. The coffin was perfectly rotten and the little bones disconnected, but I was able to gather them *all*, even the little ribs and joints of the arm being perfect and nearly sound. After breakfast I will take them to Midway and lay them in the bosom of dear little Joseph Henry my first born and tenderly beloved son. Strange that the *Infant of hours* even speaking through its feeble dust after the lapse of *many years* can arouse so deeply the feelings, regrets and love of the parent's heart. I was surprised at my own emotion; the *mother* and others of the family still repose in their beds and know not what I was doing at that early hour. Thus am I preparing step by step to depart from scenes hallowed by the memories and events of the past, yet wearing an aspect funereal and gloomy. Still my heart clings to them, and *this* in after life, will be my *Mecca*, to which sad, yet pleasing pilgrimages shall be made.[14]

In such a way, Henry prepared to leave the Retreat with its Rice Hope lands where his grandfather, the first John Jones, had laid the foundation for the family's fortune in the years before the American Revolution.

While the preparations for the move were going forward, Henry's new home in Walthourville was nearing completion. Then suddenly word came to the Retreat that the house had burned down, a complete loss. The cause of the fire was unknown, but its origins were suspicious. Some months later, Henry received from his brother-in-law Joseph Anderson, the alcoholic widower of his sister Evelyn, an urgent request to meet him in Riceboro. Putting aside other business, Henry rushed to the little boro, where he learned the astonishing news that his young nephew, Charles Berrien, Jr., had been the arsonist who set the Walthourville house ablaze. Charles Berrien's fifteen-year-old cousin, Bessie Anderson, while not actually setting the blaze, had been an accomplice. Overwhelmed by remorse, she had confessed to her father. More details soon emerged. The instigator had been none other than Marion Anderson Jones, the mother of young Charles Berrien. She had, Henry later wrote John Jones in a confidential letter, "invented falsehoods of the most malignant and ingenious character to induce the children to hate *me* their uncle and true friend." Henry prevailed upon Bessie to go with him to Montevideo and make a full confession before Charles and Mary. They were horrified.

As Bessie talked, she made an additional confession. Her Aunt Marion had attempted, after the Walthourville fire, to get Bessie and a slave to go to the Retreat at night and burn it down while Henry and his family slept. This Bessie had refused to do, although her aunt threatened her with dire consequences. "Is it not enough," Henry wrote John, "to freeze the blood with horror?" Bessie also reported that for some years her Aunt Emma Jones Harris had been "incessant in her endeavors to poison her mind" against her Uncle Henry. And Emma had told Bessie that Charles and Mary had prevented Emma from receiving Joseph's blessing "on his death bed when he was constantly calling for her by *name.*" Moreover, Emma insisted that Henry, Charles, and Mary were "the means of her *disinheritance.*" All of this was soon confessed as well by young Charles Berrien. Later Charles and Mary talked "much and seriously" with their niece and nephew, prayed with them, and read Psalm 51: "Have mercy upon me, O God, according to thy lovingkindness: according unto the multitude of thy tender mercies blot out my transgressions."[15]

Joseph Anderson and Charles Berrien's new stepfather, Dr. Benjamin King, offered to pay Henry for the loss of his house, but Henry refused. Henry wrote John: "I do forgive and endeavor to pray for those who have so cruelly wronged me, and in this matter will seek to heap coals of fire upon their heads." Henry and Mary agreed that "the first cause of hate grew out of the events following Emma's elopement." But they also agreed that the "matter must be kept a *profound secret* to shield from utter ruin the young, unfortunate victims of an unnatural relative." Henry believed, however, that the immediate family must be told in order "that they may no longer be deceived or influenced by the *really* guilty party."[16] So the young people and the reputation of the Jones family were protected as the secret was kept, and the bitter memory was suppressed, and the details were not mentioned in any correspondence except Henry's letter to his brother John. But beneath this public appearance, Joseph's family continued to break apart and fall away from one another into a deepening alienation.

The final scattering of the settlement at the Retreat was only one of many scatterings that broke over Liberty County's Gullah community during the closing years of the 1850s. And many were the husbands and wives—like Prince and Venus—who found themselves being forcefully torn apart. Plenty James, who lived at old Liberty Hall, was a leader in the church and had been for years the driver for Nathaniel Varnedoe. When Varnedoe died in 1856, his will declared: "I will and bequeath to my true and faithful servant driver Plenty one hundred dollars in money." Plenty had taken half the money and gone to Charles with a request. Charles wrote Charlie about it: "I have $50 for one of my Black friends to invest for him. Can you see if I can invest it in the Savings Bank in my own name in trust for him? And what is the interest allowed? And how can the principal be withdrawn if required?" Charles invested the money for Plenty, as he did for Cato, old Niger, and a few others with substantial cash, and paid them interest on the savings before Mary finally settled the accounts and closed the books on "Negro Money."[17]

But even Plenty, as one who was relatively privileged, was not protected from a bitter sale. When the Varnedoe estate was settled, Plenty's wife, Flora, was sold to southwest Georgia. The old man tried to keep in touch with her by going to Savannah and getting his former pastor at Midway, I. S. K. Axson, to write to her for him. And he took some of his money and made the dangerous trip during the Christmas holidays to the little village of Albany, where his wife now lived. On the trip he met John Jones, who was taking eight slaves from Bonaventure to his new plantation in Baker County. John took Plenty in his care to protect the old man from the troubles that might come from a slave traveling alone. "Old Plenty," John wrote Mary, "is to be pitied. He utters not a word of reproach against his master who certainly was wrong in reducing the old man to his widowed condition in his old age."[18]

Plenty's efforts to overcome the separation from Flora were part of a pattern of husbands and wives trying desperately to stay together in spite of the power of whites to divide them. The same was true of unmarried young adults who had fallen in love. Ben Lowe, a slave of Joseph Anderson's in Sunbury, was courting Porter and Patience's daughter Beck when he was rented out to the railroad and sent to the village of Quitman in South Georgia. Evidently with the help of a white friend, he wrote Beck:

> Dear Rebecca
>   The conversation that took place Between us the Sunday night I seen you last I have not forgot. I intend Doing what I promised and I hope you will as you promised. Rebecca I love you as I Ever loved you and Intend doing so until life leaves. Rebecca I Expect seeing you at Christmas and Then I intend asking your masters consent—give my Respects to your Father and Mother
>   I Remain your Lover
>   Ben Lowe *servant*

The next Christmas, when Ben was back in Sunbury, Anderson wrote Charles saying that he had given permission to Ben to marry Beck if it "is not contrary to your rule." Anderson added: "He is honest and industrious in past and I can safely and do cheerfully vouch for his good character." Charles noted on the letter: "Request granted." So in spite of the distance, and the likelihood that they would see each other only once a year at Christmas, Ben and Beck married.[19]

Others, however, felt the full power, anguish, and finality of family separations. Andrew and Mary Ann's daughter Dinah had grown up in the settlement at Maybank overlooking the Medway marshes and had become a lively and attractive young woman. She was, Charles said, "the life of the place." In 1850, when she was twenty-two, she married Abram, who lived at nearby Woodville. He too had grown up on the island—he had belonged to Julia King's father, Audley Maxwell—and like Dinah he knew the smell of the marsh in summer and the sound of the surf on a stormy day. Together they had four children—Harry, Silvia, Little Abram, and Dublin. A few months after their son Dublin was born, the Roswell King estate put up some eighty slaves for sale. King, in spite of his practical ways, had left a cranky and much dated will that had finally been invalidated by the court. The family had agreed that in order to settle the estate among the heirs, some slaves must be sold, and Abram was among those chosen. He was taken from the island; from his old parents at Woodville; from his wife, Dinah, and from his children at Maybank; and, with others from South Hampton, he was carried to Savannah. There he was held in Wright's slave jail, the same bitter place that Phoebe and Cassius and their children had been held, awaiting a buyer.[20]

Dinah was devastated and she beseeched Mary to help her. Mary wrote Charlie and her brother Henry asking whether they could find a buyer in Liberty County. Charlie wrote back:

> Abram is in Wright's office for sale, and in a very distressed frame of mind, not knowing who will be his purchaser, and with the probability staring him in the face of his being carried far away from his wife and children, to whom he appears to be sincerely attached. It is a hard case, and I would in a moment purchase and send him to the Island was such a thing practicable. As it is, we can only regret the sad fact of his being thus parted without the means of preventing the separation.

Henry wrote back, after conferring with Norman Gignilliat of neighboring McIntosh County, who had purchased forty-eight of the King slaves:

> I send you a line in haste simply to acknowledge the reception of your kind note and to state that I communicated immediately with Mr. Gignilliat in reference to the case of Abram. Mr. G. seems unwilling to purchase but upon my offering to release him for *one* year from the payment of the thousand dollars on his *notes* due to Helen, he consented for me to take steps to ascertain the

price at which the Boy is held. I accordingly addressed a letter to Mr. Wright
and received for reply that the Boy was still in his office, but the *owners* had
left for the West. He promised however to write me *forthwith* and learn the
value placed upon Abram, and then to notify me of the same. I cannot hold
out much encouragement however that Mr. Gignilliat will take him. I have
sought industriously for a purchaser elsewhere, thus far without success.

And then a letter came to Dinah from Abram himself:

> My dear wife I take the pleasure of writing you these few [lines] with much re-
> gret to inform you that I am Sold to a man by the name of Peterson atreader
> and Stays in new orleans. I am here yet But I expect to go before long but when
> I get there I will write and let you know where I am. My Dear I want to Send
> you Somethings but I do not know who to Send them By but I will thry to get
> them to you and my children. Give my love to my father and mother and tell
> them good Bye for me. and if we Shall not meet in this world I hope to meet
> in heaven. My Dear wife for you and my Children my pen cannot Express the
> griffe I feel to be parted from you all
>   I remain your truly husband until Death
>   Abream Scriven

Mary wrote at the bottom of Abram's letter: "Answered for her by her mistress."[21]
    Abram and Dinah never saw each other again. A few years later, Abram learned
from another Jones slave that Dinah had died.[22]

    While Abram and Dinah's marriage was being broken apart, Joe had assumed
his new position as professor of chemistry at the Medical College of Georgia.
Not long after his arrival in Augusta, he had begun courting Caroline Davis, a
charming young woman and a member of one of the most distinguished families
in Georgia. The young couple had much in common. Her father was also a Presbyterian minister, a graduate of Middlebury College and Princeton Theological
Seminary, and her mother was a Cumming and thus related through marriage
to Joe's aunt Susan Jones (Maxwell) Cumming. Caroline and her three sisters
were known "for their remarkable intellect, taste, and charm." Charlie had visited
with the family several years earlier and had noted that "The young ladies are all
well educated, intelligent, and studious in their habits, with fine conversational
powers." When their engagement was announced, Charles and Mary were delighted. Charles believed that "the match is purely a love match" on Joe's part
and "equally so on the other side." And, wrote Charles, "from all I can learn,
Carrie will take a great interest in his pursuits and pride in his advancement, and
will exert herself to render his home happy." Charles was particularly pleased

"to learn also that she is both industrious and economical and fond of reading, which in my experience are invaluable traits in a wife." "Your own dear mother," he told Charlie, "is a model wife in all these and many other particulars too numerous for me to mention."[23]

Increasingly at the center of Mary's life—and of Charles's too—were the grandchildren, who seemed to them to be amazing gifts in their old age. After the birth of Mary Jones Mallard in 1858, another little girl had arrived, Charlie and Ruth's firstborn, whom they named Julia Berrien after her maternal grandmother. In 1860 the first grandson was born—a fine little fellow whose proud parents named him Charles Colcock Mallard. Then a year after Joe and Caroline married they had a little boy—Samuel Stanhope Davis Jones—born a few months after his cousin Charles. So by Christmas 1860 Charles and Mary had four grandchildren—Mary, Julia, Charles, and Stanhope. They were the delight of their grandparents, and when they were brought for a visit to Montevideo or Maybank, the old places seemed to radiate a deep joy, and Charles and Mary remembered with gratitude the years when their own children were gathered around them at home.

Charles continued, of course, to be industrious in his retirement years. He preached as often as he could to the slaves at his old preaching stations—at the stand at Midway, at the Sunbury and North Newport Baptist Churches, and at Pleasant Grove. And when his strength allowed, he preached in the village churches at Dorchester and Walthourville and on occasion from the old pulpit at Midway.[24]

But most of his energy had gone into the writing of his history of the Christian church. It was a daunting task under any circumstances, but especially so at isolated plantations along the Georgia coast. He had pressed ahead, however, using his personal library and ordering books as needed. His vision of church history was both broad and narrow—broad in his understanding of the church's origins with Abraham and the people of Israel, and narrow in the sense of isolation from the massive historical works—especially among the Germans—of the nineteenth century. By the summer of 1860 he had begun negotiations with Charles Scribner to have the book published.[25]

The difficulty that Charles faced, however, was that his handwriting had deteriorated to such an extent that he needed someone to copy the manuscript in a neat hand for publication. In what appeared to Charles as a providential development, a young man who was visiting the island that summer, William States Lee, volunteered to be his scribe. Lee had grown up on Edisto Island, South Carolina, where his father was the longtime pastor of the Presbyterian Church. Although a New Englander by birth and education, the father had become a fire-eater for secession. His Edisto congregation was composed of a few wealthy planting families and several hundred African-American slaves.[26] If anything, Edisto was more isolated than Colonel's Island, for it was reached only by boat. Its wealth, isolation, and large Gullah population had no doubt shaped the way young Lee saw the world and his place in it. In 1860 he was in the process of establishing a new school in Columbus, Georgia, but he spent several months that summer living at Maybank, copying out the manuscript day by day. Patience was sick much of the summer, and so others had to take her heavy responsibilities for the kitchen. Among them was Peggy, an attractive young slave who was being trained to be a domestic servant.[27]

30

SOUTHERN ZION

A few weeks after William States Lee left Maybank in the late summer of 1860, Charlie was elected mayor of Savannah. He was only twenty-eight years old, the youngest man ever to be elected the city's mayor. "It is a high honor," Charles wrote his son, "coming unsolicited, and the expression of the confidence of a majority of your fellow citizens." Your parents, Charles wrote, are "gratified that your conduct and character have been such as to attract to you their suffrages, which place you in the highest office in their gift." But Charles was not one to give such praise without a parental admonition: "We sincerely hope," he told his eldest son, that the citizens of Savannah "may not be disappointed in their expectations of you, but that you will conscientiously seek to discharge your very responsible and in many respects difficult duties with all sobriety, industry, impartiality, justice, and integrity, and with kindness and decision and intelligence." Charles and Mary, drawing on their Calvinist ethic, had educated each of their children's "mind and heart and manners" for "usefulness in society." Charlie now seemed on his way to a particularly brilliant career in the public sphere, where he would be of eminent service to his homeland.[1]

By the time of Charlie's election, however, the nation was already moving rapidly toward the crisis of secession. A civil war seemed increasingly likely, and the rhetoric of war was nowhere more intense than in the low country, with its elegant little cities of Charleston and Savannah and its heated atmosphere and noxious miasmas. Like distant thunder rumbling across the Medway marshes, war talk began to intrude into what Charles and Mary regarded as the peace and harmony of their low-country home.

From his student days in New England, Charles had long admired much about the North, especially New England's pious and orderly ways. With his colleagues in Columbia and Charleston—Howe, Thornwell, and Smyth—he had long been a Unionist in sentiment. When South Carolina had threatened secession in 1850, Charles had written John Jones from Philadelphia: "South Carolina has gone beyond reason. I was going to say *politically mad*: she will pitch Georgia into the sea if we break her hopes a second time. We did so in nullification days. She remembers it." He believed during his years in Philadelphia that "*the people of the United States*—North, East, South, and West—are true to the Union. It is the *ultras*, the factionists—few in comparison to the masses—that create excitements by their noise and impudence. I am still of the opinion all will come right."[2]

As sectional tensions had built, however, Charles's views had begun to shift. John Brown's raid on Harper's Ferry in 1859 had been particularly infuriating. Charles had become livid—not over the possibility that the raid might have let loose a slave insurrection, for he dismissed a slave rising as improbable. Rather, the raid seemed to pull back a curtain for Charles and reveal to him the intentions of growing numbers in the North. "The whole abolition crusade," he wrote Charlie, "which has been preached for thirty years *ends in the sword*." Charles believed there was still time to avert a disaster, but he thought the conservative forces of the North must act decisively to avoid the ruin of the republic. If they failed to put down "this spirit of treasonable and violent aggression" against the South, then they too would drink the bitter dregs of a national disaster.[3]

One year later, however, the nation seemed to be moving irreversibly toward civil war. In mid-October 1860, Charlie wrote his parents: "The election of Lincoln seems now almost a fixed fact, in view of the recent advices received from Pennsylvania, Ohio, and Indiana. The Republicans claim New York by a clear majority of forty thousand." Charlie warned that if Lincoln were elected, "the action of a single state, such as South Carolina or Alabama, may precipitate us into all the terrors of intestine war." And then he added, almost as a postscript: "I sincerely trust that a kind Providence, that has so long and so specially watched over the increasing glories of our common country, may so influence the minds of fanatical men and dispose of coming events as to avert so direful a calamity."[4]

Charles himself fluctuated—sometimes he thought the election of Lincoln would mean war, and sometimes he thought not. In late October, as the election drew near, he wrote Charlie: "I do not apprehend any very serious disturbance in the event of Lincoln's election and a withdrawal of one or more Southern states, which will eventuate in the withdrawal of all." On what ground, he wondered, "can the free states found a military crusade upon the South?" The self-interest of the North, he thought, was with peace. And he asked: "Is not the right of self-government on the part of the people the cornerstone of the republic?" But even if the southern states had the right to withdraw, Charles prayed that God would "avert such a separation, for the consequences may in future be disastrous to both sections. Union if possible—but with it we must have *life, liberty, and equality.*"[5]

In early November, the die was finally cast and Lincoln was elected. In less than a week the "politically mad" Charlestonians were in Savannah making their appeal for concerted action. Charlie, as mayor of the city, hosted them and gave the opening address at a grand gathering at the Pulaski Hotel. Not unexpectedly, he called for the defense of southern rights and southern honor. Mary read the account of the meeting and wrote Charlie that she and his father "felt honored that our son bore so high a place." And Charles wrote his son that he "was much gratified with your speech at the dinner to the Charlestonians in Savannah."[6]

That same week a "Southern Rights Meeting" was called for the citizens of Liberty County. Charles hurried to the county seat at Hinesville to take part, and Mary went with him. She went, she said, "*to represent her father*, being the oldest child of his family now living." "You know her patriotism," wrote her proud husband to Charlie. Moreover, wrote Charles, she "has taken possession of your pistol with the shooting apparatus underneath, and Gilbert is ordered to clean and put it in perfect order."[7]

The meeting in Hinesville proceeded as expected—the right of a state to withdraw from the Union was said to be a fundamental right of the republic, and the idea of the North attempting to coerce the South was ridiculed. Henry Hart then moved that a committee be appointed to draw up a resolution for the citizens of Liberty County. Charles was among those on the committee who soon reported back to the meeting. The resolution noted the "repeated aggressions on the part of the North upon our constitutional rights, and the institution of slavery," declared that the election of Lincoln "ought not to be submitted to," and resolved "that we cordially approve of the action of the legislature in regards to the call for a state convention, and in sustaining the decision of which, we pledge our lives, our fortunes, and our sacred honor."[8]

While Charlie and his parents were making clear their position on Lincoln's election and on secession, Joe was busy preparing for a major address to the Cotton Planters Convention during the second week of December. For months he had been traveling the state collecting and analyzing data about the condition of agriculture in Georgia. He had prepared a 312-page report that examined the state's agricultural resources and that called for various reforms. Joe was asked to give a summary address to the convention. The invitation was considered a high honor since the convention drew planters from all over the state and had as its president the U.S. secretary of the treasury, Howell Cobb. As circumstances would have it, Joe's address fell at the same time Charlie was to preside over a secession meeting in Savannah. Mary hurried to Macon in the middle of the state to hear Joe's address, while Charles made the trip into Savannah to be present at the city's historic meeting.[9]

Joe began his address before the packed convention by summarizing his findings. He did not, however, go far in his address before he launched into a fiery appeal for secession. Lincoln's election, he declared, marked the triumph of a sectional party "sworn to subvert our institutions, and excite our slaves to rebellion and murder; and which would not merely make us dream of fire, poison, and murder in our sleep, but would surround us with a wall of fire, and apply the torch of incendiary to our cities, our farm-houses and our dwellings." The studious and hardworking Joe, using the most inflammatory rhetoric available to him, cast his lot for his southern home and its enslavement of all who lived in the settlements and quarters of the South.[10]

In Savannah, meanwhile, a large crowd gathered at city hall. Charles, as an elderly gentleman and father of the mayor, was given a front row seat. The crowd overflowed from the hall into the surrounding streets. Charlie gave an opening address that was "rapturously applauded." Resolutions and nominations to the state secession convention were prepared. Those in the hall emptied into a sea of people on the streets. Charlie went out on a balcony to put the resolutions and nomination to the multitude. There was a "universal hurrah of ayes," a cannon went off, and rockets flew into the sky "illuminating the scene." There was a pause. Charlie then put the next question: "'Contrary minds, no!' A dead silence—when one man cried out: 'There's *narra no*, Mayor Jones!'"[11]

So Charles and Mary, Charlie and Joe played out their parts in the secession of their state. They were, they thought, not only acting in good faith but also following a well-worn path of duty and civic responsibility. They believed that they were defending their home and homeland against a ruthless enemy, that they were acting as any patriotic and courageous people would act, and that their deepest commitments impelled them to take their stand on the side of the South and human slavery. They could not conceive at the time, of course, how much blood would flow in the defense of their homeland. Nor could they imagine how their good intentions would help bring them unexpected and unwanted results. But they had intimations of what was to come when, in the spring of 1861, shots were finally fired at Fort Sumter in Charleston harbor.

The Southern victory at Fort Sumter seemed to Charles a providential act. "Whoever read or heard," he declared, "of so important and desperate a battle as that of Fort Sumter without the loss of a man on the side of the victors or on the side of the vanquished?" And he prayed that the victory was but a foretaste of others to come. But the battle itself seemed to have broken a restraining barrier within Charles. The old ethic of moderation and prudence that had for so long guided him, and the old feelings for the Union that went back to his student days in New England, all these restraints now seemed to have been breached, and through the breach flowed a long-repressed rage. He wrote Charlie:

> I never believed we should have war until after Lincoln's inaugural address— and not altogether then, thinking that there were some preventing consider- ations of interest and self-preservation, and some residuum of humanity and respect for the opinions of the civilized world in the Black Republican party. But in this I have been mistaken. Christianity with its enlightening and soft- ening influences upon the human soul—at least so far as the great subject di- viding our country is concerned—finds no lodgment in the soul of that party, destitute of justice and mercy, without the fear of God, supremely selfish and arrogant, unscrupulous in its acts and measures, intensely malignant and vitu- perative, and persecuting the innocent even unto blood and utter destruction. That party is essentially *infidel!* And these are our enemies, born and reared in our own political family, for whom we are to pray, and from whom we are to defend ourselves.

From now on the North would be "our malignant, unscrupulous, and deter- mined enemy," and the conduct of the United States government "a disgrace to the civilization and Christianity of the age, and an outrage on the great prin- ciples of political and civil liberty upon which our former government was laid and upon which it has stood for eighty years." These were the shared sentiments of all the Jones family and of their white friends in Liberty County.[12]

The summer following the battle of Fort Sumter, as armies were gathering in the North and the South, Charlie's wife, Ruth, and their little daughter Julia re- turned to Savannah following a visit to a plantation in Burke County. Ruth was approaching the ninth month of pregnancy, and scarlet fever had been reported in Savannah. Not long after their return to the city little Julia came down with the fever. Mary—leaving Charles too weak to travel—rushed from Maybank to be with her grandchild and the ailing mother. As Julia struggled against the ravages of the disease, her mother gave birth to another little girl. Charlie wrote his father:

> Ruth was this morning at nine o'clock delivered of a fine little daughter. Her previous sufferings were not protracted, but after the birth of the child she was brought to death's door in consequence of the failure of the womb to contract, and the enormous effusion of blood. This has been stopped, but will have to remain perfectly quiet for hours to come.
> Julia, we hope, is better. The febrile action is diminished somewhat, but she

continues quite restless. I do not know what we would have done in the absence of dear Mother. She is better this morning, and I sincerely trust that her
exertions may not induce a return of her fever.

Soon Charlie was himself taken by the fever, and Joe came hurrying down from
August to attend to the sick family. Henry also arrived to be of what help he could,
and Charlie soon began to recover his strength enough to be with his ill child.
He was beside her when she died. Mary wrote Charles:

> Our little sufferer died this morning about nine o'clock. The physicians decide
> that there must be an early interment—this evening about seven o'clock. From
> the nature of the disease and poor Ruth's situation this is necessary. She lies ex-
> tremely ill—often wandering but mostly unconscious of surrounding objects,
> but rational when roused, and able to nurse her little babe. Joe thinks her in a
> very critical situation. She has as yet no symptoms of scarlet fever, but decided
> ones of puerperal fever. The infant, too, has ulcerated sore-throat and a little
> rash, which we hope may not move into scarlet fever. Charles has been very
> sick with sore throat and fever—threatened almost with suffocation; can now
> scarcely speak or swallow. Truly the hand of our God is upon us. Oh, that we
> may feel and act aright under the rod! We can only have prayer offered ere our
> dead is removed; Ruth is too ill for any service.[13]

Charles, weighed down with grief, responded immediately in a letter to his
eldest:

> My dear Son,
>   Gilbert has just come, and I cannot express to you my sympathy and grief
> at the loss of dear little Julia and the extreme illness of your affectionate and
> devoted wife, my dear Ruth.
>   Sweet child! A child of the covenant, and removed, we trust and believe, to
> be with God. She is not dead, but sleepeth. We must think of her as with the
> spirits of the redeemed in heaven. Your heart is torn; you feel what you never
> felt before. It is a great affliction; I wish I knew how to bear it for you. That
> sweet child was given you by the Lord, and *He has removed her.* Acknowledge
> His right, and humbly pray to Him for submission to His will, and that He may
> bless the stroke to your own eternal welfare. He alone can bind up the broken-
> hearted.

Ruth fought the infection that was slowly spreading through her body. She was
a strong young woman with everything to live for. But the poison did its work,
and soon the mother joined the beloved daughter in death. Mary took the in-

fant granddaughter—Charlie named her Mary Ruth—back to Maybank to care for her and to raise her as her own for the next few years. And from Savannah Charlie wrote his parents: "What I have suffered is known only to my desolate heart. Everything around me appears invested with the habiliments of the grave."[14] Shortly thereafter, he announced that he would not run for reelection. Alone and in deep sorrow, Charlie experienced a new tenderness coming into his life. And while he did not have a conversion experience that would bring him into the church as a full member, he did feel a new dependence on God. In the days ahead, he became less pompous and began to exhibit a kindness that showed his struggle to go beyond a sense of duty to a genuine empathy for the sorrows and sufferings of others.

Charles sent word to Cato that Peggy was to come to Maybank to help with the care of Mary Ruth. Earlier in the summer Peggy had given birth to a little girl, and Charlie and Mary decided that Peggy would be the best servant to nurse their new granddaughter. When Peggy arrived at Maybank, Charles and Mary discovered to their horror that her little girl was a mulatto. They questioned the nineteen-year-old Peggy carefully. The father, she confessed, was none other than William States Lee. He had, she said, seduced her shortly after he arrived at Maybank in late summer of 1860 and for weeks thereafter had continued his relations with her. She did not accuse him of forcing her, but she insisted that he was the father.[15]

Charles was incensed and wrote a blistering letter to Lee in Columbus, where he had begun his school for young women. "You had my confidence," he declared, "as unreservedly as any stranger possibly could have, and enjoyed the kind hospitality of my family from the day you entered to the day you left it." Yet in spite of this hospitality, you "debauched a young Negro girl" and "continued your base connections with this Negro woman week after week until you took your final leave!" Not only had Peggy been abused, but Charles felt abused as well. You are, Charles wrote in outrage, "the only man who has ever dared to offer to me personally and to my family and to my neighbors so vile and so infamous an insult. You are the only man who has ever dared to debauch my family servants—it being the only instance that has occurred—and to defile my dwelling with your adulterous and obscene pollutions."

Charles then spelled out in his letter the proof of Lee's "criminality," which, he said, was "so clear a character as to remove all doubt." There was first of all, "*the free, unconstrained confession of the Negro woman herself in full detail; there is the correspondence between the time of your connection with her and the birth of the child—a mulatto, now some time born; and there is a resemblance to you beyond mistake.*" The case, Charles declared, "is amply sufficient to warrant the submission of the case to the session of the Columbus church for action."[16]

Lee, upon receiving the letter, immediately showed it to two elders of the Columbus church—one a judge and clerk of the session, the other a wealthy merchant. Lee vigorously denied the charges. Since the Columbus pastor was away, the two elders sought to handle the matter with discretion. Before presenting the case to the entire session and thereby jeopardizing Lee's reputation and the work of his school, they insisted that while "it is our duty to look closely to all offenders, yet it is no less our duty to protect and defend innocent members of the church." They consequently raised several issues with the evidence presented by Charles. Most telling was their questioning of the reliability of the mother. "It is the opinion of some of our ablest legal men," they solemnly declared, "who have had much experience in the investigation of cases of bastardy that the propensity in woman is to conceal the true father." The charges made by the woman, legal experts have found, "usually arise from a sprit of revenge for what the woman considers a breach of promise, false pretenses, etc." Some of our lawyers and judges, the elders wrote with self-assurance, have been so strongly impressed with "these facts that some effort has been made in the general assembly of the state to have the law so altered as to make the mother incompetent for a witness unless the complaint be made at the time or very soon after the illicit intercourse."[17]

Charles answered their letter point by point, arguing with all the zeal of his righteous indignation and with all the forcefulness and clarity of one deeply familiar with church law. In particular, he insisted that "servants are not always liars, and are particularly slow to father their children upon white men without the best of reasons, and because of the humble and exposed condition are more open to the seductions of their superiors (not in character but in station in society)." Furthermore, Charles said that he had discovered that Lee "had been charged by a Negro girl in the village where he taught school in our country with having had criminal connection with her and with being the father of the child with which she was then pregnant; that he had denied the charge before the trustees of the academy and demanded that the Negro should be punished, which punishment was inflicted previously to the birth of the child; and the trustees acquitted him, there being no evidence but that of the Negro girl against him." Later, however, the child was born a mulatto, and the young mother "persists in the charge to this day." Some in the village, Charles admitted, still believe him innocent, but others believe him guilty. "Now," he said, "here are two Negro women living twenty miles apart, without any knowledge of or correspondence with each other, preferring the same charge against the same man holding to it." Charles was clear about his own position: "My own belief," he wrote, "is settled, which I pronounce with sorrow: that with all the circumstances and evidences before me, he is a guilty man." And he added: "Nor am I alone in that belief."[18]

A few weeks later another letter arrived from the clerk of the session containing a sworn statement from Lee: "I do hereby solemnly deny the truth of such charges and do pronounce them to be utterly false and unfounded." The clerk, at the pastor's request, asked for Charles to "reply as early as convenient," and asked that Charles, from "your extensive experience and observation in church judicature . . . please suggest what course should be adopted here by session." Will you, they asked Charles, "become prosecutor, or can the case be so made out that the session of this church can take action upon it?"[19]

Charles was clearly disgusted with the casuistry of their responses and with their avoidance of duty. "I have laid pretty fully all the evidence relating to it before you," he wrote in a brief letter to the clerk of the session, "and upon which, with the first six chapters of our book of discipline in your hands, you are well able of yourselves, independent of all assistance, to decide what course should be pursued without the intervention of any prosecutor at all."[20]

The matter, so threatening to the reputation of Lee and his school for young women, was never taken before the session. But Peggy did not change her story. She named the little girl Eva, after the child's maternal grandmother, and Lee, after the young white man who had spent several months under the hospitable roof of Charles and Mary Jones.[21]

As for Charles, Lee's behavior represented a profound betrayal not only because it broke rules of hospitality and moral rectitude but also because it betrayed a long-cherished image of a quiet and peaceful home. This betrayal evoked bitter rage in Charles, for it threatened to undercut the very foundations of Maybank and Montevideo as sacred places held in the memory and imagination of his heart. How was he to think of his low-country home now that he knew all too well that his dwelling had been defiled by "adulterous and obscene pollutions"?

While the letters were going back and forth between Charles and the elders in Columbus, preparations were going forward for the first meeting of the General Assembly of the Presbyterian Church in the Confederate States of America. In May 1861, only a few weeks after the battle of Fort Sumter, the General Assembly of the still united Presbyterian Church had met in Philadelphia. A few southern commissioners had attended, but a resolution had been passed that called on the church to "Promote and perpetuate, so far as in us lies, the integrity of these United States, and to strengthen, uphold, and encourage, the Federal government in the exercise of all its functions under our noble constitution: and to this constitution in all its provisions, requirements, and principles, we profess our

unabated loyalty." In Charleston, Thomas Smyth, an old moderate and Unionist, declared that the General Assembly had "willingly, willfully and wickedly"
severed the last link that held the North and South together. Charles agreed that
the resolution was nothing less than treason against the church, against the Gospel, and against Christ, and he joined in a call for the organization of a Southern
Presbyterian Church.[22]

Arrangements were soon made for a meeting of a Southern Presbyterian General Assembly to be held in Augusta in December 1861, and Charles was determined to attend. His health, however, was now in a serious decline. When he
preached, he had to do so sitting down, and when he made any physical exertion, he was soon out of breath. His "creeping palsy" was doing its slow but steady
work of disabling him; his heart was weakening and his strength was fast ebbing.
Nevertheless, Charles made his plan to go to the assembly.

Meanwhile, Joe had joined the old Liberty Independent Troop—the one his
grandfather Joseph had commanded during the War of 1812—and was stationed
at Sunbury as the troop's surgeon. At his father's request, he obtained a furlough
in order to accompany Charles to Augusta and to have a quick visit with Carrie
and little Stanhope. They caught the train into Savannah, and from there they
took the train to Augusta. Whenever he moved about, Charles had to lean on
Joe's arm for support.[23]

In Augusta, Charles found many of his old friends gathering for the assembly. Howe and Thornwell were there from Columbia with their colleague Joseph
Wilson. I. S. K. Axson, the former pastor at Midway, had ridden up from Savannah. (In a few years Axson's granddaughter would be married to Wilson's son
Woodrow.) Benjamin Morgan Palmer came from New Orleans, and John Leighton Wilson—whose reports and letters from Africa had been so important to
Charles—came from New York to join in the Southern cause. These and other
friends and colleagues gathered at Augusta's First Presbyterian Church. Palmer
was elected moderator and preached the opening sermon. But Thornwell was
the real leader of the assembly, and it was he who articulated a brilliant generation's considered thought on secession and its fundamental cause—human
slavery. Secession and the creation of the Confederacy provided, they believed,
a critical moment for the creation of a new social order. The North represented a
social system where capital and labor were divided—a system so oppressive to the
laboring classes that a revolution was likely to occur. Thornwell was convinced
that the only way to prevent such a bloody revolt by the masses of oppressed
workers was to convert "the labourer into capital; that, is by giving the employer
a right of property in the labour employed; in other words, by Slavery." Against
the social order that they saw rising in the North, Thornwell and his colleagues

envisioned the Confederacy as an alternative class-stratified society that would stand against the increasing anarchy of the modern world. The new Confederacy was to be a commonwealth that was both capitalistic and hierarchical. Such a commonwealth would be not a society of democratic capitalism committed to an equality of opportunity, but a commonwealth whose capitalism would be controlled by a commitment to what they called "regulated liberty"—and those whose liberty would be most carefully regulated were black slaves.[24]

If Thornwell articulated the assembly's theological and ideological position on secession and slavery, Charles was the one who captured the assembly's imagination and evoked deep images of the South as home, where old times were not forgotten and where duty and social place were inescapably linked. Charles was asked to speak to the assembly on the religious instruction of the slaves. So once again—and for the last time—he rose to address the subject that had been the great passion of his life. Though weak, he spoke for an hour on the responsibilities of the white South for the religious instruction of slaves. And he remembered with longing his labors among those who lived at Carlawter and at Lambert and at the old Mallard Place and at all the other settlements of his low-country home:

> Yes, my brethren, there is a blessing in the work. How often, returning home after preaching on the Sabbath-day, through crowds of worshippers—sometimes singing as they went down to their homes again; or returning from plantation meetings held in humble abodes, late in the star-light night, or in the soft moonlight, silvering over the forests on the roadside, wet with heavy dews, with scarcely a sound to break the silence, alone but not lonely—how often has there flowed up in the soul a deep, peaceful joy, that God enabled me to preach the Gospel to the poor. . . .[25]

31

INDIANOLA

The terrible costs of civil war had become apparent months before Charles traveled to Augusta to speak of "plantation meetings held in humble abodes." Shortly after Fort Sumter, great armies had begun to gather in both the North and the South. Throughout the spring and early summer of 1861, volunteer regiments from all over the North had moved toward Washington, and young recruits from all over the South had moved toward Virginia in anticipation of a great battle. Among the Southerners were many Georgians, and among the Georgians were many friends and relatives of Charles and Mary.[1]

Cousin Mary Robarts wrote describing a scene that was happening, with local variations, all across the South. Three companies were raised from Marietta, Roswell, and surrounding farms. The women of Marietta, taking advantage of the newly developed sewing machine, quickly made the uniforms for the recruits. Then, on the day of departure for Virginia, the troops assembled in front of the courthouse. A local minister "addressed them in a most impressive manner," and the women presented each soldier with a New Testament. Thus spiritually fortified and blessed, the young recruits marched toward the depot singing "Dixie," with a great crowd following them. Reaching the waiting train, they were allowed to break ranks "to say last words to weeping mothers and sisters and perhaps sweethearts." Flowers, bouquets of them, were pressed upon these sons, brothers, and sweethearts, and frequently there was "a tear in their eye." Then they were on the train, and with the sound of the whistle, they were off to Virginia for battles whose horrors they could not imagine. "Poor fellows," wrote Mary Robarts, as she thought of them going off to war.[2]

The Marietta troop was soon joined by companies raised in Rome, who had been sent on their way with "a solemn, affecting, and eloquent" sermon preached by John Jones. Standing among the Rome recruits to hear the sermon was Dunwody Jones, who had spent so many happy days at Maybank and Montevideo. As a lanky nineteen-year-old, Dunwody was a long way from maturity—indeed he was a young man whose parents continued to hover around their "wayward boy." Shortly after he left for Virginia, John and Jane Jones anxiously followed him to Richmond so that they could be close to their boy if he needed them. They arrived in the Confederate capital two days before the raw recruits, North and South, clashed near a rail junction named Manassas and around a sluggish little river about twenty miles south of Washington named Bull Run.[3]

The Confederate victory at Manassas—or Bull Run, as the Yankees called it—caused a great celebration throughout the South. In Savannah, Charlie thought that "surely the Lord of Hosts is with us," and everywhere across the South many believed the victory meant that Southern independence had been won. But there was a growing recognition that the victory had been won at a great price. "Our hearts are filled with gratitude to God for our victory over our enemies," wrote Mary from Maybank, "and at the same time we weep at the costly sacrifice." And John wrote from Richmond of the cries of the wounded, of the dreadful stench from the battlefield, and of his own desperate search for Dunwody among the dead and the wounded and "in a wilderness of camps and tents and soldiers," until finally "I found our boy and ran and threw my arms around his neck and kissed him as one lost and dead suddenly found again."[4]

During the coming months and bitter years, as other greater and more costly battles would be fought, hopes would rise among the Joneses and their friends when Southern armies defeated Yankee foes; but hopes would fall with Southern defeats, and despair would grow as a rising tide of blood and destruction threatened to overwhelm a southern homeland and southern home. A year and a half after Manassas, Charles wrote: "I can only repeat our daily prayer that God would take our cause into His own almighty hand, and humble us for our sins and judge between us and our enemy."[5]

In the meantime, with white troops boarding trains for Virginia and other battlefronts, the immediate concern to the master and mistress of Maybank and Montevideo was the defense of the Georgia coast. The Sea Islands and river plantations seemed easy prey to Yankee warships, which could shell the islands, and to Yankee gunboats, which could make quick raids up dark rivers. And Charles and Mary wondered not only about Yankees but also about the black men and women who lived in the settlements. These Gullahs knew how to follow secret trails through woods and deep swamps when the moon had sunk from sight. And they knew how to float a bateau on an ebb tide and move like a shadow without sound along winding creeks of the marsh to open water, deserted islands, and freedom. From long experience, Charles and Mary knew that the people of the settlements would be watching, listening, and whispering in the night. What were they saying about the war as they sat around their evening fires staring into the flames? Were they plotting how to make a break for freedom? Would they abandon their owners and even their own families and friends and go over to an unknown but seductive enemy? These were questions that troubled Charles and Mary as they prepared in the late fall of 1861 to leave Maybank for Montevideo, for they were questions about commitment, loyalty, and trust. They were at their heart questions about Charles and Mary's pleasant life by the North Newport and the Medway marshes. Had it really been built upon shared trust and mutual obligations of responsible masters and faithful servants? Or had they somehow dreadfully deceived themselves? Had their life together—with their daily commitments and routines and their feelings of immeasurable responsibility and duty to their slaves—had all this been nothing more than an illusion, a mere façade that hid the raw power of whites that kept Charles and Mary comfortably situated in the plantation house at Montevideo and kept Cato and Porter and Patience and all the others in the slave cabins at Carlawter?[6]

The move from Maybank to Montevideo in the fall of 1861 did not follow the familiar pattern of earlier moves. To be sure, after the first frost Gilbert and Charles brought their creaking oxcarts to the door of Maybank as they had in earlier years. But this year there was more, much more, to carry down the high steps and load in the carts. And this year the November move was but the first of many a long trek to Montevideo and back to Maybank. During the coming months dining room table and chairs, sofas and carpets, bureaus and desks, medicines and food, dishes, pots, and pans, the mirror stove brought from Philadelphia, and all the contents of the island home were systematically removed to Montevideo for safekeeping. As news of the war made its way to Liberty County, Charles and Mary seemed to know intuitively that their summer home, with all of its cherished memories, would no longer be theirs. Patience would be serving no more tea on the Maybank piazza. Niger would be bringing no more shrimp and crabs and oysters up from the creeks. And there would be no more visiting with friends as the light lingered over the marsh and the wind brought the sound and fragrance of a low-country night.[7]

In February 1862 Charles wrote in his journal: "Rode with M. to Maybank. House much dismantled: things moved up [to] M. video." Only Old Andrew and Mary Ann, together with a daughter Delia and grandchildren, remained at the settlement. Everyone else had been removed to Montevideo, but there was much that held Andrew and Mary Ann to their home by the marsh, where they had lived for so many years. Near their cabin under the surrounding oaks and palmettos was the recent grave of their daughter Dinah. Two years after her husband Abram Scriven had been sold off the island, she had married James, a man from Palmyra plantation across the marsh from Maybank. (James's first wife had been sent away to work on the railroad, and it was said that there was no chance she would ever be returned to her husband.) The new couple had had only a few months of married life together before Dinah had died of typhoid fever. She had been buried in her sandy grave near the Maybank settlement, and when her parents and her sister and children were finally removed in late 1862, only yucca and wild myrtle would remain as her memorial. Everything, Charles wrote of Maybank, was "moved away and house locked up and left so."[8]

Those who went off to defend the cause of the Confederacy were not only white volunteers but also black slaves who were requisitioned to do much of the hard labor of building defenses for Southern armies and cities. In March 1862 Charles received from the military authorities in Savannah a requisition for able-bodied men to work on the river defenses of the city. Charles selected July and Sam, sons of his old nurse Rosetta and her husband, Sam; Little Adam, who was Cato's brother and the youngest child of Old Lizzy; Young Pulaski (named after the old driver at the Retreat) and his brother Wally, "a faithful young servant man"; and Joe and Tyrone, two strong young field hands. Charles made July the foreman of the company and sent them all to Savannah on the train.[9]

Never before had Charles sent anyone from the settlements to do such work or to labor in another planter's rice or cotton fields. To be sure, Phoebe had worked for Julia King as a seamstress when Charles and Mary had been away in Columbia, and the plantation carpenters had helped to build barns and houses on other plantations, but it had all been under the close supervision of well-known white neighbors. Charles felt too much his own responsibility for those whom he owned and he worried too much about the treatment they might receive from unscrupulous overseers to rent out any of "his people" for field labor or work on the railroads. But now under the pressure of war, he sent these men to do the wretched work of building earthen defenses on the muddy banks of the Savannah. The results were disastrous.[10]

Within weeks they were all back, and all but Pulaski were dangerously ill. River cholera had struck, with its cramps, vomiting, and violent diarrhea. Wally died first. Then Joe. And finally Tyrone. But to make matters worse, they apparently brought back with them a deadly form of measles. Before the epidemic was over, the measles had killed nine in Carlawter, including Patience and Porter's daughter Beck. She had been brought to the washhouse that had been made into a little hospital behind Montevideo. There the plantation doctor tried to

Old Quarterman, born in slavery in Liberty County (Margaret Davis
Cate Collection, courtesy Georgia Historical Society, Savannah, Ga.)

stop the ravages of the disease, and Patience served as her nurse. Perhaps as Beck
struggled against her fever and the pneumonia that followed the measles, she
remembered the tender letters from Ben Lowe, who had promised to love her
"until life leaves." Their marriage had been short—three Christmases were all
the time they had had together—and now Ben would never have a chance to
know his infant son, who died beside his mother.[11]

Joe, who was stationed with the Liberty County Independent Troop at Sunbury, had set up his surgery in one of the old homes in the little village. With limited military responsibilities, he was using all his skills as a physician that spring
of 1862 to tend the sick at Carlawter and at other places around the county. In
late April he was at Arcadia seeing after the sick in its settlement when word came
that two Yankee gunboats were off Colonel's Island. They appeared to be threat-

ening Woodville and Social Bluff. Joe raced to Montevideo to spread the alarm. While his mother packed some rations for him, Joe took out his grandfather's double-barreled shotgun—the old silver-mounted one that his grandfather John Jones had carried with him on his fateful ride in 1805. With this relic of long-forgotten hunts, Joe rode off to the island to fight the Yankees. To his disappointment, he had no chance to send buckshot their way. But the Yankee gunboats did not appear to be intimidated by Joe and his silver-mounted shotgun or by the other rebels who rushed to defend the island. Rather, they steamed steadily up the river and were stopped only by an ebbing tide. They did no harm to the estates along the river, but a crew loading cotton at a wharf scuttled their little ship, and on the threatened plantations there was a great rushing to and fro to escape a possible shelling. Nowhere was the rushing more vigorous or orderly than at Montevideo. Charles and Mary, seeking to protect their most precious possessions, sent a steady stream of mules with loaded wagons and oxen with wobbling carts to Arcadia, whose location some distance from the river seemed more secure. The Yankee gunboats, however, soon turned around, went downstream, exchanged a few shots with the rebels on Half Moon Bluff, and then steamed off to more serious business.[12]

When the excitement had died down, Charles wrote Charlie a long letter giving all the details. Charlie, after completing his term as mayor, had enlisted in the Chatham Artillery and was serving as its first lieutenant. He was busy learning all that he could about artillery, a complicated science far removed from the study of Latin or law. But Charlie was bright and inquisitive, and he was fast becoming an accomplished artillery officer—in a few months he would be promoted to lieutenant colonel of artillery and assigned to duty as chief of artillery for the military district of Georgia, with headquarters in Savannah. When Charlie received his father's letter and learned of the gunboats on the North Newport and of his brother's rush to defend the homeland with the old shotgun, he was amused. And he wished that a section of his artillery battery had been at Half Moon to treat "the Lincolnites to a dose of shell and canister." Charles, on his part, now greatly relieved with the disappearance of the gunboats, wrote Charlie: "I think when peace comes we must have the Chatham Artillery—officers, at least, at Montevideo on a picnic."[13]

The arrival of the Yankees off the coast of Liberty County had been noted not only in the plantation houses, of course, but also in the slave settlements. And there the reaction was more ambiguous and mixed. The Yankees, after all, were also white, and generations of Gullah wisdom had taught that all whites were dangerous, that none could be trusted, and caution and care were imperative when dealing with whites. Moreover, masters and mistresses had done everything they could to impress upon their slaves that Yankees were their enemies too, that Yankees promised one thing and delivered something quite different. So many in the settlements were afraid of the Yankees and their marauding. Most were inclined, for the time being at least, to follow the old Gullah tale—to act "Jes like the tarpins or turtles: jes stick our heads out to see how the land lay." But some were bolder, and when they looked around them and saw white masters and mistresses fleeing the Yankees, they saw a chance for a longed-for freedom.[14]

Those who made their plans for escape knew that the old, well-established slave community of Liberty County—so long in the building—was already being violently broken apart. Ironically, the movement of slaves to southwest Georgia and points west had loosened one of the most powerful forces that might have kept some slaves from running away. A sense of belonging to a tightly knit community composed of husbands and wives, aunts and uncles, parents and grandparents, and friends from youth had been dramatically weakened during the preceding decade. When ties of family and friendship were broken by the removals, the ties with a home place—so long under attack—were weakened even more and the magnetic pull of freedom was strengthened. So it was not simply the nearness of Federal forces, nor the longing for freedom, nor an accumulation of rage that encouraged some to make a break for freedom. All of these factors were no doubt important in whispered plans and no doubt played their role as sources that led to flight. But surely there was also a deep sense that many of the ties that had bound a Gullah community together had already been broken and that something new was on the horizon.

The lines of secret communication between the settlements now began to hum. What was the best way to make a break for freedom? What should one take from storehouses and barns for the flight? What hidden trails were safest to follow through the woods and swamps? What boats were easily taken or could be found concealed in swamp or marsh? What island offered the best hopes of freedom?

A few weeks after the gunboats stirred the waters up and down the North Newport, Charles wrote his Aunt Eliza Robarts in Marietta: "Some Negroes (not many) have run away and gone to the enemy, or on the deserted sea islands. How extensive the matter may become remains to be seen. The temptation of change, the promise of freedom and of pay for labor, is more than most can stand; and no reliance can be placed *certainly* upon any."[15]

But already others were planning their escape. Five days after writing his aunt, Charles wrote Charlie with alarming news: "*Fifty-one* have already gone from this county. Your Uncle John has lost five. *Three* are said to have left from your Aunt Susan's and Cousin Laura's; one was captured, two not; and one of these was *Joefinny!*" The flight of Joefinny was particularly distressing because he was a trusted personal servant who had worked for years at Social Bluff, serving tea on its piazza and seeing after the orderly management of the household servants. He had been a frequent visitor to Maybank and Montevideo and was married to Flora, Patience's apprentice. Charles had even performed their wedding in the chapel at Montevideo and had made arrangements for him to have a kind of honeymoon with Flora by remaining at Montevideo for several months after the wedding. Clearly a privileged slave, he had been watching for his chance to run.[16]

When Charles and Mary had closed down Maybank, Sister Susan, with Laura and David Buttolph and their children, had evacuated Social Bluff and had temporarily moved to a rented house in Dorchester. There Joefinny plotted his escape. He drew into his plans two of his brothers who were working at Lambert plus a young nephew who had been named after Cato. They tried to get their brother-in-law, Young Andrew—the son of Old Andrew and Mary Ann—to join in their scheme, which was a mistake. He appeared horrified by such an idea and reported on them, but he was careful not to do so until they had made their break for freedom. The two youngest were caught and immediately taken to Savannah and shipped to the up-country of Georgia to be rented for fifteen dollars a month doing hard labor. But Joefinny and his brother Isaac made good their escape to Colonel's Island, where they had an intimate knowledge of the woods and ridges, the isolated hammocks and surrounding marshes. From his hiding place, Joefinny apparently stayed in touch with Flora. "I would keep an eye on Flora," warned Laura. "She might go too."[17]

David Buttolph, as the pastor of Midway, was perplexed and mortified that a faithful servant had chosen to hide in the woods as a free man rather than remain under the kind care of a paternalistic master. He wrote to John Jones, now back in Rome, that Joefinny's

> leaving was the hardest blow which could be given. I do not remember that I ever gave him a cross word. Indeed, I never had any occasion to do it, for he was a most faithful and willing servant. If he wanted anything, he had only to ask for it. I have felt deeply hurt and mortified at Joe's leaving, more so than if the whole plantation had left.[18]

Charles, for his part, felt no mortification but only anger at such a betrayal. He wrote Charlie that he thought those caught must be turned "over to the proper authorities to be tried and dealt with as the public welfare may require." He was determined that "some example must be made of this matter. They are traitors who may pilot an enemy into your *bedchamber!* They know every road and swamp and creek and plantation in the country, and are the worst of spies." So

Charles moved quickly from thinking that runaways were naïve persons yielding to the temptations of Yankee freedom to believing them traitors who were
betraying a land and a people to whom they owed loyalty. Moreover, they were
traitors who might lead the enemy during the night into the very bedchambers of
their white masters and mistresses, there to commit some heinous crime. And so
some example must be made of these traitors—and soon the example was made,
as ringleaders of plots and escapes began to be hanged in Hinesville, and others
who were caught were whipped and sent off to hard labor.[19]

As tensions grew on the coast, Charles and Mary began to consider a removal
of the people from the settlements to a more secure location. As early as November 1861, Charles had written, "We are thinking of removing a part of our people
up the country."[20] By the end of the summer of 1862, Charles and Mary, together
with their children, were clear that such a move was necessary. Charlie began
an intense search during short leaves of absence from his military duties. After
investigating a number of possibilities, he settled on a fourteen hundred–acre
plantation in Burke County in middle Georgia. Charlie thought it "without exception the best place" he had seen, with fine forests, fertile fields, and a good
location on Buckhead Creek, a broad stream that would provide a steady supply
of water. He named the place Indianola.[21]

In this way preparations began for the removal of people from Carlawter and
the settlement at Arcadia. They had, of course, been moved around before at the
whim of whites. But those moves had been within the circle of a familiar Liberty
County community. This move involved a radical relocation to middle Georgia. Charles had no illusions about its implications, for he had already written
Charlie before Indianola had been purchased that he considered "the removal
pretty much a permanent one, for by the time the war is ended the people will
be so well fixed wherever they go that it will be a losing business to break them
up again. And the places in this county, if retained, will have to be worked by
small forces until increase comes to our aid."[22]

With an increasing sense of urgency—Lincoln had already declared his intention to emancipate the slaves in the rebelling states—decisions began to be
made about who would be sent and who would stay. Because they thought of
themselves as kind and benevolent owners, the Joneses did not want to divide
any families. Charles, after all, had preached and written against such divisions
for years. But that policy was now easier said than done. It had been one thing to
move people from Montevideo to Arcadia. Husbands could still visit their "wife
house" on Saturday nights. But shipping people from Liberty County to middle
Georgia was another thing, especially since many of those who lived at Carlawter

or Arcadia were married to people on other plantations. What were Charles and Mary to do with Clarissa? She had already had her mother, Phoebe, sold away. Now she was faced with being separated from her husband, Patrick, who lived at a nearby plantation. Or what about Martha, whose husband, Peter, lived at one of the Fleming plantations? Was she to be sent far from him? Was Peggy, with her little girl Eva Lee, to be separated from Henry, whom she had so recently married and who belonged to a neighboring planter? Or what about Cato's brother Lymus, whose wife of many years lived at the Chapman place? Or Cato's brother Daniel, whose wife lived at South Hampton? Or Elsey, whose carpenter husband, Syphax, lived at Lambert? Or Patience and Porter's daughter Miley, whose husband lived at old Liberty Hall? And what about those who had a husband or wife who belonged to Sister Susan and Laura and David Buttolph—the carpenter William Pitt, Little Andrew, Little Titus, and Betty? What was to be done with all of these people and these families for whom the Joneses believed they had responsibility? Hasty negotiations began to be made to try to keep families together. Sister Susan allowed Tom to go with Betty and his family, but she said she would not send Syphax to Indianola with Elsey if she were sent, since his skills as a carpenter were needed, and besides he was not well. And Susan agreed to rent William Pitts's wife to Charles so that his family could be kept together. But all of these negotiations were complicated by the plans to empty the settlements at Lambert and White Oak by moving Susan's and the Buttolphs' slaves to a plantation in south Georgia, and by other settlements' being desolated by deportations. So of the twenty-one Jones slaves who faced separation of families, only a few—generally through their own pleading—were able to take a spouse from another plantation with them to Indianola.[23]

It was decided that of the 129 Jones slaves, 71 would go to Indianola. Stepney, the driver at Arcadia and Patience's brother, was selected to be the driver at the new plantation—a source of great sorrow for his father, Daddy Robin, who remained with only a handful of others at Arcadia. Cato was kept at Carlawter with a small work force—only 11 full hands to keep the plantation going. Old Tony remained and continued to look after the gardens at Montevideo, and Rosetta kept an eye on the few children who were still in the settlement, and Gilbert was kept to drive the carriage and help around the house. And of course Patience remained with her young children, although Porter was sent to Indianola for a few months to help build new slave cabins. Old Andrew and Mary Ann, together with their daughters and grandchildren, were sent to John Jones's Bonaventure to boil the briny water of the Medway River to make salt. There they found Bonaventure largely deserted, since John had carried most of his slaves to his plantation in southwest Georgia. They did find Mom Sylvia there, she having been moved in her old age from the Retreat, where she had raised John Jones and his sister Mary. She was lonely and angry with John for sending her children and grandchildren to southwest Georgia and leaving her in Liberty. He told her that she would be more comfortable at Bonaventure than in the new plantation in a rough, recently settled area, but she continued to complain until John made arrangements for his Old Momma to join her family.[24]

Once Charles and Mary had completed their calculations—who was going to Indianola and who was staying—and the negotiations were completed with other owners, the logistics of the move began to be addressed. Those who were selected to go began to sell most of their pigs and cows and other livestock they could not easily take with them. Four boxcars were ordered for the people and their possessions, and all those being removed were brought to the Arcadia settlement. There on 18 November 1862 they gathered for their last worship service with their master, whom whites had for some years been calling the "Apostle to the Negro Slave." After the service, they moved down the Arcadia avenue in a great procession of people, baggage, and remaining livestock, turned right at the road, and went to the rail station, which was a few miles distant. Arriving at the station, they found the cars waiting for them. They loaded their baggage, their reluctant livestock, their children, and themselves into the cars, and when they were all in, there was little room left. With the sound of the whistle, those who had lived all their lives in Liberty County were on their way to a cotton plantation in middle Georgia.[25]

That evening Charles wrote in his journal a brief description of the day's events. "The people," he wrote, had gone to the new plantation "for quiet and safety from the enemy's raids upon the coast. They all went cheerfully—a few leaving husbands and wives for the present, until matters become more settled." Believing that he had acted responsibly, he wrote: "This removal involving great expense we have undertaken from a conviction of duty and with much pain at the separation from the people and pray God's blessing and that it may issue in his glory and our good."[26]

A few days later, Charles and Mary rode over to White Oak "to see sister's people and tell them goodbye." The people of the settlement, and all but a few at Lambert, were preparing to leave the next day for southwest Georgia. As Charles and Mary moved among them saying their goodbyes, they saw the descendants of Old Jupiter, who had blown the conch-shell horn for Charles's father at Liberty Hall, and of his wife, Blind Silvey—their grandchildren, great-grandchildren, and great-great-grandchildren. There was Prince, who had followed his father, his uncle, and his grandfather as driver. His wife, Venus, had died shortly after the breakup of the Retreat settlement, when she had been carried to north Georgia to be sold. And there was Peggy, who had a family by Cassius and who had, years earlier, been so jealous of Phoebe that she had reported her theft of keys. And there were others—but no Joefinny, nor his brother Isaac, who had made their break for freedom. Around them all, many memories must have swirled for Charles and Mary, for with these men, women, and children much of their lives had been lived.[27]

These Gullah people who were being shipped from Montevideo and Arcadia, from White Oak and Lambert, and from the surrounding plantations to distant places were part of families who had lived in Liberty for generations. They were the ones who had built the dikes and plowed the fields, cooked the meals, and fished the rivers and marshes. They had driven oxcarts and carriages, had walked the land and winnowed the rice and carried the cotton. They knew Liberty County like few if any of the whites. They had been born here, they had courted and married here, they had struggled here to keep their families together, they had walked the sandy roads on Saturday nights, and they had buried their loved ones here. Yet most did not weep when they were taken from this land that they and their ancestors knew so well. They did struggle to keep their families together, and they used all the resources of the weak to persuade the whites that it was the right thing to do to keep them together. But when they went together, they went cheerfully as if some new thing was in the air, a long-expected liberation that they had prayed for and hoped for. To be sure, there were anxieties, because the separations were real and the cotton plantations toward which they traveled hardly seemed like the Promised Land.[28]

But the power of white owners was clearly being challenged as never before. Those who went off to interior counties knew that the Federal fleet was off the coast and that raiders had come up the dark rivers. And they knew that some of their own had made their breaks for freedom, some paying for it with their lives, but others having reached safety on the other side. Even the proud and pious claims that had been used to justify slavery—that whites were kind and benevolent owners who regarded their people as part of their households—were being exposed as mere bombast and fraud as the settlements were emptied and the train whistles sounded. So those who were sent on their way went cheerfully, for they sensed that they were on the road to something different from the slavery they had known in Liberty County. What they didn't know was how long the road was going to be.[29]

On the November day when the people were shipped to Indianola, Charles acknowledged to himself: "My weakness is becoming so great that I cannot longer look after the temporal affairs of the family as formerly." His creeping palsy was now moving rapidly toward its victory. As Charles felt his body giving up its remaining strength, he knew that he was fast approaching the dark valley. He had been able to resist the ravages of his disease for a remarkable period of time. His long walks, his concern about his diet, his horseback riding when the walks became too much, and his happy home life by the river and the marsh—all of this had no doubt contributed to his resistance and perhaps added to his years. But now in late 1862 and the early months of 1863, he saw his low-country world breaking apart, and he sensed that all the Confederate solders and all the sacrifices of brave men and women could not bring back a vanishing world. Everywhere he looked, he saw abandoned plantations and felt the absence of families who had made the Midway congregation and Liberty County such a distinguished community. Charles was not sentimental—he was too much a Calvinist for that—but the breakup of his world seemed to be hastening the final collapse of his body.[30]

Joe came to give him what medical attention he could in the midst of his military responsibilities. And Charlie managed to come out for a visit, and later wrote his father from Savannah: "I am very much pained, my dear father, to hear that you are still so weak. All I can do is to hope and pray that you may soon be better, and that it would please God in tender mercy to us all to prolong your days, so precious to us all."[31] But such was not to be the case.

Charles and Mary had spent the summer of 1862 in Walthourville with Mary Sharpe and Robert, but after the first frost they had moved to Arcadia. There Charles had settled in for his last days. His books had been brought from Montevideo, and he had a pleasant library on the west side of the house, where he enjoyed studying surrounded by the authors he loved. The library had a fireplace, and he would sit reading in a rocker before it. When an early spring came in March, the windows were opened and he could hear a mockingbird singing from morning until night, and sometimes even in the night. And he could feel and smell the delights of a low-country spring that he loved, and he had Mary close by him and Sister Susan too. But he wrote in his journal: "My disease appears to be drawing to its conclusion! May the Lord make me in that hour to say in saving faith and love: 'Into thine hand I commit my spirit: thou hast redeemed me, O Lord God of truth' (Psalm 31:5). So has our Blessed Saviour taught us by His own example to do; and blessed are they who die in the Lord."[32]

Early on the morning of 16 March, as the sky began to grow pale in the east, Charles rose, carefully dressed himself in black with a "pure white cravat," and went downstairs. Patience had prepared breakfast, which he ate with Mary and Susan. Then he went for a short walk on the front lawn, but returned greatly fatigued. After lunch, he sat in the study with his wife and sister. They realized that he was dying. Mary began the ritual of guiding him through the lonesome valley. She repeated some of the promises of the Savior "that He would be present with those who trust in Him, even when called to pass through the dark valley of the shadow of death." Charles responded: "In health we repeat these promises, but now they are realities." Mary said: "I feel assured the Saviour is present with you." Charles answered: "Yes. I am nothing but a poor sinner. I renounce myself and all self-justification, trusting only in the free and unmerited righteousness of the Lord Jesus Christ." Charles believed that death would bring not oblivion but an encounter with the Holy One, the Creator of the heavens and the earth, the God of Israel before whom there could be no pretense, no self-deception, but only truth. Yet as he felt this moment approaching, he felt no terror, for he put his trust in Jesus Christ, the one whom he had loved and sought to serve. Charles believed in the depth of his being that Christ was his Savior, and he believed that this Righteous One would stand for him, in Charles's place, before God's judgment seat. This was Charles's hope as he saw death standing at the door looking at him—that when death finally came in and ushered him before the High and Holy One, God would see not Charles the poor sinner but Jesus, who was without spot or blemish.[33]

Mary and Susan helped Charles upstairs to his bedroom. There, as he lay on his bed fully dressed, with Mary and Susan beside him, death came into the room for him. That night Mary wrote in her journal:

> His death, it was not death, it was gently going away, passing into the heavenly light. The inexpressible peace which marked his whole countenance as he breathed his last seemed to say "My beloved is mine and I am His forever!" There were no death sounds; no contortions of muscles or limb or cries from the Monster's sting; no lingering shivering on the brink, no fearful passage through the dark valley, no shadow of death.[34]

His funeral was held at old Midway "in the presence of a large concourse of citizens and of Negroes." Charles's body lay before the pulpit in a coffin built by Porter. A grieving David Buttolph preached. God's sovereignty, David said, means that God is working God's purposes out in human history. "There can be no refuge, no solace, no comfort in such a bereavement as this, if we do not find them in the assurance that God rules in the Kingdom of Providence, and that He will make all things work together for good to them who love God, who are called according to his purpose."[35]

32

THE REFUGE

Three months after Charles's death, Robert Mallard wrote in his journal: "I have this day written to Atlanta accepting a call to the Central Presbyterian Church of that city." The call was to be the pastor of a large and influential congregation in Georgia's rapidly growing metropolis, and there could be no doubt of the importance of such a pastorate. But the call, however important or whatever its promise for usefulness, was also a call for Robert and Mary Sharpe to move with their children away from Liberty County, away from Montevideo and the old Mallard Place, and away from a grieving Mary.[1]

With Mary Sharpe and Robert making plans to move away with the children, Mary was undecided about where she was to stay and what she was to do during the summer of 1863. She still had responsibility for Charlie's daughter Mary Ruth—"my dear little baby," Mary called her, for she had come to think of the motherless child as her own, a gift given her in the midst of deep sorrow and the turmoil of war. She knew that she had to find "some resting place for my dear little baby and self during the summer," and she trusted that the Lord would provide and lead her in the way that she should go. But she clearly missed Charles. It had been their custom to talk through important decisions and to pray together and seek divine guidance before deciding on what course to follow. Now that the "great separation day" had come and Charles was no longer there, she had to decide by herself. "For thirty-two years," she wrote Charlie, "I have had a strong arm to lean upon—a wise head to guide, a heart all love and tenderness to bless and make me happy." Now her constant prayer was that she "not be permitted to murmur or repine, and that what of life remains to me here may be spent in the discharge of duty, in the love and service of my God and Saviour, and in preparation for the solemn hour of death." So Mary prepared to do her duty as she had so often sought to do in the past, only this time she faced her duty with the loneliness of a widow.[2]

Charlie in his Confederate uniform (courtesy Hargrett Rare Book and
Manuscript Library, University of Georgia)

Fortunately for Mary, the ecclesiastical machinery of the Presbyterian Church
moved slowly, and it was the end of summer before Robert's presbytery met to
approve his call to Atlanta. In the meantime, with the season of miasmas and
fevers approaching, Mary gladly accepted the invitation to spend the summer in
Walthourville with Mary Sharpe and Robert. There she threw herself into long
days of work and worry, as supplies became increasingly short and the needs of
the people at Montevideo, Arcadia, and Indianola pressed heavily upon her. But
in the evenings, when she had retired to her room alone, she poured out her grief
in her journal, and she read and reread the letters of condolence that had been
sent to her. Her brothers, who called Charles "brother," wrote long, loving letters. John had written of Charles: "I loved him more than any man on earth; he
came very near to my own father. I know that I have lost my best male friend—
my ever kind faithful brother, on whom I have leaned with filial confidence from
early youth to the present time." Henry Hart had written in a similar vein, and

Joe in his Confederate uniform (Joseph Jones Collection,
Tulane University Manuscript Department)

George Howe too, as Charles's closest ministerial friend. But perhaps the most
unusual of all the letters Mary received was one addressed to John from Joseph
Williams, a free black preacher in Athens. He wrote that he had seen in a paper
an announcement of "the death of my dear old worthy friend Dr. C. C. Jones."
"I have known the Dr. for thirty odd years," wrote the black preacher, "but I shall
see him no more untill we meet in the final assemaly there I hope to see mis
mary not as his widow but as the sister of Christ."[3]

While Mary was spending the summer with Mary Sharpe and Robert, Joe and
Charlie were in the midst of the war. The previous fall Joe had received an ap-
pointment as a surgeon in the Confederate Army with the rank of major. And to
his great surprise and delight, the surgeon general of the Confederacy assigned
him to investigate the diseases that were rampant in the country's hospitals and
prisons. Professionally, it was an important assignment, but he quickly learned
that war was not glorious but horrifying. "We know but little of war," he wrote,
"when we view it from the battle field covered with glory, and rendered attractive
by deeds of valor." Rather, the true nature of war could be seen in the hospitals,
where the "victories of disease exceed ten fold those of the sword." Joe quickly
encountered traumatic tetanus, typhoid, and pneumonia among the wounded,

The Reverend John Jones (courtesy Hargrett Rare Book and
Manuscript Library, University of Georgia)

and above all he found the wounded suffering with a gangrene that ate away
their flesh. Using the observational skills he had first learned in the little museum at Maybank, he meticulously recorded his exposure to the horror of rotting
flesh: "When I plunged my lancet into this elevated purplish and greenish putrid-
looking mass, it encountered no resistance; the integuments and tissues appeared
to be completely dissolved, and a dark greenish and purplish, horribly offensive
matter, mixed with numerous bubbles of air, poured out in large quantity."

Later in the war, he went to Andersonville, the infamous Confederate prison
in south Georgia where ten thousand Union solders died during the first seven
months of its establishment. There Joe found Dunwody serving as a guard among
the wretched, having secured, through the efforts of his father, John Jones, what
he had hoped was a less dangerous assignment than the battlefields of Virginia.
Joe was moved deeply at Andersonville by the suffering of the prisoners, who
were dying like flies. In the filth of the crowded stockade, they had little chance
in the south Georgia heat to escape from deadly attacks of diarrhea, dysentery,
scurvy, and gangrene. Joe threw himself into his investigations, and for days in an
unventilated room he performed "*post-mortem* examinations of the thoroughly
poisoned and rapidly decomposing bodies" of Union soldiers. When Joe finally
left the hellhole, he sent meticulous reports to the surgeon general in hopes that

Dunwody Jones (courtesy Hargrett Rare Book and
Manuscript Library, University of Georgia)

there might be some relief from the suffering. But none came until Union troops
swept through Georgia, and then Joe's reports would come back to haunt him.
As for Dunwody, he later tried to explain what had happened at the stockade he
had guarded: "Andersonville was no worse than northern prisons. There was suffering at Andersonville; there was also suffering at Johnson's Island; there were
hardships in all prisons." But Joe, as long as he lived, would remember how

> the haggard, distressed countenance of these miserable, complaining, dejected
> living skeletons crying for medicine and food, and cursing their government
> for its brutality in refusing to exchange prisoners, and the ghastly corpses with
> their glazed eyeballs, staring up into vacant space, with the flies swarming down
> their open and grinning mouths, and amongst the sick and dying formed a pic-
> ture of helpless, hopeless misery which it would be impossible to portray by
> words or by the brush.[4]

Charlie on his part was busy with the defense of the coast, dashing here and
there trying to check on the readiness of widely scattered forces. In late August
1863 he was ordered to South Carolina to take command of light artillery and
to resist any attack that might come to the islands south of Charleston. He had
six batteries of four guns each under his command and about six hundred men

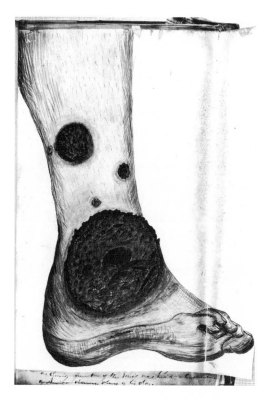

Sketch by Joe of gangrenous foot (Joseph Jones Collection,
Tulane University Manuscript Department)

ready to move quickly to any place threatened by enemy forces. The Federals, after throwing the full weight of a sustained naval attack against Charleston and its surrounding forts, were unable to take the city.[5]

By November 1863 Charlie was able to take leave from his command for a few days to go to Augusta and marry a young woman whom he described to his mother as "absolutely attractive in every particular," with a "heart as pure and tender and full of affection as dwells in woman's breast." Eva Berrien Eve was the cousin of Charlie's first wife, Ruth Berrien Whitehead, and Ruth had not been dead long before Eva had begun to show kind attention to Charlie. She had been to school in Pennsylvania and Washington, D.C., had been a seventeen-year-old bridesmaid in Ruth and Charlie's wedding, and moved in the highest social circles in Georgia. Living a "life of cultivated leisure" in Augusta, "indulging her taste for art and books," she—and her mother—had evidently seen in Charlie the grieving widower a most promising prospect for a husband. When Charles had attended the meeting of the Presbyterian General Assembly in Augusta in 1861, a few months after Ruth's death, he had written Charlie that "Mrs. and Miss Eve" had called on him twice, and then the week following he had been invited "to dine at Mrs. Eve's—one I never saw nor knew before! And putting one thing with another, I could not divine the intent of these attentions." The intent of the attentions, as Charles had known only too well, was not the father but the son. At any rate, two years after Ruth's death, Charlie was speaking of "my dear Eva." He had little resistance to her charms, for although he had been through deep waters and much sorrow, her flirting and fawning appealed to him.[6]

Eva was ten years younger than Charlie, and she was a "southern belle" of the most saccharine type. Shortly after their marriage, she wrote Mary Sharpe a silly letter—that of an educated but immature young woman. She had received, she wrote, letters from her brother Edgeworth:

> happy gleesome letters, written in the offhand nonchalant spirit of a gay boy cavalier. I wish you knew "our Edge"—the merriest young captain in Virginia, and you see I *don't* think you are such a "sober old lady"—fie, my new sister and my *only* one—as you suppose—you are Charlie's sister and I feel as though I know you—and if my pen grows jubilant and runs off into dives small extravagancies which it sometimes *will* do, when I am trying to look as grave and proper as Charlie does *himself* when he puts on his "company manners"— why, at least kindly remember I am not responsible for such a wayward pen![7]

Mary Sharpe left no indication of what she thought of such a letter, written as it was in the middle of a brutal war. But surely she must have sensed that Charlie's marriage to Eva pointed to a fundamental shift in values for part of the Jones family. Sentimentality and nostalgia would increasingly mark Charlie and Eva's life together, just as a Calvinistic piety had marked the marriage of Charles and Mary. To be sure, Charlie would be responsible and highly disciplined in his work, and Eva would in time leave behind her immature and silly ways. But their sense of duty and the ethical standards that governed their lives would be cut loose from the religious commitments that had been nurtured in Charles and Mary and that had informed their way of seeing the world and their place in it. For Charlie and Eva, such religious commitments would be largely replaced by a comfortable Victorian respectability.[8]

While the war raged and the Jones clan sought to make their way dutifully through these heart-shaking times, the people at Indianola, Arcadia, and Carlawter watched and waited and thought about what was happening around them as they went about their work and their lives.

By the summer of 1863 Cato was essentially running Montevideo by himself with his small workforce. A neighboring planter had been secured as an overseer, but he was old and in poor health, and his supervision was minimal. So Cato was making decisions about what to plant, when to plant, and how much to plant. When Mary rode over occasionally to check on the crops and the people, Cato would faithfully give her his report. But on one visit, when she counted the cattle, she noted that there was "quite a discrepancy" between Cato's account and what Charles had recorded before his death. She instructed him to have the pastures thoroughly searched and all cattle brought up to the cow pen and recounted, but she apparently did not suspect that Cato might have requisitioned some of the cattle for one of his barbeques in the woods.[9]

Stepney, for his part, was making regular trips between Liberty County and the new Jones plantation in Burke County. He had been made the driver for Indianola and sent off with the first group that had left by train in the fall of 1862. When he returned for the first time three months later, his father, Old Robin, "laid his hands upon him and sobbed aloud," having feared that he would never see his son again. But Stepney was learning much about travel and distance that would later serve him well; he was also learning how to negotiate and buy supplies for the people under his care, and that too would later serve him well.[10]

Stepney's sister Patience was busy making Arcadia her new home. She was happy to be with Daddy Robin, and Porter was doing most of his work using Arcadia as a base. She had her cooking to do when Mary was at Arcadia, but when Mary went to Walthourville for the summer of 1863, Patience was left behind to do various domestic chores and to help look after the house at Arcadia. She had lost some of her energy after the death of her daughter Beck and Beck's infant child from the measles, and then several of her adult children had been among those sent to Indianola. Even Patience's long years of faithful service and her careful watch over her children had not been enough to keep her family from being separated when there was a threat of Federal gunboats coming up the North Newport. Patience would have several long bouts of illness during the coming winter—perhaps her losses made her more vulnerable. But both her body and spirit had reserves of strength, and she would soon be up again, ready to face a new day.[11]

In early September 1863, Robert Mallard left Liberty County for Atlanta to assume his duties as the new pastor of Central Presbyterian Church and to make preparations for his family to join him. He quickly became involved not only in the work of his new pastorate but also in work among refugees and the wounded.

He spent long hours seeking shelter and food for those who had fled the fighting, and he went day after day into crowded military hospitals seeking to bring some comfort and hope among those who were terribly wounded or were suffering the ravages of some dreadful disease.[12]

In November, Robert brought Mary Sharpe and the children to Atlanta. Their departure left Mary feeling lonely and depressed, and she was soon writing Mary Sharpe: "I really feel that I can hardly undertake what I have been doing, for my strength and—what is more, I often fear—my nervous system are failing. Oh, my daughter, the desolation of heart which I feel is beyond expression!" To make matters worse for her, Charlie soon came and took Mary Ruth to Savannah for a short visit with him and "Mama Eva." The removal of her "darling baby" was, Mary thought, "the entering wedge" that would lead to Mary Ruth's eventual separation from her, and such thoughts deepened her sadness.[13]

Robert and Mary Sharpe brought with them to Atlanta Charles and Lucy, their daughter Tenah, and Kate, the eighteen-year-old daughter of Elsey and Syphax. With them was Charles's nephew young Abram, whose father, Abram Scriven, had been sold as a part of the Roswell King estate and whose mother, Dinah, lay buried under the oaks and palmettos at Maybank. Tenah's husband, young Niger, would join them later. He had had to give up his fishing, shrimping, and crabbing when the Federals began to threaten Maybank and its settlement. He and Tenah had married at Christmas 1861—over the protests of Mary Sharpe that it was a "most inconvenient arrangement." Six weeks after Tenah arrived in Atlanta in 1863, she gave birth to their child Cinda, and Niger was hired out to an Atlanta tannery.[14]

As they were all learning to find their way around Atlanta, Mary Sharpe wrote her mother of a remarkable encounter by Charles. He had apparently been sent to run some errand in the city when he met his former brother-in-law, Abram Scriven. Mary Sharpe wrote:

> Do tell Daddy Andrew that Charles has seen Abram, poor Dinah's former husband. He was working some miles from this place, and Charles met him once when he came in town. He had not heard of Dinah's death, and said he had never married until pretty recently, for he had always hoped something would turn up and he would be able to go back to Liberty. He sent a great many howdies to Mom Mary Ann and Daddy Andrew.[15]

So Abram learned of Dinah's death, and he remembered the earlier death of their marriage when he had been sold. Charles no doubt told Abram about his children—Harry, Silvia, and Dublin, who were with their grandparents Old Andrew and Mary Ann at Bonaventure. And perhaps Charles told him that his son Little Abram was in Atlanta.

Two weeks after the Mallards and their slaves arrived in Atlanta, the Yankees won a victory at Missionary Ridge outside of Chattanooga, and General William T. Sherman began to make plans for his drive toward Georgia's largest city. During the spring of 1864, Sherman successfully outflanked the Confederate defenses at Dalton, Resaca, Cassville, and Allatoona Pass as he moved steadily toward Atlanta. By early June, Sherman's troops were poised to attack the Confederate defenses at Kennesaw Mountain, at the edge of Marietta. Eliza Robarts, with her daughters and grandchildren, fled south to a relative's plantation in the south central part of the state. On their way they stayed a few days with the Mallards in Atlanta. With them were five domestic servants, including "Daddy Sam." So as the Robartses and Mallards huddled together in Atlanta before the advancing Federal armies, blacks from Liberty County were reunited in the Mallard slave quarters. For a few evenings Sam could sit with his daughter Lucy and his granddaughter Tenah and hold his new great-granddaughter Cinda. And he could ask about Rosetta and how she was bearing up, and about their children and grandchildren who had been sent to Indianola, and about their daughter Fanny, who was married to Gilbert and was still with Rosetta at Montevideo. And no doubt there were some opportunities to talk with hushed voices about the meaning of the war and the rumored promises of freedom for slaves.[16]

On 27 June, Sherman sent several Federal divisions against the entrenched Confederates at Kennesaw. In savage fighting in hundred-degree heat, they were beaten back, but Sherman responded by once again outflanking the Confederates, and soon both sides were preparing for the battle of Atlanta. As anxiety and fear of the approaching battle grew, and as the two armies maneuvered in anticipation of an imminent attack, the Mallards prepared to leave the city. They hastily packed all their belongings for shipment to Augusta. But as they were rushing to the depot, the little cart in which they were riding broke loose and ran up upon the horse. Startled, the horse began to run, violently rocking the cart and throwing the family out upon the street. Robert and the children escaped serious injury, but Mary Sharpe's collarbone was dislocated. Robert drew her shoulder back, which "put the bones in position," and they pressed ahead to the depot. This time when the train whistle blew, the white family was riding with their slaves in a boxcar. Robert opened bedding on the floor of the car and made a pallet for Mary Sharpe and fixed a rocking chair so she could sit down more comfortably. But her pain was intense as the train rocked and lurched toward Augusta.[17]

In the meantime, Mary had left Liberty County and was headed for Atlanta, thinking that she could be of help as the family prepared to leave. With her was Flora, whose husband Joefinny had made his escape early in the war. Arriving in the city, they found the house empty, the family gone, and the city in a panic, so they too joined the exodus of frightened people fleeing the approaching battle. The trip to Augusta was a nightmare for them. Wrecked freight cars on the tracks stopped the train in the middle of nowhere. "My stock of provisions," Mary later wrote, "had been completely exhausted before I left Atlanta. We stopped where not a drop of water could be had. I found a crust of bread in the lunch basket, which was shared with Flora." They had to get out of the train in the middle of the night and walk quite a distance "up embankments and down in ditches" to reach a relief car. Finally, thirty-six hours after they left Atlanta, they reached Augusta, exhausted and hungry. There Mary found that Robert had headed back to Atlanta to stay with the people of his congregation who remained in the city and to work among the wounded until there was an order for a general evacuation. Such was the confusion and the fear as the harsh realities of war drew near.[18]

By the middle of October, Mary and the Mallards were back in Liberty County. Mary had returned to Arcadia, and the Mallards were staying in Walthourville, where they had rented rooms in the old academy so that Mary Sharpe, now seven months pregnant, could be near a doctor. Sister Susan was nearby in the little village of Flemington with Laura and David Buttolph and their children. Julia King and Mary King Wells had moved to Taylor's Creek in the interior of the county, and William Maxwell, grown old and increasingly feeble, was living at his Springfield plantation across the marsh from Maybank. They, with others in Liberty County, awaited with growing fear the arrival of Sherman's army.[19]

Atlanta had fallen, and with its fall had come great destruction—the train depots and sheds, the rolling mills and machine shops, the foundries and the arsenals had all been put to the torch, and going up in the flames with them had been hotels, churches, businesses, and between four thousand and five thousand homes. In nearby Roswell, textile mills and tanneries built by Kings and Dunwodys, by Bullochs and Pratts were burned to the ground—although the elegant homes were saved—and the poor white women who worked in the mills were sent with their children to Marietta, where they were shipped north on trains before the tracks between Atlanta and Chattanooga were torn up and twisted.[20]

With Atlanta in ruins, Sherman plunged into middle Georgia on a brilliant and daring march to the sea. He had with him some sixty thousand men, twenty-four thousand horses, and twenty-five hundred wagons, each pulled by six mules. Allowing his supply lines and all communications with the North to be cut, he moved his great army toward Savannah, declaring that the army would live off the land—and live off the land it did. Foragers were organized and sent out each day to scour the countryside, to ransack plantations and farms, and to bring back with them whatever they could find to feed and support an army. And so the foragers—bummers, they came to be called—went out and came back with horses and cattle, with mules pulling wagons loaded down with corn, peas, and sweet potatoes, with ham, bacon, and barrels of molasses, and with squawking chickens and squealing pigs. And in their wake there went up the smoke of burning barns and rebel houses.[21]

The army left Atlanta on 16 November and rumbled steadily toward the sea. Among the plantations in Sherman's path was Indianola. As the first troops approached on 2 December 1864, the overseer hastily led all from the settlement to a hiding place in a nearby swamp. They took with them two horses—including Stepney's mare—and sixteen mules, hoping to keep them out of the hands of the Yankees. But a young slave betrayed their location, and the raiders came swooping down on their hiding place, forcing them all back to the plantation. Wave after wave of plunderers then passed over the plantation for three long days, and when they finally left they had confiscated not only the horses and mules but ten oxen, seventy-two hogs, three wagons, four thousand bushels of corn, two hundred bushels of rice, and all the potatoes and molasses they could find. They left behind them twenty-five bales of burning cotton and the ashes of the cotton gin and barns. Joe rode out from Augusta for a quick visit to assess the destruction. The Yankees, he said in disgust, were nothing but "degraded wretches." As for those who lived in the settlement, they refused to join the thousands of slaves who were now jubilantly following the liberation army. For the present, Stepney and the others would stay at Indianola and try to support themselves with the provisions that had escaped confiscation. Perhaps they anticipated the way the Yankees would leave the slaves vulnerable to the devastating attacks from Confederate troops attempting to harass Sherman's army from the rear.[22]

By early December, Sherman was near Savannah as he moved his forces along the banks of the Ogeechee in order to make contact with the Federal fleet in Ossabaw Sound. On 10 December the plantation that had been home to Thomas Clay and his sister Eliza went up in flames. Richmond-on-the-Ogeechee had been one of the most beautiful and affluent plantations of the South, and for more than a generation the Clays had sought to make it a center for the enlightened and benevolent management of slaves. Now it too was ashes. Three days later, Yankee foragers were in Liberty County. They would be not a quickly passing storm but a storm that stalled and lingered over the land.[23]

As Sherman's forces drew near, Mary decided that Montevideo was safer than Arcadia.[24] So once again the process began of hastily moving what was regarded as most valuable and what was thought most likely to be taken by those who would come to plunder. On the morning of Tuesday, 13 December, Mary rode from Montevideo to Arcadia to gather a number of household items. Believing that the Yankees were still some distance away, she lingered until late in the afternoon before setting out for Montevideo, with Patience's son Jack driving the carriage. They traveled down a sandy road through thick woods where the limbs of oaks draped with Spanish moss stretched out to mingle with one another and form a canopy that obscured the sky. Suddenly a "Yankee on horseback sprang from the woods and brought his carbine to bear upon Jack, ordering him to halt. Then, lowering the carbine, almost touching the carriage window and pointing into it," he demanded of Mary what she had in the carriage. She replied, "Nothing but my family effects." He asked her where she was going, and she said to her home. "Where is your home?" he asked. "Near the coast." "How far is the coast?" "About ten miles." He then told her that he would not like to harm a lady, but he warned her that more Yankees were just ahead and that they would take her horses and search her carriage. He advised her to turn around immediately and take a different route. She thanked him and ordered Jack to do so. For the next few hours they dodged Yankees as they made their way down little sandy roads in the fading light until they finally arrived at Montevideo.[25]

Later that evening, sometime after ten o'clock, Robert arrived. He was riding a mule, having given his fine horse to his brother Cyrus, who was serving picket duty for the little Confederate force that was in the county. Earlier in the day, Robert had abandoned his clergy position as a noncombatant by taking up a musket at Confederate headquarters. The musket was in Robert's possession for only a few hours before he gave it to a soldier who needed one, but they were hours that cost him dearly. Now at Montevideo he talked with Mary and Mary Sharpe, delaying his departure as long as possible. He read aloud from the eighth chapter of Romans—"Who shall separate us from the love of Christ? Shall tribulation, or distress, or persecution, or famine, or nakedness, or peril, or sword?" He went upstairs and kissed the children, and then after Jack had signaled all was clear, he departed on a trail through the woods.[26]

Late the next afternoon, Charles, who had been in Walthourville with his wife, Lucy, suddenly came into the parlor and burst into tears. He had come walking and sometimes jogging all the way from Walthourville. "Oh," he cried, "very bad news! Master is captured by the Yankees, and says I must tell you keep a good heart." When Yankees had arrived in Walthourville early that morning, they had questioned Robert, and when they learned that he had taken up a gun, if only for a few hours, it was enough to have him arrested and sent to a prison camp by the Ogeechee.[27]

The next morning, while Mary was outside walking on the lawn that ran down toward the river and Mary Sharpe was in the dining room, Elsey came running to say that the Yankees were coming. Three men rode up and dismounted by the stable. They demanded of Mary, "Where are your horses and mules? Bring them out!" Quickly the men ran toward the house, burst in on Mary Sharpe and began shouting for whiskey. Then they began to run through the house, poking into closets, going through drawers, prying open that which did not readily yield to keys, taking what they wanted. Later in the day, more men came. They ran everywhere through the house, cursing and screaming, hoping as had early arrivals to find something of value. When they finally left, they took with them the horses and a mule, but the old mule they soon turned loose, and it made its way back to the stable.[28]

On Friday, 16 December, Prophet the carpenter from South Hampton came to the house and said that Audley King's wife, Kate, was alone and terrified at South Hampton and wanted to come and stay at Montevideo. Audley had taken to the swamps to avoid capture. Armed with two navy revolvers, a huge bowie knife, and a double-barreled shotgun, he would spend the next month dodging Yankees and would use all his skills as a woodsman to help feed refugees as they went streaming south to the Confederate lines on the other side of the Altamaha River. Mary wrote Kate to come immediately to Montevideo. With fear and trembling, Kate came hurrying down the narrow road that led to the Montevideo avenue.[29]

Later that afternoon, there was a sudden great "clash of arms and noise of horsemen," as forty or fifty men came riding into the yard at Montevideo. These were the serious foragers, the bummers, who came to take all that they could find. They stormed into the house, "flying hither and thither, ripping open the safe with their swords and breaking open the crockery cupboards." Mary, as a precaution, had had some chickens and ducks roasted and put in a food safe. "These the men seized whole, tearing them to pieces with their teeth like ravenous beasts." And all the time they were clamoring for whiskey. They yelled, cursed, quarreled, and ran from one room to another in wild confusion. "Such [were] their blasphemous language, their horrible countenances and appearance," Mary Sharpe felt that they were like the damned, "the lost in the world of eternal woe. Their throats were open sepulchers, their mouths filled with cursing and bitterness and lies." They stripped the house of all the food they could find, carrying out bags of meal and flour from the pantry and the attic, loading them into a wagon they had brought with them and a wagon they took from the place. Mary pleaded with them to leave some of the meal and flour for the women and children, but her pleas fell on deaf ears.[30]

Early on Saturday morning, about four o'clock, there was a sound of horses. Mom Sue, who worked in the kitchen, came running upstairs "breathless with dismay" and reported that raiders, after asking her whether there were any young women in the family, had sent her to say that the women were going to be raped. "Oh," Mary later wrote, "the agony—the agony of that awful hour no language can describe! No heart can conceive it. We were alone, friendless, and knew not what might befall us." Mary, Mary Sharpe, and Kate King knelt down around the bed and began praying. And the children, hearing their voices, got up and knelt down beside them. They could hear the sounds of more squads arriving. Finally the women and children rose from their knees and "sat in darkness, waiting for the light of the morning to reveal their purposes, but trusting in God for our deliverance." In the gray twilight of the morning, they looked "out of the window and saw one man pacing before the courtyard gate between the house and the kitchen." Later they learned that "he had voluntarily undertaken to guard the house. In this," wrote Mary, "we felt that our prayers had been signally answered."[31]

During the next week, one raiding party followed another. Smokehouse, corn crib, rice house, all were stripped bare. The carriage was brought out of the carriage house, filled with chickens, and driven away down the Montevideo avenue, followed by wagons loaded with barrels of sugar and molasses. As the raiders left, they shot sheep in the pastures and left them to rot.

Meanwhile, in Savannah the Confederate forces, badly outnumbered, slipped out of the city in order to join up with a Confederate army. Among those leaving was Charlie with his light artillery. On 21 December, Sherman telegraphed Lincoln, presenting "as a Christmas-gift the city of Savannah, with one hundred and fifty heavy guns and plenty of ammunition, also about twenty-five thousand bales of cotton." To the blacks of the city, Sherman appeared as Moses the liberator of slaves. "I'd always thought about this, and wanted this day to come, and prayed for it and knew God meant it should be here sometime," a Savannah slave declared in disbelief, "but I didn't believe I should ever see it, and it is so great and good a thing, I cannot believe it has come now; and I don't believe I ever shall realize it, but I know it has though, and I bless the Lord for it."[32]

The fall of Savannah did not mean, however, the end of the raiding parties plundering Montevideo. Day by day they arrived looking for anything that had been left by earlier bummers.

On 4 January at daylight, Mary Sharpe told her mother that she was going into labor. Mary sent Charles through the woods to get Dr. Raymond Harris. The old man was the father of the late Dr. Stephen Harris who had eloped with Emma Jones years before. The father had bought the Retreat from Henry Hart Jones and was now living at the plantation where Joseph had once ruled the roost and from which he had banished the young couple for disobedience and impertinence. Now in response to Mary's plea, the elder Dr. Harris followed Charles as they slipped quietly through the woods on paths that linked the settlement at the Retreat to Carlawter. He found Mary Sharpe in a most critical condition, and he told Mary that she "must be prepared for the worst." He said that if "he did not succeed in relieving the difficulty, her infant at least must die." Mary responded, "Doctor, the mother first." "Certainly," he replied. And so the old doctor began to do what he could to save Mary Sharpe's life, and if possible to preserve the life of the child. While Mary Sharpe labored in great agony, struggling to give birth to her infant, band after band of Yankee raiders arrived, shouting and cursing and ransacking the place in the hopes that something of worth might still be on the plantation. Kate King met them alone at the door and pleaded with them not to come into the house or to make such a racket outside the widows. But the shouting went on. One Yankee pushed past Kate and came into the house but did not go into the bedroom where Mary Sharpe was fighting for her life and the life of her child. Finally, through her own courage and with the skill of the doctor and the prayers of her mother, Mary Sharpe gave birth to a "well-formed infant—a daughter."[33]

The next evening as night closed in, Mary walked alone up and down the front piazza. For years she had viewed her low-country world from this vantage point. Here she had been surrounded by loved ones; here she had looked out on a world of great beauty and much delight. Here on the piazza Jack and Lizzy, Phoebe and Patience, Lucy and Peggy had served her tea and had responded to her every wish. And year by year her memories of this place had deepened as all her senses told her that this was her earthly home. But now in early January 1865, as she listened to the sounds of the river flowing and felt a cold night wind rising, she struggled to comprehend the bitter changes sweeping over the land. Now on this evening she saw her plundered life illumined by low lingering flames. Departing Yankees were setting ablaze neighboring plantation houses and barns. As she identified points of light in the darkening sky, she looked with fear and trembling in the direction of the venerable old church at Midway, for already the Baptist Church at Sunbury had been burned as a signal fire. That evening, however, no light from Midway reached out into the engulfing darkness.[34]

Word gradually trickled into Montevideo on the extent of Yankee depredations. South Hampton was stripped; the Retreat was robbed of everything from bedclothes to provisions; Arcadia and White Oak, Riceboro, Walthourville, and Dorchester, all were overrun by Yankee raiders pillaging the wealth of past summers. More than a thousand Yankees camped at the old Mallard Place, turning it into a wasteland. Others camped at Lambert, where they "killed the cattle, sheep, geese, leveled the fences and burnt the cotton-house." And everywhere the proud whites of Liberty County struggled to survive the onslaught of destruction and dispossession.[35]

William Maxwell, now eighty years old, had thought that he would ride out the storm by staying on the coast at his Springfield plantation. But the storm struck him with particular fury. Hordes of Yankees camped at nearby Sunbury and regularly "entered his dwelling and pillaged every part of it before his face, taking food, bedding, bed clothing, silver, knives, forks, books, and every particle of his wearing apparel except the suit on his person." They knocked out windows and left doors broken open so that the winter wind blew through the house. Trying to stay warm, he built a fire in the parlor and hung his cloak over the back of his chair to try to block the wind. While he was bending over to tend the fire, a young Yankee came up and seized the cloak and ran away. "Insulting foe," wrote Mary in her journal, "wherever you now are, know that although no visible mark of God's displeasure may rest upon you, the reward of such a dastardly act surely awaits you at the bar of eternal justice."[36]

The old man was forced to leave Springfield and to set out on foot for Dorchester, six miles away. As he walked slowly past the Springfield settlement, he knew not only the humiliation of defeat but also the bitterness of illusions unveiled. "So completely," wrote Mary, "had the Yankees poisoned the minds of this venerable gentleman's servants who had all been raised with the tenderness and comfort of children around him, they stood up and saw him depart alone from his own dwelling without offering the slightest assistance and it has been said even laughed as with feeble steps in thin garments he was driven from his own home on a cold winter's day." Only Miley—who had been blinded by her husband's abuse and nursed by Betsey Maxwell—"came out of her house as she heard his passing step and threw her arms around him and with streams of tears told him of her love and devotion to him."[37]

All over Liberty County, some of the newly freed African-American men and women would demonstrate loyalty to former owners as Miley demonstrated loyalty to William Maxwell. But more would demonstrate no loyalty and offer no assistance. They would simply stand in their new freedom and watch their former owners struggle with the new realities that had broken over the low country. And among those who stood and watched, some would laugh as they saw the strong made weak and the proud brought low.

Sherman's raiders did not simply plunder plantation houses; they also ransacked the settlements. They rode into Carlawter, pointed a gun at Cato, and demanded the keys to the corn house, which they promptly emptied of all of the provisions. They searched the cabins "within and without and under"; they took the chickens and pigs, the cows, horses, and wagons that belonged to the people of the settlement. They took "Gilbert's knife and watch and chain, July's pants and blankets, George and Porter's blankets and clothes, the women's pails, piggins, spoons, buckets, pots, kettles, etc. etc." They found a ham at Sue's cabin, and when they discovered that it was old, they chopped it up and flung it to the dogs as Sue exclaimed: "Massa! You do poor Niggers so?"[38]

As they pillaged, the raiders also mistreated and roughed up the women of the settlement. One attempted to drag Sue into her room, but she escaped when another soldier protested. The "horrible creature" then went after Rosetta, who rebuffed him with courage, declaring with disgust that he had "no manners." Young Kate, the daughter of Elsey and Syphax, was at Montevideo when Yankees came bursting in, terrifying her. She fled into a downstairs room and locked the door. The men thundered at the door, and when she came out she had transformed herself. "From being a young girl she had assumed the attitude and appearance of a sick old woman, with a blanket thrown over her head and shoulders, and scarcely able to move."[39]

The young men of the settlement were commandeered to drive the carts, wagons, and carriages loaded with the spoils of war. Some went to the Yankee encampments near Midway; others went as far as the Ogeechee, where they saw Robert Mallard being held prisoner there. They came trickling back to Montevideo, reporting what they had seen and heard, and in this way Carlawter became the center of communication with the outside world. "Our servants keep up communication with their neighbors around," wrote Mary. But it was otherwise for those huddled in the plantation house. "In our captivity," Mary noted, "we are in utter ignorance of all without."[40]

Among the reports brought back to Carlawter were stories of the way Yankees were treating slaves and robbing them of all their possessions all over the county. At South Hampton one hundred and fifty men swooped down on the settlement. They took three months' allowance of corn that had been distributed among the families, killed forty or fifty hogs, took seven beef cattle, stole all the syrup and sugar in the settlement, took the people's clothing, and crawled "under their houses and beds searching for buried articles." At Abial Winn's plantation near Dorchester, they took from the driver Davy three horses, two wagons, two cows, three hogs, twenty bushels of rice, and fifteen bushels of corn. They took from the driver at George Howe's plantation a horse and buggy, twenty cows, thirty hogs, forty beehives, eighteen ducks, and fifty chickens. And so it went at the Mallard Place, at Laurel View and Lambert, at Liberty Hall and the LeConte plantations. Even Toney Stevens, the black preacher, did not escape the pillaging. He had been sick and bedridden for some time when the Yankees arrived. They "robbed him of everything—even his blankets. He pleaded hard for his horse and wagon, but to no avail."[41]

Such pillaging, however, did not stop the Gullah people of Liberty County from taking early steps toward their own freedom. Mary wrote her brother John: "The foundations of society are entirely broken up and although the Negroes have suffered every form of injury from the enemy in their persons and property, they yet regard them as their best friends and under their influence have thrown off all control and now believe themselves perfectly free. The consequence is they are idly wandering about from place to place and must soon come to want." Old ways and old assumptions would not immediately vanish from Montevideo or Carlawter, but it was becoming increasingly clear that great changes were taking place in the social landscape of the low country. Mary thought the changes meant anarchy. The people in the settlements thought the changes meant freedom. During the days ahead all would have to find their way forward into a new low-country world that was being born in deep anguish for whites and much anticipation for blacks.[42]

In early March 1865 John Jones finally made his way to Montevideo. John insisted that all those huddled at Montevideo come to the Refuge, his plantation in Baker County in southwest Georgia, which had escaped the raids of Yankee plunderers. Mary Sharpe left almost immediately with her uncle, taking with her the children, including her newborn babe. With them went Patience and Porter, Lucy and Elsey. Soon after they left, torrential rains began falling, and the little party found itself stuck in the great swamps that surround the Altamaha. The swamp waters began rising, and the old mules and oxen, already gaunt and now worn out by their efforts, seemed unable to take another step. The exhausted travelers were perplexed about which way to go through the swamp, as dry streambeds became swirling currents that blocked their way, and they wondered where they might find a ferry that could safely carry them across the swollen river. Finally, through great exertion and with the help of some other refugees, they managed to extract themselves and make their way to a ferry that carried them over the muddy waters of the Altamaha to the safety of a train.[43]

Joe arrived at Montevideo shortly after his uncle and sister had left with those going to the Refuge, and immediately he began to make plans to take his mother there. Arrangements had to be made with a neighboring planter to oversee Montevideo in the midst of all the disorders and dangers of an enemy occupation. And Mary had to decide what to try to take to the Refuge and what to leave. To her great distress, she realized that she would have to leave behind the family letters and Charles's papers, which she valued "above all things." "My heart," she wrote Susan, "is very sad. But God reigns!"[44]

Joe planned to take his mother and her little party of servants a less direct but safer route than the one taken by his uncle and sister. They would swing far to the west, going by Taylor's Creek to Reidsville in Tattnall County before turning south and crossing the Altamaha far upstream at a less dangerous point, then finally reaching the railroad at Blackshear. It would be a long and exhausting trip with a buggy and oxcart and would involve relying on the hospitality of families along the way that were struggling to meet their own needs; when no hospitable home could be found, they would have to camp out in some pasture or grove along the road. At first William Maxwell planned to go with them, but he was feeling his years, and he did not want to risk dying far from home. So the decision was made that he would stay behind and meet on familiar ground whatever might come his way. While these preparations for departure went forward, to their joy Robert Mallard arrived from Savannah. He had been paroled at last, and he was eager to get to his family at the Refuge. They quickly decided that Joe would go with them as far as the train in Blackshear, where he would leave them to return to his family in Augusta, and Robert would escort them the rest of the way to the Refuge.[45]

As Mary prepared to leave Montevideo, she sat at her desk one evening while gathered memories slipped out of deep places to speak in the silence of the night. She wrote in her journal:

> What a skeleton world has this now become to me. The bright promises of hope which once encircled every object and gilded every scene have faded tint by tint until dark shadows are resting where sunbeams played. Of earthly possessions and enjoyments, I have seen an end of perfection here below. Riches have taken to themselves wings and flown away. I am a captive in the home I love and soon must wander from it an exile in my native land. Memory's buried stores lie all exhumed before my eye.

Images of Charles rose up before her and touched her "withered heart." She remembered his "precious words of love" and how he had brought her to Montevideo a young and happy wife. Images of the children appeared. She remembered their school and museum, their laughter, songs, and sports. She remembered the garden, how it had once been a wilderness, and how it had grown and flowered and brought delight. And she remembered servants who used to wait faithfully and pleasantly upon her family—how many there had been: Jack and Old Lizzy, Pulaski and Mom Sylvia at the Retreat, Patience and a host of others. And perhaps Mary remembered Phoebe, how she had served her so many years, and how she had looked as she rode off with her family down the avenue. But now, Mary wrote, all things were altered. "The enemy has destroyed every living thing; even the plainest food is made scanty. His robberies and oppressions force me from my beloved home, where it is no longer safe or prudent to remain. And I must leave it in my advancing years, knowing not where the gray hairs which sorrow and time have thickly gathered will find a shelter, or the fainting heart and weary body a resting place, or any spot that I may ever again on earth call home."[46]

33

———————•—•———————

THE PROMISED LAND

While Mary was huddled with other refugees in southwest Georgia, she received a letter from Laura: "You will grieve to hear that all of our Island homes are in ashes." Maybank, Woodville, and Social Bluff—all had been burned, and all that was now left of these places of deep memory were charred timbers and scorched bricks. Yankee raiders had not set the fires but rather members of a fishing party that had come across the sound from St. Catherine's Island. A colony of runaways—of freed people—had gathered on St. Catherine's during the closing days of the war, and the fires they set at Maybank and the other island homes had been kindled by long smoldering rage and apparently by the hope to possess abandoned lands.[1]

The burning of their island homes was for their owners but one more bitter experience of loss and humiliation. Such experiences provided moments of vulnerability when disturbing questions could break through Southern defenses and threaten to overwhelm a belief in the justice and righteousness of the Southern cause. When Chattanooga had fallen to the Yankees, Mary had written: "We cannot pretend to fathom the designs of Infinite Wisdom touching our beloved and suffering Confederacy. It may be our sins will be scourged to the severest extremity—and we deserve it all. But I also believe when that wicked people have filled up the cup of their iniquity, God will take them in hand to deal with them for their wickedness and to reward them according to their transgressions." And when Atlanta was besieged, John Jones had written: "Let us daily and hourly commit our cause, ourselves, our all to Him who doeth all things well. Surely we are not to be overwhelmed in utter ruin, poverty, and disgrace!" And as Yankees had come storming across Georgia toward the low country, Robert Mallard had confided to his journal that one of the distressing effects on him was the temptation "to think hard of Providence." "I know," Robert had confessed, that what God "does is and must be right but when I see a cruel and wicked foe prospering and penetrating farther and farther into the very vitals of our country and when the prayers of God's people seem utterly fruitless in arresting them, I am perplexed and were I to listen to the Tempter, I would be disposed to question the utility of prayer at least for this object." But now in the summer of 1865, when utter defeat had arrived and their Southern Zion was desolate, John Jones thought hard truth must be faced. He confessed, "However we may be able to prove the wickedness of our enemies, we must acknowledge that the providence of God has decided against us in the tremendous struggle we have just made for property rights and country. The hand of the Lord is upon us!" And he prayed "for grace to be humble and behave aright before *Him* until these calamities be overpassed!"[2]

What seemed the most pressing calamity to Mary in the summer of 1865, as she made her way slowly back toward Montevideo, was the emancipation of her slaves. As she returned to the ruins of Atlanta with the Mallards and pressed on alone to Augusta, she was beginning an intense struggle to understand at some deep level that she could no longer control as she once had controlled Cato or Patience or Porter or Stepney or Charles or Lucy or Mom Rosetta or any of the others who had lived at Carlawter or at the old settlement by the Medway marshes or at Arcadia. When she would say, "Come, serve tea on the piazza," they would not have to come; and when she would say, "Go, work the rice in the fields," they would not have to go. Word had already gone out from Federal authorities that white planters would have to negotiate contracts with the freed people. The contracts would mean an end to the old arrangements of slavery and would call into question the assumptions and practices of the old paternalism that had justified holding in bondage the men and women of the settlements. But Mary had already begun, with other white southerners, the process of reworking an old ideology that had once undergirded slavery. This reworked ideology was intended to meet the dangers brought to a "southern way of life" by emancipation. Yankee military power may have abolished slavery, but a powerful racism would serve to keep freed people in their place under the control of whites. While Yankee raiders were ransacking Montevideo, Mary had written in her journal:

> The workings of Providence in reference to the African race are truly wonderful. The scourge falls with peculiar weight upon them: with their emancipation must come their extermination. All history, from their first existence, proves them incapable of self-government; they perish when brought in conflict with the intellectual superiority of the Caucasian race. Northern philanthropy and

cant may rave as much as they please; but *facts* prove that in a state of slavery such as exists in the Southern states have the Negro race increased and thriven most.[3]

Under the threatening new reality of emancipation, Mary abandoned the class analysis that Charles had used when discussing African Americans—that they were to be understood as one laboring class among the many of the earth. In its place she lodged a racial argument that had long been used by the most radical proslavery people who had most vigorously opposed Charles's missionary labors.[4]

When Mary returned to Montevideo in the fall of 1865, she found that the freed people in the county were also struggling to understand the radical changes that had swept over their world. They were in the midst of the momentous experience of moving from slavery to freedom. Cato and those who lived at Carlawter could remember only a time of slavery and how they had struggled within its bondage and against its oppression. Suddenly they were learning that they were no longer slaves, that they could now say openly what they had dared to say only secretly, that they could leave their former owners if they wished, that they could send their children to one of the freedmen's schools that was opening around the county, and that they could call upon the federal government for help in enforcing the new order of things. But they were also learning that the Yankees could turn against them and act like their old owners in order to maintain order and stability.[5]

Cato had quickly grasped that old ways had died and that new ways were being born. When Mary had departed Montevideo in spring of 1865, she had secured as the overseer John Fennell, a small farmer in poor health who was also serving as the county sheriff. Cato had long dealt with weak and largely absent overseers. He knew how to act in a submissive manner before them and create an atmosphere of trust that left him free to manage the plantation according to his own judgments. Now, however, such rituals of subordination could be cast aside, the mask of the faithful servant that he had worn so well and so long could be torn off, and the things that had been said only quietly around settlement fires could now be said publicly to the white overseer. When Fennell gave instructions about how the plantation was to be run, Cato apparently told him that the people of the settlement no longer had to follow the instructions of former owners or of their overseers. Fennell had been so frustrated that he had called in the Yankees stationed at Riceboro to quell the disorder. They had threatened Cato and the others with swift punishment if they did not obey the overseer, and for a while there was calm at Montevideo. But Mary, when hearing from Fennell, was out-

Carlawter settlement, 1891 (Charles Colcock Jones Papers,
Tulane University Manuscript Department)

raged by Cato's behavior. "Cato," she wrote Charlie, "has been to me a most in-
solent, indolent, and dishonest man; I have not a shadow of confidence in him,
and will not wish to retain him on the place."[6]

So when Mary finally arrived back at Montevideo in November 1865, Cato departed. He left behind him Carlawter and all the familiar places he and Cassius
had first explored when they were boys too young to be put to work in the fields.
He left the dikes, dams, and canals that had been built under his supervision and
that he had thought of as in some way his own. He left the plantation where for
twenty-five years he had been the driver, the boss, who had walked a fine line
as a buffer between those who sat around the fires of Carlawter and those who
had tea on the piazza at Montevideo. And he left the cemetery where ancestors
rested, where his mother, old Lizzy, lay in the dark ground with so many others
who had come to call Carlawter home. So Cato, who had so often expressed his
loyalty, love, and gratitude to his old master, left in November 1865 the place so
closely and intimately associated with his life of slavery. And the reason he left
was to claim a new life of freedom.[7]

Niger Fraser, far right, at Carlawter, 1891 (Charles Colcock Jones Papers, Tulane University Manuscript Department)

The following January, Cato received from Mary fifty dollars plus interest—money he had given Charles years earlier to invest for him. Shortly thereafter Cato departed Liberty County for Savannah with his wife, Jane, and an eagerness to start a new life. The old couple was part of a movement to the city by a number of Liberty County blacks. Among those going to Savannah from Carlawter was Peggy, the mother of Eva Lee. Not long after she arrived in the city, Peggy contracted smallpox and died a lonely death in great wretchedness. Mary wondered what became of the five-year-old Eva Lee, mulatto child of a Maybank guest.[8]

While Cato was making his plans to leave Montevideo and Liberty County, others were trying to make their way back to Liberty County. Among those who had been taken to Indianola, some wanted to go back to Carlawter. Phoebe's daughter Clarissa wanted to return with her children, as did Rosetta and Sam's son Sam and his family. Miley, Patience and Porter's daughter, wanted to go home to Liberty County with her family, and so did Sylvia, Andrew and Mary Ann's daughter. Stepney wanted to go back to Arcadia, where his father, Robin, was still living. Some wanted to go to White Oak. Most of the others did not know exactly where they would go, wrote Charlie, but "all nearly decide upon a return to Liberty." They would soon be on the road to the low country, part of a massive movement of freed people moving about across the South—some would be looking for a spouse who had been "sold away"; some, having been carried away to a distant place, would be trying to make their way back to remembered homes where family and friends lived; and others would be simply trying to get as far away as possible from former owners. They all had to struggle with difficult issues that swirled around a central question: Where were they to live now that freedom had come? Were they to break all ties with their former owners and find some new place to live? If so, where? Where could they find food and shelter? Where could they find work, and what kind of work could they do? Or were they to stay with a former owner in a familiar place? And if they stayed, how would they protect themselves from falling back into former patterns of bondage and dependence?[9]

Old Sam had little trouble deciding what he was going to do. He had been the indispensable servant for the Robartses in their Marietta home, but they would have to learn to get along without him. He headed for Liberty County and Car-lawter to be finally reunited with Rosetta so that they could live out their last days together. Their daughter Lucy made the same decision—she wanted to be with her husband Charles, who had not gone with her when she had been carried by the whites fleeing to the Refuge. Tenah and Niger soon followed from Atlanta, where they had gone with the Mallards—Niger's skills as a fisherman would be a help as deep want began to stalk the county. So Rosetta and Sam had around them at Carlawter not only their children but also their grandchildren and great-grandchildren. Rosetta, however, lived only a few months with such freedom. She died in the spring of 1866. "Her aged husband was with her and all her children but one." Mary talked with her before she died and asked her the familiar questions about her faith, and Rosetta "expressed her entire reliance upon the Lord Jesus Christ. Said she hoped her peace was made with God through Christ." Sam died the next spring, never having made a confession of faith. "We can only leave him in the hands of God," wrote Mary. And from Marietta, Mary Robarts wrote: "If all servants were as faithful as he was, slavery would have been a pleasant thing to master and servant."[10]

Old Andrew and Mary Ann moved to the settlement at Carlawter. They and their children were to be the most faithful to Mary of all her former slaves. Gilbert in particular would be "irreproachable in word, look or manner. He has never," wrote Mary, "shown me the least disrespect and serves cheerfully and faithfully." For years he had driven the carriage and the buggy, had gone for the mail at Rice-boro, and had delivered messages from Charles and Mary to different plantations in the county. His son Young Gilbert was to follow in his father's footsteps, in time becoming the "rider" for a grandchild of Charles Berrien Jones, going for the mail well into the twentieth century.[11]

Charles and Lucy also were to prove themselves faithful to their old mistress. But perhaps it was not so much faithfulness as it was a desire to live in the familiar surroundings of Carlawter with their parents, their children, and grandchildren, together with Charles and Lucy's brothers and sisters. Their decision to return to Carlawter was made with a new freedom and no doubt with an eye to the economic realities of the poverty and struggle that was before the freed people in Liberty County. Old loyalties lingered, but they were also new because they were in a context of a freedom to say "yes" to a different future. So a little community of overlapping families once again took up residence at Carlawter, but now they were struggling to realize what their new freedom meant and how they might relate to their old mistress with some independence.[12]

The contracts that were negotiated at Montevideo required Mary to supply housing for those at Carlawter, all the wood they needed for "fencing, general repairs, fuel, and cooking," and all the land they desired for cultivation of their own crops. Any crops they grew "were to be managed and disposed of as they may desire." In return, each adult living at Carlawter was to work for Mary one and a half acres of cotton and a half-acre of corn. They were to "perform all labor that may be deemed necessary in splitting rails, in making up fences, in repairing dams, in general repairs about the Plantation, and generally in such services as may be beneficial for the best interests and successful cultivation of the said Plantation." Mary was to provide the "plough animals and farming utensils." Such contracts were at first agreeable to all the parties involved, but it soon became clear that they were too vague, and differing expectations caused tensions to arise between Mary and those who lived at Carlawter. As a result the contracts shifted so that Mary began to pay a wage for specific work. These arrangements were part of negotiations going on all over the county between the white owners of the land and the freed people. At White Oak, Sister Susan simply rented the land to the descendants of Old Jupiter and Blind Silvey, who once again gathered in the plantation settlement. At other plantations, a system was negotiated where the freed people would work two days for the white landowners in return for certain rights—including the right to work land for their own crops.[13]

Immediately after the war's end, Patience and Porter were stuck for a time at the Refuge. Mary appealed to the Federal authorities for passes for them on the railroad, and after much effort was successful. But she wrote John at the Refuge:

And now my dear brother, before this transportation is furnished, or they are permitted to return, *I must get you to bind* them by a *written contract* to *remain with me for one year at least—subject to my direction and control.* Please make them understand that I will not allow any one to return to Montevideo or remain on the place if they are not respectful, obedient, and industrious. But if they conduct themselves as they ought, I will do my part faithfully by them.

Mary then added, as if nothing had changed: "Tell Porter and Patience I put my trust in them and do not expect them to disappoint me."[14]

Mary was apparently the only one surprised by Porter and Patience's resistance to such a proposal. Porter and Patience were themselves in the middle of a rebellion by all of the former slaves of John Jones, who had declared they would no longer work at the Refuge and had simply packed up and left. Even Sylvia, John and Mary's Old Momma, who for years had run the kitchen at the Retreat and had been so intimately connected with Joseph's family—she was the only slave to whom Mary had ever sent her love—even she left the Refuge, with her son Joe and his family. Whatever her affection for her "white children," Sylvia now was able in her old age to show where her deepest loyalties lay.[15]

Mary was perplexed by Porter and Patience's response and wrote John once again to explain her "feelings and views about Porter and Patience." They have been, she wrote, "faithful servants in days and years that are past and now that a change of condition has come over them, I do not desire to be hard in my judgments of them but to assist them. Such was my confidence in their good feelings towards myself, knowing that I had been a friend to them." Mary wrote that she had nursed Patience for months when she was sick, and Mary thought "they would wish to return to my service." She had consequently "obtained at much trouble and expense too," their transportation papers. "Of course," Mary wrote, "if they refuse to form a contract with me, they cannot return either to Montevideo or Arcadia and Porter must see that all my carpenter's tools in his possession are returned to me, besides those bought for his use." Perhaps the tone of the letter was conciliatory enough to convince Porter and Patience—and Elsey too, who was with them—that they should accept Mary's offer. Or perhaps John thought nothing could be gained by keeping them at the Refuge. At any rate, they were all back in Liberty County by early December 1865. But Patience stayed only a few days at Montevideo before she left to take up permanent residence at Arcadia. She intended to set "up for herself," and consequently she "settled herself at Arcadia," where her labors and her kitchen art would be used to sustain her own family.[16]

Patience and Porter would not entirely break their ties with Mary and Montevideo, but they were clearly establishing their independence at Arcadia, where Daddy Robin's family, together with other freed people, were creating a new community. Patience's brother Stepney soon took over the management of Arcadia and helped to transform it into a Gullah community that rented land from their former owners. With their hard work, they would in time begin to buy the land they had once labored upon as slaves. What Porter, Patience, Stepney, and others wanted was autonomy. Their history of owning pigs and cows, horses and buggies, chickens and ducks, together with their experience of raising their own corn, rice, and vegetables and of hunting and fishing, had provided them resources to become subsistence farmers who rented land or owned their own. By the time of the 1870 census, Porter and Patience owned their own small farm near Arcadia and valued at two hundred dollars. And Porter, with his skills as a carpenter, was earning extra income to supplement what cash they got from selling an occasional pig or a little corn and cotton. In such a manner, and in contrast with much of the rest of the South, the Gullah people in Liberty County largely avoided becoming sharecroppers.[17]

Mary and Patience thus parted ways. When they looked out on the world of Liberty County in 1865, each saw a different world and each sought to make her own way in her own world. Mary saw a world of chaos and anarchy. Patience saw a new world of freedom being born. Their different ways of seeing Liberty County were rooted not only in their competing self-interests but also in their different memories.

To be sure, Mary and Patience shared memories as they had shared, or had in common, the experience of living together in a particular place and a particular time. Patience knew, as Mary knew, the flow of the North Newport, and they had both heard its lapping at the banks of their lives. The Gullah woman as well as the white mistress had felt the morning wind blowing in from the sea, had smelled the scented rain on the river, and had breathed deeply of the hot fragrance of the marsh. The low country was the land where both had been born, and the land's character was deeply imprinted in all their senses and lodged in their most distant memories. They had sung hymns together, had prayed together at Midway and in the plantation chapel, and had cried together as they had buried loved ones. Moreover, Mary had gently nursed Patience when she was dangerously ill, and Patience had done the same for Mary, rubbing her back and soothing her aching muscles; so Mary knew the feel of Patience's black body, and Patience knew the feel of Mary's white body, and in their touching each had reached toward some connection with the other's world.

If they had been together in all of these shared experiences, however, they had also been apart. A great distance had separated them even in the most human moments of touch and healing. That distance had been most visible when together they had seen old man Jackson come for Phoebe and Cash and the chil-

dren, and they had heard the cries of separation and the rattle of the wagon as it
moved down the long road toward Savannah and its slave market. Such a distance
marked the world of a mistress and the world of a slave, and the great space between their two worlds meant—in spite of all that they shared—that their memories were different. Mary's memory flowed from the piazzas and dining rooms
of Maybank and Montevideo; Patience's memory flowed from the kitchens at
Maybank and Montevideo and from the cabins of the settlements.[18]

Because their memories were different, because their memories emerged out
of two different if overlapping spheres, they saw different worlds in 1865 and interpreted their present moment in different ways. As Mary watched Patience
and others assert their independence, she wrote: "My heart is pained and sickened with their vileness and falsehood in every way. I long to be delivered from
the race." Mary, however, still felt a sense of duty toward the black people who
surrounded her, and she would struggle with stoic fortitude to do her duty for
a people she was convinced were finally unable to take care of themselves. Patience, on her part, looked at the world of 1865 and saw freedom and an opportunity to be faithful to a new future. Her memory would challenge what Mary
remembered about how things had been at Montevideo and Maybank in "happier days," and Patience's independence would assert that she did not need or
want Mary's dutiful care.[19] Each woman's memory thus acted for its possessor as
a filter through which to interpret the war, Yankee victory, and emancipation.
Now at the beginning of a new day, the two women, each guided by her memory, responded in different ways to the strange events unfolding around them.[20]

Patience and Porter, Charles and Lucy, Niger and Tenah, together with the
other Gullah people of the county, found themselves not only struggling over
labor and land, but also forging new ways for themselves in other areas of their
lives. Almost immediately they began to assert their freedom by claiming family
names and family histories. Before emancipation they had been called only Patience or Porter, Stepney or Charles, Lucy or Tenah. To be sure, there had been
an occasional last name when needed for identification—Sandy Maybank the
carpenter had needed to be distinguished from Sandy Jones the carpenter. But
for the great majority of slaves, there was only a first name. This use of first names
only had been a powerful instrument of control by whites, for it said that slaves
had no family and no history, only an immediate relationship to white owners.
Consequently in the records of Midway Church, Charles was "Charles, servant
of the Rev. C. C. Jones"—not Charles the son of Andrew and Mary Ann, not
Charles the husband of Lucy, not Charles the father of Tenah, only "Charles,
the servant of . . ."[21]

Of all those who had lived at Carlawter or at the Maybank or Arcadia settlements, only a few of Old Lizzy and Robinson's descendants took the name of Jones. Most of the people took names that linked them to a more distant past, often to earlier owners who were remembered in secret traditions and whose names marked the beginning of an African-American family tradition. Old Andrew and Mary Ann, together with their children, took the family name of Lawson; when they came to put their mark on their contracts, they marked Gilbert Lawson and Charles Lawson and George Lawson. Niger and Tenah took the name Fraser. Porter and Patience claimed Way as their family name and history, while Old Robin and Stepney claimed West as theirs. Some of Sam and Rosetta's children took the name Reese at first, while others took Roberts, which soon became the family name for all. At White Oak, the descendants of Old Jupiter and Blind Silvey claimed Stewart. Other families claimed the name Anderson, or Bacon, or Holmes. And so it went as freed people publicly declared that they had a history, that they and their ancestors were linked through hard trials and a Gullah culture, and that at the deepest level of self-identity they knew who they were.[22]

As they claimed their names, they also began to assert their independence in regard to religious matters. In the early days following emancipation, the old patterns persisted. Mary would attend on occasion, with a few other whites, the North Newport Baptist Church, where there was still a white preacher for the large African-American congregation. And blacks continued to come to Midway, where David Buttolph was preaching. But change was in the air. Mary noticed it first when she dutifully tried to gather her usual Sunday class. "I have never been without my Sabbath class of young and old," she wrote in her journal, "until this emancipation has separated them spiritually as well as temporally from us. I have invited but they do not appear disposed to come." She tried to console herself by remembering that she no longer occupied "the responsible position of mistress," which had "so long weighed heavily upon my spirit." She would simply wash her hands of those who lived at Carlawter and feel free to leave them with "those who have created this separation and made a break which is likely to become only a yawning gulf of ignorance and misery." But in spite of such resolutions, she felt betrayed, as if her years of teaching, counseling, and encouragement had been dismissed and were of no value. So that Sabbath she wrote in her journal: "Let not the infidelity and neglect of servants, from whom I am assured I have the right to expect different treatment, mar my peace this day."[23]

The "spiritual separation" was soon to come to the churches in the county. The black membership of Midway was soon dismissed to a newly established Midway Presbyterian Church under the leadership of Joseph Williams, the black

preacher who had written such a kind note when Charles died. Under his leadership, the congregation was united with the Northern Presbyterian Church and
quickly grew to more than six hundred members. They continued at first to use
the familiar Midway building, but in time they built a church north of Midway
and made its cemetery the Old Field where Sharper, the black preacher who
had taught Charles so much, had been buried among his ancestors on a moonlit
night.[24]

At North Newport Baptist Church the twelve whites who were members soon
left to join other congregations. And black preachers began to be called to lead
the congregation where Charles had so often preached and where Paris, the
driver at South Hampton, had been the lead watchman. In the years ahead, the
North Newport congregation, together with Midway Presbyterian and the other
black congregations of the county, were to become centers of African-American
life.[25]

These black congregations were not new institutions that suddenly arose with
emancipation; rather, they were communities of faith that already had long histories in 1865. Much of their history had been open for whites to see at Midway
and North Newport, at Sunbury and Pleasant Grove. But much of their history
had also been secret, rooted in the bush arbors and in little gatherings around
settlement fires. Their history included the work of earlier black preachers—
Toney Stevens and Sharper, Jack Salturs and Mingo—and of such black religious leaders as Paris the driver at South Hampton, who had once thrown an
intruding dog out of the church window, and Major the leading watchman at
Midway, and Bess the church "Mother" who started the Female Prayer Service at
the Mallard Place. But the histories of these communities of faith also included
the work of Charles Colcock Jones, the white preacher and pastor, who for years
preached and taught on the Sabbath and who, during the evenings of the week,
after the people's work was done, visited in the settlements. In the years ahead,
there would be signs that some of the Gullah people of Liberty County had internalized at a deep level what they had learned from this white preacher. He had
sought to touch their hearts and their minds, to shape their religious feelings and
imaginations, and to inculcate an evangelical faith and worldview. And some
had responded positively, for they found good news in what he taught. But there
would be signs, too, that others rejected and dismissed his teaching and preaching as nothing more than the self-serving and empty words of a slave owner. In
any case, the Gullah people had now been "spiritually emancipated," and their
religious life and decisions would reflect a new context of freedom.[26]

In perhaps unexpected ways, the new schools for the freed people helped to
reinforce much of what Charles had taught during the years of his work for the

"religious instruction of the Negro." Almost as soon as freedom arrived, African Americans began to establish schools with help from Northern denominations and the federal government's Freedmen's Bureau. And many of the places where they established schools were the old stations where Charles had first gathered slaves for worship and instruction. A little primary school was started at Hutchinson Station, where Charles had taught his catechism and the hymns of an evangelical faith. Others schools were started in the churches at Midway, North Newport, and Pleasant Grove, and there was also a little school at Lodebar plantation, where Charles had been a regular visitor. But of all the schools, none was to be more influential than Dorchester Academy, established across the road from Acadia.[27]

New England Congregationalists, proud of Midway's history and the fame of Charles's work, were determined to build a fine academy for the freed people. Led by the Reverend Floyd Snelson, a black Congregational missionary, the academy was established on eighty-seven acres—enough land for a farm where the students could raise the food they ate and also livestock for help with the school's expenses. For the next seventy years, Dorchester Academy was to be the single most important institution in the Gullah community of Liberty County.[28]

While all of the schools sought to help their students prepare for a life of freedom, the teachers and curriculum at Dorchester sought with particular intensity to overcome "the corrupting and degrading" influences of slavery. The hope was that the academy would instill Calvinistic virtues into the Gullah people as the necessary foundation for their new freedom. Teachers wanted their students to internalize a new personal discipline, and they tried to instill—down into the psychic depths of their students—the virtues of modesty, industry, sobriety, self-control, and godliness. Such concerns were not distant from Charles's efforts through the Liberty County Association for the Religious Instruction of Slaves, or from the efforts of the coterie of white teachers who had taught for years in the Sunday Schools scattered around the county. But unlike Charles's classes and those taught by white planting families, the academy nurtured a democratic spirit and a love of liberty and encouraged an admiration for the history of the Gullah people who had been traveling a long road together.[29]

While Patience and Porter and other freed people were working to make a new life for themselves in Liberty County, many of the white families were giving up any hope for the old community that had been built around the Midway congregation. Few of those who had moved to southwest Georgia for new lands and safety showed an interest in returning to the coast. The rice economy had largely collapsed during the war, and the river plantations close to Midway had lost much of their economic viability with the reluctance of freed people to work in the rice fields. How many freed people, after all, wanted to wade into the mire of a rice field in July to chop weeds for a white land owner when they could hope to own their own land and grow a little cotton, corn, and peas?[30]

Almost as soon as the war was over, Charlie began to seek buyers for Arcadia, Montevideo, and Maybank. But no one was interested in purchasing the plantations. The land seemed of little value with no substantial labor force to work it. Mary had no objections to selling Arcadia; she even thought it a good idea, and apparently she was willing to sell a burned and desolated Maybank. But Montevideo was another matter. After months of struggling to reestablish a working plantation at Montevideo, Mary wrote Mary Sharpe: "I sometimes feel I must sink under the various perplexities of this situation, and know that if God should withdraw the hope and confidence which I trust He permits me to entertain in His infinite wisdom and special guidance, that I should be truly desolate and miserable." Yet in the face of "severe losses" and "sad reverses," Mary was trying to cling to her plantation home. "I have tried to live here," she wrote, "that I might protect and not sacrifice this our home from any feeling of loneliness or isolation, or from motives of ease and deliverance from care." She had, she mused, "labored to preserve it as my only home, and what might in God's providence be a home to my dear children. And even now I am not willing, if I can prevent it, to have it sacrificed."[31]

Even Mary could see, however, that there was little chance that her children would ever return to Montevideo or would ever want to take up their residence in a part of the country increasingly dominated by its black population. A few months after the end of the war, Charlie had announced that he was going to New York, of all places, to practice law. He had accepted an invitation to be a co-partner with his old Savannah law partner John Ward. Both men had extensive contacts in the North, and they intended to focus on representing the legal interests of southerners. Charlie wrote his mother: "The prospects for success, under God, appear flattering." It seemed strange for a Confederate army officer and defender of the Southern cause to move so quickly and with such apparent ease to the Yankee metropolis. But Charlie had spent years in the North studying at Princeton and Harvard, and in spite of his years of fighting Yankees, he felt no great cultural divide. Like many other southerners, he was able to come back into the Union and think of himself as an American patriot. After all, he thought that the South had been fighting to preserve the true nature of the old American Republic. Besides, he had a pragmatic approach: he knew that money could be made in New York, while Savannah was impoverished.[32]

Among the advantages Charlie found in the city was the opportunity to indulge his old passion for history and archaeology that had been first nurtured in the little school and museum at Maybank. In the evenings, after busy days in his law office, he would write about the history of his native state and about the aboriginal people who had once lived by the marshes and rivers of Georgia. New York University later awarded him the honorary degree of doctor of laws for his efforts. In 1877 Charlie and his family returned to the South and took up residence in a fine antebellum mansion near Augusta. But he remembered with pleasure his time in New York. "My eyes were opened," he wrote his daughter Mary Ruth in 1888, "my ideas enlarged, and aspirations elevated. I will always be glad of this northern residence at this special epoch in my life. The good results linger with me to the present time, and the associations then formed are even now pleasurable and profitable."[33]

Mary was glad for Charlie's growing success in New York, but what was most difficult for her was the removal of her "darling baby," Mary Ruth. The child had been a great comfort to Mary during the hard days of the war, especially after Charles's death. When Ruthie left to join her father and her stepmother, Mary had written in her journal that the little girl had been a "Sweet Comforter in hours of widow'd woe," had won her grieving grandmother "back to life," and had made Mary feel "that one sweet living tie still bound me here."[34]

The greatest pain for Mary, however, came not simply with the separation from Ruthie but with the growing alienation she felt from Eva Jones, who was herself uneasy with the role of a stepmother. Eva would call herself an "ugly stepmother" and "wicked stepmother," and then after such self-depreciation, she would quickly say how much love and attention she was giving Ruthie and how she was showering gifts of dolls and other toys upon the child. Publicly, all remained proper and pleasant between Mary and her daughter-in-law, but Eva left the city the day after Mary came for her one visit to New York, and Mary discreetly wrote Mary Sharpe, after what she considered a serious slight from Eva: "There are wounds in life very painful."[35]

Shortly after Charlie moved to New York, Mary Sharpe and her family moved to New Orleans, where Robert had accepted a call to become the pastor of the Prytania Street Presbyterian Church. Central Church in Atlanta had vigorously resisted the loss of their pastor, but the presbytery had approved the call, and the family had moved to the booming southern city in 1866. New Orleans had not suffered the devastations of Atlanta or the economic depression of Savannah, and the call was in every way a most attractive one for Robert. The church was large and influential, away from the old French Quarters and in the "American" part of the city, and the salary was substantial—especially for an impoverished family. But the move was hard for Mary, alone in Liberty County, in spite of her thinking that Robert must try to follow God's will in the matter. As Robert was considering the move, Mary had written Mary Sharpe: "I shall feel if you go to New Orleans that I shall hardly ever see you, if I am spared to live longer in Liberty." And Laura had written Mary Sharpe from Flemington: "If you go to New Orleans, Aunt Mary's children will be scattered, and it will require time to journey from one to the other." [36]

As the Mallards were preparing for their move to New Orleans, Joe was accepting a position in the medical school at the University of Nashville. Immediately after the war, he had been summoned to Washington to testify in the trial of Henry Wirz, the commander of the Confederate prison at Andersonville. Joe felt that his reports about the wretched conditions at Andersonville were distorted in the trial, and he was outraged that the court ignored what he regarded as the federal government's role in the horrors of Andersonville, for Washington had refused to exchange prisoners as the exhausted Confederacy had stumbled toward utter collapse. The conviction and execution of Wirz—the only Confederate officer executed for war crimes—left Joe dejected and bitter. The call to the professorship in Nashville, however, revived his spirits. He stayed there two years before accepting another call, this one to the University of Louisiana (later Tulane University) in New Orleans. There, near his sister's family, he was to build his reputation as one of the nation's leading authorities on tropical diseases. [37]

In this way, Mary found herself increasingly isolated at Montevideo and distant from those whom she loved. But it was not only those who moved away who left her struggling alone at her beloved home.

William Maxwell came to stay at Montevideo. He was a comfort to Mary, and she to him. She poured on him all the attention she had given Charles as his health had declined, and she gave him all the affection she had given Ruthie when the child came motherless to Montevideo. William was now in his eighties, and Mary's kind attentions helped to ease the aches and pains of his old age. Once again, as so often in the past, they would sit on the piazza and have tea and talk as afternoon shadows lengthened and the sounds of approaching night drifted up from the river. Looking across the lawn, the two old friends could see egrets flying homeward, their white plumage reflected in the dark river waters until they finally disappeared in the evening light.

In late spring 1866 Mary told William that she was going to New York for a visit with Charlie and his family and to see her precious Ruthie. As they sat together on the piazza, "his eyes filled with tears and his lips quivered as he said, 'Mary, I am afraid I shall never see you again.'" And he said to her, "When you come back you will shed a silent tear over my grave." He felt sad not only at Mary's leaving but also at his leaving Montevideo, although he was going to stay with dear friends.[38] It came as no surprise, then, a few months later for Mary to receive a letter in New York from Laura:

> My beloved Aunt,
>   My heart fails me when I think of the pain you will feel on the reception of the sad bereavement which is pressing like lead upon my heart. Dear Uncle William was called to his heavenly home yesterday the 20th at one o'clock.

William had spent some time on Colonel's Island with Audley and Kate King after Mary had left—Audley had rebuilt at Woodville a simple but adequate cottage. The island was filled with many memories and so many associations for William, but as he felt his weakness growing, he was eager to go to Dorchester, to the home of his closest friend, Abial Winn, where dear Betsy had died. Not long after he arrived at the Winns', he fell ill with a fever. Julia King came, as did other friends. He died, wrote Laura, where he wanted to die, "under the roof where dear Aunty breathed her last ten years and one month ago."[39]

So when Mary returned to Montevideo in the fall of 1866, she returned to a home that was empty. Moreover, she returned to a shattered community that was struggling to find its way into the future. Friends would come for a visit, trying to reestablish old patterns of hospitality—Julia King was never far away at South Hampton, but times were hard for the Kings, and Julia was grieving the death of her son Willie, killed in battle three days before Lee's surrender at Appomattox Courthouse. Eliza Clay came for a visit. Her new home was a simple affair at Richmond-on-Ogeechee, and she and her extended family were depending much on the hunting prowess of the young men in the family, who, when they had time, brought home deer and wild turkeys shot in the river swamps and ducks shot at dawn over old rice fields. Sister Susan would come with Laura and the children from Flemington—they all loved Montevideo and were devoted to Mary. But the underlying economic and social structures that had supported such practices of hospitality and that had been the basis for the community at Midway, those structures had largely collapsed. And with their collapse came the end of the Midway congregation.[40]

Trouble had been brewing at Midway for years. Not only had white members been moving out of the county, they had also been moving for some time to the little summer villages in the county and establishing permanent homes there. So daughter churches had been established—Walthourville Presbyterian, Dorchester Presbyterian, and Flemington Presbyterian. By 1867 only a few families remained close enough to Midway to attend regularly, and they were having great difficulty providing the necessary support for the life of the church. In the fall of 1867, David Buttolph accepted a call to become the pastor of the Presbyterian

Church in Marietta. It was a devastating blow to the congregation and the community.

People came from far and wide for the last communion service in the old church. The long thin table was once again stretched across the front of the sanctuary, and the Midway families came in turn to sit at the table and receive the sacrament of the Lord's Supper from their pastor. Mary wrote in her journal that it was an occasion of deep solemnity as they all realized that for the first time in its history Midway would be "without the living teacher." Even during the "first Revolution" arrangements had been made "at least for a pastoral ministration of the word." Now, however, "the wants and depressions and positive poverty are so great that this church and people have not the means to support the Gospel. This greatest of all their calamities, a destruction of the word of life, is thus laid upon them." Mary wondered to herself whether the future was only one of desolation. She did not flinch but asked herself: "Will God yet arise for our Zion or are the great purposes of Jehovah accomplished in and through us! Has Christ's mission through and by this church been fulfilled and must it now sit solitary and alone—or are we thus rebuked for pride and self-sufficiency?"[41]

Shortly before she pondered these questions, Mary had written Mary Sharpe in New Orleans: "I feel my child that I cannot live away from you. I want you to write me fully and freely."[42] The decision made, Mary began preparations to leave Montevideo for the same city where Phoebe and her family had disappeared into a slave market. Cattle and sheep were sold, as was the little cotton and corn that had been harvested. A caretaker was secured for the next year, and Mary's plans were explained to those living at Carlawter. Boxes were packed, trunks filled, and carpets rolled up for the long trip. And then one night, in the midst of all of this preparation, Mary rose and threw "wide the closed shutters of my chamber window" that she "might look upon my beautiful earthly home." The moon was full, and countless stars lit the winter night and illumined a world that was fast receding into the chambers of Mary's memory and heart. "Nature below," she wrote in her journal, "is in perfect repose."

> Not the faintest zephyr stirs the sleeping forest leaves. Not a waving shadow breaks the entire outline of houses and groves. The giant oaks and lofty pines are perfectly daguerreotyped upon the lawn, whose even surface, still thickly strewed with autumnal leaves, reflects a golden tint; whilst the pure white walks of the garden stand out like silvery highways.

In the profound stillness of the night, Mary felt as if she alone were "awake in the vast universe around and above. And yet," she wrote, "I know that I am not alone: I feel encompassed by countless evidences of an omnipotent, omniscient, omnipresent Deity." And within, she felt the "witness of the Blessed Spirit, witnessing with my spirit" to the sustaining love of God. "Oh, the sweet and precious consolations that have often flowed into my soul—far from living friends and kindred and all the joys and supports and sweet sympathy of my beloved children! Yes, here in this utter solitude my Heavenly Father hath given me songs of rejoicing even amid the utter loneliness and desolation of a widow's heart and a widow's home." [43]

As the days of her departure approached, Mary struggled mightily with the sense that her beloved Montevideo, in spite of its beauty and past associations, was finally empty without the people she loved and the work that had informed her life as a plantation mistress. As she walked through gardens or looked around at the familiar rooms of the house, she began to feel that Montevideo had been home for her not because of its beauty or geographical location but because it had been a place occupied with loved ones and because she had felt here a deep sense of duty, a vocation, to look after and care for the Gullah people who had made this spot on the earth a place of such beauty and comfort. Now with loved ones gone or scattered and with the freed people rejecting her proffered care and claiming their own independence, Montevideo seemed a mere reminder of days gone by when it had been her happy home.

Mary's growing awareness of the present emptiness of Montevideo kept her love for her low-country world from finally collapsing into romanticism and melancholy. She did not try to deny her love for the beauty of slow flowing rivers and marshes, of carefully developed gardens and vistas. She thought, after all, that the natural world possessed its own integrity as the handiwork of the Creator. But what she found in her loneliness was that Montevideo needed human habitation and association in order to be for her a living place. To be sure, it was not any human habitation that she missed but the habitation of family and of old friends; and the association that she missed was with servants for whom she felt a deep sense of responsibility. Without loved ones to share Montevideo's beauty, without duty that called for purposeful activity at her plantation home, only a romanticism of the rootless, only its longings, remained to this lovely place. Such romanticism could not sustain Mary in her loneliness, and in her vulnerability she confessed that her true home was with God and that no place could finally hold her widow's heart except the heart of God.

A few days before her departure, she wrote of her ending days at Montevideo: "I have felt that it might be the very last I should ever spend at my once happy and privileged home, which now appears more like the grave of my buried hopes and affections than as the dwelling place of living and attractive associations. The scenes of the past have been coming up in rapid review. They are so painful in contrast with the great changes that are now upon my heart and life!"

As she remembered the past, she prayed to "the Greater Searcher of hearts" and asked for pardon for her sins as she "tried to acknowledge and repent of them in all the relations of life" which she had sustained at Montevideo—"as a wife, a mother, a mistress, a professing Christian, a neighbour, and member of society. In each and all," she wrote in her journal, "I have been an unprofitable servant to the Great Master who appointed my work and way on earth." She asked God's forgiveness through the love and grace of Jesus Christ.[44]

Mary left for her New Orleans home in January 1868. Shortly before she left, Charles Scribner had published, after Charlie's tireless editorial work, the first volume of Charles's *History of the Church of God*. The publication had been an obsession for Mary, and while the volume would quickly pass into obscurity, seeing it in print brought a deep satisfaction to her, as if Charles's last precious years were somehow caught up and bound in the volume itself. Now what remained for her was seeing that Charles's grave was marked with a proper gravestone and inscription. Before she had left Liberty County, she had purchased bricks from Dr. Raymond Harris, who now owned the Retreat. The old plantation home had been burned in the spring of 1866, apparently set on fire by thieves, and while the graveyard had not been damaged, all else had been consumed, even the great oaks and gardens that surrounded the house. The chimneys and brick columns that supported the house had been left a rubble, and from this Retreat rubble had been selected bricks to build a base for a marble slab over Charles's grave. The bricks had been carried to Midway and stacked in the cemetery to await Mary's return and the arrival of the slab.[45]

In December 1868 Mary made the long trip back from New Orleans to Montevideo. Charlie came down from New York and met her. Gilbert went to the depot and brought the marble slab in his oxcart to Midway. Audley King came to the cemetery to help with the brickwork. Porter and Stepney came from Arcadia and joined Gilbert and Charles from Carlawter. They all worked together, this remarkable little group—Audley King and Charlie Jones, Porter Way, Stepney West, Gilbert Lawson, and Charles Lawson—in mixing an oyster-shell mortar and laying the Retreat bricks, and placing the white marble slab over the tomb.[46]

Mary made a quick visit to the island with Julia King and found all the Kings struggling to make their way in a new world. Only Mary King Wells seemed to be thriving. She was busy and "says she never was happier in her life althou she

Broken monument to Joseph Jones in the Retreat cemetery,
late twentieth century (author's collection)

has not a dollar she can command of her own. Works hard, sleeps well, has no headaches now and God blesses her with a grateful, cheerful spirit." On their return from Woodville, Mary and Julia stopped and "looked upon the ruins of Maybank." And from Montevideo, Mary wrote Mary Sharpe: "The place is beautiful, but O! how sad! And every day some new perplexity. My child! Be thankful your lot has been cast elsewhere."[47]

Mary returned to New Orleans, and there, on 23 April 1869, she died after a short illness. Mary Sharpe asked her mother in her final hours whether she wished to be buried at old Midway. Mary had replied: "I have always said, 'Where I die, there let me be buried'; for 'at the last day we shall all be raised in a moment, in the twinkling of an eye.' My whole trust is in the Saviour. I stand in his righteousness, my righteousness is as filthy rages." So Mary chose as an act of freedom and faith to be buried in a distant place far from Montevideo and the marshes of Medway and all their sacred memories.[48]

A few months after Mary's death Robert Mallard returned to Liberty County for a visit with his brothers and sisters and to see after some business matters. He stopped at Midway and wandered in the cemetery beneath the ancient oaks. There he found a new marble slab with an inscription that read in part:

Joe Jones, Stepney West, and probably Elsey Maxwell at the grave of
Charles Colcock Jones (1804–1869) (Charles Colcock Jones Papers,
Tulane University Manuscript Department)

Sacred
to the memory of
Revd Charles Colcock Jones D.D.
Born in Liberty County, Georgia
December 20th 1804,
Departed this Life at Arcadia Plantation
March 16th 1863
. . . . .
The devoted Husband and Father, the firm friend &
Kind Master, the public Benefactor, the zealous
Evangelist, the profound Theologian, the learned
Author, the pure Patriot, and the exalted Christian.
In his Character were combined all those virtues and traits
Which dignify, ennoble, and benefit mankind.

Robert went to Arcadia, and "all there expressed sorrow" over Mary's death. He
rode to Montevideo. He wrote Mary Sharpe what he found:

The people were in the field opposite the cedars and soon discovered and came
to the road to greet me. In the van were Tenah and Charles. Found Lucy at

Reading Guide
Erskine Clarke, Dwelling Place: A Plantation Epic, 345-465

26. Slave Market. What does the sale of Phoebe, Cassius, and their children tell us about that family, and also about Charles, Mary, and the slave system?

27. Patience's Kitchen. You are what you eat! Contrast the difference between Patience and her sister Phoebe.

28. Montevideo. Love and marriage for Mary Sharpe.

29. The Retreat III. Another possible case of infanticide. Arson. Family separations.

30. Southern Zion. Mayor Charlie, the Secession crisis, death, and the conduct of William States Lee.

31. Indianola. Marching to war, and the disruptions of war. Where are people's loyalties?

32. The Refuge. Pay attention to the experiences of the three children of Charles and Mary during the Civil War.

of an era.

the house. All were in good keeping. Lucy rather thinner than when you saw her last. They were sincerely glad to see me. I am sure I was to see them. Little Abram came to the buggy to meet me.

He found that Tenah had another child, "a pretty little girl" named Lucy, after her grandmother. "They all made inquiries after you and the children," Robert wrote Mary Sharpe, "and sent a 'tousand howdyes.'"

Robert walked around the house and then went out and sat for a while in the garden on a rustic seat where the cedars ran down to the river. And there he remembered "the scene of a youthful and happy pair admonished in the gathering gloom of twilight by a kind voice saying 'I Wisdom dwell with Prudence.'" And he recalled "the wedding feast and the wedding night which united my earthly destinies with a dear one for whom respect and love only grow with the flying years." [49]

Six months earlier, in late January 1869, at the courthouse in Hinesville, a young Cash Jones was married in a simple service to Rachael Stevens. Young Cash had made his way back to Liberty County from the distant place to which he had been sold with his mother, Phoebe, and his father, Cassius. [50]

Principal Characters

Names in **bold** are principal characters. The principal characters among African Americans are all slaves of Charles Colcock Jones (1804–1863) and Mary Jones (1808–1869) unless otherwise noted.

AFRICAN AMERICANS

ABRAM SCRIVEN, husband of **Dinah.** He had been a slave of **Audley Maxwell (1766–1840)** and was inherited by **Julia Maxwell King** following her father's death in 1840. He and Dinah both lived on Colonel's Island—he at the Woodville settlement, she at the Maybank settlement. They had four children: Harry, Sylvia, Abram, and Dublin. When the **Roswell King (1796–1854)** estate was settled in 1858, the elder Abram was sold in Savannah to a slave trader from New Orleans. In 1863 he was living in Atlanta, where he had remarried. There is some indication that he returned to Liberty County after the Civil War. Name sometimes spelled "Abream."

ABREAM SCRIVEN. See **Abram Scriven.**

ADAM (1825–1863), youngest son of **Lizzy** and **Robinson** and brother to **Lymus, Cato, Cassius (Cash),** and **Porter**—see genealogical chart "Lizzy and Robinson." Not to be confused with Big Adam, the husband of Adam's sister Sina. He was often called Little Adam and sometimes Old Block. He was an agricultural laborer. In 1858 he married a woman who was a slave of the Reverend **Isaac Stockton Keith Axson.** In the early days of the Civil War, Adam was sent with seven others from Carlawter to work on the river fortifications of Savannah. While there, he contracted river cholera and died from its lingering effects at Carlawter in the fall of 1863.

ANDREW (1800–1870+), husband of Mary Ann. He and Mary Ann, together with their four children, were bought by **Andrew Maybank** at an auction in Riceboro in 1828. Charles and Mary Jones inherited the family when Andrew Maybank died in 1834. Andrew and Mary Ann lived from 1828 until 1863 in the Maybank settlement. Andrew was the driver at Maybank during this entire period. They were members of the Sunbury Baptist Church and had seven children, including **Dinah, Charles, Gilbert,** and **Little Andrew.**

See genealogical chart "Andrew and Mary Ann Lawson." In 1863 the couple was moved to Bonaventure plantation on the Medway River. Following the Civil War, they lived at Carlawter with several of their children and their families. They adopted Lawson as their family name.

BECK (1842–1862), daughter of **Porter** and **Patience**. She grew up at Maybank and Carlawter following her mother, who moved between the two plantations as the chief cook for the Jones family. See genealogical charts "Robin and Lizzy West" and "Lizzy and Robinson." Beck married Ben Lowe, a slave of a neighboring planter, during the Christmas holidays 1860. She died in June 1862 of dysentery following a severe case of measles.

BEN LOWE. See **Beck**.

CASH. See **Cassius**.

CASH JONES (1837–1869+), the son of **Cassius** and **Phoebe**. He was often called Young Cassius, or Young Cash.

CASSIUS (1811–1857+), third son of **Lizzy** and **Robinson**, and husband of **Phoebe**. He was named for his maternal uncle and often went by Cash. Cassius was the brother of **Lymus, Cato, Porter,** and **Adam**. See genealogical chart "Lizzy and Robinson." He was moved with his parents and siblings to Carlawter in 1817 and lived there until 1856. He became a "good fieldhand, basketmaker, and handy at jobs," but also gained, in contrast to his brothers Cato and Porter, a reputation as a rogue and troublemaker. He married Phoebe in 1837, and they had ten children, including Young Cassius (or **Cash Jones**), **Jane,** and LaFayette. Cassius had a son, James, by **Peggy**, the daughter of **Hamlet** and **Elvira**, and a daughter, Nanny, by a slave of **Roswell King** (1796–1854). He and Phoebe were sold in Savannah with their children in 1856.

CATO (1809–1866), the second son of **Lizzy** and **Robinson**. He was moved with his parents and siblings to Carlawter in 1817 and lived there until 1865. Cato was the brother of **Lymus, Cassius (Cash), Porter,** and **Adam**. See genealogical chart "Lizzy and Robinson." He was the driver at Montevideo from 1840 until 1865, and a watchman for the North Newport Baptist Church. In 1839 he married Betsy (1820–1854), the daughter of **Jack** and **Marcia**. He and his brother Cassius were thus married to half-sisters: Betsy and **Phoebe**. Betsy was owned by **Joseph Jones** (1779–1846) and lived at the Retreat settlement until Joseph Jones's death, when she became a slave of **Charles Berrien Jones**. She was moved to Walthourville in 1854. Cato and Betsy had three children, including twins Rinah and Ned (1843–?). Cato married second Jane, who was owned by the estate of Joseph Bacon. They adopted Holmes as their family name.

CHARLES (1820–1870+), oldest son of **Andrew** and **Mary Ann**, and husband of **Lucy**. He was the brother of **Dinah, Gilbert,** and **Little Andrew**. See genealogical chart "Andrew and Mary Ann Lawson." He should not be confused with his master **Charles Colcock Jones** (1804–1863), who was also called Charles, or with **Charles Colcock Jones** (1831–1893), who was called Charlie. Charles and Lucy married in 1840 and had their only child, **Tenah**, in 1841. Charles moved between Montevideo, Maybank, and Arcadia as he was assigned work as an oxcart driver. Lucy generally remained at Montevideo and Maybank working as a domestic servant to Mary Jones. He became a member of Midway in 1852. When **Mary Sharpe Jones** married **Robert Quarterman Mallard,** Lucy and Charles became, with Tenah, the property of Mary Sharpe Mallard. In 1863, when the Mallards moved to Atlanta, Charles and Lucy were carried with them, together with Tenah and her new husband, **Niger** (1839–1891+). After the Civil War, Charles and Lucy lived at Carlawter with other members of their extended families and declared their family name to be Lawson.

CLARISSA (1766–1856), an old slave bought from the **Andrew Maybank** estate by **Charles Colcock Jones** (1804–1863) in order for her to remain at the Maybank settlement and at the Retreat. She was often call Old Clarissa or Mom Clarissa and should not be confused with **Phoebe**'s daughter **Clarissa** (1825–1865+). She had come to Maybank in 1794 with her mistress Elizabeth Girardeau Maybank, the maternal aunt of Charles Colcock Jones. "Mom Clarissa" would become a source of genealogical information and family tradition for the Charles Colcock Jones family. She spent her last days at the Retreat, where her daughters Sally and Sue cared for her.

CLARISSA (1825–1865+), the daughter of **Phoebe** and an unknown father. She was the half-sister of **John** and of the children of Phoebe and **Cassius**. She is not to be confused with **Clarissa** (1766–1856). She apparently remained at Carlawter when her mother was working in Savannah in 1831 as the personal servant of **Mary Jones**. While she spent most of 1838 in Columbia working as a young domestic under the supervision of her grandfather **Jack**, she became a field worker and a rather marginal figure in the slave community at Carlawter. Her first child, Phoebe, was born in 1848 of an unknown father after Clarissa had been moved to Arcadia. She married Patrick, a slave of a neighboring planter in 1851. Their first child, Jane, had been born the year before. She became a member of the Midway congregation in 1853. She and Patrick had three more children before Clarissa was sent to Indianola in 1863 and Patrick married another woman. By 1865 Clarissa was married to Pulaski, a carpenter who had also been sent to Indianola. They returned to Carlawter immediately after the Civil War and took Fraser as their family name.

DADDY JACK. See **Jack**.

DADDY ROBIN. See **Robin**.

DINAH (1828–1861), the daughter of **Andrew** and Mary Ann, sister of **Charles** and **Gilbert**. See genealogical chart "Andrew and Mary Ann Lawson." She lived all her life at Maybank. In 1850 she married **Abram Scriven**, a slave of **Julia Maxwell King**. He lived in the settlement at Woodville. They had four children — Harry, Silvia, Little Abram, and Dublin. When Abram Scriven was carried to Savannah to be sold in 1858, Dinah tried desperately but unsuccessfully through **Mary Jones** to have him purchased by someone who would return him to Colonel's Island and his family. In the spring of 1861 she married James, a slave of W. C. Stevens of Palmyra plantation. She died of typhoid fever in the fall of 1861 and was buried in the slave cemetery at Maybank.

DR. HARRY. See **Harry Stevens**.

ELSEY (1809–1891+), daughter of **Robin** and Lizzy, sister of **Stepney** and **Patience**, and wife of **Syphax**, a carpenter who lived at White Oak plantation. See genealogical chart "Robin and Lizzy West." Her name was often spelled "Elsie." She worked closely with her sister Patience as a domestic servant and cook for **Mary Jones**. When **Mary Sharpe Jones** married **Robert Quarterman Mallard** in 1857, Elsey and six children and one grandchild became the property of the Mallards. In the spring of 1865 she went with Mary Jones to the Refuge in southwest Georgia, returning some months later to Liberty County, where she and Syphax adopted the family name of Maxwell and rented and then purchased land at Arcadia. She was a member of the North Newport Baptist Church.

ELSIE. See **Elsey.**

ELVIRA (1798?–1826), born in Africa. She was brought on a slave ship with her mother, **Fanny,** and younger brother Marcus to the United States in 1803. **John Jones (1772–1805)** purchased the family, and Elvira and Marcus were deeded to Jones's infant daughter **Susan [Mary Jones Maxwell Cumming].** Elvira married **Hamlet** around 1812, and they had their first child, **Syphax,** in 1813. See genealogical chart "Jupiter and Silvey." She died in childbirth at Carlawter in 1826.

FANNY (1778?–1850), born in Africa. She was brought on a slave ship with her two children, **Elvira** and Marcus, to the United States. **John Jones (1772–1805)** purchased the family in 1803. She became a slave of **Joseph Jones (1779–1846)** in 1808, although during the last years of her life she lived at Carlawter. She should not be confused with the Fanny who was a part of the **Andrew Maybank** estate and was the wife of **Prime,** or with Fanny who was the daughter of **Sam** and **Rosetta** and the wife of **Gilbert.** While Fanny had difficulty mastering the Gullah dialect, she was probably a major conveyor of African traditions within the Gullah settlements at Carlawter and White Oak. She was a member of the Sunbury Baptist Church.

FLORA (1790–1851), the matriarch of a large family at Carlawter. She came to the Jones family in 1806, when her mistress Sarah Anderson married **Joseph Jones (1779–1846).** When Sarah Anderson's estate was divided in 1830, Flora became the slave of **Mary Jones.** Flora's husband is unknown, but he probably lived at the Retreat settlement as a slave of Joseph Jones. They had seven children and thirty-seven grandchildren. See genealogical chart "Flora." She was often called in her later years Old Flora and should not be confused with her granddaughter **Flora (1839–1868+).** In the 1840s and until her death in 1851, she was a nurse looking after the children in Carlawter. She was a member of the North Newport Baptist Church.

FLORA (1839–1868+), the daughter of Eve and William (a slave of **Roswell King [1796–1854]**). She is not to be confused with the Flora who married Young Gilbert. Her maternal grandmother was **Flora (1790–1851),** the matriarch of a large family at Carlawter. See genealogical chart "Flora." Her paternal grandmother was **Phillis,** who was for years a cook for **Julia Maxwell King.** In 1857 Flora married, in the chapel at Montevideo, **Joefinny,** a house servant of the **David Lyman Buttolphs.** When Joefinny ran away during the early days of the Civil War, there was concern among the Buttolphs and Joneses that Flora might try to join him. She was the personal servant of **Mary Jones** and traveled with her during the war to southwest Georgia, Atlanta, and Augusta. Mary Jones dismissed Flora in late 1865 for being "disrespectful." Flora joined Joefinny in Savannah in 1866, although she later returned to Liberty County and worked as a domestic servant for a Mrs. Anderson.

GILBERT (1824–1885), the son of **Andrew** and Mary Ann and the brother of **Dinah** and **Charles.** See genealogical chart "Andrew and Mary Ann Lawson." He married in the early 1840s Fanny, the daughter of **Sam** and **Rosetta.** Gilbert's brother **Charles** married Fanny's sister **Lucy.** Gilbert was a carriage and buggy driver and general handyman around Montevideo and Maybank. Gilbert and Fanny had seven children, including

Little Gilbert. During and after the Civil War, Gilbert was "irreproachable in word, look or manner" in his relationship to **Mary Jones.** After the war, he and Fanny declared their family name to be Lawson.

HAMLET (1769–1839), son of **Jupiter** (1740?–1812?) and Silvey, and brother of **Jupiter** (1760?–1840). He married **Phillis.** They had three children, including Little Hamlet and **Prince.** He then married **Elvira,** and they had six children, including **Syphax.** See genealogical chart for "Jupiter and Silvey." Hamlet belonged to **John Jones** (1749–1779) and John Jones (1772–1805). He was among those slaves purchased by **Joseph Jones** (1779–1846) in Riceboro in 1808 and given back to the widow and children of Jones's brother **John Jones** (1772–1805). He was part of the joint property of **Charles Colcock Jones** (1804–1863) and his sister **Susan Mary Jones Maxwell Cumming** until a division of their property in 1839. He followed his father, Jupiter, and his brother Jupiter as a driver. Hamlet's son **Prince** followed him as the driver at White Oak.

HARRY STEVENS (?–1856+), a skilled carpenter and healer and widely respected slave of **Thomas Mallard.** He was also skilled in the construction of dams and canals for rice production. Often called Dr. Harry, he was a member of Midway Congregational Church. **Charles Colcock Jones** (1804–1863) regarded him as his "good friend." Through his personal efforts and the contributions of a number of planters, Harry Stevens bought his freedom and the freedom of his family and took them to the colony of freed people in Liberia, where, wrote **Robert Quarterman Mallard,** "he became a citizen of the free African Republic!"

JACK (1750–1850), the husband first of Lizett and second of **Marcia.** He was the brother of **Robin** and the father of **Phoebe.** He should not be confused with Jack, his great-nephew and namesake, the son of **Patience** and **Porter.** The personal servant of Sarah Anderson, he came with her when she married **Joseph Jones** (1779–1846) in 1806. A man of great personal integrity and widely admired wisdom, Jack became not only the majordomo at the Retreat, overseeing with **Sylvia** the running of the house, but also a patriarch, storyteller, and dentist in the Gullah community of Liberty County. When the estate of Sarah Anderson Jones was divided in 1830, he became the slave of **Mary Jones.** He was a member of the Sunbury Baptist Church. In 1837–1838 and again in 1848–1850 he lived in Columbia, where he managed the **Charles Colcock Jones** (1804–1863) household. He and Marcia died in Columbia a few days apart in the spring of 1850.

JACOB (?–?), carpenter and slave of **John Jones** (1772–1805). He was a part of a developing tradition of carpentry among certain skilled Gullah artisans. **Sandy Jones** apparently was an apprentice with him. He should not be confused with the Jacob who was a part of the **Andrew Maybank** estate or the Jacob who was a carpenter at South Hampton.

JAMES (1842–1865+), the son of **Cassius** and **Peggy** (1815–1865+). While Cassius was married to **Phoebe** at the time of James's birth, he acknowledged James as his son and left some of his possessions to him in 1856. See genealogical chart "Jupiter and Silvey."

JANE (1838–1857), the daughter of **Phoebe** and **Cassius,** half-sister of **Clarissa** (1825–1865), **John,** and **James.** See genealogical chart "Lizzy and Robinson." She spent 1848–1850 in Columbia, where she was learning, under the direction of her grandfather **Jack,** the work of a domestic servant. In 1851, however, she was put to work in the fields at Montevideo, where her uncle **Cato** was the driver. **Charles Colcock Jones** (1804–1863) found her increasingly obstinate and surly. She may have been married to **Titus** (1826–1865+). She managed to run away to Savannah in 1856, probably by hiding on one of the small sloops that sailed the inland waters between Riceboro and Savannah. She disguised herself in Savannah and worked for several months as a domestic for hire. Discovered, captured, and sold, she died in New Orleans the next year of pleurisy or consumption.

JOEFINNY (1831–1866+), the son of Zipporah, a slave of **Audley Maxwell** (1766–1840). He was deeded with his mother and siblings to Maxwell's grandchildren **Laura Elizabeth Maxwell** and **Charles Edward Maxwell**. Joefinny spent most of his early years on Colonel's Island. Trained as a domestic servant, he became the greatly respected and trusted butler and manager of the household for Laura Maxwell and **David Lyman Buttolph** after their marriage. He married **Flora** (1839–1868+) in the chapel at Montevideo in 1857. Shortly after the Buttolphs fled their island home during the early days of the Civil War, Joefinny escaped and apparently hid on Colonel's Island for the duration of the war. In 1865 he and Flora were reunited in Savannah.

JOHN (1830–1854), son of **Phoebe** and **Sandy Jones**, half-brother to **Clarissa** (1825–1865+) and **Jane**. He spent 1848–1850 in Columbia, where he was learning, under the direction of his grandfather **Jack**, the work of a domestic servant. On his return to Carlawter in 1850, however, he was put to work in the fields. He resisted the orders of the white overseer and his uncle **Cato**, and shortly after his return to Carlawter received from the overseer a flogging. On **Mary Jones**'s return to Montevideo in 1853, she found John to be a "prayerless, wicked, profane, Sabbath breaker and immoral boy and he seemed insensible to his sins and their consequences." In 1851 he married a woman at Carlawter, but he left her the next year. He died in 1853 from hemorrhaging of the lungs. During his violent illness, he repented of his sins and confessed that he "could look only to Christ."

JUPITER (1740?–1812?), the husband of Silvey and father of **Jupiter** (1760?–1840) and **Hamlet** (1769–1839). He was the driver for **John Jones** (1772–1805) at Rural Felicity and Liberty Hall plantations. In 1808 he and his family were sold in Riceboro in order to settle the estate debts of his master. They were purchased by **Joseph Jones** (1779–1846) and given back as a gift to the widow and children of John Jones. Jupiter and his wife, Silvey (also called in her last years Blind Silvey), were the progenitors of a large and influential family at Carlawter and White Oak. See genealogical chart "Jupiter and Silvey."

JUPITER (1760?–1840), the son of **Jupiter** (1740?–1812?) and Silvey, and brother of **Hamlet**. See genealogical chart "Jupiter and Silvey." He served as the first driver at Carlawter and was followed by his brother Hamlet and at White Oak by his nephew **Prince**. If he had a wife, she lived on another plantation. He is not to be confused with his father or his nephew, the son of his sister Hannah.

LIZZY (1784–1837), wife of **Robinson** and mother of **Lymus, Cato, Cassius, Porter,** and **Adam**. She was the personal servant of Susannah Girardeau and became a slave of the Jones family when her mistress married **John Jones** (1772–1805). **Charles Colcock Jones** (1804–1863) inherited Lizzy from his mother. Lizzy and Robinson were the progenitors of a large and influential family. See genealogical chart "Lizzy and Robinson." She was a cook. In her later years she was often called Old Lizzy. At her death, Charles Colcock Jones described her as "a quiet, faithful Negro, & one of the oldest on the plantation."

She should not be confused with several of her granddaughters who were named for her or with Lizzy the wife of **Robin.**

LUCY (1820–1891+), the daughter of **Rosetta** and **Sam,** wife of **Charles,** and mother of **Tenah.** See genealogical charts "Rosetta and Sam Roberts" and "Andrew and Mary Ann Lawson." She was trained from an early age by her parents to be a domestic servant. She spent 1837–1838 in Columbia, where she worked under the supervision of **Jack.** She married Charles in 1840, and they moved back and forth between Carlawter and Maybank according to the needs of their owners. She became a member of Midway Congregational Church in 1851. When **Mary Sharpe Jones** married **Robert Quarterman Mallard** in 1857, Lucy, Charles, and Tenah became the property of the Mallards. When the Mallards moved to Atlanta in 1863, Lucy, Charles, and Tenah, together with Tenah's husband, **Niger** (1839–1891+), were carried with them. They were all at Montevideo during the weeks in 1864–1865 when it was pillaged by Union troops. Lucy and Charles signed contracts with **Mary Jones** after the war and continued living at Carlawter. Lucy and Charles served for a number of years after 1868 as the primary caretakers for Montevideo. They declared their family name to be Lawson.

LYMUS (1804–1864?), the oldest son of **Lizzy** and **Robinson,** the brother of **Cato, Cassius, Porter,** and **Adam.** He was married to a woman owned by Elijah Chapman, whose plantation was near Montevideo. Lymus was an agricultural worker and was regarded by whites as having a close relationship with **Charles Colcock Jones** (1804–1863). He apparently died at Carlawter in late 1863 or 1864.

MARCIA (1795–1850), second wife of **Jack.** She belonged to **Joseph Jones** (1779–1846), who rented her to **Mary Jones** in the 1830s so that she might live with her husband. In 1842 Mary Jones gave Joseph Jones the slave Jenny in exchange for Marcia. Jack and Marcia had four children and seven grandchildren living at the Retreat at the time of the exchange. One daughter, Betsy, was the wife of **Cato.** Marcia spent 1837–1838 in Columbia, where she was the chief cook for the family of **Charles Colcock Jones** (1804–1863). She returned to Columbia with the Jones family in 1848 and died there a few days after Jack's death in 1850.

MARY ANN. See **Andrew** and genealogical chart "Andrew and Mary Ann Lawson." She is not to be confused with Mary Ann, the daughter of **Sharper** and the wife of **Sandy Maybank.**

MILEY (?–1865+), a slave and house servant of **William Maxwell.** Her husband, Isaac, was a slave on a neighboring plantation. In the 1840s he had an affair with Louisa, another domestic servant of the Maxwells, that resulted in the two of them being excommunicated by Midway Congregational Church. In 1851 Isaac beat Miley so badly that she lost the sight in one eye. **Elizabeth Jones Maxwell** took her to Savannah for treatment by a doctor and nursed her through her recovery from the beating. When Federal troops forced William Maxwell from his Springfield plantation in early 1865, Miley was the only Maxwell slave who showed concern for Maxwell's welfare.

MOMMA. See **Sylvia.**

NIGER (1803–1862), husband of **Phillis.** See genealogical chart "Flora." He came to the Jones family in 1806, when his mistress Sarah Anderson married **Joseph Jones** (1779–1846).

When a final settlement was made of Sarah Anderson's slaves in the early 1840s, he became a slave of **Mary Jones**. He and Phillis had eight children, including **Niger** (1839–
1891+). While he was involved in a variety of agricultural work, his primary responsibility
was to drive one of the oxcarts. In 1854 he was bitten by a rattlesnake and almost died, but
"with much presence of mind," he "took out his knife and scarified the wound and put
his foot into cold water and bound up the leg." He and Phillis were members of Midway
Congregational Church. A very careful reading of sources is required to avoid confusion
with his son, and with **Niger** (1832–1865+).

NIGER (1832–1865+), the son of Fanny and **Prime**. He was with his parents and siblings part
of the **Andrew Maybank** estate that went to **Charles Colcock Jones** (1804–1863) and
Mary Jones. The family adopted the name Stevens after the Civil War. See genealogical
chart "Prime and Fanny Stevens." In 1852 Niger was moved with his parents and siblings
from Maybank to Arcadia. He married sometime before 1862 Rhina, a slave of **William
Maxwell**. In 1862 he was among those sent to Indianola in Burke County. His wife was
rented from William Maxwell in order to accompany him. After the Civil War he and
Rhina returned to Liberty County. A very careful reading of sources is required to avoid
confusion with **Niger** (1803–1862) or with **Niger** (1839–1891+).

NIGER (1839–1891+), son of **Niger** (1803–1862) and **Phillis**, and husband of **Tenah**. He spent
much of his early life at Maybank, where he developed an intimate knowledge of the
Medway marsh and became a skilled fisherman. When he asked to marry Tenah in 1861,
Mary Sharpe Jones [Mallard], her mistress, told him, "I did not think the arrangement
would suit me at all, for I did not want Tenah to marry." He, however, "seemed to think
there could be no valid objections." They were married a few weeks later in the chapel at
Montevideo in a double ceremony with Niger's sister Judy and Sam, Tenah's uncle. See
genealogical charts "Flora" and "Rosetta and Sam Roberts." When the Mallards moved
to Atlanta in 1863, Niger and Tenah were carried with them, returning to Liberty County
as Union troops began their attack on the city. After the war, Niger and Tenah remained
at Carlawter, where they were paid a wage for specified work and had land to farm on
their own. They adopted first Bacon and then Fraser as their family name. A very careful reading of sources is required to avoid confusing this Niger with **Niger** (1803–1862)
or with **Niger** (1832–1865+).

OLD MOMMA. See **Sylvia**.

PARIS (?–1851), driver at South Hampton plantation from the 1830s until his death and slave
of **Roswell King** (1796–1854). A large man, greatly respected in both the Gullah and
white communities of Liberty County, he was the chief watchman at the North Newport Baptist Church and the sexton at the Pleasant Grove Presbyterian Church. He was
frequently called upon to negotiate disputes among slaves of different plantations. He
is not to be confused with Paris the driver of G. W. Walthour's Richmond plantation.
Julia Maxwell King wrote of his death: "Our good faithful Paris is no more. His parting
words to those around him were 'do not fret for me, the way is open before me and I am
safe.' His end was peaceful." A King slave remarked that Paris's death "was not like death
but only going out of one house into another." He was, said his mistress, "a true friend;
one who prayed for us and our children nor did he forget the poor Negro's friend"; many
times he called on his death bed for **Charles Colcock Jones** (1804–1863).

PATIENCE (1817–1870+), the daughter of **Robin** and Lizzy, sister of **Elsey** and **Stepney,** and wife of **Porter.** See genealogical charts "Robin and Lizzy West" and "Lizzy." Patience was trained from an early age to be a cook as she worked under **Lizzy, Marcia,** and **Sylvia.** By the 1850s Patience had become a cook highly skilled in the preparation of food from the fields, woods, and waters of the low country. Patience spent 1837–1838 in Columbia, working under the supervision of her uncle **Jack.** She and Porter married Christmas 1838 and had nine children, including **Titus** and **Beck.** She and Porter were both members of the Midway congregation for more than thirty years. While Patience and her cousin and sister-in-law Phoebe resisted in different ways the oppression of slavery and had markedly different personalities, they worked closely together for years in the kitchen and house at Montevideo and Maybank. After the Civil War, Patience and Porter settled near Arcadia, where they first rented land and then purchased their own small farm. They adopted Way as their family name.

PEGGY (1815–1865+), the daughter of **Hamlet** and **Elvira.** See genealogical chart "Hamlet." She was part of the joint property of **Charles Colcock Jones (1804–1863)** and his sister **Susan Mary Jones Maxwell Cumming** until a division of their property in 1839, when she moved to White Oak plantation. She should not be confused with **Peggy (1842–1866).** She was an early competitor with **Phoebe** for the affection of **Cassius** and had a child, **James,** by Cassius after he and Phoebe were married and after Peggy was married to Simon, a slave from a neighboring plantation. She and Simon had four children.

PEGGY (1842–1866), the daughter of Eve and William (a slave of the **Roswell King**s). See genealogical chart "Flora." She should not be confused with **Peggy (1815–1865+).** She was trained from an early age to be a seamstress and maid and worked for **Mary Jones** at Montevideo and Maybank. In 1860 she was "debauched" by William States Lee, a white guest at Maybank, and had his child, Eva Lee, the next year. She served as the wet nurse for **Mary Ruth Jones,** the motherless child of **Charles Colcock Jones (1831–1893),** and married in 1862 Henry, a slave from a neighboring plantation. In 1866 Peggy "died of small pox and in great want and neglect in Savannah."

PHILLIS. There are five women named Phillis who need to be distinguished, although each has a minor role in the narrative. (1) Phillis the first wife of **Hamlet** and mother of **Prince.** A slave of **John Jones (1772–1805),** she died in 1812. See genealogical chart "Jupiter and Silvey." (2) Phillis who was a plantation nurse at the Retreat between 1800 and 1810 and was owned by **Joseph Jones (1779–1846).** (3) Phillis (1811–1862+), a daughter of **Flora** (1790–1851). This Phillis was married to **Niger (1803–1862)** and was the mother of **Niger** (1839–1891+). See genealogical chart "Flora." (4) Phillis, daughter of Fanny and **Prime,** who was born in 1829, married first to Paul, a slave on a neighboring plantation, and then in 1853 to Sam, a child of **Sam** and **Rosetta.** See genealogical charts "Prime and Fanny Stevens" and "Sam and Rosetta Roberts." And (5) Phillis, a cook for **Julia Maxwell King.** This Phillis died in 1858 and had been an "old friend" to Mary Jones. She was the grandmother of **Flora (1839–1868+).**

PHOEBE (1809–1857+), the daughter of **Jack** and Lizzett. Raised under the tutelage of her father and her mistress Sarah Anderson Jones. She was given when she was seventeen to **Mary Jones,** who was eighteen, to be her personal servant. The previous year she had given birth to **Clarissa (1825–1865+)** by an unknown father. Phoebe soon became an accomplished seamstress and an indispensable servant to Mary Jones. Phoebe married in 1828 **Sandy Jones,** a carpenter. They had one child, **John.** In 1831 Phoebe was carried to Savannah when **Charles Colcock Jones (1804–1863)** and Mary Jones moved there. When **Charles Colcock Jones (1831–1893)** was born, Phoebe slept on the floor beside Mary Jones in order to care for the child. She had had to leave her own children at Carlawter under the care of others. She became a member of the Midway congregation in 1832. When Sandy Jones was away from Carlawter doing carpentry work in 1835, Phoebe began an affair with **Cassius.** They were both excommunicated from the Midway congregation in 1836. That year their first son was born, Young Cassius (or **Cash Jones**). Phoebe and Cassius had nine more children, including **Jane.** Phoebe chafed under the oppression of slavery and struggled to keep her rage from flaring in dangerous ways as she sometimes came close to open defiance. Charles Colcock Jones (1804–1863) did not trust her although he knew that his wife Mary was deeply dependent on her. As long as Phoebe's father, Jack, was alive, he provided Phoebe some protection from her master's distrust and growing frustration with her behavior. In 1856 Phoebe and Cassius were sold in Savannah with their children.

PLENTY JAMES (1800?–1865+), the driver for Nathaniel Varnedoe at Liberty Hall plantation. He was sometimes called Plenty Varnedoe. He was married to a woman who lived at Liberty Hall, but he was suspended in 1846 for a year from the Midway congregation because he had been "living illicitly" with another woman. When his master died in 1856, his will stated, "I will and bequeath to my true and faithful servant driver Plenty one hundred dollars in money." The driver gave the money to **Charles Colcock Jones (1804–1863)** and asked him to invest it for him, which he did at 6 percent interest. Plenty James was apparently a person of some means within the Gullah community. He sold a buggy to **Cassius** in the early 1850s. Shortly after Varnedoe's estate was settled, Plenty James's wife was sold to a planter in Albany, Georgia. The old man was able to visit her at least on one occasion through the help of his former pastor at Midway, the Reverend **Isaac Stockton Keith Axson.**

POMPEY (1803–1873+), the driver for **Thomas Mallard** at the Mallard Place and a watchman for Midway Congregational Church. He was married to Bella, who also lived at the Mallard Place. Pompey was a highly respected driver who was allowed by his master to rent himself out to other planters for various tasks associated with plantation management. He was also able to work as much land as he could, and he frequently hired other slaves to work for him. As a watchman he was deeply involved in adjudicating disputes among slaves of surrounding plantations. After the Civil War, he and Bella took Bacon as their family name, and Pompey made claims to the United States government for substantial losses of livestock and other property taken by Federal troops when they pillaged Liberty County.

PORTER (1817–1881), son of **Lizzy** and **Robinson,** brother of **Cato** and **Cassius,** and husband of **Patience.** See genealogical chart "Lizzy and Robinson." From an early age he was trained to be a carpenter by working as an apprentice to **Sandy Jones** and **Sandy Maybank.** He was noted for his reliability and for his development as a highly skilled carpenter. He and Patience married Christmas 1838 and had nine children, including **Titus (1839–1870+)** and **Beck.** He and Patience were both members of the Midway congregation for more than thirty years. After the Civil War, while continuing his work as a carpenter, he became a prosperous small farmer, owning land near Arcadia plantation. He and Patience adopted Way as their family name.

PRIME (1798–1865+), a slave of **Andrew Maybank** and husband of Fanny, another Maybank slave. At Maybank's death in 1834, Prime and Fanny were left in Maybank's will to **Charles Colcock Jones (1804–1863)** and **Mary Jones**. Prime and Fanny had five children, including **Titus (1826–1865+)** and **Niger (1832–1865+)**. Prime is not to be confused with Prime, the son of **Cassius** and **Phoebe**. See genealogical chart "Prime and Fanny Stevens." In 1852 Prime and his family were moved from the settlement at Maybank to Arcadia. Prime was an agricultural worker, but he was also a woodsman and often had the task of cutting and splitting wood for shingles, fencing, and fires. He owned his own shotgun and became a successful hunter of ducks. In 1862 he and his family were sent to Indianola plantation in Burke County. At the end of the Civil War, he and his family returned to Liberty County and took Stevens as their family name.

PRINCE (1804–1866+), son of **Hamlet** and **Phillis**. He was born at Liberty Hall and spent time at the Retreat settlement, at Carlawter, and White Oak. He was part of the joint property of **Charles Colcock Jones (1804–1863)** and Jones's sister **Susan Mary Jones Maxwell Cumming** until a division of their property in 1839, when he became the sole property of Susan Maxwell Cumming. See genealogical chart "Jupiter and Silvey." In 1839 Prince followed in the footsteps of his grandfather **Jupiter (1740?–1812?)** and his father, Hamlet, by becoming the driver at White Oak. He was married to Venus, a slave of **Joseph Jones (1779–1846)**. When her master died in 1846, she became, through a division of property, the slave of **James Newton Jones**. Three years after James Newton Jones died in 1854, Venus was carried to north Georgia, where she was sold to a stranger. She died shortly after her sale and the trauma of her removal from her husband. In 1863, under the threat of Federal raids, Prince was removed with other slaves from White Oak and sent to southwest Georgia. After the war, he returned to Liberty County, rented land at White Oak, and took Stewart as his family name.

PULASKI (1779–1852), the husband of Affee (1782–1857+) and a slave of **Joseph Jones (1779–1846)**. Pulaski was born the same year as his master, grew up with him, and became the driver at the Retreat in the 1790s, a position he kept for almost sixty years. Joseph Jones held Pulaski in high regard as together they led in the development of the Retreat into one of the largest and most prosperous plantations of the Georgia low country. Master and driver met regularly in the evenings in the Retreat study to plan the next day's work. In spite of such a close relationship, there was no question who was the master and who was the slave. When Joseph Jones died, he left special instructions that the old driver and his wife were not to be removed from their home at the Retreat and that Pulaski was to be given annually "an extra suit of union clothing and six dollars." Pulaski and Affee had six children and more than fifteen grandchildren. Their son Young Pulaski became a driver for a plantation of the Joseph Jones estate and was sold a year after Old Pulaski died. Neither Old Pulaski nor Young Pulaski should be confused with Pulaski the carpenter who was the son of **Niger (1803–1862)** and **Phillis** and was sent to work on the Savannah fortifications.

ROBIN (1778–1870+), the brother of **Jack.** He came to the Jones family in 1806, when his mistress Sarah Anderson married **Joseph Jones** (1779–1846). When Sarah Anderson's estate was divided in 1830, Robin and his wife, Lizzy, became the slave of **Mary Jones.** He and Lizzy had three children—**Elsey, Stepney,** and **Patience**—and became the progenitors of one of the most important families in the Gullah community of Liberty County. See genealogical chart "Robin and Lizzy West." Lizzy died in 1832 after having broken her thigh. She had been, noted **Charles Colcock Jones** (1804–1863), a "faithful servant," a Christian who "died in hope." She should not be confused with **Lizzy,** wife of Robinson. Robin was apparently a remarkably strong person who lived at least into his nineties. When he was in his seventies, he was still active as a woodsman, cutting fence rails and shingles. In 1846 he was moved from Carlawter to Arcadia, where his son Stepney was the driver. After the Civil War, he remained at Arcadia, where Stepney coordinated the renting of much of the old plantation, and Patience and her husband, **Porter,** bought land and established themselves on a nearby small farm. Robin and Stepney declared West to be their family name.

ROBINSON (1780?–1850+), the husband of **Lizzy,** and father of **Lymus, Cato, Cassius, Porter,** and **Adam.** See genealogical chart "Lizzy and Robinson." He was a slave of **Eliza Greene Low Robarts.** As a young man, he had smallpox, which left him both scarred and immune from the disease. Eliza Robarts's slaves were often mingled with those of **Charles Colcock Jones** (1804–1863), so Robinson and Lizzy lived together in Sunbury, in Greensboro, at the Retreat, and at Carlawter. They were separated in 1833 when **Joseph Jones** (1779–1846) bought Hickory Hill plantation for his sister **Eliza Greene Low Robarts** and gave her part of the Montevideo plantation to **Mary Jones.** Thereafter, Robinson had to make the Saturday afternoon trip from Hickory Hill to his "wife house" at Carlawter until Lizzy's death in 1837. When Eliza Robarts moved to Marietta in 1849, she made arrangements for Robinson to live at the Retreat settlement. In 1850 he served as a nurse to those who had smallpox and were being held in quarantine in Riceboro.

ROSETTA (1800–1866), the wife of **Sam.** She was born a slave of John Bohum Girardeau and was willed shortly after her birth to **Susannah Girardeau Jones,** who willed her to her son **Charles Colcock Jones** (1804–1863). When Susannah Girardeau Jones died in 1810, Rosetta was carried, with her master, to Greensboro, where she lived and worked in the household of her master's aunt, **Eliza Greene Low Robarts.** There she got to know Sam, who was being trained to be a domestic servant for the Robartses. Rosetta was herself trained to be a domestic under the tutelage of **Lizzy.** When Eliza Robarts returned to Liberty County, Rosetta lived first at the Retreat and then at Carlawter. She and Sam married in 1818 and had five children, including **Lucy,** Fanny (the wife of **Gilbert**), and Sam (the husband of **Phillis**). After the Civil War her family took the name Roberts. See genealogical chart "Rosetta and Sam Roberts." Rosetta's work involved a variety of domestic tasks, including spinning, churning butter, cleaning the house, and, in her old age, watching after the slave children at Carlawter. She became a midwife and was implicated in the 1850s for concealing an infanticide by one of the Robarts slaves. When Eliza Robarts moved to Marietta in 1849, Sam was taken away from Rosetta and his family in order to function as the butler and manager of the Robarts household. He was allowed to return each winter to Liberty County for about six weeks, but Rosetta grieved deeply over the separation and worried that he would find another wife in northern Georgia.

After the Civil War, Sam returned to Carlawter and lived with his wife and children. Rosetta died a few months after his return, surrounded by her children, and confessing her confidence in God's goodness and grace.

SAM (1798?–1867), husband of **Rosetta** and progenitor with her of a large and influential family. See genealogical chart "Rosetta and Sam Roberts." He was owned by **Eliza Greene Low Robarts** and was, from an early age, trained to be a domestic servant. He quickly became an indispensable and respected manager of the Robarts household. In 1849, when his mistress moved to Marietta, he was separated from his family. While he was allowed to return to Liberty County every Christmas and to stay for about six weeks, the separation was particularly painful for Rosetta. In Marietta his reputation as a wise and dependable servant continued to grow. When the Robartses fled the approaching Union troops in 1864, Sam went ahead of them to middle Georgia to make arrangements for their move. He returned to Liberty County after the war to be with his wife and family. Rosetta died shortly after his return, and he died the following year. They had declared their family name to be Roberts. He is not to be confused with Sam, the black preacher who followed **Sharper**, or with his own son Sam.

SANDY JONES (1793?–1843), a highly skilled carpenter who was owned by **John Jones** (1772–1805). He was among those slaves purchased by **Joseph Jones** (1779–1846) in Riceboro in 1808 and given back to the widow and children of his brother John. He was part of the joint property of **Charles Colcock Jones** (1804–1863) and his sister **Susan Mary Jones Maxwell Cumming** until a division of their property in 1839. In 1828 he married **Phoebe.** They had one son, **John.** After the younger Phoebe had an affair with **Cassius** and married him, Sandy Jones's health began a steady decline. He died of "inflamed lungs" after having been "in feeble health" for several years. He was a member of the Midway congregation and died with "good hope."

SANDY MAYBANK (?–1861), a carpenter and slave of **Andrew Maybank** who became the property of **Charles Colcock Jones** (1804–1863) and **Mary Jones** when Andrew Maybank died in 1834. Of all the carpenters owned by various members of the Jones family, he was the most skilled and valuable, bringing the highest wages when he was rented to neighboring planters. He learned to read and write at an early age and was consequently able to carry with him instructions about the work that he was to do. He was married to Mary Ann, the daughter of **Sharper.** She was owned by **Joseph Jones** (1779–1846) and lived at the Retreat settlement. In 1842, while he was working at the plantation of William Quarterman Baker, he had an affair with Baker's slave Mag. The next year the Midway congregation suspended him for adultery. He and Mag had two children, and Sandy continued to have two families for a number of years. In the early 1850s he stopped living with Mag and began living only with Mary Ann, although he continued to see and support his Baker family. He was consequently received back into full communion with the Midway congregation. When his health began to fail in the late 1850s, he was sent to Augusta to be under the treatment of Dr. **Joseph Jones** (1833–1896) and for "a change of air" in the hopes that "his health may be improved thereby." He died in 1861 of pneumonia. His funeral was in the chapel at Montevideo, and he was buried in the slave cemetery at Carlawter. Charles Jones called him "our old friend and faithful servant."

SHARPER (?–1833), a slave preacher hired from his owner by the Midway congregation to preach and minister among the slaves of Liberty County. For more than two decades, he rode from three to seven miles in the evenings to preach and visit in the settlements of Liberty County. In the early 1830s, **Charles Colcock Jones (1804–1863)** believed him to be the most influential person in the Gullah community. His freedom to move about among the various settlements provided him an intimate knowledge of the Gullah people and their traditions. He was an important mentor for Jones in his missionary work. Sharper's wife belonged to **Joseph Jones (1779–1846)** and lived at the Retreat, and his daughter Mary Ann was the wife of **Sandy Maybank**. Sharper was a man of a little "below middling stature," with a "smooth, benevolent forehead, and of a pleasant countenance." When he preached, a slight impediment gave a distinctive character to his speech and "added to the interest of his address." His prayers were elegant and deeply moving. He died in 1833 after eating green plums. His funeral, held at night on the green before Midway Church, was attended by hundreds of slaves. He was buried about a mile north of Midway Church in an old slave cemetery.

SILVEY (1740?–1812?), see **Jupiter (1740?–1812?)**.

STEPNEY (1812–1898+), the son of **Robin** and Lizzy and the brother of **Elsey (1809–1870+)** and **Patience**. When **Charles Colcock Jones (1804–1863)** purchased Arcadia in 1846, he selected Stepney to be its driver. Stepney proved to be a good driver and helped to turn Arcadia into the most prosperous of the Joneses' plantations. He was married first to Cate, a slave of **Susan Mary Jones Maxwell Cumming**. She was allowed to live at Arcadia but became a "clay eater" in the early 1850s. She was sent to Maybank, where it was hoped that a better diet and the threat of an iron mouthpiece would cure her of the dangerous practice. While she was at Maybank, Stepney had an affair with Daphne, who was seventeen years younger than he, lived in the Arcadia settlement, and was the daughter of **Flora (1790–1851)**. Their son Pharaoh was born the year after Cate was sent to Maybank. Stepney and Daphne married three months after Cate died in 1853. Stepney was admitted to membership of the Midway congregation in 1859. He owned his own horse and buggy and his own shotgun and was known for his ability as a duck hunter. He was sent in 1863 to Indianola, where he was the driver. He made numerous trips by himself between Burke County and Liberty County during the Civil War. After the war, he took over the management of Arcadia and then coordinated the renting and then purchasing by freed people of much of the land of the old plantation. He and father Robin claimed West as their family name.

STEVENS, HARRY. See **Harry Stevens**.

STEVENS, TONEY. See **Toney Stevens**.

SYLVIA (1785–1866+), the cook and primary manager of the household at the Retreat plantation from 1806 to 1856. She came to the Jones family in 1806, when her mistress Sarah Anderson married **Joseph Jones (1779–1846)**. She was a person of remarkable strength, personal integrity, and organizational ability. When the Reverend **John Jones (1815–1893)** received his share of his mother's estate in 1842, Sylvia became his slave although she continued to stay and work at the Retreat. Both **Mary Jones** and John Jones regarded her as their "Momma," as she had been their primary nurse when they were young. They held her in great affection and sought to meet her expressed needs and wishes. She was the only slave to whom Mary Jones ever sent her love. Both John and Mary Jones referred to her in her old age as "My old Momma." While she fit many of the stereotypes of a "Mammy," she asserted her independence and primary commitments to her own family after the Civil War. She should not be confused with Sylvia who was a part of the **Andrew Maybank** estate that came to **Charles Colcock Jones (1804–1863)** and Mary Jones.

SYPHAX (1813–1870+), son of **Hamlet** and **Elvira** and husband of **Elsey.** He and Elsey married in 1832 and had eight children. See genealogical charts "Jupiter and Silvey" and "Robin and Lizzy West." Syphax was trained to be a carpenter under the tutelage of **Sandy Jones** and **Sandy Maybank.** He was part of the joint property of **Charles Colcock Jones (1804–1863)** and his sister **Susan Mary Jones Maxwell Cumming** until a division of their property in 1839. Syphax was then moved to White Oak, while Elsey stayed nearby at Carlawter. He did carpentry work on a number of surrounding plantations, often for hire. When **Mary Sharpe Jones** married **Robert Quarterman Mallard** in 1857, Elsey and six children and one grandchild became the property of the Mallards and moved to Walthourville. When Elsey was moved to Indianola in 1863, Syphax stayed at White Oak although Susan Cumming allowed him to make the trip to Burke County to visit his wife and children. After the Civil War, he and Elsey lived at Arcadia, where they rented and then bought land. Several of their children and grandchildren lived nearby. They adopted Maxwell for their family name.

TENAH (1841–1884), the daughter of **Charles** and **Lucy,** granddaughter of **Andrew** and Mary Ann and of **Rosetta** and **Sam,** and wife of **Niger (1839–1891+).** See genealogical charts "Andrew and Mary Ann Lawson," "Rosetta and Sam Roberts" and "Flora." She grew up at Carlawter and Maybank. When **Mary Sharpe Jones** married **Robert Quarterman Mallard,** she became with her parents the property of Mary Sharpe Mallard. She married Niger, the fisherman at Maybank, in 1861. Her mistress gave her a Swiss muslin dress for the wedding and had a special cake baked. The wedding was held in the chapel at Montevideo at the same time that Tenah's uncle Sam was marrying Niger's sister Judy. When the Mallards moved to Atlanta in 1863, Tenah and Niger were taken with them. They returned to Liberty County as Union troops began their attack on the city. After the war, Tenah and Niger remained at Carlawter, where they were paid a wage for specified work and had land to farm on their own. They adopted first Bacon and then Fraser as their family name.

TITUS (1826–1865+), son of **Prime** and Fanny. He is often called Big Titus and should not be confused with **Titus (1839–1870+),** who was often called Little Titus. He was, with his parents and siblings, part of the **Andrew Maybank** estate that went to **Charles Colcock Jones (1804–1863)** and **Mary Jones.** The family adopted the name Stevens after the Civil War. See genealogical chart "Prime and Fanny Stevens." In 1852 Big Titus was moved with his parents and siblings from Maybank to Arcadia. He may have been the husband of **Jane.** He was included in the first listing of slaves to be sold by Charles and Mary Jones in 1856, but his name was later removed from the list. When most of the Jones slaves were removed to Indianola in Burke County, Big Titus remained at Arcadia with **Robin.** After the Civil War he was among those who, under the leadership of **Stepney,** rented and farmed land that was a part of Arcadia.

TITUS (1839–1870+), son of **Patience** and **Porter.** He was often called Little Titus and should not be confused with **Titus (1826–1865+),** who was Big Titus. See genealogical charts

"Robin and Lizzy West" and "Lizzy and Robinson." When he was twelve, he was moved to Arcadia, where his uncle **Stepney** was the driver and grandfather **Robin** was living. The next year he asked for permission to marry Rachael, who lived at Lambert and was a slave of **Susan Mary Jones Maxwell Cumming. Charles Colcock Jones (1804–1863)** wrote from Philadelphia refusing to allow the thirteen-year-old to marry the fourteen-year-old Rachael, but they nevertheless married later in the year. Titus was made the personal servant of Dr. **Joseph Jones (1833–1896)** in 1856, a position that apparently pleased him and his mother, who immediately began teaching him to cook and wash. He moved to the Savannah home of his new master and during the next few years followed him to Athens and Augusta, returning to Liberty County regularly. In 1858 he made a profession of faith at the same time as his master and joined the First Presbyterian Church, Athens. He was often with his master Dr. Joseph Jones as Jones investigated the hospitals and prisons of the Confederacy. After the Civil War, Titus and Rachael lived at Arcadia plantation and rented and purchased land with other members of his extended family. They adopted Way as their family name.

TONEY STEVENS (1787–1866), a son of Jack Salturs, who had been one of the slave preachers appointed by Midway Congregational Church in the early part of the nineteenth century to minister among the slaves of Liberty County. The father had been bought by the congregation so that he might work full-time in his ministry. Toney Stevens joined the Midway congregation in 1807, the same year he married. He was owned by Miss Mary Mell, who rented him to the Midway congregation in the late 1830s as the congregation's black preacher to slaves. He worked closely with **Charles Colcock Jones (1804–1863)** during the time of Jones's missionary labors. The congregation provided a horse for him to make his regular rounds to the surrounding plantations, although he later owned his own horse and wagon. When the watchmen at Midway Congregational Church and at the North Newport Baptist Church were organized in the 1840s into a kind of church court, meeting regularly to hear reports about the spiritual life of the congregations and adjudicating disputes and cases of discipline, Toney Stevens was the most influential member. From the late 1830s until the beginning of the Civil War, he conducted many of the marriages in the Gullah community of Liberty County. By 1864 he was in declining health and unable to perform many ministerial functions. When Federal troops began pillaging in Liberty County, he was confined to his bed. They took all that he owned, even his blankets, and, in spite of his protests, they confiscated his horse and wagon. He should not be confused with **Tony.**

TONY (1775?–1865), the husband of **Willoughby.** He came to the Jones family in 1806, when his mistress Sarah Anderson married **Joseph Jones (1779–1846).** When Sarah Anderson's estate was divided in 1830, he became the slave of **Mary Jones.** After Willoughby died in 1840, he married a woman from a neighboring plantation. In his old age he became the gardener at Montevideo and a conveyor of information about earlier generations of whites and blacks. His name was sometimes spelled "Toney." He should not be confused with **Toney Stevens.**

YOUNG CASH. See **Cash Jones (1837–1869+).**

WILLOUGHBY (1779–1840), the sister of **Lizzy** and wife of **Tony.** She was the slave of Susannah Girardeau and became a slave of the Jones family when her mistress married **John**

Jones (1772–1805). **Charles Colcock Jones (1804–1863)** inherited her from his mother. Willoughby and Tony had three children, including Tom who married Betty, the daughter of **Flora.** See genealogical chart "Flora." She should not be confused with Maum Willoughby, who was the cook at the Mallard Place.

EUROPEAN AMERICANS

ADGER, JAMES (1777–1858), wealthy Charleston merchant, banker, and cotton broker. His daughter Margaret Milligan Adger was the wife of **Thomas Smyth.** His son John Bailey Adger was a missionary to Armenia, pastor of the Anson Street Presbyterian Church for slaves in Charleston, and successor to **Charles Colcock Jones (1804–1863)** as professor of ecclesiastical history at Columbia Theological Seminary.

ANDERSON, EVELYN ELOUISA JONES (1822–1849), daughter of **Joseph Jones (1779–1846)** and **Elizabeth Screven Lee Hart Jones** and half-sister of **Mary Jones** and **John Jones (1815–1893).** She accompanied the family of **Charles Colcock Jones (1804–1863)** on a trip to the North in 1839 in an attempt to improve her health. In 1843 she married Joseph Andrew Anderson. Her health continued to decline after her marriage, and she visited various hot springs and baths in the hope of some improvement, but to no avail. After her death in 1849, her daughters Elizabeth (Bessie) Mary Emma Anderson (1844–1879), and Evelyn (Eva) Josephine Anderson (1848–1930) spent much time at Montevideo and Maybank. Joseph Andrew Anderson suffered for years from alcohol and possibly opium abuse.

ANDERSON, JOSEPH ANDREW (1820–1866). See **Anderson, Evelyn Elouisa Jones.**

AXSON, ISAAC STOCKTON KEITH (1813–1891), Presbyterian minister and pastor of Midway Congregational Church (1836–1853), and Independent Presbyterian Church, Savannah (1857–1891). His wife, Rebecca Longstreet Randolph, was the sister of Mrs. Nathaniel Varnedoe of Liberty Hall plantation. Axson was a strong supporter of **Charles Colcock Jones (1804–1863)**'s missionary labors and a close personal friend, although Jones frequently criticized him and other pastors for not paying enough attention to the slave members of their congregations. In 1885, in the manse of the Independent Presbyterian Church, Axson officiated at the marriage of his granddaughter Ellen Louise Axson to Woodrow Wilson, future president of the United States.

BERRIEN, CHARLES. See **Jones, Charles Berrien.**

BUTTOLPH, DAVID LYMAN (1822–1905), a native of Norwich, New York, and a Presbyterian minister. He graduated from Williams College and from Columbia Theological Seminary and served as assistant to **Thomas Smyth** at the Second Presbyterian Church, Charleston, before becoming in 1854 pastor of Midway Congregational Church. He married **Laura Elizabeth Maxwell** in 1856. Her slaves and plantations, it was said, made her "one of the fattest lambs of his flock." They made Social Bluff plantation their home and had five children, four of whom lived to maturity. After the Civil War, he struggled to continue his ministry at Midway, but the changing social and economic conditions of the region made it impossible for the dwindling congregation to support him. He accepted a call to the First Presbyterian Church, Marietta, Georgia, in 1867, and with his departure from Liberty County the white Midway congregation soon came to an end.

BUTTOLPH, LAURA. See **Maxwell, Laura Elizabeth.**

CHARLES. See **Jones, Charles Colcock (1804–1863).**

CHARLES EDWARD. See **Maxwell, Charles Edward.**

CHARLIE. See **Jones, Charles Colcock (1831–1893).**

CLAY, ELIZA CAROLINE (1809–1895), daughter of the Honorable Joseph Clay and sister of **Thomas Savage Clay.** After the death of her brother Thomas in 1849, she became deeply involved in the management of Richmond-on-Ogeechee plantation in Bryan County, Georgia, issuing orders to her overseers about slave life and the cultivation of rice. She and her brother's family generally spent the summer and fall in New England, returning to their beautiful plantation home for the winter and spring. In Georgia she was part of a cluster of wealthy slave owners who belonged to the Bryan Neck Presbyterian Church. She was a close friend to **Mary Jones** and **Charles Colcock Jones (1804–1863)** and frequently corresponded with them.

CLAY, THOMAS SAVAGE (1801–1849) wealthy planter and social reformer and brother of **Eliza Caroline Clay.** His father, Joseph Clay, a federal district judge, had abandoned his legal career and had become the pastor of the First Baptist Church, Boston. Thomas Savage Clay consequently grew up in New England before moving back to Georgia to supervise extensive planting interests in Bryan County. Tall and handsome, he was regarded as refined and engaging. He married in 1836 Matilda Willis McAllister of Strathy Hall plantation in Bryan County. Clay's plantation, Richmond-on-Ogeechee, was noted for its beautiful setting and was the arena for an extensive experiment in the paternalistic management and religious instruction of slaves. Clay was closely associated with **Charles Colcock Jones (1804–1863)** in attempts to reform slavery and to encourage the religious instruction of slaves. He was an elder in the Bryan Neck Presbyterian Church.

CUMMING, SUSAN MARY JONES MAXWELL (1803–1890), daughter of **John Jones (1772–1805)** and **Susannah Hyrne Girardeau Jones** and sister of **Charles Colcock Jones (1804–1863)**, who often called her Sister Susan. She married James Audley Maxwell (1796–1828) in 1823. They had two children who lived to maturity: **Laura Elizabeth Maxwell** and **Charles Edward Maxwell.** In 1838 Susan married Joseph Cumming (1790–1846). Through a gift of her uncle **Joseph Jones (1779–1846)**, she became the owner of White Oak plantation. Her children received from their grandfather **Audley Maxwell** Social Bluff plantation and adequate funds to purchase Lambert plantation. An attractive woman, she had many friends and the deep affection of her family. In Savannah, where she often lived, she moved in the highest social circles. In contrast to **Mary Jones,** who was always ready to make decisive judgments about many matters, she had little business sense, especially in regard to the management of a plantation. She and her children spent many years as guests in the home of her uncle Joseph Jones, her sister **Elizabeth Jones Maxwell,** and her brother Charles Colcock Jones. When Laura Maxwell married **David Buttolph,** Susan Cumming made her home with them at Social Bluff. After the Civil War, she moved with her daughter's family to Marietta, Georgia, where she died in 1890.

DAVID. See **Buttolph, David Lyman.**

DUNWODY. See **Jones, James Dunwody.**

DUNWODY, JOHN (1786–1858), planter and capitalist and early supporter of the religious instruction of slaves. He was the uncle of Jane Dunwody Jones, wife of **John Jones (1815–**

1893). He moved his family to Roswell, Georgia, in 1837 and participated in its development as a manufacturing center. He sold Arcadia plantation to **Charles Colcock Jones** (1804–1863) in 1846. Jones was, with his family, a frequent visitor to Dunwody's home in Roswell, called at first Dunwody Hall, then Phoenix Hall, and later renamed Mimosa Hall. John Dunwody was a founding elder in the Roswell Presbyterian Church.

HARRIS, EMMA ADELAIDE JONES (1827–1913), daughter of **Joseph Jones** (1779–1846) and **Elizabeth Screven Lee Hart Jones,** and half-sister of **Mary Jones.** She eloped with Stephen Nathan Harris (1823–1854) in June 1846. For this act of disobedience, her father disinherited her. Mary Jones and **Charles Colcock Jones** (1804–1863) considered her irresponsible and self-centered. She felt bitterly alienated from them and from her brother **Henry Hart Jones.** In an extended family dispute, she was allied with her mother and with Marion Anderson Jones, the unstable widow of **Charles Berrien Jones.** In 1858 she married Columbus Starnes Harris, the younger brother of her first husband.

HART, HENRY. See **Jones, Henry Hart.**

HOWE, GEORGE (1802–1883), Presbyterian minister and professor of oriental literature and Biblical criticism at Columbia Theological Seminary from 1831 to 1883. While Howe was not the first professor at Columbia, he was through his long tenure and distinguished scholarship the true founder of the seminary. He and **Charles Colcock Jones** (1804–1863) were close colleagues in the Presbyterian ministry. He married in 1836 Sarah Ann Walthour of Liberty County, the widow of Dr. Robert C. McConnell. Originally from Massachusetts, Howe became through his marriage a large slave owner. In 1860 he had two plantations in Liberty County.

JIMMA. See **Jones, James Newton.**

JOE. See **Jones, Joseph** (1833–1896).

JONES, CHARLES BERRIEN (1820–1857), son of **Joseph Jones** (1779–1846) and **Elizabeth Screven Lee Hart Jones,** half-brother of **Mary Jones** and **John Jones** (1815–1893), and husband of Marion Susan Anderson (1823–1888). Known for his pompous ways, he lacked the drive and business acumen of his brother **Henry Hart Jones** and the winsome spirit of his brother **James Newton Jones.** He was particularly close to his mother and took her part in family disputes. His wife was the sister of Joseph Andrew Anderson and shared with her brother a certain instability of character.

JONES, CHARLES COLCOCK (1804–1863), Presbyterian minister, evangelist to the Gullah people of Liberty County, Georgia, professor at Columbia Theological Seminary, and social reformer. He was the son of **John Jones** (1772–1805) and **Susannah Hyrne Girardeau Jones.** His uncle **Joseph Jones** (1779–1846), his aunt **Eliza Greene Low Robarts,** and his older half-sister **Elizabeth Jones Maxwell** raised him after the death of his mother. Educated in the North, he came to regard slavery as a great evil that threatened the future of the country. After struggling with his sense of vocation in the face of such an evil, he decided to return to Georgia to work as a missionary among the slaves of his home county. He soon became a leading advocate for the reform of slavery in an attempt to make the system of slavery more humane. He married his first cousin **Mary Jones** in 1830. They had three children who lived to maturity: **Charles Colcock Jones** (1831–1893), **Joseph Jones** (1833–1896), and **Mary Sharpe Jones.** Through gifts from two uncles and from his marriage to Mary Jones, he became a wealthy slave owner and eventually the master of three plantations—Montevideo, Maybank, and Arcadia. Throughout this narrative, he is referred to as Charles in distinction from his son, who is called Charlie. He should not be confused with his slave **Charles,** the son of **Andrew** and **Mary Ann Lawson** and husband of **Lucy.**

JONES, CHARLES COLCOCK (1831–1893), lawyer, archaeologist, and historian. The eldest son of **Charles Colcock Jones (1804–1863)** and **Mary Jones,** he was educated at the plantation school at Maybank and Montevideo, at South Carolina College, Princeton, and Harvard. He married Ruth Berrien Whitehead (1837–1861) in 1858. They had one child, **Mary Ruth Jones,** who lived to maturity. In 1863 he married Eva Berrien Eve (1841–1890). He was mayor of Savannah at the beginning of the Civil War. He served as a lieutenant colonel of artillery in the Confederate Army. After the Civil War he practiced law in New York City for a number of years before settling in Augusta, Georgia. He wrote extensively on the history of his native state and pioneered in the archaeological examination of Native American history. While he was a faithful supporter of the Presbyterian Church, he never had a personal religious experience or made the public confession of faith that was necessary for church membership—a source of concern and sorrow for his parents. Throughout this narrative, he is referred to as Charlie in distinction from his father, who is called Charles.

JONES, ELIZABETH SCREVEN LEE HART (1801–1870), third wife of **Joseph Jones (1779–1846)** and mother of fourteen children, of whom ten lived to maturity. See genealogical chart "John and Mary Jones." Elizabeth Jones was the stepmother of **Mary Jones** and **John Jones (1815–1893).** She and Mary Jones lived with a suppressed tension as long as Joseph Jones was alive. After his death, Mary Jones never again called her mother but simply referred to her as Mrs. Jones.

JONES, HENRY HART (1823–1893), planter and son of **Joseph Jones (1779–1846)** and **Elizabeth Screven Lee Hart Jones.** As a teenager, he had two children by a young slave woman. He married Abigail (Abby) Sturges Dowse in 1846. They had eleven children, only five of whom lived past childhood. A successful planter and respected political figure in Georgia, he and his family lived at Lodebar plantation (1846–1856) and then at the Retreat (1856–1862). In 1850 he and his wife hosted a wedding—to which whites and blacks were both invited to Lodebar—for the slave mother of his children. His new and unfinished house in Walthourville was burned in 1859 as the result of deep alienation with his sister-in-law Marion Anderson Jones, the unstable widow of **Charles Berrien Jones.** He moved most of his slaves in 1859 to Baker County in southwest Georgia, where he owned two plantations. In 1863 he and his family moved to Cuthbert, Georgia. He was often called Henry Hart.

JONES, JAMES DUNWODY (1842–1904), eldest son of **John Jones (1815–1893)** and Jane Adaline Dunwody. He may have been dyslexic and was always something of a difficult child for his parents. They constantly worried about him and sought, through their influential connections, to ease his way into maturity. During the Civil War he fought in several of the early battles in Virginia, and while he showed much bravery, it was an experience he was eager not to repeat. Late in the war, he was made a guard at the infamous Andersonville Prison in south Georgia. After the war, he attempted unsuccessfully to plant and manage his father's Bonaventure plantation in Liberty County. He moved to Atlanta in

1871 and assumed an eccentric and flamboyant role as a former Confederate officer mysteriously promoted to the rank of colonel.

JONES, JAMES NEWTON (1825–1854), planter, son of **Joseph Jones** (1779–1846) and **Elizabeth Screven Lee Hart Jones**, and half-brother of **Mary Jones** and **John Jones** (1815–1893). He became engaged in 1845 to the lively **Mary Elizabeth King [Wells]**. She broke the engagement a few months later, an action that appeared scandalous to friends and family. In 1851 he married Sarah Jane Norman, a beautiful and affectionate daughter of a neighboring planter. Among all the children of Joseph Jones and Elizabeth Hart Jones, he was best known for his gentle and generous character. After his father's death, he became the guardian of his younger brothers and sisters and managed the Retreat plantation. He was called James Newton by his family and often referred to as Jimma. In 1854, at the request of his sister **Emma Jones Harris,** he went to Savannah during a yellow fever epidemic in the city to secure some of her personal papers. He contracted the fever and died in his wife's arms at Lodebar plantation.

JONES, JOHN (1749–1779), father of **John Jones** (1772–1805) and **Joseph Jones** (1779–1846). His plantation Rice Hope, together with his mercantile business in Sunbury, established the foundation for his descendants' wealth. He died a Revolutionary War hero at the battle of Savannah.

JONES, JOHN (1772–1805), owner of Liberty Hall plantation and much land throughout coastal Georgia. He married Elizabeth Stewart (sister of General Daniel Stewart), by whom he had **Elizabeth Jones Maxwell** and John Jones, Jr. (1798–1813). After his first wife's death, he married **Susannah Hyrne Girardeau Jones,** by whom he had **Susan Mary Jones [Maxwell Cumming]** and **Charles Colcock Jones** (1804–1863). He apparently enjoyed acting the role of an English country gentleman. He served several terms in the state legislature. At the time of his death he had incurred substantial debts by the purchase of slaves and land.

JONES, JOHN (1815–1893), Presbyterian minister and son of **Joseph Jones** (1779–1846) and Sarah Anderson (1783–1817). He was the brother of **Mary Jones** and the half-brother of the children of Joseph Jones and **Elizabeth Screven Lee Hart Jones**. Shortly after he graduated from Columbia Theological Seminary, he married Jane Adaline Dunwody (1820–1884), niece of **John Dunwody** and granddaughter of **James Smith**. They had four children, including **James Dunwody Jones.** Jane Jones brought thirty slaves into their marriage and later inherited additional slaves and land from her grandfather. With these slaves and through inheritance from his mother, John Jones became a large slave owner, although throughout his life he had deep reservations about the viability of slavery as an economic system. Shortly after his marriage, he sold to his father for $8,500 twenty-three of the slaves he had inherited from his mother's estate. A greatly beloved pastor in a number of Presbyterian churches, he was particularly gifted in his ability to enter deeply into the sorrows of others and to offer them through his words and presence Christian hope. He was the owner of Bonaventure plantation in Liberty County and the Refuge in Baker County, as well as extensive property in Atlanta. His cheerful and gracious ways drew many friends to him in spite of their frustrations over his habitual procrastination. After the Civil War, as his eyesight began to fail, he served for a number of years as the chaplain to the Georgia senate.

JONES, JOSEPH (1779–1846), son of **John Jones** (1749–1779) and Mary Sharpe (1753–1798).
He was the master of the Retreat and a number of other Liberty County plantations and
was for forty years the patriarch of the Jones family. He married in 1799 Mary Maybank
(1781–1804). Of their four children, only **Joseph Maybank Jones** lived to maturity. In
1806 he married Sarah Anderson (1783–1817). Of their eight children, only **Mary Jones**
and **John Jones** (1815–1893) lived to maturity. In 1820 he married **Elizabeth Screven Lee
Hart Jones.** They had fourteen children, ten of whom lived to maturity. See genealogical
chart "John and Mary Jones." He was often called Captain Jones for his service as captain of the Liberty Independent Troop during the War of 1812. While he was famous for
his business acumen and personal discipline, he was also known for his generosity to his
family and friends and to needy whites of Liberty County. Having already given slaves
and land to his older children, he left at his death 208 slaves and more than five thousand acres to be divided among his heirs. Throughout this narrative, he is referred to as
Joseph in distinction from his grandson **Joseph Jones** (1833–1896), who is called Joe.

JONES, JOSEPH (1833–1896), physician and educator, son of **Charles Colcock Jones** (1804–
1863) and **Mary Jones.** He was educated at the plantation school at Maybank and Montevideo, then at South Carolina College, Princeton, and the Medical College of the University of Pennsylvania. From an early age he developed great personal discipline and
an intense interest in the natural world of the low country. Before his thirtieth birthday
he had become an expert on the various fevers and diseases that afflicted much of the
nineteenth-century South. After serving briefly at the beginning of the Civil War with the
Liberty Independent Troop, he was commissioned as a surgeon with the rank of major
and assigned to investigate the medical conditions in the armies, hospitals, and military
prisons of the Confederacy. His work on gangrene was particularly important, especially
with his emphasis on sanitation and prevention. In 1868 he was called to the Medical
Department of the University of Louisiana (later Tulane). There he gained an international reputation for his study of tropical diseases. He married in 1859 Caroline Smelt
Davis (1832–1868) of Augusta, Georgia. They had four children. In 1870 he married
Susan Rayner Polk, daughter of the Right Reverend Leonidas Polk (1806–1864), Episcopal bishop of Louisiana and lieutenant general in the Confederate Army. They had three
children. Joseph Jones was an elder in the Presbyterian Church and reflected throughout
his life the piety and values of his parents. Throughout this narrative, he is referred to as
Joe in distinction from his grandfather, **Joseph Jones** (1779–1846), who is called **Joseph.**

JONES, JOSEPH MAYBANK (1804–1831), son of **Joseph Jones** (1779–1846) and Mary Maybank (1781–1804), and half-brother to **Mary Jones** and **John Jones** (1815–1893) and the
children of **Joseph Jones** (1779–1846) and **Elizabeth Screven Lee Hart Jones.** The gift
of slaves to him by his father precipitated a family crisis among the heirs of Joseph Jones.

JONES, MARY (1808–1869), daughter of **Joseph Jones** (1779–1846) and Sarah Anderson, sister of **John Jones** (1815–1893), half-sister of **Henry Hart Jones** and the other children
of Joseph Jones and **Elizabeth Screven Lee Hart Jones.** She married her first cousin
Charles Colcock Jones (1804–1863) in 1830. They had three children who lived to maturity: **Charles Colcock Jones** (1831–1893), **Joseph Jones** (1833–1896), and **Mary Sharpe
Jones.** She functioned as a strong mother figure not only for her children but also for her
brother and her half-brothers and sisters. At the time of her marriage she received from

her mother's estate a number of slaves who would become, with the slaves inherited by her husband and the slaves received from **Andrew Maybank**'s estate, the foundation of the family's wealth. By 1854 Mary and Charles Jones owned jointly 128 slaves. She was highly disciplined, literate, and deeply pious, and she sought to be a thoughtful adviser and support to her husband in his ministry and in his management of their slaves. She had a profound love for her plantation homes, Montevideo and Maybank. She reflected throughout her life a sense of great privilege as a slave owner and great responsibility for the welfare of her family's slaves. After the Civil War she struggled for several years to maintain her plantation home, but finally felt compelled to move to New Orleans, where her daughter's family lived. She died there in 1869.

JONES, MARY RUTH (1861–1934), daughter of **Charles Colcock Jones** (1831–1893) and Ruth Berrien Whitehead (1837–1861). When her mother died a few days after Mary Ruth's birth, her grandmother **Mary Jones** took her to Maybank and Montevideo to rear her as "my darling baby" during the hard days of the Civil War. Family called her Ruthie. When Ruthie went to the home of her father and her stepmother, Eva Berrien Eve (1841–1890), after the war, Mary Jones felt the removal of her granddaughter as a great personal loss.

JONES, MARY SHARPE (1835–1889), the daughter of **Charles Colcock Jones** (1804–1863) and **Mary Jones**. Throughout this narrative she is referred to as Mary Sharpe in distinction from her mother, who is called Mary. She was educated at the plantation schools at Maybank and Montevideo and at a private school in Philadelphia. Bright and articulate, she was never able as a woman to gain the academic and professional status of her brothers **Charles Colcock Jones** (1831–1893) and **Joseph Jones** (1833–1896). She married **Robert Quarterman Mallard** in 1857. They had five children. See genealogical chart "John and Mary Jones." When her husband was called in 1863 to be the pastor of Central Presbyterian Church, Atlanta, she and her children moved to Atlanta a few months before the arrival of the Union Army at the outskirts of the city. When the battle of Atlanta began, she and the children fled to Liberty County, where her husband later joined them. She gave birth at Montevideo to a daughter as Federal troops were in the midst of plundering the plantation. A few weeks later, she fled to southwest Georgia as a refugee. She never again returned to Liberty County. In 1866 she moved to New Orleans, where her husband had accepted a call to be the pastor of a congregation.

JONES, SUSANNAH HYRNE GIRARDEAU (1778–1810), second wife of **John Jones** (1772–1805) and mother of **Susan Mary Jones** [Maxwell Cumming] and **Charles Colcock Jones** (1804–1863). When her husband died in a hunting accident in 1805, his brother **Joseph Jones** (1779–1846) became her guardian and the guardian of her children. She lived at Liberty Hall and at a summer home in Sunbury.

JOSEPH. See **Jones, Joseph** (1779–1846).

KING, BARRINGTON (1798–1866), planter and manufacturer and brother of **Roswell King**. In 1822 he married Catherine Margaret Nephew (1804–1887), who brought into their marriage a number of slaves and South Hampton plantation. He developed South Hampton into a prosperous rice plantation before selling it and forty-two slaves to his brother Roswell in 1838. Barrington King, together with a few other low-country capitalists, developed the town of Roswell in the former Cherokee territory of Georgia. Flour and textile mills were established, and Barrington Hall, a Greek Revival mansion, was built as his family's residence. **Charles Colcock Jones (1804–1863)** and **Mary Jones** often visited Barrington's family when they were in Roswell.

KING, JAMES AUDLEY MAXWELL (1829–1920), planter, son of **Roswell King** and **Julia Rebecca Maxwell King**. He was a childhood friend of **Charles Colcock Jones (1831–1893)**, **Joseph Jones (1833–1896)**, and **Mary Sharpe Jones** and attended with them the plantation school at Maybank and Montevideo. After his father's death, he managed the family's South Hampton and Woodville plantations. He married Elizabeth Catherine (Kate) Lewis (1839–1920) in 1860. Noted for his neat and orderly ways, he possessed a generous personality and a kind and winsome manner.

KING, JULIA REBECCA MAXWELL (1808–1892), daughter of **Audley Maxwell**, and wife of **Roswell King**. Her brother James Audley Maxwell (1796–1828) was married to **Susan Mary Jones Maxwell [Cumming]**. She brought into her marriage Woodville plantation and a number slaves, and she inherited additional land and slaves at the death of her parents. She and **Mary Jones** were close friends and neighbors. She and Roswell King had eleven children, nine of whom lived to maturity, including **James Audley Maxwell King** and **Mary Elizabeth King Wells**. Kind, affectionate, and genteel, she often appeared a counterpoint to her eccentric and often blunt husband.

KING, ROSWELL (1796–1854), planter, son of Roswell King (1776–1839), and husband of **Julia Rebecca Maxwell King**. Through his own business acumen and the lands and slaves of his wife, he became a large and successful rice planter. For a number of years he managed the vast holdings of Pierce Butler on the Georgia coast, where he fathered several slave children. He bought South Hampton plantation and forty-two slaves from his brother **Barrington King** in 1838. Pragmatic and eccentric, he was something of a "know-it-all" who delighted in his plainspoken and vivid language. He was a close friend to **Charles Colcock Jones (1804–1863)** and **Mary Jones**, although he did not share their religious commitments. When he died in 1854, his will was long out of date; it was eventually annulled by the court. When his estate was finally settled, seventy-eight slaves were sold in order to divide his property among his heirs.

MALLARD, ROBERT QUARTERMAN (1830–1904), Presbyterian minister, son of **Thomas Mallard** and Rebecca Eliza Burnley Mallard (1789–1861). He grew up at the Mallard Place and his family's summer home in Walthourville. After graduating from Columbia Theological Seminary, he became pastor of the Walthourville Presbyterian Church. In 1857 he married **Mary Sharpe Jones.** Through his own inheritance and his marriage, he became the owner of a number of slaves. Tall and handsome, he was widely regarded as a fine preacher and excellent pastor. In 1863 he was called to be the pastor of Atlanta's Central Presbyterian Church. He was involved in extensive relief efforts among prisoners and the wounded until the evacuation of the city. Taking refuge with his family in Liberty County, he was captured when Federal troops arrived in Walthourville. He spent several months in Savannah as a prisoner of war. After the Civil War, he and his family moved to New Orleans when he was called to be the pastor of the Prytania Street Presbyterian Church.

MALLARD, THOMAS (1778–1861), planter and husband of Rebecca Eliza Burnley (1789–1861). They had nine children, eight of whom lived to maturity, including **Robert Quarterman Mallard.** For years they moved between their winter residence, the Mallard

Place, and their summer residence in Walthourville, before they made their home in Dorchester in the early 1850s. Thomas Mallard was a leader in Midway Congregational Church and was an active supporter of the religious instruction of slaves. Having already given a number of slaves to his children, he left at his death 135 slaves to be divided among his heirs.

MARY. See Jones, Mary.

MAXWELL, AUDLEY (1766–1840), planter and father of James Audley Maxwell (1796–1828) and **Julia Rebecca Maxwell King.** He gave as gift and inheritance to his grandchildren **Laura Elizabeth Maxwell** and **Charles Edward Maxwell** a number of slaves and Social Bluff plantation. Other slaves and land went to his daughter, Julia.

MAXWELL, CHARLES EDWARD (1826–1852), son of James Audley Maxwell (1796–1828) and **Susan Mary Jones Maxwell [Cumming],** and brother of **Laura Elizabeth Maxwell.** His father died when Charles Edward was two, and for the next ten years he and his mother and sister lived in Savannah or with relatives in Liberty County. Much time was spent in the homes of his great uncle **Joseph Jones** (1779–1846), his aunt **Elizabeth Jones Maxwell,** and his uncle **Charles Colcock Jones** (1804–1863). When his mother married Joseph Cumming in 1838, the family resided in Savannah. When Joseph Cumming died in 1846, the family resumed the practice of moving between a residence in Savannah and the plantation homes of relatives. In such an environment of mutual commitments and affections, cousins seemed as brothers and sisters, and aunts and uncles regarded their nieces and nephews with parental care. Charles Edward Maxwell showed great promise as a student and was admitted to Princeton as a sophomore. In 1848 he entered the Medical College of the University of Pennsylvania, graduating in early spring 1852. A few days later, he started toward Savannah, where he intended to begin his medical practice. In Morristown, New Jersey, he contracted a severe case of diarrhea. Charles and **Mary Jones** rushed from Philadelphia to his side and secured the best doctors they could find, but to no avail. His body was returned to Liberty County and buried in the cemetery at Midway.

MAXWELL, ELIZABETH JONES (1794–1856), daughter of **John Jones** (1772–1805) and his first wife, Elizabeth Stewart, sister of General Daniel Stewart. She married in 1811 **William Maxwell** (1785–1866). They had no children, but they thought of her half-sister **Susan Mary Jones [Maxwell Cumming]** and half-brother **Charles Colcock Jones** (1804–1863) as in some ways their children. Family and friends knew her as Betsy. She was much loved by a wide circle of relatives and friends and was a person of remarkable good humor, hospitality, and Christian graces. While well connected to some of the most socially prominent families of the low country, she was fundamentally a countrywoman who enjoyed church, good food, visiting with friends, and talking about the weather. The children of Susan Maxwell Cumming and Charles Colcock Jones regarded her as a grandmother figure.

MAXWELL, LAURA ELIZABETH (1824–1903), daughter of James Audley Maxwell (1796–1828) and **Susan Mary Jones Maxwell [Cumming],** and sister of **Charles Edward Maxwell.** Her father died when she was four, and for the next ten years she and her mother and brother lived in Savannah or with relatives in Liberty County. Much time was spent in the homes of her great uncle **Joseph Jones** (1779–1846), her aunt **Elizabeth Jones Maxwell,** and her uncle **Charles Colcock Jones** (1804–1863). When her mother married Joseph Cumming in 1838, the family resided in Savannah. When Joseph Cumming died in 1846, the family resumed the practice of moving between a residence in Savannah and the plantation homes of relatives. Some time was spent in Philadelphia when her brother was in medical school and the family of her uncle Charles Colcock Jones was resident in the city. Laura Maxwell received from her grandfather **Audley Maxwell** a number of slaves and inherited with her brother Social Bluff plantation on Colonel's Island. Lambert plantation was purchased for her and her brother following her grandfather's death in 1840. Laura Maxwell had a playful spirit and a happy and affectionate relationship with her extended family. As a young woman, she was known for her beauty and for her lively wit, which drew to her many suitors. In 1856 she married **David Lyman Buttolph,** the pastor of Midway Congregational Church. They made Social Bluff their home. They had five children, four of whom lived to maturity. When Federal gunships threatened the Georgia coast, they abandoned Social Bluff and moved to the interior of the county. In 1867 David Buttolph accepted a call to become pastor of the First Presbyterian Church, Marietta, Georgia. Shortly after his departure, the white Midway congregation was disbanded.

MAXWELL, WILLIAM (1785–1866), planter and husband of **Elizabeth Jones Maxwell.** He grew up in Sunbury, where he had extended family connections both in the village and on surrounding plantations. William Maxwell's father died when he was two, and his mother died when he was eight. In his early years he had a quick temper that could be ignited with any hint of disrespect, and he drank more whiskey than was good for him. He married Elizabeth Jones in 1811 and was deeply devoted to his "Betsy." Childless, they helped to raise the orphaned **Charles Colcock Jones (1804–1863)** and **Susan Mary Jones [Maxwell Cumming].** They moved about often, buying and selling plantations— Orange Grove, Laurel View, Lodebar, and Springfield. Maxwell was often in debt to his friend **Joseph Jones (1779–1846),** but he had the affection and respect of a wide circle of friends. They elected him the captain of the Liberty Independent Troop, and when he was hurting financially, they elected him the county sheriff, a position that brought a small but steady income. He was called Colonel Maxwell for his service in the War of 1812—a promotion that can be accounted for by some esoteric procedure used by a certain class of southerners. In the late 1830s he had a conversion experience and became a member of the Midway congregation. If his impulsive ways never left him, they were tempered—as was his drinking. In his later years, he became increasingly known for his kindness and his deep loyalty to family and friends. When his wife died, a new loneliness arrived, but he gave increased attention to those whom he loved. When he died, he died, as Betsy had, in the home of a friend.

MAYBANK, ANDREW (1768–1834), planter and philanthropist. He married in 1794 Elizabeth Girardeau, sister to **Susannah Hyrne Girardeau Jones,** the second wife of **John Jones (1772–1805).** His younger sister, Mary Maybank Jones (1781–1804), was the first wife of **Joseph Jones (1779–1846).** He willed a number of slaves to **Charles Colcock Jones (1804–1863)** and **Mary Jones,** as well as the plantation that came to be called Maybank. He left in his will, through the sale of slaves and land, a large endowment for Columbia Theological Seminary.

McWHIR, WILLIAM (1759–1851), Presbyterian minister and educator. Born in Ireland, he had smallpox as a child that left him pockmarked and blind in one eye. He was for many years the headmaster of Sunbury Academy, where he had **Charles Colcock Jones (1804–1863)** as a student. Well known as a progressive educator and disciplinarian, he evoked lifelong admiration and affection among many of his students. Jones called him "the most perfectly social man that I have ever known" and noted that McWhir was "warm and sincere in his attachments" and that he found "heartfelt pleasure" to be "in the society of his friends." While "not celebrated for his beauty," McWhir was said to be "an entertaining, instructive, and interesting companion" full of anecdotes and jokes in which he did not spare himself. He lived until he was ninety-one, when he died at South Hampton plantation surrounded by grieving friends.

RAHN, IRWIN (1806–1891), farmer, craftsman, and plantation overseer, he managed Arcadia plantation for **Charles Colcock Jones (1804–1863)** from 1848 through 1853. He was known locally for his skills as a carpenter, but he was rather indifferent in his care for and management of slaves.

ROBARTS, ELIZA GREENE LOW (1785–1868), daughter of Philip Low (1735–1785) and his second wife, Mary Sharpe (1753–1793), widow of **John Jones (1749–1779)**. She was a half-sister to **John Jones (1772–1805)** and **Joseph Jones (1779–1846)** and was consequently an aunt to both **Charles Colcock Jones (1804–1863)** and **Mary Jones.** Married and widowed three times before her twenty-eight birthday, she had three children: Mary Eliza Robarts (1805–1878), Joseph William Robarts (1811–1863), and Louisa Jane Robarts (1813–1897). After her last husband's death, she and her family moved between Joseph Jones's home, the Retreat, and her summer home at Sunbury. In 1849 she and her daughters, together with the four motherless children of her son Joseph, moved to Marietta, Georgia, where they had a large and comfortable home. She left a number of her slaves in the low country, where they were rented to various family members. Throughout this narrative, she is frequently called Aunt Eliza. She evoked deep affection and intense loyalty not only from her children but also from her nieces and nephews.

SHARPE, MARY. See **Jones, Mary Sharpe.**

SHEPARD, THOMAS (1803–1873), farmer and plantation overseer, he managed Montevideo for **Charles Colcock Jones (1804–1863)** and White Oak for **Susan Mary Jones Maxwell Cumming** from 1848 through 1852. While Charles Jones was not always satisfied with the results of Shepard's management, Shepard was a careful and honest overseer of the plantations and their slave populations.

SISTER SUSAN. See **Cumming, Susan Mary Jones Maxwell.**

SMITH, JAMES (1766–1854), planter, a wealthy neighbor and hunting companion of **John Jones (1772–1805)**, and the maternal grandfather of Jane Adaline Dunwody (1820–1884), wife of **John Jones (1815–1893)**. James Smith owned plantations in Liberty County and in neighboring McIntosh County. In 1793 raids by the Creeks carried off a number of his slaves. In 1837 he joined the little exodus of low-country families moving to the former Cherokee country. **Charles Colcock Jones (1804–1863)** and **Mary Jones** often visited in his home Welham, near Marietta, which was described as "a quiet, delightful home; its inmates kind, cheerful, and affectionate. The mansion is the perfection of cottage beauty, and the outer buildings admirably correspond. The whole presents the appearance of order, neatness, and comfort." James Smith maintained his low-country plantations Hope Still and Sidon, where his family often spent winters. At his death, his will stipulated that his estate was to be held together in perpetuity because no one heir would be able to buy out the others, and because Smith abhorred splitting up slave families. According to his will, slaves born after his death had at the age of eighteen the possibility of being freed and sent to Liberia. The court annulled the will.

SMYTH, THOMAS (1808–1873), Presbyterian minister and pastor of Second Presbyterian Church, Charleston. In 1832 he married Margaret Milligan Adger, the daughter of **James Adger**. A prolific writer, Smyth published more than thirty volumes on theological matters and contemporary social and cultural issues. A substantial part of his personal library of twenty thousand volumes was sold to Columbia Theological Seminary. He was a strong ally with **Charles Colcock Jones (1804–1863)** in advocating religious instruction of slaves.

STEWART, DANIEL (1761–1829), army officer, planter, and close friend of **John Jones (1772–1805)**. He joined the colonies' army during the Revolution when he was fifteen and fought under General Francis Marion in South Carolina. He distinguished himself in the "Indian wars" after the Revolution, especially against the Creeks in Georgia, and again in the War of 1812. He was promoted to brigadier general. He served in the Georgia legislature for a number of years. His sister Elizabeth was the first wife of John Jones and the mother of **Elizabeth Jones Maxwell**. General Stewart was thus the uncle of "Betsy" Maxwell and was regarded by her half-brother **Charles Colcock Jones (1804–1863)** as his uncle as well. Fort Stewart, Georgia, is named after Daniel Stewart.

THORNWELL, JAMES HENLEY (1812–1862), Presbyterian minister, theologian, and educator. He was professor of logic and belles lettres at South Carolina College during **Charles Colcock Jones (1804–1863)**'s first term as a professor at Columbia Theological Seminary (1837–1838) and was professor of sacred literature and evidence of Christianity at South Carolina College during Jones's second term as a professor at Columbia (1848–1850). A brilliant theologian, Thornwell sought a middle way on the question of slavery between extreme proslavery advocates and those calling for the immediate abolition of slavery. He served a term as a popular president of South Carolina College before accepting a call as a professor of theology at Columbia Theological Seminary. While he and Jones were friends and he was a strong supporter of Jones's work for the religious instruction of slaves, Thornwell was much more the sophisticated theologian, while Jones was more the practicing missionary pastor among the Gullah people.

WELLS, MARY ELIZABETH KING (1827–1871), daughter of **Roswell King** and **Julia Rebecca Maxwell King**. She was noted for her lively and winsome ways as a young woman. **Elizabeth Jones Maxwell** described her as "gay as a lark and at the head of all mischief and fun." In 1845 she broke her engagement to **James Newton Jones**, which seemed scandalous to many friends and relatives. In 1849 she married Dr. Charlton Henry Wells (1822–1854), a young and promising physician. After his death from yellow fever, she was devastated, "having loved him with the most uncontrolled affection," and began to suffer severe headaches. Travel to hot springs and the North occasionally helped with her headaches, but they disappeared only after the Civil War, when it was reported that she "works hard, sleeps well, has no headaches now and God blesses her with a grateful, cheerful spirit."

GENEALOGICAL CHARTS

Jupiter and Silvey

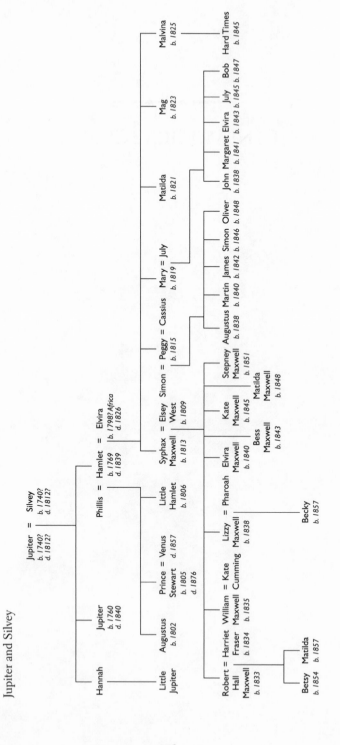

Robin and Lizzy West

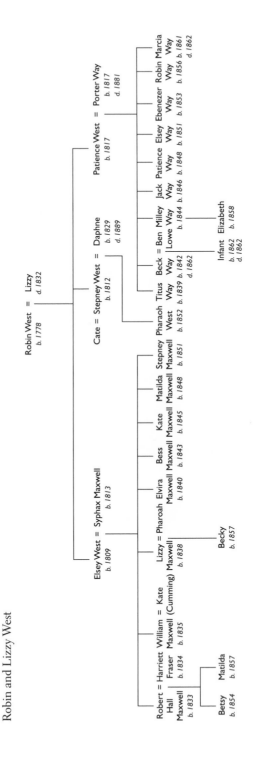

Lizzy and Robinson

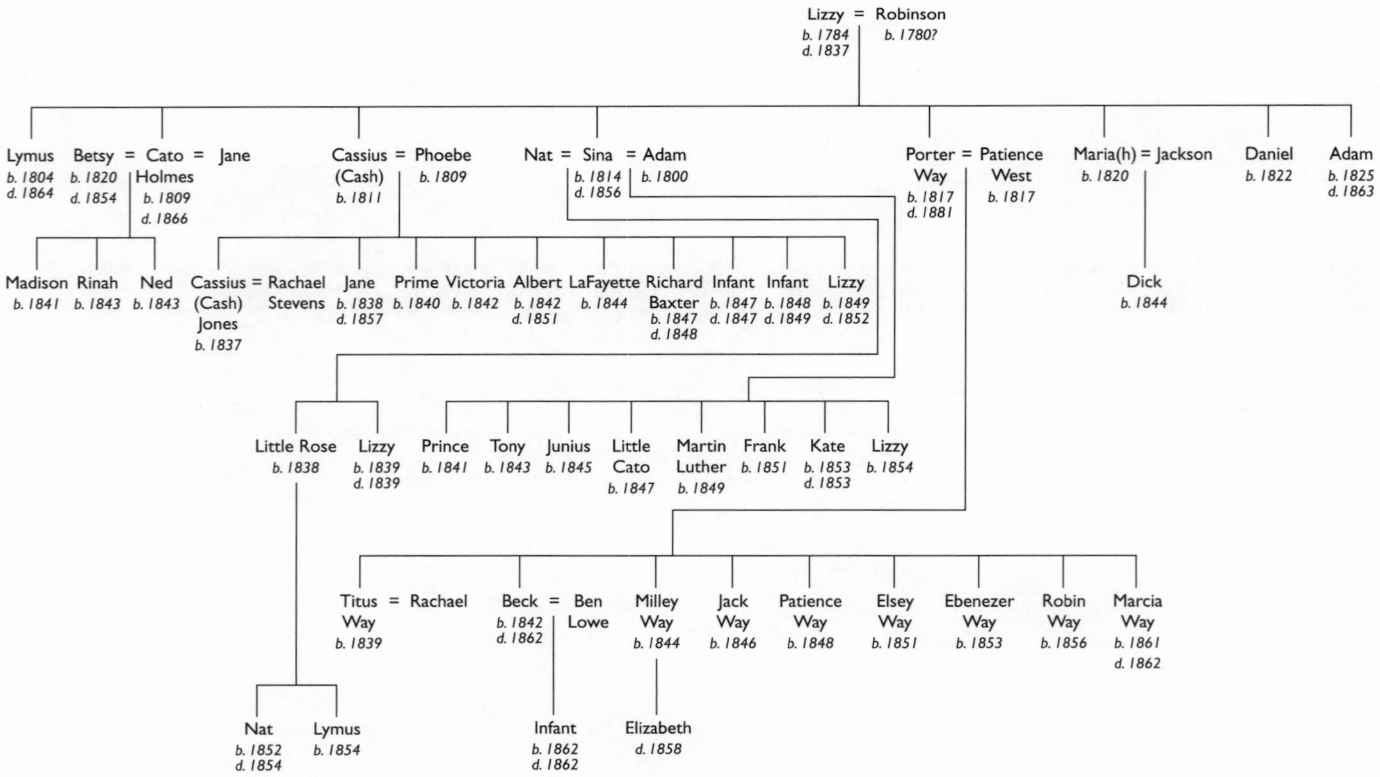

Flora

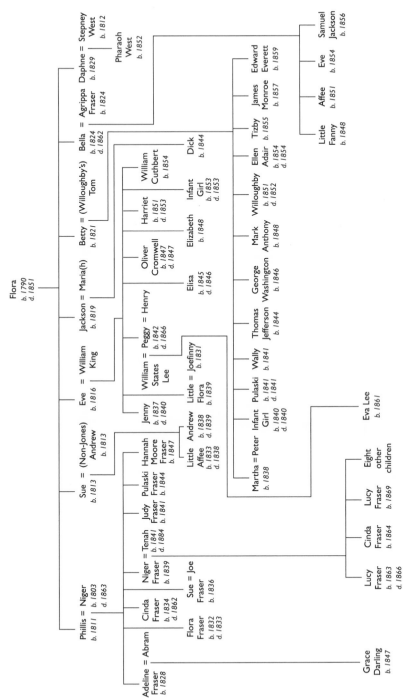

Prime and Fanny Stevens

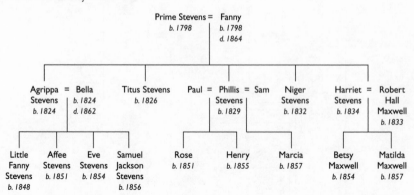

Prime Stevens = Fanny
b. 1798   b. 1798
               d. 1864

Agrippa = Bella   Titus Stevens   Paul = Phillis = Sam   Niger   Harriet = Robert
Stevens   b. 1824   b. 1826   Stevens   Stevens   Stevens   Hall
b. 1824   d. 1862   b. 1829   b. 1832   b. 1834   Maxwell
                                                                                                  b. 1833

Little   Affee   Eve   Samuel   Rose   Henry   Marcia   Betsy   Matilda
Fanny   Stevens Stevens Jackson   b. 1851   b. 1855   b. 1857   Maxwell   Maxwell
Stevens b. 1851 b. 1854 Stevens   b. 1854   b. 1857
b. 1848   b. 1856

Rosetta and Sam Roberts

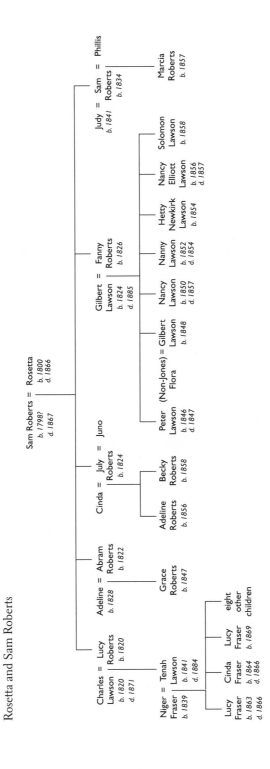

Andrew and Mary Ann Lawson

Andrew Lawson = Mary Ann
b. 1800   b. 1801

Children:

Charles = Lucy
Lawson   Roberts
b. 1820 b. 1820
d. 1871

Cuffee = Sylvia = Billy
Lawson
b. 1822

Gilbert = Fanny
Lawson   Roberts
b. 1824 b. 1826
d. 1885

Abram (Abream) = Dinah = James
Scriven   Lawson   Stevens
= 1850   b. 1828 = 1861
                 d. 1861

George = Rose
Lawson
b. 1830

Delia = Alfred
        Lawson
        b. 1833

Little = Jenny
Andrew
Lawson
b. 1820

Niger = Tenah
Fraser Lawson
b. 1839 b. 1841
        d. 1884

Mary Ann
Lawson
b. 1840

Peter (Non-Jones) = Gilbert
Flora   Lawson
b. 1846   d. 1847
d. 1847

Gilbert
Lawson
b. 1848
d. 1857

Nancy
Lawson
b. 1850
d. 1857

Nanny
Lawson
b. 1852
d. 1854

Hetty
Newkirk
Lawson
b. 1854

Nancy
Elliott
Lawson
b. 1856
d. 1857

Solomon
Lawson
b. 1858

Harry
Scriven
b. 1851

Silvia
Scriven
b. 1853

Abram
Scriven
b. 1855

Dublin
Scriven
b. 1857

Lucy   Cinda   Lucy   eight
Fraser   Fraser   Fraser   other
b. 1863   b. 1864   b. 1869   children
d. 1866   d. 1866

Ancestry for Tenah's "pretty little girl named Lucy"

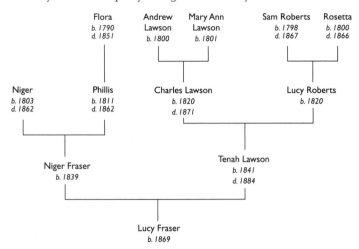

Flora
b. 1790
d. 1851

Andrew
Lawson
b. 1800

Mary Ann
Lawson
b. 1801

Sam Roberts
b. 1798
d. 1867

Rosetta
b. 1800
d. 1866

Niger
b. 1803
d. 1862

Phillis
b. 1811
d. 1862

Charles Lawson
b. 1820
d. 1871

Lucy Roberts
b. 1820

Niger Fraser
b. 1839

Tenah Lawson
b. 1841
d. 1884

Lucy Fraser
b. 1869

John and Mary Jones

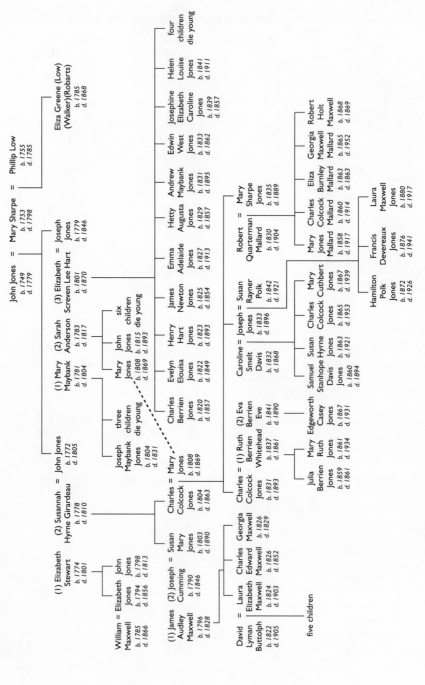

PLANTATIONS

ARCADIA—Plantation home of John Dunwody until his move to Roswell in 1838. It contained approximately 2,000 acres used for raising inland swamp rice and Sea Island cotton. Charles Colcock and Mary Jones purchased Arcadia in 1845. People from Maybank and Montevideo were moved into its settlement where Stepney [West] was the driver. The Jones family used Arcadia as a regular residence only during the Civil War.

BONAVENTURE—A Sea Island cotton plantation of some 2,800 acres purchased by the Reverend John Jones in 1845. Jones never lived at Bonaventure, but he moved a number of his slaves to the plantation shortly after its purchase. Jones's son, Dunwody Jones, tried unsuccessfully to plant there after the Civil War.

CARLAWTER—See **Montevideo**

LAMBERT—A rice and Sea Island cotton plantation owned in the eighteenth century by John Lambert. At Lambert's death in 1786, he left the plantation and thirty-one slaves in trust for philanthropic purposes. The plantation became the center of the Gullah community in Liberty County and was home of a number of early slave preachers. In 1839 the trustees of the estate sold the Lambert slaves and invested the funds in railroad and other stock. Lambert plantation was purchased in 1846 by Susan Jones Maxwell Cumming for her children Laura and Charles Edward. Thirty-eight slaves were moved to Lambert from White Oak plantation shortly after its purchase.

LAUREL VIEW—A 2,500-acre Sea Island cotton plantation owned by Joseph Jones (1779–1846) and located near Dorchester. Its lands reached to the Medway River. Andrew Maybank Jones inherited the plantation in 1846. People from the Retreat settlement were the primary laborers at Laurel View.

LIBERTY HALL—A rice and Sea Island cotton plantation located near Riceboro and owned by John Jones (1772–1805). Jupiter (1740?-1812?) was the longtime driver on the plantation. Elizabeth (Betsy) Jones Maxwell, Susan Jones Maxwell Cumming, and Charles Colcock Jones (1804–1863) were all born at Liberty Hall. After the death of Susannah Hyrne Girardeau Jones in 1810, the plantation was sold, its slaves were moved to the Retreat, and the plantation passed into the hands of Nathaniel Varnedoe.

LODEBAR—A Sea Island cotton plantation located near Dorchester. It was the home in the 1830s of William and Betsy Maxwell. Joseph Jones (1779–1846) purchased the plantation from the Maxwells in the 1840s and gave it to his son Henry Hart Jones. A number of slaves were moved from the Retreat settlement to Lodebar when it was purchased by Jones. Henry Hart Jones sold the plantation in 1856. After the Civil War a freedman's school was established at the plantation.

MALLARD PLACE—A Sea Island cotton and rice plantation located east of the Midway Congregation Church. Thomas Mallard owned the plantation for more than forty years, until his death in 1861. The Reverend Robert Quarterman Mallard spent the winter and spring months of his youth at the plantation. A large slave community lived in its settlement, including the driver Pompey and the carpenter and healer Dr. Harry Stevens.

MAYBANK—A 700-acre Sea Island cotton plantation and summer home located on Colonel's Island and overlooking the Medway marshes. Andrew Maybank in his will left the plantation to Charles Colcock Jones (1804–1863) and Mary Jones in 1834 with fifteen slaves. Andrew [Lawson] was the driver at Maybank for more than thirty years. The Jones family used the plantation as their summer home, staying there from early June until the first frost in the fall. Marauders burned the plantation house shortly after the end of the Civil War.

MONTEVIDEO—A 936-acre rice and Sea Island cotton plantation located on the North Newport River near Riceboro. Originally composed of three tracts, the plantation was a gift to Charles Colcock Jones (1804–1863) and Mary Jones from Joseph Jones (1779–1846). In 1839 a southern section of the plantation, some 400 acres, was broken off to form White Oak plantation, owned by Susan Jones Maxwell Cumming. Additional land was purchased to enlarge the plantation to approximately 900 acres. Montevideo was the primary residence and home of the Jones family. The section of Montevideo on which its slave settlement was located was known as Carlawter. Jack Anderson was the butler at Montevideo; Lizzy Jones and Patience [Way] were the primary cooks; Phoebe [Anderson Jones] was the seamstress; and Cato [Holmes] was the driver.

RETREAT—A rice and Sea Island cotton plantation located near Riceboro that eventually came to include more than 4,000 acres. The Retreat had originally been a part of Rice Hope plantation developed by John Jones (1749–1779), but Joseph Jones (1779–1846) greatly expanded its size and the production of its crops. Pulaski (1779–1852) was the driver at the Retreat for more than sixty years. During Joseph Jones's lifetime, the plantation was the center of the extended Jones family and the place of residence for many. After Joseph Jones's death, the plantation was managed by his son James Newton Jones, then purchased in 1856 by James Newton's brother Henry Hart Jones. The Retreat was sold out of the Jones family in the early 1860s. The Retreat house was burned shortly after the Civil War.

SOCIAL BLUFF—A Sea Island cotton plantation located on Colonel's Island overlooking the mouth of the North Newport River. The plantation had long been in the Maxwell family when Audley Maxwell left it to his grandchildren Laura and Charles Edwards Maxwell. The plantation was sometimes known as Point Maxwell or Point Prospect. When Laura Maxwell married the Reverend David Buttolph, Social Bluff became their home. Joefinny was the butler for the Buttolphs. Marauders burned the plantation house shortly after the end of the Civil War.

SOUTH HAMPTON—A rice and Sea Island cotton plantation of approximately 1,950 acres located on the North Newport River east of Montevideo. Barrington King developed the plantation from 1822 to 1838, when he sold South Hampton to his brother Roswell King. Paris was the longtime driver at the plantation. After Roswell King's death in 1854, the plantation was managed by his son James Audley King.

SPRINGFIELD—A plantation on the mainland overlooking the Medway marshes with a view of Colonel's Island. The Reverend William McWhir owned Springfield in the early decades of the nineteenth century. Later it was the plantation home of William Maxwell, who lived there until he was driven from it by Federal troops when they entered Liberty County in December 1864.

WHITE OAK—Originally a part of Montevideo plantation known as the Cooper tract, White Oak was formed as a distinct plantation of some 400 acres in 1839, when it became the sole property of Susan Jones Maxwell Cumming. There was no plantation house at White Oak, but an important slave settlement was located on the property. Prince was the driver at White Oak from 1839 until the removal of the people to southwest Georgia during the Civil War. After the war a number of the former slaves who had lived at White Oak returned to its settlement and rented the land from their former owner.

WOODMANSTON—The plantation, located near Bull Town Swamp, was the home of the LeConte family. Woodmanston was famous for its botanical garden and in particular for its extensive collection of camellias. The plantation was the childhood home of the scientists Joseph and John LeConte.

WOODVILLE—A Sea Island cotton plantation and summer home on Colonel's Island that was a part of the Audley Maxwell estate. When Maxwell died, his daughter Julia Maxwell King, wife of Roswell King, inherited Woodville. The plantation house overlooked the mouth of the North Newport River. The Kings used it as their summer home, staying there from early June until the first frost in the fall. Marauders burned the plantation house shortly after the end of the Civil War.

NOTES

Individuals and Institutions

CCJ—Charles Colcock Jones
CCJj—Charles Colcock Jones, Jr.
CTS—Columbia Theological Seminary
EHJ—Elizabeth Screven Lee Hart Jones (1801–1870)
EM—Elizabeth Jones Maxwell (1794–1856)
HHJ—Henry Hart Jones (1823–1893)
JJ—Joseph Jones (1833–1896)
JoJ—John Jones (1815–1893)
JosJ—Joseph Jones (1779–1846)
MJ—Mary Jones
MSJ—Mary Sharpe Jones; after April 22, 1857, Mary Sharpe Jones Mallard
MSJM—Mary Sharpe Jones Mallard; before April 22, 1857, Mary Sharpe Jones
RQM—Robert Quarterman Mallard
SJMC—Susan Jones Maxwell Cumming
TS—Thomas Shepard
WM—William Maxwell (1785–1866)

Document Sources

CJUG—Charles Colcock Jones, Jr., Collection, Special Division, University of
    Georgia Libraries
CO—*Charleston Observer*
CPB—Carlawter Plantation Book, JTU
GHS—Georgia Historical Society, Savannah, Ga.
JDU—Charles Colcock Jones, Jr., Collection, Duke University
JJUG—The Rev. John Jones Collection, University of Georgia

JTU—Charles Colcock Jones Papers, Howard-Tilton Memorial Library, Tulane
   University
MPB—Maybank Plantation Book, JTU
PHSM—Presbyterian Historical Foundation, Montreat, N.C.
PCLC—Probate Court, Hinesville, Liberty County, Ga.
SCLC—Office of the Clerk of Superior Court, Liberty County, Ga.
UGA—Special Division, University of Georgia Libraries

1. LIBERTY HALL

1. For Jupiter as the driver at Liberty Hall, see John Jones to Elizabeth Jones, 9 February 1796, JTU; John Jones Daybook, 1805, JTU. For Lizzy and Lymus see John Jones
   Daybook, 1805, JTU; Plantation Book for Carlawter, 8, JTU. Except where otherwise
   noted, "John Jones" citations refer to the master of Liberty Hall who lived from 1772 to
   1805. For slave driver as "caller" in the early morning, see William L. Van DeBurg, *The
   Slave Drivers: Black Agricultural Labor Supervisors in the Antebellum South* (Westport,
   Conn., 1979), 11. For the use of conch-shell horns, see Duncan Clinch Heyward, *Seed
   from Madagascar* (Chapel Hill, 1937), 179. Such a horn can be seen in the Charleston
   Museum, Charleston, S.C. For slave clothing, see John Jones Daybook, 1803–1805,
   JTU; Estate Papers of John Jones, PCLC.
2. Mary Jones Low to John Jones, 15 February 1784, JTU.
3. John Jones, "A List of My Negroes for the Year 1805 per my Tax returns," JTU; Philip D.
   Morgan, *Slave Counterpoint: Black Culture in the Eighteenth-Century Chesapeake
   and Lowcountry* (Chapel Hill, 1998), 104–122; Robert Ascher and Charles H. Fairbanks, "Excavation of a Slave Cabin: Georgia, U.S.A.," *Historical Archaeology* 5 (1971):
   3–17; Theresa Ann Singleton, "The Archaeology of Afro-American Slavery in Coastal
   Georgia: Regional Perception of Slave Household and Community Patterns" (Ph.D.
   diss., University of Florida, 1980); Leland Ferguson, *Uncommon Ground: Archaeology
   and Early African America, 1650–1800* (Washington, D.C., 1992), 63–82; Julia Floyd
   Smith, *Slavery and Rice Culture in Low Country Georgia* (Knoxville, 1985), 119–130;
   John Michael Vlach, *Back of the Big House: The Architecture of Plantation Slavery*
   (Chapel Hill, 1993), 153–167.
4. John Jones to Elizabeth Jones, 25 January, 1796, JTU; John Jones to Elizabeth Jones,
   16 January, 1795, JTU; Elizabeth Jones to John Jones, 1 January, 1797, JTU; John Jones
   to Elizabeth Jones, 29 January, 1796, JTU.
5. For slave drivers, see Morgan, *Slave Counterpoint*, 218–225; Peter Kolchin, "Reevaluating the Antebellum Slave Community: A Comparative Perspective," *Journal of American History* 70, no. 3, (1983): 595–596; Frederick Law Olmsted, *The Cotton Kingdom:
   A Traveller's Observations on Cotton and Slavery in the American Slave States,* ed.
   Arthur Schlesinger (New York, 1953), 186–187; James M. Clifton, "The Rice Driver:
   His Role in Slave Management," *South Carolina Historical Magazine* 82 (Oct. 1981):
   331–353; William L. Van DeBurg, *The Slave Drivers: Black Agricultural Labor Supervisors in the Antebellum South* (Westport, Conn., 1979).

6. Plantation Book for Carlawter, 8, JTU; John Jones to Elizabeth Jones, 7 February 1796, JTU; John Jones to Elizabeth Jones, 9 February 1796, JTU.

7. John Jones, "A List of My Negroes for the Year 1805 per my Tax returns," JTU; John Jones (1749–1779) Daybook, "A List of Negroes for the Year 1778," JTU; Will of John Bohum Girardeau, 11 November 1800, Will Record, 1790–1823, PCLC.

8. John Jones Daybook, 1803–1805, JTU.

9. For African origins of Fanny, Marcus, and Elvira, see MPB, 50b. Marcus, the child of Fanny and younger brother of Elvira, is listed as "from Africa." For Fanny's difficulty in learning to speak Gullah English, see Thomas Shepard to C. C. Jones, 14 November 1850, JTU. For Gullah as a language and bearer of culture, see Morgan, *Slave Counterpoint*, 559–580; Sidney W. Mintz and Richard Price, *An Anthropological Approach to the Afro-American Past: A Caribbean Perspective* (Boston: 1992), 20–22.

10. For the task system and the classification of "hands," see Morgan, *Slave Counterpoint*, 179–187; Philip D. Morgan, "Work and Culture: The Task System and the World of Lowcountry Blacks, 1700 to 1880," *William and Mary Quarterly*, 3rd ser., 39 (October 1982): 563–599; J. W. Joseph, "Pattern and Process in Plantation Archaeology of the Lowcountry of Georgia and South Carolina," *Journal of the Society for Historical Archaeology* 23, no. 1 (1989): 57–68; Larry E. Hudson, Jr., *To Have and to Hold: Slave Work and Family Life in Antebellum South Carolina* (Athens, Ga., 1997); William A. Noble, "Antebellum Hopeton and Current Altama Plantations in Georgia: A Study in Contrasts," in *One World, One Institution: The Plantation*, Proceedings of the Second World Plantation Conference, ed. Sue Eakin and John Tarver, Shreveport, La., October 6–10, 1986 (Baton Rouge, 1989), 71–91. For "weapons of the weak," see James C. Scott, *Weapons of the Weak: Everyday Forms of Peasant Resistance* (New Haven, 1985), 1–47.

11. Morgan, *Slave Counterpoint*, 180.

12. Ibid., 11, 113–116, 358–376. For personal property of slaves in the Georgia low country, see Betty Wood, *Women's Work, Men's Work: The Informal Slave Economies of Lowcountry Georgia* (Athens, Ga., 1995); Thomas F. Armstrong, "From Task Labor to Free Labor: The Transition Along Georgia's Rice Coast, 1820–1880," *Georgia Historical Quarterly* 64, (1980): 432–437; Philip D. Morgan, "The Ownership of Property by Slaves in the Mid-Nineteenth Century Low Country," *Journal of Southern History* 49, no. 3 (1983): 399–420; Dylan Penningroth, "Slavery, Freedom, and Social Claims to Property Among African Americans in Liberty County, Georgia, 1850–1880," *Journal of American History* 84 (September 1997): 405–435. For comparable developments in the Caribbean, see B. W. Higman, *Montpelier, Jamaica: A Plantation Community in Slavery and Freedom, 1739–1912* (Kingston, Jamaica, 1998), 191–257; Orlando Patterson, *Slavery and Social Death: A Comparative Study* (Cambridge, Mass., 1982), 182.

13. C. C. Jones, Jr., to Mary Ruth Jones, 11 May 1888, JDU; Estate Papers of John Jones, PCLC.

14. C. C. Jones, Jr., to Mary Ruth Jones, 11 May 1888, JDU; George White, *Historical Collections of Georgia* (New York, 1855), 537.

15. Robert Long Groover, *Sweet Land of Liberty: A History of Liberty County, Georgia*

(Roswell, Ga., 1987), 234; White, *Historical Collections*, 527–529; John Jones (1772–1805) Daybook, 1803, JTU.

16. James Stacy, *History of the Midway Congregational Church, Liberty County, Georgia* (Newnan, Ga., 1899), 1–20; Erskine Clarke, *Wrestlin' Jacob: A Portrait of Religion in the Old South* (Atlanta, 1979), 5–6.

17. Stacy, *History of Midway*, 27–34.

18. Robert Manson Myers, ed., *The Children of Pride: A True Story of Georgia and the Civil War* (New Haven, 1972), 8. For the strength of Calvinism in the South Carolina low country, see Erskine Clarke, *Our Southern Zion: A History of Calvinism in the South Carolina Low Country, 1690–1990* (Tuscaloosa, 1996).

19. John Jones Daybook, 1803, JTU.

20. C. C. Jones, Jr., to Mary Ruth Jones, 11 May 1888, JDU; Bills paid to Dr. North for "attendance John Jones (last illness)," Estate Papers of John Jones, PCLC.

21. For Jacob and Sandy as carpenters, see John Jones Daybook, 1803–1805, JTU. For the practice of slave carpenters building coffins, see RQM, *Plantation Life Before Emancipation* (Richmond, 1892), 25.

22. William Bartram, *Travels Through North and South Carolina, Georgia, East & West Florida, the Cherokee Country, the Extensive Territories of the Muscogulges, or Creek Confederacy, and the Country of the Chactaws* (1791; rpt. New York, 1988), 36–37.

23. Prayer by John Jones, John Jones Daybook, n.d., JTU.

24. Transcribed from the Midway Cemetery, Liberty County, Ga.

25. Joseph Jones, "Memorandum to Capt. Swain," 1805, JTU; Cf. David E. Stannard, *The Puritan Way of Death: A Study in Religion, Culture, and Social Change* (New York, 1977), 122–134, 167–196.

2. RICEBORO

1. Will of John Bohum Girardeau, 11 November 1800, Will Record, 1790–1823, PCLC; 1800 Tax Return for Sunbury District, SCLC.

2. For the fear and uncertainty slaves experienced around the prospects of a sale and removal, see Frederick Douglass, *Life and Times of Frederick Douglass* (New York, 1962), 97. Cf. CCJj to CCJ and MJ, 24 August 1854, JTU.

3. John Jones Daybook, 1803–1805, JTU.

4. For Rice Hope plantation, see Indenture Between Mary Jones and Philip Low, Record B, 348–351, SCLC. For the relationship of Rice Hope to the Retreat, see John Jones (1749–1779) Daybook, 1778, JTU; C. C. Jones, Jr., to Mary Ruth Jones, 11 May 1888, JDU; JosJ, Notes on Births and Deaths, n.d., CJUG. For patriarchalism, see Philip D. Morgan, "Three Planters and Their Slaves: Perspectives on Slavery in Virginia, South Carolina and Jamaica, 1750–1790," in *Race and Family in the Colonial South*, ed. Winthrop D. Jordan and Sheila L. Skemp (Jackson, Miss., 1987), 37–79; Philip D. Morgan, *Slave Counterpoint: Black Culture in the Eighteenth-Century Chesapeake and Lowcountry* (Chapel Hill, 1998), 274–284. For patriarchalism and the role of an uncle in providing protection and guardianship, see Catherine Clinton, *The Plantation Mistress: Woman's World in the Old South* (New York, 1982), 36–57.

5. JosJ, Estate John Jones in a/c Current, JosJ Administrator, 1805, 1806, PCLC. For medicines used at Liberty Hall, see ibid. and John Jones Daybook, passim.
6. For the hurricane of 1804, see CCJ, "Funeral Service of Mrs. John Ashmore, June 1847," JTU. For the plantation expenses at Liberty Hall and the growing financial crisis, see JosJ, Estate John Jones in a/c Current, 1805–1808, PCLC.
7. Robert Manson Myers, ed. *The Children of Pride: A True Story of Georgia and the Civil War* (New Haven, 1972), 12; "Sheriff's Sale," *Georgia Gazette* (Savannah), 26 July 1798; MJ to CCJ, 27 October 1827, JTU.
8. Kenneth Coleman, "1775–1820," in Kenneth Coleman, ed., *A History of Georgia* (Athens, Ga., 1977), 96–97, 101.
9. "Sheriff's Sale," *Georgia Gazette* (Savannah), 26 July 1798.
10. See, e.g., *Georgia Gazette* (Savannah), 16 August 1798, 18 October 1798, 1 December 1799, 8 May 1802; *Columbian Museum and Savannah Advertiser*, 10 November 1799.
11. Real Estate Division, County Record E, 194–195, 227–228, 239–240, SCLC. Headright was a land-grant system for able-bodied men dating back to the early 1600s in the Virginia colony and adapted throughout the South and later Texas. Up to one thousand acres per family, including fifty to one hundred acres per wife, child, and slave, sometimes at minimal extra cost per acre, might be granted the applicant by the state to encourage the settlement and working of the land.
12. Real Estate Division, County Record F, 11–12, 18–19, 54–56, SCLC; John Jones Daybook, 1803–1805, JTU; Appraisal of the Estate of John Jones, 14 October 1805, Will Record A, 1790–1823, PCLC.
13. Virginia Fraser Evans, "Riceboro," in *Liberty County, Georgia: A Pictorial History*, compiled by Virginia Fraser Evans (Statesville, N.C., 1979), 38–41; William C. Fleetwood, Jr., *Tidecraft: The Boats of South Carolina, Georgia, and Northeastern Florida, 1550–1950* (Tybee Island, Ga., 1995), 45–121. For the transatlantic economy, see Robert Harms, *The Diligent: A Voyage Through the Worlds of the Slave Trade* (New York, 2002).
14. Evans, "Riceboro," 38–39; JosJ, Estate John Jones, 1805–1808, SCLC.
15. For the purchase of rum, see John Jones Daybook, 1803–1805, JTU. On rum use and slave health, see Robert William Fogel, *Without Consent or Contract: The Rise and Fall of American Slavery* (New York, 1989), 153; and Morgan, *Slave Counterpoint*, 134–143. For the decades-long controversy between planters and shopkeepers in Riceboro, see CCJ to Thomas Shepard, 23 August 1849, JTU.
16. For the role of a village in a plantation setting and for the tensions between shopkeepers and planters, see Larry E. Hudson, Jr., "'All That Cash': Work and Status in the Slave Quarters" in Larry E. Hudson, Jr., ed., *Working Toward Freedom: Slave Society and Domestic Economy in the American South* (Rochester, 1994), 77–94; Philip D. Morgan, "The Ownership of Property by Slaves in the Mid-Nineteenth Century Low Country," *Journal of Southern History* 49, no. 3 (1983): 399–420. For ways in which Riceboro could function as a scene of conflict between white planters and slaves with their boro allies, see James C. Scott, "Making Social Space for a Dissent Subculture" in *Domination and the Art of Resistance: Hidden Transcripts* (New Haven, 1990), 120–124.

17. For a particularly brutal court sentence requiring the whipping of a slave in Riceboro in 1809, see Ralph Betts Flanders, *Plantation Slavery in Georgia* (Chapel Hill, 1935), 262.
18. For traditional locations in Riceboro of slave sales, see Sale of Certain Negroes to Joseph Bacon, County Record F, 197, SCLC; *Savannah Republican*, 20 June 1816.
19. For examples of the familiar questions asked in slave sales, see Michael Tadman, *Speculators and Slaves: Masters, Traders, and Slaves in the Old South* (Madison, Wis., 1989), 83–108.
20. Lydia Parrish, *Slave Songs of the Georgia Sea Islands* (1942; rpt. Athens, Ga., 1992), 196.
21. Sale of Certain Negroes to Joseph Bacon, County Record F, 197, SCLC; Sale of Certain Negroes to Capt. P. H. Wilkins, County Record F, 197, SCLC.
22. See James Stacy, *History of the Midway Congregational Church, Liberty County, Georgia* (Newnan, Ga., 1899), 30; County Record H, 13, SCLC; Sale of Certain Negroes to Col. Joseph Law, County Record F, 198, SCLC. See also PBC, 5.
23. See PBC, 5; Indenture between JosJ and Susannah Jones, Elizabeth Jones, John Jones, Susanna Mary Jones, and CCJ, 16 June 1808, County Record F, 211, SCLC.
24. John Jones Daybook, 1803–1805, JTU; Will of Susannah Jones, 5 October 1810, Will Record A, 1790–1823, PCLC.

3. SUNBURY

1. Sale of Certain Negroes to Col. Joseph Law, County Record F, 198, SCLC. See also CPB, 5. For slave nurses of slave children, see William A. Noble, "Antebellum Hopeton and Current Altamaha Plantations in Georgia: A Study in Contrasts," in *One World, One Institution: The Plantation,* Proceedings of the Second World Plantation Conference, ed. Sue Eakin and John Tarver, Shreveport, Louisiana, October 6–10, 1986 (Baton Rouge, 1989), 78–79. For work of slave children, see Elizabeth Fox-Genovese, *Within the Plantation Household: Black and White Women of the Old South* (Chapel Hill, 1988), 151–159; Philip D. Morgan, *Slave Counterpoint: Black Culture in the Eighteenth-Century Chesapeake and Lowcountry* (Chapel Hill, 1998), 197–198, 252–253. A note, evidently by MJ, written on the back of a letter from Jos. P. Eryles to CCJ, 1 November 1847, JTU, provides information on Rosetta's role as CCJ's early nurse and on CCJ's early history. Hereafter referred to as MJ Note on Early History of CCJ, JTU.
2. JosJ, Estate John Jones in a/c Current, JosJ Administrator, 1805–1808, PCLC; MJ Note on Early History of CCJ, JTU; RQM, *Montevideo-Maybank: Some Memoirs of a Southern Christian Household in the Olden Time; or, The Family Life of the Rev. Charles Colcock Jones, D.D., of Liberty County, Ga.* (Richmond, 1898), 34–36.
3. CCJ to CCJj, 20 April 1854, CJUG.
4. Journal of MJ, 1863, JTU.
5. Ibid.; CCJ to CCJj, 20 April 1854, CJUG.
6. John M. B. Harden, M.D. "Observations on the Soil, Climate and Diseases of Liberty County, Georgia," in *Southern Medical and Surgical Journal,* new ser., 1, no. 10 (October 1845): 555–557.
7. JosJ, Estate John Jones, 1808, PCLC.

8. John McKay Sheftall, *Sunbury on the Medway: A Selective History of the Town, Inhabitants, and Fortifications* (Norcross, Ga., 1995), 14–16; William Bartram, *Travels Through North and South Carolina, Georgia, East & West Florida, the Cherokee Country, the Extensive Territories of the Muscogulges, or Creek Confederacy, and the Country of the Chactaws* (1791; rpt. New York, 1988), 32–33; Charles C. Jones, Jr., *Dead Towns of Georgia* (1878; rpt. Savannah, 1997), 173–174.

9. Jones, *Dead Towns of Georgia*, 210–223.

10. The lots were numbers 29 and 30. See Appraisal of the Estate of John Jones, 14 October 1805, Will Record A, 1790–1823, PCLC. For the location of the lots, see the town plat in Jones, *Dead Towns of Georgia*, 141. For the regular movement of the family between Sunbury and Rice Hope, see, e.g., Mary Low to John Jones, 28 March 1785, and Mary Low to John Jones, 25 April 1795, JTU. For the burial place of Mary Low behind the Jones house in Sunbury, see Last Will and Testament of JosJ, Will Record, 1824–1850, PCLC; John Jones Daybook, 1804–1805, JTU.

11. JosJ, Estate John Jones, 1808, PCLC. Jones, *Dead Towns of Georgia*, 215.

12. Indenture Between Sarah Anderson and JosJ, County Record F, 134, 1806, SCLC; JosJ, Notes on Births and Deaths, n.d., CJUG.

13. For the Robarts house on lot 6, see Sheftall, *Sunbury on the Medway*, 186. Robert Manson Myers, ed., *The Children of Pride: A True Story of Georgia and the Civil War* (New Haven, 1972), 27, 1658.

14. JosJ to Sarah Jones, 6 July 1808, JTU.

15. CCJ, *The Religious Instruction of the Negroes in the United States* (Savannah, 1842), 110–111. For everyday forms of slave resistance, see James C. Scott, *Weapons of the Weak: Everyday Forms of Peasant Resistance* (New Haven, 1985), 28–47.

16. For Robinson as Lizzy's husband and the father of her children, see Thomas Shepard to CCJ, 16 December 1850, JTU.

17. For slave "visiting," "abroad wives," and "wife house," see RQM, *Plantation Life Before Emancipation* (Richmond, 1892), 51; Morgan, *Slave Counterpoint*, 524–525; Paul D. Escott, *Slavery Remembered: A Record of Twentieth-Century Slave Narratives* (Chapel Hill, 1979), 52.

18. Indenture Between Sarah Anderson and JosJ, 1806; An Inventory and Appraisement of the Goods and Chattels of JosJ of Liberty County, 15 December 1846, County Record M, 413, PCLC; MJ to CCJj, 29 May 1863, JTU; MJ to JoJ, 18 September 1865, JJUG. For the Mammy figure, see Deborah Gray White, *Ar'n't I a Woman? Female Slaves in the Plantation South* (New York, 1985), 27–51; and Elizabeth Fox-Genovese, *Within the Plantation Household: Black and White Women of the Old South* (Chapel Hill, 1988), 291–292.

19. Indenture Between Sarah Anderson and JosJ, 1806, SCLC. For the "slave in the middle," see Morgan, *Slave Counterpoint*, 334–353. For the larger context of acculturation to a Western worldview as a way to resist the power of the West, see Theodore H. Von Laue, *The World Revolution of Westernization: the Twentieth Century in Global Perspective* (New York, 1987).

20. Jack, as the patriarch of his community and the one in charge of household affairs for

the CCJ family, was apparently the primary storyteller who supplied the young CCJj with the folktales he later published as *Negro Myths from the Georgia Coast Told in the Vernacular* (1888; rpt. Columbia, S.C., 1925). For the role of folktales as conveying strategies for resistance, see James C. Scott, *Domination and the Art of Resistance: Hidden Transcripts* (New Haven, 1990), 162–166; Charles Joyner, *Down by the Riverside: A South Carolina Slave Community* (Urbana, Ill., 1984), 172–195; Lawrence W. Levine, *Black Culture and Black Consciousness: Afro-American Folk Thought from Slavery to Freedom* (Oxford, 1977), 97–101. For the West African tradition of a clever trickster, see Will Coleman, *Tribal Talk: Black Theology, Hermeneutics, and African/American Ways of "Telling the Story"* (University Park, Pa., 2000), 20–23.

21. Bartram, *Travels*, 33–35.
22. Jones, *Dead Towns*, 157, 169, 171, 217; John Jones (1749–1779) Daybook, 1777–1778; Myers, *Children of Pride*, 1658.
23. Myers, *Children of Pride*, 1621.
24. CCJ, Journal, 2 June 1860, JTU; RQM, *Montevideo-Maybank*, 10–11.
25. Audley King to CCJ, 17 October 1853, JTU. For slaves claiming surnames of earlier owners, see Eugene D. Genovese, *Roll, Jordan, Roll: The World the Slaves Made* (New York, 1974), 445–447; Herbert G. Gutman, *The Black Family in Slavery and Freedom, 1750–1925* (New York, 1976), 230–256, esp. 252; Morgan, *Slave Counterpoint*, 555–558.
26. Will of John Bohum Girardeau, 11 November 1800, Will Record 1790–1823, PCLC. For the role of seafood, see Elizabeth J. Reitz, Tyson Sibbs, Ted A. Rathbun, "Archaeological Evidence for Subsistence on Coastal Plantations," in *The Archaeology of Slavery and Plantation Life*, ed. Theresa A. Singleton (Orlando, 1985), 163–186; Morgan, *Slave Counterpoint*, 134–143.
27. Jones, *Dead Towns*, 171, 212.
28. CPB, 64, JTU.
29. For Jack and Lizett as husband and wife and as parents of Phoebe, see Indenture Between Sarah Anderson and JosJ, County Record F, 134, 1806, SCLC; CPB, 9, 67; and Appraisement and Division of Negroes between JosJ and CCJ on behalf of his Wife, 23 February 1831, CJUG. John C. Inscoe, "Carolina Slave Names: An Index to Acculturation," *Journal of Southern History* 49, no. 4 (November 1983): 535; Cheryll Ann Cody, "There Was No 'Absalom' on the Ball Plantations: Slave-Naming Practices in the South Carolina Low Country, 1720–1865," *American Historical Review* 92, no. 1 (February 1987): 573, 579.
30. Will of Susanna H. Jones, 10 May 1810, Will Record A, 1790–1823, PCLC.
31. Journal of MJ, 1863, JTU. Myers, *Children of Pride*, 13. Cf. Joseph LeConte, *The Autobiography of Joseph LeConte* (New York, 1903), 6–7.
32. JosJ, Estate John Jones, 1810–1811, PCLC.
33. MJ Note on Early History of CCJ, JTU. This note gives a different account of the years 1810–1813 from the one in Myers, *Children of Pride*, 13.
34. MJ Note on Early History of CCJ, JTU.
35. CPB, 64.
36. Myers, *Children of Pride*, 13, 1658.

4. THE RETREAT

1. For the relationship of Rice Hope to the Retreat, see John Jones (1749–1779) Daybook, 1778, JTU; EGR to CCJ, 21 February 1859, JTU.
2. Plat of the Retreat Plantation, Liberty County, Georgia, CJUG; Last Will and Testament of JosJ, Will Record, 1824–1850, PCLC. For examples of loans by JosJ, see JosJ's loan of $1,800 to Colonel Joseph Law, County Record H, 13, SCLC; and Inventory, Appraisement, and Division of Estate of Jos. Jones, Will Record, 1824–1850, PCLC. For the role of capitalism generally in the plantation South, see Robert William Fogel, *Without Consent or Contract: The Rise and Fall of American Slavery* (New York, 1989), 64–72; Peter A. Coclanis, *The Shadow of a Dream: Economic Life and Death in the South Carolina Low Country, 1670–1920* (New York, 1989).
3. MJ Note on Early History of CCJ, JTU (see Chapter 3, note 1). John Jones died on November 24, 1813.
4. Inscription transcribed from Midway cemetery.
5. Description of the avenue at the Retreat is drawn from Plat of the Retreat Plantation, Surveyed March 19, 1827, by Robert Hendry, Jr., Co. Surveyor, Grant Record Book I, 182–183, SCLC; a composite map of the Retreat by F. M. Martin, III, October 1985, in Liberty County file, GHS; Last Will and Testament of JosJ, Will Record, 1824–1850, PCLC; and CCJ, "Account of My Dear and Honored Father's Death," 1846, JTU. For the use of "threshold devises" on a plantation avenue, see John Michael Vlach, *Back of the Big House: The Architecture of Plantation Slavery* (Chapel Hill, 1993), 5.
6. For the ideological role of the plantation house, see Vlach, *Back of the Big House*, 1–12; Rhys Isaac, *The Transformation of Virginia, 1740–1790* (Chapel Hill, 1982), 32–42.
7. Description of the Retreat plantation house is drawn from MJ to CCJ, 11 June 1829, JTU; CCJ to MJ, 22 November 1829, JTU; CCJ to MJ, 16 July 1830, JTU; CCJ, "Account of My Dear and Honored Father's Death," 1846, JTU.
8. JosJ, Notes on Births and Deaths, n.d., CJUG; MJ to CCJj, 7 July 1858, CJUG. For pregnancy and pregnancy rates of white plantation women, see Brenda E. Stevenson, *Life in Black and White: Family and Community in the Slave South* (New York, 1996), 101–105; and Fogel, *Without Consent or Contract*, 114–116.
9. For Sylvia and Jack as special servants of Sarah Anderson Jones before her death in 1817 and for their responsibilities at the Retreat, see CPB, 64; CCJ, "Account of My Dear and Honored Father's Death," 1846, JTU.
10. JosJ, Estate John Jones in a/c Current, JosJ Administrator, 1811–1812, PCLC; Indenture between JosJ and Susannah Jones, Elizabeth Jones, John Jones, Susanna Mary Jones, and CCJ, 16 June 1808, County Record F, 211, SCLC. For Hamlet's marriage to Elvira and the birth of Syphax, see CPB, 12. For the interaction of African and European cultures on slaves such as Syphax, see Peter Wood, *Black Majority: Negroes in Colonial South Carolina from 1670 through the Stono Rebellion* (New York, 1974), 196–217; Michael Gomez, *Exchanging Our Country Marks: The Transformation of African Identities in the Colonial and Antebellum South* (Chapel Hill, 1998), 186–243; Sterling Stuckey, *Slave Culture: Nationalist Theory and the Foundations of Black America* (New York, 1987), 3–27.

11. For landscape's role in shaping human perspectives and emotions, see Benjamin Z. Kedar and R. J. Zwi Werblowski, *Sacred Space: Shrine, City, Land* (New York, 1998); Frederick Turner, *Spirit of Place: The Making of an American Literary Landscape* (San Francisco, 1989); Wendell Berry, *What Are People For?* (Berkeley, 1996). For the role of landscape in plantation societies, see B. W. Higman, *Montpelier, Jamaica: A Plantation Community in Slavery and Freedom, 1739–1912* (Kingston, Jamaica, 1998), 297–300; William M. Kelso and Rachel Most, eds., *Earth Patterns: Essays in Landscape Archaeology* (Charlottesville, 1990); John Michael Vlach, "Plantation Landscapes of the Antebellum South," in *Before Freedom Came: African-American Life in the Antebellum South*, ed. Edward D. C. Campbell, Jr., and Kym S. Rice (Charlottesville, 1991). For CCJ's continuing interest in hunting on an occasional basis, see CCJ to MJ, "Our Tenth Wedding Day, December 21, 1840," JTU; and CCJ to CCJj, 3 January 1853, CJUG; and cf. Joseph LeConte, *The Autobiography of Joseph LeConte* (New York, 1903), 17–28. For CCJ's lifelong love of nature, see Journal of MJ, 1863, JTU; and David Buttolph, "Funeral Sermon of CCJ," 18 March 1863, JTU.

12. CCJ to MJ, 8 January 1828, and CCJ to MJ, 22 November 1829, JTU. Journal of MJ, 1863, JTU.

13. CCJ to MJ, 8 January 1828, JTU; and CCJ, "Account of My Honored Father's Death," 1846, JTU.

14. Philip D. Morgan, *Slave Counterpoint: Black Culture in the Eighteenth-Century Chesapeake and Lowcountry* (Chapel Hill, 1998), 27–95; Daniel C. Littlefield, *Rice and Slaves: Ethnicity and the Slave Trade in Colonial South Carolina* (Baton Rouge, 1981); Julia Floyd Smith, *Slavery and Rice Culture in Low Country Georgia, 1750–1860* (Knoxville, 1985); and Judith A. Carney, *Black Rice: The African Origins of Rice Cultivation in the Americas* (Cambridge, Mass., 2001).

15. John M. B. Harden, M.D., "Observations on the Soil, Climate, and Diseases of Liberty County, Georgia," *Southern Medical and Surgical Journal*, new ser., 1, no. 10 (October 1845): 546–549; JJ, M.D., *Agricultural Resources of Georgia: Address Before the Cotton Planters Convention of Georgia at Macon, December 13, 1860* (Augusta, Ga., 1861), 6–7. For inland swamp cultivation of rice, see Charles H. Fairbanks, "The Plantation Archaeology of the Southeastern Coast," *Historical Archaeology* 18 (1984): 6–7; Douglas C. Wilms, "The Development of Rice Culture in Eighteenth Century Georgia," *Southeastern Geographer* 12 (1972), 45–57; Carney, *Black Rice*, 86–89.

16. For the development of river swamp cultivation, utilizing the influence of the tide, see Morgan, *Slave Counterpoint*, 155–159; Joyce E. Chaplin, "Tidal Rice Cultivation and the Problem of Slavery in South Carolina and Georgia, 1760–1815," *William and Mary Quarterly*, 3rd Ser., 49 (1992): 29–61.

17. MJ Note on Early History of CCJ, JTU.

18. Ibid.; Robert Manson Myers, ed. *The Children of Pride: A True Story of Georgia and the Civil War* (New Haven, 1972), 13.

19. For the character of the Sunbury Academy and its curriculum, see advertisements in the Savannah papers, e.g.: *Columbia Museum and Savannah Advertiser*, 13 August 1799; and *Savannah Republican*, 15 January 1818. Cf. Charles C. Jones, Jr., *Dead Towns of Georgia* (1878; rpt. Savannah, 1997), 214–216.

20. T. B. Smith, Essays, in T. B. Smith Papers, item no. 56, GHS.
21. Ibid., 30–36.
22. Malcolm Bell, Jr., *Major Butler's Legacy: Five Generations of a Slaveholding Family* (Athens, Ga., 1987), 170–172.
23. Jones, *Dead Towns*, 219–220. For Jupiter as body servant, see CCJj, *The Negro Myths from the Georgia Coast: Told in the Vernacular* (1888; rpt. Columbia, S.C., 1925), 177.
24. Bell, *Major Butler's Legacy*, 172; George White, *Statistics of the State of Georgia* (Savannah, 1849), 288; John Solomon Otto, *Cannon's Point Plantation, 1794–1860: Living Conditions and Status Patterns in the Old South* (Orlando, 1984).
25. Quoted in Bell, *Major Butler's Legacy*, 182.
26. For the story of what happened to those going to Nova Scotia, see ibid., 182–191.

5. CARLAWTER

1. JosJ, Estate John Jones in a/c Current, JosJ Administrator, 1811–1812, PCLC.
2. For the purchase and gift of the Carlawter and Cooper tracts, see County Record H, 66–67, SCLC. For the purchase and gift of the Lambright tract, see County Record H, 226–227, SCLC. For summaries of these transactions, see CPB, 1–4.
3. For the details of the tracts, see plat surveyed by Wm. Cundiff 2 October 1798, and plat surveyed by Robert Hendry 5 March 1812, in box 21, folder 8, CJUG.
4. CPB, 4–6.
5. For the ages of those moved to Carlawter, see CPB, 12–13. For slaves passing skills and positions to their children, see Philip D. Morgan, *Slave Counterpoint: Black Culture in the Eighteenth-Century Chesapeake and Lowcountry* (Chapel Hill, 1998), 545.
6. For Robinson's work as a nurse in a later outbreak of smallpox, see Thomas Shepard to CCJ, 16 December 1850. Cf. Elizabeth A. Fenn, *Pox Americana: The Great Smallpox Epidemic of 1775–82* (New York, 2001).
7. CPB, 12–13.
8. For Sam's role in the Robarts household, see, e.g., Eliza Robarts to MJ, 16 January 1858, JTU. For "life in the big house" for house servants generally, see Eugene D. Genovese, *Roll, Jordan, Roll: The World the Slaves Made* (New York, 1974), 328–365.
9. Cf. William Dusinberre, *Them Dark Days: Slavery in the American Rice Swamps* (New York, 1996), 84–121.
10. For Willoughby, Tony, and their children, see Indenture between JosJ and Susannah Jones, Elizabeth Jones, John Jones, Susanna Mary Jones, and CCJ, 16 June 1808, County Record F, 134 and 211, SCLC; CPB, 12–13; and MPB 50a. For Fanny and her children, see CPB, 7.
11. Cf. Morgan, *Slave Counterpoint*, 519–530; and Dusinberre, *Them Dark Days*, 84–121.
12. For plantations as "so many little villages," see CCJ, *Seventh Annual Report of the Association for Religious Instruction of the Negroes in Liberty County, Ga. Together with the Address to the Association by the President, The Rev. Josiah Spry Law. The Constitution of the Association. And the Population of the County for 1840.* (Savannah, 1842), 10.
13. For Liberty Hall's location in relation to Carlawter, see County Record H, 66–67, SCLC; County Record K, 129, SCLC.

14. See Thomas Shepard to CCJ, 6 August 1851. For the relationship of African Americans to the natural world, see Ras Michael Brown, "'Walk in the Feenda': West-Central Africans and the Forest in the South Carolina–Georgia Lowcountry," in *Central Africans and Cultural Transformations in the American Diaspora*, ed. Linda M. Heywood (Cambridge, 2002), 289–318.

15. Cato later was able to taste the river water to see whether it was fresh enough to flood the rice fields. See HHJ to CCJ, 1 July 1857, JTU.

16. For slaves' fishing in the rivers of the low country and use of boats and canoes, see Elizabeth J. Reitz, Tyson Sibbs, Ted A. Rathbun, "Archaeological Evidence for Subsistence on Coastal Plantations," in *The Archaeology of Slavery and Plantation Life*, ed. Theresa A. Singleton (Orlando, 1985), 163–186; Morgan, *Slave Counterpoint*, 134–143; RQM, *Plantation Life Before Emancipation* (Richmond, 1892), 25–26.

17. For the role of trails and an "alternative territorial system," see Rhys Isaac, *The Transformation of Virginia, 1740–1790* (Chapel Hill, 1982), 52–57; and Higman, *Montpelier, Jamaica*, 99–100. For whites knowing about such trails and the uses to which they could be put, see CCJ to CCJj, 10 July 1862, CJUG. For an example of slaves at Carlawter killing and butchering a cow in a secret place, see Elija Chapman to CCJ, 17 November 1855, JTU

18. In South Carolina, Lambert had been a member of the Bethel Pon Pon Presbyterian Church that was visited by Whitefield. Bethel Pon Pon Presbyterian Church, Session Minutes, 1740–1770, PHSM.

19. Will of John Lambert, Papers of the Estate of John Lambert, GHS.

20. Inventory and Appraisement of the Goods and Chattels of John Lambert Deceased, Estate of John Lambert; and Estate of John Lambert, II, Papers of the Estate of John Lambert, GHS. List of Negroes, Estate of Lambert, 1837, JJUG. Estate of John Lambert, II and IV, Papers of the Estate of John Lambert, GHS.

21. Estate of John Lambert, II, 4 January 1806. CCJ, *Tenth Annual Report of the Association for the Religious Instruction of the Negroes, in Liberty County, Georgia* (Savannah, 1945), 6.

22. For Jack, see Estate of John Lambert, II, 11 April 1810, 14 February 1812, 16 December 1813, GHS. For Sharper and his wife, see Last Will and Testament of JosJ, Will Record, 1824–1850, PCLC; Journal of CCJ, 25 April 1858, JTU; and CCJ, *Tenth Annual Report*, 8.

23. Estate of John Lambert, II, 18 December 1805, 11 January 1815, 28 June 1805, 9 June 1805, GHS. For slave doctors and nurses and the use of folk medicines, see Betty Wood, *Slavery in Colonial Georgia, 1730–1775* (Athens, Ga., 1984), 152–154; Lawrence W. Levine, *Black Culture and Black Consciousness: Afro-American Folk Thought from Slavery to Freedom* (Oxford, 1977), 63–66.

24. Works Projects Administration, *Drums and Shadows: Survival Studies Among the Georgia Coastal Negroes* (Athens, Ga., 1940), 112–132; Michael Mullin, *Africa in America: Slave Acculturation and Resistance in the American South and the British Caribbean, 1736–1831* (Urbana, Ill., 1992), 68–72; Morgan, *Slave Counterpoint*, 615–625; Albert J. Raboteau, *Slave Religion: "The Invisible Institution" in the Antebellum South* (New York, 1978), 80–86, 275–288; Theophus H. Smith, *Conjuring Culture: Biblical For-*

mations of Black America (New York, 1994), 140–158; John W. Blassingame, *The Slave Community: Plantation Life in the Ante-Bellum South* (New York, 1972), 1–40.

25. Weak remnants of a European tradition of magic may have lingered among some white planters of Liberty County at the beginning of the nineteenth century, but I have found no indication in the letters and papers of whites of a belief in the occult. See Diane Purkiss, *The Witch in History: Early Modern and Twentieth-Century Representations* (New York, 1996); Robin Briggs, *Witches and Neighbors: The Social and Cultural Context of European Witchcraft* (New York, 1998).

26. For the cultural and religious assumptions that informed a national proslavery argument rooted in a conservative republicanism, see Larry E. Tise, *Proslavery: A History of the Defense of Slavery in America, 1701–1840* (Athens, Ga., 1987), 347–362. Cf. CCJ, *Tenth Annual Report*, 12.

27. For slave resistance, see Robert William Fogel, *Without Consent or Contract: The Rise and Fall of American Slavery* (New York, 1989), 154–198. For the creation of a coherent culture as "*the* most significant act of resistance in its own right," see Morgan, *Slave Counterpoint*, xii. Cf. James C. Scott, *Weapons of the Weak: Everyday Forms of Peasant Resistance* (New Haven, 1985), 314–318.

28. *Savannah Republican*, 3 January 1820. On runaways, see John Hope Franklin and Loren Schweninger, *Runaway Slaves: Rebels on the Plantation* (New York, 1999); Blassingame, *The Slave Community*, 104–131.

29. *Savannah Republican*, 18 July 1816. CCJ, *Tenth Annual Report*, 12.

6. SAVANNAH

1. John M. B. Harden, M.D., "Observations on the Soil, Climate and Diseases of Liberty County, Georgia," in *Southern Medical and Surgical Journal*, new ser., 1, no. 10 (October 1845): 552–556. JJ, *Medical and Surgical Memoirs: Containing Investigations on the Geographical Distribution, Causes, Nature, Relations, and Treatment of Various Diseases* (New Orleans, 1887), 501–502.

2. See Andrew Spielman and Michael D'Antonio, *Mosquito: A Natural History of Our Most Persistent and Deadly Foe* (New York, 2003); and Margaret Humphreys, *Yellow Fever and the South* (Baltimore, 1992), 37–38.

3. Cf. Harden, "Observations," 557; and J. Hume Simons, M.D., *Planter's Guide, Family Book of Medicine: For the Instruction and Use of Planters, Families, Country People, and All Others Who May Be Out of the Reach of Physicians, or Unable to Employ Them* (Charleston, S.C., 1848), 72–82. Peter H. Wood, *Black Majority: Negroes in Colonial South Carolina from 1670 Through the Stono Rebellion* (New York, 1974), 87–88.

4. James Stacy, *The Published Records of Midway Church* (Newnan, Ga., 1894), 151; JJ, *Medical and Surgical Memoirs*, 502.

5. Simons, *Planter's Guide*, 72–74.

6. JosJ, Notes on Births and Deaths, n.d., CJUG.

7. MJ to CCJj, 7 July 1858, CJUG.

8. Eliza Ferguson to JosJ, 5 October 1818, 3 March 1819, JTU.

9. Susan Jones to JosJ, 24 February 1818, 4 April 1818, 26 December 1818; Eliza Ferguson

to JosJ, 11 December 1819, JTU. For the social and political leadership concentrated in Circular Congregational Church, see Erskine Clarke, *Our Southern Zion: A History of Calvinism in the South Carolina Lowcountry, 1690–1990* (Tuscaloosa, 1996), 142–159.

10. Journal of MJ, 1863, JTU.

11. For an example of JoJ's affection for Sylvia as his "old Momma," see JoJ to MJ, 19 May 1863, JTU.

12. Robert Manson Myers, ed., *The Children of Pride: A True Story of Georgia and the Civil War* (New Haven, 1972), 1569–1570; George White, *Historical Collections of Georgia* (New York, 1855), 534.

13. Myers, *Children of Pride*, 1573.

14. MJ to CCJ, 2 September 1830, JTU. For MJ referring to her stepmother as "Mrs. Jones," see, e.g., MJ to MSJM, 31 July 1862, JTU.

15. *Savannah Republican*, 14 December 1816. JosJ to MJ, 27 September 1820, JTU. MJ to MSJM, 15 August 1862; MJ to JosJ, 12 August 1822, JTU.

16. Phinizy Spalding, "The Colonial Period" in *A History of Georgia*, ed. Kenneth Coleman (Athens, Ga., 1977), 19–21.

17. Richard C. Wade, *Slavery in the Cities: The South, 1820–1860* (New York, 1964), 8–9.

18. "Rev. Charles Colcock Jones, D.D.," *Southern Presbyterian*, 4 June 1863; Myers, *Children of Pride*, 13.

19. Betty Wood, *Women's Work, Men's Work: The Informal Slave Economies of Lowcountry Georgia* (Athens, Ga., 1995), 131.

20. *Savannah Republican*, 17 August 1817. Cf. Wood, *Women's Work, Men's Work*, 80–100. *Savannah Republican*, 17 August 1818.

21. Wade, *Slavery in the Cities*, 73–74. Wood, *Women's Work, Men's Work*, 101–121.

22. *Savannah Republican*, 2 Feb. 1818.

23. Wade, *Slavery in the Cities*, 327, 249–252; Ira Berlin, *Slaves Without Masters* (New York, 1974); Philip D. Morgan, *Slave Counterpoint: Black Culture in the Eighteenth-Century Chesapeake and Lowcountry* (Chapel Hill, 1998), 285–297.

24. Alan Gallay, *The Formation of a Planter Elite: Jonathan Bryan and the Southern Colonial Frontier* (Athens, Ga., 1989), 52–53. James M. Simms, *The First Colored Baptist Church in North America, Constituted at Savannah, Georgia, January 20, A.D. 1788, with Biographical Sketches of the Pastors* (Philadelphia, 1888), 72–73.

25. Janet Duitsman Cornelius, *Slave Missions and the Black Church in the Antebellum South* (Columbia, S.C., 1999), 104–106;

26. Simms, *The First Colored Baptist Church*, 79–84; Cornelius, *Slave Missions and the Black Church*, 105–106. See *Savannah Republican*, 17 January 1818.

27. For Jones's relationship with Henry Cunningham and Jones's preaching in the Second African Baptist Church, see CO, 28 September 1833.

28. Journal of MJ, 1863, JTU.

29. Stacy, *Records of Midway Church*, 123.

30. James Stacy, *History of the Midway Congregational Church, Liberty County, Georgia* (Newnan, Ga., 1899), 27–38; Midway Congregational Church, Session Minutes, 1827–1840, PHSM.

31. Stacy, *Records of Midway Church*, 161.
32. Carol A. Pemberton, "Lowell Mason," in *American National Biography*, ed. John A. Garraty and Mark C. Carnes (New York, 1999), 14: 656–657. Lowell Mason to CCJ, 28 May 1857, JTU.
33. Lowell Mason to CCJ, 14 February 1859, JTU.
34. Journal of MJ, 1863, JTU.

7. SCATTERED PLACES

1. See MJ to JosJ, 9 December 1823, JTU; MJ to JosJ, 10 January 1824, JTU.
2. MJ to JosJ, 9 December 1823, JTU. Tabby was a cement incorporating oyster shells that was used along the South Carolina and Georgia coasts in the eighteenth and nineteenth centuries, and, by extension, a building made with that cement.
3. See Will of J. Audley Maxwell, recorded 11 January 1841, Will Record B, 1824–1850, PCLC; Malcolm Bell, Jr., *Major Butler's Legacy: Five Generations of a Slaveholding Family* (Athens, Ga., 1987), 532.
4. Cf. MJ to JosJ, 10 January 1824, JTU. Laura Maxwell to MJ, 16 May 1851, JTU. CCJ to EM, 24 November 1824, JTU.
5. Cf. James C. Scott, *Domination and the Arts of Resistance: Hidden Transcripts* (New Haven, 1990), 47–48.
6. Journal of MJ, 1863, JTU. CCJ to EM, 17 August 1827; RQM, *Plantation Life Before Emancipation* (Richmond, 1892), 11. Glenn T. Miller, *Piety and Intellect: The Aims and Purposes of Ante-Bellum Theological Education* (Atlanta, 1990), 68–69. CCJ to MJ, 7 September 1853, JTU.
7. See the extensive treatment of the Roswell Kings, Sr. and Jr., in Bell, *Major Butler's Legacy*, esp. 223–226.
8. For the shift from patriarchalism to paternalism, see Philip D. Morgan, *Slave Counterpoint: Black Culture in the Eighteenth-Century Chesapeake and Lowcountry* (Chapel Hill, 1998), 273–274, 284–296. For the long history of patriarchy, see Gerda Lerner, *The Creation of Patriarchy* (Oxford, 1986).
9. Roswell King, Jr., "Letter to the Editor," *Southern Agriculturalist* 1 (December 1828): 523, 528. For Roswell King, Jr., as an overseer, see Charles H. Fairbanks, "The Plantation Archaeology of the Southeastern Coast" *Historical Archaeology* 18 (1984): 1–14; Bell, *Major Butler's Legacy*, 234–239; William Dusinberre, *Them Dark Days: Slavery in the American Rice Swamps* (New York, 1996).
10. CCJ to EM, 4 October 1825, JTU. See also Bell, *Major Butler's Legacy*, 219, 515–516.
11. Indenture between Roswell King and Julia Rebecca Maxwell, County Record I, 156–157, SCLC. List of Negroes of Mrs. Julia R. King, July 1854, by Joseph E. Maxwell, Trustee, Midway Museum, Liberty County, Ga. Bell, *Major Butler's Legacy*, 280–281.
12. Robert Manson Myers, ed., *The Children of Pride: A True Story of Georgia and the Civil War* (New Haven, 1972), 1573. Cf. Charles Berrien Jones to CCJ, 17 July 1854, JTU; Charles Berrien Jones to MJ, 24 July 1856, JTU.
13. CCJ to EM, 9 October 1832, JTU.

14. Joseph Maybank Jones to JosJ and JosJ's note on the letter, 26 November 1827, CJUG; Joseph Maybank Jones to MJ, 7 December 1827, JTU; CCJ to R. M. Charlton and William Law, 4 November 1848, CJUG.

15. CCJ to CCJj, 4 October 1856, CJUG.

16. Cf. Scott, _Domination and the Arts of Resistance_, 36–44, esp. 37.

17. For the childbearing patterns for slaves in the low country, see Morgan, _Slave Counterpoint_, 87–92. By the 1830s the average age for females at first birth was about twenty-one. See Robert William Fogel, _Without Consent or Contract: The Rise and Fall of American Slavery_ (New York, 1989), 152. For Phoebe's age at the time of Clarissa's birth, see CPB, 67, JTU. Rosetta was twenty at the birth of her first child, Lucy, who was twenty-one at the birth of her first child. Sina, Lizzy's oldest daughter, born in 1814, was twenty-four when she had her first child in 1838.

18. For the Jezebel figure, see Deborah Gray White, _Ar'n't I a Woman? Female Slaves in the Plantation South_ (New York, 1985), 27–51; Elizabeth Fox-Genovese, _Within the Plantation Household: Black and White Women of the Old South_ (Chapel Hill, 1988), 291–292.

19. CCJ to EM, 4 October 1825. JTU

20. Ibid.

21. CCJ to EM, 16 November 1828, JTU.

22. CCJ to EM, 4 October 1825, JTU.

23. CCJ to EM, 14 April 1826, JTU.

24. Ibid.

25. Ibid.

26. CPB, 63–78.

27. For WM's altercation with the rider, see WM, Sworn Statement, 18 November 1817, Record Book G, SCLC. For JosJ's loan to WM, see WM mortgage to JosJ, 8 January 1825, County Record I, SCLC.

28. CCJ to WM, 4 March 1826, JTU.

29. CCJ to EM, 17 August 1827, JTU.

30. CCJ to MJ, 11 September 1827, JTU; MJ to CCJ, 27 October 1827, JTU.

31. CCJ to MJ, 11 September 1827, JTU; MJ to CCJ, 27 October 1827, JTU.

32. MJ to CCJ, 30 May 1828, JTU.

33. CCJ to MJ, 8 January 1828, JTU; CCJ to MJ, 19 September 1828, JTU.

34. Ralph Waldo Emerson, "Self-Reliance," in _Essays: First Series_ (Boston, 1841).

35. On CCJ's concerns about Audley Maxwell, see CCJ to MJ, 22 July 1829, JTU.

36. CCJ to MJ, 22 November 1829, JTU; CCJ to MJ, 8 May 1830, JTU; MJ to CCJ, 19 May 1830, JTU; MJ to CCJj, 4 April 1863, CJUG.

37. CCJ to JosJ, 19 May 1829, JTU.

38. MJ to JosJ, 27 May 1829, JTU.

39. JosJ to MJ, 30 May 1829, JTU.

40. CCJ to EM, 20 June 1829, JTU; CCJ to MJ, 10 June 1829, JTU.

41. CCJ to MJ, 30 May 1829, JTU.

8. PRINCETON

1. CCJ to MJ, 10 June 1829, JTU.

2. For Catharine Beecher as a social reformer and feminist, see Kathryn Kish Sklar, *Catharine Beecher: A Study in American Domesticity* (New Haven, 1973), esp. 59–77; Jeanne Boydston, Mary Kelley, and Anne Margolis, *The Limits of Sisterhood: The Beecher Sisters on Women's Rights and Woman's Sphere* (Chapel Hill, 1988), esp. 1–8.

3. CCJ to MJ, 20 June 1829, JTU. Quoted in Boydston, Kelley, and Margolis, *Limits of Sisterhood*, 133.

4. CCJ to MJ, 20 June 1829, JTU. Harriet Beecher Stowe, *A Key to Uncle Tom's Cabin; Presenting the Original Facts and Documents Upon Which the Story is Founded, Together with Corroborative Statements verifying the Truth of the Work* (1853; rpt. Port Washington, N.Y., 1968), see esp. 199–200, 246–247.

5. CCJ to JosJ, 20 July 1829, JTU; CCJ to MJ, 22 July 1829, JTU.

6. MJ to CCJ, 27 October 1827, JTU.

7. See CCJ to MJ, 2 October 1829, JTU; CCJ to MJ, 24 June 1830, JTU.

8. MJ to CCJ, 16 October 1829, JTU.

9. MJ to CCJ, 3 December 1829, JTU; CCJ to MJ, 1 January 1830, JTU.

10. MJ to CCJ, 6 November 1829, JTU.

11. CCJ to MJ, 24 October 1829, JTU.

12. MJ to CCJ, 24 November 1829, JTU. For the larger context of MJ's position on slavery, see David Brion Davis, *The Problem of Slavery in Western Culture* (Ithaca, N.Y., 1966); and David Brion Davis, *In the Image of God: Religion, Moral Values, and Our Heritage of Slavery* (New Haven, 2001), 123–136.

13. Quoted in James O. Farmer, *The Metaphysical Confederacy: James Henley Thornwell and the Synthesis of Southern Values* (Macon, Ga., 1986), 52.

14. Sydney E. Ahlstrom, *A Religious History of the American People* (New Haven, 1972), 403–414.

15. CCJ to MJ, 8 December 1829, JTU.

16. CCJ to MJ, 3 February 1830, JTU.

17. Ibid.

18. CCJ to MJ, 9 July 1829, JTU.

19. CCJ to MJ, 18 May 1830, JTU.

20. Ibid.

21. CCJ to MJ, 5 June 1830, JTU.

22. Ibid.

23. CCJ to MJ, 24 June 1830, JTU; CCJ to MJ 23 July 1830, JTU.

24. CCJ to MJ, 24 June 1830, JTU.

25. Ibid. For the African colonization movement, see P. J. Staudenraus, *The African Colonization Movement, 1816–1865* (Princeton, 1961).

26. CCJ to MJ, 16 July 1830, JTU.

27. CCJ to MJ, 23 July 1830, JTU.

28. Ibid. For a biography of John Ross and the story of the Cherokee removal, see Gary E. Moulton, *John Ross, Cherokee Chief* (Athens, Ga., 1978), esp. 34–53.

29. MJ to CCJ, 5 July 1830, JTU.
30. MJ to CCJ, 4 August 1830, JTU. For Thomas Spalding, see E. Merton Coulter, *Thomas Spalding of Sapelo* (Baton Rouge, 1940).
31. CCJ to MJ, 25 August 1830, JTU.
32. Ibid. For a biography of Lundy, see Merton Dillon, *Benjamin Lundy and the Struggle for Negro Freedom* (Urbana, Ill., 1966); Jane H. Pease and William H. Pease, *Bound with Them in Chains* (Westport, Conn., 1972).
33. CCJ to MJ, 25 August 1830, JTU.
34. CCJ to MJ, 6 September 1830, JTU.
35. CCJ to MJ, 18 September 1830, JTU.
36. CCJ to MJ, 8 September 1829, JTU.

9. SOLITUDE

1. MJ to CCJ, 8 January 1830, JTU. For Sandy's age and work as a carpenter, see John Jones Daybook, 1802, JTU. For a description of the long-standing practice of slave carpenters' having Saturdays for themselves, see CCJ to Thomas Shepard, 13 February 1852, JTU. For slave carpenters as apprentices and their work generally, see Philip D. Morgan, *Slave Counterpoint: Black Culture in the Eighteenth-Century Chesapeake and Lowcountry* (Chapel Hill, 1998), 214–215, 347–353. For Sandy as a church member, see Session Minutes, Midway Congregational Church, 26 August 1842, PHSM; CPB, 64, JTU. For slave weddings, see CCJ, *The Religious Instruction of the Negroes in the United States* (Savannah, 1842), 132–133; Albert J. Raboteau, *Slave Religion: "The Invisible Institution" in the Antebellum South* (New York, 1978), 228–230; Eugene D. Genovese, *Roll, Jordan, Roll: The World the Slaves Made* (New York, 1972), 475–482. On expectations in regard to marriage for members of Midway Congregational Church, see Session Minutes, Midway Congregational Church, passim, PHSM. PBC, 67, JTU.
2. This is a composite picture drawn from a number of sources. See CCJ to MJ, "Our Tenth Wedding Day, December 21, 1840," JTU; EM to CCJ and MJ, 19 March 1838, JTU; CCJ to CCJj, 24 December 1860, CJUG; and, for arrangements used in nineteenth-century plantation weddings, an interview with Elizabeth Warren, Middleton Place Plantation, Charleston, S.C., 25 January 2002.
3. CCJ to CCJj, 24 December 1860, CJUG.
4. CPB, 66, JTU; CCJ to EM, 17 April 1850, JTU.
5. CCJ to MJ, 2 January 1831, JTU; CCJ to MJ, 4 January 1831, JTU.
6. CCJ to MJ, 25 December 1829, JTU.
7. CCJ to MJ, "Our Tenth Wedding Day, December 21, 1840," JTU.
8. For an example of earlier opposition in general to any instruction of slaves, but esp. religious instruction, see "Schools for the Instruction of Slaves, etc.," *Savannah Republican*, 14 August 1817. For direct opposition to Jones's proposals for religious instruction of slaves, see CCJ, *Tenth Annual Report of the Association for the Religious Instruction of the Negroes, in Liberty County, Georgia* (Savannah, 1845), 18.
9. Indenture Between Sarah Anderson and Joseph Jones, County Record F, 134, 1806,

SCLC; Appraisement and Division of Negroes for Mrs. Mary Jones the Wife of the Rev. C. C. Jones, 23 February 1831, CJUG. For prenuptial agreements and separate estates for wives with property, see Brenda E. Stevenson, *Life in Black and White: Family and Community in the Slave South* (New York, 1996), 63–94.

10. Appraisement and Division of Negroes for Mrs. Mary Jones the Wife of the Rev. C. C. Jones, 23 February 1831, CJUG.

11. These included the slaves of Charles Jones, his sister Susan Jones, his aunt Eliza Robarts, and his wife, Mary Jones. For Hamlet as the driver and Ashmore as the overseer, see CPB, 20–22, JTU.

12. CCJ to MJ, 18 May 1830, JTU.

13. For the Liberty County Temperance Society, see "Liberty County Temperance Society," *Charleston Observer*, 17 May 1834. For Library Society and Education Society, see "Midway and Newport Library Society," JTU and *Charleston Observer*, 16 October 1839. Part of the following description and analysis of Jones's proposal was originally published in Erskine Clarke, *Wrestlin' Jacob: A Portrait of Religion in the Old South* (Atlanta, 1979), 21–29.

14. CCJ, *Tenth Annual Report*, 14. CCJ, "Annual Report of the Missionary to the Negroes, in Liberty County (Ga.)," *Charleston Observer*, 15 March 1834.

15. CCJ, *The Religious Instruction of the Negroes, A Sermon, Delivered before Associations of Planters in Liberty and McIntosh Counties, Georgia*, 4th ed. (Princeton, 1832), 6–7. CCJ's view of the "condition" of African Americans was widespread in both the North and South. See, e.g., David Brion Davis, "The Culmination of Racial Polarities and Prejudice," in *In the Image of God: Religion, Moral Values, and Our Heritage of Slavery* (New Haven, 2001), 323–342.

16. Cf. CCJ, *Eleventh Annual Report of the Association for the Religious Instruction of the Negroes, in Liberty County, Georgia* (Savannah, 1846), 14, 17–18; CCJ, "Religious Instruction of the Negroes: Third Annual Report of the Missionary to the Negroes in Liberty County, Ga.," *Charleston Observer*, 17 September 1836; CCJ, *Tenth Annual Report*, 39. The most extensive treatment of the proslavery argument is Larry E. Tise, *Proslavery: A History of the Defense of Slavery in America, 1701–1840* (Athens, Ga., 1987).

17. CCJ, *The Religious Instruction of the Negroes, A Sermon*, 18–19.

18. CCJ to MJ, 3 February 1830, JTU.

19. CCJ, *The Religious Instruction of the Negroes, A Sermon*, 25–28. For the "face-grows-to-fit-the-mask" theory, see James C. Scott, *Domination and the Arts of Resistance: Hidden Transcripts* (New Haven, 1990), 70–107, esp. 76.

20. Ibid., 29–30. See also CCJ, *The Religious Instruction of the Negroes in the United States* (Savannah, 1842), 208–210.

21. CCJ, *The Religious Instruction of the Negroes, A Sermon*, 30–32.

22. This first call was extended by the Midway Domestic Missionary Society in cooperation with the new association. CCJ to MJ, 8 September 1829, JTU.

23. CCJ, *Thirteenth Annual Report of the Association for the Religious Instruction of the Negroes, in Liberty County, Georgia* (Savannah, 1848), 61; CCJ, *Tenth Annual Report*, 15–18.

24. Robert Manson Myers, ed., *The Children of Pride: A True Story of Georgia and the Civil War* (New Haven, 1972), 1585–1586; CCJ to MJ, 14 January 1832, JTU.

25. See "Journal of a Missionary to the Negroes in the State of Georgia," *Charleston Observer*, 28 September 1833 and 14 March 1835. For the Sunbury Baptist Association, see Mechal Sobel, *Trabelin' On: The Slave Journey to an Afro-Baptist Faith* (Westport, Conn., 1979), 316–329, 357–362; Janet Duitsman Cornelius, *Slave Missions and the Black Church in the Antebellum South* (Columbia, S.C., 1999), 27–29, 106–107.

26. MJ to EM, 26 July 1831, JTU; Mary Robarts to MJ, 10 September 1831, JTU.

27. CCJ to MJ, 14 January 1832, JTU.

28. CCJ to MJ, 3 December 1831, JTU.

29. Ibid.; Minutes of the Synod of South Carolina and Georgia, 3 December 1831, PHSM.

30. "Report of the Committee, to whom was referred the subject of the Religious Instruction of the Colored Population, of the Synod of South Carolina and Georgia, at its late Session in Columbia, S.C.," *Charleston Observer*, 29 March 1834. The report had to work its way through the procedures of the synod and was not published until 1834.

31. Ibid.

32. CCJ to MJ, 6 December 1831, JTU.

33. Ibid.

34. George Howe, "History of Columbia Theological Seminary," in *Memorial Volume of the Semi-Centennial of the Theological Seminary at Columbia, South Carolina* (Columbia, S.C., 1884), 140.

35. CCJ to MJ, 6 December 1831, JTU.

36. MJ to CCJ, 6 January 1832, JTU; MJ to CCJ, 23 January 1832, JTU; MJ to CCJ, 8 August 1832, JTU.

37. CCJ to Betsy, 9 October 1832, JTU.

38. Session Minutes, Midway Congregational Church, 23 November 1832, PHSM.

10. MONTEVIDEO AND MAYBANK

1. Map of Montevideo and Carlawter, JTU. See also map in County Record H, 226–227, SCLC. For the memory of planning the house and for the hopes for the garden at Montevideo, see CCJ to MJ, "Our Tenth Wedding Day, December 21, 1840," JTU; CCJ to MJ, 5 November 1838, JTU. For some details of the house and garden, see RQM, *Montevideo-Maybank: Some Memoirs of a Southern Christian Household in the Olden Time; or, The Family Life of the Rev. Charles Colcock Jones, D.D., of Liberty County, Ga.* (Richmond, 1898), 9–10.

2. Cf. MJ, Journal, 9 December 1867 and 12 January 1868, JTU.

3. CPB, 1–4.

4. MJ to Joseph Jones, 11 March 1834, JTU.

5. CPB, 3.

6. Ibid., 2, 64; MJ to CCJ, 17 May 1837, JTU. For Lizzy's lingering illness see MJ to CCJ, 17 May 1837, JTU.

7. "Accounts," in CPB, 18. Sandy was one of the most valuable slaves at Montevideo in the 1830s. In 1837 he was valued at $1,000. For Syphax and Porter as carpenters, see ibid., 7.

8. Ibid., 18–26. For the wharf see CCJ to MJ, 13 November 1841, JTU.

9. Rodris Roth, "Tea Drinking in 18th Century America: Its Etiquette and Equipage," in *Contributions from the Museum of History and Technology*, bulletin 225, paper 14 (1961). See also Charles E. Orser, Jr., "On Plantations and Patterns," *Journal of the Society for Historical Archaeology* 23, no. 2 (1989): 28–40.

10. For landscape's role in shaping human perspectives and emotions, see Chapter 4, note 11.

11. For the "hidden transcripts" of the slave settlements, see James C. Scott, *Domination and the Art of Resistance: Hidden Transcripts* (New Haven, 1990), 1–16.

12. Cf. "The Negro Spirituals," *Atlantic Monthly* 19 (June 1867): 685; "Slave Songs on a Mission," *Southern Christian Advocate* 7 (29 December 1843): 114.

13. For slaves' attachment to the places where they "were born and brought up," and the reasons for such attachments, see Frederick Douglass, *Life and Times of Frederick Douglass* (1881; rpt. New York: 1962), 97.

14. Cf. B. W. Higman, *Montpelier, Jamaica: A Plantation Community in Slavery and Freedom, 1739–1912* (Kingston, Jamaica, 1998), 297–300; Rhys Isaac, *The Transformation of Virginia, 1740–1790* (Chapel Hill, 1982), 32–42; David N. Livingston, "Hallowed Ground: Mapping the Geography of the Sacred," *Books and Culture* 6 (May–June 2000): 36–39.

15. Robert Manson Myers, ed. *The Children of Pride: A True Story of Georgia and the Civil War* (New Haven, 1972), 1621.

16. An Inventory and Appraisement of the Goods and Chattel of the late Andrew Maybank, deceased, of Liberty County, 17 March 1843, County Record L, PCLC; [Andrew Maybank,] A List of Slaves on Col. Island Plantation, Jan. 1833, JTU.

17. Myers, *Children of Pride*, 1621.

18. Will of Andrew Maybank, 13 January 1834, Will Record, 1824–1850, PCLC.

19. Ibid.

20. Ibid. JosJ bought Maybank's Cherry Hill plantation near Midway Church. See Last Will and Testament of JosJ, Will Record, 1824–1850, PCLC.

21. CCJ to MJ, 22 July 1829, JTU.

22. MPB, 4.

23. Executor's Sale, Andrew Maybank Estate Papers, JTU; Will of John Bohum Girardeau, 11 November 1800, Will Record 1790–1823, PCLC; Audley King to CCJ, 17 October 1853, JTU; Will of Andrew Maybank, 13 January 1834.

24. Estate of Andrew Maybank in Account Current with C. C. Jones, Executor, Accounts Book, 1831–1838, PCLC. The Maybank Endowment, like most of the endowment of Columbia Theological Seminary, was lost in the Civil War and its aftermath.

25. MPB, 1–3.

26. CCJ, Journal, 2 June 1860, JTU.

27. Myers, *Children of Pride*, 1574–1575.

28. Mortgage of James Holmes to Andrew Maybank, 18 November 1823, County Record I, SCLC; Sheriff's Titles to Andrew Maybank, Esq., for Driver Andrew, his wife, Mary Ann, and Their Three Children: Charles, Silvia, and Gilbert, 14 September 1826, CJUG.

29. Audley King to CCJ, 21 July 1857, JTU.
30. Notice on Jacob, 24 February 1823, Andrew Maybank Jones Collection, UGA.
31. For the history and geology of the Georgia Sea Islands, see James D. Howard, Chester B. Depratter, and Robert W. Frey, "Excursions in Southeastern Geology: The Archaeology-Geology of the Georgia Coast," Guidebook 20, 1980 Annual Meeting, Geological Society of America, Atlanta; Elizabeth J. Reitz, Tyson Sibbs, Ted A. Rathbun, "Archaeological Evidence for Subsistence on Coastal Plantations," in *The Archaeology of Slavery and Plantation Life*, ed. Theresa A. Singleton (Orlando, 1985), 163–186.
32. William Bartram, *Travels Through North & South Carolina, Georgia, East & West Florida, the Cherokee Country, the Extensive Territories of the Muscogulges, or Creek Confederacy, and the Country of the Chactaws* (1791; rpt. New York, 1988), 33–35.
33. For the character of salt marshes and the cordgrass *Spartina alterniflora*, see John and Mildred Teal, *Life and Death of the Salt Marsh* (New York, 1971); Jennifer Ackerman, *Notes from the Shore* (New York, 1996).
34. MJ to Joseph Jones, 9 December 1823, JTU.
35. For CCJ's experience of the sublime at sea, see CCJ to MJ, 6 October 1829, JTU. For MJ's experience of the sublime on Sapelo Island, see MJ to CCJ, 4 August 1830, JTU.
36. Cf. EM to CCJ and MJ, 31 August 1846, JTU; CCJ to Laura Maxwell, 5 October 1846, JTU; CCJ, Journal, 29 August 1860, JTU.
37. Cf. CCJ's rejection of a "sickly sentimentalism" in CCJ to MJ, 22 November 1829, JTU.
38. These theological convictions are found throughout CCJ's sermons and lectures. See, e.g., CCJ, "Nineteen Lectures on the Epistle to the Romans," JTU; and "Thirteen Lectures on Genesis," 1833, JTU.
39. There is a huge body of literature on the ways in which religion is a reflection of a social context. See, e.g., Ludwig Feuerbach, *The Essence of Christianity*, trans. George Eliot (1841; rpt. New York, 1957); Karl Marx and Friedrich Engels, *On Religion* (Moscow, 1957), esp. 37–38; Maurice Bloch, *Marxism and Anthropology* (Oxford, 1983), esp. 17–18. More recently, some anthropologists have argued for the reciprocal relationship between a religious tradition and a particular social and cultural context. See Clifford Geertz, "Religion as a Cultural System," in *The Interpretation of Cultures: Selected Essays*, 193–223 (New York: 1973). Cf. also Paul Ricoeur, *Lectures on Ideology and Utopia*, ed. George H. Taylor (New York, 1986), 183–197; Michael Walzer, *The Revolution of the Saints: A Study in the Origins of Radical Politics* (Cambridge, Mass., 1965), esp. 19.
40. For the functions of ideology, see Geertz, "Ideology as a Cultural System"; Ricoeur, *Lectures*, 3, 185, 254–266.
41. For the utopian character of this alternative vision, see Ricoeur, *Lectures*, xvi, xxi–xxiii, 15–17, 269–314; Karl Mannheim, *Ideology and Utopia*, trans. Louis Wirth and Edward Shils (New York, 1936), 208. Mannheim and Ricoeur emphasize that utopian visions, rather than legitimating an existing social order, challenge it.

11. THE STATIONS

1. "Journal of a Missionary to the Negroes in the State of Georgia," *CO*, 6 July 1833.
2. Eliza Sumner Martin, "Flemington" in *Liberty County, Georgia: A Pictorial History*, Virginia Fraser Evans, compiler (Statesville, N.C., 1979), 79. CCJ, Thirteen Lectures to the Negroes of Liberty County with Dates and Places, JTU. "Annual Report of the Missionary to the Negroes, in Liberty County (Ga.)," *CO*, 15 March 1834.
3. "Journal of a Missionary," *CO*, 6 July 1833.
4. Ibid.
5. CCJ, *A Catechism for Colored Persons* (Charleston, S.C., 1834), iii–vii. Cf. Janet Duitsman Cornelius, *Slave Missions and the Black Church in the Antebellum South* (Columbia, S.C., 1999), 124–158.
6. "Journal of a Missionary," *CO*, 27 July 1833.
7. "Journal of a Missionary," *CO*, 6 July 1833; CCJ, Lecture 2: Sabbath, Marriage, Primitive Condition of Man—Genesis 2:1–13, JTU.
8. "Journal of a Missionary," *CO*, 6 July 1833. For a review of the scholarly debate on what Herbert Gutman called a wholesome "pre-nuptial intercourse" and what E. Franklin Frazier called "slave licentiousness," see David Brion Davis, *In the Image of God: Religion, Moral Values, and Our Heritage of Slavery* (New Haven, 2001), 278–289.
9. CCJ, Lecture 2, Genesis 2, 10–13, JTU.
10. Ibid., 11.
11. See CCJ, *A Catechism*, iii–vii; cf. Sylvia R. Frey, *Water from the Rock: Black Resistance in a Revolutionary Age* (Princeton, 1991), 284–325; Cain Hope Felder, ed. *Stony the Road We Trod: African American Biblical Interpretation* (Minneapolis, 1991), esp. 40–56.
12. CCJ, Lecture 2, Genesis 2, 13–14, JTU.
13. Ibid., 15–16.
14. "Journal of a Missionary to the Negroes in the State of Georgia," *CO*, 6 July 1833, 27 July 1833, 17 August 1833, 24 August 1833, 31 August 1833, 7 September 1833, 21 September 1833, 28 September 1833.
15. CCJ, Lecture 4, History of Cain and Abel, Genesis 4, 5; Lecture 6, Noah, Genesis 6, 7; Lecture 9, Building Babel, Genesis 11, 6; Lecture 12, History of Abraham, Genesis 12, 7.
16. CCJ, Lecture 13, Genesis 13, 14, 15, 16, 31–35, JTU.
17. CCJ to MJ, 22 July 1829, JTU; and "Report of the Committee, to whom was referred the subject of the Religious Instruction of the Colored Population, of the Synod of South Carolina and Georgia, at its late Session in Columbia, S.C.," *CO*, 29 March 1834. James C. Scott, *Weapons of the Weak: Everyday Forms of Peasant Resistance* (New Haven, 1985), 17–44.
18. CCJ, Eight Lessons on the Epistle to the Hebrews, Lesson 1, 1, JTU.
19. Cf. MJ, Journal, 1863, JTU.
20. CCJ, *Second Annual Report of the Association for the Religious Instruction of the Negroes, in Liberty County, Georgia* (Savannah, 1834), 1–2; and CCJ, *Tenth Annual Report of the Association for the Religious Instruction of the Negroes, in Liberty County, Georgia* (Savannah, 1845), 22.

21. CCJ, *Second Annual Report*, 3; CCJ, *Tenth Annual Report*, 25; CCJ, *Second Annual Report*, 2; CCJ, *Eleventh Annual Report of the Association for the Religious Instruction of the Negroes, in Liberty County, Georgia* (Savannah, 1846), 15–16; CCJ, *Twelfth Annual Report of the Association for the Religious Instruction of the Negroes, in Liberty County, Georgia* (Savannah, 1847), 13.

22. Cornelius, *Slave Missions and the Black Church*, 128–131; and Albert J. Raboteau, *Slave Religion: The "Invisible Institution" in the Antebellum South* (New York, 1978), 161–162; and Larry E. Tise, *Proslavery: A History of the Defense of Slavery in America, 1701–1840* (Athens, Ga., 1987), 295–301.

23. CCJ, *A Catechism for Colored Persons*, iii.

24. "Historical Catechism: Part I. Of John the Baptist," *CO*, 17 September 1836. See also *CO*, 10 September 1836, 1 October 1836, 5 November 1836.

25. "Historical Catechism: Part II. Of Our Lord and Saviour Jesus Christ," *CO*, 12 November 1836, 19 November 1836. CCJ interrupted the publication of the "Historical Catechism" for three years and then resumed it in 1839. See "Historical Catechism: Part II. Of Our Lord and Saviour Jesus Christ," *CO*, 9 March 1839, 16 March 1839, 6 April 1839, 20 April 1839, 27 April 1839, 11 May 1839.

26. "The Rev. Charles Colcock Jones, D.D." *Southern Presbyterian*, 4 June 1863; John B. Adger, *My Life and Times, 1810–1899* (Richmond, 1899), 100–101.

27. Parts of the following analysis were originally published in Erskine Clarke, *Wrestlin' Jacob: A Portrait of Religion in the Old South* (Atlanta, 1979), 35–58.

28. CCJ, *A Catechism of Scripture, Doctrine and Practice: For Families and Sabbath Schools, Designed also for the Oral Instruction of Colored Persons*, 3rd ed. (Savannah, 1845), 69. Cf. Margaret Washington Creel, *"A Peculiar People": Slave Religion and Community Culture Among the Gullahs* (New York, 1988), 211–251.

29. Ibid., 127–131.

30. Cf., e.g., Raboteau, *Slave Religion*, 294; and Scott, *Weapons of the Weak*, 115–118. But Larry Tise, in a "comparison of one of the popular New England catechisms of the early nineteenth century with one of the so-called catechisms for slaves reveals an extraordinary similarity of content." Tise uses the catechism of a South Carolina Episcopal bishop for comparison, but the same may be said of CCJ's catechism—there is an extraordinary similarity of content with popular catechisms used in New England. See Tise, *Proslavery*, 418 n. 20.

31. CCJ, *The Religious Instruction of the Negroes in the United States* (Savannah, 1842), 256, 252.

32. CCJ, *Suggestions on the Religious Instruction of the Negroes in the Southern States; Together with an Appendix Containing Forms of Church Registers, form of a Constitution, and Plans of Different Denominations of Christians* (Philadelphia, 1847), 14.

33. CCJ, *The Religious Instruction of the Negroes in the United States*, 261, 110–111.

34. Hampden C. DuBose, *Memoirs of Rev. John Leighton Wilson, D.D., Missionary to Africa, and Secretary of Foreign Missions* (Richmond, 1895), 97–105. For Wilson's letters, see, e.g., *CO*, 28 September 1833, 8 November 1834, 9 May 1835, 1 September 1835, 7 May 1836. J. Leighton Wilson, *Western Africa: Its History, Condition, and Prospects* (New York, 1856).

35. Cf. CCJ, *The Religious Instruction of the Negroes in the United States,* passim.
36. "Journal of a Missionary," *CO,* 31 August 1833.
37. For Mary Ann as Sharper's daughter and Sandy Maybank's wife, see CCJ, Journal, 25 April 1858, JTU. For Sharper staying with his family regularly at his "wife house," see "Journal of a Missionary," *CO,* 21 February 1835.
38. "Journal of a Missionary," *CO,* 31 August 1833.
39. CCJ, *The Religious Instruction of the Negroes in the United States,* 261.
40. Ibid., 256; CCJ, *Suggestions on the Religious Instruction of the Negroes,* 14.
41. CCJ to MJ, 26 June 1837, JTU.
42. CCJ, *The Religious Instruction of the Negroes in the United States,* 255.
43. CCJ to MJ, 8 December 1829, JTU.
44. CCJ, *The Religious Instruction of the Negroes in the United States,* 255, 262; cf. CCJ, *Suggestions on the Religious Instruction of the Negroes,* 15; and *Tenth Annual Report,* 41–42.
45. CCJ, sermon file, 1832–1838, JTU.
46. CCJ, *Third Annual Report of the Missionary to the Negroes, in Liberty County, Ga. Presented to the Association, Riceborough, January 1836* (Charleston, 1836), 13.
47. CCJ, "Eliezer, Gen. 24:1–67," sermon written 15 March 1834, JTU; CCJ, "Character of Gehazi, Servant of Elisha, the *Man of God,*" sermon written 12 July 1833, JTU. Cf. Eugene D. Genovese, *Roll, Jordan, Roll: The World the Slaves Made* (New York, 1974), 202–206.
48. "Journal of a Missionary," *CO,* 21 September 1833.
49. Ibid. I have used this version of what happened with the sermon on Onesimus rather than the better-known account written years later in *Tenth Annual Report,* 24–25. Cf. Raboteau, *Slave Religion,* 294; and Scott, *Weapons of the Weak,* 115–118.
50. CCJ, "Religious Instruction of the Negroes," *CO,* 17 September 1836.
51. CCJ, *Tenth Annual Report,* 24; CCJ, *Third Annual Report,* 24.

12. THE MALLARD PLACE

1. CCJ to MJ, 1 April 1833, JTU.
2. Ibid.; *Minutes of the Sunbury Baptist Association, Convened at the Newington Church, Screven County, Georgia, Nov. 1829* (Savannah, 1829); *Minutes of the Sunbury Baptist Association, Convened at Walthourville, Liberty County, Georgia on Friday and Saturday, November the 11th and 12th, 1836* (Savannah, 1836); MJ to CCJ 8 February 1830, JTU; "Watchmen in Newport Church, 1843," JTU.
3. CCJ to MJ, 1 April 1833, JTU; Robert Manson Myers, ed. *The Children of Pride: A True Story of Georgia and the Civil War* (New Haven, 1972), 1648.
4. CCJ to MJ, 10 April 1833, JTU. For the island plantations, see Malcolm Bell, Jr., *Major Butler's Legacy: Five Generations of a Slaveholding Family* (Athens, Ga., 1987), 106–107, 147, 477; Margaret Davis Cate, *Early Days of Coastal Georgia* (St. Simons Island, Ga., 1955); Leland Ferguson, *Uncommon Ground: Archaeology and Early African America, 1650–1800* (Washington, D.C., 1992), 63–82.
5. CCJ to MJ, 4 April 1839, JTU. [Jane Wood Pratt], "Scripture Sketches for Colored Per-

sons," *CO*, 29 June 1833, 3 August 1833, 10 August 1833, 17 August 1833, 31 August 1833. For the identification of Jane Wood Pratt as the author of these sketches, see CCJ, *The Religious Instruction of the Negroes in the United States* (Savannah, 1842), 79; see also "A Letter on Dreams" *CO*, 25 January 1834.

6. [Pratt], "Scripture Sketches," 27 July 1833, 31 August 1833.
7. CCJ, "The Moral and Religious Condition of our Coloured Population," *CO*, 10 October 1833, 2 November 1833, 9 November 1833, and 16 November 1833.
8. John Winn, "Thomas S. Clay," 8 September 1888, GHS.
9. Thomas S. Clay, "Detail of a Plan for the Moral Improvement of Negroes on Plantations. Read before the Georgia Presbytery. By Thomas S. Clay of Bryan County, Ga.," *CO*, 8 February 1834.
10. Thomas S. Clay, "Detail of a Plan for the Moral Improvement of Negroes on Plantations. Read before the Georgia Presbytery. [Continued]," *CO*, 22 February 1834. Cf. Janet Duitsman Cornelius, *Slave Missions and the Black Church in the Antebellum South* (Columbia, S.C., 1999), 85–87.
11. CCJ, *The Religious Instruction of the Negroes in the United States*, 267. Parts of the following analysis were originally published in Erskine Clarke, *Wrestlin' Jacob: A Portrait of Religion in the Old South* (Atlanta, 1979), 59–81.
12. RQM, *Plantation Life Before Emancipation* (Richmond, 1892), 16–17.
13. "Minutes of the Watchman's Meeting for Midway Church," JTU; "Minutes of the Session, Midway Congregational Church," 26 November 1830, PHSM.
14. "Minutes of the Watchman's Meeting for Midway Church," JTU; Claim of Pompey Bacon, Liberty County, Georgia, Case Files, Southern Claims Commission, Records of the 3rd Auditor, Allowed Case Files, Records of the U.S. General Accounting Office, RG 217 (National Archives, Washington, D.C.). See also Dylan Penningroth, "Slavery, Freedom, and Social Claims to Property among African Americans in Liberty County, Georgia, 1850–1880," *Journal of American History* 84 (September 1997): 405–435.
15. See Journal of CCJ, 19 February 1860, JTU.
16. RQM, *Plantation Life*, 48; CCJ to Thomas Shepherd, 23 December 1848, JTU; Eliza Mallard to RQM, 2 June 1854, JTU; Edward Harden to CCJ, 2 November 1854, JTU.
17. "Minutes of the Session, Midway Congregational Church," 15 February 1845, PHSM; RQM, *Plantation Life*, 51–57.
18. Cf. Philip D. Morgan, *Slave Counterpoint: Black Culture in the Eighteenth-Century Chesapeake and Lowcountry* (Chapel Hill, 1998), 441.
19. CCJ, *Tenth Annual Report of the Association for the Religious Instruction of the Negroes, in Liberty County, Georgia* (Savannah, 1845), 23; CCJ, *Third Annual Report of the Missionary to the Negroes, in Liberty County, Ga. Presented to the Association, Riceborough, January 1836* (Charleston, 1836), 4.
20. CCJ, "Annual Report of the Missionary to the Negroes, in Liberty County (Ga.)," *CO*, 15 March 1834; CCJ, *Eighth Annual Report of the Association for the Religious Instruction of the Negroes, in Liberty County, Georgia; together with the Address to the Association by the President the Rev. I. S. K. Axson* (Savannah, 1845), 4; CCJ, *Tenth Annual Report*, 41.
21. CCJ, *Eleventh Annual Report of the Association for the Religious Instruction of the*

Negroes, in Liberty County, Georgia (Savannah, 1846), 20; CCJ, "Journal of a Missionary to the Negroes in the State of Georgia," *CO*, 31 August 1833.

22. CCJ, "Journal of a Missionary to the Negroes in the State of Georgia," *CO*, 31 August 1833. For the chapel at Montevideo, see CPB, 95; CCJ to Jane Dunwody Jones, 10 September 1846, JJUG; CCJ to MJ, 24 December 1851, JTU. For plantation chapels, see Cornelius, *Slave Missions and the Black Church*, 89; and Frederick Law Olmsted, *A Journey in the Seaboard Slaves States: In the Years 1853–1854, With Remarks on Their Economy* (New York, 1856), 80.

23. "Minutes of the Session, Midway Congregational Church," 1833–1838, PHSM.

24. CCJ, *First Annual Report*, 8; CCJ, *Tenth Annual Report*, 23; CCJ, *The Religious Instruction of the Negroes in the United States*, 17, 268; RQM, *Plantation Life*, 105.

25. RQM, *Plantation Life*, 29–31, 17–19.

26. CCJ to MJ, 19 April 1830, JTU. CCJ, "Journal of a Missionary to the Negroes in the State of Georgia," *CO* 31 August 1833. CCJ, *Suggestions on the Religious Instruction of the Negroes in the Southern States: Together with an Appendix containing Forms of Church Registers, Form of a Constitution, and Plans of Different Denominations of Christians* (Philadelphia, 1847), 17.

27. "Journal of a Missionary to the Negroes in the State of Georgia," *CO*, 24 August 1833.

28. Ibid.

29. Ibid.

30. CCJ, *The Religious Instruction of the Negroes in the United States*, 16; CCJ, *Thirteenth Annual Report of the Association for the Religious Instruction of the Negroes, in Liberty County, Georgia* (Savannah, 1848), 13–16; RQM, *Plantation Life*, 20–30.

31. CCJ, *The Religious Instruction of the Negroes in the United States*, 115–116; RQM, *Plantation Life*, 32.

32. CCJ, *Suggestions on the Religious Instruction of the Negroes in the Southern States*, 35; and cf. RQM, *Plantation Life*, 31–32.

33. CCJ, *Suggestions on the Religious Instruction of the Negroes in the Southern States*, 35. Cf. CCJ, *Second Annual Report of the Association for the Religious Instruction of the Negroes, in Liberty County, Georgia* (Savannah, 1835), 9; CCJ, *The Religious Instruction of the Negroes in the United States*, 241.

34. See CCJ, *The Religious Instruction of the Negroes in the United States*, 209, 242; CCJ, *A Catechism of Scripture, Doctrine and Practice: For Families and Sabbath Schools, Designed also for the Oral Instruction of Colored Persons*, 3rd ed. (Savannah, 1845), 128; CCJ, *Suggestions on the Religious Instruction of the Negroes in the Southern States*, 35.

35. CCJ, *A Catechism of Scripture, Doctrine and Practice*, 128.

36. For encouragement by agricultural journals of providing good housing and care for slaves, see Kenneth Stampp, *The Peculiar Institution* (New York, 1956), 293.

37. For household codes, see Wayne A. Meeks, *The Origins of Christian Morality* (New Haven, 1993), esp. chapter 3; David C. Verner, *The Household of God: The Social World of the Pastoral Epistles*, SBL Dissertation Series 71 (Chico, Calif., 1983); David Balch, *Let Wives Be Submissive: The Domestic Code in 1 Peter*, SBL Monograph Series 26 (Chico, Calif., 1981). Colossians 4:1.

13. THE ARBORS

1. CCJ, "Journal of a Missionary to the Negroes in the State of Georgia," *CO*, 31 August 1833, 21 February 1835.
2. Savannah Unit, Georgia Writers' Project, Work Projects Administration, *Drums and Shadows: Survival Studies Among the Georgia Coastal Negroes* (Athens, Ga., 1986), passim, esp. 116.
3. Lydia Parrish, *Slave Songs of the Georgia Sea Islands* (1942; rpt. Athens, Ga., 1992), 45–47. For Dublin Scribben belonging to Benjamin Scriven, see census of church members by CCJ in 1845 entitled "Return of Members," JTU.
4. See, e.g., the *Savannah Republican*, 10 November 1820, 20 December 1820. See also Michael Gomez, *Exchanging Our Country Marks: The Transformation of African Identities in the Colonial and Antebellum South* (Chapel Hill, 1998).
5. Robert William Fogel, *Without Consent or Contract: The Rise and Fall of American Slavery* (New York, 1989), 17–21, 29–34. CCJ, "Journal of a Missionary to the Negroes in the State of Georgia," *CO*, 7 September 1833. Sterling Stuckey, *Slave Culture: Nationalist Theory and the Foundations of Black America* (New York, 1987).
6. For the debate among historians over "African survivals" in the slave communities of the Western world, see Sidney W. Mintz and Richard Price, *An Anthropological Approach to the Afro-American Past: A Caribbean Perspective* (Boston: 1992); John Thornton, *African and Africans in the Making of the Atlantic World, 1400–1800* (Cambridge, 1992); Ira Berlin, *Many Thousands Gone: The First Two Centuries of Slavery in North America* (Cambridge, Mass., 1998).
7. There is a massive anthropological literature that seeks to understand or explain witchcraft, conjurers, and magic. A good entry point into the literature is Brian Morris, *Anthropological Studies of Religion: An Introductory Text* (Cambridge, 1987).
8. CCJ, *The Religious Instruction of the Negroes in the United States* (Savannah, 1842). I have not included under the category of "conjurer" the healers, like Dr. Harry at the Mallard Place, who drew on traditions of African medicine and on an African-American pharmacology. My reasons for this are that the two are clearly separated in the primary sources before me. See, however, Theophus Smith, *Conjuring Culture: Biblical Formations of Black America* (New York, 1994), esp., 5–6.
9. CCJ, "Samuel Elliott's Funeral Sermon," *CO*, 13 October 1838. For CCJ's comments on conjuring in light of Vesey and Turner, see "Journal of a Missionary to the Negroes in the State of Georgia," *CO*, 21 September 1833.
10. CCJ, *CO*, 13 October 1838. See also CCJ, *CO*, 22 September 1838, 6 October 1838.
11. Work Projects Administration, *Drums and Shadows*, 112–119. Cf. Robin Briggs, *Witches and Neighbors: The Social and Cultural Context of European Witchcraft* (New York, 1998).
12. CCJ, "Journal of a Missionary to the Negroes in the State of Georgia," *CO*, 21 February 1835.
13. Ibid. See also for the leadership role of the black preacher Eugene D. Genovese, *Roll, Jordan, Roll: The World the Slaves Made* (New York, 1974), 255–279.

14. CCJ, "Journal of a Missionary to the Negroes in the State of Georgia," *CO*, 21 September 1833.

15. Work Projects Administration, *Drums and Shadows*, 114, 124–125.

16. See James C. Scott, *Domination and the Art of Resistance: Hidden Transcripts* (New Haven, 1990), 142–143. For slave use of poisons in the low country, see Philip D. Morgan, *Slave Counterpoint: Black Culture in the Eighteenth-Century Chesapeake and Lowcountry* (Chapel Hill, 1998), 614–618.

17. CCJ, *Thirteenth Annual Report of the Association for the Religious Instruction of the Negroes, in Liberty County, Georgia* (Savannah, 1848), 22. For the cultural significance of slave dancing, see Morgan, *Slave Counterpoint*, 581–588, 592–593.

18. Work Projects Administration, *Drums and Shadows*, 118. CCJ, "Journal of a Missionary to the Negroes in the State of Georgia," *CO*, 25 January 1834. CCJ, *Thirteenth Annual Report*, 22.

19. Malcolm Bell, Jr., *Major Butler's Legacy: Five Generations of a Slaveholding Family* (Athens, Ga., 1987), 151–152.

20. For the development of the banjo, see Dena J. Polachek Epstein, "The Folk Banjo: A Documentary History," *Ethnomusicology* 19, no. 3 (1975): 347–371. Morgan, *Slave Counterpoint*, 585.

21. Cf. Morgan, *Slave Counterpoint*, 580–581.

22. See MJ to MSJ, 12 June 1850, JTU. Cf. Lawrence W. Levine, *Black Culture and Black Consciousness: Afro-American Folk Thought from Slavery to Freedom* (New York, 1977), 6; and Dena J. Polachek Epstein, *Sinful Tunes and Spirituals: Black Folk Music to the Civil War* (Urbana, Ill., 1977).

23. Laura Maxwell Buttolph to MJ, 15 July 1857, JTU.

24. "Watchmen in Newport Church, 1843," JTU; "Watchmen in Midway Church, 1843," JTU. For bush arbors and hush arbors, see Albert J. Raboteau, *Slave Religion: The "Invisible Institution" in the Antebellum South* (New York, 1978), 212–288; Janet Duitsman Cornelius, *Slave Missions and the Black Church in the Antebellum South* (Columbia, S.C., 1999), 8–12; Margaret Creel, *"A Peculiar People": Slave Religion and Community-Culture Among the Gullah* (New York, 1988), 276–302.

25. Parrish, *Slave Songs*, 161.

26. "Slave Songs on a Mission," *Southern Christian Advocate* [Charleston, S.C.], 29 December 1843.

27. William Francis Allen, ed. *Slave Songs of the United States* (New York, 1867), 53.

28. Parrish, *Slave Songs*, 165.

29. Cf. Raboteau, *Slave Religion*, 251–263.

30. Thomas Wentworth Higginson, *Army Life in a Black Regiment* (Boston, 1870), 203.

31. Allen, *Slave Songs*, 55.

32. See W. E. B. DuBois, "The Sorrow Songs" in *Souls of Black Folk* (1902; rpt. Greenwich, Conn., 1961). See also Howard Thurman, *Deep River* (New York, 1945), 36.

33. Parris, *Slave Songs*, 56–57.

34. Ibid., 71–72. See also for the ring dance, Gomez, *Exchanging Our Country Marks*, 244–263.

35. See "Minutes of the Session, Midway Congregational Church," 1831–1832, PHSM. CCJ, "Journal of a Missionary to the Negroes in the State of Georgia," CO, 17 August 1833, 7 March 1835, 25 January 1834. Cf. Clifton H. Johnson, ed. *God Struck Me Dead: Religious Conversion Experiences and Autobiographies of Ex-Slaves* (Philadelphia, 1969), 169–171.

36. CCJ, "Journal of a Missionary to the Negroes in the State of Georgia," CO, 17 August 1833, 25 January 1834.

37. CCJ, "Journal of a Missionary to the Negroes in the State of Georgia," CO, 17 August 1833.

38. CCJ, "Simon the Sorcerer," sermon preached 28 March 1834, JTU.

39. CCJ, "Journal of a Missionary to the Negroes in the State of Georgia," CO, 7 March 1835, 17 August 1833.

40. CCJ, "Journal of a Missionary to the Negroes in the State of Georgia," CO, 25 January 1834, 7 March 1835. For CCJ's definition of a "new heart," see CCJ, *A Catechism for Colored Persons* (Charleston, S.C., 1834), 99. A "new heart" involves both feelings and actions. Erskine Clarke, *Our Southern Zion: A History of Calvinism in the South Carolina Low Country, 1690–1990* (Tuscaloosa, 1996), 9–23.

41. CCJ, "Journal of a Missionary to the Negroes in the State of Georgia," CO, 14 March 1835. For membership in the Societies, see CCJ, *Eleventh Annual Report of the Association for the Religious Instruction of the Negroes, in Liberty County, Georgia* (Savannah, 1846), 19. For sacred meals among the Yoruba of west Africa, see J. Omosade Awolalu, *Yoruba Beliefs and Sacrificial Rites* (Essex, United Kingdom, 1979), esp. 134–182. For ritual as social drama, see Victor Turner, *Dramas, Fields, and Metaphors: Symbolic Action in Human Society* (Ithaca, N.Y., 1974).

42. "Journal of a Missionary to the Negroes in the State of Georgia," CO, 21 February 1835.

43. CCJ, "Journal of a Missionary to the Negroes in the State of Georgia," CO, 28 February 1835. For slave funerals, see Raboteau, *Slave Religion*, 44–45, 71–72, 83–85; Morgan, *Slave Counterpoint*, 640–645; Creel, "A Peculiar People," 313–317. Cf. Awolalu, *Yoruba Beliefs and Sacrificial Rites*, 53–68.

14. COLUMBIA

1. See Estate of Andrew Maybank in Account Current with C. C. Jones, Executor, Accounts Book, 1831–1838, PCLC. Minutes of the Board of Directors of the Theological Seminary, 1, 1827–1861, archives CTS.

2. CCJ to William Plumer, 24 January 1835, 23 February 1835, PHSM. See "Proposed Society for the Religious Instruction of the Colored Population," CO, 30 May 1835, 26 September 1835.

3. CCJ to MJ, 2 November 1835, JTU.

4. CCJ to MJ, 2 November 1835, JTU. CCJ to William Plumer, 28 June 1834, PHSM.

5. Erskine Clarke, *Our Southern Zion: A History of Calvinism in the South Carolina Low Country, 1690–1990* (Tuscaloosa, 1996), 144, 188–189.

6. *Liberator*, 1 January 1831.

7. Larry E. Tise, *Proslavery: A History of the Defense of Slavery in America, 1701–1840* (Athens, Ga., 1987), 269–272.

8. "Voice of the People," *CO*, 11 August 1835. See Tise, *Proslavery*, 308–346.

9. Whitemarsh B. Seabrook, *An Essay on the Management of Slaves, and Especially, on their Religious Instruction: Read before the Agricultural Society of St. John's Colleton* (Charleston, 1834), 13–26.

10. Cf. Tise, *Proslavery*, 317–318; Duitsman Cornelius, *Slave Missions and the Black Church in the Antebellum South* (Columbia, S.C., 1999), 91–97.

11. For the social location and political and economic influence of Circular Congregational Church, see Clarke, *Our Southern Zion*, 142–164, 346–347; William H. Pease and Jane H. Pease, *The Web of Progress: Private Values and Public Styles in Boston and Charleston, 1824–1843* (New York, 1985). CCJ to MJ, 6 November 1835, JTU.

12. CCJ to MJ, 5 November 1835, JTU.

13. See Tise, *Proslavery*, 308–346; William Sumner Jenkins, *Pro-Slavery Thought in the Old South* (Chapel Hill, 1935), 242–284. See responses of two Charleston clergy to claims of a dual origin of the races: Thomas Smyth, *Unity of the Human Races* (New York, 1850); John Bachman, *The Doctrine of the Unity of the Human Race Examined on the Principles of Science* (Charleston, S.C., 1850).

14. CCJ to MJ, 5 November 1835, JTU.

15. CCJ to MJ, 11 November 1835, JTU.

16. CCJ to MJ, 16 November 1835, JTU; CCJ to William Plumer, 8 December 1835, PHSM.

17. CCJ to William Plumer, 8 December 1835, PHSM; CCJ to MJ, 16 November, 1835, JTU.

18. MJ to CCJ, 17 May 1837; CCJ to MJ, 23 May 1837; CCJ to MJ, 2 June 1837, JTU.

19. CCJ to MJ, 18 November 1836, JTU; MJ to CCJ, 21 November 1836, JTU.

20. CCJ to MJ, 19 May 1837, JTU. See also The Museums at Stony Brook, *19th Century American Carriages: Their Manufacture, Decoration and Use* (Stony Brook, N.Y., 1987), 34–65. CCJ to EM, 8 February 1837, JTU; CCJ to EM, 14 May 1838, JTU.

21. Robert Manson Myers, ed., *The Children of Pride: A True Story of Georgia and the Civil War* (New Haven, 1972), 1555–1556. Louis C. LaMotte, *Colored Light: The Story of the Influence of Columbia Theological Seminary, 1828–1936* (Richmond, 1937), 43. See Will of Andrew Walthour, Will Record, 1824–1850, PCLC for Sara Ann Walthour's inheritance from her father. By 1860, Howe owned with Sara Ann eighty-six slaves and property valued at $60,000 in Liberty County. See Joseph Karl Mann, "The Large Slaveholders of the Deep South, 1860" (Ph.D. diss., University of Texas, 1964), 739.

22. CCJ to EM, 8 February 1837, JTU.

23. CCJ to EM, 25 March 1837, JTU; CCJ to MJ, 22 May 1837, JTU. The son of the town's mayor, Campbell Bryce, stabbed an Irishman during a brawl between college students and some workmen. Bryce was found not guilty. See also CCJ to MJ, 21 October 1837, JTU; CCJ to EM, 25 March 1837, JTU; CCJ to MJ, 21 October 1837, JTU.

24. CCJ to MJ, 3 November 1838, JTU; CCJ to MJ, 22 May 1837; CCJ to MJ, 29 May 1837.

25. CCJ to MJ, 12 June 1837, JTU; CCJ to EM, 25 April 1837, JTU; CCJ to MJ, 19 May 1837, JTU; MJ to CCJ, 15 June 1837, JTU; CCJ to MJ, 3 July 1837, JTU.
26. Sara Ann Walthour Howe to MJ, 30 August 1837.
27. CCJ to MJ, 26 October 1837, JTU; CCJ to MJ, 21 October 1837, JTU.
28. CCJ to EM, 24 December 1837, JTU.
29. MJ and CCJ to JosJ, 15 March 1838; CCJ to EM, 14 May 1838; CCJ to EM, 26 May 1838, JTU.
30. EM to CCJ, 29 March 1838, JTU.
31. Erskine Clarke, "The Strange Case of Charleston Union Presbytery," *Affirmation*, Fall 1993, 41–58. CCJ to MJ, 8 November 1838, JTU.
32. CCJ to EM, 18 October 1838, JTU; CCJ to MJ, 8 November 1838, JTU.

15. CARLAWTER II

1. Cf. CCJ to EM, 8 February 1837, JTU.
2. "Accounts" in CPB, 28–32.
3. Cf. CCJ to MJ, 25 May 1837, JTU.
4. See CCJ to MJ, 5 November 1838, JTU. MJ, Journal, March 1865, JTU.
5. For slave families and kinship networks, see Robert William Fogel, *Without Consent or Contract: The Rise and Fall of American Slavery* (New York, 1989), 162–168; Philip D. Morgan, *Slave Counterpoint: Black Culture in the Eighteenth-Century Chesapeake and Lowcountry* (Chapel Hill, 1998), 498–558, esp. 530–558; Herbert G. Gutman, *The Black Family in Slavery and Freedom, 1750–1925* (New York, 1976).
6. CPB, 64, JTU; CCJ to Cato, 28 January 1851, JTU; Cato to CCJ, 3 March 1851, JTU; Cato to CCJ, 3 September 1852, JTU.
7. For Cassius as a basket maker, see CCJ to CCJj, 2 October 1856, CJUG. For the price he received for his stick baskets and for his accumulated possessions, see "Account of Property belonging to Cassius left to be given away and to be sold as he desired by his former Master," attached to letter CCJj to CCJ, 20 March 1857, JTU. For techniques of basket making in the low country, see Margaret Davis Cate, *Early Days of Coastal Georgia* (St. Simons Island, Ga., 1955), 157. Dale Rosengarten, "Spirits of Our Ancestors: Basket Traditions in the Carolinas," in *The Crucible of Carolina: Essays in the Development of Gullah Language and Culture*, ed. Michael Montgomery (Athens, Ga., 1994), 133–157, esp. 146–156; John Michael Vlach, *The Afro-American Tradition in Decorative Arts* (Cleveland, 1978), 7–19; Morgan, *Slave Counterpoint*, 232–233. For Cassius's temper, see CCJ to Thomas Shepard, 24 March 1849, JTU.
8. "Maybank Plantation in Account Current with C. C. Jones," MPB.
9. CCJ to MJ, 18 November 1836, JTU; MJ to CCJ, 15 June 1837, JTU; CPB, 24–26.
10. Cf. MJ to CCJ, 5 January 1852, JTU; CCJ to Thomas Shepard, 13 February 1852, JTU. For slave carpenters hiring themselves out, see Philip D. Morgan, *Slave Counterpoint*, 352.
11. CPB, 64, JTU.
12. See "Photograph File," JTU.
13. CPB, 12.

14. CCJ to MJ, 16 November 1836, JTU; CCJ to MJ, 1 November 1838, JTU.

15. "Accounts" in CPB, 28–32; "Maybank Plantation in Account Current with C. C. Jones," MPB, 14–31; CCJ to Thomas Shepard, 24 October 1848, JTU.

16. MJ to CCJ, 30 May 1851, JTU; CCJ to Thomas Shepard 8 April 1851, JTU; CCJ to Thomas Shepard, 24 October 1848, JTU.

17. CPB, 9, 67.

18. Cf. RQM, *Plantation Life Before Emancipation* (Richmond, 1892), 55.

19. "Minutes of the Session, Midway Congregational Church," 14 December 1833, PHSM; CPB, 67, JTU.

20. MJ to CCJ, 15 June 1837, JTU; CPB, 64.

21. CCJ to MJ, 16 May 1837, JTU.

22. MJ to CCJ, 17 May 1837, JTU.

23. CCJ to MJ, 23 May 1837, JTU.

24. MJ to CCJ, 15 June 1837, JTU.

25. MJ to JoJ, 20 April 1841, JJUG.

26. CCJ to EM, 24 December 1837, JTU.

27. For Cassius's other children, see "Account of Property belonging to Cassius left to be given away and to be sold as he desired by his former Master," attached to letter CCJj to CCJ, 20 March 1857, JTU; Phoebia and Cash to Mr Delions, 17 March 1857, JTU; CPB, 7; MPB, 46.

28. MJ to CCJ, 17 May 1837, JTU.

29. CCJ to MJ, 25 May 1837, JTU.

30. See Margaret Washington Creel, "Gullah Attitudes Toward Life and Death," in *Africanisms in American Culture*, ed. Joseph E. Holloway (Bloomington, Ind., 1990), 69–97.

31. "Minutes of the Session, Midway Congregational Church," 21 February 1835, PHSM.

32. MJ to CCJ, 3 December 1861, JTU; CCJ to CCJj and JJ, 16 June 1837; HHJ to MJ, 9 May 1846, JTU; MJ to Laura Maxwell, 17 August 1848, JTU; MJ to EM, 30 August 1849, JTU.

33. RQM, *Montevideo-Maybank: Some Memoirs of a Southern Christian Household in the Olden Time; or, The Family Life of the Rev. Charles Colcock Jones, D.D., of Liberty County, Ga.* (Richmond, 1898), 37.

34. For the "Mammy" figure, see Deborah Gray White, *Ar'n't I a Woman? Female Slaves in the Plantation South* (New York, 1985), 27–51; Elizabeth Fox-Genovese, *Within the Plantation Household: Black and White Women of the Old South* (Chapel Hill, 1988), 291–292.

35. For Betsy as Cato's wife and as Jack's daughter, and for Betsy's age and work as a domestic, see C. B. Jones to CCJ, 9 April 1854, JTU; CCJ to CCJj, 6 September 1854, CJUG; CCJ to MSJM, 23 December 1859, JTU; Inventory, Appraisement, and Division of Estate of Jos. Jones [esp. slaves numbered 37–48, for Jack and Marcia's children and grandchildren], Will Record, 1824–1850, PCLC. For Cato's age, see CPB, 64, JTU. For Marcia, see CPB, 17.

36. CPB, 12; "List of Negroes belonging to Mrs. S. M. Cumming at White Oak Plantation, May 1, 1848," MPB, 46.

16. SOUTH HAMPTON

1. Betsy Maxwell to MJ, 29 March 1838, JTU; see Bill of Sale, Barrington King to Roswell King, Jr., 23 February 1838, SCLC, Real Estate Division, County Record Book K, 470–473.

2. For the Cherokee removal, see Gary E. Moulton, *John Ross, Cherokee Chief* (Athens, Ga., 1978); Michael D. Green, ed., *The Cherokee Removal: A Brief History with Documents* (Boston, 1995).

3. Clarence Martin, *A History of the Roswell Presbyterian Church* (Dallas, 1984), 17–21. JoJ to MJ, 19 July 1847, JTU; Robert Manson Myers, ed., *The Children of Pride: A True Story of Georgia and the Civil War* (New Haven, 1972), 1680.

4. See George White, *Statistics of the State of Georgia: Including an Account of its Natural, Civil, and Ecclesiastical History; Together with a Particular Description of Each County, Notices of the Manners and Customs of Its Aboriginal Tribes, and a Correct Map of the State* (Savannah, 1849), 87–93.

5. See Bill of Sale, Barrington King to Roswell King, Jr., 470–473; Indenture between Barrington King and Roswell King, Jr., 26 February 1838, SCLC, Real Estate Division, County Record Book K, 474–475.

6. For a description of the rice fields at South Hampton, for identifying boundaries, and for Jacob and Peter as carpenters, see Indenture between Barrington King and Roswell King, Jr., 473.

7. For contemporary accounts of rice production on river swamps, see Frederick Law Olmsted, *A Journey in the Seaboard Slave States in the Years 1853–1854, With Remarks on Their Economy* (New York, 1856), 94–123; Eliza Clay to MJ and CCJ, 17 March 1856, JTU. For the development of river swamp cultivation utilizing the influence of the tide, see Philip D. Morgan, *Slave Counterpoint: Black Culture in the Eighteenth-Century Chesapeake and Lowcountry* (Chapel Hill, 1998), 155–159; Joyce E. Chaplin, "Tidal Rice Cultivation and the Problem of Slavery in South Carolina and Georgia, 1760–1815," *William and Mary Quarterly*, 3rd ser., 49 (1992): 29–61.

8. See Bill of Sale, Barrington King to Roswell King, Jr., 470–473; Indenture between Barrington King and Roswell King, Jr., 474–475. These sales included thirty slaves (nine belonging to Catherine King) who were a part of the sale of the plantation for $17,200. An additional twelve slaves, owned by Catherine King, were purchased by Roswell King, Jr., for $4,800. For the relationship between profits drawn from slavery and the development of the Industrial Revolution, see Eric Williams, *Capitalism and Slavery* ([1944]; rpt. New York, 1966); Hugh Thomas, *The Slave Trade: The Story of the Atlantic Slave Trade, 1440–1870* (New York, 1997); David Brion Davis, *In the Image of God: Religion, Moral Values, and Our Heritage of Slavery* (New Haven, 2001), 151–164.

9. See, e.g., Malcolm Bell, Jr., *Major Butler's Legacy: Five Generations of a Slaveholding Family* (Athens, Ga., 1987), 250. Roswell King, Jr., "Letter to the Editor," *Southern Agriculturalist* 1 (December 1828), 525–527.

10. Bell, *Major Butler's Legacy*, 245; William Dusinberre, *Them Dark Days: Slavery in the American Rice Swamps* (New York, 1996), 253.

11. The story of the mulatto children of Roswell King, Jr., is a complicated and disputed

history. See Bell, *Major Butler's Legacy*, 280–281, 550; Dusinberre, *Them Dark Days*, 248–250, 507 n. 1. For the construction of "whiteness," see Theodore W. Allen, *The Invention of the White Race*, 2 vols. (New York, 1994).

12. EM to Laura Maxwell, 5 September 1845, JTU.

13. Roswell King to CCJ, 8 October 1851, JTU.

14. EM to MJ, 25 May 1853, JTU.

15. See RQM, *Montevideo-Maybank: Some Memoirs of a Southern Christian Household in the Olden Time; or, The Family Life of the Rev. Charles Colcock Jones, D.D., of Liberty County, Ga.* (Richmond, 1898), 43–44.

16. For Julia King's character, see, e.g., Julia King to MJ, 20 August 1846, 27 June 1851, 27 July 1858, 29 July 1858, JTU. RQM, *Montevideo-Maybank*, 44.

17. Will of Audley Maxwell, 27 March 1834, Will Record 1824–1850, PCLC.

18. Ibid. In 1854, when Roswell King had 179 slaves, Julia had an additional 52 in her own name. See Bell, *Major Butler's Legacy*, 532.

19. Will of Roswell King, Jr., 9 May 1840, Will Record 1850–1863, PCLC. For Paris's character, see MJ, Journal, 16 March 1863, JTU. For other prominent slaves at South Hampton, see Julia King to MJ, 29 July 1858, JTU.

20. Myers, *Children of Pride*, 1499.

21. Cf., e.g., Susan Jones Maxwell to Joseph Jones, 30 January 1833, JTU; SJMC to CCJ, 6 November 1847, JTU; CCJ to SJMC, 31 May 1848, JTU; CCJ to SJMC, 13 December 1852, JTU. For the varied responsibilities of slaveholding women and for the gender conventions association with them, see Elizabeth Fox-Genovese, *Within the Plantation Household: Black and White Women of the Old South* (Chapel Hill, 1988), 116–145, 192–197.

22. Cf., e.g., SJMC to MJ, 19 March 1862, 10 December 1864, 15 April 1865, JTU; MJ to SJMC, 9 December 1864, 12 December 1864, JTU.

23. CCJ to WM, 5 May 1849, JTU. Cf. CCJ to Laura Maxwell and Charles Edward Maxwell, 26 May 1838, JTU.

24. Myers, *Children of Pride*, 1499.

25. CPB, 3–4, 7–9; MPB, 50, 38–39.

26. Cf., for CCJ's relationship to Cato and for Cato's character, CCJ to MJ, 3 September 1842, JTU; CCJ to TS, 24 October 1848, 1 February 1849, JTU; CCJ to Cato, 28 January 1851, JTU; Cato to CCJ, 3 March 1851 and 3 September 1852, JTU; S. S. Barnard to CCJ, 19 December 1857, JTU. For a "slave in the middle," between master and those who lived in the settlements, see James C. Scott, *Domination and the Art of Resistance: Hidden Transcripts* (New Haven, 1990), 106–107. For the "cotton planter," see RQM, *Plantation Life Before Emancipation* (Richmond, 1892), 40–41.

17. MIDWAY

1. CCJ to MJ, 26 October 1838, JTU.

2. CCJ to MJ, 22 January 1830, 19 April 1830, 17 August 1830, JTU. See also CCJ to MJ, 20 February 1830, 14 June 1830, 7 July 1830, 6 August 1830, JTU. CCJ's views on marriage reflect a Puritan — or more broadly a Calvinist — perspective that was widespread

in the low country. See John Demos, *Past, Present, and Personal: The Family and the Life Course in American History* (New York, 1986); Erskine Clarke, *Our Southern Zion: A History of Calvinism in the South Carolina Low Country, 1690–1990* (Tuscaloosa, 1996).

3. MJ to CCJ, 2 September 1830, 8 April 1830, 30 May 1828, JTU; CCJ to MJ, 6 March 1830, JTU.
4. Obituary for MJ written by John Jones, JJUG. Cf. Catherine Clinton's position in *Plantation Mistress: Woman's World in the Old South* (New York, 1982), 16–35; Jean E. Friedman, *The Enclosed Garden: Women and Community in the Evangelical South, 1830–1900* (Chapel Hill, 1985), 3–53.
5. For household codes, see Wayne A. Meeks, *The Origins of Christian Morality* (New Haven, 1993), esp. chapter 3; David Balch, *Let Wives Be Submissive: The Domestic Code in 1 Peter*, SBL Monograph Series 26 (Chico, Calif., 1981). See Ephesians 5:22 and 6:5.
6. MJ to CCJ, 8 January 1830, 5 January 1852, JTU.
7. CCJ to MJ, 21 December 1840, 12 June 1837; 3 November 1837, JTU; MJ to CCJ, 5 January 1852, JTU.
8. "Rev. C. C. Jones' Report," *CO*, 18 April 1840.
9. Ibid.
10. CCJ to EM, 16 May 1839, JTU.
11. CCJ to EM, 10 July 1839, JTU.
12. CCJ to EM, 3 August 1839, JTU.
13. "Rev. C. C. Jones' Report," *CO*, 18 April 1840.
14. Ibid.
15. "Minutes of the Session, Midway Congregational Church," passim, PHSM; *Minutes of the Sunbury Baptist Association, Convened at the Newington Church, Screven County, Georgia, Nov. 1829* (Savannah, 1829); *Minutes of the Sunbury Baptist Association, Convened at Walthourville, Liberty County, Georgia on Friday and Saturday, November the 11th and 12th, 1836* (Savannah, 1836).
16. "Minutes of the Watchman's Meeting for Midway Church," 8 March 1840, JTU.
17. CCJ, *Tenth Annual Report of the Association for the Religious Instruction of the Negroes, in Liberty County, Georgia* (Savannah, 1845), 24–25.
18. "Minutes of the Watchman's Meeting for Midway Church," 3 May 1840, 7 February 1841, JTU.
19. For the developing patterns of family life in the settlements of the low country, see Philip D. Morgan, *Slave Counterpoint: Black Culture in the Eighteenth-Century Chesapeake and Lowcountry* (Chapel Hill, 1998), esp. 3–4, 498–558; Herbert G. Gutman, *The Black Family in Slavery and Freedom, 1750–1925* (New York, 1976); Margaret Washington Creel, *"A Peculiar People": Slave Religion and Community-Culture Among the Gullahs* (New York, 1988), esp. 244–249, 265–270; David Brion Davis, *In the Image of God: Religion, Moral Values, and Our Heritage of Slavery* (New Haven, 2001), 278–289.
20. Janet Duitsman Cornelius, *Slave Missions and the Black Church in the Antebellum South* (Columbia, S.C., 1999), 36–45. See also Janet Cornelius, "Slave Marriage in a

Georgia Congregation," in *Class, Conflict, and Consensus: Antebellum Southern Communities*, ed. Orville Vernon Burton and Robert C. McMath (Westport, Conn., 1982), 128–145. "Minutes of the Session, Midway Congregational Church," 11 April 1841; 1827–1864, passim, e.g., 29 February 1830 [*sic*], 14 November 1846, PHSM.

21. "Minutes of the Session, Midway Congregational Church," 17 February 1843, 26 August 1843, 15 February 1844, 15 May 1852, PHSM. CCJ to Sandy Maybank, 15 August 1853, JTU.

22. CCJ to EM, 10 July 1839, JTU. "Minutes of the Watchman's Meeting for Midway Church," 3 May 1840, JTU. "Minutes of the Session, Midway Congregational Church," 16 May 1840, 5 December 1840, 27 February 1841, PHSM. Charles Edward Maxwell to MJ, 5 September 1851, JTU; CCJ to CCJj and JJ, 19 August 1851, JTU.

23. CCJ, *Seventh Annual Report of the Association for the Religious Instruction of the Negroes, in Liberty County, Georgia* (Savannah, 1842), 4–5.

24. CCJ, "The Marriage State: The Nature and Honor of It, Hebrews 13:4," JTU.

25. CCJ, "Duties of Husbands, Ephesians 5:22, 33," JTU.

26. Ibid.

28. CCJ, *Thirteenth Annual Report of the Association for the Religious Instruction of the Negroes, in Liberty County, Georgia* (Savannah, 1848), 15–16.

28. Ibid., 16–17; CCJ to MJ, 22 July 1829, JTU.

18. MAYBANK

1. CCJ to MJ, 16 November 1841, JTU; CCJj to SJ MC, 21 April 1842, JTU; Robert Manson Myers, ed., *The Children of Pride: A True Story of Georgia and the Civil War* (New Haven, 1972), 1508–1509.

2. For the landscape, the travel time between Montevideo and Maybank, and the use of oxcarts, see CCJ to MSJM, 15 June 1858, JTU; CCJ to CCJj, 9 August 1859, CJUG; RQM, *Plantation Life Before Emancipation* (Richmond, 1892), 15–19.

3. RQM, *Montevideo-Maybank: Some Memoirs of a Southern Christian Household in the Olden Time; or, The Family Life of the Rev. Charles Colcock Jones, D.D., of Liberty County, Ga.* (Richmond, 1898), 10–11; MPB, 22–27; CCJ, Journal, 5 September 1862, JTU.

4. CCJ to MJ, 21 June 1851, JTU; EM to MJ, 29 July 1853; RQM, *Montevideo-Maybank*, 11–12; CCJj to Mary Ruth Jones, 11 May 1888, JDU; John M. B. Harden, M.D. "Observations on the Soil, Climate and Diseases of Liberty County, Georgia," *Southern Medical and Surgical Journal*, new ser., 1, no. 10 (October 1845): 553.

5. CCJj to JJ, 10 September 1841, JTU; Audley Maxwell King to CCJj, 6 May 1850, JTU.

6. CCJj to Mary Ruth Jones, 11 May 1888, JDU; James William Berry, "Growing Up in the Old South: The Childhood of Charles Colcock Jones, Jr." (Ph.D. diss., Princeton University, 1981), 317–342; Daniel J. Pfeifer, "Charles C. Jones, Jr.: Resilient Southerner" (M.A. thesis, Georgia Southern University, 1997), 11–21.

7. Cf. MJ to MSJM, 22 April 1867, JTU.

8. See Joseph LeConte, *The Autobiography of Joseph LeConte* (New York, 1903), 8–18, 21–36.

9. Cf. ibid. and CCJj to Mary Ruth Jones, 11 May 1888, JDU.

10. CCJj to Mary Ruth Jones, 11 May 1888, JDU.

11. Ibid.; see also Audley Maxwell King to CCJj, 6 May 1850, JTU.

12. RQM, *Montevideo-Maybank*, 14; CCJ to CCJj and JJ, 12 September 1850, JTU.

13. Harden, "Observations," 547; CCJj, *Antiquities of the Southern Indians, Particularly of the Georgia Tribes* (1873; rpt. Tuscaloosa, 1999), 454–456, 157. See also RQM, *Montevideo-Maybank*, 82.

14. Laura Maxwell to MJ, 25 December 1828, JTU.

15. Frank T. Schnell, Jr., Introduction, to CCJj, *Antiquities*, xxv, xix. For JJ's medical and scientific career, see James O. Breeden, *Joseph Jones, M.D., Scientist of the Old South* (Lexington, Ky., 1975); Margaret Humphreys, *Yellow Fever and the South* (Baltimore, 1992).

16. MSJM to MJ, 16 October 1860, JTU. Cf. CCJj to CCJ and MJ, 10 October 1857, JTU.

17. CCJ, *The Religious Instruction of the Negroes in the United States* (Savannah, 1842).

18. MJ to CCJj, 22 May 1851, CJUG; MJ to MSJ, 10 December 1852, JTU; MJ to MSJM, 26 June 1857, JTU.

19. CCJ to CCJj, 27 February 1852, CJUG; MJ to Laura Maxwell, 18 February 1850, JTU.

20. For EM's writing, see EM to CCJ, 17 June 1850, JTU; John Jones to CCJ, 8 October 1856, JTU. For EM's relationship with her nieces and nephews, see CCJ to EM, 14 May 1838, JTU; EM to Laura Maxwell, 5 September 1845, JTU; EM to CCJ, 31 August 1846, JTU.

21. CCJj to Mary Ruth Jones, 11 May 1888, JDU.

22. MJ to CCJ, 5 November 1835, JTU. For MJ's concern for the conversion of her children, see MJ to MSJ, 11 June 1847, JTU; MJ to CCJj 28 October 1850, CJUG.

23. Cf. Audley Maxwell King to CCJj, 6 May 1850, JTU. For the Calvinist emphasis on "ordinary life," see Charles Taylor in *Sources of the Self: The Making of the Modern Identity* (Cambridge, Mass., 1989), 211–233.

24. See MPB, 10, JTU; CCJ to MJ, 2 April 1845, 17 April 1845, 10 February 1846, JTU; CCJ to WM, 3 April 1849, JTU.

25. Cf. Paulo Freire, *Pedagogy of the Oppressed*, trans. Myrna Bergman Ramos (New York, 1970).

26. Leon F. Litwack, *Been in the Storm so Long: The Aftermath of Slavery* (New York, 1979), 450–456; Jacqueline Jones, *Soldiers of Light and Love: Northern Teachers and Georgia Blacks* (Chapel Hill, 1980); Robert C. Morris, *Reading, 'Riting, and Reconstruction: The Education of Freedmen in the South, 1861–1870* (Chicago, 1981).

27. CCJ to MJ, 2 April 1845, 17 April 1845, 10 February 1846, JTU.

28. For the character of oxen used in the rice-growing regions of South Carolina and Georgia, see Martin A. Garrett, Jr., "Evidence on the Use of Oxen in the Postbellum South," *Social Science History* 22, no. 2 (Summer 1998). For the number of oxen at Montevideo, Maybank, and Arcadia during the 1850s, see, e.g., CCJ, "Stock on the three Plantations," Almanac, June 1855, JTU.

29. See "Photograph File," JTU; CCJ to CCJj, 4 August 1858, CJUG; CCJ to CCJj, 10 May 1862, JTU; MJ, Journal, 4 January 1865, JTU.

30. CCJj to Mary Ruth Jones, 11 May 1888, JDU; cf. CCJj's account of Indian fishing in

Antiquities, 332–340. For the tradition of slave fishermen in the low country, see Peter Wood, *Black Majority: Negroes in Colonial South Carolina from 1670 Through the Stono Rebellion* (New York, 1974), 201; Philip D. Morgan, *Slave Counterpoint: Black Culture in the Eighteenth-Century Chesapeake and Lowcountry* (Chapel Hill, 1998), 240–242. CCJ to MJ, 20 October 1856, JTU.

31. For the work of slave women generally in the low country, see Morgan, *Slave Counterpoint*, 194–203.

32. CCJ, *Eleventh Annual Report of the Association for the Religious Instruction of the Negroes, in Liberty County, Georgia* (Savannah, 1846), 9; Journal of MJ, 4 November 1866, JTU. See, e.g., CO, 12 October 1839, 26 October 1839, 12 September 1844, 19 October 1844, 16 November 1844.

33. Lawrence W. Levine, *Black Culture and Black Consciousness: Afro-American Folk Thought from Slavery to Freedom* (New York, 1977), 99–100. CCJ, *Religious Instruction of the Negroes in the United States*, 130.

34. James C. Scott, *Domination and the Art of Resistance: Hidden Transcripts* (New Haven, 1990), 3–4, 31–36. CCJ, *Religious Instruction of the Negroes in the United States*, 110.

35. Scott, *Domination and the Art of Resistance*, 157–166. Ras Michael Brown, "'Walk in the Feenda': West-Central Africans and the Forest in the South Carolina–Georgia Lowcountry," in *Central Africans and Cultural Transformations in the American Diaspora*, ed. Linda M. Heywood (Cambridge, 2002), 301–302.

36. CCJj, *Negro Myths from the Georgia Coast, Told in the Vernacular* (1888; rpt. Columbia, S.C., 1925), 1–3. Levine, *Black Culture and Black Consciousness*, 81–133, and Scott, *Domination and the Art of Resistance*, 162–166, have been particularly helpful for my analysis of these folktales.

37. CCJj, *Negro Myths*, 50, 52, 37, 67.

38. Ibid., 12–14, 64.

39. For the trickster, see Will Coleman, *Tribal Talk: Black Theology, Hermeneutics, and African/American Ways of "Telling the Story"* (University Park, Pa., 2000), 20–23.

40. CCJj, *Negro Myths*, 29–33. Cf. Levine, *Black Culture and Black Consciousness*, 111; Scott, *Domination and the Art of Resistance*, 163.

41. CCJj, *Negro Myths*, 108–110.

42. Cf. Thomas L. Webber, *Deep Like the Rivers: Education in the Slave Quarter Community, 1831–1865* (New York, 1978), 131–139; Wilma King, *Stolen Childhood: Slave Youth in Nineteenth-Century America* (Bloomington, Ind., 1995); Marie Jenkins Schwartz, *Born in Bondage: Growing Up Enslaved in the Antebellum South* (Cambridge, Mass., 2000), 75–107.

19. ARCADIA

1. Note by JoJ, 16 February 1840, JJUG.

2. See Martha Bulloch to JoJ, 15 December 1836, JJUG; JoJ to Martha Bulloch, 1 February 1837, JJUG; Till Bulloch to JoJ, 4 August 1837, JJUG.

3. Frederick Law Olmsted, *A Journey in the Seaboard Slave States in the Years 1853–1854, With Remarks on Their Economy* (New York, 1856), vol. 2, 44–45. See also Carolyn

Clay Swiggart, *Shades of Gray: The Clay and McAllister Families of Bryan County, Georgia, During the Plantation Years* (Darien, Conn., 1999) 13–26;

4. John Dunwody to Eliz. Smith Dunwody, 22 December 1840, JJUG.
5. Births, deaths, and genealogical information found in JosJ, Notes on Births and Deaths, n.d., CJUG; Bessie Anderson, "Grandmother's Drawer," July 1869, JTU.
6. Cf. CCJ to EM, 7 April 1832, JTU.
7. JosJ to JoJ, 21 October 1832, JJUG.
8. Mathew 6:19–21. Those gathered included JosJ, CCJ, JoJ, WM, Thomas Clay, James Smith, George Washington McAllister, Richard J. Arnold, Henry M. Stevens, and John S. Maxwell. See JoJ to Jane Dunwody Jones, 28 April 1842, JJUG. For the size of their slave holdings, see Federal Census, 1840, Bryan County, Ga.; Federal Census, 1840, Liberty County, Ga.
9. JoJ to Jane Dunwody Jones, 28 April 1842, JJUG; Obituary for MJ written by JoJ, JJUG.
10. Note by JoJ, 14 May 1842, JJUG; CPB, 17. Cf. JoJ to MJ, 1 October 1850, JTU.
11. County Record M, part 2, 600–603, SCLC; Bonaventure Plantation file in JJUG. See also James Newton Jones to JoJ, 19 February 1845, JJUG; CCJ to Jane Dunwody Jones, 10 September 1846, JJUG; MJ to JoJ, 30 July 1847, JJUG.
12. See Last Will and Testament of JosJ, Will Record, 1824–1850, PCLC; Inventory, Appraisement and Division of the Estate of Jos. Jones, Will Record, 1824–1850, PCLC.
13. For the record of births and deaths at Carlawter and Maybank, see CPB, 64–73. For the births and deaths of slaves of SJMC, Laura Maxwell, and Charles Edward Maxwell, see MPB, 39–40, 46–47. For a statistical summary, giving age, gender, and month of births and deaths at Montevideo, see "Statistics of Montevideo drawn up by JJ, May 16, 1861," CPB. For overviews of demographic studies on slave populations, see Robert William Fogel, *Without Consent or Contract: The Rise and Fall of American Slavery* (New York, 1989), 114–153; William Dusinberre, *Them Dark Days: Slavery in the American Rice Swamps* (New York, 1996), 410–416, 441–451; Philip D. Morgan, *Slave Counterpoint: Black Culture in the Eighteenth-Century Chesapeake and Lowcountry* (Chapel Hill, 1998), 79–95.
14. Will of Audley Maxwell, 27 March 1834, Will Record 1824–1850, PCLC. For the purchase of Lambert, see County Record O, 12–14, SCLC.
15. "Minutes of the Session, Midway Congregational Church," 1830–1840, PHFM. "A List of Negroes and other personal property of Estate John Lambert, 29th June 1837," JJUG. For the act of the Georgia legislature allowing the sale of the Lambert Estate and the investment of the funds "in stocks, or such other property, as in their discretion they may deem best," see *Acts of the General Assembly of the State of Georgia Passed in Milledgeville at an Annual Session in November and December 1838* (Milledgeville, 1839), 148–149.
16. "List of Negroes at Lambert Plantation, May 1, 1848," MPB, 39–40; Will of Andrew Maybank, 13 January 1834, Will Record, 1824–1850, PCLC; Will of Audley Maxwell, 27 March 1834, Will Record 1824–1850, PCLC.
17. "List of Negroes belonging to Mrs. S. M. Cumming at White Oak Plantation, May 1, 1848," MPB, 46–47.
18. For the details on Arcadia, see "Tax Returns of CCJ and Wife MJ for the year 1847,"

CPB, 59; CCJ to JoJ, 26 March 1846, JJUG. Plat of Arcadia, drawn by W. Hughes, 25 August 1856, CJUG.

19. "Statistics of Arcadia drawn up by JJ, May 16, 1861: Population January 1846," CPB; CCJ to WM, 21 September 1848, JTU; MJ to CCJj, 19 February 1863, CJUG; MJ to JoJ, 1 December 1865, JJUG; MJ to MSJM, 9 December 1865, JTU.

20. Robert Manson Myers, ed. *The Children of Pride: A True Story of Georgia and the Civil War* (New Haven, 1972), 1567; MSJM to MJ, 18 March 1865, JTU; HHJ to JoJ, "Confidential Note," 6 February 1860, in JJUG.

21. CCJ to MJ, 5 October 1844, 5 August 1845, JTU; Evelyn Jones Anderson to MJ, 6 September 1845, JTU; MJ to CCJj, 11 May 1854, CJUG; CCJ to CCJj, 17 March 1860, CJUG; SJMC to "Dear Cousin," 12 April 1866, JTU.

22. Myers, *Children of Pride*, 1571–1572; JoJ to MJ, 9 April 1851, JTU; James Newton Jones to JoJ, 13 June 1853, JJUG; CCJ to CCJj, 9 October 1854, CJUG. EM to Laura Maxwell, 5 September 1845, JTU. Julia King to MJ, 9 November 1845, JTU. James Newton Jones to MJ, 24 September 1845, JTU.

23. Charles Edward Maxwell to MJ, 27 November 1845, JTU. A copy of MJ's response to Julia King was written on Julia King's letter to MJ, 9 November 1845, JTU. Myers, *Children of Pride*, 1571–1572, 1721.

24. See Laura Maxwell to MJ, 23 October 1844, 31 October 1844, 17 August 1847, JTU.

25. HHJ to MJ, 8 May 1844, JTU.

26. Rebecca Mallard to RQM, 30 January 1850, JTU.

27. Henry Hart Jones to MJ, 19 August 1848, JTU. For a careful exploration of the dynamics of sex and race in the antebellum South, see Catherine Clinton, "Caught in the Web of the Big House: Women and Slavery," in *Women and the Family in a Slave Society*, ed. Paul Finkelman (New York, 1989), 9–24.

28. Myers, *Children of Pride*, 1570–1571. Rebecca Mallard to RQM, 5 March 1850, JTU.

29. Myers, *Children of Pride*, 1544.

30. Julia King to MJ, 20 August 1846, JTU.

31. MJ to EM, 24 September, 1846, JTU; Last Will and Testament of JosJ, Will Record, 1824–1850, PCLC.

32. See Susan Cumming to MJ, 16 September 1851, JTU.

33. The account of JosJ's accident and death is drawn from the nineteen pages of CCJ, "Some Account of my Dear & Honored Father's Death," 21 October 1846, JTU. See also CCJ, "Obituary of Capt. JosJ," 18 October 1846, JTU.

34. JoJ to MJ, 12 October 1847, JTU.

35. JoJ to MJ, 9 April 1851, JTU.

20. THE RETREAT II

1. *Proceedings of the Meeting in Charleston, S.C., May 13–14, on the Religious Instruction of the Negroes, Together with the Report of the Committee, and the Address to the Public* (Charleston, 1845), 3, 4. See Erskine Clarke, *Wrestlin' Jacob: A Portrait of Religion in the Old South* (Atlanta, 1979), 100–107; Barbara Bellows, *Benevolence Among Slaveholders: Assisting the Poor in Charleston, 1670–1860* (Baton Rouge, 1993).

2. William McWhir to MJ, 15 May 1845, JTU.

3. Quoted in Richard C. Wade, *Slavery in the Cities: The South 1820–1860* (New York, 1967), 10–12.

4. For the Charleston slave trade and the importance of Chalmers Street in the trade, see Frederic Bancroft, *Slave Trading in the Old South* (New York, 1931), 165–196.

5. For the expansion of slavery to the western states, see Robert William Fogel, *Without Consent or Contract: The Rise and Fall of American Slavery* (New York, 1989), 64–72; Ira Berlin, *Generations of Captivity: A History of African-American Slaves* (Cambridge, Mass., 2003), 161–244.

6. *Charleston Mercury*, 12 May 1845.

7. *Proceedings of the Meeting in Charleston, S.C.*, 15.

8. Ibid.

9. Ibid. CCJ to MJ, 18 May 1830, JTU. Drayton Grimké was the brother of the abolitionists Sara and Angelina Grimké. See Catherine H. Birney, *The Grimké Sisters: Sara and Angelina Grimké, the First American Women Advocates of Abolition and Woman's Rights* (Westport, Conn., 1969).

10. *Proceedings of the Meeting in Charleston, S.C.*, 15.

11. Ibid., 15–17.

12. CO, 24 May 1845; *Proceedings of the Meeting in Charleston, S.C.*, 18.

13. CCJ, *Eleventh Annual Report of the Association for the Religious Instruction of the Negroes, in Liberty County, Georgia* (Savannah, 1846), 34. For CCJ's reflections on the changes in the South during the previous ten years, see ibid., 23; *Thirteenth Annual Report of the Association for the Religious Instruction of the Negroes, in Liberty County, Georgia* (Savannah, 1848), 57. See also Janet Duitsman Cornelius, *Slave Missions and the Black Church in the Antebellum South* (Columbia, S.C., 1999), 103–123.

14. John Jones, "Memorial of Charles Colcock Jones, D.D.," in *Memorial Volume of the Semin-Centennial of the Theological Seminary at Columbia, South Carolina* (Columbia, 1884), 197; CCJ, *Eleventh Annual Report*, 21; CCJ, *Thirteenth Annual Report*, 58–67. Cf. also Donald G. Mathews, "Charles Colcock Jones and the Southern Evangelical Crusade to Form a Biracial Community," *Journal of Southern History* 41 (August 1975): 299–320; Eduard N. Loring, "Charles C. Jones: Missionary to Plantation Slaves 1831–1847" (Ph.D. diss., Vanderbilt University, 1976), 152–290.

15. CCJ, *Tenth Annual Report of the Association for the Religious Instruction of the Negroes, in Liberty County, Georgia* (Savannah, 1845), 24–36; CCJ, *Eleventh Annual Report*, 7–10; CCJ, *Twelfth Annual Report of the Association for the Religious Instruction of the Negroes, in Liberty County, Georgia* (Savannah, 1847), 4–9; CCJ, *Thirteenth Annual Report*, 4–10. CCJ, *Tenth Annual Report*, 6; "Minutes of the Session, Midway Congregational Church," 18 February 1839, 15 August 1840, PHSM; "Minutes of the Watchman's Meeting for Midway Church," 8 March 1840, JTU.

16. CCJ, *Twelfth Annual Report*, 11–12.

17. CCJ, "Return of Members," 1846, JTU; CCJ, *Twelfth Annual Report*, 11–12.

18. CCJ, "Return of Members"; CCJ, *Twelfth Annual Report*, 13.

19. CCJ, *Twelfth Annual Report*, 13. Cf. CCJ, *Seventh Annual Report*, 5. For white members in Midway, see "List of Church Members" and "Deaths" in James Stacy, *The Pub-*

lished *Records of Midway Church* (Newnan, Ga., 1894), 144–154, 157–163. The total number at any one period does not exceed 350. For the few white members of the Baptist Churches during this period, see *Minutes of the Thirty-First Anniversary of the Sunbury Baptist Association, Convened at Walthourville Baptist Church, Liberty County, Georgia* (Savannah, 1848), 5.

20. CCJ, *Eleventh Annual Report*, 16.
21. CCJ, *Twelfth Annual Report*, 14–17. For property owned by slaves in Liberty County, see Philip D. Morgan, "The Ownership of Property by Slaves in the Mid-Nineteenth Century Low Country," *Journal of Southern History* 49, no. 3 (1983): 399–420; Dylan Penningroth, "Slavery, Freedom, and Social Claims to Property Among African Americans in Liberty County, Georgia, 1850–1880," *Journal of American History* 84 (September 1997): 405–435. CCJ, *Twelfth Annual Report*, 17–18.
22. CCJ, *Thirteenth Annual Report*, 14–15.
23. For the larger nineteenth-century context of CCJ's reform and benevolent efforts, see Gertrude Himmelfarb, *Poverty and Compassion: The Moral Imagination of the Late Victorians* (New York, 1991); Gertrude Himmelfarb, *The De-Moralization of Society: From Victorian Virtues to Modern Values* (New York, 1995).
24. Last Will and Testament of Joseph Jones, Will Record, 1824–1850, PCLC.
25. Inventory, Appraisement, and Division of the Estate of Joseph Jones, 15 December 1846, Will Record, 1824–1850, PCLC.
26. CCJ to Elizabeth S. L. Jones, 21 December 1846, JTU; CCJ to R. N. Charlton and William Law, 4 November 1848, CJUG.
27. Last Will and Testament of Joseph Jones, Will Record, 1824–1850, PCLC.
28. CCJ to James Newton Jones, 6 March 1847, JTU; CCJ, "Memorandum" 1847, JTU. CCJ to EM, 29 July 1849, JTU; MJ to MSJM, 31 July 1862, JTU.
29. C. B. Jones to MJ, 27 December 1851, 17 June 1854, JTU.

21. COLUMBIA II

1. CPB, 64–73; "List of Negroes on Lambert Plantation, May 1, 1848," "List of Negroes Belonging to Mrs. S. M. Cumming at White Oak Plantation, May 1, 1848," MPB, 39–46.
2. Robert Manson Myers, ed. *The Children of Pride: A True Story of Georgia and the Civil War* (New Haven, 1972), 1674–1675.
3. Eliza Sumner Martin, "Flemington," in *Liberty County, Georgia: A Pictorial History* compiled by Virginia Fraser Evans (Statesville, N.C., 1979), 79–94. Undated note on death of Rahn child, apparently 1849, from Ezra Stacy to CCJ, JTU. MJ to CCJ, 5 January 1852, JTU.
4. Cf. Audley King to CCJ, 21 July 1857, JTU. See, e.g., CCJ to WM, 2 February 1849, JTU.
5. CCJ, *Thirteenth Annual Report of the Association for the Religious Instruction of the Negroes, in Liberty County, Georgia* (Savannah, 1848), 10.
6. Ibid., 67; Rebecca Eliza Mallard to RQM, 22 January 1848, JTU; Papers of the Estate of John Lambert, IV, 1847–1851, GHS. Myers, *Children of Pride*, 1735.
7. CPB, 68; MJ to Laura Maxwell, 17 August 1848, JTU; CPB, 67–68.

8. CCJ to TS, 14 December 1848, JTU; CCJ to William and Betsy Maxwell, 17 April 1850, JTU; CCJj to Mary Ruth Jones, 11 May 1888, JDU.

9. CCJ to William and Betsy Maxwell, 17 April 1850, JTU. For slaves' recognition of white dependence, see Sidney W. Mintz and Richard Price, *An Anthropological Approach to the Afro-American Past: A Caribbean Perspective* (Boston, 1992), 6, 27; cf. also Philip D. Morgan, *Slave Counterpoint: Black Culture in the Eighteenth-Century Chesapeake and Lowcountry* (Chapel Hill, 1998), 334–337.

10. MPB, 4.

11. JoJ to MJ, 27 October 1847, JTU.

12. JoJ to MJ, 19 July 1847, JTU.

13. JoJ to MJ, 1 June 1848, JTU.

14. JoJ to MJ, 19 August 1847, JTU.

15. JoJ to MJ, 28 April 1848, JTU; CCJ to MJ, 23 July 1830, JTU. For John Ross's home on the Coosa, see Gary E. Moulton, *John Ross, Cherokee Chief* (Athens, Ga., 1978). For Elizur Butler, see Jill Norgren, *Cherokee Cases: Two Landmark Federal Decisions in the Fight for Sovereignty* (Norman, Okla., 2004).

16. JoJ to MJ, 27 October 1847, JTU; CCJ to Mary Robarts, 4 May 1849, JTU.

17. Federal Census, 1840, Liberty County, Ga. For Eliza Robarts's slaves who remained in Liberty County, see TS to CCJ, 16 December 1850, JTU; EM to MJ, 10 January 1850, JTU; Eliza Robarts to CCJ, 22 January 1859, JTU. Eliza Robarts to CCJ, 18 December 1847, JTU. CPB, 64–71.

18. CCJ to TS, 26 January 1850, JTU; Eliza Robarts to MJ, 25 December 1854, JTU; Mary Robarts to MJ, 6 January 1855, JTU; Eliza Robarts to MJ, 10 November 1856, JTU; CCJ to Eliza Robarts, 13 December 1862, JTU.

19. CCJ to Betsy and William Maxwell, 4 October 1848, JTU.

20. JJ and MSJ to EM, 11 November 1848, JTU.

21. CCJ to WM, 2 February 1849, JTU

22. CCJ to Betsy and William Maxwell, 4 October 1848, JTU; CCJ to TS, 14 December 1848, JTU.

23. CCJ to WM, 2 February 1849, JTU; Myers, *Children of Pride*, 1663; JJ and MSJ to Betsy Maxwell, 11 November 1848; CCJ to JoJ, 2 April 1849, JJUG.

24. CCJ to Mary Robarts, 4 May 1849, JTU; Daniel W. Hollis, *The University of South Carolina*, 2 vols. (Columbia, 1951), 1: 161–162. See also Daniel W. Hollis, "James Henley Thornwell and the South Carolina College," *Proceedings of the South Carolina Historical Association*, 1953, 17–36.

25. MJ to MSJ, 11 June 1847, JTU. For Cocke's Alabama experiment, see Randal Miller, ed., *Dear Master: Letters of a Slave Family* (Ithaca, N.Y., 1978). For Cocke's visits with the Jones family, see CCJ to WM, 23 December 1848, JTU; CCJ to MSJ, 24 December 1849, JTU.

26. CCJ to WM, 23 December 1848, JTU; CCJ to Mary Robarts, 4 May 1849, JTU.

27. CCJ to JoJ, 2 April 1849, JJUG.

28. CCJ to TS, 24 October 1848, JTU.

29. CCJ to TS, 14 December 1848, JTU; CCJ to WM, 2 February 1849, JTU. On masters' care for elderly slaves, see Morgan, *Slave Counterpoint*, 334.

30. CCJ to TS, 2 May 1849, 26 June 1849, JTU.
31. CCJ to Betsy and William Maxwell, 4 October 1848, JTU; CCJ to WM, 2 February 1849, JTU; CCJ to TS, 26 January 1850, JTU.
32. CCJ to TS, 23 December 1848, 24 March 1849, JTU.
33. For slave resistance generally, see Robert William Fogel, *Without Consent or Contract: The Rise and Fall of American Slavery* (New York, 1989), 154–198. Eliza Robarts to JoJ, 8 July 1847, JJUG. On runaways, see John Hope Franklin and Loren Schweninger, *Runaway Slaves: Rebels on the Plantation* (New York, 1999); John W. Blassingame, *The Slave Community: Plantation Life in the Ante-Bellum South* (New York, 1972), 104–131.
34. CCJ to WM, 2 February 1849, JTU; CCJ to TS, 24 March 1849, JTU; CCJ to Betsy Maxwell, 29 July 1849, JTU; Laura Maxwell to MJ, 25 April 1850, JTU.
35. CCJ to EM, 19 May 1849, JTU; CCJ to William and Betsy Maxwell, 18 June 1849, JTU; CCJ to TS, 20 July 1849, JTU.
36. MJ to EM, 30 August 1849, JTU.
37. CCJ to TS, 26 June 1849, JTU; CCJ to EM, 5 July 1849, JTU.
38. CCJ to William and Betsy Maxwell, 19 August 1849, 28 September 1849, JTU.
39. J. H. Thornwell, B. M. Palmer, and Georgia Howe to CCJ, 26 April 1850, together with attached apology from Howe for being so late in giving the invitation and CCJ's penciled note of indignation. For the theology of a "middle way," see Erskine Clarke, *Our Southern Zion: A History of Calvinism in the South Carolina Low Country, 1690–1990* (Tuscaloosa, 1996), 165–181. See also E. Brooks Holifield, *The Gentlemen Theologians: American Theology in Southern Culture, 1795–1860* (Durham, N.C., 1978). Cf. Eugene Genovese, *The Southern Tradition: the Achievement and Limitations of an American Conservatism* (Cambridge, Mass., 1994).
40. CCJ to William and Betsy Maxwell, 17 April 1850, JTU; Laura Maxwell to MJ, 25 April 1850, JTU.
41. CCJ to William and Betsy Maxwell, 23 April 1850, JTU.
42. In MJ's hand, note dated 9 October 1857, Maybank.
43. "Inventory of Marcia's and Jack's Clothing," May 1850, JTU.
44. "Inscription for Jack and Marcia," 20 April 1850, in JTU.

22. PHILADELPHIA

1. J. J. Janeway to CCJ, 8 May 1850, JTU; "For the Anniversary of the Board of Domestic Missions, October 17, 1850," JTU.
2. For classic accounts of the "Protestant Empire" and its assumptions, see Martin E. Marty, *Righteous Empire: the Protestant Experience in America* (New York, 1970); Sydney E. Ahlstrom, *A Religious History of the American People* (New Haven, 1972), esp. 403–471.
3. CCJ to MJ, 30 May 1850, JTU.
4. Ibid.; MJ to CCJ, 5 June 1850, JTU.
5. MSJ to CCJ, 10 June 1850, JTU; JoJ, 29 June 1850, JTU; EM to CCJ, 17 June 1850, JTU; CCJ to The Presbyterian Board of Missions, 10 July 1850, JTU.
6. MJ to CCJ, 12 June 1850, JTU; EM to CCJ, 17 June, 1850, JTU.

7. MJ to CCJ, 12 June 1850, JTU.
8. MJ, Journal, 1 June 1850, JTU.
9. CCJ and MJ to CCJj and JJ, 26 July 1850, CJUG.
10. Cf. James William Berry, "Growing Up in the Old South: The Childhood of Charles Colcock Jones, Jr.," (Ph.D. diss., Princeton University, 1981), esp. 266–294; James O. Breeden, *Joseph Jones, M.D., Scientist of the Old South* (Lexington, Ky., 1975),13–20.
11. CCJ to CCJj and JJ, 12 September 1850, JTU; Audley Maxwell King to CCJj, 6 May 1850, JTU. See also Robert Manson Myers, ed. *The Children of Pride: A True Story of Georgia and the Civil War* (New Haven, 1972), 1581, 1586. Laura Maxwell to MJ, 10 February 1855, JTU.
12. Laura Maxwell to MJ, 24 June 1850, 27 July 1850, JTU; MJ to CCJj and JJ, 1 October 1850, CJUG.
13. MJ to CCJj and JJ, 7 October 1850, CJUG; JoJ to MJ, 1 October 1850, JTU.
14. "For the Anniversary of the Board of Domestic Missions, October 17, 1850," JTU. For the nineteenth century as a period of Protestant expansion, see Kenneth Scott Latourette, *A History of Christianity* (New York, 1953), esp. chapter 45.
15. Cf. Benjamin Gildersleeve to CCJ, 6 June 1850, JTU; Robert Manson Myers, *A Georgian at Princeton* (New York, 1976), passim; CCJ, "Report to the Board of Domestic Missions," 23 May 1853, JTU.
16. CCJ to MJ, 7 May 1850, JTU; CCJ to CCJj and JJ, 8 May 1850, CJUG.
17. CCJ to MJ, 10 May 1851, 27 May 1851, JTU.
18. CCJ to MJ, 17 May 1851, JTU.
19. See J. D. B. DeBow, *Statistical View of the United States* (Washington, D.C., 1854). CCJ to CCJj and JJ, 29 May 1851, CJUG.
20. CCJ to MJ, 17 June 1851, JTU. See also Myers, *A Georgian at Princeton*, 159–187.
21. MJ to CCJ, 5 May 1851, JTU.
22. CCJ to MJ, 21 June 1851, JTU.
23. CCJj to CCJ, 19 July 1851, CJUG.
24. MJ to CCJ, 12 May 1851, JTU.
25. MJ to MSJ, 12 November 1851, JTU; CCJ to MSJ, 17 November 1851, JTU.
26. CCJ to CCJj and JJ, 19 November 1851, CJUG. JoJ to MJ, 29 August 1851, 19 May 1853, 17 October 1853, 10 January 1847, JTU. For indications of learning disabilities, see letters of Dunwody Jones in JJUG and JTU, e.g., JoJ to MJ, 12 May 1864, JTU; Dunwody Jones to JoJ, 8 April 1867, JJUG.
27. CCJ to MSJ, 1 December 1851, JTU.
28. MJ to CCJj, 25 December 1851, CJUG; Sarah Howe to CCJ, 31 October 1854, JTU.
29. JoJ to MJ, 9 April 1851, JTU; James Newton Jones to JoJ, 13 June 1853, JJUG; CCJ to CCJj, 9 October 1854, CJUG.
30. CCJ to MSJ, 1 December 1851, JTU; CCJ to MSJ, 26 November 1851, JTU. See also CCJ to CCJj, 1 December 1851, CJUG; CCJ to MSJ, 1 December 1851, JTU.
31. CCJ to MSJ, 1 December 1851, JTU.
32. MJ to CCJ, 20 December 1851, 22 December 1851, 23 January 1832, JTU.
33. CCJ to MJ, 21 December 1851; CCJ to JoJ, 31 January 1852, JTU.
34. MJ to CCJ, 5 June 1850, JTU.

35. MJ to CCJ, 5 January 1852, JTU. See also MJ to CCJ, 13 January 1852, JTU.

36. MJ to CCJ, 14 January 1852, JTU. For the evangelical impulse that led many women to "witness," see Nancy A. Hardesty, *Women Called to Witness: Evangelical Feminism in the Nineteenth Century* (Nashville, 1984).

37. MJ to CCJ, 5 January 1852, JTU; MJ to JoJ, 7 March 1856, JJUG; Obituary for MJ written by JoJ, JJUG. For the varied responsibilities of slaveholding women and for the gender conventions association with them, see Elizabeth Fox-Genovese, *Within the Plantation Household: Black and White Women of the Old South* (Chapel Hill, 1988), esp. 116–145, 192–197.

38. CCJ to MJ, 13 January 1852, 23 January 1852, JTU. See Lois A. Boyd and R. Douglas Brackenridge, *Presbyterian Women in America: Two Centuries of a Quest for Status* (Westport, Conn., 1983); Rosemary Skinner Keller, "Protestant Laywomen in Institutional Churches," in *In Our Own Voices: Four Centuries of American Women's Religious Writing*, ed. Rosemary Skinner Keller and Rosemary Radford Ruether (New York, 1995), 61–108.

39. MJ to CCJj, 25 December 1851, CJUG; MJ to CCJ, 13 January 1852, JTU.

40. MJ to CCJ, 16 January 1852, JTU.

41. CCJ to MJ, 26 January 1852, JTU. Cf. CCJ to JoJ, 31 January 1852, JJUG.

42. MJ to CCJ, 16 January 1852, 26 January 1852, 30 January 1852, JTU.

43. See Minutes of the General Assembly, Presbyterian Church in the U.S.A., 1840–1852, PHSM; DeBow, *Statistical View*. For the expansion of Protestantism generally, see Curtis D. Johnson, *Redeeming America: Evangelicals and the Road to Civil War* (Chicago, 1993).

44. MJ to CCJj, 17 February 1852, CJUG.

45. SJMC to Charles Edward Maxwell, 22 March 1852, JTU.

46. MJ to Laura Maxwell, 23 March 1852, JTU; Telegram, Charles Edward Maxwell to CCJ, 30 March 1852, JTU.

47. CCJ to CCJj and JJ, 31 March 1852, CJUG; CCJ to CCJj and JJ, 1 April 1852, 2 April 1852, JTU.

48. CCJ to SJMC, 3 April 1852, JTU; MJ to CCJj and JJ, 26 April 1852, CJUG.

49. Mary Robarts to CCJ and MJ, 27 April 1852, JTU; JoJ to CCJ and MJ, 7 May 1852, JTU.

50. JoJ to MJ, 23 April 1853, 17 October 1853, JTU.

51. Charles West to CCJ, 28 November 1852, JTU.

52. CCJ to J. J. Janeway and Members of the General Assembly's Board of Missions, 2 December 1852, JTU; R. Happersett to CCJ, 14 December 1852, JTU; CCJ to CCJj, 29 December 1852, CJUG; Eliza Mallard to RQM, 19 January 1853, JTU.

53. CCJ, Report to the Board of Domestic Missions, 25 May 1853, JTU. See CCJ to MJ, 1 January 1852, JTU; Henry Foote to CCJ, 26 February 1853, JTU; CCJ to CCJj and JJ, 26 November 1851, CJUG; CCJ to MJ, 5 January 1852, JTU. Thomas Fleming to CCJ, 19 August 1852, JTU; CCJ to SJMC, 13 December 1852, JTU. Note on Retirement, Spring of 1853, JTU. Action of the Board of Missions in Relation to the Health of C. C. Jones, 13 June 1853, JTU.

54. CCJ to MJ, 10 June 1853, JTU.

55. CCJ to MJ, 10 July 1853, 11 July 1853, 13 July 1853, 16 July 1853, 20 July 1853, JTU.

56. CCJ to MJ, 20 July 1853, JTU; MJ to CCJ, 22 July 1853, JTU.
57. *The Papers of Frederick Law Olmsted*, ed. Charles Capen McLaughlin, vol. 2, *Slavery in the South*, ed. Charles E. Beveridge, Charles Capen McLaughlin, and David Schuyler (Baltimore, 1981), 162, 166, 168. Cf. Julia Floyd Smith, *Slavery and Rice Culture in Low Country Georgia* (Knoxville, 1985), 66.
58. CCJ, *Thirteenth Annual Report of the Association for the Religious Instruction of the Negroes, in Liberty County, Georgia* (Savannah, 1848), 14–15; *Olmsted Papers*, 2: 173–177. Cf. marginal notes by CCJ in letter from Isaac Brown to CCJ, 31 July 1854, JTU.
59. See Lori Merish, "Sentimental Consumption: Harriet Beecher Stowe and the Aesthetics of Middle-Class Ownership," *American Literary History* 1, no. 1 (1996): 1–33; Andrew Burstein, *Sentimental Democracy: The Evolution of America's Romantic Self-Image* (New York, 1999).
60. Harriet Beecher Stowe, *A Key to Uncle Tom's Cabin; Presenting the Original Facts and Documents upon which the Story is Founded* (1853; rpt. Port Washington, N.Y., 1968), 67.
61. See, e.g., ibid., 39, 42, 127–129, 199–200, 244–250.
62. Ibid., 42, 244, 127, 244.

23. CARLAWTER III

1. MJ to CCJj, 31 January 1856, CJUG; CCJ to TS, 26 January 1850, JTU.
2. RQM, *Plantation Life Before Emancipation* (Richmond, 1892), 39–40; cf. Robert William Fogel, *Without Consent or Contract: The Rise and Fall of American Slavery* (New York, 1989), 47. For Cato's ownership of two horses, see "Negro Money" in CCJ, "Memoranda Book," JTU. For slave ownership of horses and cattle in Liberty County, see Philip D. Morgan, "The Ownership of Property by Slaves in the Mid-Nineteenth Century Low Country," *Journal of Southern History* 49, no. 3 (August 1983): 399–420; Larry E. Hudson, Jr., "'All That Cash': Work and Status in the Slave Quarters" in *Working Toward Freedom: Slave Society and Domestic Economy in the American South*, ed. Larry E. Hudson, Jr. (Rochester, 1994): 77–94; Thomas F. Armstrong, "From Task Labor to Free Labor: The Transition Along Georgia's Rice Coast, 1820–1880," *Georgia Historical Quarterly* 64 (Winter 1980): 432–437.
3. TS to CCJ, 23 October 1853, 10 November 1851, JTU. Cf. Irwin Rahn to CCJ, 3 November 1851, JTU. Cf. also Philip D. Morgan, *Slave Counterpoint: Black Culture in the Eighteenth-Century Chesapeake and Lowcountry* (Chapel Hill, 1998), 200–201.
4. CCJ to TS, 23 December 1848, 23 August 1849, JTU; James Newton Jones to CCJ, 30 April 1850, JTU; TS to CCJ, 29 April, 1850, JTU.
5. TS to CCJ, 23 December 1850, 4 January 1851, 22 January 1851, 17 March 1851, JTU. Cf. Morgan, *Slave Counterpoint*, 179–187.
6. TS to CCJ, 17 March 1851, JTU.
7. TS to CCJ, 29 November 1850, 16 December 1850, JTU; WM to CCJ, 2 December 1850, JTU; CCJ to TS, 4 December 1850, JTU; EM to MJ, 10 December 1850, JTU.
8. TS to CCJ, 16 December 1850, 29 November 1850, 23 December 1850, JTU; EM to MJ, 10 December 1850, JTU; HHJ to CCJ and MJ, 7 April 1851, JTU.

9. HHJ to CCJ and MJ, 7 April 1851, JTU.

10. For an earlier expression of the controversy between planters and the Riceboro merchants, see CCJ to TS, 23 August 1849, JTU. For the broader conflict between merchants and planters see Morgan, "Ownership of Property"; Morgan, *Slave Counterpoint*, 300–317, 412–420. Cf. also James C. Scott, "Making Social Space for a Dissent Subculture," in *Domination and the Art of Resistance: Hidden Transcripts* (New Haven, 1990), esp. 120–124.

11. CCJ to Cato Jones, 28 January 1851, JTU.

12. For the driver's role and relationship with white masters, see Morgan, *Slave Counterpoint*, 218–225; Peter Kolchin, "Reevaluating the Antebellum Slave Community: A Comparative Perspective," *Journal of American History* 70, no. 3, (1983): 595–596; James M. Clifton, "The Rice Driver: His Role in Slave Management," *South Carolina Historical Magazine* 82 (October 1981): 331–353; William L. Van DeBurg, *The Slave Drivers: Black Agricultural Labor Supervisors in the Antebellum South* (Westport, Conn., 1979).

13. Cato Jones to CCJ, 3 March 1851, 3 September 1852, JTU.

14. Cato's letters to CCJ provide an excellent example of what James C. Scott has called "the public transcript" between dominant elites and subordinates. See Scott, "The Public Transcript as a Respectable Performance," in *Domination and the Art of Resistance*, 45–69, and ibid., 1–16.

15. CCJ, *The Religious Instruction of the Negroes in the United States* (Savannah, 1842), 110. Cf. Scott, *Domination and the Art of Resistance*, 70–107.

16. For the relationships between white mistresses and personal servants, see Catherine Clinton, *The Plantation Mistress: Women's World in the Old South* (New York, 1982); Elizabeth Fox-Genovese, *Within the Plantation Household: Black and White Women of the Old South* (Chapel Hill, 1988), esp. 157–167, 178–186. For owners having a particularly close relationship with slaves with whom they have spent much of their adult lives, see Morgan, *Slave Counterpoint*, 334–335.

17. CCJ to EM, 24 December 1837, JTU; EM to CCJ, 29 March 1838, JTU; Laura Maxwell to MJ, 25 April 1850, JTU; MJ to MSJ, 12 June 1850, JTU; MJ, Journal, 1850, JTU.

18. For Cassius's ownership of a mare and a buggy, see CCJ to CCJj, 18 March 1857, CJUG; CCJ, "Account of Property belonging to Cassius left to be given away and to be sold as he desired by his former Master," note attached to CCJj to CCJ, 20 March 1857, JTU.

19. CCJ to TS, 12 February 1851, JTU. See also MJ to CCJ, 30 May 1851, JTU.

20. TS to CCJ, 29 October 1850, 14 November 1850, JTU.

21. TS to CCJ, 14 November 1850, JTU; Cato Jones to CCJ, 3 March 1851, JTU.

22. CCJ to TS, 8 April 1850, JTU; MJ to CCJ, 30 May 1851, JTU.

23. TS to CCJ, 27 August 1851, JTU.

24. Irwin Rahn to CCJ, 1 September 1851, JTU; TS to CCJ, 13 October 1851, 4 November 1851, JTU.

25. TS to CCJ, 14 July 1851, 6 August 1851, JTU; CCJ to TS, 23 August 1851, JTU.

26. TS to CCJ, 6 September 1851, 22 January 1851, JTU; CCJ to TS, 26 January 1850, 12 February 1851, 6 March 1851, JTU.

27. TS to CCJ, 25 September 1851, 23 October 1851, JTU; CPB, 68–69, JTU.

28. JJ, M.D., "Outline of Investigations into the Nature, Causes and Prevention of Endemic and Epidemic Diseases, and More Especially Malarial Fever, During a Period of Thirty Years," in *Medical and Surgical Memoirs: Containing Investigations on the Geographical Distribution, Causes, Nature, Relations, and Treatment of Various Diseases, 1855–1890* (New Orleans, 1890), 3: n.p.

29. See Fogel, "Fetal and Childhood Malnutrition and Their Affect on Slave Mortality," in *Without Consent or Contract*, 142–147.

30. For the synergistic interaction of diet, worms, malaria, and other diseases, see Kenneth F. Kiple and Virginia Himmelsteib King, *Another Dimension to the Black Diaspora: Diet, Disease, and Racism* (Cambridge, 1981), 113–116.

31. For slave hunting and fishing in the low country, see Ras Michael Brown, "'Walk in the Feenda': West-Central Africans and the Forest in the South Carolina–Georgia Lowcountry," in *Central Africans and Cultural Transformations in the American Diaspora*, ed. Linda M. Heywood (Cambridge, 2002), 305–317.

32. RQM, *Plantation Life Before Emancipation* (Richmond, 1892), 26.

33. TS to CCJ, 27 August 1851, JTU; Laura Maxwell to MJ, 13 August 1853, JTU; Laura Maxwell Buttolph to MJ, 5 September 1859, JTU; RQM, *Plantation Life Before Emancipation*, 27. Cf. Thomas S. Baker to RQM, 5 May 1849, JTU.

34. TS to CCJ, 23 December 1850, JTU; CCJ to MSJ, 26 November 1850, JTU; MJ to CCJ, 13 January 1852, JTU; CCJ to MSJM, 6 December 1862, JTU. For slave ownership of guns in the low country, see Robert Ascher and Charles H. Fairbanks, "Excavation of a Slave Cabin: Georgia, U.S.A.," *Historical Archaeology* 5 (1971): 3–17.

35. For slave utilization of wild foods in the low country, see Josephine A. Beoku-Betts, "'She Make Funny Flat Cake She Call Saraka': Gullah Women and Food Practices under Slavery" in Hudson, *Working Toward Freedom*, 211–231; Kiple and King, *Another Dimension to the Black Diaspora*, 79–95; Elizabeth J. Reitz, Tyson Gibbs, and Ted A. Rathbun, "Archaeological Evidence for Subsistence on Coastal Plantations," in *The Archaeology of Slavery and Plantation Life*, ed. Teresa A. Singleton (Orlando, 1985), 163–187; Morgan, *Slave Counterpoint*, 134–143.

36. MJ to CCJ, 30 May 1851, JTU. This Titus had come to Carlawter in 1847 from the Retreat. He had been among the slaves Mary had inherited from her mother, but he had been kept at the Retreat until after Joseph Jones's death. MJ to CCJ, 30 May 1851, JTU; Charles Edward Maxwell to MJ, 25 May 1851, JTU.

37. For the continuing claims of "culturalists" that "clay eating was essentially a cultural trait or habit passed along from generation to generation," see Kiple and King, *Another Dimension to the Black Diaspora*, 119–122.

38. See Roswell King, Jr., "Letter to the Editor," *Southern Agriculturalist* 1 (December 1828): 525–527. John LeConte, "Observations on Geophagy," *Southern Medical and Surgical Journal* 1 (1845): 427–444. MJ to CCJ, 30 May 1851, JTU; Charles Edward Maxwell to MJ, 25 May 1851, JTU. For a discussion of pica or geophagy, see Kiple and King, *Another Dimension to the Black Diaspora*, 113, 119–123.

39. CCJ to TS, 8 April 1851, JTU. For the corn and rice patches of those who lived in the settlements, see EM to CCJ and MJ, 19 April 1850, JTU; Irwin Rahn to CCJ, 3 Novem-

ber 1851, JTU; CCJ to MJ, 17 June 1851, JTU; Andrew [Lawton] to CCJ, 9 October 1852, JTU.

40. Cato Jones to CCJ, 3 September 1852, JTU; TS to CCJ, 27 September 1852, JTU.

41. Phoebe and Cassius Jones to Mr. Delion [Frederick Ransom Lyons], 17 March 1857, JTU. See "Statistics of Montevideo—drawn up by JJ," in CPB, n.p. See also Fogel, "The Population Question," in *Without Consent or Contract*, 114–153; Morgan, *Slave Counterpoint*, 92–101. Cf. William Dusinberre, *Them Dark Days: Slavery in the American Rice Swamps* (New York, 1996), 235–247, for the dismal record of infant mortality on other low-country plantations.

24. ARCADIA II

1. Irwin Rahn to CCJ, 3 November 1851, JTU. See also plat of Arcadia drawn by W. Hughes, 25 August 1856, CJUG.

2. See Schedule of Tax Returns for 1847–1854 for Arcadia, Maybank, and Montevideo, CPB, 59–84.

3. CCJ to MJ, 13 January 1852, JTU.

4. Will of John Bohum Girardeau, 11 November 1800, Will Record 1790–1823, PCLC; Will of Andrew Maybank, 13 January 1834, Will Record, 1824–1850, PCLC; MPB, 10.

5. CPB, 76.

6. Ibid., 63–78.

7. Ibid., 18–84.

8. Ibid., 68–69; CCJ, "Return of Members" 1846, JTU.

9. See Irwin Rahn to CCJ, 15 July 1851, 11 August 1851, 1 September 1851, 23 September 1851; CCJ to MJ, 13 January 1852, JTU. "Minutes of the Session, Midway Congregational Church," 14 February 1852, PHSM; CPB, 69.

10. MPB, 4, JTU; CCJj to CCJ and MJ, 11 September 1858, JTU; Will of Audley Maxwell, 27 March 1834, Will Record 1824–1850, PCLC; Abream Scriven to Dinah Jones, 19 September 1858, JTU.

11. TS to CCJ, 19 July 1852, JTU.

12. For black-white sexual relations and abuse of black women by whites, see Eugene D. Genovese, *Roll, Jordan, Roll: The World the Slaves Made* (New York, 1974), 413–431; John W. Blassingame, *The Slave Community: Plantation Life in the Ante-Bellum South* (New York, 1972), 81–85; Elizabeth Fox-Genovese, *Within the Plantation Household: Black and White Women of the Old South* (Chapel Hill, 1988), 325–326, 379–380; Robert William Fogel, *Without Consent or Contract: The Rise and Fall of American Slavery* (New York, 1989), 181–182.

13. Rebecca Mallard to RQM, 30 January 1850, JTU.

14. Robert Manson Myers, ed. *The Children of Pride: A True Story of Georgia and the Civil War* (New Haven, 1972), 1713–1714; Rebecca Mallard to RQM, 5 March 1850, JTU.

15. CCJ to MJ, 19 April 1830, JTU; James C. Scott, *Weapons of the Weak: Everyday Forms of Peasant Resistance* (New Haven, 1985), 17–44, and esp. 142–143.

16. Cf. Philip D. Morgan, *Slave Counterpoint: Black Culture in the Eighteenth-Century*

Chesapeake and Lowcountry (Chapel Hill, 1998), xxii; and see Margaret Washington Creel, *"A Peculiar People": Slave Religion and Community-Culture Among the Gullahs* (New York, 1988), 239–240.

17. For the larger picture of the movement of slaves westward from the old seaboard, see Fogel, *Without Consent or Contract*, 65–72; Ira Berlin, *Generations of Captivity: A History of African-American Slaves* (Cambridge, Mass., 2003). Berlin describes the movement of nearly one million slaves from the seaboard to the interior of the South as a "Second Middle Passage." For Liberty County, see CCJ, Journal, 20 January 1859, JTU, for recitation of those having moved or moving out of the county by the end of the decade.

18. See F. N. Boney, "The Emerging Empire State," in *A History of Georgia*, ed. Kenneth Coleman (Athens, 1977), 157–162; Buddy Sullivan, *Early Days on the Georgia Tidewater: The Story of McIntosh County and Sapelo* (Daren, Ga., 2001), 258–259. See also, e.g., MSJM to Mary Jones Taylor, 14 December 1857, JTU.

19. Eliza Robarts to CCJ, 22 January 1859, JTU; CCJ, Journal, 21 December 1859, 6 January 1860, JTU; Plenty Varnadoe to CCJ, 19 August 1859, JTU.

20. See "Minutes of the Session, Midway Congregational Church,"1850–1854, PHSM, for the number of persons, black and white, joining Midway. See esp. 19 November 1853, 17 February 1854. CCJ to Irwin Rahn, 12 February 1851, JTU.

21. CCJ to MJ, 21 June 1851, JTU; "Minutes of the Session, Midway Congregational Church," 15 May 1852, 14 February 1852, PHSM; MJ to CCJj and JJ, 10 June 1852, CJUG.

22. "Minutes of the Session, Midway Congregational Church," 15 May 1852, PHSM; RQM, *Plantation Life Before Emancipation* (Richmond, 1892).

23. Rebecca Mallard to RQM, 8 December 1852, JTU. On runaways generally, see John Hope Franklin and Loren Schweninger, *Runaway Slaves: Rebels on the Plantation* (New York, 1999); Blassingame, *Slave Community*, 104–131. One important source for evaluating runaways in Liberty County over an extended period of time is "Minutes of the Session, Midway Congregational Church," passim, PHSM. Slaves members were disciplined—suspended or excommunicated—for running away.

24. MJ to CCJj, 12 March 1852, CJUG; CCJ to CCJj, 21 February 1854, CJUG.

25. TS to CCJ, 28 June 1852, JTU; Irwin Rahn to CCJ, 2 July 1852, 10 August 1852, JTU; John Stevens, 15 July 1852, JTU. See also, for details of the murder, *Savannah Georgian*, 21 July 1852; Sullivan, *Early Days on the Georgia Tidewater*, 238, 808, 813.

26. For black-on-black violence, see Charles C. Jones, *The Religious Instruction of the Negroes in the United States* (Savannah, 1842), 136; Morgan, *Slave Counterpoint*, 471–476. The "Minutes of the Session, Midway Congregational Church," passim, PHSM, contains numerous accounts of slaves disciplined for fighting, for disputes with other slaves, and for quarreling.

27. CCJ, Journal, 21 April 1858, JTU; CCJ to CCJj, 18 March 1854, CJUG.

28. TS to CCJ, 10 June 1852, JTU.

29. CCJ to TS, 14 June 1852, JTU. Later generations of southern whites would call upon a southern way of life to protect a valued black worker. In a novel by Walker Percy, the Louisiana planter Lancelot pleads to the Klansman J. B. Jenkins, "Yeah, but he's *my*

nigger, J.B. He's been working for us for forty years and you know that." *Lancelot* (New York, 1977), 99.

30. See CCJ to TS, 24 March 1849, 16 December 1850, JTU.
31. Elijah Chapman to CCJ, 17 November 1855, JTU.

25. MAYBANK II

1. SJMC to MJ, 16 September 1851, JTU.
2. Cf. CCJ to MJ, 26 January 1852, JTU.
3. Inventory, 25 October 1853, JTU; Packing lists, October 21–24, 1853, JTU.
4. See notes attached to "Directions" for unpacking of piano, 9 November 1853, JTU; CCJ to Capt. Grovenstine, 9 November 1853, JTU.
5. CCJ to Sandy Maybank, 15 August 1853, JTU.
6. See, e.g., CCJ to MJ, 5 November 1838, JTU; Jane LeConte Harden to MJ, [?] May 1848, JTU; Rebecca Eliza Mallard to RQM, 28 March 1848, JTU; CCJ to TS, 20 July 1849, 11 January 1851, JTU; Laura Maxwell to MJ, 25 April 1850, 1 May 1851, JTU.
7. See CCJ to WM, 2 February 1849, JTU; CCJ to MJ, 21 June 1851, JTU.
8. CCJ to CCJj, 22 May 1854, CJUG.
9. Cf., for the role of the ordinary in the imagination, Charles Taylor, *Sources of the Self: The Making of the Modern Identity* (Cambridge, Mass., 1989), 211–233.
10. John Colcock to CCJ, 25 December 1852, JTU; Audley King to CCJ, 17 October 1853, JTU; CCJ to MSJ, 12 November 1852, JTU. Cf. Philip D. Morgan, *Slave Counterpoint: Black Culture in the Eighteenth-Century Chesapeake and Lowcountry* (Chapel Hill, 1998), 334–336.
11. CCJ to CCJj, 20 April 1854, CJUG.
12. CCJ to CCJj, 7 August 1854, CJUG; Roswell King to CCJ, 8 October 1851, JTU; MJ to CCJj, 7 August 1854, CJUG; CCJ to CCJj, 6 September 1854, CJUG. King's *"Touch of the Times"* is apparently a reference to Laura's menstrual period.
13. CCJ to CCJj, 11 September 1854, CJUG; MJ to CCJj, 14 September 1854, CJUG.
14. MJ to CCJj, 14 September 1854, CJUG; CCJ to CCJj, 11 September 1854, CJUG. See also, CCJ, Journal, 2 June 1860, JTU.
15. For a history of yellow fever epidemics in the nineteenth-century South, see Margaret Humphreys, *Yellow Fever and the South* (Baltimore, 1999), 5, 45–76. See also Joseph Ioor Waring, *A History of Medicine in South Carolina*, 2 vols. (Columbia, S.C., 1964–1967), 1: 48–61, 147–149. MJ to CCJj, 14 September 1854, CJUG; Sarah Howe to CCJ, 31 October 1854, JTU.
16. Robert Manson Myers, ed. *The Children of Pride: A True Story of Georgia and the Civil War* (New Haven, 1972), 1544.
17. For a contemporary description of the symptoms of yellow fever, see J. Hume Simons, M.D., *Planter's Guide, Family Book of Medicine: For the Instruction and Use of Planters, Families, Country People, and All Others Who May Be Out of the Reach of Physicians, or Unable to Employ Them* (Charleston, S.C., 1848), 82–84. CCJ to CCJj, 9 October 1854, CJUG.
18. CCJ to CCJj, 9 October 1854, CJUG.

19. See Frank T. Schnell, Jr., Introduction to Charles C. Jones, Jr., *Antiquities of the Southern Indians, Particularly of the Georgia Tribes* (1873; rpt. Tuscaloosa, 1999), xviii–xix. James O. Breeden, *Joseph Jones, M.D., Scientist of the Old South* (Louisville, Ky., 1975), 36.

20. EM to MJ, 29 July 1853, JTU; Rebecca Eliza Mallard to RQM, 1 December 1854, JTU.

21. MJ to Laura Maxwell, 19 May 1856, JTU.

22. MJ to CCJ, 7 May 1851, JTU; MJ to CCJj, 6 March 1856, 25 June 1856, CJUG; SJMC to MJ, 5 April 1856, JTU.

23. CCJ, "Mrs. Elizabeth Jones Maxwell," 24 July 1856, CJUG.

24. Betsy Maxwell's death and funeral stand in contrast to the Victorian funeral and the sentimental gravestones described by David E. Stannard in *The Puritan Way of Death: A Study in Religion, Culture, and Social Change* (New York, 1977), esp. 167–196.

26. SLAVE MARKET

1. Benjamin Allen to CCJ, 19 September 1853, JTU. I have not been able to identify John's wife.

2. MJ to CCJ, 26 December 1853, CJUG. For the health of slaves, see Julia Floyd Smith, *Slavery and Rice Culture in Low Country Georgia, 1750–1860* (Knoxville, 1985), 113–140; Ted A. Rathbun, "Health and Disease at a South Carolina Plantation: 1840–1870," *American Journal of Physical Anthropology* 74 (1987): 239–253; Joseph I. Waring, "Colonial Medicine in Georgia and South Carolina," *Georgia Historical Quarterly* 59 (1975): 141–159.

3. CCJ to CCJj, 2 February 1854, CJUG. See also MJ to CCJ, 5 February 1854, JTU.

4. CCJ to CCJj, 21 February 1854, CJUG.

5. Ibid. For a comparison to other slave funerals in the low country, see Margaret Washington Creel, *"A Peculiar People": Slave Religion and Community-Culture Among the Gullahs* (New York, 1988), 201–202, 313–317; William Dusinberre, *Them Dark Days: Slavery in the American Rice Swamps* (New York, 1996), 227, 277–278.

6. MJ to CCJj, 31 January 1856, CJUG. See also CCJ to CCJj, 17 January 1856, CJUG.

7. See John Hope Franklin and Loren Schweninger, *Runaway Slaves: Rebels on the Plantation* (New York, 1999), 125–148. Franklin and Schweninger present Jane as having run away before. I find no evidence of that and believe that they have misread CCJj to CCJ, 1 October 1856, JTU, as printed in *The Children of Pride: A True Story of Georgia and the Civil War*, ed. Robert Manson Myers (New Haven, 1972), 240–243.

8. CCJ to CCJj, 2 October 1856, CJUG. See, for the role of sailors and watermen in helping slaves to escape, David S. Cecelski, *The Waterman's Son: Slavery and Freedom in Maritime North Carolina* (Chapel Hill, 2001), esp. 121–151. CCJj to CCJ, 1 October 1856, CJUG.

9. CCJj to CCJ, 1 October 1856, CJUG.

10. CCJ to MJ, 23 October 1856, JTU.

11. CCJj to CCJ, 1 October 1856, CJUG.

12. Ibid.

13. CCJ to CCJj, 2 October 1856, CJUG.

14. There is confusion about the identity of Big Titus in "The Index: The Slaves," in Myers, *Children of Pride*, 1845. See TITUS (1826–1865+) in List of Principal Characters: African Americans. The Myers index apparently collapses "Big Titus" and "Little Titus" into one. See CPB, 15, MPB, 10.

15. CCJj to CCJ, 4 October 1856, CJUG.

16. CCJ to MJ, 23 October 1856, JTU.

17. Notes from "Memoranda, October, 1852, Bank Account, etc," 6 March 1855, JTU. The mortgage, with the State Bank of Georgia, was for $1,500.

18. MJ to CCJj, 9 October 1856, CJUG.

19. MJ to John Jones, 30 July 1847, JJUG; CCJ to John Jones, 2 March 1848, JJUG; CCJ to CCJj, 20 April 1854, CJUG; S. S. Barnard to CCJ, 17 September 1857, JTU.

20. CCJ to CCJj, 1 November 1856, CJUG.

21. Ibid. Cf. Phoebia and Cash to Mr. Delions [Frederick Ransom Lyons], 17 March 1857, JTU.

22. "Account of Property belonging to Cassius left to be given away and to be sold as he desired by his former Master," note written by CCJ and attached to CCJj to CCJ, 20 March 1857, JTU. A piggin was a type of bucket.

23. CCJ to CCJj, 17 November 1856, 2 October 1856, CJUG.

24. CCJ to CCJj, 1 November 1856, CJUG.

25. MJ to CCJj, 20 November 1856, CJUG; CCJ to CCJj, 29 November 1856, CJUG; CCJ to MJ, 10 December 1856, JTU. For the rise in slave prices during the antebellum period, see William Fogel, *Without Consent or Contract: The Rise and Fall of American Slavery* (New York, 1989), 64.

26. MJ to CCJ, 10 December 1856, JTU; "Memoranda, October, 1852, Bank Account, etc," 11 December 1856, 15 December, 1856, JTU; "Settled with Sandy and Porter for their Saturdays from March 10, 1855 to Jan. 10 1857." See "Bill," in CCJ, Almanac, 1857, 30 January 1857, JTU. MJ to MSJ, 22 December 1856, JTU.

27. CCJ to MJ, 18 May 1830, JTU.

28. See CCJ, "Slavery," in *Southern Presbyterian Review* 9 (January 1856): 345–364; and cf. CCJ, *Religious Instruction of the Negroes. An Address Delivered before the General Assembly of the Presbyterian Church, at Augusta, Ga., December 10, 1861* (Richmond, n.d.).

29. Harriet Beecher Stowe, *A Key to Uncle Tom's Cabin; Presenting the Original Facts and Documents upon which the Story is Founded* (1853; rpt. Port Washington, N.Y., 1968), 127.

30. CCJ to CCJj, 18 March 1857, and note attached, CJUG.

31. CCJ to CCJj, 26 March 1857, CJUG. I have been unable to locate the correspondence with Palmer.

32. See HHJ to CCJ and MJ, 7 April 1851, JTU, for a report of Lyons's selling whiskey to slaves.

33. Phoebia and Cash to Mr. Delions [Frederick Ransom Lyons], 17 March 1857, JTU.

34. Other slaves addressed in the letter were "Aunt Affee," the widow of Pulaski at the Retreat; Sina, the sister of Cassius; Judith at Carlawter, who was married to Pulaski Jr. at the Retreat, and their two sons Milton and Little Pulaski; Charles, the oxcart driver,

husband of Lucy; Phillis and her husband, Niger; and Becky and Miley, the daughters of Patience and Porter.

35. Cf. Genesis 50:20.

36. For the New Orleans slave market and the concern to feed slaves well before their sale, see Walter Johnson, *Soul by Soul: Life Inside the Antebellum Slave Market* (Cambridge, Mass., 1999), 119.

37. CCJ to CCJj, 26 March 1857, CJUG.

27. PATIENCE'S KITCHEN

1. CCJ to Betsy Maxwell, 17 April 1850, JTU; CPB 68; MJ to EM, 30 August 1849, JTU.

2. Cf. Audre Lorde, "Eye to Eye: Black Women, Hatred, and Anger," in *Sister Outsider: Essays and Speeches* (New York, 1984), 145–175, esp. 167.

3. Cf. James C. Scott, *Domination and the Art of Resistance: Hidden Transcripts* (New Haven, 1990), 17–44, esp. 35.

4. MJ to Laura Maxwell, 17 August 1848, JTU. Cf. Deborah Gray White, *Ar'n't I a Woman? Female Slaves in the Plantation South* (New York, 1985), 27–51; Elizabeth Fox-Genovese, *Within the Plantation Household: Black and White Women of the Old South* (Chapel Hill, 1988), 291–292; Scott, *Domination and the Art of Resistance*, 17–44. For the Mammy figure, see Patricia Hill Collins, "Mammies, Matriarchs, and Other Controlling Images," in *Black Feminist Thought: Knowledge, Consciousness, and the Politics of Empowerment* (New York, 1991), 67–90.

5. RQM, *Plantation Life Before Emancipation* (Richmond, 1892), 18; RQM, *Montevideo-Maybank: Some Memoirs of a Southern Christian Household in the Olden Time; or, The Family Life of the Rev. Charles Colcock Jones, D.D., of Liberty County, Ga.* (Richmond, 1898), 37. For the character of the plantation kitchen with its equipage, see John Michael Vlack, *Back of the Big House: The Architecture of Plantation Slavery* (Chapel Hill, 1993), 43–47. See, for the tradition of African cuisine, Josephine A. Beoku-Betts, "'She Make Funny Flat Cake She Call Saraka': Gullah Women and Food Practices Under Slavery," in *Working Toward Freedom: Slave Society and Domestic Economy in the American South*, ed. Larry E. Hudson (Rochester, 1994), 211–231. Beoku-Betts emphasizes the ways Gullah women resisted, through their culinary practices, the white social order.

6. For vegetables, see CCJ, Almanac, 1857, JTU. For strawberries at Montevideo and Maybank, see, e.g., Rebecca Eliza Mallard to RQM, 28 March 1848, JTU; CCJ to MJ, 24 April 1860, JTU. For the fame of the Maybank melons, see CCJ to EM, 5 July 1849, JTU; Laura Maxwell to MJ, 6 August 1851, 13 August 1853, JTU. For pickling melons, see MJ to EM, 30 August 1849, JTU.

7. For smokehouses, see John Michael Vlack, *Back of the Big House: The Architecture of Plantation Slavery* (Chapel Hill, 1993), 63–76. For hog killing, see Rahn to CCJ, 21 February 1851, JTU; RQM, *Plantation Life Before Emancipation*, 22. For the "large sausage stuffer," see CCJ and MJ to MSJ, 12 December 1853, JTU.

8. For syrup making, see Irwin Rahn to CCJ, 4 January 1851, JTU; MJ to CCJj, 7 December 1854, CJUG; and cf. William A. Noble, "Antebellum Hopeton and Current Altama

Plantations in Georgia: A Study in Contrasts," in *One World, One Institution: The Plantation: Proceedings of the Second World Plantation Conference*, ed. Sue Eakin and John Tarver (Baton Rouge, 1989), 71–85.

9. See, e.g., MJ to MSJM, 22 May 1857, JTU; MJ to CCJj, 16 July 1860, CJUG.

10. Quotations from Karen Hess, *The Carolina Rice Kitchen: The African Connection* (Columbia, S.C., 1992), 17, 26. For the difference between the Chinese and Indian ways of preparing rice, see ibid., 25–35. For the African connection to the low-country rice kitchen, see also Daniel C. Littlefield, *Rice and Slaves: Ethnicity and the Slave Trade in Colonial South Carolina* (Baton Rouge, 1981), 80–88; Judith A. Carney, *Black Rice: The African Origins of Rice Cultivation in the Americas* (Cambridge, Mass., 2001), 112–115.

11. For pilaus, see Hess, *Carolina Rice Kitchen*, 36–83. Examples of recipes used for pilau at Montevideo and Maybank can be found in a collection of recipes in JTU (hereafter given as "Recipes," JTU). These recipes, and many others in the collection, were written down by Mary Jones. Patience as the cook, however, made most use of the recipes. A number were apparently the result of Patience's own experimenting in the kitchen.

12. "Rice Cake," "Rice Bread," in "Recipes," JTU.

13. "Sea Foam Cake," "Plain Pound Cake," "Pound Cake," and "Fruit Cake," ibid. See also, e.g., Laura Maxwell to MJ, 29 December 1847, JTU.

14. "Cora's Light Rolls," in "Recipes," JTU.

15. "Oyster Soup," ibid. For fish, see MJ to CCJj, 21 August 1854, CJUG; CCJ to CCJj, 30 July 1858, CJUG; CCJ to MSJM, 20 August 1858, JTU. For crabs, see MJ to CCJj, 11 May 1854, CJUG.

16. From a facsimile of Mrs. Samuel G. Stoney, *Carolina Rice Cook Book* (Charleston, S.C., 1901), 4, in Hess, *Carolina Rice Kitchen*. For game, see Julia King to MJ, 20 August 1855, JTU; MJ to CCJj, 7 December 1854, CJUG; CCJ to MSJ, 26 November 1850, JTU; CCJ to CCJj, 29 December 1852, CJUG; MJ to CCJ, 13 January 1852, JTU.

17. MJ to CCJj and Ruth Jones, 20 September 1860, CJUG; CCJ to MSJ, 12 November 1852, JTU; CCJ to MJ, 20 October 1856, JTU; MJ to CCJj, 11 May 1854, CJUG; MJ to CCJ, 13 January 1852, JTU; Frederick Law Olmsted, *A Journey in the Seaboard Slaves States: In the Years 1853–1854, With Remarks on Their Economy* (New York, 1904), 2: 34. Cf. Hess, *Carolina Rice Kitchen*, 5.

18. Cf. B. W. Higman, *Montpelier, Jamaica: A Plantation Community in Slavery and Freedom, 1739–1912* (Kingston, Jamaica, 1998), 206–210.

19. See CCJ to TS, 22 November 1848, 26 June 1849, JTU; CCJ to WM, 23 December 1848, JTU; TS to CCJ, 29 April 1850, JTU; EM to CCJ and MJ, 19 April 1850, JTU; Irwin Rahn to CCJ, 3 November 1851, JTU; CCJ to CCJj, 6 September 1854, CJUG; S. S. Barnwell to CCJ, 5 November 1856, JTU; RQM, *Plantation Life Before Emancipation*, 31–32. For archaeological evidence of slave use of wild foods in the Georgia low country, see Elizabeth J. Reitz, Tyson Giggs, and Ted A. Rathbun, "Archaeological Evidence for Subsistence on Coastal Plantations," in *The Archaeology of Slavery and Plantation Life*, ed. Teresa A. Singleton (Orlando, 1985), 163–187.

20. "Account of Property belonging to Cassius," note written by CCJ and attached to CCJj to CCJ, 20 March 1857, JTU; RQM, *Plantation Life Before Emancipation*, 30.

21. MJ to SJMC, 2 December 1852, JTU. For slave food generally in the low country, see Patricia Samford, "The Archaeology of African-American Slavery and Material Culture," *William and Mary Quarterly*, 3rd ser., 53, no. 1 (January 1996): 95–97; Leland Ferguson, *Uncommon Ground: Archaeology and Early African America, 1650–1800* (Washington, D.C., 1992), 93–99; Beoku-Betts, "'She Make Funny Flat Cake'"; Philip D. Morgan, *Slave Counterpoint: Black Culture in the Eighteenth-Century Chesapeake and Lowcountry* (Chapel Hill, 1998), 134–143. For a general assessment of slave diets, see Robert William Fogel, *Without Consent or Contract: The Rise and Fall of American Slavery* (New York, 1989), 132–142.

22. For hoppin' john, see Hess, *Carolina Rice Kitchen*, 93–110; and Morgan, *Slave Counterpoint*, 141.

23. Cf. MJ to CCJj, 26 September 1859, CJUG.

24. See Hess, *Carolina Rice Kitchen*, 111–113, for the widespread use of okra in the African diaspora. For the use of okra soup in the settlements, see Roswell King, Jr., "Letter to the Editor," *Southern Agriculturalist* 1 (December 1828): 525–527.

25. See CCJ, "Stock on the three Plantations," Almanac, June 1855, JTU. Cf. CCJ, Almanac, November 1857, JTU. For the purchase of pork for the settlements, see Benjamin Allen to CCJ, 11 April 1853, JTU; Irwin Rahn to CCJ, 19 May 1853, JTU; Montgomery Cumming to CCJ, 22 April 1854, JTU. For the use of beef in slave diets in the low country, see Fogel, *Without Consent or Contract* 136–137. CCJ to TS, 26 June 1849, JTU. For the killing of cattle for the people in the settlements, see CCJ to TS, 22 November 1848, 23 August 1849, JTU; Andrew [Lawson] to CCJ, 10 September 1852, JTU; CCJ to MJ, 25 November 1859, JTU. For Cato's cattle, see CCJ, Almanac, November 1857, JTU.

26. Fogel, *Without Consent or Contract*, 137–147; MJ to CCJ, 5 January 1852, JTU; CCJ to MJ, 24 April 1860, JTU; Eliza Clay to MJ, 30 April 1860, JTU.

27. Cf. Scott, *Domination and the Art of Resistance*, 33.

28. CPB, 67–69, 72, 78.

28. MONTEVIDEO

1. Charles and Mary Jones moved into the old section of Montevideo in January 1856, following a short stay at Arcadia. See MJ to CCJj, 18 December 1855, CJUG; CCJ to MSJ, 10 January 1856, JTU.

2. See CCJ to Wm. Patterson, 29 August 1856, JTU for details of the renovated Montevideo plantation house.

3. See Robert Manson Myers, ed., *The Children of Pride: A True Story of Georgia and the Civil War* (New Haven, 1972), 18, for this undated note by MJ found in JTU.

4. Cf. for the layout of plantations and varying perspectives, John Michael Vlach, *Back of the Big House: The Architecture of Plantation Slavery* (Chapel Hill, 1993).

5. See, e.g., Eliza Robarts to MJ, 10 November 1856, JTU; CCJ, Almanac 1857, 8 March 1857, JTU; CCJ to MJ, 20 October 1856, JTU; CCJ to MSJM, 7 December 1857, JTU.

6. CCJ, Almanac 1858, 15 July 1858, JTU; MJ to CCJj, 11 May 1854, JTU; Myers, *Children of Pride*, 1691.

7. MSJ to MJ and CCJ, 18 November 1852, JTU; Luther James to CCJ, 2 July 1853, JTU.

8. MSJ to JJ, 21 December 1853, JTU; Myers, *Children of Pride*, 1478.

9. See Rebecca Mallard to RQM, 12 April 1849, 23 May 1849, JTU.

10. Ethel Davis Hack Martin, Jane Hack Allen, Lillian Norman Boroughs, "Walthourville," in *Liberty County, Georgia: A Pictorial History*, compiled by Virginia Fraser Evans (Statesville, N.C., 1979), 53–78.

11. CCJ to MSJ, 22 October 1855, JTU; MJ to MSJ, 10 March 1855, 3 October 1855, JTU; RQM, *Plantation Life Before Emancipation* (Richmond, 1892), 20–28.

12. MSJ to Mary Jones Taylor, 5 November 1856, JTU; T. S. Baker to RQM, 25 August 1846, JTU; MJ to CCJ, 26 May 1852, JTU; "Minutes of the Session, Midway Congregational Church," May 1852, PHSM.

13. RQM to MSJM, 13 July 1869, 4 September 1856, JTU. A number of the love letters between RQM and MSJ are in Myers, *Children of Pride*; see, e.g., 231–235, 251–253, 258–260, 271–272, 280–281, 283–286.

14. MJ to CCJj, 2 April 1857, CJUG; Sarah Howe to MJ, 10 April 1857, JTU; John H. Cocke to CCJ, 14 April 1857, JTU.

15. CCJ, Almanac 1857, 15 January 1857, 8 March 1857, JTU; CCJj to CCJ, 14 March 1857, JTU; CCJ to CCJj, 2 October 1856, CJUG.

16. Isabel King to MJ, 15 April 1857, JTU.

17. CCJ, Almanac 1857, 4 April 1857, 22 April 1857, JTU; RQM to MSJM, 13 July 1869, JTU; MJ to SJMC, 9 April 1857, JTU.

18. CCJ to CCJj, 27 April 1857, CJUG; CCJ, Almanac 1857, 27 April 1857, JTU.

19. See Indenture Between MSJ and RQM, County Record O, 316, 1857, SCLC.

20. Ibid.

21. "Tax Returns for C. C. Jones, Jun., Joseph Jones, and M. S. Jones for 1857," 1 April 1857, JTU.

22. For the character of Charles Berrien Jones and his relationship with CCJ and MJ, see MJ to CCJ, 5 January 1852, JTU; EM to CCJ, 8 March 1852, JTU; C. B. Jones to CCJ, 11 July 1852, JTU; CCJ to CCJj, JJ, and MSJ, 10 January 1853, CJUG; MJ to CCJj, 29 March 1854, CJUG; C. B. Jones to MJ, 24 July 1856, JTU; MSJM to MJ, 18 March 1865, JTU.

23. HHJ to JoJ, 6 February 1860, JJUG; MJ to EM, 24 September 1846, JTU; HHJ to CCJ, 4 May 1857, JTU.

24. MJ to MSJM, 22 May 1857. See also *Minutes of the General Assembly of the Presbyterian Church in the United States of America with an Appendix* (Philadelphia, 1857).

25. MJ to MSJM, 10 July 1857, 1 August 1857, JTU.

26. JoJ to CCJ and MJ, 1 June 1857, JTU; Myers, *Children of Pride*, 1573; Joseph Lumpkin to CCJ, 26 April 1858, JTU.

27. Myers, *Children of Pride*, 1568.

28. JoJ to CCJ, 4 May 1858, JTU; MJ to JJ, 13 May 1858, JTU. I have concluded by reviewing the ages of the children at Montevideo that Porter and Patience's Robin was the child nursed by Mary Sharpe Mallard. See CPB, 73.

29. MJ to CCJj, 19 June 1858, CJUG.

30. See, e.g., MJ, Journal, 21 October 1860, JTU.

29. THE RETREAT III

1. CCJ to MSJ, 29 December 1856, JTU; Last Will and Testament of Joseph Jones, Will Record, 1824–1850, PCLC; "White Oak Plantation (S. M. Cumming) in Account Current with CCJ," MPB, 49; Eliza Robarts to SJMC, 5 November 1857, JTU.

2. "Facts Respecting the Case of Infanticide on Montevideo Plantation," enclosure in letter CCJ to CCJj, 10 November 1859, CJUG. See also Dr. Thomas Middleton Stuart to CCJ, November 1859, JTU.

3. CCJ, *The Religious Instruction of the Negroes in the United States* (Savannah, 1842), 135; CCJ, Almanac 1859, 3 November 1859, JTU.

4. CCJj to CCJ, 11 November 1859, 23 November 1859, CJUG; MJ to CCJ, 25 November 1859, JTU.

5. CCJ to CCJj, 10 December 1859, CJUG.

6. For the record of Lucy's whipping, see the notes by CCJ on the back of "Facts Respecting the Case of Infanticide on Montevideo Plantation," enclosure in letter CCJ to CCJj, 10 November 1859, CJUG. For an earlier and particularly brutal whipping ordered by the court in Liberty County, see Ralph Betts Flanders, *Plantation Slavery in Georgia* (Chapel Hill, 1935), 262. For the use of the whip on plantations, see Laura to CCJ, June, 1852, JTU; and cf. William Dusinberre, *Them Dark Days: Slavery in the American Rice Swamps* (New York, 1996), 126–128, 254–260; Philip D. Morgan, *Slave Counterpoint: Black Culture in the Eighteenth-Century Chesapeake and Lowcountry* (Chapel Hill, 1998), 266–267.

7. CCJj to CCJ, 12 December 1859, CJUG. Cf. Martha Hodes, *White Women, Black Men: Illicit Sex in the Nineteenth–Century South* (New Haven, 1997), 52, 82, 137, 150.

8. CCJ, Almanac 1859, 19 December 1859, 21 December 1859, JTU; and see MJ to CCJj, 20 September 1863, 15 December 1859, CJUG.

9. MJ to MSJM, 9 December 1858, JTU; HHJ to MJ, 25 March 1863, JTU; Abby Jones to MJ, 8 January 1859, JTU; CCJ, Almanac 1859, 3 January 1859, JTU.

10. JoJ to MJ, 16 January 1859, JTU; John Jones to MJ, 16 July 1859, JTU; CCJ, Almanac, 6 January 1860, JTU.

11. See Ira Berlin, *Generations of Captivity: A History of African-American Slaves* (Cambridge, Mass., 2003), 161–244, for the massive movement of slaves out of the old seaboard to the west.

12. Eliza Robarts to CCJ, 22 January 1859, JTU.

13. HHJ to MJ, 4 November 1854, JTU. See gravestones of children of Henry Hart Jones and Abigail Jones in Midway cemetery.

14. CCJ, Almanac, 23 March 1859, JTU; HHJ to JoJ, 25 April 1859, JJUG.

15. HHJ to JoJ, 6 February 1860, JJUG.

16. Ibid. See also HHJ to Thomas King, 13 April 1860, JJUG, in which HHJ refers to the written confessions of the children; CCJ to MJ, 24 April 1860, JTU.

17. Last Will and Testament of Nathaniel Varnedoe, Will Record, 1850–1863, PCLC, 232–233; CCJ to CCJj, 24 April 1856, CJUG. See "Negro Money" in CCJ, "Memoranda Book," JTU.

18. Plenty Varnedoe to CCJ, 19 August 1859, JTU; JoJ to MJ, 16 January 1859, JTU.

19. Ben Lowe to Beck [Jones], 21 October 1860, 23 July 1860, JTU; J. A. Anderson to CCJ, 26 December 1860, JTU.

20. CCJ to CCJj, 3 October 1861, CJUG. See Will of A. Maxwell, Will Record, 1824–1850, 11 January 1841, PCLC; "List of Negroes of Mrs. Julia King, 1854," Roswell King file, Midway Museum, Midway, Ga.; CCJ to CCJj, 6 September 1854, CJUG; Will of Roswell King, Jun., Will Record, 1824–1850, 4 September 1854, PCLC; CCJ, Almanac 1859, 20 January 1859, JTU.

21. CCJj to CCJ and MJ, 11 September 1858, JTU; HHJ to MJ, 11 October 1858, JTU; Abream Scriven to Dinah Jones, 19 September 1858, JTU.

22. MSJM to MJ, 10 March 1863, JTU.

23. Robert Manson Myers, ed. *The Children of Pride: A True Story of Georgia and the Civil War* (New Haven, 1972), 1505–1506; CCJ to CCJj, 19 October 1859, CJUG.

24. See, e.g., CCJ, Almanac 1859, passim, JTU.

25. Charles Scribner to CCJ, 9 July 1860, JTU.

26. For William States Lee, Sr., and the character of the Edisto Island Presbyterian Church, see Erskine Clarke, *Our Southern Zion: A History of Calvinism in the South Carolina Low Country, 1690–1990* (Tuscaloosa, 1996), 126, 225, and 305.

27. MJ to CCJj, 16 July 1860, CJUG.

30. SOUTHERN ZION

1. CCJ to CCJj, 15 October 1860, CJUG; and cf. James William Berry, "Growing Up in the Old South: The Childhood of Charles Colcock Jones, Jr." (Ph.D. diss., Princeton University, 1981), 266–294; James O. Breeden, *Joseph Jones, M.D., Scientist of the Old South* (Lexington, Ky., 1975), 13–20.

2. CCJ to JoJ, 11 November 1850, JJUG; MJ and CCJ to CCJj and JJ, 21 November 1850, CJUG; and cf. CCJ to MJ, 11 July 1853, JTU.

3. CCJ to CCJj, 7 November 1859, CJUG.

4. CCJj to CCJ and MJ, 18 October 1860, CJUG.

5. CCJ to CCJj, 27 October 1860, CJUG.

6. MJ to CCJj, 15 November 1860, CJUG; CCJ to CCJj, 15 November 1860, CJUG.

7. CCJ to CCJj, 19 November 1860, CJUG.

8. Robert Long Groover, *Sweet Land of Liberty: A History of Liberty County, Georgia* (Roswell, Ga., 1987), 147–148.

9. Breeden, *Joseph Jones*, 68–87.

10. JJ, *Agricultural Resources of Georgia: Address Before the Cotton Planters Convention of Georgia at Macon, December 13, 1860* (Augusta, Ga., 1861), 10.

11. CCJ to MSJM, 13 December 1860, JTU.

12. CCJ to CCJj, 20 April 1861, 10 July 1862, CJUG; CCJ to David Porter, 30 April 1861, JTU.

13. CCJj to CCJ, 25 June 1861, in Robert Manson Myers, ed., *The Children of Pride: A True Story of Georgia and the Civil War* (New Haven, 1972), 701; MJ to CCJ, 2 July 1861, JTU.

14. CCJ to CCJj, 2 July 1861, CJUG; CCJj to CCJ and MJ, 29 July 1861, in Myers, *Children of Pride*, 723.
15. CCJ to William States Lee, 26 August 1861, JTU.
16. Ibid.
17. John Johnson and A. G. Redd to CCJ, 24 September 1861, JTU.
18. CCJ to John Johnson and A. G. Redd, 16 October 1861, JTU.
19. John Johnson to CCJ, 18 November 1861, JTU.
20. CCJ to John Johnson, 25 December 1861, JTU. Cf. Catherine Clinton, "Caught in the Web of the Big House: Women and Slavery," in *Women and the Family in a Slave Society*, ed. Paul Finkelman (New York, 1989), 9–24.
21. Minutes of the Session, First Presbyterian Church, Columbus, Ga., 1861–1863, PHSM. See CPB,72; MJ to CCJj, 19 March 1866, CJUG.
22. Erskine Clarke, *Our Southern Zion: A History of Calvinism in the South Carolina Low Country, 1690–1990* (Tuscaloosa, 1996), 210–215; CCJ to David Porter, 30 April 1861, JTU.
23. MJ to CCJj, 3 December 1861, CJUG.
24. Clarke, *Our Southern Zion*, 207–215.
25. CCJ, *Religious Instruction of the Negroes. An Address Delivered before the General Assembly of the Presbyterian Church, at Augusta, Ga., December 10, 1861* (Richmond, n.d.), 24.

31. INDIANOLA

1. James M. McPherson, *Battle Cry of Freedom: The Civil War Era* (New York, 1988), 308–336.
2. Mary Robarts to MJ, 31 May 1861, JTU.
3. Ibid.; JoJ to CCJ and MJ, 31 July 1861, JTU.
4. Robert Manson Myers, ed., *The Children of Pride: A True Story of Georgia and the Civil War* (New Haven, 1972), 725; MJ to CCJj, 25 July 1861, CJUG; JoJ to CCJ and MJ, 31 July 1861, JTU.
5. CCJ to CCJj, 8 December 1862, CJUG. For the role of religion in the Civil War, see Randall M. Miller, Harry S. Stout, and Charles Reagan Wilson, eds., *Religion and the American Civil War* (New York, 1998); James W. Silver, *Confederate Morale and Church Propaganda* (Gloucester, Mass., 1964); James H. Moorhead, *American Apocalypse: Yankee Protestants and the Civil War, 1860–1869* (New Haven, 1978).
6. CCJ to CCJj, 11 September 1861, CJUG; CCJ to RQM, 30 November 1861, JTU; Malcolm Bell, Jr., *Major Butler's Legacy: Five Generations of a Slaveholding Family* (Athens, Ga., 1987), 352–371.
7. MJ to CCJj, 3 December 1861, CJUG; CCJ, Almanac 1862, 25 February 1862, 17 March 1862, JTU; CPB, "List of People, March 25, 1862," JTU.
8. CCJ, Almanac 1862, 25 February 1862, 31 December 1862, JTU; Wm. C. Stevens to CCJ, 30 March 1861, JTU; CCJ to CCJj, 3 October 1861, CJUG.
9. CCJ, Almanac 1862, 5 March 1862, JTU.
10. For the mobilization of slaves for the Confederate war effort, see Thomas C. Bryan,

Confederate Georgia (Athens, Ga., 1953), 132–133; Bell Irvin Wiley, *Southern Negroes, 1861–1865* (New Haven, 1938), 114–122.

11. CCJ, Almanac 1862, 4 April 1862, 3 October 1862, 19 October 1862, JTU; MJ to CCJj, 16 April 1862, CJUG; CCJ to CCJj, 14 June 1862, CJUG.

12. CCJ to CCJj, 28 April 1862, CJUG; James O. Breeden, *Joseph Jones, M.D.: Scientist of the Old South* (Louisville, Ky., 1975), 118–121.

13. CCJj to CCJ, 30 April 1862, CJUG; CCJ, Almanac 1862, 26 April 1862; CCJ to CCJj, 28 April 1862, CJUG.

14. Lawrence W. Levine, *Black Culture and Black Consciousness: Afro-American Folk Thought from Slavery to Freedom* (New York, 1977), 100; CCJ, Almanac 1862, 26 April 1862.

15. CCJ to Eliza Robarts, 5 July 1862, JTU.

16. CCJ to CCJj, 10 July 1862, CJUG; Laura Maxwell Buttolph to MJ, 12 December 1857, JTU; CCJ, Almanac, 26 December 1857, JTU.

17. CCJ to CCJj, 10 July 1862, JTU; Laura Maxwell Buttolph to MJ, 7 August 1862, JTU.

18. David Buttolph to JoJ, 28 July 1862, JJUG.

19. CCJ to CCJj, 10 July 1862, CJUG; David Buttolph to JoJ, 28 July 1862, JJUG; CCJ, Almanac, 1 August 1862, 18 August 1862, 14 September 1862, JTU; Laura Maxwell Buttolph to MJ, 7 August 1862, JTU; CCJ to MSJM, 23 September 1862, JTU; and cf. James C. Scott, *Domination and the Art of Resistance: Hidden Transcripts* (New Haven, 1990), 197; Leon F. Litwack, *Been in the Storm So Long: The Aftermath of Slavery* (New York, 1979), 55.

20. CCJ to CCJj, 11 November 1861, CJUG. Cf. CCJ to JoJ, 15 September 1862, JJUG.

21. CCJj to CCJ, 16 October 1862, CJUG.

22. CCJ to CCJj, 30 September 1862, CJUG.

23. CCJ to JoJ, 15 September 1862, JJUG; Irwin Rahn to CCJ, 23 September 1851, JTU; MJ to CCJj, 24 September 1863, CJUG. A note in CCJ's hand lists those going to Indianola and those staying in Liberty County, box 20, folder 4, JTU. SJMC to CCJ, 14 November 1862, JTU; CCJ, Almanac, 18 November 1862, JTU.

24. CCJ to CCJj, 10 November 1862, CJUG; CCJj to CCJ, 10 November 1862, CJUG; CCJ to David Buttolph, 14 November 1862, JTU; "Indianola List," JTU; CCJ, Almanac, 18 November 1862, JTU; JoJ to MJ, 19 May 1863, 16 June 1863, 7 December 1863, JTU; MJ to John Jones, 15 April 1864, JJUG.

25. CCJ, Almanac, 18 November 1862, JTU.

26. Ibid.

27. CCJ, Almanac, 8 December 1862, JTU; CCJ to CCJj, 8 December 1862, CJUG. For the movement of slaves around the South in response to Federal threats, see Litwack, *Been in the Storm So Long,* 30–36.

28. For the extent of the breakup of the settlements in Liberty County, see CCJ to Eliza Robarts, 13 December 1862, JTU.

29. Litwack, *Been in the Storm So Long,* 104–166; Ira Berlin and Leslie S. Rowland, eds., *Families and Freedom: A Documentary History of African-American Kinship in the Civil War Era* (New York, 1997), 21–54.

30. CCJ, Almanac, 18 November 1862, JTU.

31. CCJj to CCJ and MJ, 3 March 1863, CJUG.
32. CCJ, Almanac, 12 March 1863, JTU.
33. MJ to Mary Jones Mallard, 30 March 1863, JTU; CCJj to George Howe, 19 March 1863, in Myers, *Children of Pride,* 1041–1044.
34. MJ, Journal, 16 March 1863, JTU.
35. Myers, *Children of Pride,* 1042; David Buttolph, "Funeral Sermon for the Rev. Charles Colcock Jones," JTU.

32. THE REFUGE

1. RQM, "Common Place Book," 18 June 1863, PHSM; CCJj to MJ, 3 April 1863, CJUG.
2. MJ to CCJj, 5 June 1863, CJUG.
3. JoJ to MJ, 24 March 1863, JTU; HHJ to MJ, 25 March 1863, JTU; George Howe to MJ, 28 March 1863, JTU; Joseph Williams to John Jones, 26 April 1863, JJUG.
4. James O. Breeden, *Joseph Jones, M. D.: Scientist of the Old South* (Lexington, Ky., 1975), 125, 127, 159, 198. Joseph Jones, *Medical and Surgical Memoirs,* vol. 3 (New Orleans, 1890), 405–418, contains JJ's medical investigations at Andersonville, together with sketches of arms and legs infected with gangrene. See also Horace H. Cunningham, *Doctors in Gray: The Confederate Medical Service* (Baton Rouge, 1958), esp. 239–244. Dunwody Jones is quoted in James M. McPherson, *Battle Cry of Freedom: The Civil War Era* (New York, 1988), 801–802.
5. CCJj to MJ, 31 August 1863, 12 October 1863, CJUG.
6. Robert Manson Myers, ed., *The Children of Pride: A True Story of Georgia and the Civil War* (New Haven, 1972), 1516; CCJ to CCJj, 20 December 1861, CJUG; CCJj to MJ, 4 August 1863, CJUG.
7. Eva Eve Jones to MSJM, 23 April 1864, JTU.
8. Cf. Anne C. Rose, *Victorian America and the Civil War* (New York, 1992).
9. MJ to CCJj, 29 May 1863, CJUG.
10. CCJ to CCJj, 27 January 1863, 23 February 1863, CJUG; CCJj to CCJ and MJ, 14 February 1863; CCJ, Almanac 1863, 16 February 1863, 24 February 1863, JTU.
11. MJ to MSJM, 5 March 1864, 16 March 1863, 30 March 1863, JTU.
12. RQM to MSJM, 23 September 1863, 30 September 1863, 6 October 1863, JTU; RQM, "Record of Pastor," 1863, PHSM.
13. MJ to MSJM, 8 December 1863; RQM to MSJM, 21 January 1863, JTU.
14. MSJM to MJ, 11 December 1863, 20 December 1860, 8 February 1864, JTU.
15. MSJM to MJ, 10 March 1864, JTU.
16. Stanley P. Hirshson, *The White Tecumseh: A Biography of General William T. Sherman* (New York, 1997), 207–223; MSJM to MJ, 27 May 1864, 7 June 1864, 11 June 1864, 23 June 1863, JTU.
17. McPherson, *Battle Cry of Freedom,* 749–750; Hirshson, *White Tecumseh,* 223–224. Cf. JoJ to MSJM, 1 July 1864, JTU; and see MSJM to Laura Maxwell Buttolph, 18 July 1864, JTU.
18. MJ to SJMC, 22 July 1864, JTU; RQM, "Record of Pastor," 19 July 1864, PHSM.

19. RQM, "Common Place Book," 7 September 1864, PHSM; CCJ to Eliza Robarts, 13 December 1862, JTU; MSJM to MJ, 19 October 1864, 26 August 1864, JTU.

20. Hirshson, *White Tecumseh*, 252–253; Sarah Blackwell Temple, *The First Hundred Years: A Short History of Cobb County, Georgia* (Atlanta, 1935), 332–334, 534.

21. Hirshson, *White Tecumseh*, 252–253.

22. Breeden, *Joseph Jones*, 164.

23. Carolyn Clay Swiggart, *Shades of Gray: The Clay and McAllister Families of Bryan County, Georgia, During the Plantation Years (ca. 1760–1888)* (Darien, Conn., 1999), 32.

24. The following account of Yankee raids of Montevideo is drawn largely from the overlapping diaries of MJ and MSJM. For a textual analysis of the diaries, see David Gruning, "A Note on the Civil War Diaries in the Charles Colcock Jones Collection," JTU. Hereafter given as MJ and MSJM, Diaries. The page numbers refer to the typed copy of the diaries in JTU.

25. MJ and MSJM, Diaries, 1–2.

26. Ibid., 4.

27. Ibid., 5; RQM, "Common Place Book," 7 September 1865.

28. MJ and MSJM, Diaries, 5–11.

29. Ibid., 11. For Audley King, see Joseph LeConte, *'Ware Sherman: A Journal of Three Months' Personal Experience in the Last Days of the Confederacy* (Berkeley, 1937), 24–25, 51.

30. MJ and MSJM, Diaries, 11–13.

31. Ibid., 14.

32. Ibid., 14–29; Hirshson, *White Tecumseh*, 264; Leon F. Litwack, *Been in the Storm So Long: The Aftermath of Slavery* (New York, 1979), 122.

33. Raymond Harris to MJ, 25 November 1867, JTU; MJ and MSJM, Diaries, 33–35.

34. MJ and MSJM, Diaries, 37. See also LeConte, *'Ware Sherman*, 43, for light from burning plantations.

35. MJ and MSJM, Diaries, 23, 41; Margaret Rebecca Miller, "Diary," in Robert Long Groover, *Sweet Land of Liberty: A History of Liberty County, Georgia* (Roswell, Ga., 1987), 171–175; RQM, *Plantation Life Before Emancipation* (Richmond, 1892), 230.

36. MJ, Journal, [22 December? 1864], JTU.

37. Ibid.

38. MJ and MSJM, Diaries, 18, 25, 33.

39. Ibid., 23, 30.

40. Ibid., 42–43.

41. Ibid., 23; Claim of Davy Stevens and Claim of Linda Roberts, Liberty County, Georgia, Case Files, Southern Claims Commission, Records of the 3rd Auditor, Allowed Case Files, Records of the U.S. General Accounting Office, RG 217 (National Archives, Washington, D.C.). For an analysis of the claims of former slaves in Liberty County against the U.S. government for confiscation of their property by Union troops, see Dylan Pennigroth, "Slavery, Freedom, and Social Claims to Property Among African Americans in Liberty County, Georgia, 1850–1880," *Journal of American History* 84

(1997): 405–435; Philip D. Morgan, "The Ownership of Property by Slaves in the Mid-Nineteenth-Century Low Country," *Journal of Southern History* 49 (August 1983): 399–420. For Toney Stevens, see Groover, *Sweet Land of Liberty*, 49.

42. MJ to JoJ, 30 January 1865, JTU. Cf. Pennigroth, "Slavery, Freedom, and Social Claims to Property," 406.

43. MSJM to MJ, 8 March 1865, JTU.

44. MJ to SJMC, 25 March 1865, JTU.

45. MJ, Journal, April 1865, JTU.

46. MJ, Journal, March 1865, JTU.

33. THE PROMISED LAND

1. Laura Buttolph to MJ, 30 June 1865, JTU. This letter in Laura Buttolph's hand, with the date written later, is not the same letter written by Buttolph to MJ on the same date that is in Robert Manson Myers, ed., *The Children of Pride: A True Story of Georgia and the Civil War* (New Haven, 1972), 1277. Much of the content and language of the two letters are the same. For the colony of freed people on St. Catherine's Island, see Robert Long Groover, *Sweet Land of Liberty: A History of Liberty County, Georgia* (Roswell, Ga., 1987), 51–52.

2. MJ to CCJj, 18 September 1863, CJUG; JoJ to MSJM, 1 July 1864, JTU; RQM, "Common Place Book," 7 August 1864, PHSM; JoJ to MJ, 21 August 1865, JTU.

3. See note 24 in chapter 32 above. MJ and MSJM, Diaries, 43–44.

4. For an example of CCJ's class analysis, see CCJ, *Eleventh Annual Report of the Association for the Religious Instruction of the Negroes, in Liberty County, Georgia* (Savannah, 1846). For racism in proslavery thought, see Larry E. Tise, *Proslavery: A History of the Defense of Slavery in America, 1701–1840* (Athens, Ga., 1987).

5. Leon F. Litwack, *Been in the Storm So Long: The Aftermath of Slavery* (New York, 1979), 167–220.

6. MJ to JoJ, 18 September 1865, JJUG; MJ to CCJj, 6 September 1865, CJUG; Groover, *Sweet Land of Liberty*, 51. Cf. also James C. Scott, *Domination and the Art of Resistance: Hidden Transcripts* (New Haven, 1990), 45–69.

7. Except for the next reference, Cato disappears from the Jones materials at Tulane and the University of Georgia after November 1865.

8. "Negro Money" in CCJ, "Memoranda Book," 24 January 1866, JTU; Nancy to Julia King, 5 April 1866, Midway Museum, Midway, Georgia; MJ to MSJM, 14 May 1866, JTU.

9. MJ to CCJj, 26 November 1865, JTU; cf. Litwack, *Been in the Storm So Long*, 292, from which the above point is drawn. See also Elizabeth Regosin, *Freedom's Promise: Ex-Slave Families and Citizenship in the Age of Emancipation* (Charlottesville, 2002).

10. MJ, Journal, 16 March 1866, JTU; Mary E. Robarts to MJ, 11 April, 1867.

11. MJ to JoJ, 1 December 1865, JJUG; Mrs. LeCounte Baggs, interview by author, Liberty County, Ga., 12 May 2002.

12. For those living at Carlawter, see "Memorandum of Agreement, Montevideo Plantation," 1866 and 1867, CJUG.

13. "Memorandum of Agreement, Montevideo Plantation," 1866, 1867, CJUG; Office of B.R.F. and A. L., Walthourville, to July [Reece] and Jesse [Reece], 23 April 1866, JTU; MJ to SJMC, 1 May 1866, JTU; MJ to CCJj, 28 May 1866, CJUG; "Memorandum of Agreement, White Oak Plantation," 1870, CJUG.

14. MJ to JoJ, 18 September 1865, JJUG.

15. Ibid.; JoJ to MJ, 9 January 1866, JTU.

16. MJ to JoJ, 1 December 1865, JJUG; MJ to MSJM, 9 December 1865, JTU.

17. MJ, Journal 21 November 1867, JTU; MJ to MSJM, 4 March 1867, JTU. For the renting of land at Arcadia by former Jones slaves, see "Memorandum of Agreement, Arcadia Plantation," 1866, CJUG. In 1868 MJ paid Porter $150 to repair buildings at Montevideo. See note signed by "Porter Way, January 4, 1868," JTU. See also Thomas F. Armstrong, "From Task Labor to Free Labor: The Transition Along Georgia's Rice Coast, 1820–1880," *Georgia Historical Quarterly* 64 (Winter 1980): 432–437. A number of contracts between white plantation owners and freed people in Liberty County can be found in "Records of the Bureau of Refugees, Freedmen, and Abandoned Lands," Record Group 105, National Archives, Washington, D.C. Included are contracts for the Retreat, South Hampton, and Laurel View.

18. MJ to MSJM, 9 December 1865, JTU.

19. Ibid.

20. For the ways in which memory can shatter the ideological claims of a dominant class, see Michael Walzer, *Interpretation and Social Criticism* (Cambridge, Mass., 1987); Hans-Georg Gadamer, *Truth and Method* (New York, 1984), esp. "Hermeneutics and Historicism," 460–491; Paul Ricoeur, *The Conflict of Interpretations* (Evanston, Ill., 1974).

21. "Minutes of the Session, Midway Congregational Church," 21 May 1852, PHSM. For the implication of surnames for slaves, see Herbert G. Gutman, *The Black Family in Slavery and Freedom, 1750–1925* (New York, 1976), 230–256.

22. The surnames are given in "Memorandum of Agreement, Montevideo Plantation," 1866, 1867, 1869, and in "Memorandum of Agreement, White Oak Plantation," 1870, CJUG.

23. MJ, Journal, 4 November 1866, JTU.

24. Charles A. H. Maxwell, *Advance Through Storm: History of Midway First Presbyterian Church* (Pembroke, Ga., 1966), 7–11; *Fifth Annual Report of the General Assembly's Committee on Freedmen, of the Presbyterian Church, in the United States of America* (Pittsburgh, 1870), 17, 28; *Third Annual Report of the [Northern] Presbyterian Committee of Missions for Freedmen, to the General Assembly of the Presbyterian Church* (1873), 8, PHSM; Groover, *Sweet Land of Liberty*, 53.

25. *Minutes of the New Sunbury Association, Held with Jones' Creek Church, Liberty County, Ga., November 24, 25, and 26, 1866* (Savannah, 1867); Molene Herbert Chambless Burke, interview by author, Walthourville, Ga., 14 March 1997.

26. For a positive appraisal of CCJ's continuing influence among the blacks of Liberty County, see Lillie Walthour Gillard, "A Chronicle of Black History in Liberty County, Georgia," in *Liberty County, Georgia: A Pictorial History*, compiled by Virginia Fraser Evans (Statesville, N.C., 1979), 113–114. For a critical view, see Mrs. Walthour, Liberty

County, Ga., interview by Andrew Polk Watson, Fisk University Social Science Institute, 1930.

27. See "Teacher's Monthly School Report," 1867–1869, Liberty County, Ga., in Freedmen's Bureau Records, National Archives, Washington, D.C.

28. "Documents Illustrating the Historical Development of Dorchester Academy and Dorchester Center, Parts I and II, selected by The Amistad Research Center, New Orleans, Louisiana, from Archives of the American Missionary Association."

29. Litwack, *Been in the Storm So Long*, 451–501; and cf. Edmund L. Drago, *Initiative, Paternalism, and Race Relations: Charleston's Avery Normal Institute* (Athens, Ga., 1990).

30. For the decline of rice as an important crop in the low country, see Peter A. Coclanis, *The Shadow of a Dream: Economic Life and Death in the South Carolina Low Country, 1670–1920* (New York, 1989).

31. CCJj to MJ, 16 November 1865, JTU; MJ to MSJM, 8 January 1867, JTU.

32. CCJ to MJ, 15 November 1865, JTU.

33. CCJ to Ruth Jones, 11 May 1888, Rare Book, Manuscript, and Special Collections Library, Duke University.

34. MJ, Journal 28 July 1865, JTU.

35. Eva Jones to MJ, [?] March 1866, 26 June 1866, JTU.

36. Moses Greenwood to RQM, 13 January 1866, 21 May 1866, JTU; B. M. Palmer to RQM, 19 May 1866, JTU; MJ to MSJM, 20 June 1866, JTU; Laura Buttolph to MSJM, 17 July 1866, JTU; RQM, "Commonplace Book," 27 August 1866, PHSM.

37. James O. Breeden, *Joseph Jones, M.D.: Scientist of the Old South* (Lexington, Ky., 1975), 169–175.

38. MJ to MSJM, 28 May 1866, JTU.

39. Laura Buttolph to MJ, 21 August 1866, JTU.

40. MJ to MSJM, 4 March 1867, 15 May 1867, JTU; Eliza Clay to MJ, 9 January 1867, JTU.

41. MJ, Journal, 31 November [*sic*] 1867, JTU.

42. MJ to MSJM, 1 October 1867, JTU.

43. MJ, Journal, 9 December 1867, JTU.

44. Ibid., 12 January 1868.

45. R. Harris to MJ, 25 November 1867, JTU;

46. MJ to MSJM, 8 January 1869, JTU.

47. Ibid.

48. MJ to SJMC, 24 April 1869, JTU.

49. RQM to MSJM, 13 July 1869, JTU.

50. "Record of Marriages of Colored Persons, 1866–1874," PCLC.

INDEX OF NAMES

Notes: GC and LPC (always at end of main entry) indicate references in the Genealogical Charts and the List of Principal Characters, respectively. **Boldface type** indicates a photograph.

Titus (1826–1865) (Stevens) (Big), 117, 317–318, 350, 352; GC, 500; LPC, 481
Titus (1839–1870+) (Way) (Little), 317, 352, 354, 384, 417, 563n14; GC, 497, 498; LPC, 481–482
Toney Stevens. *See* Stevens, Toney
Tony (1775?–1865): gardener, 269, 291, 309, 417; husband to Willoughby, 46, 100; LPC, 482
Turner, Nat, 153

Venus, 386, 391, 417, 477; GC, 496
Victoria, 315, 350, 352, 360–361; GC, 498

William (driver at Lambert), 237
William (husband of Eve), 332
Williams, Joseph (Reverend), 424, 453
Willoughby (sister of Lizzy), 3, 10, 46, 185–186, 482–483
Willoughby, Maum (cook at Mallards), 144, 146–147, 151, 200, 483

E U R O P E A N   A M E R I C A N S

Adger, James, 168, 288, 383, 483
Anderson, Bessie, 390–391
Anderson, Evelyn Elouisa Jones, 71, 206–207, 239, 258, 382, 390; LPC, 483
Anderson, Joseph, 239, 382, 390–393, 483
Axson, Rev. I. S. K., 244, 289, 392, 406; LPC, 483

Barnwell, Robert, 176, 249–250
Barnwell, William, 171, 249
Bartram, John, 376
Bartram, William, 7, 21, 121
Beecher, Catharine, 83–85, 101, 103, 298, 525n2
Beecher, Harriet. *See* Stowe, Harriet Beecher
Beecher, Lyman, 83, 87, 91, 101, 116
Berrien, John M., 91–92, 384
Bess, 144, 151
Brown, John, 398

Bulloch, James Stephens, 191–193
Bulloch, Martha Stewart, 191
Bulloch, Mittie, 376
Bullock, James Stevens, 101
Butler, Pierce, 42, 69, 157, 314
Buttolph, David: marriage of, 340, 343, 375, 415, 417, 432; ministry, 389, 421, 453, 459–460; LPC, 483
Buttolph, Laura Elizabeth Maxwell: child of Susan and James Audley, 68, 75, 78–79, 85, 116–117, 120, 196, 198–200, 222, 237, 294–295, 339, 341–342, 375, 459; correspondence, 262, 275, 443, 458–459, 574n1; description of, 336, 340, 561n12; marriage, 340–343, 415, 417, 432; slaves, relationship with, 354, 414; visits, 268, 284; LPC, 491–492

Calhoun, John C. 93, 249
Capers, William, 109, 249
Chapman, Elijah, 328–329, 372
Clay, Eliza, 63, 297, 375, 433, 459, 484
Clay, Thomas: friend of Charles Jones, 63, 200, 433; ministry, support of, 142–143, 148, 167, 170, 174, 233–235, 247–248, 534nn9–10; plantation owner, 234, 250; LPC, 484
Cocke, John (General), 267–269, 379
Colcock, Charles Jones (Judge), 57, 108, 168–169, 171, 247
Colcock, John, 335
Cooper, Thomas, 108, 172, 247
Couper, John, 41
Cumming, Joseph, 199–200, 237, 260, 340
Cumming, Susan Jones Maxwell: "Aunt Susan," 339, 394; childhood of, 1, 18, 19–22, 28, 30–34, 38–39, 44–45, 57, 64, 115–116; children of, 240, 293–295, 340–341, 449; in-laws of, 132, 341–343 James Maxwell, marriage to, 68, 75, 78–79; Joseph Cumming, marriage to, 199–200; plantation owner, 112, 260, 414; "Sister Susan," 168, 175, 196, 198–199, 257, 279, 294, 330, 336, 362, 375,

General Index

Abolitionism, 95, 169–171, 206–207, 299, 398
Acculturation, 26–27, 209, 263, 307
African influences, 26–27, 29, 51, 150, 152–166, 181. *See also* Slaves: as basket makers, and dance, names and naming practices of
African slaves, 3, 41, 152–153, 310
Altahama river, 6, 42, 70, 140–141, 195, 440–441
American Board of Commissioners for Foreign Missions, 92, 116
American Colonization Society, 89, 92
American Home Missionary Society, 91
Andersonville Prison Camp, 425–426, 458
Andover Theological Seminary, 69, 84, 87, 207, 265
Antiquities of the Southern Indians, Particularly of the Georgia Tribes, 221
Antislavery, 83–84, 91
"Apostle to the Negro Slaves," 251
Arcadia plantation, 101, 191, 234, 238, 323, 326, 337, 379, 382, 420, 432; breakup of settlement, 417–419; description of, 505; and final visits, 464; and freed people, 447, 451; overseers, 261, 317; plundered by Yankees, 437; settlement at, 238, 317–319, 323
Athens, Ga., 384, 424

Atlanta, 264, 422, 429–432; Central Presbyterian Church, 422, 429, 457
Augusta, Ga. 200, 406, 427

Baker County, Ga., 388–389
Baltimore, 94–95
Banjoes and fiddles, 157
Baptism, 64, 163, 282, 323–324
Baptists, 140, 249–250. *See also under specific titles*
Barsden Bluff, 59
Bonaventure plantation, 236, 257, 389, 417–418, 505
Bush and hush arbors: and freed people, 454; for religious gatherings, 51, 138–139, 146, 158–161; and Societies and sacred meals, 164
Byan Neck Presbyterian Church, 142, 143, 235–236

Calvinism: character of, 87–88, 126–129, 218, 273–274, 290–291, 344, 397; and admonitions to children, 281–282; and freed people, 455; replaced by Victorian respectability and sentimentality, 428; and the value of ordinary life, 223
Carlawter settlement, 44–54, 75, 100, 112, 150, 180–189, 236, 300–316, 327, **446**, 447; and freed people, 445–450; and

590